N.C.WYETH

SELF PORTRAIT (1913)
Oil on canvas, h:18¼, w:12¼
Unsigned
Courtesy of Mr. & Mrs. Nicholas Wyeth

N.C. WYETH

THE COLLECTED
PAINTINGS, ILLUSTRATIONS AND MURALS

—— • ——

By Douglas Allen and Douglas Allen, Jr.

WITH A FOREWORD BY PAUL HORGAN
AND AN INTRODUCTION BY RICHARD LAYTON

CROWN PUBLISHERS, INC. · NEW YORK

Also by Douglas Allen

Frederic Remington and the Spanish-American War
Frederic Remington's Own Outdoors

© 1972 by Douglas Allen and Douglas Allen, Jr.

Library of Congress Catalog Card Number: 71–168323

ISBN: 0-517-50054X

ISBN: 0-517-501589

Printed in the United States of America

Published simultaneously in Canada by
General Publishing Company Limited

DESIGNED BY GEORGE HORNBY

Composition by Hallmark Typographers, Inc.
Color Plates and Printing by Davis-Delaney-Arrow, Inc.
Black and White Plates and Printing by
Halliday Lithograph Corp.

THIS BOOK IS DEDICATED to the memory of two departed friends—the late Helen L. Card and E. Walter Latendorf. They devoted themselves to the advancement of American illustration as a great art. Their like will not be seen again.

ROMANCE OF ADVENTURE
National Association of Book Publishers poster
    for Children's Book Week © 1928

Contents

Preface

THERE WERE three basic reasons for my attempting a book on N. C. Wyeth.

The first was my long-standing interest in the works of that large group of artists who devoted their lives to making the pictures that, reproduced on the printed pages of books and magazines, have given such great pleasure to countless people over the years.

The second was my admiration for N. C. Wyeth, not only as an artist but as a man. He was deeply dedicated to his profession, his home, his friends, and especially to his family, a family that has carried on in his tradition, thereby tendering him a greater memorial than monuments, plaques, or mere words.

The third reason was more personal. It is a part of my own life. Some twenty or more years have passed since I was suddenly exposed to the art of N. C. Wyeth under somewhat different circumstances. Previously I had known of his work only through his brilliant illustrations for the Scribner Illustrated Classics, that library of great books especially selected as outstanding literature for young people. In those days, my special hobby was—it still is—the great artists who portrayed the Old West: in particular, Frederic Remington. In my frequent trips to bookshops specializing in the old and rare, in search of new finds to add to my own collection, I was at times accompanied by a young boy, who delighted in the browsing and rummaging as much as I did. One of these outings resulted in his discovering a copy of the limited edition of James Boyd's *Drums*, a Scribner Illustrated Classic, signed both by the author and by the illustrator, N. C. Wyeth.

Buying that book was my undoing. From that time on, there had to be other trips for other books and other periodicals and other prints—my young son's Wyeth collection became bigger and bigger. My own dream of someday owning an original Remington went aglimmer as they became ever scarcer and more costly.

The young boy has grown to manhood now, and his N. C. Wyeth collection has grown with him. And, as the years passed, I too developed a constantly increasing appreciation for the magnificent contribution N. C. Wyeth had made to the field of American illustration and art.

One fine day the inevitable happened. We discussed doing a book on N. C. Wyeth. The idea had considerable appeal. However, the little I knew about him and his work had been picked up casually through friends who dealt in books and art—it was hardly enough on which to base a comprehensive presentation. There followed years of library research by both of us, innumerable visits to art galleries, and constant reference to my son's extensive collection—before we came to this: our book on N. C. Wyeth and his art.

My son worked on the Bibliography for ten years to make it the most comprehensive source of information about N. C. Wyeth's work that seems possible. Meanwhile, as I worked on the text, I realized that N. C. could speak best for himself in so many instances that I have quoted him freely. My son and I hope that our joint efforts to present a thorough, rounded view of N. C. Wyeth and his art will enable the reader to share our enthusiasm and admiration.

DOUGLAS ALLEN

[9]

LONG JOHN SILVER AND HAWKINS (*To me he was unweariedly kind; and always glad to see me in the galley.*)
Oil on canvas, h:48, w:40
Signed upper left: N. C. Wyeth
Treasure Island, by Robert Louis Stevenson
Charles Scribner's Sons, 1911
Courtesy of Mrs. Andrew Wyeth

Foreword

I

THIS IS a lifetime we are looking at.

II

N. C. Wyeth was most widely known as an illustrator. For years there poured forth from his workshop series after series of pictures dramatizing high moments out of classic tales for young people. Through the technique of color reproduction, these works reached an enormous public. They were all characterized by admirable draughtsmanship, pleasure in the dramatic range of human character, and above all, a powerful sense of mood. Wyeth was unique in the most distinctive quality of his story pictures, and that was a most beguiling sense of conviction. By the magic of his rich nature, he was able to imagine himself *there*, in whatever situation his author set forth. This gave him a delightful authority by which he transcended the disadvantages of never personally having been in Sherwood Forest, or at the Admiral Benbow Inn, or in that little Austrian town where the Angel Satan* came in the guise of a beautiful youth to play his melancholy role of detached observer of the woes of men and women.

It was a fine achievement to have educated with his fond and exciting images of storied life the imaginations of the children of his time. He played, really, an educational role in them, which was the expression of his conscience, and in it there are three fine values which moved him powerfully. The first of these was his love for America. He loved it for its landscape, its spiritual belief in the individual human being, and for any separate expression of that belief, however (and even especially) original or outlandish it might be. The second of the values which moved him as he re-created the past was his joy in the trappings of historical period. He was an exhaustive student of historical periods, and loved accuracy of detail with a scholar's respect for the facts. Some accident of his taste made him especially effective in two periods, the medieval time and the American Colonial era. But to say this is not to depreciate his virtuosity in such affairs as giants, all kinds of ships, or the limning of the fabulous. The third of his moving values was his love for the beauty of humanity, the face, the form, and the attitude of man and woman.

* In *The Mysterious Stranger*, by Mark Twain.

And it is with that value that his work as illustrator merges into his work as a painter of freer subject matter. For he drew incessantly, at the proper study of mankind. The largeness of spirit visible in even his less important illustrations called for a larger expression than their subject matter sometimes might suggest. He painted many murals, some on an heroic scale. Like most of the murals in the world including the very greatest, they were larger illustrations than those found in the pages of a book. This is not to confuse or interchange the way murals and book illustrations are conceived. It is only to say that it is historically absurd to exclude a painter who is a first class illustrator from the company of more serious or abstract painters on the grounds that he is merely an illustrator. It is essentially an illustrative function to arrest in painting a great episode in spiritual or political history for the celebration of the past and the inspiration of the future. Wyeth in his murals—most of them, so far as I know, painted on canvas and later applied to the wall—treated many moments of American history, and otherwise celebrated symbolically the course of human life. Such works are mentioned here primarily to compose the opposite points of view which are held about the dignity of the illustrator's role. What is relevant finally is just this: whether the illustrator is or is not a good artist. With the evidence increasing in every phase of his growth, up to the very last, it is clear through the range of his lifetime's work that Wyeth was indeed a very good artist and possibly a great one.

III

It is interesting to speculate for a moment upon what formed the style of this painter. Even in its experimental phases it is a curiously consistent style, it has a signature in every line and reach of light that is unmistakably his. His color is rich, warm, and freshly harmonious. He has an extraordinary skill at capturing the quality of light itself, not merely its symbolic representation in the arrangement of planes and their shadows, and he exercised it to the fullest, with an almost offhand delight in his mastery. His compositions are massive, with the play of great bodies, or loom of rock, or rise of tree, or the bulk of something fashioned by builders. There is substance to his forms and reality to his objects.

And in the mood in which these components are brought together there is an unstated spiritual quality which sets us to thinking that with all his remarkable power and command of his craft, he was always, even in his least serious work, seeking to say more than could meet the eye.

That, indeed, is the grand element in his personal style. It is what spoke to the countless youth in his paintings of mood and action, and it is what he triumphantly realized in his last, most personal works—that power of both representing and commenting upon human life which has always been to their varying degrees the characteristic of true artists in all media.

Because his style has two major aspects, we will look in perhaps contrasting directions to find their origins.

When he was a very young man, Wyeth spent a year or so in the American Southwest. I feel this experience had much to do with how he ever afterward saw Nature. He saw it there, under the sun which so vastly plays light upon mountains, and plains, and continents of clouds, in a grand abstraction. That light and that landscape became his symbols for fabled places when later he needed to represent them.

His apprenticeship as a painter was served in Wilmington and Chadds Ford under Howard Pyle whose powerful personality drew a whole school of American illustrators to him. Pyle's vision of romance and dramatic composition marked Wyeth's development very plainly. We see Pyle now as a period artist, with respect for his fine craftsmanship, and with the extent of his growth historically plain. Nearer to Wyeth, we see in him a far greater range than Pyle commanded, even as we acknowledge the younger man's debt to the older.

Philosophically, Wyeth drew much of his sense of people from the faith of the New England transcendentalists. He was a New Englander all his life, of the temper of Emerson and Thoreau. When he idealized his human subjects, they often came out with the calm of a rather bleak faith in their faces, a Sunday afternoon excellence which undoubtedly was nearer to the American experience than the baroque conceits of the European masters. Among these masters, on the other hand, he revered Michelangelo above everyone else; and it is paying tribute in both directions to note that there is evidence of that respect in Wyeth's heroic handling of the figure in many of his works.

The affirmative, the optimistic flavor proper to the illustrative works is drawn, then, from the inexhaustible sunlight of the Southwest, from the studio experience under Pyle, and from the faith of the New England tradition. But there is another view to be had of experience and the likeness of life if we follow Wyeth's eye as he searches for expression which will unlock that which is not visible, and reveal the great theme of life under God. And here we find him in the company of those artists who, like Beethoven, spend themselves in the holy task of trying to release such beauty, form, and affirmation as dwell in the commonplace and the familiar, and give them noble substance worthy of their Creator. He avowed no religion altogether, though the dignity and plainness of the Quaker beliefs spoke to him. But his intensity of emotion and the respect he gave to the accessible world had much religious character, which meant endless search for two truths—his own, and Nature's.

No less a motive than that empowered Wyeth to grow and grow, in his last paintings, until his technical mastery came to serve rather than dominate; and his lifelong love of the human condition yielded him, and us, the fulfillment of its quest.

IV

They are paintings of the American places and people he knew best . . . the Pennsylvania countryside and the Maine coast. They are painted in a technique which he undertook relatively late in his life: egg tempera on gesso panels, where heretofore he had worked in oil on canvas. In tempera, he found a new clarity and crispness. Its lucidity, and the quality of the plasterlike surface of gesso, had much to do with the sudden release of a vein of his thought and feeling long recognized but not delivered. With his familiar expertness, he mastered expression in the technique new to him and applied it both to illustrative work and to the more personal painting of his last few years.

In those paintings there is a contemplative mood which somehow carries the thought beyond the immediate subject matter. Their sombre lyricism is perhaps the truest echo of Wyeth's personality to be found in all his work. They give rise to such feeling and thought as we look at them that we are moved to say, while regarding his image of the world, "Here is what a man of very large nature had to say as he followed his task of celebrating and praising life through art: in every object or person there is beauty to be discovered, though now it prove to be tragic, or again innocent and hopeful; but in all things there is dignity, and it is my task that I find it, and set forth my view of life in such a way that those who look on what I have done will know that harmony I have sought to find between God's inscrutable designs and our daily course on earth; and all this with all my strength, my conscience and my spirit."

In so daring to paraphrase an artist's credo, I have here the advantage of long intimate years of friendship with Wyeth, and have heard his words on the subject. Yet I do not rely too heavily on that rich experience to make the conclusion. The evidence is there in the late pictures. It is there in terms of the color, in the massiveness of the designs, in the enchantments of his technical devotion to every problem of surface and of form; and again and above all, it speaks from the temper of the works, grave, exalted, attentive and at times almost worshipful or rapturous, as in the *Summer Night;* or the *Island Funeral,* with its godlike view; or the *Spring House,* with its little poems of natural joy in leaf and stone and flower all miraculously drawn, and clustered around the central homely splendor of the gorgeous milk, symbol of sustenance, pouring from the pail like light itself.

He loved the moment, the place, the person so much that in a period of art whose fashion it was to paint abstractions of the ego, he spent himself at the job representing truly that which he loved, while he served respect for the values of abstraction through respect for the art of design and composition. Light itself, weather, the atmosphere and its myriad spells, these seem to live a captured life in his pictures; not just their symbols and conventional signs. It is an American light, off the coast of Maine, or over the mellow Brandywine whose every change of daily mood he knew from living there. This is a quality which one day will be regarded as equal in interest and significance, in discovering Wyeth's place in American art, as it was in appraising the values of the French Impressionists' rediscovery of the properties of light in the atmosphere.

V

All his various activities as are represented in this collection of his lifetime's growth sprang from a superb vitality. He was a big man, with an heroic head. His face was massively modelled, deeply marked by the wonders and doubts of his inner experience. His eyes were brilliant, and the play of his expression had a flashing range, from the merriment and charm with which he talked with friends and charged the characters of his large family, to a profound earnestness, a tragic and powerful look which could make a trivial topic suddenly assume a new and enlightening importance. His conversation was energizing. He was wonderfully articulate, playing through a vocabulary which had as many rich and colorful and striking notes as his palette. The variety of his work was honestly come by, for his personality, his mind, his interests, had countless aspects, all of them of that sort of versatility which reinforces rather than contradicts the central character of the man. He embodied goodness and generosity, tolerance and respect and encouragement, love for the simplest humanity of man, and impatience with nonsense or self-indulgence, and he worshipped the best he saw in Nature, humanity, and art.

Life was profuse wherever he made himself felt, and seemed better than it was, and more worthy of hard work and deserving of joy. He took great draughts of comfort and confirmation from music and literature as well as from the mightiest of his predecessors in the world of painting. He challenged his own spirit with the power and the compassion which he found in Beethoven, Michelangelo, and Shakespeare. As I have noted elsewhere,° Wyeth was quick to recognize and

° *Encounters With Stravinsky*, pp. 62 ff.

proclaim the true masters of new styles in his own century—such artists in music as Igor Stravinsky and Alban Berg, for example. A work he often had reference to was *The Dynasts*, by Thomas Hardy. He found in its godlike view and melancholy courage some grand statement of his own character. And on the other hand, he was ribald and hilarious among his family and friends. At the head of his table, he was a master of bounty, surrounded by children and grandchildren and friends and neighbors, with dogs under the chairs, and a profusion of foods on the board, and a riot of harmony in the air. Giving so much, he contained more than he could give.

It was, among other things, what made him so magnetic and powerful a teacher. Not only a teacher of his own art, but of those responsibilities of spirit and action which life itself demands and does not always see fulfilled. He did teach many artists, notably his own son Andrew, his daughters Henriette and Carolyn, and his sons-in-law, Peter Hurd and John McCoy II. But there were others, and of them all he demanded imitation not of his work, but of his love of work; and to them all he gave his full sense of how all that there is of life can pertain to a single act of art.

In other words, he had greatness as a man, in which his powers as an artist were deeply and securely rooted, and by which they were ever refreshed.

VI

As an illustrator, he was head and shoulders above his contemporaries.

As "pure" painter, he left a rich legacy of works which celebrate his own image of his country. When we see it as he saw it, we will see him more truly—for so by the interaction of a creative interpreter and the places and conditions of his life we come to know, from his particular spiritual and physical experience passionately recorded, the universal values that abide in those acts of art which live long after the mortal span of the artist himself. He will be rediscovered in terms which were for the most part denied him during his lifetime.

Until then, his country inherits his beautiful tributes to the earthly likeness of mankind as he knew it.

PAUL HORGAN

Introduction

With pictures by N. C. Wyeth. These words, appearing on the covers and pages of scores of magazines and books, have served to quicken the hearts and raise the expectations of young readers for three generations. To all of us as parents, librarians, or students of history, the name N. C. Wyeth has stood as a hallmark of special merit. In very large measure, it was his hand that gave form to our earliest concepts of heroism and adventure.

During the "golden" years of illustration in America, from the mid-1870s through the first decades of this century, many capable and creative talents found their way into print. Fewer were the really great ones, such as Winslow Homer, Howard Pyle, or Frederic Remington. Certainly, Newell Convers Wyeth was one of the "greats." Through forty-two years of illustrating, from 1903 until his death in 1945, Wyeth created a large body of important and lasting works—nearly four thousand in all. We now have at hand a valuable and comprehensive record cataloguing the products of this remarkable career, a career well worth examining.

When N. C. Wyeth arrived at Wilmington, Delaware, in 1902, the Howard Pyle School of Art had already gained wide and enthusiastic acclaim in the two short years since its inception. Pyle soon found in his new pupil an enthusiasm for learning coupled with a youthful impatience to put that learning to practical use. In the master, Wyeth found a rare individual of uncommon understanding and noble ideals.

At the very heart of Pyle's teaching was his concept of "Mental Projection." It was through this means, potentially, that one might sense fully whatever needed portraying on canvas. "One must live in the picture," Pyle stressed. Later, in his own teaching, Wyeth was to convey the same idea with expressions such as, "Don't just paint a sleeve—become the arm!" Something of the difference in the personalities of the two men is perhaps suggested in those brief statements, as well as a hint at the qualities that might be anticipated in their works. In Pyle's art can be perceived a distillation of the intellect; Wyeth's, on the other hand, seems forged by inner blows of an emotional urge. We might look, for comparison, to the separate series of masterful illustrations each did for the rollicking tales of *Robin Hood,* and perhaps find there those individual qualities. Nevertheless, like his mentor, Wyeth loved accuracy and authenticity in recording historical fact, but never became pedantic or a slave to mere detail. He always placed spirit above clinical fact.

N. C. Wyeth joyfully embraced life's daily experiences with an exuberance that is unmistakable, as is revealed in his art. Even as a boy, he enjoyed the labors that exposed him to the forces of nature. "My brothers and I were brought up on a farm, and from the time I could walk I was conscripted into doing every conceivable chore that there was to do about the place. This early training gave me a vivid appreciation of the part the body plays in action. Now, when I paint a figure on horseback, a man plowing, or a woman buffeted by the wind, I have an acute bodily sense of the muscle-strain, the feel of the hickory handle, or the protective bend of head and squint of eye that each pose involves. After painting action scenes, I have ached for hours because of having put myself in the other fellow's shoes as I realized him on canvas."

Because of his intense concentration on working from the costumed figure during his student years and after, Wyeth rarely needed to use models in his later work. Instead, he used his own figure to work out the needed expression or stance. An example that clearly demonstrates this is in one of the illustrations for *Drums,* in which the story's main character, Johnny Fraser, is depicted standing "On the Sea Wall with John Paul Jones." There, back to us, is the figure of the artist himself!

When the occasion did require a model, the individual was most often a member of the artist's family. As the family expanded, the choice of age and subject type increased, providing a convenient pool of readily-available assistants. The smiling Priscilla portrayed in *The Courtship of Miles Standish* and the beautiful dark-haired heroine of *Vandemark's Folly* are one and the same model, the patient and cooperative *Mrs.* N. C. Wyeth. And the handsome young gallant striking the required poses for *Anthony Adverse* is son Andrew, who gained through such experiences much helpful insight, soon to be similarly employed in his own celebrated works.

As N. C. Wyeth's art gained national recognition, marked especially by the advent of the great *Treasure Island* series in 1911, and with the issuing of each succeeding title of the Scribner's Classics, it is not surprising that he frequently was called upon to present his personal views on art and his advice to young illustrators. This he did, as Pyle had done before him, with a deep sense of responsibility. Fortunately, he had developed the ability of expressing himself in words almost as vividly as in pictures. On one occasion he remarked, "To a great number, art is principally an escape from life (a very sterile pleasure indeed) and they fail lamentably to grasp the fact that the cultivation of life through the arts is a vital need to inspired living." In a writing directed to students, he advised, "The genuineness of the artist's work depends upon the genuineness of the artist's living. In other words, art is not what you do, it is what you are. We cannot in art produce a fraction more than what we are."

In all that he did, he evidenced a profound reverence for the simple, familiar, and common things and experiences, finding fresh inspiration in his daily contacts with all life around him.

With this almost mystical view, and having spent his boyhood near Concord, it is not surprising that as he matured he was drawn strongly to the writings of Thoreau. This devotion continued throughout the greater part of his life. "Thoreau's tremendous force to me as an artist," he wrote to a friend, "lies within his ability to boil up the little into the big! He demonstrates the fact that to elevate the little into the great is genius."

N. C. Wyeth's art was ever evolving. In scanning the scope and changing style of his works, from first to last it is nothing short of remarkable. The talent which in its youth gave us "The Indian in His Solitude" and the memorable images of Bill Bones and Blind Pew was the same expansive genius that later could forge onto canvas the "Battle of Wilson's Creek" and "Wallace's

Vision"—and later still—"Walden Revisited" and "Nightfall." The record of his career provides an exciting view of a magnificent performance.

Just as N. C. Wyeth was a vital force in illustration, illustration has been a major force in American art, contributing much of what can be identified as genuinely original or innovative in painting idioms. Its position no longer needs defending.

Illustration today, however, is languishing, pale in the shadow of the vitality imparted by Homer, Remington, Pyle, and Wyeth. It has either lost or deserted its public, a public sated with overexposure to glossy photographic images.

In the face of the current dissipation and the plight of publishing generally, it is perhaps a phenomenon worth noting that the Wyeth-illustrated classics are still being reissued through popular demand, and rare first editions are sought by an ever-increasing number of avid collectors.

Though N. C. Wyeth spent the major portion of his life painting in the Brandywine country he most loved, he has passed on to us a testament of steadfast devotion to the highest of ideals in his art. His works will stand the test of time.

RICHARD LAYTON
Wilmington, Delaware
May 1972

N.C.WYETH

Howard Pyle at his easel (1898)
Courtesy of the Delaware Art Museum

1

Howard Pyle's World of Illustration

No ATTEMPT can be made to write about Newell Convers Wyeth without mention of the man who gave so much of himself in molding the character and creative gifts of the many young people associated with him in those years often termed the Golden Age of American Illustration.

During this period that had known Frederic Remington, A. B. Frost, E. W. Kemble, Charles Dana Gibson, and many other notable illustrators, one man stood apart. That man was Howard Pyle, renowned artist, classic writer, and profound student. His accomplishments were great and varied, but small when compared to his unselfish dedication to the schooling and training of a group of young, enthusi-astic, and talented budding artists who were destined to make a priceless contribution to American art for decades.

Howard Pyle was at his productive peak that October of 1894 when he agreed to give "A Course in Practical Illustration" at the Drexel Institute of Art, Science and Industry in Philadelphia. At the time he had more commitments than he could handle and was absorbed in ideas for future projects as well. Why, then, did he decide to devote precious and lucrative time to training young people in the field of art? There were a number of reasons.

Pyle was wholeheartedly dedicated to his profession. He had noted with concern that many an apparently gifted young man and

←

THE GIANT
Oil on canvas, h:72, w:60
Signed lower left: N. C. Wyeth 1923
Courtesy of the Westtown School, Westtown,
 Pennsylvania
The children (*from left*) are William Clothier Engle
 (in whose memory the mural was painted), Henriette
 Wyeth, Ann Wyeth, Andrew Wyeth, Nathaniel Wyeth,
 and Carolyn Wyeth.

woman made an artistic debut in a flame of brilliance that all too soon flickered and faded. He felt that this decline was basically due to a lack of sound training, for he firmly believed that talent alone, without the basics of an education in the field of illustration, could not bring success in that profession. The underlying fault, he thought, was that the art schools of that period believed in the routine of endless hours spent copying from the classic plaster cast and drawing from the model. This method might produce skilled artists and be a necessary part of training, but it did not produce the creativity that was all important for an illustrator. So, with his vast experience and his resolve to help young people get started on the right road, Pyle set out to develop a course that could produce men "who would paint living pictures rather than dead, inert matter in which there was not one single spark of real life."[1]

Steadfast in his belief that illustration was the basic art and the one that must be conquered before an artist could reach out and specialize, Pyle said: "Today I often find that the word 'illustrator' is regarded with contempt by a few who claim a higher position as being 'painters'. Such an attitude I cannot respect."[2]

The course at Drexel began on a simple note, a once-a-week gathering on Saturday afternoons at two o'clock. Only advanced students were accepted, and only after an evaluation of their ability. Approximately thirty students attended the initial course. Among them were three who were, within the not too distant future, to become outstanding in the field of illustration. Surprisingly for that day, two of these were women, Jessie Wilcox Smith and Elizabeth Shippen Green. The lone male in the trio was the fabulous Maxfield Parrish.

For its first two years, the Howard Pyle course was largely a trial run, but its success was so astounding that the circular of the School of Illustration for the 1896/7 semester announced:

After two years of experiment in conducting a class in Illustration at the Drexel Institute, under the direction of Mr. Howard Pyle, the results have been such as to warrant the Institute in extending considerably the scope of this branch of its work in the Art Department.[3]

Pyle's original intent had been to teach a small group for a few hours once a week—such a schedule would permit him to carry out his commitments to his publishers. But the course grew like the legendary beanstalk. The enlarged curriculum for the year 1896/7 dropped the original Saturday class and replaced it with Monday and Friday classes. Why was the course so successful? Originally, it may have been merely the magic of the Howard Pyle name that drew students, but as the aspiring illustrators promptly became aware of the high standards of performance demanded by their teacher, they recognized how uniquely valuable the course might prove to their future work.

Though the course was radical for its time, the principles it adhered to were simple. As already mentioned, the pupil gained admittance by passing an examination of his drawing ability; he was supposed to know the techniques of draftsmanship already. Beyond that, it was Pyle's main objective to teach his students how to project themselves, to put mind and body completely into the story to be told on canvas. Only in this way, Pyle was convinced, could the student create and not imitate. A second and no less important part of the course was mastering the technique of composition. His own experience had taught him that this was all-important for success.

Perhaps the most valuable contribution Howard Pyle made to his young charges was his own nature and character. His personality, his dedication to his art, and his deep spiritual sincerity influenced and inspired all those who studied under him. He was far more than a great teacher. He was counselor, guide, and—most important—a sincere friend.

Under Pyle's influence, the School of Illustration at Drexel soon expanded to the point where he felt he could no longer carry on the high ideals and standards that were his original intent. The classes grew too large, and he felt that only a minority of the students really had the qualities to carry on in the illustrating profession. He could not give these few the attention they merited without being accused of showing favoritism, and this he could not abide. In February of 1900 he wrote his resignation:

My time is very valuable, and now that I feel myself quite matured in my art knowledge, I think it both unwise and wrong to expend my time in general teaching. The great majority of a class as large as that which I teach at the Drexel Institute is hopelessly lacking in all possibility of artistic attainment. There are only one or two who can really receive the instruction which I give. To impart this instruction to these two or three who can receive it appears to be unfair to the others who do not receive such particular instruction. This apparent favoritism upon my part must inevitably tend to disrupt the Art School or to make the large majority discontented with the instruction which they receive in contrast with that which the few receive; nor is it possible to assure such discontented pupils that that which I give them is far more abundant and far more practical than that which they would receive from any other Art Institute—the fact remains in their minds that they are not given that which I give to the other pupils and that apparently there is favoritism in the class.[4]

When Howard Pyle resigned from Drexel, he had already formulated plans to open his own school in Wilmington, Delaware. The new school was to be built around those few exceptional young people who had studied under him at Drexel. By his personal invitation they followed him to Wilmington—Stanley Arthurs, Philip Hoyt, James McBurney, Ethel Franklin Betts, Sarah Stillwell, Ellen Thompson, and Frank E. Schoonover.

The program he intended to follow at Wilmington was basically the same as the one he had so successfully formulated at Drexel. He was, however, determined that the enrollment would remain limited to a carefully selected few. Those young artists who were capable of absorbing his theories of mental projection and of composition would have the greatest chance of working under his guidance. There were no entrance examinations as such. The student was simply advised to submit "examples" of his work: "When you apply for admission to the school, don't send me 'samples' of your work, send 'examples'. There are no 'samples' of art."[5]

These examples were carefully reviewed by Howard Pyle personally. If they showed "imagination and enthusiasm, artistic ability and drawing technique," the student could consider himself fortunate. This was the entrance examination, and as simple as it appeared on the surface it was an exacting test to meet. Of the hundreds of young people who applied to him for admittance, few were accepted.

It is our gain that one who was, was Newell Convers Wyeth.

RIP VAN WINKLE

Wyeth's Student Years

NEWELL CONVERS WYETH was born in Needham, Massachusetts, on October 22, 1882.

Needham shared the colonial flavor of nearby towns whose names are better known because of historical events that brought them into more prominent focus—Plymouth, Salem, Lexington, Concord, and, of course, Boston. In the time of Wyeth's childhood, Needham was still a quiet suburban community, agricultural in flavor. The Wyeth farm, nestled on the banks of the Charles, had been operated by succeeding generations of the family ever since the homestead had been built in 1730.

Of his early life on the farm, Wyeth later recalled:

One of the greatest assets in my life has been the early training I received at home. My brothers and myself were expected to do every conceivable form of work about the home and in it. I find the earliest years of my life are the source of my best inspiration.[1]

The "chores" young Newell performed as a boy were to prove invaluable in his work in later

Sketchbook Self-portrait (circa 1896)
Drawing on paper, h:7, w:4½
Unsigned
Courtesy of Mr. & Mrs. Anton Kamp

SELF-PORTRAIT (1900)
Oil on canvas, h:24½, w:19½
Unsigned
Courtesy of Andrew Wyeth

years: he knew from personal experience the arrangement of a saddle on a horse, how to hold a scythe or wheat cradle, the proper method of log splitting and plowing.

Like most children, young Wyeth displayed an early interest in drawing pictures, but unlike most youngsters, who gradually are diverted to other pursuits, he continued to draw.

> It's a strange thing, but I seemed to lack all that imaginative stuff that most kids have. I was quiet and my mother said I was observant, but I saw things as they were, and not as the fairy tales paint them.[2]

By the time Newell had reached his mid-teens, he knew that he wanted to be an artist. He must certainly have discussed this with those closest to him, but it was his mother who was the most sympathetic of anyone. When he was sixteen he was about to be sent off to New Hampshire to work as a farmhand, but she intervened and insisted that he be given an opportunity to develop his talent, and she prevailed. He was sent to the Massachusetts Normal Art School. There, Richard Andrew recognized the boy's natural inclination toward illustration and encouraged him in that direction. Wyeth said later:

> I rose to his advice like a trout to a straw and soon attached myself to C. W. Reed, who was a book illustrator with a studio on West Street.[3]

Next the young man attended the Eric Pape School of Art, and in the spring of 1902 he began to study with Charles H. Davis in Mystic, Connecticut. However, though he had both talent and motivation, in his inexperience he did not realize that he was not receiving the proper training in the art of illustration. Twenty years later he was to mention this in an article he wrote:

> To destroy individuality seems to be the main function of the illustrating class-room today. To turn the embryo mind face to face with technical methods, style, and the restrictions of publishing processes which all figure so prominently in composition, before he is able to feel the divine urge which comes only from a sound initiation into nature's truths is, to my mind, the

HOWARD PYLE'S STUDIO (March 1903)
Oil on canvas, h:12, w:8
Unsigned
Courtesy of Mr. & Mrs. Richard Layton

principal reason why such a tragic percentage of art students fail.

> I know from experience what it means to answer that premature call for pictures. The second week I spent in an art school I was requested to do this as part of the routine, and how I suffered for that entire year. I noted that cleverness was rewarded, stunty and affected methods got the applause, so naturally I concluded that my salvation lay in my ability to develop a new "stunt".

Then he reflected back through the years to the time he was given the opportunity to study under Howard Pyle, and continued:

> Only rarely does a fortunate student happen upon a helpful mind, one sufficiently strong and sympathetic to help him back into the real light.[4]

While Wyeth was a student at the Eric Pape School of Art, two of his close friends and classmates, Clifford Ashley and Henry Peck, were accepted as trial students in the Howard Pyle School of Art in Wilmington. They urged him to send some of his work to Pyle for evaluation. Because of the limitations Pyle placed on the size of his class, young Wyeth felt he had little hope of acceptance, but he sent his drawings anyhow. To his delight, he was summoned to Wilmington.

It was "one of those blue and golden days in October. The air was sharp and keen,"[5] and it was also his twentieth birthday, October 22, 1902, a day he would long remember.

My most vivid recollecton of Howard Pyle was gained during the first five minutes I knew him. He stood with his back to the blazing and crackling logs in his studio fireplace, his legs spaced apart, his arms akimbo. His towering figure seemed to lift to greater heights with the swiftly ascending smoke and sparks from the hearth behind him.

I was young, ambitious and impressionable. For years, it seemed, I had dreamed of this meeting. Success in winning this master's interest and sympathy to the cause of my own artistic advancement seemed so much to ask, so remote, such a vain hope. But here I was at last, seated before him in the very room in which were born so many of the pictures I had breathlessly admired from boyhood. Paintings and drawings that had long since become a living and indispensable part of my own life.

And as Howard Pyle stood there, talking gently but with unmistakable emphasis, his large and genial countenance hypno-

tized me. My rapid reflections were swept beyond the actual man. It was bewildering. I heard every modulation of his voice and I took note of his every word. Occasionally I would answer a question. I remember all this clearly.

I had come to him, as many had before me, for his help and guidance, and his first words to me will forever ring in my ears as an unceasing appeal to my conscience: "My boy, you have come here for help. Then you must live your best and work hard!" His broad, kindly face looked solemn as he spoke these words, and from that moment I knew that he meant infinitely more to me than a mere teacher of illustration.[6]

The interview ended, and Wyeth was accepted as a pupil on probation.

I speculated for a week and then decided to stay on with him and was assigned a place to live and work. I had expected to hear Howard Pyle enthuse over my drawings, and to find him pass over them casually just about knocked the props from under me. The one note of encouragement was his interest in my background of New England living and the amount of enthusiasm I showed in wanting to come to him.[7]

The Howard Pyle School of Art was born of a thorough conviction that young people who had a truly earnest desire should be given the opportunity to benefit from the guidance and experience of one of the most highly respected and sought-after illustrators of the day. Pyle's motives were completely unselfish. There were no entrance fees or tuition at his school. The cost of materials and studio rental were nominal. But the requirements were stringent—imagination, artistic ability, a sense of color and drawing, youth, intelligence, and earnestness of purpose. Howard Pyle demanded hard work, but he also had a deep understanding of the needs of the young.

Howard Pyle (center) with a group of his students in 1903: George Harding, Gordon McCouch, Thornton Oakley, N. C. Wyeth, and Allen True. Courtesy of the Delaware Art Museum

There are many in this world who radiate the feeling of love and earnestness of purpose, but who have not the faculty or power to impart the rudiments of accomplishment. There is nothing in this world that will inspire the purpose of youth like the combined strength of spirituality and practical assistance. It gives the young student a definite clue, as it were, to the usefulness of being upright and earnest. Howard Pyle abounded in this power and lavished it upon all who were earnest.[8]

Mr. Pyle's inordinate ability as a teacher lay primarily in his sense of penetration; to read beneath the crude lines on paper the true purpose, to detect therein our real inclinations and impulses. Wretched, unstable drawing would quickly assume coherent shape and character; raw and uncouth conceptions would become softened and refined, until in a marvelously short time the student would find himself and emerge upon that elevation of thinking and feeling which would disclose before him a limitless horizon of possibilities.

The most striking feature of Mr. Pyle's teaching was his composition class. It met Monday evenings and each student was expected to bring a composition. This was a rough charcoal drawing made without

MAN WITH A PISTOL (1903)
Oil on canvas, h:29, w:22½
Signed lower right: N. C. Wyeth
Courtesy of Mrs. A. J. Sordoni, Jr.

models and intended to indicate a picture we wished to paint.[9]

The power of Howard Pyle stemmed from his wonderful interest in life: whether you painted it, or wrote about it, or lived it, the result must be vital, red-blooded, worthwhile. This love of life came through clearly in his work and in his teaching. According to former students, he used to tell them:

"It is easy enough to learn to draw; it is very difficult to learn to think." What he meant to express was, for us younger art students, the enormous difficulty of putting into a picture the essential qualities of deep feeling, sympathy and sincerity [that] far outweighed the lesser difficulty of accurately

Howard Pyle and students gathered in front of the old gristmill, Chadds Ford. Summer instruction was held here from 1898 to 1903.
Courtesy of the Delaware Art Museum

INTO TOWN FROM THE SOUTH
"Working for Fame," by John M. Oskison
Leslie's Popular Monthly, August 1903

learning to draw. Picture-making to Mr. Pyle was not making pictures of life but really putting down the life itself. He used to urge us to write as well as paint. "If you can picture life," he would say, "you can describe it."[10]

For the next four months young Wyeth put all his energies into his work. His reward came when his teacher informed him that his probation days were over and that he was now a full-fledged member of the Howard Pyle School. The young student was elated, but in sober reflection he later recalled little incidents that were especially meaningful in his striving to succeed and be accepted as a student under Pyle:

Who of his associates can forget the sombre hours in the gloaming when, after a hard day's work before our easels, we sat in the class studio, watching with blissful content the fading square patch of the skylight, warm with the light of the after-glow, violet, then a dim, dusty gray? Who of us did not thrill in those moments when suddenly we heard the dull jar of the master's door, the slight after-rattle of the brass knocker as it closed, and the faint sound of his foot-steps on the brick walk? And then, as we had hoped, our own door was opened and he entered in the dim light and sat among us.

I can see him now, the soft overhead light faintly modeling his large, generous features, his massive forehead and deep-set eyes and the prominent cheek-bones. Breaking the tense silence he would talk in a soft, hushed voice of art, its relation to life, his aspirations, his aspirations for us. Only too soon he would say goodnight and leave us in the darkness, and, as we felt for our hats and coats, each one knew that every jaw was set to do better in life and work in some measure to express our deep gratitude to the one who had inspired us.[11]

Once young N. C. Wyeth had become an accepted member of the Howard Pyle School of Art, he took more time to look around. Older students, he noted, were already starting to carve profitable careers for themselves as illustrators, and so he decided to make an effort in that direction himself. He did a rough in oil in the grand manner—a wild bronco, pitching and twisting to unseat his rider—and from it made a finished canvas. This he submitted to the Curtis

AS BROADWELL RACED WEST
"Working for Fame," by John M. Oskison
Leslie's Popular Monthly, August 1903

BRONCO BUSTER
Oil on canvas, h:26, w:18
Signed lower right: Sketch 1902
Courtesy of the Delaware Art Museum

Publishing Company. On January 8, 1903, he could write: "The *Post* went wild over my cover and gave me $60 for it."

Several weeks later, he was disappointed to receive a check for $50 instead of the amount agreed upon, but his disappointment was short-lived when his painting finally appeared as the cover for *The Saturday Evening Post* of February 21, 1903. In the exuberance of youth, he felt he had arrived. Indeed, to have had a cover accepted and published by *The Saturday Evening Post* was no small accomplishment by any standard.

Wyeth did not rest on his laurels. He kept busily at work on other illustrations for other periodicals, and they were being accepted. The

March 1903 issue of *Success* published a story, "The Romance of the 'C.P.'," by Edwin Markham with an accompanying illustration by Wyeth. Untitled, it represented two surveyors at work during the construction of the Central Pacific Railroad, the theme of the story. The November and December issues of *Success* also contained Wyeth illustrations, as did the August 1903 issue of *Leslie's Popular Monthly*, for the story "Working for Fame" by John M. Oskison. This prompt recognition did not go to young Newell's head, however—he was well aware he still had much to learn from Howard Pyle.

Some of Wyeth's warmest memories pertained to this period of his life. There were parties. There were excursions into the surrounding area to rummage through old furniture and antique shops in search of interesting props and seasoned mahogany panels to paint upon. And there were frequent trips, especially in the warmer weather, to Mr. Pyle's home at Chadds Ford, Pennsylvania, where the students could roam the hills and woods of the historic Brandywine valley.

It was this remote village that brings back the fondest memories to the most of us. In a large roomy house that nestled in the trees beneath a great hill, within a stone's throw of General Lafayette's headquarters and surrounded by his wife and family of six children, I have the keenest and most enjoyable remembrances of him. Many, many jolly evenings did we spend before his crackling log fire, eating nuts, telling stories, or best of all listening to reminiscenses of his own or accounts from his vast store of knowledge of history and of people. His intimacy with colonial his-

tory, and his sympathetic and authentic translations into pictures of those times are known and loved the world over.

How can I tell in words the life of the thirty or more of us who lived in these historic, rolling hills, working in the spacious and grain scented rooms of an old grist mill. To recall the unceasing rush of the water as it flowed over the huge, silent wheel beneath us thrills me through. And here the teacher kept his class intact for five glorious summers.[12]

Let it not be thought that the students in the Howard Pyle School of Art were different from other youths in their late teens and early twenties. They had their escapades too. One such incident was recalled by Wyeth during an interview in later years. It involved a fountain in Wilmington containing a sculptured cupid and a crane. In their "experienced minds," the students considered it bad art, badly proportioned and rather stupid looking.

So they improved its strangeness by adding a gay ballet skirt in many colors. Now there were certain authorities who did not approve of Cupids in ballet skirts and they took it upon themselves to analyze the paint thereon. Plainly it was from an artist's pallet, so the next thing the Cupid knew, a more or less contrite circle of art students, overseen by several laymen of the community, was industriously hiding the ballet skirt under a generous coat of white paint. The application of this paint was done so thoroughly that in a few days both Cupid and Crane were a mass of leprous-looking blisters. The very words are painful to think of, how much more so than the fountain itself. So of course there was nothing to be done but for the students to snatch it from its moorings and suspend it from a bridge over the river. The police, fearing that Cupid and his Crane might fall someday on a small foot-bridge that was nearby, cut the rope. Thus it came about that the fountain was assigned to complete and irretrievable oblivion.[13]

THE ROMANCE OF THE "C.P."
EDWIN MARKHAM

TWO SURVEYORS
"The Romance of the 'C.P.'" by Edwin Markham
Success, March 1903

N. C. Wyeth in the costume of Little John at the Howard Pyle Studio, March 4, 1904. The occasion was a banquet the students gave their teacher. From the Blanche Swayne Collection, Brandywine River Museum

FIGHTING THE FIRE FROM THE TELEPHONE POLES
Charcoal on paper
Signed lower right: Wyeth/Balto.
Feb–1904–
"The Great Baltimore Fire"
Collier's Weekly, February 13, 1904

AN EXHIBITION OF SELF EFFACEMENT . . .
"Take at the Flood," by Vincent Harper
The Saturday Evening Post, June 3, 1905

Howard Pyle believed in practical experience as part of the maturing process. An occasion to put this belief into practice came about quite suddenly. The disastrous Baltimore fire, which occurred in the early part of February 1904, was headline news. The Sunday morning of the fire a half dozen of the students were grouped around Mr. Pyle on the steps of his studio discussing the conflagration when he suddenly hit upon the idea of their going to Baltimore. As Wyeth later wrote, "If it became his impulse to carry out an idea, a scheme in our

THE MINUTE MEN
"Here once the embattled farmers stood and fired
the shot heard round the world."–Emerson
The Delineator, October 1905

. . . TRADING FROM THE BATTLEMENTED WALLS . . .
"An Antiente Greate Companie," by Arthur E. McFarland
The Saturday Evening Post, November 1905

behalf, a trip, a banquet, nothing could stand in his way to accomplish it."[14]

Howard Pyle went to the phone, called the Collier office in New York, and arranged that his students cover the fire as sketch artists for the magazine. He put seventy-five dollars into their hands and they were shortly on their way.

Wyeth later commented: "Our sketches did not prove of any great value, although several were published, but our friend had thrust us in the way of some unique and valuable experience."[15]

An examination of numerous copies of *Collier's Weekly* issued during that period failed at first to bring to light any sketches of the Baltimore fire by the students. However, a drawing

by N. C. Wyeth was printed in the magazine on February 13, 1904. Its rarity is due to the fact that it appeared in a separate supplement, and apparently fewer of these supplements were saved than of the regular issues.

The year 1904 was a relatively successful one for the young illustrator. His work also appeared in *Leslie's Popular Monthly, Metropolitan, The Saturday Evening Post, Scribner's,* and *Success.* One painting he began early that year merits special mention, though it did not appear in a magazine until the following year. Of it, he wrote: "I'm now deep in a successful picture of 'How the embattled farmers stood and fired the shot heard round the world.' I never enjoyed making a picture more in my life."

N. C. Wyeth, Stanley Arthurs, and Frank E. Schoonover were photographed in Atlantic City, New Jersey, by Allen True in 1906.
Courtesy of Frank E. Schoonover

THE BALL . . . ROLLED STRAIGHT TOWARD THE GOAL
Oil on canvas, h:34, w:24
Signed lower right: N. C. Wyeth '04
"Skiffington's Pony," by George Hibbard
The Metropolitan, October 1904
Courtesy of Kennedy Galleries, Inc., New York

This picture appeared in *The Delineator* in October 1905, but the appeal of the subject apparently remained with Wyeth, for he painted a strongly similar scene for one of the U.S. Treasury Department (bank holiday) posters he illustrated nearly two decades later.

The first book to contain Wyeth illustrations—*Boys of St. Timothy's* by Arthur Stanwood Pier—also made its appearance in 1904, but that year was memorable for other reasons too. In August he was graduated from the Howard Pyle School of Art and on his own, and in September he made his first trip west.

The Saturday Evening Post had commissioned Wyeth to illustrate a western story, and Howard Pyle also managed to convince *Scribner's Magazine* that the down-to-earth experience of a western trip for Wyeth might eventually prove advantageous to them, since he would be better able to provide authentic west-

ern illustrations for the magazine on future assignments. The result was that the *Post* and *Scribner's* jointly sponsored Wyeth's trip, an investment that ultimately more than paid for itself. His later illustrations for stories dealing with the West were without parallel for years, with the possible exception of the work Frederic Remington did exclusively for *Collier's Weekly.* It must be remembered, however, that the Remington paintings appearing in this magazine were, for the most part, documentary representations of an era long past.

The next chapter dwells on the work Wyeth did in the field of western illustration. His return East after the months spent in the Southwest did not affect his continuing in Wilmington under the guidance of Howard Pyle. For the next several years, in fact, he remained a member of that close-knit group of former students who were becoming well-known professionals.

Four Navajo studies young Wyeth made in November 1904.
Courtesy of Mrs. Andrew Wyeth

ROPING HORSES IN THE CORRAL
Oil on canvas, h:22, w:32
Signed lower left: N. C. Wyeth/Hash-knife Ranch/Colo
    1904
Courtesy of Dr. & Mrs. William A. Morton, Jr.

3

N.C.'s West

Anyone familiar with the entire span of
N. C. Wyeth's work cannot fail to be aware that
even in his earliest drawings he showed a decided liking for picturing the Old West as he
visualized it in his imagination. Like so many of
us, he was completely fascinated by that era
of American history.

It is reasonable to suspect that Wyeth's
early inspiration for depicting the Old West
may have been that great artist of the western
scene Frederic Remington. Certainly, during his
growing-up years, young Newell must have been
exposed to many of Remington's pictures, for
that indefatigable artist produced an endless
stream of illustrations for all the leading periodicals of the day—*Harper's Weekly, Harper's
Monthly, Century, Scribner's, Outing, Cosmopolitan, Youth's Companion,* and others. Later,
while Wyeth was a student at the Howard Pyle
School of Art, Remington's greatest works were

AN ALMIGHTY EXCITING RACE
"Arizona Nights," by Stewart Edward White
McClure's Magazine, March 1906

HAHN PULLED HIS GUN AND SHOT HIM THROUGH
THE MIDDLE
"Arizona Nights," by Stewart Edward White
McClure's Magazine, April 1906

appearing as full-color reproductions in *Collier's Weekly*. During those years too, it is known that whenever Wyeth had one of his infrequent opportunities to travel to New York, he never missed the chance to visit art galleries or the current exhibits, which at times were devoted exclusively to Remington's paintings.[1]

Although most of Wyeth's own first published works were strictly western in character, he had never been to the West to absorb its flavor and atmosphere and to gain the firsthand knowledge necessary to paint it with complete assurance and authenticity. Quite naturally, therefore, he welcomed the opportunity to make the western trip mentioned at the end of the preceding chapter, and he set out promptly in the latter part of September, the month following his graduation. For practical purposes, there was nothing else he could have done that would have proved more valuable, particularly since he

then seemed determined to do illustrations for western stories. By going there himself, he could observe with the keen eye of a good artist the people, the color, and the landscape.

During his visit in the West, he followed the trails into the mountains and the cattle country. He took part in all its work and pleasures, and managed to get a real taste of all the activities available, from carrying the mail and driving a stage to riding the range. He spent time at remote trading posts and with various Indian tribes, absorbing their customs and way of life and making careful observations of all he saw. And when he returned home, not only were his portfolios crammed with sketches; he also brought back saddles, bridles, guns, rugs, costumes, and regalia of all sorts for use in painting future pictures.

In the January 1906 issue of *Scribner's Magazine* it was noted that Mr. Wyeth had just

I SAW HIS HORSE JUMP BACK DODGIN' A
RATTLESNAKE OR SOMETHIN'
Oil on canvas, h:36, w:23¾
Signed lower left: N. C. Wyeth '05
"Arizona Nights," by Stewart Edward White
McClure's Magazine, April 1906
Courtesy of Southern Arizona Bank & Trust Company, Tucson

LISTEN TO WHAT I'M TELLIN' YE!
"Arizona Nights," by Stewart Edward White
McClure's Magazine, May 1906

N. C. Wyeth on horseback in Colorado, October 1904.
Courtesy of Frank E. Schoonover

returned from the West. The story of his experiences "in the cattle country engaged in the work of a cowboy in order to become thoroughly familiar with his subject" would be published in the not too distant future, the magazine promised. In strict accuracy, however, it must be pointed out that Wyeth had not "just returned from the West." He had returned at the end of December 1904.

Wyeth's article "A Day with the Round-Up" appeared in the March 1906 issue. Its color illustrations established him as a first-rate portrayer of the western scene, and his narrative proved him to be equally adept at writing. On the pages immediately following are reproduced both "A Day with the Round-Up" and the fine paintings that accompanied it in that memorable issue of *Scribner's Magazine.*

[35]

THE LAST STAND
Oil on canvas, h:50⅛, w:34
Signed lower left: N. C. Wyeth '06
"The Story of Montana," by C. P. Connolly
McClure's Magazine, September 1906
Courtesy of Southern Arizona Bank & Trust Company,
    Tucson

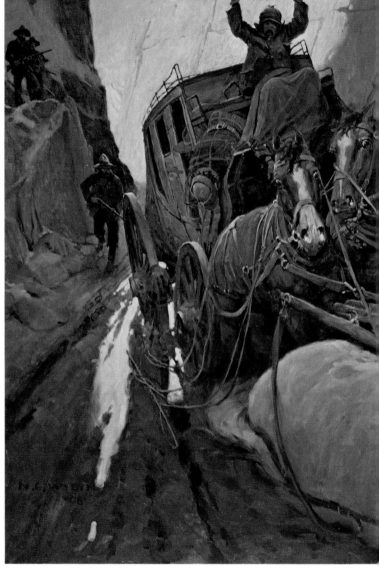

HANDS UP (*Holdup in the Canyon*)
Oil on canvas, h:43, w:30
Signed lower left: N. C. Wyeth '06
"The Story of Montana," by C. P. Connolly
McClure's Magazine, August 1906
Courtesy of Walter Reed Bimson, Valley National Bank,
    Phoenix, Arizona

THE PROSPECTOR
Oil on canvas, h:47, w:29¾
Signed lower left: N. C. Wyeth '06
"The Story of Montana," by C. P. Connolly
McClure's Magazine, September 1906
Courtesy of Southern Arizona Bank & Trust Company, Tucson

I HEREBY PRONOUNCE YUH MAN AND WIFE!
Oil on canvas, h:38, w:25
Signed lower left: N. C. Wyeth '07
"The Misadventures of Cassidy," by Edward S. Moffat
McClure's Magazine, May 1908
Courtesy of Mr. & Mrs. Joseph E. Levine

THE ADMIRABLE OUTLAW (My English friend thought
    it was a hold-up)
Oil on canvas, h:38, w:23½
Signed lower right: N. C. Wyeth, '06
"The Admirable Outlaw," by M'Cready Sykes
Scribner's Magazine, November 1906
Courtesy of the National Cowboy Hall of Fame and Western
    Heritage Center, Oklahoma City

[37]

RACING FOR DINNER

THE LEE OF THE GRUB-WAGON

ABOVE THE SEA OF ROUND, SHINY BACKS
THE THIN LOOPS SWIRLED

A Day with the Round-Up *

GROPING and feeling my way out from beneath three or four thick blankets and turning back to the stiff dewy tarpaulin, I peered into the gloom of early morning. The sweeping breeze of the plains brushed cool and fresh against my face. Shapeless forms of still sleeping men loomed black against the low horizon. Near by I saw the silhouetted form of the cook's thick legs and a big kettle swing before the light of the breakfast fire. I stared in wonderment about me—then my confused mind cleared and I remembered that it was the cow-camp of the night before.

I hurriedly pulled on my boots and rolled the great pile of still warm blankets into a huge bundle and tied them so with two shiny black straps. Dark figures were moving about the camp—some crawling from beneath heaps of tangled beds, others trundling their big ungainly rolls, lifted high on their backs, to the bed-wagon. And so I carried mine, joining the silent processions that moved, a vague, broken line in the growing light of the early morning. . . .

Then I joined the dark mass of men around a tin pail of water. The cow-punchers do not wash very much on the round-up. A slap of water to freshen the face, a vigorous wipe with a rough, wearisome towel, and the men were ready for their breakfast.

I joined them—a crowd seated in the lee of the grub-wagon. Everything was very quiet, save now and then the click of the

* The illustrations used here appeared with the original article published in *Scribner's Magazine,* March 1906.

[38]

spoons on the tin cups. They ate in silence, all unconscious of the rich yellow glow that was flooding the camp.

Then the quiet of the morning was broken by a soft rumbling that suddenly grew into a roar, and from a great floating cloud of golden dust the horse herd swung into the rope corral.

The men tossed the tin cups and plates in a heap near the big dish-pan. There was a scuffle for ropes and the work started with a rush. In the corral the horses surged from one side to the other, crowding and crushing within the small rope circle. Above the sea of round, shiny backs, the thin loops swirled and shot into volumes of dust; the men wound in and out of the restless mass, their keen eyes always following the chosen mounts. Then one by one they emerged from the dust, trailing very dejected horses. The whistling of ropes ceased, and with a swoop the horse herd burst from the corral to feed and rest under the watchful eye of the "wrangler."

By now we had all "saddled up" and mounted save "The Swede." . . .

We watched him as he led his mount into "open country," for the horse was known to be "bad." His name was "Billy Hell," and he looked every bit of that. He was white, of poor breed, and probably from the North.

"The Swede" walked to the nigh side of his horse and hung the stirrup for a quick mount. . . . The horse stood perfectly still, his hind legs drawn well under him; his head hung lower and lower, the ears were flattened back on his neck, and his tail was drawn down between his legs. "The Swede" tightened his belt, pulled his hat well down on his head, seized the cheek-strap of the bridle with one hand, and then carefully fitted his right over the shiny metal horn. For an instant he hesitated, and then, with a glance at the horse's head, he thrust his boot into the iron stirrup and swung himself with a mighty effort into the saddle.

The horse quivered and his eyes became glaring white spots. His huge muscles gathered and knotted themselves in angry response to the insult. Then with his great brutish strength he shot from the ground, bawling and squealing in a frantic struggle to free himself of the human burden. It was

like unto death. Eight times he pounded the hard ground, twisting and weaving and bucking in circles. The man was a part of the ponderous creaking saddle; his body responded to every movement of the horse, and as he swayed back and forth he cursed the horse again and again in his native tongue.

Then it was over. The cow-punchers nodded in approval and one of them dropped from his saddle and picked up "The Swede's" hat.

"Rounding-up" means to hunt and to bring together thousands of cattle scattered over a large part of the country known as the free range. For convenience in hunting them, the free range is divided into a number of imaginary sections. Into these sections the "boss" of an outfit sends the score or more of punchers, divided into squads of twos and threes, each squad covering a given section. This is called "riding the circle." . . .

[One] morning I started out with the others on the trail of some four or five hundred cattle.

We rode many miles, finding every little while a few of the cattle, some three or four, perhaps, standing quietly together in a gully. And as we pushed our way toward the distant camp of the outfit that had moved to the farther end of the section since we left, our herd gradually increased. With the added numbers the driving became difficult and we had to crowd our horses into the rear of the sullen and obstinate herd. We crossed, recrossed, and crossed again, yelling and cursing and cutting them with our quirts. The herd slowly surged ahead, above them floating a huge dense cloud of silvery dust that seemed to burn under the scorching sun of the plains.

It was well-nigh to noon before we saw a sharp dark line on the horizon that appeared and disappeared as we rose and fell along the undulating creek bottom. We knew the dark line to be the cattle already rounded up, and that we were late. But we had ridden the big circle that morning.

Our cattle soon saw the larger herd, and their heads went up, their tails stiffened, and they hurried to join the long dark line that began slowly to separate itself, as we drew nearer, into thousands of

BUCKING

ROUNDING-UP

cattle. And as we approached the main herd our cattle became more quiet. From the distant waiting multitude, as if in greeting, came a low, rumbling moan. The sound was faint; it became audible as the hot wind of the plains blew against my face, then it died away again—even as the wind spent itself on the long stretch of level plain.

Soon our cattle were on the run, and from a distance we stopped and watched the two herds merge one into the other. We were late, and the cow-punchers greeted us with jibes of all sorts, but we did not mind them, for the day's drive was over. To the right of the herd, some six hundred yards, stood the grub-wagon. Near by it I saw the smoke slowly rising from the cook's fire, and my appetite was made ravenous. Someone called, "Who says dinner?" and with that came the stinging crack of many quirts, the waving of hats, the whirling of ropes, and with the cow-boys' yells . . . there followed a wild, spectacular race for dinner. My horse was tired and streaked with sweat and white dust, his ears drooped, his tail hung limp, and he breathed hard, but I found myself in the first "bunch" at the finish. I jumped to the ground and hurriedly loosened the saddle and the soaking wet blanket from the horse's back and threw them on the ground to dry. Then I made for the soap-box of tin dishes and heaped my tin plate with meat and potatoes, and afterwards, by way of dessert, I had a small can of tomatoes. We sat in the shade of the grub-wagon, and along with the eating the men told of a large herd of antelope they had seen and of an unbranded cow they had brought in.

The "wrangler" ended the dinner. Into the camp he drove the horse herd, and from it fresh mounts were roped for the afternoon's work of "cutting out."

Cutting out is a hard, wearisome task. There were some six thousand cattle in the herd that had been rounded up that morning, and it was the work of the men to weave through that mass and to drive out certain brands known as the "Hash Knife," the "Pot Hook," the "Lazy L," and the like.

The herd that had been quiet was again in a turmoil, bellowing and milling, but it was kept within limited bounds and well "bunched" by the score or more of punchers outside.

My roan was well trained. He seemed to know by my guiding which cow I was after, and with incredible twisting and turning, well-directed kicks and bites, we would separate our cow from the writhing mass. I could faintly see my fellow-workers, flat silhouettes in the thickening dust, dodging and turning through the angry mass of heads and horns. My throat grew parched and dry, and the skin on my face became tight and stiffened by the settling dust. . . .

And so the afternoon passed quickly. I rode for the last time into the sullen herd, carefully watching for any remaining cows with the brand of the "Hash Knife." But I did not find any; my work was finished and I rested in the saddle, watching the remaining men complete their "cutting out," helping them now and then with a stray cow.

The sun was low and very red, the shadows were long and thin. The afternoon's work was completed, and I was glad. From across the plain I saw the red dust of a small herd that had already left camp on their long night journey to the home pasture, and I heard the faint yelps of the cowboys who were driving them. I dismounted

and with the knotted reins thrown over my arm, slowly walked back to the grub-wagon.

Some of the beds had already been unrolled, and I spread mine in a good level place. The ground was still hot and dry, but the air was rapidly becoming cooler, and the dew would soon fall.

In twos and threes the men came into camp, tired and dusty. We grouped about the wagons, sitting on the tongues, on unrolled beds, anywhere, perfectly contented, watching the cook prepare the evening meal. The odor of coffee scented the air, and I was hungry and tired as I never was before.

After the supper, a circle of men gathered about the camp-fire. The pulsing glow of many cigarettes spotted the darkness; the conversation slowly died with the fire, and one by one the dark, sombre faces disappeared from the light.

I was the last to leave. I crawled into my blankets and lay for a moment looking into the heavens and at the myriads of stars. I pulled the blankets up to my chin and then I felt the warmth of the ground creep through them. As I lay there I heard the faint singing of a night herder floating across the plains, and—for an instant—I thought of the morrow.

CUTTING OUT

A NIGHT HERDER

BILLY THE KID and BOB OLLINGER
Headpiece pen-and-ink drawings
"The Imitation Bad Man," by Emerson Hough
The Saturday Evening Post, January 20, 1906

The illustrations accompanying Wyeth's first-person narrative "A Day with the Round-Up" must have been to some extent responsible for the subsequent constant demand for his talents in the field of western illustration. But even before that article was published in 1906, commissions for western pictures had poured in. In fact, from the time he returned from the West at the end of 1904, publishers had besieged him with requests.

The Saturday Evening Post, which had helped to finance the western trip, engaged Wyeth to illustrate three stories by Emerson Hough. The first, titled "The Wasteful West," appeared in the issue of October 14, 1905. "The Imitation Bad Man" and "The Tenderfoot" appeared in the issues of January 20 and February 10, 1906, respectively.

Stewart Edward White's great western classic *Arizona Nights,* illustrated by Wyeth,

was originally published in three consecutive issues of *McClure's Magazine* in 1906. The first installment came out the same month as "A Day with the Round-Up"; the others, in the two months immediately following. Other notable Wyeth-illustrated short stories published in 1906 included "Bar 20 Range Yarns" by Clarence Edward Mulford (*Outing Magazine*) and "The Admirable Outlaw" by M'Cready Sykes (*Scribner's Magazine*).

Unlike *Arizona Nights,* which first appeared serially in a magazine and then was published as a book, four great western stories that Wyeth illustrated appeared only in book form. Two of these, *The Throwback* by Alfred Henry Lewis and *Whispering Smith* by Frank H. Spearman, were published in 1906; the other two, *Langford of the Three Bars* by Kate and Virgil D. Boyles and *Beth Norvell* by Randall Parrish, appeared in 1907. However, in spite of his prodigious output of western illustration from 1905 through 1907, he still found time to illustrate numerous other works that were not western in character.

Wyeth undertook the only other trip he ever made into the Far West in the early part of 1906. Of short duration, it was sponsored by *Outing Magazine,* for Wyeth to do a series of paintings for an article, "How They Opened the Snow Road," by W. M. Raine and W. H. Bader. Four color plates accompanied the article in the January 1907 issue of that magazine. (They are reproduced here in black and white in Chapter 8.)

Of the other great western illustrations Wyeth made over the next few years, some were done for stories and others stood by themselves as frontispiece color plates. Several of the best of these are reproduced in this chapter.

In the January 1909 issue of *Scribner's Magazine,* Wyeth's second autobiographical narrative appeared—"A Sheep-Herder of the South-West." This was drawn from recollections of his first trip west in 1904. The narrative was supplemented by several of his finest western works, more easel art than illustration.

HUNGRY, BUT STERN, ON THE DEPOT PLATFORM
"The Imitation Bad Man," by Emerson Hough
The Saturday Evening Post, January 20, 1906

A PARTNERSHIP FOR THE SAKE OF GREATER
    SAFETY
Oil on canvas, h:16, w:36
Signed lower left, Wyeth '05
"The Wasteful West," by Emerson Hough
The Saturday Evening Post, October 14, 1905

[43]

THE PAY STAGE
Oil on canvas, h:38, w:26½
Signed lower right: N. C. Wyeth, March '09
Scribner's Magazine, August 1910
Courtesy of Southern Arizona Bank & Trust Company, Tucson

NAVAJO HERDER IN THE FOOTHILLS
Oil on canvas, h:37¼, w:28¼
Signed lower right: N. C. Wyeth '08
Collection of Douglas Allen, Jr.

A Sheep-Herder of the South-West*

TWO GRAY HILLS," a remote Navajo Indian trading-post in New Mexico, looks for all the world like a play-village of tiny squared mud-cakes, built on a vast, undulating play-ground of sand hills, with a long, low strip of blue-paper mountains slid in behind it. And not until you get within calling distance of the "Post" can you fully determine its identity. In reality it is mud, with a few small windows pierced in three of its sides resembling port-holes, and a dirt roof, growing a veritable garden of grass and weeds, out of which peeps the top of a gray stone chimney. To the right of the

building stand two low adobe barns, and to the left a long, flat sheep-shed, fraying off into a spindly corral.

As I came upon "Two Gray Hills" one warm October afternoon, after two days of slow, thirsty travel across the desert from Farmington, Sel Ritchie, trader, received me with the hearty hospitality so characteristic of these remote merchants of the desert; and after I explained to him my great interest in the Indians and anxiety to see something of their life, he instantly invited me to make his "Post" my headquarters.

What a remarkable vantage-point it was! Surrounding us and extending endlessly to the east lay the great gray desert, the sky-line broken by freakish shapes of earth and rock and the tumbled ruins of

---

* The illustrations accompanying this narrative by N. C. Wyeth appeared with the original article in *Scribner's Magazine*, January 1909.

[45]

ancient Pueblo dwellings that bore strange tales of superstition and encounter; and hidden below the gray levels, in the canyons and arroyos, were mysterious caves, poisonous springs, and enchanted pools, the sight and scene of many Indian festivities and ceremonies.

And to the west of the "Post," not half a day's ride, stretched the Pine Ridge, an imposing range of jagged mountains, the home of many cold, sparkling brooks, grassy uplands, shady groves of cottonwoods, fragrant pine forests, and great spreading groups of nut-laden piñon trees.

Hidden amidst this abundance are sequestered many Navajo settlements of dome-shaped huts, built of mud and logs; thatch-roofed sheep-barns, large corrals of gnarled roots and brush; and like gems laid deep in slumbrous colors, one would often come upon blanket weavers seated before ponderous looms, upon which would be stretched blankets of brilliant scarlet and black, or blue and white; and mingled with the chatter of the weavers or the calls of the children one could always hear the distant musical tinkle of the sheep-bells, as the many herds wandered above and below on the steep slopes of the mountain-sides.

This remote tinkle of bells was from the first fascinating and alluring to me; so one morning, while roaming around the mountains, I decided to hunt out one of the roving bands and its keeper. For three hours I climbed over ledges, crawled through thickets, crossed innumerable mountain streams, toward that always far-away tinkle; but not until the noon-day sun threw its shortest shadows did I discover that my quest was an echo; that I had climbed the wrong side of the ravine.

It was too late that day to resume the search, but on the morrow, after a delightful night's sleep under the venerable roof of a mighty pine grove, I found my will-o'-the-wisp.

From my night's resting-place, in the cool morning shadows at the base of the long deep slope, I could distinctly hear the silvery ring of that elusive bell from far above where the morning sun shone and where the dews sparkled. How I wished I could be invisibly and silently placed amid that mountain pastoral, without disturbing the unconscious peacefulness of it all; could absorb that vision of poetry without intruding my commonplace self to disconcert the herder, to frighten the sheep, and arouse the watchful dog.

As I feared, my entrance upon the scene spoiled it all. But, thanks to my almost noiseless approach, I was able first to get at least a glimpse of the life with all its charm.

Before a small fire, its thin, blue skein of smoke floating upward on the light morning air, kneeled a Navajo boy; he was about twelve years old, his bobbed hair hung down to his shoulders in a dense mass, which was held back from his eyes with a deep crimson "bandy" of silk tied around his head. He wore a faded blue blouse, belted in very low on the hips with a frayed sash. Tight trousers, split from the knee down on the outside, a little the worse for wear, and a pair of smoke-tanned moccasins completed his costume. Beside him, in a heap, lay his blanket of many colors, and upon it his bow and quiver of arrows. On a long, slender spit he was roasting a piece of meat, which was eagerly watched by a big, shaggy dog seated close at his side. Behind this group and running at a slant up the mountain-side were the sheep, busily feeding. The bell, even at so close range, sounded soft and muffled, and I wondered that the sound could carry as far as I knew it did.

But this fragment of unconscious beauty lasted but a brief moment. My presence was discovered. The dog barked and bounded toward me, the boy jumped to his feet and gathered his blanket about him, the sheep ceased their quiet feeding and disappeared into the thickets. The dog's threatening behavior occupied my attention for a few moments; meanwhile the boy, my prize, had fled; and when the dog discovered that he was left alone with me, he turned and scampered likewise.

For a long time I sat there and listened to the diminishing sound of the bell, until finally, far up in the heights, I heard the slow, uneven chime telling me that peace and quietude reigned once more. I hadn't courage to molest them again, so retraced my tracks down the mountain, took my horse at one of the settlements at its base, and reached "Two Gray Hills" that evening. Of course I related my experience to Ritchie, and it apparently struck him as being wholly to be expected. He related similar experiences of his own, and practically discouraged me from ever trying to become in the least familiar with the Indians.

One morning, not long after, I was in the corral trying to rope an old, scraggly, moth-eaten looking burro. I had caged my droll target, and resolved to practise a new throw upon it until I at least understood the method. I had made about half a dozen very crude and unsuccessful attempts, and was preparing my rope for the next one when my captive made a run for the gate. The bar I knew was too high for the stiff-legged burro to jump—but lo and behold! he made a sort of running slide and rolled under it. I saw his trick quick enough to make a ragged, awkward cast, and as luck would have it, my loop made fast to a kicking hind leg just as he rolled under the bar. This sudden success came as a surprise, but the surprise that immediately followed had it "beaten a mile"—his triphammer kicks jerked the rope out of my hand, and away he galloped, stiff-legged and awkward like a calf, with my new hemp and horse-hair rope dangling and snapping after him. I watched him with disgust until he disappeared in a cloud of dust, my chief thought being a hope that no one had witnessed this "tenderfoot" predicament; but no sooner had it flashed through my mind than I heard behind me a shrill, boyish laugh, and, turning, whom should I see, looking through one of the larger openings, but my sheep-herder from the mountains. I felt humiliated. I tried to intercept his continued laughter with an explanation, but he wouldn't listen, and suddenly left me and disappeared in the big door of the "store".

Disgusted, I made a detour of the post buildings, thinking perhaps that I might locate the burro on the near-by sandhills; but he had fled from sight, so I, too, strolled

into the store, determined to face out my discomfiture. There were a number of Indians inside, and when I entered they greeted me with broad, knowing grins and started talking about me among themselves. I felt like a spanked child. The boy stood over behind the big chunk-stove, his black eyes sparkling with delight. I smiled at him, and he grinned back, disclosing two rows of handsome teeth that looked like pearls against the mahogany-copper colored skin of his face, and his hair looked blacker than ever. His shining eyes followed every movement I made, and I perceived that he was intently looking at my watch-fob, a miniature stirrup of silver.

The older Indians, as they finished the bargaining, departed one by one, and finally there remained only the trader, the boy and myself. Now was my chance! I asked Ritchie

THE PLAINS HERDER
Oil on canvas, h:37¼, w:28¼
Signed lower left: N. C. Wyeth 1908
Courtesy of Southern Arizona Bank & Trust Company, Tucson

at Ford Defiance for two years, and could talk freely if he wanted to.

Further efforts proved useless, but Begay continued to follow me around, always placing himself within sight of the silver stirrup dangling from my watch-pocket. At last I hit upon a plan. I would give him the stirrup. To see his face light up, to watch his big black eyes dance with pleasure, was worth fifty watch-fobs. With a grunt of satisfaction, he snatched the treasure from my hand, and concealing it in his blouse dashed out of the store.

It was only after a long search that I found him seated on the ground behind the wood-pile, gazing at the trinket with all his eyes, placing his finger in the tiny stirrup, holding it up by the strap with the other hand, and turning it in the sun to see it shine and glisten. His face this time met mine with a gracious smile; little by little I urged him to talk; and before the afternoon wore away we became fast friends.

That night Ritchie told me that the boy was about to trail a thousand sheep twenty-five miles across the desert to "Nip" Arment's, a sheep buyer and cattle dealer, just off the reservation; and had come, in anticipation of his trip, to make arrangements to corral and feed the sheep for one night, as he expected to make "Two Gray Hills" his first stopping place.

Such an undertaking for so young a boy seemed to me incredible, but I was told that he had accomplished the same thing for the two previous years, and once with two thousand sheep. And, furthermore, he always went on foot, which to me made the achievement even more remarkable. Ritchie could not understand my desire to accompany the lad on such a wearisome journey, but, according to my wishes he promised to "fix it up" so that I could go.

Three evenings later, a thin drift of dust appeared directly in the light of the setting sun, and by eight o'clock a thousand bleating sheep were driven into the cedar corral for the night. Many loosened bales of alfalfa were thrown in for them to eat, and the long, shallow troughs were filled with water. The boy was accompanied by his father to this point, who stopped only long

to explain to the boy who I was and in some way break the ice toward an acquaintance. At this request Ritchie laughed and the boy grinned. "He kin talk Americano as good as you and me kin; go ahead an' hit up a pow-wow with him," said Ritchie, and added, "His name is Begay."

At this glad news I turned to Begay and burst into a flow of explanations and questions. The boy stood mute, looking at me blankly, and after a long pause he answered in a soft half-whisper: "No savvy." I tried in every way to induce him to talk, but these were the only words he would utter. His continued silence and occasional solemn glances at Ritchie almost convinced me that the "trader" was playing a little joke on his guest; but I was reassured that the boy had attended the government school enough to see the sheep safely corralled, and with a few parting words to Begay disappeared into the night toward his distant cornfields in the bottom-lands, where his squaws had already started the harvesting.

We started two hours before sun-up. The bars of the corral were lifted out, the dog wormed his way among the still sleeping herd, and suddenly the dim, gray mass poured out of the gate, turned a sharp angle to the left and streamed off into the darkness. A few quick, mysterious words from the boy sent the dog hurtling after. Begay, his blanket girded about his loins with an old cartridge-belt, a small haversack of buckskin hung over one shoulder, and a curious stick from which dangled a number of empty tomato-cans, suspended by thongs, left us without a word in the direction of the vanished herd; and with a hurried "so long" to Ritchie I followed him.

The long, hard journey had begun. Dust arose from the herd in clouds; I could not see it, but could feel it sift against my face, and I could taste the peculiar, sweet flavor of alkali. Frequent calls from the boy to his dog, punctuated by the occasional clatter of the tin cans on the stick was all that broke the silence beyond the soft, quivering rustle made by thousands of feet as they plodded through the sand.

The level horizon of the desert lay before us, toward which we slowly trudged through endless stretches of loose sand, around the bases of towering buttes and down into and out of many dry arroyos. It was in these places that I saw Begay put the mysterious stick with its jingling cans into effective use. To drive the sheep over the banks and down into the dry river beds was an easy matter, but to force them up the sharp acclivity on the opposite side required considerable strategy. As the herd approached the embankment, it would invariably turn either to the right or left and run along the base of it, vainly searching for easier footing. At a word from Begay, the well-trained dog would dash to the front of the bunch, frantically jumping and barking, nipping the legs of the leaders, and eventually turning the entire herd in

NOTHING WOULD ESCAPE THEIR BLACK, JEWEL-LIKE, INSCRUTABLE EYES
Oil on canvas, h:46½, w:37½
Signed lower left: N. C. Wyeth
"Growing Up," by Gouverneur Morris
Harper's Monthly Magazine, November 1911
Courtesy of Edward Eberstadt & Sons, New York

the opposite direction. Then the boy from his position between the sheep and the open stretch of the arroyo, waving his blanket and hissing loudly, would hurl his stick and jingling cans in front of the sheep fast escaping through the unguarded side. The cans would jangle and crash on the stones and hard gravel, and the panic-stricken animals, frightened by the noise, would scramble up the bank, Begay would recover his "tanglang" as he called it, and we would laboriously crawl up after them.

The trip had been one of very few words; those that had passed between us could be numbered on the fingers of one hand. Twice, with solemn gesture, he pointed out distant landmarks, and explained, in short, quick accent, "Toh," meaning water; and another time he fondly pulled the silver stirrup from inside his blouse, and, holding it up, smiled and questioned, "To qui?" meaning "how much?" I did not comprehend exactly what he meant, although I could interpret the words. Finally I answered, fully an hour later, "Peso," meaning one dollar. At this he smiled a broad, pleased smile, and from then on he would take out the ornament again and again, and holding it in the sunlight would watch it glisten, casting laughing sidelong glances at me.

Except for these few moments of slight diversion, Begay's attention was fixed steadfastly on his sheep, his eyes always watchful of the condition of the trail ahead. Toward the end of the afternoon he urged the sheep on at a faster pace, and frequently looked at the position of the sun.

His anxiety evidently grew greater as it neared the horizon, and once I questioned him about the distance to water, but he was silent and seemed not to be conscious of my presence.

The slow, steady walking since four o'clock that morning, with not even a halt for noon lunch, through heavy sands, up steep slopes, and over rough mounds of shale-rock and loose gravel, began to tell on me. My thighs at times became cramped and stiff, and for miles I would walk stooped in order to proceed at all. And now, as the herd increased its speed to almost double, I was gradually left behind. Begay appeared as fresh as in the early morning. He walked with perfect ease and grace, his long, slender legs measuring off the distance in rhythmic steps, his body bent slightly forward, one arm clasping his blanket and "tanglang," and the other swinging free like a pendulum.

I managed to stagger along for an hour more with the herd well in the lead; the sun had disappeared behind a deep purple horizon, and the afterglow flooded the desert with a radiant, liquid light. All the earth glowed as though lighted from within, the very sands at my feet looked a stained

orange, and the few clumps of dry, dusty sage-brush fairly burned in the weird light; while far ahead, just over the margin of a low hill, a great, red, golden cloud of dust told the tale of the fast-moving herd.

Twenty minutes of weary, anxious plodding brought me to the summit; the light was growing dim, but I could vaguely see, 'way down the gentle slope, a fringe of cedar clumps, and from beyond them I could hear the faint murmur of the sheep, like distant strains of many bagpipes. I knew they were nearing water; and I felt so relieved at the thought that it was comparatively near that I lay down in my tracks, and in perfect contentment watched the stars as they appeared one by one.

I don't know how long it was before I was suddenly conscious of a distant call; the sound drew nearer until I recognized the boyish voice of Begay. He had returned to find me, and as we slowly made our way in the dark, he told me in his own quaint way the reason of his anxiety and hurry: "Sheep no drink for long time—dark come quick—afraid for no find trail to water in deep hole—sheep run and fall on rock—get kill." And with a long impressive pause, "Me no want kill sheep—Savvy?"

I understood, but I understood far better when we cautiously picked our way down one of the most precipitous trails I ever saw. How he managed to get those thousand restless, thirsty sheep down into that canyon, fully two hundred feet deep, unscathed, as they proved to be, is far beyond my imagination. It was incredible!

We ourselves crawled down, and frequently I lighted matches to see where to place my foot next, sick, dizzy, to see the edge of the trail not a foot away disappearing into a chasm of blackness. Now and then a loose piece of shale would slide off into space, and it seemed minutes before the dry click sounded as it struck the bottom.

Once at the base, Begay led me to a large log "hogan," similar to the dome-shaped huts I had seen in the mountains. We crawled through the low door, and soon had a cheery fire of crackling cedar logs burning in the center of the floor, the smoke rising and disappearing out of the large vent in the roof. This shelter had been built for the use of any-one who found it

MEXICAN SHEPHERD
Oil on canvas, h:28¼, w:37¼
Signed lower left: N. C. Wyeth 1908
Courtesy of Southern Arizona Bank & Trust Company, Tucson

necessary to spend the night in the canyon. On one side were piled two or three dozen ragged and worn sheep skins for bedding, and alongside, piled in a heap on the ground, were a number of blackened and dented tin dishes. In the center sat a great pile of wood-ashes, telling the tale of many camp-fires, and over the low door hung a tattered piece of buckskin. We made a pot of strong, black coffee from the muddy water, from which a stench of sheep now rose, and with a large can of veal-loaf and some pilot bread we ate ravenously until barely enough was left for breakfast. With the last mouthful swallowed, the boy dragged four or five skins to the fire, and wrapping himself in his blanket threw himself upon them, and immediately fell into a sound sleep. The night promised to be a sharp, frosty one, so I dragged a huge cedar root on to the dying embers, and preparing in my turn a bed of skins was soon dead to the world.

It seemed hardly an hour's time before I was aroused by the bark of the dog and the bleating sheep. I crawled out of the hut wrapped in my blanket; it was still dusk, but the sky was rapidly brightening. A sharp, cutting wind swept through the canyon, and I could hear Begay down at the water-hole cracking the ice with a stick. The high rock walls that hemmed us in loomed gigantic and black in the gloom; they resembled the ruins of mighty castles, fringed at the top with the silhouettes of tufted cedar. The steady increasing gray light sifted down upon us, disclosing enormous rounded boulders, jagged pinnacles of rock, mysterious caves, gnarled and twisted cedars through which the winds moaned and sighed, drifting the loose sands in tiny eddies into caves and crevices or piling it in fantastic mounds on the open stretches. Directly behind the hut, and protected by a projecting ledge, nestled the corral enclosing the sheep, and beyond, at the foot of a long, gentle incline, lay the precious pool of water.

A light breakfast eaten and the sheep watered, we started the second and last lap of our journey. Unlike the descending trail of the previous night, the way out of the

canyon was comparatively easy, except that we had to be very cautious and evade the many soft and treacherous sand-drifts. I asked Begay what time he expected we would reach our destination; he replied by pointing to the sun and following its orbit till its position indicated three o'clock.

It was about that time when we descended into the bottom-lands of the Rio Las Animas, where lay "Nip" Arment's thriving trading-post.

The sheep moved slowly, and the dog, his services unneeded, lagged behind. We were seen long before we reached the post, and upon our arrival a dozen Indians aided Begay to count and corral the sheep. I stood apparently unnoticed, until, as all were walking toward the "store," Begay flourished the silver stirrup; a brief explanation followed and all eyes were turned on me.

A moment later "Nip" Arment appeared upon the scene, and with a hearty welcome led me to his house. The home was lavish in comforts; many Navajo rugs adorned the floors, numberless trophies of the hunt and rare relics from the desert hung on the walls; but I missed my new friend. That night I talked long and late with the trader, and once in bed I fell into a sound, sound sleep. I did not wake before noon; but then I dressed hurriedly and rushed out in search of Begay. A group of Indians were playing cards behind the "store" in the warm sun, and I asked them where to find him. One of them, a tall, sinister fellow, slowly and solemnly arose, and coming over to where I was standing, placed one hand on my shoulder and pointed with a long, dark finger at two disappearing specks on the western horizon. They were Begay and his dog.

CALLING THE SUN DANCE
Oil on canvas, h:35½, w:26½
Signed lower left: N. C. Wyeth '08
Courtesy of W. S. Farish III

Shortly after returning from his journey to Colorado in 1906, Wyeth felt the urge to settle down in his own peaceful area of Chadds Ford, Pennsylvania. The West had been good for him and for his pursuit, but the lengthy absences from home and family made him long for a more settled way of life.

> ... with five years of almost incessant work, mostly western in character, I have experienced a remarkable change. My ardor for the West has slowly, but with increasing impetus, been dwindling, until my desires to go there to paint its people are already lukewarm. The West appealed to me as it would to a boy; a sort of external effervescence of spirit seemed to be all that substantiated my work.[2]

But the demand for his western illustrations was to plague him for years to come. Publishers continued to vie for his talents in this field, and he was sometimes deluged with requests to illustrate books and stories in periodicals and to make western-type pictures for commercial art commissions as well. Among the books for which he painted western scenes were *Reminiscences of a Ranchman* by Edgar Beecher Bronson (1910), *Letters of a Woman Homesteader* by Eleanor Pruitt Stewart (1914), *Nan of Music Mountain* by Frank H. Spearman (1916), *Vandemark's Folly* by Herbert Quick (1922), *The Oregon Trail* by Francis Parkman (1925), and *Ramona* by Helen Hunt Jackson (1939). The western classic *Cimarron* by Edna Ferber, which was published serially by *Woman's Home Companion* from November 1929

[53]

THE ORE WAGON
Oil on canvas, h:38, w:25
Signed lower right: N. C. Wyeth '07
"The Misadventures of Cassidy," by Edward S. Moffat
McClure's Magazine, May 1908
Courtesy of Southern Arizona Bank & Trust Company, Tucson

I'VE SOLD THEM WHEELERS
"The Misadventures of Cassidy," by Edward S. Moffat
McClure's Magazine, May 1908

A FIGHT ON THE PLAINS
Oil on canvas, h:32, w:40
Signed lower right: To Mr. and Mrs. Harlan Pyle/from
  N. C. Wyeth
"The Great West That Was," by Col. William F. Cody
Hearst's Magazine, September 1916
Courtesy of Andrew Wyeth

SITTING UP CROSS-LEGGED, WITH EACH HAND
  HOLDING A GUN . . .
Oil on canvas, h:37, w:26
Signed lower right: N. C. Wyeth 1906
"Bar 20 Range Yarns," by Clarence Edward Mulford
The Outing Magazine, May 1906
Courtesy of Alexander F. Treadwell

through May 1930, was also handsomely illustrated by N. C. Wyeth.

Once, when asked why he had given up the comforts of home and friends to travel into the West, to sleep on the ground or in the Indian hogan, to battle the heat of the desert or the icy cold of the mountains, Wyeth replied, after some reflection:

Every man, whether he is an artist or not, has what is commonly called a soul. Sooner or later he yearns to express his soul in some way. He may start out in search of the unusual, the novel or the bizarre, and if he is an artist, he may find certain satisfaction in the theatrical—the great western plains, for instance, where you see a speck on the horizon, and have to travel all day to reach it or you see a mountain that looks a few hours journey off, and you ride three days to get to it. You may have the greatest sympathy for the people you meet, for the picturesqueness of their life and their traditions and clothing—but the time comes when his soul gets restless, and he finds that he has been enjoying a show in which he really has no fundamental part.

He finds that in order to express himself fully, he has got to come back to the soil he was born on, no matter where it is—it may be the glorious White Mountains of New Hampshire, or the woods of Needham—the call is imperative, he has got to answer it. There is something in his bones that comes right out of the soil he grew up on—something that gives him a power and contract communion with life which no other place gives him.[3]

THE WAR CLOUDS
Scribner's Magazine (frontispiece), March 1909

THE MYSTERY TREE
Oil on canvas, h:35½, w:25½
Signed lower left: N. C. Wyeth '08
Reminiscences of a Ranchman, by Edgar Beecher Bronson
George H. Doran Company, New York, 1910
Courtesy of J. N. Bartfield Art Galleries, Inc., New York

THE HUNTER

THE SOLITUDE SERIES
The Outing Magazine, June 1907

THE MAGIC POOL

4

The Indian in His Solitude

THE American Indian—what images the phrase conjures up! It brings to mind those brilliant horsemen of the Plains, the Cheyenne; the Sioux warrior chief resplendent in his magnificent warbonnet; the Apache, scourge of the Southwest, lurking in his stronghold amid the rocks and cactus of his desert country. These and more automatically come into mental focus at the mere mention of the phrase, for to most of us the Indians who figured so prominently in the young nation's push westward personify that colorful era, which in reality was not so very far in the past.

To N. C. Wyeth, however, the American Indian he found of greatest interest was the Indian of longer ago, the Indian faced by our forefathers when they first came to this land to settle. He was the Iroquois, the Huron, the Mohawk, and the Seneca. He was not the Indian of the vast plains, the mountains, or the desert. He was the Indian of poetry—the Woodland Indian of the Northeast.

As ferocious as his counterpart in the Far West, the Woodland Indian fought with as much dedication to preserve his land and the way of life that was rightfully his. The forces of nature played a major role in determining his every act, and in painting him Wyeth took account of that fact. With deep feeling and sensitive understanding, he depicted the Woodland In-

THE MOOSE CALL
Scribner's Magazine, October 1906

Preliminary Study for *The Indian in His Solitude*
Charcoal on paper, h:25½, w:16¼
Signed lower right: N.C.W. 1906
Collection of Douglas Allen, Jr.

dian, not as the gaudily painted warrior bent on massacre, but as a child of nature, whose moods dictated his day-to-day existence from birth to death.

In 1904, while studying at the Howard Pyle School, Wyeth painted one of the most popular of his Indian canvases, *The Moose Call,* which was subsequently reproduced in *Scribner's Magazine,* October 1906. To coincide with its appearance in the magazine, Scribner's also published the picture as a mounted print, which met with immediate success. It signaled Wyeth's emergence as one of America's foremost painters of nature and the unspoiled wilderness.

During 1906, Wyeth painted a number of other pictures of the Woodland Indian. Five of these appeared in the June 1907 issue of the old *Outing Magazine,* reproduced in full color with the title *The Indian in His Solitude.* They represent some of his finest work. Soon afterward, the magazine advertised that *The Indian in His Solitude* series was available as color prints, each measuring twelve by sixteen inches, mounted on heavy board and enclosed in an attractive box. Although this advertisement appeared regularly over a span of years, one mys-

tery remains. Our long-term research into the work of American illustrators brought to light only one complete set of the "Solitude" series and one single print.

Again in *Scribner's Magazine,* October 1907, the tranquil *Silent Fisherman* appeared. Painted in 1906, it may originally have been intended for the *Solitude* series, for it clearly interprets the feeling of solitude, showing the silent water and an Indian alone in contemplation. Some two years later, Wyeth made a series of four Indian paintings for *Scribner's Magazine.* These were reproduced in the December 1909 issue, to accompany a group of poems—"The Moods"—dedicated to the four seasons, written by George T. Marsh. This group of pictures served as the theme for what was to be Wyeth's first venture into the field of mural painting, in 1911: four decorative panels for the new Hotel Utica.

Perhaps one of the most beautiful portrayals of the Woodland Indian ever painted was Wyeth's *A Primitive Spearman. Scribner's,* always eager to provide their subscribers with the best in art and illustration, reproduced this painting as the frontispiece in October 1913 issue.

THE SILENT FISHERMAN (*The Lone Fisherman*)
Scribner's Magazine (frontispiece), October 1907

HIAWATHA'S FISHING
The Children's Longfellow
Houghton Mifflin Company, Boston, 1908

A WYETH PORTFOLIO

THE BEST OPPORTUNITY

EVER OFFERED DISCERNING PEOPLE TO DECORATE THE HOME, DEN, OR CLUB WITH CHOICE PICTURES BY A MASTER PAINTER

It is not going too far to say that N. C. Wyeth is to-day one of our greatest, if not our *greatest* painter of American outdoor life. It is Wyeth's faculty of getting at "the soul of things" that makes his art so appealing.

The Solitude Series

the title of the five pictures in this Portfolio, is a series of canvases depicting the American Indian in his native haunts, surrounded by the all-pervading mystery of Nature. It is the Indian as he was, owner of this vast land, that has interested Wyeth so keenly.

The bigness of the outdoors, the forests, the plains, the *vastness of things* — all these qualities are found in these wonderful pictures; and, too, besides the "spirit," there is a masterly draughtsmanship throughout — and marvelous color harmonies. The whole set is a thing of beauty and singular charm.

The Color Work

in the reproduction of these pictures has been studiously followed. Every tone, every mass of brilliancy has been faithfully adhered to. The small black and white cuts herewith shown can give the purchaser only an idea of the subject matter treated.

THE OUTING MAGAZINE

The Size

The color reproduction of this Portfolio measures 12 by 16 inches. Each picture is mounted on heavy boards (ready for framing), making them about 17 by 22 inches over all. The set of five subjects is enclosed in an attractive box.

The Price

of these Portfolios is $4.50. Purchased singly, each picture costs $1.00. As a holiday item they would be welcomed as a choice and precious gift. For wall decoration of the Home, the Den, the Club, they are incomparable.

We Have Reserved

a few sets of this beautiful work to be used for Subscription purposes in connection with *The Outing Magazine*. This offer is open to both new and old Subscribers. While the limited number lasts, we will furnish one of the portfolios with every year's subscription to *The Outing Magazine* for $6.00.

NOTE THESE FIGURES

Year's Subscription to The Outing Magazine $3.00   YOU CAN
A Wyeth Portfolio (five works of art)   -   4.50   OBTAIN ALL   **$6**.⁰⁰
                          Total $7.50   THIS FOR

Send in your
subscription
NOW
The supply of
Portfolios is ab-
solutely limited

SUBSCRIPTION DEPT., DEPOSIT, N. Y.

1907 Advertisement of *The Outing Magazine* for
Wyeth's Solitude Series portfolio.

THE SPEARMAN

IN THE CRYSTAL DEPTHS

THE SILENT BURIAL

WINTER
Oil on canvas, h:33, w:30
Signed lower left: N. C. Wyeth '09
"The Moods," by George T. Marsh
Scribner's Magazine, December 1909
Courtesy of Andrew Wyeth

SPRING

SUMMER

AUTUMN

THE MOODS
Scribner's Magazine, December 1909

A PRIMITIVE SPEARMAN
Scribner's Magazine (frontispiece), October 1913

DRIVING THE CATTLE WHERE THE MEADOW
   BROOK IS BRAWLING
"Back to the Farm," by Martha Gilbert Dickinson Bianchi
Scribner's Magazine, August 1908

5

Brandywine Country

Newell Convers Wyeth and Carolyn B. Bockius were married in April of 1906. At first they lived in Wilmington, as Wyeth continued to study under Howard Pyle and concentrated on fulfilling the many commitments that were coming his way. But, in the latter part of 1907, their first child was born, and they both felt that a family should be brought up in the country.

In seeking a satisfactory location for a permanent home, the young couple concentrated their attention on the rural area of Chadds Ford, Pennsylvania, which was a relatively short distance from Wilmington proper. They knew the area well, since Howard Pyle's summer home was there and for a number of years his art school held classes there during the warm summer months.

Wyeth was enamored of this Brandywine countryside with its rolling fields and wooded hillsides, its streams and its meadows and its farms. He loved its historical associations and its serenity. It reminded him of the country surrounding Needham, Massachusetts, where he was born and raised.

In the spring of 1908 the Wyeths moved to this Brandywine countryside and there they remained.

He once explained during an interview:

In me has revived a stronger and more vital interest and love for the life that lies about me. I am finding deeper pleasure, deeper meanings in the simple things in the country life here. Being older and more mature, I am realizing that one must go

MOWING
Oil on canvas, h:37½, w:27
Signed lower right: N. C. Wyeth, Chadds Ford, Pa.
Courtesy of Mr. & Mrs. Andrew Wyeth

beneath the surface to paint and so it is that my real loves, my real affections are reviving.[1]

In the spring of 1907 *Scribner's* had forwarded to Wyeth a copy of a poem entitled "Back to the Farm," by Martha Gilbert Dickinson Bianchi. He was so taken with the prospects it offered for picture material that he vowed he would spend the summer working on illustrations for it. His first was a delightful portrayal of a young girl holding a pitcher while a youthful scyther drank deep, for the work had been hard and the sun burned down on the landscape with a scorching heat. The painting, *Mowing*, won praise from all Wyeth's friends who saw it and a special commendation from Howard Pyle. This picture was not published in the series that appeared in *Scribner's Magazine*, August 1908. Another of similar theme took its place, but it is reproduced here along with the four that subsequently accompanied the poem, for which he also made eight charming pen-and-ink drawings.

N. C. Wyeth at work on a landscape, Chadds Ford, 1909

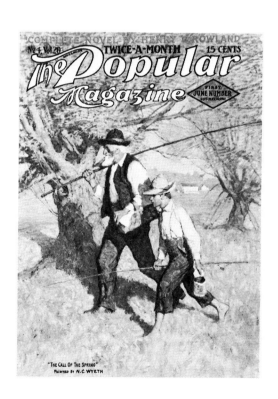

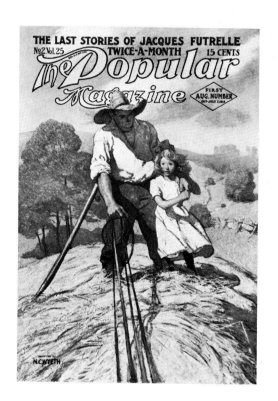

THE SCYTHERS (*Down in the hayfield where scythes
    glint through the clover . . .*)
Oil on canvas, h:37½, w:26¾
Signed lower right: N. C. Wyeth
"Back to the Farm," by Martha Gilbert Dickenson Bianchi
Scribner's Magazine, August 1908
Courtesy of University of Arizona Museum of Art, Samuel
    L. Kingan Collection

DOBBIN *(Plowing the Cornfield)*
Oil on canvas, h:37, w:28
Signed lower right: To my Chadds Ford/friend/Tinker
    Quimby/N. C. Wyeth/1907
"Back to the Farm," by Martha Gilbert Dickenson Bianchi
Scribner's Magazine, August 1908
Courtesy of Mrs. Sidney Ashcraft

Cover Illustration
The Popular Magazine, November 1913

Wyeth thrived in the Chadds Ford atmosphere. When not at work in his studio he could now often be seen somewhere about the acres of his farm discussing cabbages or cattle with his neighbors, or swinging an ax or following a plow with the best. He was absorbed in his community, his farm, and his family. Retreating

N. C. Wyeth in his apple orchard at Chadds Ford, ca. 1944.
Photograph by William E. Phelps.
Courtesy of Mrs. N. C. Wyeth

to some isolated workshop had no place in Wyeth's scheme of things. He found inspiration in his contact with the life about him, and he began to paint more of the rural scene. It was no accident that much of his finest work should result from this theme.

My brothers and I were brought up on a farm and from the time I could walk I was conscripted into doing every conceivable chore that there was to do about the place. This early training gave me a vivid appreciation of the part the body played in action.

Now, when I paint a figure on horseback, a man plowing, or a woman buffeted by the wind, I have an acute bodily sense of the muscle-strain, the feeling of the hickory handle, or the protective bend of the head or squint of eye that each pose involves. After painting action scenes I have ached for hours because of having put myself in the other fellow's shoes as I realized him on the canvas.[2]

Pen-and-ink Drawings
Susanna and Sue, by Kate Douglas Wiggin
Houghton Mifflin Company, Boston, 1909

BRINGING HOME THE PUMPKINS
Oil on canvas, h:38, w:27
Signed lower right: N. C. Wyeth '07
"Back to the Farm," by Martha Gilbert Dickinson Bianchi
Scribner's Magazine, August 1908
Courtesy of Mr. and Mrs. Curtis Hutchins

CORN HARVEST IN THE HILL COUNTRY
The Progressive Farmer, October 1945

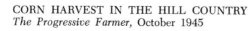

TWO BOYS IN A PUNT
Oil on canvas, h:37, w:26
Signed lower left: N. C. Wyeth
The Popular Magazine (cover),
    August 7, 1915
Courtesy of Dr. & Mrs. William
    A. Morton, Jr.

With the appearance of the illustrations for "Back to the Farm," other publishers took notice of his ability at portraying the rural scene. Soon he was busy making a series of delightful pen-and-ink drawings for a book called *Susanna and Sue* by Kate Douglas Wiggin, which appeared late in 1909.

Wyeth's versatility made it possible for him to turn to almost any subject or theme for his work, but his love of country life and the rural landscape remained apparent in many of his paintings for the rest of his life. The rural scenes that he did for periodicals were usually cover illustrations; they were made primarily for *The Popular Magazine*, *Progressive Farmer*, and *Country Gentleman*. But he painted many purely for pleasure and relaxation; these are reproduced in Chapter 11.

WHEN HE COMES HE WILL RULE OVER THE
    WHOLE WORLD
"The Lost Boy," by Henry Van Dyke
Harper's Monthly Magazine, December 1913

COME LIVE WITH US, FOR I THINK THOU ART
    CHOSEN
"The Lost Boy," by Henry Van Dyke
Harper's Monthly Magazine, December 1913

THE CHILD
The Parables of Jesus (frontispiece), by S. Parkes Cadman
David McKay Company, 1931

THE PARABLE OF THE LEAVEN
The Parables of Jesus, by S. Parkes Cadman
David McKay Company, 1931

THE BOY CHRIST IN THE CARPENTER'S SHOP
"The Man Nobody Knows," by Bruce Barton
Woman's Home Companion, December 1924

6

Religious Painting

A sign on the door of N. C. Wyeth's studio read: "I will not have Good Fortune or God's Blessing let in while I am working."

"But," he once cheerfully remarked during an interview, "it doesn't seem to work because people just say they are neither Good Fortune or God's Blessing, and they walk right in."[1]

Wyeth seems to have attempted no paintings on biblical themes before 1912. That year, in the December issue of *Scribner's Magazine*, a story by Thomas Nelson Page, "The Stable of the Inn," was illustrated by two Wyeth paintings in color, and Wyeth paintings based on biblical stories were to appear from time to time in the years that followed.

On December 25, 1923, the Unitarian Laymen's League, which had headquarters in Boston, Massachusetts, held a private showing of the first six paintings Wyeth had completed for them based on the parables of Jesus. Approximately three years before then, this Unitarian group had decided the best way to engrave the parables indelibly on the minds of children and thus make their truths a lasting influence

would be to publish them in book form, without comment or moralizing, but illustrated with imagination, sympathy, skill, and beauty. Research indicated that in all the history of art, no serious attempt had ever been made to illustrate the parables as a whole. As the possibilities were studied, the committee became more and more convinced of the merit of the idea. They felt certain that such a book would have great appeal for, as well as an unconscious influence on, not only children but all who love beauty of picture and thought. Of course, the success of the project would depend almost entirely on their securing an artist possessed of the necessary talent and vision, one who would interpret the parables unawed by orthodox opinion and portray the characters in all their native virility, uninfluenced by the conventional ascetic precedents of religious art.

The search was ended when they found such a man in N. C. Wyeth.

A commission of this kind appealed to Wyeth as an opportunity to create true masterpieces. Undertaking the task in that spirit, he

MUHAMMAD THE PROPHET
Oil on canvas, h:47, w:38
Unsigned
"The Red Star," by Arthur Conan Doyle
Scribner's Magazine, January 1911
Collection of Douglas Allen, Jr.

devoted a year to preliminary study before he began the paintings. He himself said of his interpretations:

The vitality of artistic expression is essentially auto-biographical. The creation of a picture, a poem, a musical composition, is a record of the artist's emotional and spiritual reaction to life and its traditions. This is true, whether the senses deal with beauty in the abstract or with the tangible drama and poetry of everyday existence. There is also that stimulating and valuable spirit of protest which is inevitably a factor in the agitation toward personal expression —the protest against unsatisfying existing standards or of tradition.

This spirit of protest was in a considerable measure responsible for my interest in the painting of a series of paintings to ac-

company certain of the parables of Jesus— a protest against the inanities of teaching in the Sunday School classroom as I knew it.

From earliest boyhood the attendance at Sunday School was an unutterable bore to me. Only the inherited sense of duty, fostered carefully by my father and mother, made my attendance record respectable.

The years have passed and I have often looked back upon those tedious hours and have wondered at their barrenness. Now that I am able to read the Bible with almost the same excited interest with which I can read Homer, Shakespeare or Tolstoy, I begin to perceive some of the reasons why my Sunday School experiences were all but meaningless, and why they well nigh turned me away from the Bible forever for enjoyable and profitable reading.

The stories of the Bible were invariably

THE NATIVITY
Oil on canvas, h:47, w:38
Signed lower right: N. C. Wyeth
"The Stable of the Inn," by Thomas Nelson Page
Scribner's Magazine, December 1912
Collection of Douglas Allen, Jr.

THE PARABLE OF THE NET
The Parables of Jesus, by S. Parkes Cadman
David McKay Company, 1931

THE PARABLE OF THE SEED
The Parables of Jesus, by S. Parkes Cadman
David McKay Company, 1931

used as a bludgeon to drive home a moral lesson. In the process, all traces of those transcendent qualities of dramatic story telling and vivid beauty were lost. The inevitable harangue on the ethical deductions left me in a state of mental lethargy.

Art can become invaluable propaganda, but propaganda can never become art. Revealing the dramatic power and great beauty of a story from the Bible to the young mind is the surest method of releasing its moral and ethical force. Its potentiality for good must dawn upon the youth of its own power. It is the supreme art in the parables of Christ that is most valuable. The hordes of reformers and preachers since His day have done these allegories incalculable damage by turning them into cold doctrines of conduct. To preclude art with ethics is to rob it of life.

Referring particularly to the parables, let us recognize that an outstanding dramatic feature of these symbolisms is that they deal with the common, everyday life as seen by the Master. It is as though, while preaching, He raised His eyes to the hills and saw the Harvesters at work—the spontaneous parable of The Secret Growth of the Seed came to Him. As he talked to the multitude by the shore, He glimpsed the fishermen of Galilee and the parable of The Net was born. In passing through the sunlit streets of a Judean town He saw a mother at her task of bread making—and so came The Leaven.

Not once does He refer to the legends of ancient times or remote peoples. His source of inspiration was life, life as He saw and felt it about Him.

Is it not this spirit of the magnificent romance of reality which we must cherish when we attempt to reveal His teachings? Is this not a proper feature for an artist to emphasize when presuming to place a pictorial accompaniment to His marvelous words? Not pictures which attempt to interpret or explain, but rather conceptions which become as it were an obbligato to the magical singing melody of His stories.[2]

THE LOST LAMB
Oil on canvas, h:45, w:40
Signed lower right: N. C. Wyeth
Courtesy of Colby Art Museum,
Waterville, Maine

The original plan to have the parables published in book form did not work out. Instead, a committee made up of various religious denominations promoted the paintings as Christmas cards, which were printed in twelve colors and gold. Six hundred thousand were printed and sold at fifteen cents each. There was no financial gain for anyone, but a new standard was set in the quality of Christmas cards. These cards are now rare collector's items.

Eventually, the parable paintings Wyeth had done for the Unitarian Laymen's League did appear in a book—S. Parkes Cadman's *The Parables of Jesus*, which was published in 1931. By that time, another group of Wyeth's religious paintings had already been published. He had made these to illustrate Bruce Barton's *Children of the Bible*. They appeared in all issues of *Good Housekeeping* for the year 1929. But the crowning glory of his efforts in the field of religious painting must surely be the triptych housed in the National Cathedral in Washington, D.C. This is pictured in Chapter 11—"Murals, Lunettes, and the Triptych."

CAPTAIN BILL BONES (*All day he hung round the cove,
    or upon the cliffs, with a brass telescope.*)
Oil on canvas, h:47, w:38
Signed lower left: N. C. Wyeth
Treasure Island, by Robert Louis Stevenson
Charles Scribner's Sons, 1911
Courtesy of Mrs. Brigham Britton

7

The Classics

As I contemplated the writing of this chapter, my mind went back to my childhood. When I was ten or twelve years old, I often received books as gifts on birthdays, at Christmas, or sometimes on occasions that marked no special celebration in my young life. Those closest to me, aware of what an avid reader I was, did not have to ponder long over the choice of a gift that would please me.

The name N. C. Wyeth did not mean anything to me in those years. The pictures that were a part of these books did. The images of them remained with me and were more vivid in my memory, I daresay, than the spellbinding stories they illustrated.

But now I do know of N. C. Wyeth, and I recognize what his art has meant to me. I can now look at his contribution in perspective, and it is a certainty that what he gave to me he also gave to tens of thousands of others.

Most of the Wyeth-illustrated classics were published nearly a half century ago, but they are still being printed and still being bought as gifts for children, who some forty years hence will recall them as I have done. The cycle repeats itself—the long parade of beloved characters portrayed in story and illustration goes on and on in a never-ending procession.

In 1911, Robert Louis Stevenson's unforgettable *Treasure Island* was issued by Charles Scribner's Sons as the first book in its series known as the Scribner Illustrated Classics. For N. C. Wyeth, it marked the beginning of a long list of great books that he would be commissioned to illustrate over the next thirty years. His *Treasure Island* paintings had such dynamic storytelling quality that they must surely be ranked with the story itself—a classic marriage of text and pictures, for all time. His skill in projection—the heroic quality, rich color, and

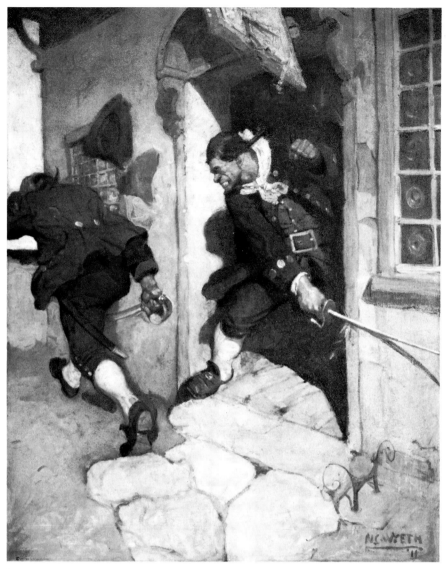

CAPTAIN BONES ROUTS BLACK DOG
Oil on canvas, h:47, w:38
Signed lower right: N. C. Wyeth
Treasure Island, by Robert Louis Stevenson
Charles Scribner's Sons, 1911
Courtesy of Mr. and Mrs. John W. McCoy II

convincing interpretations in his paintings—made the characters living, breathing people who had really existed in the past. That Wyeth was able to do this was not strange. He had been subjected to Howard Pyle's theory of projection until it had become part of his very fiber.

In my own life I try to live the life that I depict. Some may wonder how I can live the life of the 12th century, which most of my costumed romance represents. All I can say is that the elemental feelings of long ago are identical with our own. The costumes and accessories of the 12th century may be different, but the sunlight on a bronzed face, the winds that blow across the marshlands, the moon illuminating the old hamlets of medieval England, the rain-soaked travelers of King Arthur's day passing across the moors are strictly contemporaneous in feeling. The farmer swinging a scythe uses the same muscles, experiences the same sensations as we do today. But you've got to do these things to understand them.[1]

The success of *Treasure Island* as a publishing enterprise was so great, and so lavish were the praises for the illustrations that con-

OLD PEW
Oil on canvas, h:47, w:38
Signed lower right: N. C. Wyeth 1911
Treasure Island, by Robert Louis Stevenson
Charles Scribner's Sons, 1911
Courtesy of Mrs. Andrew Wyeth

PREPARING FOR THE MUTINY (*Loaded pistols were
served out to all the sure men.*)
Oil on canvas, h:47, w:38
Signed upper left: N. C. Wyeth
Treasure Island, by Robert Louis Stevenson
Charles Scribner's Sons, 1911
Courtesy of Andrew Wyeth

THE HOSTAGE (*For all the world, I was led like a dancing
bear.*)
Oil on canvas, h:47, w:38
Signed lower right: N. C. Wyeth
Treasure Island, by Robert Louis Stevenson
Charles Scribner's Sons, 1911
Courtesy of Mrs. Brigham Britton

JIM HAWKINS LEAVES HOME
Oil on canvas, h:47, w:38
Signed lower left: N. C. Wyeth
Treasure Island, by Robert Louis Stevenson
Charles Scribner's Sons, 1911
Courtesy of Wilmington Y.M.C.A., Wilmington, Delaware

Exterior and interior views of the studio N. C. Wyeth
built after his success illustrating the first of the
Scribner Classics, *Treasure Island*. The studio was completed
at the end of 1911.
Courtesy of William Penn Memorial Museum, Harrisburg

tributed to its appeal, that it did not take the Scribner organization long to formulate plans for a second book. The choice was *Kidnapped*, another Stevenson tale. When approached about the contemplated edition, Wyeth replied:

Your letter this morning affected me greatly and I am delighted. I want you to know that I have the greatest hopes, and unless I outclass Treasure Island I want you to cancel the entire scheme. Will write regarding "Kidnapped" in a few days.[2]

Kidnapped was published in 1913, and although the illustrations that were done for it did not "outclass" those done for *Treasure Island*, they stood on their own merit, as did those illustrating two more Stevenson stories that were later added to the shelf of Scribner Classics—*The Black Arrow* (1916) and *David Balfour* (1924).

His outstanding work for the series of Scribner Classics inevitably led to commissions from other publishers for illustrating juvenile books, and he threw himself wholeheartedly into all such assignments. A notable example was

MR. BALFOUR OF THE
HOUSE OF SHAWS
Kidnapped, by Robert Louis
Stevenson
Charles Scribner's Sons, 1913

Mark Twain's *The Mysterious Stranger*, which he illustrated for Harper's. Others, later, included *Robin Hood* and *Rip Van Winkle*, both for David McKay, *Robinson Crusoe* and *The White Company* for the Cosmopolitan Book Corporation, and the romantic *The Courtship of Miles Standish* for Houghton Mifflin. But the wonderful Scribner Classics went on and on too. For *The Boy's King Arthur*, he made an exciting, colorful series of pictures. The range of his

interpretations continued to be varied and powerful.

Wyeth also occasionally became involved in writing the foreword or preface for a book, or in the actual choice of a title to become a part of the Scribner Illustrated Classics series.

In making the fourteen beautiful color illustrations for Jules Verne's *The Mysterious Island*, N. C. Wyeth realized one of his dearest wishes. The idea of this edition was his own. When the question came up of what book should follow in the series of illustrated books for young readers, he proposed *The Mysterious Island,* a favorite book of his, one he had always wished to illustrate.[3]

His reaction was sometimes unpredictable, though. When asked a few years later to illustrate another book by Jules Verne, *Twenty Thousand Leagues Under the Sea,* he flatly turned it down:

I positively cannot get up the least interest in Twenty Thousand Leagues etc. I have read it twice with all the concentration I am capable of and the damn thing sickens me. . . . I find so little in it which offers itself as a sympathetic vehicle on which to carry the things I love most to express.

If on the other hand you will consider another title for me I would be made very happy if the volume of patriotic verse were to be considered again. I had made up my mind and heart on that.[4]

BEN GUNN (*I saw a figure leap with great rapidity behind the trunk of a pine . . .*)
Oil on canvas, h:47, w:38
Signed lower right: N. C. Wyeth
Treasure Island, by Robert Louis Stevenson
Charles Scribner's Sons, 1911
Courtesy of Mrs. Andrew Wyeth

ON THE ISLE OF ERRAID (. . . *as long as the light
lasted I kept a bright look-out . . .*)
Oil on canvas, h:40, w:32
Signed lower right: N. C. Wyeth
Kidnapped, by Robert Louis Stevenson
Charles Scribner's Sons, 1913
Courtesy of Mr. & Mrs. William V. Sipple, Jr.

AND LAWLESS, KEEPING HALF A STEP IN FRONT
OF HIS COMPANION . . . STUDIED OUT THEIR
PATH
The Black Arrow, by Robert Louis Stevenson
Copyright 1916 Charles Scribner's Sons;
renewal copyright 1944 N. C. Wyeth

This volume of patriotic poems was published in 1922—*Poems of American Patriotism* by Brander Matthews.

The first American classic to be undertaken for the Scribner series was James Fenimore Cooper's *The Last of the Mohicans*. Although it did not make its appearance until 1919, the planning for it went as far back as 1915. In a letter from Wyeth to Scribner's under the date April 16, 1915, he agreed to illustrate the book, and in a later letter he remarked:

I got some remarkable material in the Lake George country. Cooked my supper over a fire in "Cooper's Cave" in spite of the fact that it is right in the heart of the city of Glens Falls.

Found a rifle ball at Fort George where they are just now excavating for a R-R siding. The bullet is sponsor for one good picture idea at least.[5]

His apparent enthusiasm for illustrating *The Last of the Mohicans* turned to bitter disappointment when he received the proofs to review. In a letter to Mr. Scribner he complained:

Your letter has in turn made me feel very miserable that I have misconstrued or made so much out of what was but a pleasant effort on your part to relieve my disappointment over the Cooper reproductions. No doubt I have been feeling the failure of the platemakers too bitterly, but it is hard, after four months of intense application, to see one's efforts reduced to such pitiable terms—and to know that they will be so multiplied.[6]

From this same letter it is clear that his pain was eased somewhat by the news of the choice of another book for him to illustrate, Charles Kingsley's *Westward Ho!*, and he conveyed his pleasure:

WE MUST BE IN THE DUNGEON . . .
The Black Arrow, by Robert Louis Stevenson
Copyright 1916 Charles Scribner's Sons;
renewal copyright 1944 N. C. Wyeth

THE BLACK ARROW FLIETH NEVERMORE
Oil on canvas, h:40, w:32
Signed upper right: N. C. Wyeth
The Black Arrow, by Robert Louis Stevenson
Copyright 1916 Charles Scribner's Sons;
renewal copyright 1944 N. C. Wyeth
Courtesy of Mr. Andrew Wyeth

[91]
THE SIEGE OF THE ROUND-HOUSE (*. . . with a rush
    of feet and a roar . . .*)
Oil on canvas, h:40, w:32
Signed lower right: N. C. Wyeth
Kidnapped, by Robert Louis Stevenson
Charles Scribner's Sons, 1913
Courtesy of Mrs. Russell G. Colt

ROBIN AND HIS MOTHER GO TO NOTTINGHAM
    FAIR
Robin Hood, by Paul Creswick
David McKay, Publisher, 1917

CAPTAIN NEMO
The Mysterious Island, by Jules Verne
Copyright 1918 Charles Scribner's Sons;
renewal copyright 1946 Carolyn B. Wyeth and
Charles Scribner's Sons

I am delighted, as you must realize, that you have decided upon "Westward Ho!" I began the reading and study of this magnificent story some six weeks ago so already I have it well in hand. The Naval Bureau of Navigation in Washington has agreed to furnish me with all data concerning ships of the period, which was the main stumbling block for me.[7]

During the period when he was making the illustrations for *Westward Ho!* other projects were also under way, among them the pictures for the aforementioned *Robinson Crusoe* for Cosmopolitan Book Corporation.

The Scribner organization was anxious to proceed with *Westward Ho!* and rather concerned at the delay in getting all the finished paintings. To their inquiries on the status of the work, Wyeth replied:

Let me say right away that I am speeding up on Westward Ho! and expect to beat July 10th as a delivery date.

I am sorry that there seems to be so much concern about my behavior in doing the two books and beg to say that no favorable discrimination has been shown in either case. I would like to say here that the preparation for Westward Ho! has required more than twice as much time and money than I ever spent before, entailing two trips to Massachusetts (Haverhill and Salem libraries), also Washington and Philadelphia. The obscurity of maritime detail of 1580 is amazing. . . . The general lack of data made me recast the scheme of subjects several times in order to meet the kind of thing I could do with reasonable accuracy.

Robinson Crusoe, except for two pictures, the first and last, has required no data whatsoever except the few details I am perfectly familiar with.

The above stated facts are all that have created any discrimination in delivery dates.[8]

This was followed by a letter dated June 14 (1920):

Every hour and every ounce of energy is being directed in getting the Westward

SIR MADOR'S SPEAR BRAKE ALL TO PIECES, BUT
    THE OTHER'S SPEAR HELD
The Boy's King Arthur, edited by Sidney Lanier
Copyright 1917 Charles Scribner's Sons;
renewal copyright 1945 N. C. Wyeth

[93]

ESELDORF WAS A PARADISE FOR US BOYS
Oil on canvas, h:40, w:32
Signed upper left: N. C. Wyeth
The Mysterious Stranger, by Mark Twain.
Harper & Brothers Publishers, 1916
(Copyright 1916 by Harper & Row, Publishers, Inc.;
renewed 1944 by Clara Clemens Gabrilowitsch.)
Courtesy of Mr. & Mrs. Peter Hurd

ROBIN HOOD AND THE MEN OF THE GREENWOOD
Oil on canvas, h:40, w:32
Signed lower left: N. C. Wyeth
Robin Hood (cover design), by Paul Creswick
David McKay, Publisher, 1917
Copyright permission, courtesy of David McKay Company,
   Inc.
Courtesy of The New York Public Library

Ho! drawings completed as early as possible. Everything else is being sacrificed to do this.[9]

And on July 19 (1920):

I am trembling to tell you this but it must be said—I have withdrawn one of the Westward Ho! pictures and am doing it over again. With the set completed, the drawing showing John Brimblecombe stood out as distinctively inferior to the rest and I could not let it go through. . . .

I have thoroughly enjoyed doing the book, every minute of it, and were it not for the matter of time would feel genuinely sorry to say finis.[10]

Three Wyeth-illustrated books, in fact, were published in 1920—in addition to *Westward Ho!* and *Robinson Crusoe, The Courtship of Miles Standish* also made its appearance. *Robinson*

Crusoe had always been a particular favorite of Wyeth's, and in his preface to the book he wrote:

The outstanding appeal of this fascinating romance to me personally is the remarkably sustained sensation one enjoys of Crusoe's contact with the elements—the sea and the sun, the night and the storms, the sand, rocks, vegetation and animal life. In few books can the reader breathe, live and move with his hero so intensely, so easily and so consistently throughout the narrative. In Robinson Crusoe we have it; here is a story that becomes history, history living and moving, carrying with it irresistibly the compelling motive of a lone man's conquest over what seems to be inexorable fate.[11]

The year 1921 saw the publication of two more books with handsome illustrations by N. C. Wyeth: *Rip Van Winkle* (by the McKay organization) and *The Scottish Chiefs,* which was the eighth Scribner Illustrated Classic he had done.

In midsummer of 1921 he wrote to Scribner's of the progress being made on *The Scottish Chiefs*:

By this time, without much doubt, you have three more of the "Scottish Chiefs" drawings. More will follow soon. I hope that these come somewhere near your expectations. I am trying to keep a greater freshness of color and spontaneity of rendering, and still present considerable detail.[12]

Shortly thereafter, the work for this book was completed:

As I wired you, the last illustration for "Scottish Chiefs" was shipped in the morning of Aug. 12th. The subject is one that has given me so much difficulty from the beginning—"The Battle of Stirling Castle". I believe I have got something at last—a picture which rings with a certain historic conviction, a quality which I felt was very necessary, in that particular subject.

With reasonably good color plates, this series should take its place with the best I have done.[13]

His obvious pleasure with the results he had achieved in the illustrations done for this book inspired him to contemplate doing a num-

TREASURE ISLAND
BY
ROBERT LOUIS STEVENSON

Illustrated
By
N.C.WYETH

NEW YORK
CHARLES SCRIBNER'S SONS
M · C · M · X · I

ROBIN HOOD AND HIS COMPANIONS LEND AID
    . . . FROM AMBUSH
Oil on canvas, h:40, w:32
Signed upper left: N. C. Wyeth
Robin Hood, by Paul Creswick
David McKay, Publisher, 1917
Copyright permission, courtesy of David McKay Company,
    Inc.
Courtesy of The New York Public Library

THE BATTLE AT GLENS FALLS
Oil on canvas, h:40, w:32
Signed lower left: N. C. Wyeth
The Last of the Mohicans, by James Fenimore Cooper
Copyright 1919 Charles Scribner's Sons;
renewal copyright 1947 Carolyn B. Wyeth
Courtesy of Mrs. Russell G. Colt

THE THREE FRIENDS
The White Company, by A. Conan Doyle
Cosmopolitan Book Corporation, New York, 1922

ber of others that might fit into the Scribner series. A few days later he wrote to Joseph Chapin:

> What I want you to do now, in the course of the next three or four years, is to let me go to Scotland and gather material for a series of five or six of Scott's novels!!! following with an edition of Burns and another of James Hogg.[14]

It is not known whether any serious consideration was given to this suggestion. Suffice it to say that Wyeth did not illustrate a book by any of these three writers.

During most of the 1920s he was inundated with a constant demand for his creations, however. This was a period when his output of mural work was enormous; he also fulfilled a good many commissions for advertising art in addition to illustrating fourteen books and painting countless pictures for stories in periodicals —a prodigious volume of creative activity.

While Wyeth was working on the paintings for *The Odyssey of Homer* (Houghton Mifflin), Scribner's approached him about illustrating *Gulliver's Travels,* which they proposed to add to the Illustrated Classics series. He replied to them in June of that year (1929):

[99]

AND WHEN THEY CAME TO THE SWORD THE
HAND HELD, KING ARTHUR TOOK IT UP . . .
Oil on canvas
Signed lower right: N. C. Wyeth
The Boy's King Arthur, edited by Sidney Lanier
Copyright 1917 Charles Scribner's Sons;
renewal copyright 1945 N. C. Wyeth
Courtesy of Jack Webb

ROBIN MEETS MAID MARIAN
Oil on canvas, h:40, w:32
Signed lower left: N. C. Wyeth
Robin Hood, by Paul Creswick
David McKay, Publisher, 1917
Copyright permission, courtesy of David McKay Company,
Inc.
Courtesy of the New York Public Library

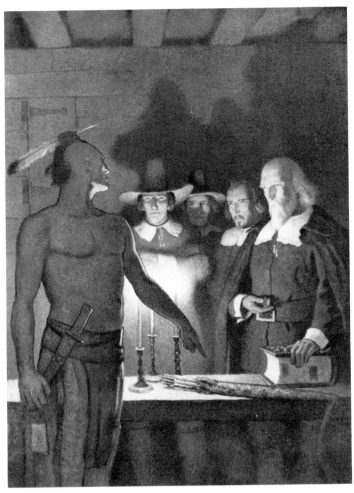

NEAR THEM WAS STANDING AN INDIAN, IN
    ATTITUDE STERN AND DEFIANT
The Courtship of Miles Standish, by Henry Wadsworth
    Longfellow
Houghton Mifflin Company, 1920

I am planning to take up Gulliver soon after I complete the Odyssey. This will be, I judge about the middle to the last of September. I am reading Gulliver now. . . .[15]

I am very tardy in acknowledging the receipt of the selected volume of Gulliver's Travels you sent to me. However, I am now prepared to report to you after a fresh reading and a reasonably careful study of the stories as material for illustration pictures.

Thirty years or more have passed since I last read the travels and it is significant to me that the first two parts remained vividly in my mind, whereas, the last parts left almost no impression at all. The voyage to Laputa leaves me cold, but I do feel the urge to do a few amusing grotesqueries for Gulliver's visit to the Houyhnhnms.

It is a pity that we cannot get out an elaborately pictured volume of just the Lilliput and Brobdingnag adventures.[16]

The Scribner plans for *Gulliver* did not conform to Wyeth's ideas. He mulled over the proposal to do the book for several months, and on August 19, 1929, he wrote:

For reasons pertaining purely to my present state of artistic transition I wish to "beg off" and so postpone "Gulliver" for a year. I shall, of course, do nothing else in

WHY DON'T YOU SPEAK FOR YOURSELF, JOHN?
The Courtship of Miles Standish, by Henry Wadsworth
　　Longfellow
Houghton Mifflin Company, 1920

KING MARK SLEW THE NOBLE KNIGHT SIR
    TRISTRAM
Oil on canvas, h:40, w:32
Signed upper left: N. C. Wyeth
The Boy's King Arthur, edited by Sidney Lanier
Copyright 1917 Charles Scribner's Sons;
renewal copyright 1945 N. C. Wyeth
Courtesy of Mr. & Mrs. Ronald Rauch Randall

THE FIGHT IN THE FOREST
Oil on canvas, h:40, w:32
Signed lower right: N. C. Wyeth
The Last of the Mohicans, by James Fenimore Cooper
Copyright 1919 Charles Scribner's Sons;
renewal copyright 1947 Carolyn B. Wyeth
From the Permanent Collection, Brandywine River Museum

competitive book illustration in the meantime. . . .

I realize how much I am disturbing your plans, but no more so than a set of perfunctory drawings which would result were I forced to go through with the work. I have tried hard, ever since reading and planning the "Gulliver" series two months ago, to see my way clear to tackle them, but I cannot arouse sufficient spirit and enthusiasm.[17]

John Fox, Jr.'s *The Little Shepherd of Kingdom Come* was published by Scribner's as an Illustrated Classic in 1931, a handsome volume, particularly the elaborately printed and bound limited edition. It was the last book Wyeth was

HE WAS . . . SURPRISED AT THE SINGULARITY OF
THE STRANGER'S APPEARANCE
Rip Van Winkle, by Washington Irving
David McKay, Publisher, 1921

THESE FOLKS WERE EVIDENTLY AMUSING
THEMSELVES . . .
Rip Van Winkle, by Washington Irving
David McKay, Publisher, 1921

[107]

JOHN OXENHAM
Oil on canvas, h:40, w:30
Signed upper left: N. C. Wyeth
Westward Ho!, by Charles Kingsley
Copyright 1920 Charles Scribner's Sons;
renewal copyright 1948 Carolyn B. Wyeth
Courtesy of George D. Beck

I STOOD LIKE ONE THUNDERSTRUCK . . .
Oil on canvas, h:40, w:30
Signed lower right: N. C. Wyeth
Robinson Crusoe, by Daniel Defoe
Cosmopolitan Book Corporation, 1920
Copyright permission, courtesy of David McKay Company,
    Inc.
Courtesy of Wilmington Institute & New Castle County
    Libraries, Wilmington, Delaware

KING EDWARD
The Scottish Chiefs, by Jane Porter
Copyright 1921 Charles Scribner's Sons;
renewal copyright 1949 Carolyn B. Wyeth

to illustrate for eight years. Then came Marjorie Kinnan Rawlings's delightful *The Yearling*, chosen as a Scribner Illustrated Classic in spite of the fact that it was a new book. To obtain authentic background material for his *Yearling* illustrations, Wyeth made a trip to Florida to study the locale firsthand:

I'm already quite saturated with the appearance of Baxter's Island clearing, the neighboring "sink" and the vast surrounding wilderness of palmetto scrub-lands.

This is a surprisingly wild country as you move back from the few main highways and the people who live on these endless sandy roads are as interesting and authentic types of American pioneers, hunters and trappers as I ever saw.

I've watched "gators" slide into the dark streams, caught a glimpse of a black bear and actually heard the scream of a panther last night. I was standing in one of those "bays" of live-oak and pines. There was a light wind which moved the Spanish

PAUL REVERE
Poems of American Patriotism, edited by Brander Matthews
Copyright 1922 Charles Scribner's Sons;
renewal copyright 1950

RIP VAN WINKLE (*It was with some difficulty that he
    found the way to his own house . . .*)
Oil on canvas, h:40, w:30
Signed lower left: N. C. Wyeth
Rip Van Winkle, by Washington Irving
David McKay Company, 1921

SIR NIGEL SUSTAINS ENGLAND'S HONOR IN THE
    LISTS
Oil on canvas, h:40, w:30
Signed lower left: N. C. Wyeth
The White Company, by A. Conan Doyle
Cosmopolitan Book Corporation, 1922
Courtesy of Mrs. N. C. Wyeth

THE MIDNIGHT ENCOUNTER
Legends of Charlemagne, by Thomas Bulfinch
Cosmopolitan Book Corporation, 1924

THE WATER-HOLE
Oil on canvas, h:28, w:36
Signed lower left: N. C. Wyeth
The Oregon Trail (end papers), by Francis Parkman
Little, Brown & Company, 1925
Courtesy of Southern Arizona Bank & Trust Company, Tucson

moss back and forth spectrally, and through this the moon-light poured. The moving shadows made the ground we were standing on writhe and undulate as though it were actually alive. The distant fearful call of that cat added the last touch of blood-chilling accompaniment to the scene.[18]

In that same year, 1939, Little, Brown and Company issued an illustrated edition of Helen Hunt Jackson's celebrated *Ramona.* This was the last outstanding literary work for which Wyeth was to paint the illustrations.

Following is a list of the great masterpieces of writing to which N. C. Wyeth contributed the illustrations:

Treasure Island by Robert Louis Stevenson
Charles Scribner's Sons, 1911.

Kidnapped by Robert Louis Stevenson
Charles Scribner's Sons, 1913.

The Black Arrow by Robert Louis Stevenson
Charles Scribner's Sons, 1916.

The Mysterious Stranger by Mark Twain
Harper & Brothers, 1916.

The Boy's King Arthur
(Edited by) Sidney Lanier
Charles Scribner's Sons, 1917.

Robin Hood by Paul Creswick
David McKay, 1917.

The Mysterious Island by Jules Verne
Charles Scribner's Sons, 1918.

The Last of the Mohicans
by James Fenimore Cooper
Charles Scribner's Sons, 1919.

Westward Ho! by Charles Kingsley
Charles Scribner's Sons, 1920.

Robinson Crusoe by Daniel Defoe
Cosmopolitan Book Corporation, 1920.

THE DUEL
Oil on canvas, h:34, w:25
Signed upper left: N. C. Wyeth
David Balfour, by Robert Louis Stevenson
Copyright 1924 Charles Scribner's Sons;
renewal copyright 1952 Carolyn B. Wyeth and
    Charles Scribner's Sons
Courtesy of Alexander F. Treadwell

THE PARKMAN OUTFIT—HENRY CHATILLON, GUIDE
    AND HUNTER
Oil on canvas, h:40½, w:29⅛
Signed lower left: N. C. Wyeth
The Oregon Trail, by Francis Parkman
Little, Brown and Company, 1925
Courtesy of Southern Arizona Bank & Trust Company, Tucson

BUFFALO HUNT
Oil on canvas, h:40, w:30
Signed lower left: N. C. Wyeth
The Oregon Trail, by Francis Parkman
Little, Brown and Company, 1925
Courtesy of J. N. Bartfield Galleries, Inc., New York

EMERGING INTO AN OPENING . . .
Oil on canvas, h:40, w:32
Signed lower left: N. C. Wyeth/To Peter/from Grandfather
The Deerslayer, by James Fenimore Cooper
Copyright 1925 Charles Scribner's Sons;
renewal copyright 1953
Courtesy of Peter Wyeth Hurd

[117]

MELISSA
The Little Shepherd of Kingdom Come, by John Fox, Jr.
Copyright 1931 Charles Scribner's Sons;
renewal copyright © 1959

The Courtship of Miles Standish
   by Henry W. Longfellow
   Houghton Mifflin Company, 1920.

The Scottish Chiefs by Jane Porter
   Charles Scribner's Sons, 1921.

Rip Van Winkle by Washington Irving
   David McKay, 1921.

Poems of American Patriotism
   by Brander Matthews
   Charles Scribner's Sons, 1922.

The White Company by A. Conan Doyle
   Cosmopolitan Book Corporation, 1922.

David Balfour by Robert Louis Stevenson
   Charles Scribner's Sons, 1924.

Legends of Charlemagne
   by Thomas Bulfinch
   Cosmopolitan Book Corporation, 1924.

The Deerslayer by James Fenimore Cooper
   Charles Scribner's Sons, 1925.

THE FIGHT WITH OLD SLEWFOOT
The Yearling, by Marjorie Kinnan Rawlings
Copyright 1939 Charles Scribner's Sons;
renewal copyright © 1967

THE DISCOVERY OF THE CHEST
Oil on canvas, h:40, w:30
Signed lower left: N. C. Wyeth
The Mysterious Island, by Jules Verne
Copyright 1918 Charles Scribner's Sons;
renewal copyright 1946 Carolyn B. Wyeth and
    Charles Scribner's Sons
Courtesy of Mrs. Arthur L. Smythe

←
DEERSLAYER THREW ALL
    HIS FORCE INTO A
    DESPERATE EFFORT
Oil on canvas, h:40, w:32
Signed lower right: N. C. Wyeth
The Deerslayer, by James
    Fenimore Cooper
Copyright 1925 Charles Scribner's
    Sons;
renewal copyright 1953
Courtesy of Mrs. N. C. Wyeth

The Oregon Trail by Francis Parkman
    Little, Brown & Company, 1925.

Michael Strogoff by Jules Verne
    Charles Scribner's Sons, 1927.

Drums by James Boyd
    Charles Scribner's Sons, 1928.

The Odyssey of Homer
    (Translated by) Charles Herbert Palmer
    Houghton Mifflin Company, 1929.

Jinglebob by Philip Ashton Rollins
    Charles Scribner's Sons, 1930.

The Little Shepherd of Kingdom Come
    by John Fox, Jr.
    Charles Scribner's Sons, 1931.

The Yearling by Marjorie Kinnan Rawlings
    Charles Scribner's Sons, 1939.

Ramona by Helen Hunt Jackson
    Little, Brown & Company, 1939.

THE ROAD TO VIDALIA
Oil on canvas, h:48¼, w:39¼
Signed lower right: N. C. Wyeth
Cease Firing, by Mary Johnston
Houghton Mifflin Company, 1912
Courtesy of James B. Wyeth

8

From Blackbeard to St. Nick

IN presenting the many types of subject matter that N. C. Wyeth painted, his works have been arranged in specific categories. To have presented them in chronological order would have resulted in a disconcerting hodgepodge. Among his book and magazine illustrations, however, are a sizable number on widely varied themes that do not readily lend themselves to such categorizing. These are grouped together here—and this chapter could aptly have been titled "Miscellaneous Book and Magazine Illustration." As might be expected, though, there is nothing "miscellaneous" about their quality.

Most of these illustrations were originally made for magazines; many appeared later as book illustrations when the stories were reprinted in book form. The authors whose tales

were made more vivid by Wyeth's pictorial skill were among the best known and most popular of the period: Peter B. Kyne, James B. Connolly, Arthur Conan Doyle, Dorothy Canfield Fisher, Edna Ferber, Ben Ames Williams, Bret Harte, Stewart Edward White, Rafael Sabatini, Harold Bell Wright, and James Oliver Curwood, to name only a few.

Nor can we ignore the dust wrapper illustrations Wyeth painted for Kenneth Roberts's historical novels—*Arundel, The Lively Lady,* and *Rabble in Arms*—or the exceptional illustrations done for his *Trending into Maine,* works so praiseworthy that several of them have been included in Chapter 11, which is devoted to his easel paintings.

The Wyeth Edition of the *Bounty* trilogy

THE FIRST CARGO
Oil on canvas, h:47, w:38
Signed lower left: N. C. Wyeth
"The First Cargo," by Arthur Conan Doyle
Scribner's Magazine, December 1910
Courtesy of The New York Public Library

brought together those three outstanding works by Nordhoff and Hall: *Mutiny on the Bounty, Men Against the Sea,* and *Pitcairn's Island.*

Last but not least were the Boston Blackie stories by none other than the great No. 6606.

Since this chapter concludes the presentation of N. C. Wyeth's work in the field of book and magazine illustration, which was certainly the field in which he was most renowned, it might be appropriate to consider briefly not only that period termed by many the Golden Age of American Illustration, but also Wyeth's personal feelings regarding his craft.

The Golden Age of American Illustration roughly covered some fifty years. Following the Civil War, the industrial revolution intensified in the United States, and with it came a phenomenal burgeoning of inventive genius. The printing industry was one of those most affected by the new developments. Practical inventions and vastly improved techniques resulted in making the printed word available to the general public more cheaply than ever before. This was especially true in the case of periodicals—their stories were supplemented by more illustrations than had been economically possible in the past. The change soon brought into prominence some of the names that became outstanding in American art and illustration—among them Winslow Homer, A. B. Frost, Edwin A. Abbey, Frederic Remington, and Howard Pyle. The best talents were commissioned by such topflight publishers as Harper's, Scribner's, and Century; the myriad of other publications that were appearing on the scene were forced to turn to the inferior ones. Even these lesser illustrators had little difficulty in getting their work accepted for publication, however, and the pages of both periodicals and books began to be filled with second-rate work.

It was for just this reason that Howard Pyle founded his courses of study in illustration at Drexel Institute and later at his own school in Wilmington. The young students who studied under him and a few of the established illustrators who came to him for guidance during the late eighteen nineties and early nineteen hundreds were, in a great measure, responsible for bringing a new quality to illustration for the remainder of the Golden Age. Of course the art of illustration did not survive only because of Howard Pyle and those who studied

[125]

MOOSE HUNTERS—A MOONLIT NIGHT
Oil on canvas, h:40, w:21½
Signed upper left: N. C. Wyeth
Scribner's Magazine, October 1912
Courtesy of Mr. & Mrs. Andrew Wyeth

FROM AN UPPER SNOW PLATFORM . . . A SECOND
    MAN HEAVED THEM OVER THE BANK
"How They Opened the Snow Road," by W. M. Raine and
    W. H. Eader
The Outing Magazine, January 1907

LONG HENRY DROVE CAUTIOUSLY ACROSS THE
    SCENE OF YESTERDAY'S ACCIDENT
"How They Opened the Snow Road," by W. M. Raine
    and W. H. Eader
The Outing Magazine, January 1907

THE EIGHT MINERS FOLLOWED THE
    TREACHEROUS TRAIL
"How They Opened the Snow Road," by W. M. Raine and
    W. H. Eader
The Outing Magazine, January 1907

HE . . . FLUNG THE SIX POUNDS OF POWERFUL
    EXPLOSIVE OUT INTO THE GREAT SNOW
    COMB
"How They Opened the Snow Road," by W. M. Raine and
    W. H. Eader
The Outing Magazine, January 1907

"The Drifts Became Heavier. There Were No Marks of Recent Travel"

THE DRIFTS BECAME HEAVIER
"A Christmas Venture," by S. Weir Mitchell
Ladies' Home Journal, December 1907

THE VEDETTE
Oil on canvas, h:48¼, w:38¼
Signed lower right: N. C. Wyeth '10
The Long Roll, by Mary Johnston
Houghton Mifflin Company, 1911
Courtesy of Mr. & Mrs. George A. Weymouth

under him. There were other great illustrators who had that special talent that enabled them to survive changes in taste and vogue. But there were many more who lacked that gift.

Like Howard Pyle, N. C. Wyeth was deeply disturbed as he contemplated the gradual deterioration of illustration as a result of the lack of sound basic training in the art schools. To be a success in the field of illustration it was not only essential that a student know how to draw, but, more important, that he be educated to project himself into the soul of the character to be depicted in an illustration. In this the teaching of young, aspiring illustrators was sadly lacking. Howard Pyle had been deeply aware of this fundamental, and he made it basic in the teaching of his own students. N. C. Wyeth had been thoroughly indoctrinated in this approach.

It is a universal opinion among discriminating readers that illustration in the majority of cases is a superimposed burden upon the story it pretends to illustrate. I am in hearty sympathy with that opinion. It is too often a detached art and makes little pretense to be in working harmony and sympathetically submissive to the spirit of the tale. In being submissive it will add

power and charm to the story but if it precludes the author's artistry by repeating in bald assertions the main incidents and characters it becomes a vital menace and detriment in the expression of any writing, be the writing ever so powerful and the pictures ever so inferior.

The artistic powers of an illustrator spring from the same source as do the powers of the painter; but the profound difference lies in the fact that the illustrator submits his inspiration to a definite end; the painter carries his into infinitude. Therefore, the work of the illustrator resolves itself into a craft and he must not lose sight of that very important factor.

To successfully illustrate he must be subjective. It is important business to use restraint, particularly in the choice of subjects. The ability to select subject matter is an art in itself and calls to action similar dramatic instincts required in the staging of

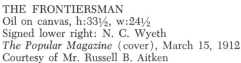

THE FRONTIERSMAN
Oil on canvas, h:33½, w:24½
Signed lower right: N. C. Wyeth
The Popular Magazine (cover), March 15, 1912
Courtesy of Mr. Russell B. Aitken

THE BATTLE
Oil on canvas, h:45¾, w:36¾
Signed lower right: N. C. Wyeth 1910
The Long Roll, by Mary Johnston
Houghton Mifflin Company, 1911
Courtesy of Mr. & Mrs. George A. Weymouth

a play. The illustrator must first feel the power of the story in all its rhythm and swing, at the same time sense just at the right moment to step in with his illustration just as the play producer endeavors to intensify and enhance the drama with his ingenious stage properties and effects. To do this requires an amount of instinctive ability, but, like everything else, it improves with experience and serious study.

By avoiding the shackles of explicit action and detail the illustrator will find a field of far greater range upon which to exercise his powers, emotional and technical, and is given a better chance to produce something of real merit.[1]

Convincing illustration must ring true to life. The characters should be of flesh and blood, not puppets who strike attitudes for the sake of composition, or manikins which serve as drapes for clothes, however effective the costumes in themselves may be.[2]

The time rapidly approached when the Golden Age of American Illustration began to come to an end. N. C. Wyeth had been a vital part of this age, and he became depressed by the changes. His thoughts turned more and more to mural painting. He also began to take on more commercial assignments. Although his output of book illustrations maintained a steady pace, his interest in purely magazine illustration took a sharp decline. In a letter to Joseph Chapin of Scribner's, dated November 11, 1919, he remarked:

GOLYER
The Pike County Ballads, by John Hay
Houghton Mifflin Company, 1912

LITTLE BREECHES
The Pike County Ballads, by John Hay
Houghton Mifflin Company, 1912

BOSTON BLACKIE FORCED DRAWER
AFTER DRAWER
"Boston Blackie Stories," by No. 6606
The American Magazine, July 1914

Headpiece Illustration
"The Quest of Narcisse LaBlanche," by George T. Marsh
Scribner's Magazine, May 1916

STONEWALL JACKSON
Oil on canvas, h:47, w:38¼
Signed lower right: N. C. Wyeth '10
The Long Roll, by Mary Johnston
Houghton Mifflin Company, 1911
Courtesy of Alexander F. Treadwell

Magazine illustration has become a very unsatisfactory job. The pay in most instances is liberal enough, but presentation to the public is rotten! One must needs work abortively to help the engraver, thus ruining the finer pleasure in making the pictures, and then one gets a bad reproduction anyway.[3]

Did Wyeth's attitude toward magazine illustration stem from emotions that may have prevailed generally at the time? Or had he

THE CARPETBAGGERS
Oil on canvas, h:49, w:39
Signed lower left: N. C. Wyeth
The Pike County Ballads (cover design), by John Hay
Houghton Mifflin Company, 1912
Courtesy of Diamond M Foundation, Snyder, Texas

JIM BLUDSOE OF THE PRAIRIE BELLE
Oil on canvas, h:32, w:24
Signed lower right: N. C. Wyeth
The Pike County Ballads, by John Hay
Houghton Mifflin Company, 1912
Courtesy of Diamond M Foundation, Snyder, Texas

THE OPIUM SMOKER (*"Finally I Became a Daily
    User of Opium"*)
Oil on canvas, h:32, w:44
Signed upper right: N. C. Wyeth 1913
"A Modern Opium Eater," by No. 6606
The American Magazine, June 1914
Courtesy of Mr. and Mrs. Dallett Hemphill

[131]

'N THERE'S A DRAGON BLACK AS INK WI' ONE EYE
Oil on canvas, h:44, w:32
Signed lower left: N. C. Wyeth
"The Rakish Brigantine," by James B. Connolly
Scribner's Magazine, August 1914
Courtesy of The Needham Public Library, Needham, Mass.

HE'D LET A ROAR OUTER HIM, AN' MEBBE HE'D
SING, "HAIL COLUMBIA, HAPPY LAND!"
"The Rakish Brigantine," by James B. Connolly
Scribner's Magazine, August 1914

N. C. Wyeth posed with the
completed illustrations for
"The Rakish Brigantine."
Courtesy of the Delaware
Art Museum

SONG OF THE EAGLE THAT MATES WITH THE
    STORM
Oil on canvas, h:40, w:32
Signed lower right: N. C. Wyeth
"The Wild Woman's Lullaby," by Constance Lindsay
    Skinner
Scribner's Magazine, December 1916
Courtesy of Thomas Gilcrease Institute, Tulsa, Oklahoma

THE DEATH OF FINNWARD KEELFARER
Oil on canvas, h:44, w:32
Signed lower left: N. C. Wyeth
"The Waif Woman," by Robert Louis Stevenson
Scribner's Magazine, December 1914
Courtesy of Mr. & Mrs. Joseph E. Levine

OH, MORGAN'S MEN ARE OUT FOR YOU; AND
    BLACKBEARD—BUCCANEER!
"The Golden Galleon," by Paul Hervey Fox
Scribner's Magazine, August 1917

simply stated a personal observation after careful consideration? The statistics are interesting. From that day in 1903 when his *Saturday Evening Post* cover appeared, to the end of 1919, a span of seventeen years, Wyeth contributed to approximately twenty-four different periodicals in 275 issues, making a total number of 561 illustrations for them. From 1920 through 1945,

an even longer span of time, the number of periodicals for which he worked dropped to nineteen; the number of issues to 100, which contained only 229 Wyeth illustrations.

In 1927 a series of articles was published about notable illustrators, and one of these was devoted to Wyeth:

THE FIGHT IN THE PEAKS
Oil on canvas
Signed lower left: N. C. Wyeth
Scribner's Magazine, February 1917
Courtesy of Mr. & Mrs. R. R. M. Carpenter, Jr.

FRONTIER TRAPPER
Oil on canvas, h:34, w:32
Signed lower right: N. C. Wyeth
Copyright by The Book House for Children, 1920; from
    My Book House
Courtesy of the United Educators, Inc.,
    Lake Bluff, Illinois

OLE ST. NICK (OLD KRIS)
Oil on canvas, h:41½, w:31
Signed lower right: N. C. Wyeth
The Country Gentleman (cover), December 1925
Courtesy of John Denys McCoy

COLUMBUS' LANDING
Essentials of American History, by
  Thomas Bonaventure Lawler
Copyright 1918 by Thomas Bonaventure Lawler; renewed
  1946 by T. Newman Lawler
Ginn and Company

A CALIFORNIA MISSION
Oil on canvas, h:39¼, w:26¼
Signed lower left: N. C. Wyeth
Essentials of American History, by
  Thomas Bonaventure Lawler
Copyright 1918 by Thomas Bonaventure Lawler; renewed
  1946 by T. Newman Lawler
Ginn and Company
Courtesy of Mr. & Mrs. Richard DeVictor

THE BOY COLUMBUS ON THE WHARF IN GENOA
New Geography, Book One, the Frye-Atwood Geographical
  Series
Copyright 1917 by Alexis Everett Frye; renewed 1945
  by Teresa A. Frye.
Ginn and Company

Cover Illustration
Ladies' Home Journal, March 1922
Courtesy of the *Ladies' Home Journal*

Unpublished Illustration
Oil on canvas, h:31¾, w:34
Signed upper right: N. C. Wyeth
Inscription lower right: To my friend Kamp from N.C.W.
Made for "Snake and Hawk," by Stephen Vincent
    Benét, a story that appeared in the *Ladies'*
    Home Journal, March 1923
Courtesy of Mr. & Mrs. Anton Kamp

BIG BLACK BEPPO AND LITTLE BLACK BEPPO
"Time and Tide," Adriana Spadoni
Woman's Home Companion, July 1924

Preliminary Study for "Sea-Fever"
Drawing on paper, h:13⅜, w:9⅝
Signed lower right: N C W
The finished illustration was used with John
    Masefield's "Sea-Fever"
World of Music Series—Discovery
Ginn & Company, 1938
Courtesy of Mr. & Mrs. Richard Layton

THERE WAS AN OLD WOMAN TOST UP IN A
    BASKET . . .
Oil on panel, h:36, w:26
Signed upper left: N. C. Wyeth
Anthology of Children's Literature, compiled by
    Edna Johnson and Carrie E. Scott
Houghton Mifflin Company, 1940
Courtesy of The Free Library of Philadelphia and
    Houghton Mifflin Company

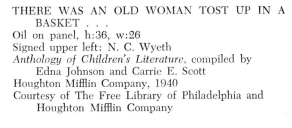

"PECULIARSOME" ABE
Oil on panel, h:32, w:24
Signed lower right: N. C. Wyeth
Anthology of Children's Literature,
comp. by Edna Johnson
and Carrie E. Scott
Houghton Mifflin Company, 1940
Courtesy of The Free Library of
Philadelphia and Houghton
Mifflin Company

Not long ago, there sat a gentleman before an open book. His manner was a sad manner. In his eye there was, perhaps, a tear.

"Where," he asked, "where is there another Howard Pyle?"

Tears are a great luxury. Likewise there is no other Howard Pyle. With him there passed a truly great illustrator. But illustration did not end there. There is, for in-stance, N. C. Wyeth. And there are some sensations we experience in Wyeth illustra-tion that few other illustrators can offer. I doubt if we find their exact counterpart in the illustration of Wyeth's principal teacher, Howard Pyle himself.

It is its own signature, and an inspiring one. There is a heroic treatment of anatomy, for example, that makes a Wyeth masculine-type so gloriously strong and virile,—you

SHE MAKES A GRAND LIGHT *(The Burning of the Bounty)*
Oil on panel, h:34, w:25
Signed lower right: N. C. Wyeth
The Bounty Trilogy, by Charles Nordhoff and James Norman Hall
Little, Brown and Company, 1940
Courtesy of The Free Library of Philadelphia and Little, Brown and Company

FIRST FARMER OF THE LAND
"The First Farmer of the Land," by Donald Culross Peattie
The Country Gentleman, February 1946
(This illustration was on Wyeth's easel, in the process of completion, at the time of his fatal accident.)

ALLONS! . . . IT IS TIME TO MAKE AN END
"The Duel on the Beach," by Rafael Sabatini
Ladies' Home Journal, September 1931
Courtesy of the *Ladies' Home Journal*

look for a new discovery and technique.
Then that romance of color, of wave, of
cloud. Of those authentic, yet fascinating
ships that toss or float over seas, fabulously
stormy or credibly calm.

In the affections of the adolescent boy,
there will be few to replace N. C. Wyeth.
To the very human critic Wyeth has an
insured niche. When one is wearied a bit
it is a pleasant relaxation to rediscover the
sheer color ecstasy and eternal decorative
beauty of an illustration by N. C. Wyeth.[4]

That accolade is just as true today as when
it was written.

UNION TROOPS BOARDING MISSISSIPPI
RIVER STEAMERS
Oil on panel, h:19½, w:14½
Signed lower right: N. C. Wyeth
"The Peach-Brandy Leg,"
by Mabel Thompson Rauch
Woman's Day, August 1945
Courtesy of Kennedy Galleries, Inc., New York

FIRST AID TO THE HUNGRY
Circa 1915 advertisement illustrated by N. C. Wyeth
Courtesy of the W. K. Kellogg Company

9 *Commercial Art*

EARLY in his career N. C. Wyeth learned that commissions for paintings to be used exclusively for advertising purposes were financially worthwhile. Following his first such assignment—for Cream of Wheat—commercial projects were offered to him in steadily increasing numbers: work for magazine advertisements, calendars, posters. He was highly sought after, and despite the large number of paintings he turned out for magazine and book illustration, his output of commercial artwork was considerable. In style, freshness, and appeal, most of his commercial creations are as alive today as they were some fifty years ago; they are not "dated," like the work of so many of the well-known commercial artists of that period.

The financial rewards of doing an abundance of commercial work were a temptation, but Wyeth was well aware of the pitfalls. His commitments for book and magazine illustration and his interest in mural painting and in improving his techniques in easel painting led him to explain his feelings to Joseph Chapin. In a letter dated November 11, 1919, he wrote:

In the meantime opportunities in the illustrating field have piled in beyond anything I ever experienced, particularly for the advertising houses. To date I have turned down all the latter with the exception of a single painting for the Winchester Rifle. In a sense it has been somewhat of an ordeal, for in several cases (three, to be accurate) the price has been 1500.00 for single drawings.

I believe that most of my friends, worthy to know this, would say, "How foolish!". To me it is not foolish, even though it may be impractical. Heaven knows! I've none too much idealism, and what little I've got must be applied. So it is that I am resolved not to be inundated with a character of work which is such an insidious antidote for the qualities within my nature which are struggling for expression. The miserable failure of the older men of my generation in illustration to advance to higher forms of artistic expression stands as an obvious and mighty lesson, and not to

NEW YEAR'S DAY

THANKSGIVING DAY

FOURTH OF JULY
Similar in content to the illustration Wyeth made
in 1904 for *The Delineator* (see Chapter 2).

CHRISTMAS DAY

BANK HOLIDAY POSTERS
(Commissioned by the United States Treasury Depart-
ment; published by The Canterbury Company, Inc.,
Chicago; copyrighted 1921 by Charles Daniel Frey
Company, New York and Chicago.)

make an effort to avoid their errors would be the height of weakness.

Advertising art has indeed progressed remarkably and on the whole is much more interesting to look at than the illustrated story section of most periodicals, but that does not justify it to the artist by any means, for the demands of the advertiser are far more confining and far more artificial than the demands of an author. The big prices offered are blinding and it is so damned easy not to see the danger.[1]

It is, of course, both impractical and impossible to reproduce here everything Wyeth did in the field of commercial art. Many of the originals have disappeared entirely; some doubtless remain in the hands of unknown owners. Others that might have been reproduced appeared originally in periodicals that used a very poor grade of paper and hence are not in good enough condition today to make satisfactory reproduction copy.

Wyeth's Cream of Wheat paintings were made in 1906 and 1907, but all were copyrighted 1907. They were frequently reproduced in the top periodicals for a number of years after their initial appearance. Originally, they were housed in the Minneapolis cereal plant of the National Biscuit Company; later they were donated to the Minneapolis Institute of Art. The painting *Alaska*, while being restored for presentation, was unfortunately destroyed by fire in 1969.

The calendar painting for Winchester Arms that Wyeth mentioned in his 1919 letter to his friend Chapin (*The Moose Hunters*) was not his only commission for that firm. He had painted another hunting scene for a Winchester Arms calendar in 1912, with a bear as the quarry.

Among the commercial work Wyeth did in 1915 was one painting quite different in mood from any commercial illustration he had done before or was to do in the future. This marching group of happy children was made for the W. K. Kellogg Company of Battle Creek, Michigan. The whereabouts of the original painting is unknown, but thanks to the medium of advertising, copies of the original advertisement still exist. Other commercial assignments of those early years included paintings for Fisk Tire, Pierce-Arrow, and Blue Buckle OverAlls (Jobbers OverAll Company, Inc.).

[143]

ALASKA
Oil on canvas
Signed lower right: N. C. Wyeth
Advertisement for Cream of Wheat
Courtesy of the National Biscuit Company

Though Wyeth had written Chapin in his November 1919 letter that he had turned down all advertising work except an assignment for Winchester Arms, he must earlier that year have completed the first of his paintings for Aunt Jemima Mills, for it appeared in national magazines that autumn. By the end of World War I, the jolly-faced Aunt Jemima known and loved by a generation of Americans had begun to lose her appeal and seemed in need of rejuvenation as an advertising symbol. James Webb Young, manager of the J. Walter Thompson Company in Chicago, planned an extensive advertising campaign using a new approach—a series of ads on the theme "The Legend of Aunt Jemima," each of which would contain a choice bit of Aunt Jemima lore in the form of

THE BEAR HUNTERS
Illustration made for 1912
Winchester Arms calendar

THE BRONCO BUSTER
Oil on canvas, h:41½, w:28⅛
Signed lower right: N. C. Wyeth '06
Advertisement for Cream of Wheat
Courtesy of The Minneapolis Institute of Arts,
Gift of The National Biscuit Company

In 1919, Wyeth made a series of illustrations
for Blue Buckle OverAlls, of which this is a representative
example.

AT THE WORLD'S FAIR IN '93
Aunt Jemima advertisement illustrated by N. C. Wyeth
Courtesy of the Quaker Oats Company

WHERE THE MAIL GOES CREAM OF WHEAT GOES
Oil on canvas, h:44¼, w:37⅞
Signed lower right: N. C. Wyeth '06
Advertisement for Cream of Wheat
Courtesy of The Minneapolis Institute of Arts,
Gift of The National Biscuit Company

WAGNER AND LISZT
Courtesy of Steinway & Sons

an interesting narrative illustrated by a handsome, specially commissioned picture. This departure from the then standard type of advertisement had a long-lasting influence on the development of creative techniques in American advertising. During the next four or five years, N. C. Wyeth made six illustrations for the Aunt Jemima campaign, which proved to be a great success.

The year 1921 saw the appearance of four delightful paintings Wyeth made for posters. They represented the four major bank holidays —New Year's Day, the Fourth of July, Thanksgiving, and Christmas—and bore slogans designed to encourage industry and thrift.

Another group of four commercial paintings made around this time can truly be classified as fine art. They were commissioned by Steinway & Sons, for use in advertising their fine piano, "The Instrument of the Immortals." The first of the group, a masterly portrayal of the two musical giants Wagner and Liszt, was reproduced in periodicals in 1919. This was followed in 1921 by a striking composition depicting Beethoven. The third and fourth paintings were based on operas: *The King's Henchman* from Deems Taylor's opera of that name and an allegorical scene from Wagner's *Die Walküre— The Magic Fire Spell*. All four are now part of a distinguished collection of musical memorabilia

THE VIKING SHIP

THE SHIPS OF COLUMBUS

THE GOLDEN GALLEON

THE CONQUEROR

SHIP CALENDAR ILLUSTRATIONS
These four illustrations were painted for the 1923 calendar
of the Berwind-White Coal Mining Company.
Courtesy of the Delaware Art Museum

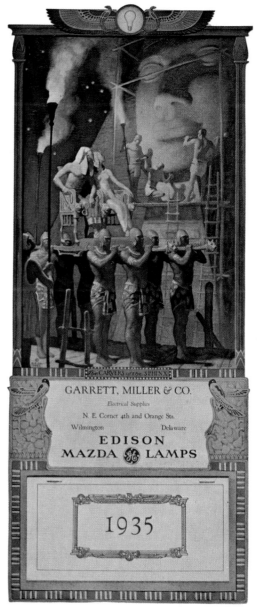

THE CARVERS OF THE SPHINX
Nela Park Division of General Electric Company 1935
    calendar
Courtesy of General Electric Company and the
    Delaware Art Museum

THE TORCH RACE
Nela Park Division of General Electric Company
    1936 calendar
Courtesy of General Electric Company and the
    Delaware Art Museum

on exhibit at Steinway Hall on West Fifty-seventh Street in New York City.

Among the many calendar illustrations Wyeth made over the years, perhaps the most beautiful and one of the most eye-appealing series is the one he made for the Berwind-White Coal Mining Company's 1923 calendar. This series consisted of four paintings of picturesque sailing ships famous for the part they played in maritime history, plus a cover illustration. It also provides an especially fine example of his talent for the effective use of scroll designs and decorative motifs.

Sometimes Wyeth's commercial work was planned to serve a dual purpose—to appear not

only in magazine advertisements but also on posters. A prime example is two large paintings he made for the Interwoven Stocking Company that appeared both in the firm's advertisements and as posters in men's haberdashery stores. These two paintings received special recognition by being reproduced in the *Annual of Advertising Art: Christmas in Old Virginia* in the Seventh Annual (1928) and *The Christmas Ship in Old New York* in the Eighth Annual (1929).

In the field of commercial illustration, one of Wyeth's first commissions in the 1930s was for the Pennsylvania Railroad (now the Penn Central Transportation Company). On May 1,

BEETHOVEN AND NATURE
Courtesy of Steinway & Sons

1930, a notice was displayed in all the railroad's stations and ticket offices advising the public that

Historical posters in full color, dealing with patriotic subjects, have been designed by a well-known painter. The purpose of the new posters is not only to interest the public in the historical significance of the scenes and events portrayed, but also to emphasize the identity of the Pennsylvania Railroad with the country's growth, and its own development as a national institution.

The notice went on to say that these patriotic posters would be twelve in number, and that each would depict an outstanding scene or event in the early history and the development of the United States. However, only four of the planned twelve posters appeared, and apparently the project was dropped.

On May 22, 1930, the first poster—*Ringing Out Liberty*—was announced. It was followed on July 30 of the same year by the second one, *In Old Kentucky*. The third, *Pittsburgh in the Beginning—Fort Prince George*, was made available on November 23. The last of the announcements appeared in an undated bulletin: "*The Building of the First White House*—one of the Pennsylvania Railroad's contributions to the Washington bicentennial year." (This painting, *Building the First White House*, appeared on the 1971 Christmas card sent by President and Mrs. Nixon.)

PUBLIC TEST OF THE WORLD'S FIRST REAPER
Courtesy of International Harvester Company of America,
Inc.

THE CHRISTMAS SHIP IN OLD NEW YORK
Courtesy of Interwoven, Division of Kayser-Roth
Corporation

RINGING OUT LIBERTY

IN OLD KENTUCKY

PENNSYLVANIA RAILROAD PATRIOTIC POSTERS
Courtesy of the Pennsylvania Railroad

PITTSBURGH IN THE BEGINNING—FORT PRINCE
GEORGE

BUILDING THE FIRST WHITE HOUSE

[151]

What whiskey was born 10 years before the first Kentucky Derby?

Paul Jones
A BLEND OF ALL STRAIGHT WHISKIES

THE FIRST KENTUCKY DERBY
Courtesy of Joseph E. Seagram & Sons, Inc.

"Nature in the Raw is seldom MILD"

No raw tobaccos in Luckies —that's why they're so mild

LUCKY STRIKE CIGARETTES

"It's toasted"
That package of mild Luckies

CUSTER'S LAST STAND
American Tobacco Company advertisement

Advertisements appearing in 1931 carried a quite different Wyeth historical picture: the first public test of the McCormick reaper at Steele's Tavern in Virginia in July of 1831. This was commissioned by the International Harvester Company to illustrate an advertisement commemorating the hundredth anniversary of the event, which had signaled the beginning of the emancipation of the American farmer. The original of this painting was destroyed in a fire.

In 1932 the American Tobacco Company launched an advertising campaign for Lucky Strike cigarettes using the slogan "Nature in the Raw is seldom Mild." The campaign included radio plugs as well as pictorial advertisements in newspapers and magazines. The paintings Wyeth made for the campaign, which really depicted "Nature in the Raw" and were definitely not "Mild," represented actual historical episodes: *The Fort Dearborn Massacre, Custer's Last Stand, The Dark and Bloody Ground, The Sea Wolf,* and *The War Whoop.*

In searching for material on N. C. Wyeth's commercial art, word-of-mouth information came to us that he had done calendar work for

General Electric Company. Then two calendars turned up in a private collection, indicating that the work had been done for General Electric's Lamp Division at Nela Park, Cleveland, Ohio.

There is an interesting bit of background information on one of these paintings. In a letter Wyeth wrote his father on September 17, 1926, he referred to having completed a calendar picture entitled *The Carvers of the Sphinx* for the Edison Mazda Company. The details he gave about it in this letter constitute an exact description of the General Electric Lamp Division calendar that came out nine years later, in 1935. *The Torch Race,* which appeared on General Electric's Lamp Division calendar in 1936, may also have been done years earlier, but there is no available documentation to support this possibility.

In the mid-thirties, Frankfort Distilleries commissioned Wyeth to paint several advertising pieces featuring their Paul Jones whiskey. The themes were related to things near and dear to Southern gentlemen and in particular to that area known as Kentucky—namely, horses and bourbon. The following titles are represen-

SAM HOUSTON
Oil on canvas, h:32, w:28
Signed lower right: N. C. Wyeth
John Morrell & Company
        calendar—"America in the
        Making," November 1940
Courtesy of Iowa State
        University, Gift of John
        Morrell & Company

tative samples: *The First Kentucky Derby; Now Major, for the best part of the game; I would like to have known my grandfather better;* and *Toby, fetch me the key to the springhouse.*

During those same years and later, Wyeth painted a number of illustrations to advertise a less potent potable, Coca-Cola. He executed no fewer than nine commissions for this company, including magazine pieces, two calendars, and several posters, among them a series of posters on the lumber and transportation industries.

During his last years, N. C. Wyeth accepted numerous calendar assignments. Those done for Hercules Incorporated and for John Morrell and Company were particularly notable; he also executed fine calendar paintings for New York Life Insurance and Brown & Bigelow, among others. His first Hercules Incorporated calendar painting, which was called *The Three Hunters,*

appeared in 1933. Those made subsequently appeared as calendars, prints, and covers for the company publication *The Hercules Mixer,* each being completed in the year immediately prior to its use. Hence, the last one, which appeared on the 1946 calendar, may well have been one of his final works of commercial art, though the painting itself bears no date. In addition to the 1933 calendar, the other Hercules Incorporated calendars were:

1934—*The Seeker*
1935—*New Trails*
1938—*The Alchemist*
1939—*A New World*
1940—*The Pioneers*
1942—*Primal Chemistry*
1944—*Sweet Land of Liberty*
1946—*The Spirit of '46*

[153]

LUMBER
One of the series of industrial posters
made for Coca-Cola in 1943
Courtesy of Coca-Cola Company

THE CONFEDERATE BATTLE FLAG—
    FAITHFUL TROOPS CHEER
    GENERAL LEE
Oil on panel, h:32, w:28
Signed lower right: N. C. Wyeth
John Morrell & Company calendar—"Flags in
    American History," November 1944
Courtesy of the United States Naval
    Academy, Annapolis, Gift of
    John Morrell & Company

THE ALCHEMIST
Hercules Incorporated 1938 calendar
Courtesy of Hercules Incorporated

[155]

FRANCISCO VASQUEZ
DE CORONADO
Oil on canvas, h:32, w:28
Signed lower right: N. C. Wyeth
John Morrell & Company
     calendar—"America in the
     Making," January 1940
Courtesy of Iowa State
     University, Gift of John
     Morrell & Company

Wyeth's first commission for John Morrell & Company of Ottumwa, Iowa, a meat-packing company, was to do one of the twelve illustrations to be used on their 1939 calendar, which was titled "Twelve Artists Depict America." This calendar was so much in demand, particularly by schools, that the company decided to follow a historical theme—"America in the Making"—for their calendar the following year, and they asked N. C. Wyeth to make the illustrations. Again in 1941, their calendar was a Wyeth exclusive—this time on the theme "The Romance of Commerce." For their 1944 calendar they turned to him once more, to illustrate "Flags in American History."

It is known that Wyeth, in the early 1940s, made a painting of Abraham Lincoln writing the famous Bixby letter (November 21, 1864), to express sympathy to the widow who had lost her five sons on the battlefields of the Civil War. Under the title *A Cherished Memory*, the painting was commissioned by the Shaw-Barton ad-

vertising agency to be used on a calendar. Subsequently, it was used as the cover illustration for the February 1944 issue of *American Legion Magazine*, but the present owner of the painting is unknown.

The records of Brown & Bigelow reveal that Wyeth executed five paintings for them that were reproduced on calendars between 1943 and 1945. The themes were chosen to emphasize the importance of the home front during World War II, as is evidenced by the following titles: *Soldiers of the Soil, The American Flag, The Returning Soldier, The Cornhusker,* and *Lift Up Your Hearts.*

The reproductions of Wyeth's commercial work presented here, though only a varied cross-section, can certainly be considered examples of some of the finest work he did in this field. His standing as a commercial artist is further attested to by the stature of the firms who commissioned his services, many the most renowned in the saga of American enterprise.

10

Murals, Lunettes, and the Triptych

Wyeth at work on *The Galleons* mural for the First National Bank of Boston. Courtesy of Mrs. N. C. Wyeth

Newell Convers Wyeth was an exceptionally energetic man—he worked hard and he played hard. But play to him was felling trees, plowing a field, or running a footrace with his younger neighbors. A good deal of this virility spilled over onto his canvases. They were consistently big—as large as he could make them within the limitations of the requirements for magazine and book reproduction.

It is not surprising, therefore, that he eventually attempted that vastly larger scale of work, the mural. This kind of painting is pretty much a field in itself, and few artists who attain fame in other types of painting can—or desire to—undertake huge panoramas. Wyeth, however, gladly accepted the challenges of mural painting and executed many outstanding murals in the course of his career.

In all probability, Wyeth's first mural painting resulted from studies he submitted to the directors of the Hotel Utica Corporation as a speculative presentation, in the hope of being commissioned to do four large decorations for the grillroom of the hotel. The basic themes for

the decorations were almost identical in content to the four paintings Wyeth did to accompany "The Moods," which appeared in the December 1909 issue of *Scribner's Magazine*.

Wyeth's preliminary studies were accepted, and the murals were completed in the latter part of 1911. The Hotel Utica (Utica, New York) opened in March 1912: the murals were installed shortly before that date.

At the beginning of the Prohibition era, the Hotel Utica murals were removed from their settings and placed in storage. After Repeal, when they were taken from storage to be remounted in their original settings, it was discovered that they had deteriorated to such an extent that they could not be restored. Probably the only extant pictures of them are reproductions in color in a rare little folder put out originally as a keepsake by the Hotel Utica on the occasion of its opening. The two murals shown here—*The Indian Fisherman* and *The Indian Hunter*—are reproduced from that folder. They duplicate in theme *Summer* and *Autumn* from "The Moods" series in *Scribner's*.

THE BATTLE OF WILSON'S CREEK

The Union forces, under Nathaniel Lyon, attempted a surprise attack on the Confederate forces commanded by General Ben McCulloch, which were encamped at Wilson's Creek, twelve miles from Springfield, Missouri. General Sterling Price is given much of the credit for the Confederate victory in this battle on August 8, 1861, one of the bloodiest in the war. Bloody Hill in the central background was the site of Totten's battery, which fired the opening guns.

Oil on canvas, h:6′, w:12′. Signed lower left: N. C. Wyeth 1920

Courtesy of the State of Missouri and the Missouri State Museum

THE BATTLE OF WESTPORT

On the morning of October 23, 1864, Colonel John F. Phillips led a spectacular cavalry charge against General Sterling Price's Confederate cavalry, which was making a desperate rush on the Union batteries. The masses of horsemen crashed at full speed with a din that could be heard above the gunfire. This battle secured Missouri for the Union.

Oil on canvas, h:6′, w:12′. Signed lower right: N. C. Wyeth 1920

Courtesy of the State of Missouri and the Missouri State Museum

An almost exact duplicate of one of the hotel murals is Wyeth's painting *The Return of the Hunter,* which was reproduced in color in the center of fine tableware made for the hotel by the Syracuse China Corporation, of Syracuse, New York. These plates, made in various sizes, were bordered with an overglaze gold band with a maroon color line. The Wyeth painting in the center was applied by decal. On the back of each plate a special backstamp indicated that it was made expressly for the Hotel Utica. The original order for the plates was entered on August 14, 1911. Replacement orders were made in August 1937 and April 1939, but there is no record of the quantities manufactured.

Following the installation of his murals in the Hotel Utica in 1912, Wyeth was approached to do an assignment for the Washington Irving High School in New York City, which did not materialize. However, in 1915 four panoramic murals by Wyeth were mounted on the walls of the Submarine Grille of the Traymore Hotel in Atlantic City, New Jersey. In early June of that year while the murals were being completed and installed, such crowds of people came to watch that the hotel owner was compelled to put a notice in the newspaper announcing that the room would be closed to the public until the pictures were completely finished and in place. After World War II the Grille was redecorated and the murals were removed. It is not known what disposition was made of them. The rare photographs from which the reproductions in this chapter were made were generously supplied by Mrs. Andrew Wyeth.

In January of 1920 interest was shown in having N. C. Wyeth paint several lunettes for the Missouri state capitol in Jefferson City. The building was new, completed only in 1918 on a bluff overlooking the Missouri River and the rich farmlands beyond. The State Capitol Decorating Committee had decided to have the corridors decorated with lunette murals six feet high by twelve feet wide depicting incidents in the history of the state, and commissioned Wyeth to do two of them. The lunettes were unveiled on January 9, 1921.

In April of 1920 there was some discussion about Wyeth's painting murals for the Buccaneer Room of the new Flamingo Hotel in Miami, but the idea apparently came to naught. However, by August he had accepted a commission to paint two murals for the Federal

THE RETURN OF THE HUNTER
Reproduced on tableware made by the Syracuse China Corporation for the Hotel Utica. The plate shown is ten inches in diameter.
Courtesy of Onondaga Pottery Company (Syracuse China Corporation).

Reserve Bank of Boston. These, each approximately twelve feet high by ten feet wide, still decorate opposite walls of the junior officers' quarters at the bank.

Even though Wyeth remained deeply involved with book illustration, more and more mural commissions came his way. A letter to his friend Joseph Chapin of Scribner's is indicative of his feelings about the work:

> Personally speaking, an outstanding event for me will be the arrangements already made to devote about ⅓ of my time to study under George Noyes (an obscure painter but a marvelous colorist). I need this help beyond words! Mural work is looming up importantly and I must know more definitely the science of color:—this knowledge added to certain instinctive feelings I have regarding it should mean much.[1]

Throughout the 1920s Wyeth turned out mural masterpieces with regularity. Although a planned assignment for the Highland Park High School in Highland Park, Illinois, was canceled, he did at least thirteen murals and panels for

THE HUNTER
Oil on canvas
Hotel Utica Mural
Courtesy of Mrs. Andrew Wyeth

THE FISHERMAN
Oil on canvas
Hotel Utica Mural
Courtesy of Mrs. Andrew Wyeth

IN THE DARK DAYS OF THE CIVIL WAR
Oil on canvas, h:12′, w:10′
Signed lower right: N. C. Wyeth 1922
The mural depicts Lincoln and Secretary of
    the Treasury Salmon P. Chase.
Courtesy of the Federal Reserve Bank of Boston

five edifices during the balance of the decade. One of these was *The Giant,* a memorial decoration made for the Westtown School of Westtown, Pennsylvania, in 1923. This large canvas, six feet high by five feet wide, embellishes the dining room of the long-established school. *The Giant* was painted as a memorial to a very popular student who had died at an early age—William Clothier Engle, a boy with high ideals, a fine sense of humor, and a distinct talent for art. When this young friend and student of N. C. Wyeth's died, Wyeth consented to do the mural and took great pains to choose a theme he felt the lad would have appreciated. The locale of the painting was Beach Haven, New Jersey, where both Engle and the Wyeth children had enjoyed summer holidays. The Wyeth children appear in the painting.

By the spring of 1924 he had completed five other murals—for the First National Bank of Boston: four ship murals and a map mural that surrounded a large impressive doorway. Of this commission Wyeth wrote:

When I was first commissioned to do the work, the portraying of incidents associated with Boston history was considered. But this seemed too local and confining. Ships and the sea had been much in my dreams for years. Visions of canvasses, alive with moving water, sailing clouds and flying ships, seemed at last within my grasp. In pondering as to what would relate to the bank's commercial activities and retain the infinite spirit of the sea, I evolved the idea of cargo carriers.

Four historic periods of shipping finally were chosen, represented by Phoenician biremes, Elizabethan galleons, clipper ships and tramp steamers.[2]

That same year (1924) saw the installation of his great mural in the Hotel Roosevelt in New York City. This consisted of three panels, the center one of which depicted the sturdy little Dutch ship *Half Moon* gliding up the Hudson before a fair autumn wind that whipped the river into serried whitecaps, with the soaring Palisades as a background. Wyeth selected this 1609 event as his theme not only for its historic aptness but as a tribute to the Dutch, for the Netherlands was the ancestral home of the world-famed American statesman and native New Yorker for whom the hotel is named. From the deck of the *Half Moon,* sailors are watching the looming highlands in wonder while, in the

AN APOTHEOSIS OF FRANKLIN
Oil on canvas, h:30', w:16'
Signed lower right: N. C. Wyeth
Courtesy of the Franklin Savings Bank, New York City

side panels, Indians gaze at the winged intruder from behind a tracery of birches, alders, and cottonwood saplings.

The year 1925 was marked by the completion of a huge mural—*An Apotheosis of Franklin* —decorating the east wall on the main floor of

Hotel Traymore Mural
Oil on canvas, h:8', w:20'
Courtesy of Mrs. Andrew Wyeth

the Franklin Savings Bank at Forty-second Street and Eighth Avenue in New York City. This was approximately thirty feet high by sixteen feet wide.

For the second floor of the National Geographic Society headquarters in Washington, Wyeth did a series of five murals, which were completed in 1927. At that time, the magazine offices were largely concentrated in the Gardner Greene Hubbard Memorial, a building dedicated in the early part of the century as a tribute to the founder of that world-renowned publication. Today, the magazine headquarters is a new steel and glass building on Seventeenth Street, behind its former location, and the Gardner Greene Hubbard Memorial is little used in comparison to former years and is virtually closed to the public. But the murals remain in place on the upper level, reached by a circular stairway. Consideration was once given to transferring them to the new building, but no suitable area was available to display them. Full-color sup-

plements reproducing the murals were published as part of the March, May, July, and November 1928 issues and the January 1929 issue of the *National Geographic Magazine*.

Toward the end of the 1920s, Wyeth wrote to Chapin at Scribner's:

Regarding Gulliver. I am selected by the Massachusetts Art Commission to execute six panels for the State House in Boston. At present, the problem is to get the Ways and Means Committee to appropriate the funds. This is a memorial to the First General Court Meeting in Massachusetts which took place in 1630; so if it goes through O.K. these panels must be done as soon as possible. Before giving you a decision on Gulliver I must await the outcome of the State House matter. I ought to hear most any day.[3]

Apparently the funds were never appropriated—at any rate, Wyeth never carried out any such assignment in the State House in Boston. However, during the 1930s he completed six more magnificent wall decorations, the first doubtless being the mural for the First Mechanics National Bank of Trenton, New Jersey (now the First Trenton National Bank). The subject was General Washington's entrance into Trenton on his way to New York to be inaugurated as our first President.

Records show that the general and his suite arrived on the opposite bank of the river at Colvin's Ferryhouse at two o'clock on the afternoon of April 21, 1789, and Patrick Colvin ferried them across the Delaware. At Trenton Landing, near the tavern of Rensselaer Williams, the party was met by leading citizens of Trenton with appropriate ceremonies, and then the assemblage escorted the travelers into the village proper. There the general and his suite mounted the horses that had been readied for them, and proceeded up the Ferry Road and thence toward the bridge over Assunpink Creek, where the matrons and young ladies of the village had superintended the erection of a beautiful arch.

Wyeth was always a stickler for historic accuracy in his paintings and researched his themes and scenes very thoroughly. A careful examination of the details in this Trenton bank mural seems to indicate he may have been influenced by a contemporary account of the arch and the details of Washington's entrance into Trenton that was published in *Columbian Magazine*, May 1789.

While Wyeth was overseeing the installation of the Trenton bank mural from a scaffold high above the marble floor, it is said that he slipped and almost fell. The frightening experience haunted him and resulted in a dream, the essence of which he put on canvas: *In a Dream I Meet General Washington*. This was awarded the fourth William A. Clarke Prize in the 1932 Corcoran Biennial.

During the years 1930 and 1931 Wyeth also worked hard on another mural—*The Apotheosis of the Family*—to have it ready in time to dedicate at the centennial of the Wilmington Savings Fund, which was founded in 1832. This, one of the largest single murals in the United States (nineteen feet high by sixty feet long), was painted on heavy canvas and mounted in five

[163]

THE PHOENICIAN BIREMES
Oil on canvas, h:15', w:12'
Signed lower right: N. C. Wyeth 1923
Courtesy of the First National Bank of Boston

THE TRAMP STEAMER
Oil on canvas, h:15', w:12'
Signed lower left: N. C. Wyeth
Courtesy of the First National Bank of Boston

THE DISCOVERER
Published March 1928
Oil on canvas, h:7'10⅜", w:30'2"
Signed lower right: N. C. Wyeth 1927
© 1928 National Geographic Society

sections spanning the entire south wall of the Wilmington Savings Fund Society building.

At first, the officers of the society had been in a quandary as to what type of decoration might be given the long blank wall. Frederic E. Stone, then the president, thought the best solution would be a large mural on a theme compatible with the business of the organization—the story of thrift as it applies to humanity—and he consulted with N. C. Wyeth, who happened to be a close personal friend. For a full year Wyeth mulled over ideas for projecting the concept of family solidarity and integrity as the basic structure upon which civilization is built. He concluded that only an allegorical painting with a theme focused on the family would be appropriate for the Savings Fund's hundredth anniversary.

After making preliminary sketches, Wyeth did a finely executed oil study to scale, and it was from this that the mural was painted. In all, it took him a year and a half to complete his grand conception. Dominating the center of the picture is the group symbolizing Home and the Family. From left to the center, and from the center to right, the seasons merge from spring to summer and from fall to winter, and so the observer's eye moves from one kind of human activity to another, ever aware of man's varied labors and of the influence of nature's fundamental forces. In its overall effect, the mural is like a symphonic presentation.[4]

Wyeth wrote a very detailed explanation of the mural he painted for the main lobby of the Penn Mutual Life Insurance Company office in Philadelphia, *William Penn, Man of Courage–Vision–Action*. This painting, completed in the fall of 1932 and mounted on the first of February the following year, is fourteen feet high by ten and a half feet wide.

Wyeth's next mural was commissioned to celebrate an anniversary—the first half century of the Silver Burdett Company's service to education. Titled *The Spirit of Education*, this painting was originally housed in the company's New York office, but when their new headquarters in Morristown, New Jersey, were completed in 1955, it was moved there, where it dominates the main entrance foyer.

By the spring of 1936, Wyeth had completed a truly magnificent mural—the triptych in the Chapel of the Holy Spirit at the Washington Cathedral (Episcopal), which is one of the great cathedrals of the world, exceeded in area by only five others. As visitors wander through this vast edifice, properly called the Cathedral

[164]

Church of Saint Peter and Saint Paul, they eventually come to the Chapel of the Holy Spirit, and after passing through iron gates and grilles lacelike in design they are confronted by beautiful oak-paneled reredos and Wyeth's triptych.

No one could better describe this great work of Wyeth's than John H. Bayless, curator at the cathedral for almost forty years. He has lived with the triptych since its inception:

I watched every stroke of his brush. The mural was painted on Gesso which Mr. Wyeth built layer by layer with painstaking effort.

The seven gifts of the Holy Spirit are symbolized by the doves at the base of the triptych. In the center panel, the figure of Christ seems almost to be moving forward suggesting the 28th verse of the eleventh chapter of the Gospel According to Saint Matthew, "Come Unto Me, All Ye That Labor and are Heavy Laden, and I Will Give You Rest". The feeling of motion is produced by the rays of glory about the Figure (strips of gilded wood glued to the wood and planed from the extremities to the point where they meet the figure flush with the surface of the painting). "I Am the True Vine and Ye are the Branches Thereof" is suggested by the motif above

the figure. The two side panels portray angels in motion, symbolic of the Holy Spirit.

In the dining room of St. Andrew's School, Middletown, Delaware, is a Wyeth mural commissioned by Mrs. Irénée duPont, who, with her brother, A. Felix duPont, donated the original funds for the school.[5] The June 6, 1936, issue of the school paper, *The Cardinal*, announced, "The mural now being executed by N. C. Wyeth will cover the east wall of the dining room." Progress was reported six months later in the January issue—the mural was "now well under way, and is expected to be finished by the dedication services, April 14th."

The headmaster's report in June of that year had this to say of it:

Mrs. Irénée duPont's fine gift of a mural for the Dining Room has been more than half finished by the painter, Mr. N. C. Wyeth, and to all who have seen it, seems a thrilling symbol of the School's conception and realization.

Over a year later came this report:

On September 1st [1938] Mr. N. C. Wyeth placed on the Dining Room wall the long

HALF MOON IN THE HUDSON (left panel)

HALF MOON IN THE HUDSON (center panel)

HALF MOON IN THE HUDSON TRIPTYCH
Oil on canvas, each panel, h:14', w:8'
Right panel signed lower right: N. C. Wyeth 1924
Courtesy of the Hotel Roosevelt

HALF MOON IN THE HUDSON (right panel)

GENERAL WASHINGTON'S ENTRANCE INTO
TRENTON
Oil on canvas, h:17½′, w:12′
Signed lower left: N. C. Wyeth 1930; lower right: ©
    First Mechanics National Bank of Trenton
Courtesy of First Trenton National Bank
Photograph courtesy of the Edward Seal Collection

THE APOTHEOSIS OF THE FAMILY
Oil on canvas, h:19′, w:60′
Signed bottom center: N. C. Wyeth 1931
Courtesy of Wilmington Savings Fund Society

MAP OF DISCOVERY—EASTERN HEMISPHERE
Published November 1928
Oil on canvas: h:7′11⅛″, w:9′3⅜″
Signed lower left: N. C. Wyeth 1927
© 1928 National Geographic Society

MAP OF DISCOVERY—WESTERN HEMISPHERE
Published January 1929
Oil on canvas, h:7′11½″, w:8′11⅞″
Signed lower right: N. C. Wyeth 1927
© 1929 National Geographic Society

Right-hand part of St. Andrew's School mural
Oil on canvas
Courtesy of St. Andrew's School and the Reverend
    Robert A. Moss, Headmaster

THE COMING OF THE MAYFLOWER
Oil on canvas, h:9', w:13¼'
Signed lower left: N. C. Wyeth
Courtesy of the Metropolitan Life Insurance Company

expected mural. This remarkable painting has exceeded even the highest expectations for it, and will be a focal point of inspiration for many generations of St. Andreans.

The left portion of the mural shows Alma Mater seated on her throne amidst the boys of St. Andrew's. It is said that at first Wyeth strove for realistic likenesses of specific students, but it was decided that anonymity was preferable. So the boys were finally painted from the artist's imagination.

The right-hand side of the mural pictures the charter trustees of the Episcopal Church School Foundation, Inc., through which Mr. duPont founded and endowed the school, and several notables who, though not of this group, were greatly engrossed in the activities. The group is depicted examining and discussing the blueprints for the school. The English cathedrals —Canterbury and St. Paul's—which appear in the misty background, represent the Anglican Church tradition on which the school's life and worship were based. The portraits of the men in the group are true likenesses. Each of them posed for Wyeth, and he also attended meetings of the trustees so that he could observe the typical role and attitude of each man.

The last mural commission Wyeth accepted was one he looked forward to doing with a very special sense of happiness and enthusiasm. The assignment was actually a series of murals on the grand scale, to serve as a graphic and dramatic expression of the spirit of New England: *The Coming of the Mayflower* and *The Departure of the Mayflower*, along with six others— *First Harvest, The Turkey Hunt, The Thanksgiving Feast, Going to Church, Priscilla and John Alden,* and *The Wedding Procession.*

Throughout his lifetime Wyeth never lost sight of or failed to convey to others his pride in his New England heritage.

New England was where I was born, raised and educated. I felt, therefore, that of all the subjects possible, this was the one I knew best. The romance of early colonization, especially that of the Pilgrims in Massachusetts, had always excited me. My ancestor, Nicholas Wyeth, came from Wales to Massachusetts in 1647. The spirit of early days on the Massachusetts coast was an oft-discussed subject in my home.

I was born in Needham, not far from the town of Plymouth, to which I made many pilgrimages during my boyhood, spending thrilling days in and around that historic territory. With this as a background,

THE TURKEY HUNT
Oil on canvas, section shown, h:7′, w:28¾′; section
    not shown, h:7′, w:13½′
Unsigned
Courtesy of the Metropolitan Life Insurance Company

THE THANKSGIVING FEAST
Oil on canvas, section shown, h:7′, w:23′; section not
    shown, h:7′, w:23⅔′
Signed lower left: N. C. Wyeth
Courtesy of the Metropolitan Life Insurance Company

THE WEDDING PROCESSION
Oil on canvas, h:7′, w:25¼′
Unsigned
Courtesy of the Metropolitan Life Insurance Company

HERONS IN SUMMER
Oil on canvas, h:6¾', w:13'
Unsigned
Courtesy of the Metropolitan Life Insurance Company

it was natural that my mind and heart should fly to Plymouth and to the Pilgrims as a fitting and appropriate subject for a series of New England paintings.

If then, the warmth and appeal of these paintings is apparent to those who study them, it is principally because they are, in some related way, a statement of my own life and heritage. All creative expression, be it in painting, writing, or music, if it pretends to appeal warmly and eloquently, must spring from the artist's own factual and emotional experience.[6]

Thus began the planning of his final work in the field of mural painting in the latter part of 1939. He was to devote much of the next six years to it, though he was not destined to see its completion. On an October morning in 1945 tragedy struck—the artist's hand was stilled forever in a railroad-crossing accident. What more fitting memorial could there have been than that Wyeth's younger son, Andrew, now America's most popular living artist, and his son-in-law John McCoy should complete the work he had begun?

MALLARD DUCKS IN SPRING
Oil on canvas, h:10½', w:13'
Signed lower right: N. C. Wyeth
Courtesy of the Metropolitan Life Insurance Company

[171]

TRIPTYCH—Chapel of the Holy Spirit
Oil on canvas
Courtesy of Eston Photo Reproductions, New York

The great panorama of the Pilgrim murals is not all the Wyeth bounty housed in the main office of the Metropolitan Life Insurance Company in New York City. There are also four handsome panels depicting aquatic and game birds.

From time to time, various articles have appeared that made reference to N. C. Wyeth's having painted other murals besides those shown and discussed here. After carefully investigating these reports, we are convinced that the paintings reproduced in this chapter represent his total output of murals—certainly a bountiful heritage from one who was at the same time steadily fulfilling book, magazine, and advertising commissions and creating numerous easel paintings that rank with the best done by his peers.

SEPTEMBER AFTERNOON (1918)
Oil on canvas, h:42, w:48
Signed lower right: N. C. Wyeth
Courtesy of Mrs. N. C. Wyeth

11 *Easel Painting*

THE name N. C. Wyeth is, by most people, instantly and invariably associated with the fine illustrations he made for books and magazines, in particular those he painted for the classics that were published by Charles Scribner's Sons, Cosmopolitan Book Corporation, and David McKay. Without doubt he is best remembered for these because they impressed young readers both consciously and subconsciously, and thereby remained with them as an integral part of the growing-up experience.

However, from his earliest days as an illustrator, Wyeth had expressed a desire to become a landscape painter, and had had many conversations about this with his teacher Howard Pyle, who encouraged him to devote part of his time

Peter Minuet

PETER MINUIT
Oil on canvas, h:42, w:30
Signed lower right: N. C. Wyeth 1926
(This portrait hung in New York's Hotel Roosevelt
and is believed to have been painted to complement
the mural *Half Moon on the Hudson.*)
Courtesy of Edward Eberstadt & Sons, New York

to such paintings. With his deep love of nature and the out-of-doors, it is easy to understand why Wyeth would find particular satisfaction in expressing these feelings in landscapes and sea-scapes depicting either his beloved Brandywine country or the environs of his summer home at Port Clyde, Maine.

Wyeth attributed much of his success in the field of both illustration and easel painting to an early teacher, Charles W. Reed, who taught him that observation must be converted to memory, for without training this faculty, mood and imagination would be lacking in the artist's work. Wyeth took this advice to heart, and later in life he said:

Every illustration or painting I have made has been done from the imagination or the memory. However, I have constantly stud-ied from the figure, from animals and from landscape, and have especially stressed the training of my memory.[1]

His many years of self-discipline in con-verting observation to memory resulted in his beautiful painting *Summer Night,* completed in 1942, to name one example. Wyeth recalled the circumstances:

One summer's night several years ago, during one of my familiar walks along the broad stretches of the Brandywine Mead-ows, I passed among a herd of dairy cows quietly standing and lying down in the bright moonlight. It was sultry, and great threatening clouds moved and lifted in

[174]

ANN STUYVESANT
Oil on canvas, h:42, w:30
Signed lower left: N. C. Wyeth 1926
(Like the portrait of Peter Minuit, this too is
believed to have been made to complement the
mural *Half Moon on the Hudson.*)
Courtesy of Edward Eberstadt & Sons, New York

STILL LIFE WITH APPLES (1918)
Oil on canvas, h:32⅛, w:40⅛
Unsigned

[175]

A MAINE SEA CAPTAIN'S DAUGHTER
Tempera on panel, h:29½, w:22¾
Signed upper left: N. C. Wyeth
Courtesy of William R. Rollins

STILL LIFE WITH BRUSH
Oil on canvas, h:16, w:20
Signed lower right: N. C. Wyeth
Courtesy of B. F. Schlimme

FENCE BUILDERS
Oil on canvas, h:37½, w:49½
Signed lower right: N. C. Wyeth 1915
Courtesy of Carl D. Pratt

LAST OF THE CHESTNUTS (*Tree Cutters*) (1917)
Oil on canvas, h:37, w:49
Signed lower right: N. C. Wyeth
Courtesy of Diamond M Foundation, Snyder, Texas

SUMMER DAYS (circa 1910)
Oil on canvas, h:16, w:20
Unsigned
Courtesy of Mr. & Mrs. Andrew Wyeth

[177]

NEWBORN CALF (*Cows in Moonlight*)
Oil on canvas, h:42, w:47
Signed lower left: N. C. Wyeth 1917
Courtesy of Mrs. Andrew Wyeth

majestic patterns across the sky line like the silent shifting of scenery on a celestial stage.

The full moon threw shafts of clear mellow light through the cloud openings which slowly swung across the dark terrain like beams from a beatific searchlight.

As I watched the impressive spectacle before me, I became conscious that one of the cows, standing apart from the main groups of reposing animals, was in labor and about to drop her calf.

I watched the progress of this miracle of birth for a long time, in fact until the new bit of life on earth finally struggled to

its feet, cast its own new shadow, and wobbled and fumbled its way to its mother's teats and drenched itself in warm milk.

Many times since then I have attempted to express the mood of this impressive experience in pattern and color.[2]

Throughout his career N. C. Wyeth was constantly referred to as an illustrator, a label he deeply resented, not because laymen used it in referring to him, but because those in the art world looked down from their ivory towers and deprecated illustration as a second-rate art form. He once wrote:

There is a very depressing belief in artistic circles, particularly among the painters themselves, that illustration is not an art but a craft, that it is not conceived from inspirational sources, but is built and fashioned as a stage setting would be around the theme of a story, or planned like an ingenious design. The painter's opinion of the illustrator's profession as compared to his own, is often very near that of contempt.[3]

In speaking before a class conducted by another renowned former student of the Howard Pyle School, Harvey Dunn, Wyeth was somewhat startled by the general attitude of the students: they wanted to be illustrators so that they could make money and become artists.

"Fine," he commented, "but the only trouble is that you've got to be an artist before you can be an illustrator."[4]

Illustration was and still remains, to a degree, an inferior form in the eyes of certain art critics, art experts, and others who consider themselves highly knowledgeable. Many of them spurn or ignore work they term "commercial" but go into ecstasies over the efforts of others made famous only through public relations media. In actuality, few are the great artists of history who were not illustrators. Their pictures told stories of the places, the customs, and the incidents in the lives of their people. Our own Winslow Homer and John Sloan were illustrators before they were "discovered" and "saved" from that stigma.

Despite Wyeth's success in the field of book and magazine illustration and his prominence as a mural painter, he constantly strove to rise above the label he so detested. He cherished the rare moments when he was free of commitments and could retire to the countryside of his beloved Chadds Ford or the Maine seacoast to sketch and paint the things that he knew best and that stirred him most—neighbors at work in the field, a rural scene, a quaint old house, a salty lobsterman—the simple native themes of his finest paintings.

In 1915, Wyeth was hard at work on a large easel painting, *The Fence Builders*. This may have been his first truly serious effort to

BUTTONWOOD FARM (1920)
Oil on canvas, h:48½, w:42½
Signed lower right: N. C. Wyeth
Courtesy of The Reading Public Museum
and Art Gallery, Reading, Pa.

CANNIBAL SHORE (1930)
Oil on canvas, h:30, w:47
Signed lower left: N. C. Wyeth
Courtesy of William A. Farnsworth Library
and Art Museum, Rockland, Maine

SOUNDING SEA (Black Head, Monhegan Island) (1934)
Oil on canvas, h:48¼, w:52¼
Signed lower left: N. C. Wyeth
Courtesy of Mr. & Mrs. Joseph E. Levine

CORN HARVEST ON THE
  BRANDYWINE (1936)
Oil on canvas, w:52, h:48
Signed lower right: N. C. Wyeth 193-
The Progressive Farmer (cover), November
  1936 & October 1946
Courtesy of the North Carolina Museum
  of Art, Raleigh

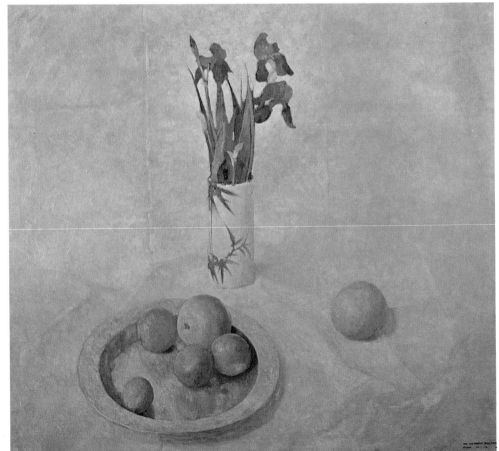

STILL LIFE WITH IRIS AND ORANGES
Oil on canvas, h:36, w:40
Signed lower right: N. C. Wyeth
Courtesy of the Delaware Art Museum

SUMMER NIGHT (1942)
Tempera on panel, h:22, w:36
Signed lower left: N. C. Wyeth
Courtesy of Mr. and Mrs. Bruce Bredin

THE HUPPER FARM (*Evening*) (1939)
Tempera on panel, h:24¾, w:39¾
Signed lower right: N. C. Wyeth
Courtesy of the Dallas Museum of Fine Arts,
    Gift of C. R. Smith

ISLAND FUNERAL (1939)
Tempera on wood, h:44, w:52
Signed upper left: N. C. Wyeth
Courtesy of Hotel DuPont, Wilmington

DEEP COVE LOBSTERMAN (1939)
Oil on panel, h:19, w:25
Signed lower right: N. C. Wyeth
Courtesy of The Pennsylvania Academy of the Fine Arts

SUN GLINT (1938)
Tempera on panel, h:25, w:31
Signed lower left: N. C. Wyeth
Courtesy of The New Britain Museum of American Art,
Harriet Russell Stanley Memorial

do a canvas that would not be associated with illustration as such. He spent the better part of the spring of that year working on it, and in letters to his family one can sense his feeling of accomplishment.

The influence of one Giovanni Segantini, whom Wyeth greatly admired, was apparent in a number of his easel paintings over the next few years. The use of pure color bordered by gradations of white heightened the brilliancy of the color pigment, and his experimentation in the technique of Segantini resulted in several outstanding paintings, among which were *Newborn Calf*, *September Afternoon*, and *Buttonwood Farm*.

To achieve recognition as a painter became an obsession. Despite the many requests he received to illustrate stories for books and magazines and anticipated commissions for mural paintings and commercial artwork, the pressures within him demanded that he strive to reach that higher pinnacle.

I have passed through two months of the worst depression I ever remember. I have been highly conscious of certain serious artistic weaknesses that stand between me and the next step ahead. Only thorough application will overcome the difficulty I guess.[5]

In yet another letter he concerned himself with the work of a well-known author of the· time, and the parallels between writing and painting.

His enthusiasm is great! and his craft is highly appealing. But this to me does not conceal a remarkable lack of earthiness—of sound basic appeal, a primal quality which must exist in an artist's work as a foundation wall exists under a house.

One can feel the very curvature of the earth's surface in John Constable's landscapes; a seemingly lost power to even our best landscapists today. Just as in Homer, Tolstoi and Whitman we can feel the earth in its cycle in spite of the sharp movements and distractions of passing human incidents.

And this power can come but from one source—from life lived deeply—from contact felt, the results of bodily feeling and not of mental conjuring. Millet's peasants work with backs bent from a toil that he had

LOBSTERING OFF BLACK SPRUCE LEDGE (1939)
Tempera on panel, h:42, w:52
Signed lower left

experienced; the hoes and mattocks they grip in their hands have the "feel" and weight that only a man who had used them could interpret. Rembrandt's heads are profound because fundamentally he loved the very structure, weight and substance of the head from the front back through the skull. There is material as well as spiritual identification required for this standard of creative art.

My axiom of art is the old, old one that we can only produce vitally what we are bodily—no more. An artificial life begets artificiality—no more, although artificiality can be superlatively dressed up on occasion I'll admit.[6]

Through the early twenties Wyeth accepted the challenge of what would seem a staggering amount of work for most artists. Mural commis-

THE LOBSTERMAN (Hauling in a Light Fog)
Trending into Maine, by Kenneth Roberts
Little, Brown and Company, 1938

CORN HARVEST (1943)
Tempera on panel, h:31, w:34
Signed lower left: N. C. Wyeth
Courtesy of the Wilmington Trust Company

sions flooded in, but with the tremendous vitality that characterized him, he turned them out one after another—and then went back to his experimentation. Painting simple still life canvases gave him a chance to test his handling of light, depth of color, and form. A demijohn, for example, taken from a shelf after years of undisturbed slumber, provided an opportunity to interpret a concrete object—its shape, the light pattern, the dust; a vase of iris and a dish of oranges—color harmony, light, and form of a different nature.

Wyeth did not find such work "stupid or pottering." He did it for "practice and self-dis-cipline, especially since such concrete work" helped him to

avoid the danger of generalizing too much in his painting. Combined with the discipline [was] the joy in feeling the form of objects, in observing the light and in knowing that such training [was] a sort of investment which [would] yield greater return by being stored up and augmented.[7]

The July 1925 issue of the *Ladies' Home Journal* contained an article about Wyeth and his art:

THE DORYMAN (*Evening*)
Oil on canvas, h:42, w:35
Signed lower right: N. C. Wyeth/Port Clyde/Maine
Trending into Maine, by Kenneth Roberts
Little, Brown and Company, 1938
Courtesy of Mrs. Norman B. Woolworth

DARK HARBOR FISHERMAN (1943)
Tempera on panel, h:35, w:38
Signed lower left: N. C. Wyeth
Courtesy of Robert F. Woolworth

MRS. CUSHMAN'S HOUSE (1942)
Tempera on panel, h:21, w:36½
Signed lower left: N. C. Wyeth
Courtesy of the New Britain Museum of American Art

N. C. Wyeth's ambition is to be a painter. He is today the most outstanding figure among the younger American decorators and an illustrator of real note. In the eyes of most, these achievements would stamp him as a painter of the first water, but that Wyeth is more exacting in his self-appraisal is characteristic of his modesty.

By the end of the nineteen twenties Wyeth's prodigious output of book and magazine illustration had dwindled to a trickle in comparison with former years. He became more and more involved with his serious painting.

The past year has been, I believe, a critical and important one for me, artistically. I have, at any rate, worked myself into a position from which I can see years of exciting and progressive adventure.[8]

Throughout the thirties and early forties, he spaced out his acceptance of commissions for murals, book illustrations, and considerable work in the field of commercial art so that, between assignments, he could devote some time to painting subjects of his own choice.

These paintings materialized, not in the rapid fashion that had marked his earlier work in illustration. Weeks, sometimes months, were spent on the preliminary composition and the preparation of the panel. For the most part done in tempera, these pictures were created by the slow and methodical buildup of color and glaze.

After all the many years of Wyeth's dedication to art he finally had his day—December 4, 1939, the opening of his first one-man show at

[186]

THE ROAD TO THE JONES HOUSE (1939)
Tempera on panel, h:22, w:40
Signed lower right: N. C. Wyeth
Courtesy of the Dallas Museum of Fine Arts, Gift
   of C. R. Smith

IN PENOBSCOT BAY
Tempera on panel, h:23¼, w:47½
Signed lower right: N. C. Wyeth 1942
Courtesy of Amanda K. Berls

THE SPRINGHOUSE
Tempera on wood, h:36, w:48
Signed lower left: N. C. Wyeth 1944
Courtesy of Delaware Art Museum

NIGHTFALL (1945)
Tempera on wood, h:31¾, w:40
Signed lower left: N. C. Wyeth
Courtesy of Robert F. Woolworth

the old MacBeth Galleries in New York City, which included a number of his finest paintings, most of them of recent vintage. The center of attraction was perhaps his recently completed *Island Funeral*, along with a number of others depicting the Maine scene.

Wyeth's son-in-law Peter Hurd, a fine artist in his own right, had this to say in his introduction to the show catalogue:

The paintings are the product of revolt against the inevitable limitation of the art of illustration which Mr. Wyeth has long served with sincerity and grace. Of the illustrator's heritage he takes freely and consciously those components which may relate to painting—a strongly dramatic presentation but one freed from the paraphernalia of archeology; an ability to establish vividly

PENNSYLVANIA FARMER *(Portrait of a Farmer)* (1943)
Tempera on panel, h:40, w:60
Unsigned
Courtesy of Robert F. Woolworth

Preliminary Study for *Pennsylvania Farmer*
(Portrait of a Farmer)
Courtesy of Mrs. N. C. Wyeth

N. C. Wyeth outside his studio, circa 1944.
Photograph by William E. Phelps
Courtesy of William Penn Memorial Museum, Harrisburg

N. C. Wyeth, 1944
Photograph by William E. Phelps
Courtesy of the Delaware Art Museum

the quality of a certain moment in which he unfolds the observer and causes him to see, to hear, and above all, to feel. He compels us to stop and ponder with him the surrounding vision of form and color, of radiance and shadow. This world of his is at once grave and lyric.

In 1941 Wyeth was recognized by those who had frowned on illustration as a second-rate art form—he was elected to the National Academy. And in June of 1945 he received a further distinction—the honorary degree of Master of Arts from Bowdoin College. In between these years, great paintings materialized: *Black Spruce Ledge, Summer Night, In Penobscot Bay, Mrs. Cushman's House, Pennsylvania Farmer, Dark Harbor Fishermen, The Spring House,* and *Nightfall.*

Since the tragic accident on that October day in 1945 that took the life of N. C. Wyeth, the years have tested his merit as an artist. His works, like the paintings of some others who were belittled as illustrators, are now diligently sought and collected by the very people who once spurned them.

N. C. Wyeth, Port Clyde, Maine
Courtesy of Mrs. N. C. Wyeth

DR. CLAPTON
Oil on canvas, h:40, w:30
Signed lower right: W
Drums, by James Boyd
Charles Scribner's Sons, 1928
Courtesy of J. N. Bartfield

*A Bibliography
of the Published Works of
N.C. Wyeth*

THIS bibliography of the published works of Newell Convers Wyeth deals with a long period of production namely, from 1903 to 1945. Throughout forty-two years as illustrator, muralist, and painter, his brush was never still. The magical illustrations he created for the Scribner's Juvenile Classics have enriched the imaginations of generations of Americans, both young and old. Yet from the outset of his career, he found that avenue which demanded his personal expression as a painter.

Wyeth was introduced to a fundamental but valued art training under various teachers in Boston; however, it is with Howard Pyle and his school of art in Wilmington and Chadds Ford that he is chiefly identified. Under the exacting tutelage of this master illustrator, Wyeth's abilities were drawn out and directed. Soon leading publishing firms vied for his talents. It was in such periodicals as *The Saturday Evening Post, Leslie's Popular Monthly*, and *Success* that Wyeth's illustrations made their first published appearances.

Wyeth was a creative artist in the truest sense; many of his works bridged the gap between illustration and the broader field of painting. Most notable examples are "The Solitude Series," "Back to the Farm," and "The Moods."

Wyeth's convincing portrayals of the protagonists in the realm of children's literature are always exciting. In his work he tried to live the life of the adventures he depicted. Immersed in the spirit of a tale, he painted characters that seem to burst from their confinement, overreaching for space. His treatment of the Stevenson classics is most remarkable. The immediate visual impact is sudden and forceful. The images of Old Pew, Bill Bones, Long John Silver, Ebenezer Balfour, and Lawless are branded in the eye of the mind.

Favoring large canvases, many times up to forty or fifty inches, Wyeth combined broad brush textures, impasto painting, scumblings, and transparent glazing. Occasionally, the palette knife was brought into play, plying the pigment where brushes failed. This tendency to paint large works naturally led to a new field of endeavor: mural decoration. His first commissions were four panels executed for the Hotel Utica in 1911. By 1941 he had completed some forty murals and large decorations for institutions, banks, and public buildings.

Between literary illustration, advertising assignments, and mural commissions, Wyeth used what precious time was left to paint the rural American scene. Unhampered by those varying limitations and restrictions placed upon him as an illustrator, he directed his efforts more and more to easel painting. An ever-consuming love for life and the out-of-doors drove him to his freer and most personal expression. The four seasons of the Brandywine Valley, its rolling hills, marshes, meadows, and forests, were captured on canvas. Summering along the coast of Maine offered, along with a picturesque environment, the changing moods of the Atlantic.

Most of Wyeth's enormous output of nearly two thousand illustrations and a like number of portraits, still lifes, and landscapes were done in oil on canvas or, in later years, oil on panel. In the late 1930s he was introduced to the medium of egg tempera. Though handed down from the Renaissance, this was a fresh technique to him. With this medium he achieved a new quality of light, depth, richness, and meticulous detail. He was a foremost exponent of a style of painting termed "magic realism," today shared by his celebrated son and grandson. In such late tempera paintings as "Dark Harbor Fishermen," "The Spring House," and "Nightfall," N. C. Wyeth achieves a complete statement about the character of rural American life. No American artist has so fully captured the spirit of his native land.

Some forty-two years ago, a brief listing of books illustrated by N. C. Wyeth appeared in *Contemporary Illustrators of Children's Books*, compiled by Bertha E. Mahoney and Elinor Whitney. In 1938 Theodore Bolton wrote *American Book Illustrators*, which contained the first major attempt at cataloguing the books illustrated by N. C. Wyeth. Not complete, but an invaluable source from which to begin, it listed forty-seven titles. In 1963, Helen L. Card, a pioneer in promoting American illustration, published her sales catalogue No. Five, which contained an extensive listing of Wyeth items. More recently, the bibliographer Jeff C. Dykes compiled another more extensive listing in the *American Book Collector*. Because of an ever-increasing interest in and demand for the works of N. C. Wyeth, a cumulative volume of his collected works was needed. The following bibliography is directed not only toward individual collectors but libraries, art galleries, and museums.

I wish to acknowledge a great debt to my mother and father, who stimulated my interest in N. C. Wyeth at an early age; the late Helen L. Card, for her encouragement and help in the development of this bibliography; Mrs. N. C. Wyeth and Mr. and Mrs. Andrew Wyeth, who generously made their private collections available to me for research and study purposes; and the Delaware Art Museum, Wilmington, Delaware, for allowing me access to their comprehensive N. C. Wyeth collection.

DOUGLAS ALLEN, JR.

A Note on the Arrangement

I. Book and Dust Wrapper Collations

The list is divided into five sections: *first,* books containing the writings and the first published appearances of illustrations by N. C. Wyeth; *second,* books containing dust wrapper illustrations by N. C. Wyeth; *third,* books containing illustrations reprinted from —or previously appearing in—books, periodicals; *fourth,* books containing biographical information and references to N. C. Wyeth; *fifth,* books published since 1946 containing illustrations by the artist.

Full collation data is given only for those books that contain the first publication of the artist's illustrations or his writings. Partial collation data is given for those books containing reprinted illustrations and dust wrappers designed by Wyeth. Books are listed alphabetically by author.

II. Periodicals

This list contains both illustrations and writings by N. C. Wyeth, plus references to the artist. Periodical titles are listed alphabetically, with the articles arranged in chronological order.

III. Newspapers

The list contains both illustrations and writings by N. C. Wyeth, plus articles and references to the artist. Since hundreds of newspaper articles mentioned Wyeth during his life and since, this compiler has omitted some, selecting only those of importance and genuine content.

IV. Prints and Portfolios

This list contains prints in color, colors (tints), and in black and white. They are arranged alphabetically according to publisher; the measurements given are height and width, respectively.

V. Posters

Here are listed posters in color, colors (tints), and in black and white. They were intended primarily for advertising purposes. They are arranged alphabetically according to publisher or company; the measurements given are height and width, respectively.

VI. Calendars

They are arranged alphabetically according to publisher or campany, and are measured by height and width.

VII. Advertisements

An alphabetical list according to the name of the company using Wyeth illustrations for advertising promotion and display.

VIII. Exhibition Catalogues

IX. Miscellaneous Catalogues

X. Exhibition Folders

XI. Folders, Brochures, Booklets, and Pamphlets

Sections VIII–XI are arranged alphabetically according to gallery, museum, advertiser, or publishing firm.

XII. Sale Catalogues

This list of catalogues published by galleries, art dealers, or auction houses describes a variety of N. C. Wyeth material. The arrangement is alphabetical according to firm name.

XIII. Cards and Postcards

Here are listed Christmas cards, advertising cards, museum picture cards, postcards, arranged alphabetically according to publisher, firm, or institution.

XIV. The Hotel Utica Plate

This rare plate fits into no specific category.

Index to Illustrations, Paintings, and Drawings

Over a period of years, many of the titles that have accompanied N. C. Wyeth's illustrations and paintings have been abbreviated, condensed, or changed for publication or exhibition purposes. In this index, these titles are referenced in their first published form; in the instance of exhibited easel paintings, the titles are those originally assigned by the artist.

This index does not include the large body of easel paintings, studies from nature, and composition drawings that, to date, remain unpublished or have never been exhibited publicly. Hopefully, someday they too will be catalogued.

NOTE: For bibliographic purposes, an asterisk (°) follows those titles that were assigned by this compiler in instances where no line of description accompanied the original published illustration. In many instances, these assigned titles are exactly those phrases followed by Wyeth in creating a particular illustration.

I. Books

Books Containing the Writings and the First Published Appearance of Illustrations by N. C. Wyeth

Abbott, Charles D.

[pictorial decoration] / HOWARD PYLE / A Chronicle / By Charles D. Abbott with / an Introduction by N. C. Wyeth / and Many Illustrations / from Howard Pyle's Works / [publisher's colophon] / Harper & Brothers Publishers / New York & London MCMXXV

Large 8 vo. Collation: Half title (with drawing); frontispiece (in color) (II); title (with pictorial decoration) (first line and publisher's colophon in red) (III); copyright (1925) (First Edition with code letters L–Z) and drawing (IV); dedication (V); drawing (VI); acknowledgments (VII); drawing (VIII); contents (IX); illustrations (XI–XIII); introduction (XIII–XIX); drawing; half title (with drawing); drawing; text (1–249).

Size of leaf trimmed 6¼ x 9⁵⁄₁₆ inches. Tinted top.

Issued in boards (gray) with cloth spine (blue black). Paper label on cover: Howard Pyle / A Chronicle / (decoration) / Charles D. Abbott (surrounded by boxed rules). Spine with paper label and stamped in gold: Howard / Pyle / A Chronicle / (ornament) / Charles D. Abbott (surrounded by boxed rules) / (at bottom in gold) (rule) / HARPERS

Introduction by N. C. Wyeth • Chadds Ford, Pennsylvania June, 1925 (XIII–XIX)

Note: A large portion of the introduction by N. C. Wyeth originally appeared in the article "Pupils of Pyle Tell Of His Teaching" by N. C. Wyeth, published in *The Christian Science Monitor*, November 13, 1912.

Allen, Hervey

ANTHONY ADVERSE / By / Hervey Allen / Illustrations by N. C. Wyeth / Pen Decorations by Allan McNab / New York / Farrar and Rinehart, Inc. / On Murray Hill / 1934

Two Volumes. Enclosed in slipcase with decorative pictorial labels in color (same) on both sides and label decoration in color on spine, designed by N. C. Wyeth.

Large 8 vo. Collation to Volume One: Half title (I); author's book list (II); frontispiece (in color) (IV); title (printed over pictorial decoration in blue) (surrounded by double boxed rules) (V); copyright 1933 (1934) and imprint (VI); dedication (VII); quotation–Sir Thomas Brown (VIII); contents (IX-XI); chapter heading (surrounded by double boxed rules) (1); text (3–592).

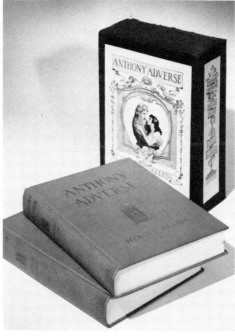

Collation to Volume Two: Half title; author's book list; frontispiece (in color); title (printed over pictorial decoration in blue) (surrounded by boxed rules); copyright 1933 (1934) and imprint; text (593–1224).

Size of leaf trimmed 6⅞ x 9¼ inches.

Issued in full cloth (green). Front cover stamped in gold with small pictorial design: ANTHONY / ADVERSE / (pictorial design) / HERVEY ALLEN. Spine with pictorial design and ornament stamped in gold: ANTHONY / ADVERSE / (pictorial design) / HERVEY / ALLEN / (ornament–star) / FARRAR & / RINEHART

Volume One
Frontispiece illustration and endpapers in color.
Anthony and Mr. Bonnyfeather
"Three mornings later Anthony emerged from his seclusion to take up his duties in the world of men."

Volume Two
Frontispiece illustration and endpapers in color.
Anthony and Neleta
"It was Neleta who had made him master of Gallegos, and Neleta was mistress of it all."

Andress, J. Mace, and Evans, W. A.

The Practical Health Series • • *Book Two* / HEALTH / AND GOOD CITIZENSHIP / By J. Mace Andress, Ph.D. / [two lines of author's credits] / and W. A. Evans, M.D. / [four lines of author's credits] / Revised Edition / [publisher's colophon] / Ginn and Company / Boston • New York • Chicago • London • Atlanta • Dallas • Columbus • San Francisco

12 mo. Collation: (publisher's book list) (II); title (III); copyright 1925, 1926, (1933) (code number 633.1) and imprint (IV); for the teacher to read (V–VIII); contents (IX–X); frontispiece (in color) (XI); text (1–388); appendix (389–407); pronouncing vocabulary and index (409–419).

Size of leaf trimmed 5½ x 7¼ inches.

Issued in full cloth (red). Front cover stamped in black with pictorial design (children carrying flags): HEALTH / AND / GOOD / CITIZENSHIP / ANDRESS • AND • EVANS (title surrounded by and enclosed in boxed rules) • Spine stamped in black: (double rules) / (double rules) / Andress And Evans • HEALTH AND GOOD CITIZENSHIP • Revised Edition Ginn and Company / (double rules) / (double rules)

Frontispiece illustration in color by N. C. Wyeth.
America's Greatest Wealth Is in Her Healthy Children

Arthurs, Stanley

THE / AMERICAN / HISTORICAL / SCENE / As Depicted by / Stanley Arthurs / and Interpreted by / Fifty Authors / [pictorial decoration] / University of Pennsylvania Press : Philadelphia / 1935

(Limited Edition of 100 copies.)
This volume contains an original water color by Stanley Arthurs.
4 to. Full levant; slipcase.
Fifty-four plates in color and black and white from paintings and illustrations by Stanley Arthurs.

One illustration in color by N. C. Wyeth.
A Portrait of Stanley Arthurs. fp 2
Article written by N. C. Wyeth titled "Quiet Custom House." (pp 130–132)

THE / AMERICAN / HISTORICAL / SCENE / As Depicted by / Stanley Arthurs / and Interpreted by / Fifty Authors / [pictorial decoration] / University of Pennsylvania Press : Philadelphia / 1935

4 to. Collation: Half title; frontispiece (in color) (II); title (sixth line in red) (III); copyright (1935) (IV); acknowledgment (V); foreword (VII); contents (IX–XIX); half title (1); text (2–151); national edition and imprints.

Size of leaf trimmed 9 x 12 inches. Cellophane wrapper.

Issued in buckram sides and morocco spine (red). Spine stamped in gold: (rule) / THE / AMERICAN / HISTORICAL / SCENE / (rule) / Stanley / Arthurs / (rule)

Fifty-four plates in color and black and white from paintings and illustrations by Stanley Arthurs.

One illustration in color by N. C. Wyeth. Same as in the Limited Edition.

Atwood, Wallace W.

Frye-Atwood Geographical Series / NEW / GEOGRAPHY / Book Two / By / Wallace W. Atwood / [design–globe] / Ginn and Company / Boston • New York [etc.]

4 to. Collation: Frontispiece (in color); title (surrounded by decorative rules) (I); preface and copyright (1920) (code number 420.4) (II); contents (III–IV); text (1–304); appendix, index, and pronunciations (I–XVI).

Size of leaf trimmed 9½ x 11¼ inches.

Issued in full cloth (olive green). Front cover with pictorial design (the caravels of Columbus) stamped in black: Frye-Atwood Geographical Series / (pictorial design) / A New World Lies Before Us / NEW GEOGRAPHY / BOOK TWO • ATWOOD / (design–globe) / Ginn and Company–Publishers (enclosed in border designs). Spine stamped in black: • NEW GEOGRAPHY • • BOOK TWO •

Illustrated from photographs and with numerous maps.

Two illustrations in color by N. C. Wyeth.
Harvest Time on an American Farm (frontispiece) 1
Modern Farming in the Fields of France 2 fp 180

Idem: Except the frontispiece 1 is replaced by the illustration 2 and the title changed to The New Farming in the Old World.

Baldwin, James

THE SAMPO / Hero Adventures From The Finnish Kalevala / By / James Baldwin / Author of "The Story of Siegfried," "A Story of The Golden / Age," "The Story of Roland," etc. / Illustrated by N. C. Wyeth / New York / Charles Scribner's Sons / 1912

8 vo. Collation: Author's book list; half title; frontispiece (with tissue inset) (II); title (III); copyright (1912) (published October, 1912) (IV); proem (V–VI); contents (VII–VIII); illustrations (IX); text (1–366); notes (367–68).

Size of leaf uncut 5¾ x 8⅛ inches.

Issued in full cloth (olive green). Front cover stamped in gold with pictorial design by Wyeth stamped in colors: THE SAMPO / By JAMES / BALDWIN / (pictorial design). Spine stamped in gold with ornamental designs stamped in black: (double rules) / THE / SAMPO / — / BALDWIN / (double rules) / (decoration) / (double rules) / SCRIBNERS / (double rules).

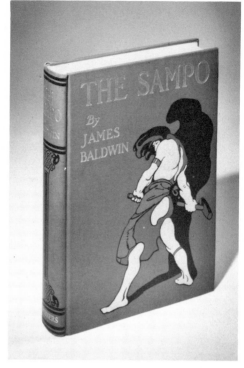

Four illustrations in color.
The Golden Maiden
    The flames died suddenly away, and out of the vessel there sprange a wonderful image —the image of a beautiful maiden. p II (frontispiece)
The Magician and the Maid of Beauty[1]
    High in the sky he saw a rainbow, and on it the Maid of Beauty. fp 16
The Hag of the Rock
    An old, old woman, gray-eyed, hook-nosed, wrinkled, was sitting on the rock and busily spinning. fp 138
The Slave Boy
    Then, at length, when all were peacefully feeding, he sat down upon a grassy hummock and looked around him, sad, lonely, vindictive. fp 262

[1] Also appears in color in *Life* magazine, December 17, 1971, for the article "The Wyeths' Kind of Christmas Magic" by Richard Meryman.

Bartlett, Frederick Orin

THE GUARDIAN / By / Frederick Orin Bartlett / Author of "The Web of the Golden Spider," "The Seventh / Noon," "The Prodigal Pro Tem," etc. / With a frontispiece by / N. C. Wyeth / [ornament] / Boston / Small, Maynard and Company / Publishers.

12 mo. Collation: Half title; frontispiece (in color); title; copyright (1912); dedication; contents; half title; text (1–470).

Size of leaf trimmed 5 x 7⅜ inches.

Issued in full cloth (dark blue). Front cover stamped in white: THE / GUARDIAN / Frederick Orin Bartlett. Spine stamped in white: THE / GUARDIAN / — / BARTLETT / SMALL / (ornament) / MAYNARD / & COMPANY

Frontispiece illustration in color.
    Description: Nat and Julie on the Summit of Eagle Mountain.

Boyd, James

DRUMS / • The Little River Country • / [pictorial design] / by James Boyd / • With

Pictures By • / N•C•Wyeth / Charles Scribner's Sons / New York : London

Large 8 vo. Collation: This Edition is Limited to Five Hundred and Twenty-Five Copies of Which Five Hundred Are For Sale (signed by the author and illustrator); half title; title (printed over two banners, the first, surrounding pictorial design in color) (first line in blue) (author, sixth and seventh lines in red) (I); copyright 1925, (1928) and publisher's colophon (II); dedication (III); author's note (V); facsimile letters of James Boyd and N. C. Wyeth (VII) (with seven pages of correspondence); illustrations (IX–XII); half title (1); text (3–409).

Size of leaf uncut 7 x 9¼ inches.

Boxed (orange) with paper label (black) stamped in gold on front. Tissue wrapper.

Issued in full cloth (orange). Pictorial cover label in color surrounded by boxed border with first line in brown, outlined in black: DRUMS / by James Boyd / Pictures by N. C. Wyeth. Spine stamped in gold: DRUMS / (ornament—crossed cannon barrels) / JAMES / BOYD / Illustrated / By / N. C. WYETH / SCRIBNERS

Seventeen illustrations in color including cover label, endpapers, and title page design.

Forty-seven illustrations (drawings) in pen and ink.

Illustrations (plates) in color:
The Little River Country (title page design) p III
The Fraser Family
    He was crammed, stiff and heated, into the old chaise between his parents. fp 20
Captain Flood
    "Never had time to follow Scripteh much, what with following the sea. But I respects a man that does." fp 54
Dr. Clapton
    He ventures no further remark, but stood there blinking and vaguely smiling. fp 68
Johnny's Fight with Cherry
    "Quit now," he managed to whisper, "if you want to." fp 84
The Indian Longthought
    "All night they drum, and never cease until the Sun, the Bloody Hunter, sets the hills on fire." fp 158

The Horse Race
Cursing and whipping like a madman, the scarlet jockey drew up on the turn, hung knee to knee, passed him by. fp 184

Captain Tennant
Sturdy, composed, unhurried, he stood on the top step in the full uniform of an officer of the line. Behind him Hoddin, uniformed as well, locked the door. fp 206

Sally Merrillee and Johnny
"I'm glad you think I'm not scared," he said. "I haven't talked like this to anybody else." fp 234

Johnny's Defeat at the Dock
He supported Johnny down the lane, the others followed, called out obscenities at Johnny in low malignant tones.[1] fp 278

With Eve in London
"Well," she said, as if this was the first moment of their meeting, "how have you been, sir?" fp 288

The Mother of John Paul Jones
A woman's drawn, sad face appeared at the door; she picked up the package, weighed it in her hand, then despite her years, shouted with extraordinary vigor at the fleeing youngster. fp 320

Sir Nat and the Horse
Johnny watched Sir Nat rub the gray muzzle, run a quick hand down the ewe neck, stand back critically and proceed to a minute and systematic inspection of the antique nag. fp 346

On the Sea Wall with John Paul Jones
For a long moment Paul Jones gazed out over the crowded shipping, down the long narrow harbor, out to the open water. He whistled dolefully between his teeth.[2] fp 354

The Fight in the Foretop
At the word three, they poured a volley into the mizzentop; pale, smoke-veiled faces withered away before it, but a volley answered them. fp 370

Illustrations (drawings) in pen and ink:

A Scribner Illustrated Classic (Limited Edition)

[1] Also appears in color in *Life* magazine, June 17, 1946, for the article "N. C. Wyeth."
[2] Appears in color in the book *Forty Illustrators and How They Work* by Ernest W. Watson, published by Watson-Guptill Publications, Inc., New York, February 1946.
[3] The illustrations also appear in the book *Everyday Things in American Life* by William Chauncy Langdon, published by Charles Scribner's Sons, New York, 1937.

DRUMS / · The Little River Country · [pictorial design] / by James Boyd / · With Pictures By · / N·C·Wyeth / Charles Scribner's Sons / New York : London

Large 8 vo. Collation: Half title (I); title (printed over two banners, the first, surrounding pictorial design in color) (first line in blue) (author, sixth and seventh lines in red) (III); copyright 1925, (1928) and publisher's colophon (IV); dedication (V); author's note (VII); illustrations (IX–XII); half title (1); text (3–409).

Size of leaf uncut 7 x 9¼ inches. Tinted top.

Issued in full cloth (black). Pictorial cover label in color surrounded by boxed border with first line in brown, outlined in black: DRUMS / by James Boyd / Pictures by N. C. Wyeth. Spine stamped in gold: DRUMS / (ornament—crossed cannon barrels) / JAMES / BOYD / Illustrated / By / N. C. WYETH / SCRIBNERS

Seventeen illustrations in color including cover label, endpapers, and title page design. The cover label is repeated as a label on the dust wrapper. The color plates are the same as those in the Limited Edition.

Forty-seven illustrations (drawings) in pen and ink. These are the same as those in the Limited Edition.

A Scribner Illustrated Classic

Boyles, Kate and Virgil D.
LANGFORD / OF THE THREE BARS / By / Kate and Virgil D. Boyles / With Illustrations in Color / By N. C. Wyeth / [publisher's colophon] / Chicago / A. C. McClurg & Co. / 1907

8 vo. Collation: Half title; frontispiece (in color) (2); title (3); copyright (1907) (published April 15, 1907) and imprint (4); dedication (5); contents (7); illustrations (9); text (11–278); recent Western Fiction, eight pages of publisher's advertising.

Size of leaf trimmed 5¼ x 7⅞ inches.

Issued in full cloth (light tan). Front cover stamped in black with pictorial design (cowboy) by Wyeth stamped in colors: LANGFORD / OF THE THREE BARS / (pictorial design by Wyeth). Spine stamped in black with decoration (rope) in brown: LANGFORD / OF THE / THREE BARS / – / BOYLES / (decoration) / A. C. / McCLURG / & CO.

Four illustrations in color.
"I take it I am the One Wanted," Said Williston. (frontispiece) p 2
The Glowing Iron Stuck in His Hand, Jesse Turned and Faced Squarely the Spot which Held the Watching Man. fp 18
Louise Loved to Climb to the Summit on One of the Barren Hills Flanking the River,

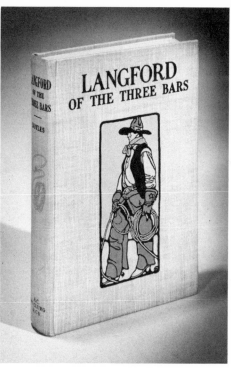

and Stand There While the Wind Blew. (repeated in orange tint on the dust wrapper) fp 146
The Little Posse Started Out on its Journey, the Wiry Marshal First. fp 258

Briggs, Thomas H.; McKinney, Isabel; and Skeffington, Florence
JUNIOR HIGH SCHOOL / ENGLISH / BOOK II / For The Eighth Grade / By / Thomas H. Briggs / Isabel McKinney / and / Florence Skeffington / NEW EDITION / [publisher's colophon] / Ginn and Company / Boston · New York · Chicago · London / Atlanta · Dallas · Columbus · San Francisco

12 mo. Collation: Frontispiece (in color); title (I); copyright (1926) (code number 326.12) and imprint (II); preface (III–V); contents (VII–XII); text and appendix (1–417); index (419–422).

Size of leaf trimmed 5 x 7¼ inches.

Issued in full cloth (tan). Front cover stamped in black with ornamental decoration (floral design): JUNIOR · HIGH · SCHOOL · ENGLISH / Book · II · / BRIGGS · McKINNEY / SKEFFINGTON (title surrounded by ornamental decoration). Spine stamped in black: JUNIOR / HIGH / SCHOOL / ENGLISH / Book · II · / Briggs / McKinney / Skeffington / (ornament) / NEW / EDITION / GINN AND / COMPANY

Frontispiece illustration in color by N. C. Wyeth.
After the Day's Work

Bronson, Edgar Beecher
REMINISCENCES OF / A RANCHMAN / By / Edgar Beecher Bronson / Author of "In Closed Territory," / "The Red-Blooded," Etc. / New Revised Edition, With New Matter and / Numerous Illustrations / New York / George H. Doran Company

8 vo. Collation: Half title; author's book list; frontispiece; title; copyright (A. C. McClurg & Co. 1910) (published September 10, 1910);

dedication; contents; illustrations; half title (1); text (3–370) including appendix.

Size of leaf trimmed 5¼ x 7¹⁵⁄₁₆ inches.

Issued in full cloth. Pictorial cover label in color: Reminiscences / Of A Ranchman / Edgar Beecher Bronson (lettering printed in green). Spine stamped in white: Reminis / cences / of a / Ranch / man / Bronson / George H. Doran / Company

Illustrated by N. C. Wyeth, W. Herbert Dunton (pictorial cover label), Maynard Dixon, W. J. Benda, etc.

Two illustrations in black and white by N. C. Wyeth.
> "Criers called the stirring news that the time for the Sun Dance had come." fp 226
> The Mystery Tree. fp 234

Idem: Except the book is published under the title *Cowboy Life on the Western Plains*, The Reminiscences of a Ranchman.

Note: The illustrations were originally intended as cover designs for *McClure's Magazine* depicting the Sioux ceremony of the Sun Dance but were never used in that form.

Bulfinch, Thomas

LEGENDS •.• OF / CHARLEMAGNE / [pictorial design in color] / • By Thomas Bulfinch • / Illustrated by N• C• Wyeth / Cosmopolitan Book Corporation •• Publishers • MCMXXIV

(The Wyeth Edition)

Large 8 vo. Collation: Half title (I); title (pictorial design in color) (III); preface (V–VI); contents (VII); N. C. Wyeth's paintings (IX–X) and artist's copyright; half title (XI); text (1–273).

Size of leaf trimmed 6⅞ x 9⅛ inches. Gilt top.

Issued in full cloth (maroon). Pictorial cover label in color: • LEGENDS • OF • / CHARLEMAGNE / (pictorial design in color) / ILLUSTRATED BY N. C. WYETH. Spine stamped in gold: LEGENDS / OF / CHARLEMAGNE / THOMAS / BULFINCH / Illustrated / By / N. C. WYETH / Cosmopolitan

Eleven illustrations in color including cover label, endpapers and title page design. The cover label illustration is repeated on the dust wrapper.

Illustrations (plates) in color:
Orlando and the Giant Farragus
> Orlando's utmost skill only availed to keep him out of the giant's clutches, but all his efforts to wound him with the sword were useless. fp 4

The Midnight Encounter
> Despiteful and terrible were the blows they gave and took by the moonlight. Agrican fought in a rage, Orlando was cooler. fp 32

The Winged Horse
> Bradamante beheld distinctly a winged horse, mounted with a cavalier in rich armor, cleaving the air with rapid flight. fp 78

The Sea-Serpent and Angelica
> The huge monster soon came in sight, part of his body appearing above the waves and part concealed. fp 98

The Fight on the Bridge
> Orlando at last had strength to lift his foe and fling him over the side, but had not wit to clear himself from him, so both fell together. fp 136

Prince Leo Presents Rogero to Charlemagne
> "Behold," Leo said, "The champion who maintained from dawn to setting sun the arduous contest; he comes to claim the guerdon of the fight." fp 184

Death of Orlando
> Orlando fixed his eyes on the hilt of his sword as on a crucifix, and appeared like a creature seraphical and transfigured, and bowing his head, he breathed out his pure soul. fp 198

Ogier and Morgana
> Ogier dismounted and took some steps along the stream, but was soon stopped by meeting a young beauty, such as they paint the Graces. fp 268

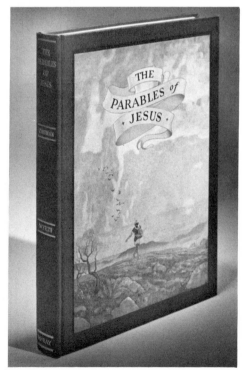

Cadman, S. Parkes

THE PARABLES OF JESUS / By / S. Parkes Cadman, D.D., LL.D., / Pastor of Central Church, Brooklyn, New York / Radio Minister of the Federal Council of Churches / of Christ in America / [ornament] / Illustrated By / N. C. Wyeth / David McKay Company / Washington Square ••• Philadelphia

Large 8 vo. Collation: Frontispiece (in color); title; copyright (1931) and imprint; dedication (1); illustrations (3); the foreword (5); the foreword–S. Parkes Cadman (7); acknowledgments (9); contents (11–12); text (13–163).

Size of leaf trimmed 7¼ x 9½ inches.

Issued in full cloth (purple). Pictorial cover label in color with decorative banner, printed in black: THE / PARABLES of / (ornament) JESUS (ornament). Spine stamped in gold: (rule) / THE PARABLES / OF / JESUS / (rule) / CADMAN / (rule) / (rule) / WYETH / (rule) / (rule) / McKAY / (rule).

Nine illustrations in color including cover label. The cover label illustration is repeated on the dust wrapper.

Endpapers illustration in pen and ink with portion printed in blue.

Illustrations (plates) in color:
The Child (frontispiece)
The Leaven. fp 34
The Hidden Treasure. fp 38
The Net. fp 42
The Secret Growth of the Seed.[1] fp 46
The Prodigal Son. fp 76
The Barren Fig Tree. fp 102
The Good Samaritan. fp 110

Idem: Except issued in full cloth (dark blue).

Note: The illustrations were conceived and printed as Religious Folders (Christmas cards) by N. C. Wyeth in 1923.
[1] Also appears in color in the book *Adventure* (The World of Music series) edited by Mabelle Glenn, Etc., published by Ginn and Company, Boston, 1938.

Cheney, Warren

THE CHALLENGE / By / Warren Cheney / Author of / The Way of the North, etc. / With Illustrations by / N. C. Wyeth / Indianapolis / The Bobbs-Merrill Company / Publishers

12 mo. Collation: Half title; frontispiece (with tissue inset); title; copyright (1906) (March) and imprint; dedication; contents; half title; text (1–386); eighteen pages of publisher's advertisements.

Size of leaf trimmed 4⅞ x 7¼ inches.

Issued in full cloth (Indian red). Front cover stamped in white with decorations stamped in gold and green: THE CHALLENGE / (ornament) Warren Cheney (ornament) / (decoration). Spine stamped in white with decoration stamped in green: THE / CHALLENGE / (decoration) / Cheney / Bobbs / Merrill

Four illustrations in black and white.
> He kept his gaze fixed as before and pointed. (frontispiece)
> "I shall pray to God that your punishment shall come!" fp 108
> The girl saw that Ivan had grappled with the floundering man. fp 170
> "I am here to give you this before you go." fp 302

(Clemens, Samuel Langhorne)

THE / MYSTERIOUS STRANGER / A Romance / By / Mark Twain / With Illustrations By / N. C. Wyeth / [publisher's colophon] / Harper & Brothers Publishers, New York and London

Large square 8 vo. Collation: Author's book list; frontispiece (in color with tissue inset); title; copyright (1916) (published October

1916) (code letters K–Q); illustrations; half title; text (1–151).

Size of leaf uncut 7 x 9⅜₆ inches. Gilt top.

Glassine wrapper with title, publisher and price printed on spine.

Issued in full cloth (black). Front cover stamped in gold with pictorial cover label in color (enclosed in box rules and borders stamped in gold): THE MYSTERIOUS / STRANG-ER • by / MARK TWAIN. Spine stamped in gold: THE / MYSTER • / -IOUS / STRAN-GER / – / MARK / TWAIN / (at bottom) HARPERS

Eight illustrations in color including cover label.

Illustrations (plates) in color:
  Eseldorf was a Paradise for Us Boys. (frontispiece)
  The Lightning Blazed Out Flash upon Flash and Set the Castle on Fire. fp 20
  On the Fourth Day Comes the Astrologer from His Crumbling Old Tower. (repeated on the cover label) fp 38
  Marget Was Cheerful by Help of Wilhelm Meidling. fp 60
  The Astrologer Emptied the Whole of the Bowl into the Bottle. fp 74
  There Was a Sound of Tramping Outside and the Crowd Came Solemnly In. fp 108
  "Life Itself Is Only a Vision, a Dream." fp 148

Note: The illustrations originally appeared in color in *Harper's Monthly Magazine*, May thru November 1916, for the story THE MYSTERIOUS STRANGER by Mark Twain.

The ADVENTURES of / TOM SAWYER / By / Mark Twain (Samuel L. Clemens) / With New and / Original Illustrations / By / Peter Hurd / The John C. Winston Company / Chicago (Philadelphia) Toronto

8 vo. Collation: Frontispiece (in color); title (surrounded by double boxed rules) (I); copyright (1931) (publisher's colophon) and imprint (II); preface (III); drawing (IV); contents (V–VI) list of illustrations (VII–VIII); text (1–264).

Size of leaf trimmed 6 x 8⅜ inches. Orange top.

Issued in full cloth (black). Pictorial cover label design with title (by Wyeth) in color surrounded by boxed rules stamped in gold: THE ADVENTURES OF / TOM SAWYER. Spine stamped in gold: (rule) / THE / AD-VENTURES / OF / TOM / SAWYER / (ornament) / MARK / TWAIN / WINSTON / (rule).

Cover label illustration in color by N. C. Wyeth (repeated in its entirety on the dust wrapper).
  Description: Whitewashing the fence.

Cody, Col. Wm. F.

The / GREAT / WEST / that / WAS / by / Col. Wm. F. Cody / Illustrated by / N. C. Wyeth / Buffalo Bill's / Life Story / Reprinted from / Hearst's / Magazine

12 mo. Collation: Copyright (1916) by The Star Company; text (1–60); imprint (Palmer & Oliver, Inc., N. Y.)

Size of leaf trimmed 5⅜ x 7½ inches.

Issued in paper wrappers. Front cover printed in orange and black (first, tenth, and eleventh lines in orange), with pictorial design (Indian aiming rifle) in colors.

Eleven illustrations in colors and black and white including cover design.
  Description: Bison approaching and drinking from water hole. p 1
  To my great joy father took me with him on his first trip into Kansas—where he was to pick out his claim and incidentally to trade with the Indians from our wagon. p 5
  Description: War-bonneted Sioux chief aiming rifle silhouetted in moon (repeated on the cover)[1] p 11
  Description: A shower of arrows rained on our dead horses from the closing circle of red-men.[1] p 19
  Description: Pursued by fifteen bloodthirsty Indians, I had a running fight of eleven miles.[1 2] p 23
  Description: It was no time for argument. I fired and killed him. (double-page vignette in black and white)[1] pp 26 & 27
  Description: He shoved a pistol in the man's face and said: "I'm calling the hand that's in your hat."[1] p 29

Description: Chief Santanta passed the peace-pipe to General Sherman and said: "My great white brothers."[1] p 39
Brigham, the most famous buffalo horse in the west.[1] p 51
Description: "I drove stage between Plum Creek and Fort Kearney, with plenty of hair-raising adventures thrown in."[1] p 55

Note: The illustrations originally appeared in *Hearst's Magazine*, August through December 1916, for the story "The Great West That Was" by Col. William F. Cody. A number of the illustrations are untitled and are described by those titles given in the *Hearst's Magazine* series.
[1] The illustrations also appeared in the book *An Autobiography of Buffalo Bill* by Colonel W. F. Cody, published by the Cosmopolitan Book Corporation, New York, 1920.
[2] Appears in color in *American Heritage*, October 1965, for the article "N. C. Wyeth" by Henry C. Pitz.

Cooper, James Fenimore

The LAST of the MOHICANS / A Narrative Of 1757 / [pictorial design] / by James Fenimore Cooper / Illustrated by N. C. Wyeth / [quotation, two lines] / New York / Charles Scribner's Sons / 1919 / Copyright 1919, by Charles Scribner's Sons

Large 8 vo. Collation: Half title (I); title (with pictorial design in color) and copyright (1919) (III); illustrations (V–VI); half title (VII); text (1–370).

Size of leaf uncut 7 x 9¼ inches. Tinted top.

Issued in full cloth (black). Pictorial cover label in color with gold inset, printed in black: THE LAST OF / THE MOHICANS / By / James Fenimore Cooper / (illustration) (all enclosed in box borders). Spine stamped in gold: THE LAST / OF THE / MOHICANS / (ornament—arrowhead) / JAMES / FENI-MORE / COOPER / Illustrated / By / N. C. WYETH / SCRIBNERS

Seventeen illustrations in color including cover label, endpapers, and title page design.
  Illustrations (plates) in color:
Uncas Slays a Deer
  Avoiding the horns of the infuriated animal, Uncas darted to his side, and passed his knife across the throat. fp 26

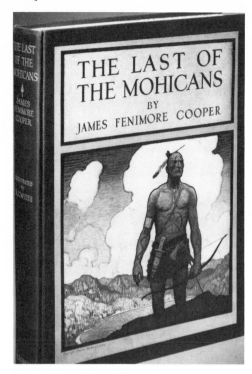

The Battle at Glens Falls
　Each of the combatants threw all his ener-
　gies into that effort, and the result was, that
　both tottered on the brink of the precipice.[1][2]
　fp 66
Captives
　When the pilot chosen for the task of guiding
　the canoe had taken his station, the whole
　band plunged again into the river, the vessel
　glided down the current and in a few mo-
　ments the captives found themselves on the
　south bank of the stream. fp 94
The Fight in the Forest
　The battle was now entirely terminated, with
　the exception of the protracted struggle be-
　tween Le Renard Subtil and Le Gros Serpent.
　fp 114
David Gamut
　Never minstrel, or by whatever more suitable
　name David should be known, drew upon his
　talents in the presence of more insensible au-
　ditors. fp 120
The Meeting of the Generals
　As soon as this slight salutation had passed,
　Montcalm moved towards them with a quick
　but graceful step, baring his head to the vet-
　eran, and dropping his spotless plume nearly
　to the earth in courtesy. fp 166
Magua Captures Alice
　He hesitated a moment; and then catching the
　light and senseless form of Alice in his arms,
　the subtle Indian moved swiftly across the
　plain towards the woods. fp 182
The Flight Across the Lake
　The scout having ascertained that the Mohi-
　cans were sufficient of themselves to maintain
　the requisite distance, deliberately laid aside
　his paddle, and raised the fatal rifle.[3] fp 214
In the Council Lodge
　A flaring torch was burning in the play, and
　sent its red glare from face to face and figure
　to figure, as it waved in the currents of air.
　fp 244
The Termagant
　Throwing back her light vestment, she
　stretched forth her long skinny arm, in deri-
　sion. fp 250
The Masquerader
　The grim head fell on one side, and in its
　place appeared the honest, sturdy countenance
　of the scout. fp 268
The Lovers
　Heyward and Alice took their way together
　towards the distant village of the Delawares.
　fp 278

The Supplicant
　Cora had cast herself to her knees; and, with
　hands clenched in each other and pressed
　upon her bosom, she remained like a beaute-
　ous and breathing model of her sex. fp 320
The Burial of Uncas
　"The boy has left us for a time; but, Saga-
　more, you are not alone." fp 368

A Scribner Illustrated Classic

Also appears in black and white in *The Artgum*
magazine, April 1926, for the article "N. C.
Wyeth, Painter and Illustrator," by Anton Kamp.
[2] Also appears in color in *Life* magazine, December 9, 1957, for the article "The Stouthearted
Heroes of a Beloved Painter." In addition, it appears in *American Heritage* magazine, October
1965, for the article "N. C. Wyeth," by Henry C.
Pitz.
[3] Appears in a number of volumes on American
history.

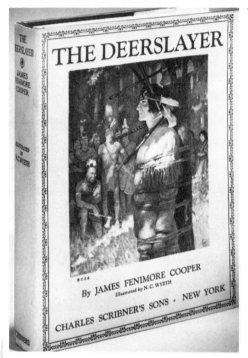

THE DEERSLAYER / Or / THE FIRST
WAR-PATH / By / James Fenimore Cooper
/ with pictures by / N. C. Wyeth / New
York / Charles Scribner's Sons / 1925

　Large 8 vo. Collation: Half title (I); title
(printed over pictorial design) (third, sixth and
seventh lines in red) (III); copyright (1925)
(publisher's colophon) (IV); preface to the
Leather-Stocking Tales (V–VIII); preface (IX–
X); illustrations (XI); text (1–462).
　Size of leaf uncut 7 x 9¼ inches. Tinted top.
　Issued in full cloth (black). Pictorial cover
label in color: DEERSLAYER / (illustration)
/ By James Fenimore Cooper / Pictures By
(red) / N. C. WYETH. Spine stamped in gold:
THE / DEERSLAYER / (ornament—Indian
design) / JAMES / FENIMORE / COOPER /
Illustrated / By / N. C. WYETH / SCRIB-
NERS

Twelve illustrations in color including cover
label, endpapers, and title page design.
　Illustrations (plates) in color:
　　. . . Emerging into an opening that appeared
　　to have been formed partly by the ravages of
　　the wind, and partly by those of fire. fp 4
　　The savage gave the yell . . . and came
　　bounding across the open ground, flourishing
　　a tomahawk. fp 92
　　All this while the canoe, with the form of

Hetty erect in one end of it, was dimly perceptible. fp 128
Judith fairly trembled, as she cast her first
glance at the interior. fp 170
Deerslayer threw all his force into a desperate
effort. fp 240
At this instant the door flew open and the
fight was transferred to the platform, the
light, and the open air. fp 278
. . . She found Chingachgook studying the
shores of the lake, the mountains, and the
heavens. fp 360
The unflinching firmness with which he faced
his assailants . . . excited a profound respect
in the spectators. (repeated as a label in
color on the dust wrapper) fp 422
"I may never see this spot again, Deerslayer,"
she said, "and it contains the bodies of my
mother and sister!" fp 454

A Scribner Illustrated Classic

Creswick, Paul

ROBIN HOOD / Illustrated By / N•C•
Wyeth / [pictorial design] / David McKay,
Publisher / Philadelphia / MCMXVII

　Large 8 vo. Collation: Half title (1); title
(pictorial design in color with lettering printed
over banner) (3); illustrations (5); half title
(7); text (9–362).
　Size of leaf trimmed 7 x 9¼ inches. Gilt top.
　Issued in full cloth (green). Front cover
stamped in gold with pictorial cover label in
color (surrounded by boxed rules and borders
stamped in gold): ROBIN • HOOD. Spine
stamped in gold: ROBIN / HOOD / (ornament—bow and arrow) / PAUL / CRESWICK
/ Illustrated / By / N•C•WYETH / DAVID
McKAY

　Eleven illustrations in color including cover
label, endpapers and title page design. The
cover label illustration is repeated on the dust
wrapper.
　Illustrations (plates with tissue insets) in
color:
Robin and His Mother Go to Nottingham Fair
　The road wound in and about the forest and
　at noon they came to a part where the trees
　nigh shut out the sky. fp 18

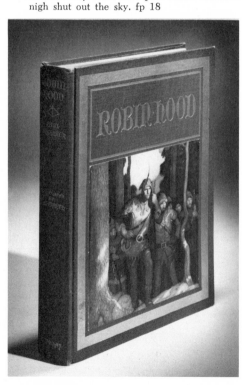

Robin Wrestles Will Stuteley at Gamewell
"Catch him by the middle," he shouted. "Now you have him, lording, fairly. Throw him prettily!" And sure enough Stuteley came down. fp 53

Robin Meets Maid Marian
But Robin, venturing all, drew nigh. He came to the edge of her box, and began to speak.[1] fp 116

Robin Hood and His Companions Lend Aid to Will o' th' Green from Ambush
Their arrows flew together, marvellous shots, each finding its prey.[1][2] fp 156

Little John Fights with the Cook in the Sheriff's House
At least he made a dart upon Roger and the chase grew furious. Dishes, plates, covers, pots and pans—all that came in the way of them went flying. fp 197

Robin Hood Defeats Nat of Nottingham at Quarter-staff
The beggar dealt his foe a back-thrust so neatly, so heartily, and so swiftly that Nat was swept off the stage into the crowd as a fly off a table. fp 257

Little John Sings a Song at the Banquet
That evening, whilst Monceux raged and stormed without, they all sat to a great feast. fp 327

The Passing of Robin Hood
Leaning heavily against Little John's sobbing breast, Robin Hood flew his last arrow out through the window, far away into the deep green of trees. fp 361

Endpaper illustration: Nottingham (title printed on banner)

Idem: Except for the tissue insets.

[1] Illustrations and cover label appear in color in *Life* magazine, December 9, 1957, for the article "The Stouthearted Heroes of a Beloved Painter."
[2] Illustration and cover label also appear in *The Mentor*, December 1923, for the article "Six Immortals and How They Grew into Books" by Arthur Bartlett Maurice. In addition, the illustration appeared in color in *Life* magazine, June 17, 1946, for the article on N. C. Wyeth. The illustration also appeared in color in the book *The Wyeths* by N. C. Wyeth (edited by Betsy James Wyeth), published by Gambit, Boston, 1971.

Defoe, Daniel

ROBINSON CRUSOE / by / Daniel Defoe / Pictures by N. C. Wyeth / New York / Cosmopolitan Book Corporation / MCMXX

Large 8 vo. Collation: Half title; frontispiece (in color with tissue inset); title (pictorial design in color with title, author and artist printed on banner); illustrator's preface; contents; the illustrations; half title, text (1–368).
Size of leaf trimmed 7 x 9⅜₆ inches. Gilt top.
Boxed with pictorial label in color.
Issued in full cloth (royal blue). Front cover stamped in gold with pictorial cover label in color (surrounded by boxed borders stamped in gold): ROBINSON / CRUSOE. Spine stamped in gold: ROBINSON / CRUSOE / DANIEL / DEFOE / Illustrated / By / N. C. WYETH / Cosmopolitan

Sixteen illustrations in color including cover label (repeated on box), endpapers, and title page design.
Illustrations (plates) in color:
"For a mile, or thereabouts, my rafts went very well—" (frontispiece)[1]
"My father, a wise and grave man, gave me serious and excellent counsel against what he foresaw was my design." fp 2
"—and making it into a great cross, I set it up on the shore where I first landed—" fp 84
"All this while I sat upon the ground, very much terrified and dejected." fp 106

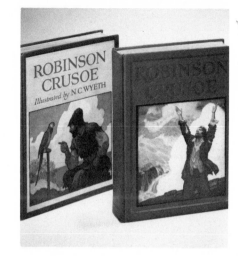

"In the morning I took the Bible; and beginning at the New Testament, I began seriously to read it—" fp 126
"I reaped it my way, for I cut nothing off but the ears, and carried it away in a great basket which I had made." fp 154
"—and thus I every now and then took a little voyage upon the sea." fp 182
"I stood like one thunderstruck, or as if I had seen an apparition."[2] fp 204
"I laid me down flat on my belly on the ground, and began to look for the place." fp 242
"—and then he kneeled down again, kissed the ground, and taking me by the foot, set my foot upon his head." fp 270
"—we cut and hewed the outside into the true shape of a boat." fp 302
"—and no sooner had he the arms in his hands but, as if they had put new vigor into him, he flew upon his murderers like a fury." fp 312
"At first, for some time I was not able to answer him one word; but as he had taken me in his arms, I held fast by him, or I should have fallen to the ground." fp 362

[1] Also appears in color in the *National Geographic Magazine*, April 1949, for the article "The British Way," by Sir Evelyn Wrench.
[2] Also appears in color in *Life* magazine, December 9, 1957, for the article "The Stouthearted Heroes of a Beloved Painter."

ROBINSON CRUSOE / by / DANIEL DEFOE / Pictures by N. C. WYETH / New York / Cosmopolitan Book Corporation / MCMXX

Large 8 vo. Collation: Half title; frontispiece (in color with tissue inset); title (pictorial design in color with title, author and artist printed on banner); illustrator's preface; contents; the illustrations; half title; text (1–368); imprint.
Size of leaf trimmed 7 x 9⅜₆ inches. Gilt top.
Issued in full cloth (maroon). Pictorial cover label in color: ROBINSON / CRUSOE / Illustrated by N. C. WYETH (lettering in blue). Spine stamped in gold: ROBINSON / CRUSOE / DANIEL / DEFOE / ILLUSTRATED / BY / N. C. WYETH / Cosmopolitan

Sixteen illustrations in color including cover label, endpapers, and title page design.

Illustrations (plates) in color: Same as those in the blue cloth edition.

Note: In this edition, the cover label illustration was changed from the original concept.

Dodge, Mary Mapes

HANS BRINKER / OR THE SILVER SKATES / By Mary Mapes Dodge / Illustrated in color by N. C. Wyeth and Peter Hurd / Copyright 1932, By Garden City Publishing Co., Inc.

8 vo. Collation: Half title; copyright and imprint; frontispiece—title (in color by Peter Hurd) (first line in white); dedication; contents; illustrations; half title; text (1–305).
Size of leaf trimmed 6⅛ x 8⅜₆ inches. Blue top.
Issued in full cloth (dark blue). Pictorial cover label in color by N. C. Wyeth (surrounded by stamped light blue borders): HANS BRINKER / Or / THE SILVER SKATES. Spine stamped in light blue with rules and design: (stamped rule) / HANS / BRINKER / Or THE / SILVER / SKATES / Mary M. / Dodge / (design–house) / (stamped rule) / Illustrated by / N. C. WYETH / and / PETER HURD / (stamped rule) / GARDEN CITY / PUBLISHING CO. / (stamped rule).

Illustrated by N. C. Wyeth and Peter Hurd.
Cover label illustration in color by N. C. Wyeth.
Description: Hans and Gretel skating. (Repeated on the dust wrapper.)

Note: Also appears in color in *Life* magazine, December 9, 1957, for the article "The Stouthearted Heroes of a Beloved Painter."

Doyle, A. Conan

THE / WHITE COMPANY / • BY • / A. CONAN DOYLE / [ornament] / Pictures By / N. C. Wyeth / Cosmopolitan Book Corporation / New York / MCMXXII

Large 8 vo. Collation: half title; title (pictorial design [banner] in color enclosing title)

(first five lines in red, remaining lines in brown); contents; the illustrations and artist's copyright; half title; text (1–363).

Size of leaf trimmed 6⅞ x 9³⁄₁₆ inches. Gilt top.

Issued in full cloth (maroon). Pictorial cover label in color with decorative scroll, printed in red and blue: The / WHITE COMPANY / by A. CONAN DOYLE / Illustrated by / N. C. WYETH. Spine stamped in gold: THE WHITE COMPANY / A. CONAN DOYLE / Illustrated / by / N. C. WYETH / Cosmopolitan.

Sixteen illustrations in color including cover label, endpapers and title page design. The cover label illustration is repeated on the dust wrapper.

Illustrations (plates) in color:

The Renegade Monk
"By the black rood of Waltham!" he roared, "if any knave among you lays a finger-end upon the edge of my gown, I will crush his skull like a filbert!" fp 8

The Wrestling Match at the "Pied Merlin"
It would have been hard that night, through the whole length of England, to set up a finer pair in face of each other. fp 50

The Three Friends
The bowman sang snatches of French love songs in a voice which might have scared the most stouthearted maiden. fp 68

The Fugitives
"This way!" the woman whispered. "Into the stream to throw the dogs off, though I think it is but a common cur, like its master." fp 82

The Sailing of the Yellow Cog
The breeze blew, the sail bellied, over heeled the portly vessel, and away she plunged through the smooth blue rollers. fp 148

The Three Knights
"It is very fitting," said Chandos, "that we should be companions, Nigel, for since you have tied up one of your eyes, we have but a pair between us." fp 178

Alleyne Fights on the Banks of the Garonne
Back and back gave Tranter, ever seeking time for a last cut. On and on came Alleyne. fp 196

Sir Nigel Sustains England's Honor in the Lists
Up and down went the long, shining blades with flash of sparks at every parry. fp 230

The Brushwood Folk and the Castle of Villefranche
High and strong the chateau, lowly and weak the brushwood hut; but God help the seigneur and his lady when the men of the brushwood set their hands to the work of revenge! fp 262

The Murder of Squire Ford
"My God!" cried Alleyne, shaking in every limb. "What devil's deed is this?" fp 284

The White Company
Day was already breaking in the east, and Sir Nigel's Company, three hundred strong, were on their way for the defile. fp 308

Alleyne's Ride with a Message for the Prince
He was dizzy, sick, faint, but he must not die, and he must not tarry, for his life meant many lives that day. fp 352

The Lovers
Her foot is on the very lintel of the church, and yet he bars the way. fp 360

Note: The endpapers illustration appears in *The Red Barrel* magazine, December 15, 1939.

Fassett, James H.

THE / CORONA READERS / EGAN • BROTHER LEO • FASSETT / SECOND READER / Based on the Beacon Second Reader / BY / JAMES H. FASSETT / [pictorial design] / GINN AND COMPANY / Boston • New York • Chicago • London / Atlanta • Dallas • Columbus • San Francisco [title surrounded by ornamental rules and decorations]

12 mo. Collation: Frontispiece (in color) (2); title (3); copyright (1920) (code number 528.3) and imprint (4); preface (5); contents (6–7); illustration (The Good Shepherd) (8); text (9–198); phonetic tables (199–224).

Size of leaf trimmed 5½ x 7¼ inches.

Issued in full cloth (light blue). Front cover stamped in dark blue with stamped pictorial design (lilies): THE CORONA / READERS / SECOND / READER. Spine stamped in dark blue: (ornament–crown) CORONA READERS : SECOND READER : GINN AND COMPANY (ornament–crown)

Frontispiece illustration in color by N. C. Wyeth.

"Suffer the Little Children to Come Unto Me"

Forester, C. S.

CAPTAIN / HORATIO / HORNBLOWER / By C. S. Forester / [drawing] / With Drawings By / N. C. Wyeth / Published in Boston by / Little, Brown and Company / 1939

Thick 8 vo. Collation: Half title; author's book list; frontispiece; title (with drawing); copyright (various dates) (1939) (published April 1939); contents; half title (1); drawing (2); text (3–662).

Size of leaf trimmed 5¹¹⁄₁₆ x 8⅜ inches. Gray green top.

Issued in full cloth (red). Front cover decoration stamped in gold. Spine stamped in gold with decorations: CAPTAIN / HORATIO / HORNBLOWER / (ornament) / C. S. / FORESTER / LITTLE, BROWN

Frontispiece illustration in color.
Description: Captain Horatio Hornblower. (repeated on the dust wrapper)
Four illustrations in pen and ink.*
Title page drawing.
Description: Sailor and cannon.
The Landfall–Captain Hornblower Aloft[1] p 2
The Sutherland–Ship of the Line[1] p 222
The Cutter–Witch of Endor[1] p 460

[1] Also appear in the three-volume set of *Captain Horatio Hornblower.*
* Contrary to the title page credit, the four pen-and-ink illustrations were drawn by Andrew Wyeth under his father's supervision.

Captain Horatio / HORNBLOWER / By C. S. Forester / I / Beat to Quarters / [publisher's colophon] / Boston / Little, Brown And Company / 1939

(Published in three volumes with glassine wrappers.)

8 vo. Collation: Half title; frontispiece (printed over tint); title (printed over tint and surrounded by double boxed rules and ornamental borders); copyright 1938 (1939) and imprint; contents; text (1–324).

Size of leaf trimmed 5¼ x 8 inches. Gray green top.

Slipcase with paper label printed in gray.

Issued in full cloth (gray green). Spine stamped in gold over black inset: Captain / Horatio / Hornblower / (ornament–anchor) / C. S. Forester / I / Beat to Quarters / (at bottom) Little, Brown / And Company / •

Frontispiece illustration in pen and ink.*
Description: The Landfall–Captain Horatio Hornblower Aloft.

Captain Horatio / HORNBLOWER / By C. S. Forester / II / Ship of the Line / [publisher's colophon] / Boston / Little, Brown And Company / 1939

8 vo. Collation: Half title; frontispiece (printed over tint); title (printed over tint and surrounded by double boxed rules and ornamental borders); copyright 1938 (1939) and imprint; text (1–323).

Size of leaf trimmed 5¼ x 8 inches. Gray green top.

Issued in full cloth (gray green). Spine stamped in gold over black inset: Captain / Horatio / Hornblower / (ornament–anchor) / C. S. Forester / II / Ship of the Line / (at bottom) Little, Brown / And Company / •

Frontispiece illustration in pen and ink.*
Description: The Sutherland–Ship of the Line.

Captain Horatio / HORNBLOWER / By C. S. Forester / III / Flying Colours / [publisher's colophon] / Boston / Little, Brown And Company / 1939

8 vo. Collation: Half title; frontispiece (printed in tint); title (printed over tint and surrounded by double boxed rules and ornamental borders); copyright 1938 (1939) and imprint; text (1–294).

Size of leaf trimmed 5¼ x 8 inches. Gray green top.

Issued in full cloth (gray green). Spine stamped in gold over black inset: Captain / Horatio / Hornblower / (ornament–anchor) / C. S. Forester / III / Flying Colours / (at bottom) Little, Brown / And Company / •

Frontispiece illustration in pen and ink.*
Description: The Cutter–Witch of Endor.

Note: The illustrations also appear in the book *Captain Horatio Hornblower* by C. S. Forester, published by Little, Brown and Company, Boston, April 1939.
* The three frontispiece illustrations were drawn by Andrew Wyeth under his father's supervision.

Fox, John, Jr.

THE LITTLE SHEPHERD / OF KINGDOM COME / By / John Fox, Jr. / A Limited Edition / With Pictures By N. C. Wyeth / [ornament] / New York / Charles Scribner's Sons / 1931

4 to. Collation: This Edition is Limited to Five Hundred and Twelve Copies, Signed by the Illustrator, Of Which Twelve are for Presentation; half title; frontispiece (in color surrounded by boxed border in gold, mounted and with tissue inset) (II); title (III); copyright 1903, (1931) (IV); title (mounted pictorial design in color) (author and illustrator in reddish brown) (V); dedication (VII); contents (IX–X); illustrations (XI); half title (1); text (3–322); imprint.

Size of leaf uncut 8⅜ x 10⅞ inches. Gilt top.

Boxed (blue) with paper label stamped in gold on front. Cellophane wrapper.

Issued in cloth sides (blue with rules) and vellum spine stamped in gold: THE / LITTLE / SHEPHERD / OF / KINGDOM / COME / (ornament–pine cone) / JOHN FOX, JR. / (at bottom) SCRIBNERS

Sixteen illustrations in color including frontispiece and title page design. The illustrations (plates) are surrounded by boxed borders in gold, mounted and with tissue insets.

Illustrations (mounted plates) in color:
"Stick to him, little un," shouted Tom. fp 22
Softly and swiftly Chad's fingers worked. fp 42
"Where are you from, little man?" fp 70
He looked at the boy a long time and fancied he could see some resemblance to the portrait. fp 86
Dan, nearly unseated, had dropped his lance to catch hold of his charger's wool. fp 114
Straight in front of the Squire gathered the Turners about Melissa and Chad and Jack as a centre. fp 130
Once the girl started through the yard as though she would rush after them and stopped at the gate. fp 148
Steadily the boy worked—and the schoolmaster helped him unwearyingly. fp 156
"I wish you could see yourself; I wish I could tell you how you look." fp 184
"Major, I'm going into the Union army." fp 198
It was not until Shiloh that Chad got his shoulder-straps, leading a charge. fp 228
"Two prisoners, sir. We captured 'em with Daws Dillon." fp 246
Rebel Jerry and Yankee Jake. fp 286
He sat there until the sun went down. fp 320

A Scribner Illustrated Classic (Limited Edition)

Note: This, the Limited Edition, lacks the endpaper illustration (Melissa and Chad) that appears in the first trade edition.

THE LITTLE SHEPHERD / OF KINGDOM COME / by John Fox, Jr. [pictorial design] / With Pictures By / N. C. WYETH / New York / Charles Scribner's Sons / 1931

Large 8 vo. Collation: Half title (I); title (pictorial design in color with titles printed over banners) (author and illustrator in reddish brown) (III); copyright 1903 (1931) (code letter A) and publisher's colophon (IV); dedication (V); contents (VII–VIII); illustrations (IX); half title (1); text (3–322).
Size of leaf uncut 7 x 9¼ inches. Tinted top.
Boxed with pictorial label on front. Cellophane wrapper.
Issued in full cloth (black). Pictorial cover label in color: THE LITTLE SHEPHERD / OF KINGDOM COME / by John Fox, Jr. Spine stamped in gold: THE / LITTLE / SHEPHERD / OF / KINGDOM / COME / (ornament—pine cone) / JOHN FOX, JR. / Illustrated / By / N. C. WYETH / SCRIBNERS

Seventeen illustrations in color including cover label, endpapers, and title page design. The cover label is repeated as a label in color on the box front.
Illustrations (plates) in color: same as in the Limited Edition. Endpaper illustrations: Melissa and Chad (titles printed on banner).
A Scribner Illustrated Classic

Franklin, Benjamin

THE / PICTORIAL LIFE / OF / BENJAMIN FRANKLIN / PRINTER / Typefounder • Ink Maker / Bookbinder • Copperplate Engraver and Printer / Stationer • Merchant • Bookseller • Author • Editor • Publisher / Inventor • Scientist • Philosopher / Diplomat • Philanthropist / and Statesman / Published in Commemoration of the 200th Anniversary of the arrival of Franklin in Philadelphia / [trade mark] / Dill & Collins Co. / Philadelphia / 1923

Thin 4 to. Collation: Frontispiece; title (fourth and fourteenth lines in orange); copyright (1923); foreword; commemorative dates; text (1–62) (unnumbered).
Size of leaf trimmed 8½ x 11 inches.
Issued in cloth sides (green simulated leather) and cloth spine (black). Front cover with decorative paper label (title surrounded by decoration): THE PICTORIAL LIFE / OF / BENJAMIN FRANKLIN.
Illustrated with numerous paintings, sculpture, engravings, photographs, etc.

Frontispiece illustration in color by N. C. Wyeth.
Franklin's Arrival in Philadelphia

Note: The illustration also appeared as a cover for the *National Republic,* March 1927.

French, Allen

By Allen French / THE / RED KEEP / A Story of Burgundy in the Year 1165 / [drawing] / Illustrations by N. C. Wyeth and Andrew Wyeth / Houghton Mifflin Company • Boston / The Riverside Press Cambridge / 1938

8 vo. Collation: Half title; frontispiece (in color); title; copyright (1938) and imprint; dedication; contents; text (1–310).
Size of leaf trimmed 5⁹⁄₁₆ x 8½ inches.
Issued in full cloth (red). Front cover stamped in black with decoration (castle): THE / RED KEEP / (decoration) / ALLEN FRENCH. Spine stamped in black with decoration (castle keep): THE / RED / KEEP / (decoration) / FRENCH / HOUGHTON / MIFFLIN CO.

Illustrated by N. C. Wyeth and Andrew Wyeth.

Frontispiece illustration in color by N. C. Wyeth.
    The fief was granted to Conan of Prigny to hold and protect for the Lady Anne. (Repeated on the dust wrapper.)

Frye, Alexis Everett

Frye-Atwood Geographical Series / NEW / GEOGRAPHY / Book One / by / Alexis Everett Frye / [design—globe] / Ginn and Company / Boston • New York • Chicago • London / Atlanta • Dallas • Columbus • San Francisco

4 to. Collation: Frontispiece; title (surrounded by decoration borders) (I); copyright 1917 (1920), and preface (II); contents (III–IV); index and colored plates (V–VIII); photograph (moon); text, photographs, maps, etc. (1–264); supplement (I–V); pronouncing word list (VI–VIII).
Size of leaf trimmed 8⅛ x 10⅛ inches.
Issued in full cloth (olive green). Front cover with pictorial design (the caravels of Columbus) stamped in black: Frye-Atwood Geographical Series / (pictorial design) / A New World Lies Before Us / NEW GEOGRAPHY / Book One • • • Frye / (design—globe) / Ginn and Company—Publishers (cover enclosed in border designs). Spine stamped in black: • NEW GEOGRAPHY • • BOOK ONE •

Illustrated in color by N. C. Wyeth and Thornton Oakley, and with numerous photographs, maps, etc.
Frontispiece illustration in color by N. C. Wyeth.
The Boy Columbus on the Wharf at Genoa

Glenn, Mabelle; Leavitt, Helen S.; Rebmann, Victor L. F.; and Baker, Earl L. [Edited by]

The World of Music / Song Programs For Youth / DISCOVERY / [decoration and rule] / Edited by / Mabelle Glenn / [credits] / Helen S. Leavitt / [credits] / Victor L. F. Rebmann / [credits] / Earl L. Baker / [credits] / Artist / N. C. Wyeth / [rule and decoration] / Ginn and Company / Boston • New York • Chicago • London / Atlanta • Dallas • Columbus • San Francisco

4 to. Collation: Frontispiece (in color); title (1); copyright (1937) (code number 837.10) (2); contents, illustrations, and instrumental themes (3); acknowledgments (4); text (5–190); alphabetical index (191–192).
Size of leaf trimmed 7¾ x 10⅛ inches.
Issued in full cloth (black). Front cover in black over stamped gold decoration and light green bands: • SONG • PROGRAMS • FOR • YOUTH • / DISCOVERY (over stamped gold decoration / • THE • WORLD • OF • MUSIC • Spine stamped in light green: THE WORLD OF MUSIC / DISCOVERY / GINN AND COMPANY

Six illustrations in color.
Discovery (frontispiece)
A Gypsy Sings to His Pony. fp 16
Indian Prayer. fp 48
The Prince. fp 64
Ballad of Robin Hood.[1] fp 128
Sea Fever. fp 144

Idem: Except for new illustration.

[1] Because of controversy involving the illustration, the Ballad of Robin Hood was eliminated after the first printing of this volume. The painting depicts Robin and Friar Tuck relieving a nobleman of his wealth. A new painting was submitted and subsequently reproduced in a new edition. This painting depicts Robin Hood and Little John walking through Sherwood Forest.

The World of Music / Song Programs For Youth / ADVENTURE / [decoration and rule] / Edited by / Mabelle Glenn / [credits] / Helen S. Leavitt / [credits] / Victor L. F. Rebmann / [credits] / Earl L. Baker / [credits] / Artist / N. C. Wyeth / [rule and decoration] / Ginn and Company / Boston • New York • Chicago • London / Atlanta • Dallas • Columbus • San Francisco

4 to. Collation: Frontispiece (in color); title (1); copyright (1938) (code number 840.2) and acknowledgments (2); contents (3–6); illustrations and instrumental themes (6); text (7–190); alphabetical index (191–192).
Size of leaf trimmed 7¾ x 10⅛ inches.
Issued in full cloth (black). Front cover in black over stamped gold decoration and light orange bands: • SONG • PROGRAMS • FOR • YOUTH • / ADVENTURE (over stamped gold decoration) / • THE • WORLD • OF • MUSIC • Spine stamped in light orange: THE WORLD OF MUSIC / ADVENTURE / GINN AND COMPANY

Six illustrations in color.
Cap'n Storm-Along (frontispiece)
The Forge. fp 16
Song of the Reapers.[1] fp 49
The Man of Wales. fp 64

The Cowboy's Life. fp 113
The Air Mail.² fp 128

¹ Illustration was originally conceived and printed in a series of Christmas cards by N. C. Wyeth in 1923. In addition, it appeared in color in the book *The Parables of Jesus* by S. Parkes Cadman, published by David McKay Company, Philadelphia, 1931.
² Also appears in black and white in *Cathedral Age*, Spring Issue 1940.

The World of Music / Song Programs For Youth / TREASURE / [decoration and rule] / Edited by / Mabelle Glenn / [credits] / Helen S. Leavitt / [credits] / Victor L. F. Rebmann / [credits] / Earl L. Baker / Artist / N. C. Wyeth / [rule and decoration] / Ginn and Company / Boston • New York • Chicago • London / Atlanta • Dallas • Columbus • San Francisco

4 to. Collation: Frontispiece (in color); title (1); copyright (1938) (code number 838.5) (2); contents, illustrations and instrumental themes (3); acknowledgments (4); text (5–190); alphabetical index (191–192).
Size of leaf trimmed 7¾ x 10⅛ inches.
Issued in full cloth (black). Front cover in black over stamped gold decoration and light purple bands: • SONG • PROGRAMS • FOR • YOUTH • / TREASURE (over stamped gold decoration) / • THE • WORLD • OF • MUSIC • Spine stamped in light purple: THE WORLD OF MUSIC / TREASURE / GINN AND COMPANY

Six illustrations in color.
The Feast of Rayni (frontispiece)
The Cobbler. fp 16
Queen Astrid Comes No More. fp 49
The Enchanted Wood. fp 64
River of Sleep. fp 113
In a Strange Land. fp 128

Hay, John

THE PIKE COUNTY BALLADS / Illustrated by / N. C. Wyeth / Houghton Mifflin Company / Boston and New York

Thin 8 vo. Collation: Title (printed over banner and pictorial design) (1); copyright (various dates) (1912) (published October 1912) (2); illustrator's preface (3–4); contents and illustrations (5); text (with illustrations) (7–47); imprint.
Size of leaf trimmed 6⅜ x 8⅝ inches. Brown top.
Boxed (tan) with pictorial label in color.
Issued in full cloth (tan). Pictorial cover label in color surrounded by stamped brown border: The / Pike County / Ballads / by John Hay (second, third and fourth lines [John Hay] in orange). Spine stamped in brown: The / Pike / County / Ballads / John / Hay / (at bottom) Houghton / Mifflin Co.

Illustrator's Preface by N. C. Wyeth.
Nine illustrations in color including cover label (repeated on box) and title page design.
Twenty-six illustrations in black and white including endpapers.
Illustrations (plates) in color:
Jim Bludso
    He weren't no saint—them engineers is all pretty much alike. fp 8
Little Breeches
    No four-year-old in the country could beat him for pretty and strong. fp 14
Banty Tim
    But he staggered up, and packed me off, with a dozen stumbles and falls. fp 20

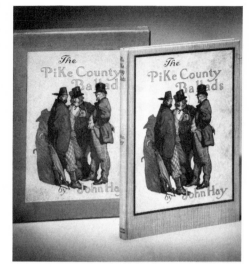

The Mystery of Gilgal
    I ax yer parding, Mister Phinn—jest drap that whisky-skin. fp 26
Golyer
    Over hill and holler and ford and creek jest like the horses had wings, we tore.¹ fp 32
The Pledge at Spunky Point
    The Deacon and Parson Skeeters in the tail game of Draw.² fp 40
Illustrations in black and white.
Descriptions:
    Jim Bludso p 7
    Jim Bludso's voice was heard . . . p 9
    In the smoke of the Prairie Bell p 12
    Little Breeches p 13
    And hell-to-split over the prairie p 15
    And sarched for 'em far and near p 17
    We looked in and seen them huddled thar, . . . p 18
    Sargeant Tilmon Joy p 19
    Ef Tim shill go or stay p 21
    Through that fire-proof, gilt-edged hell! p 24
    The Mystery of Gilgal p 25
    Tom Taggart's of Gilgal p 27
    And ca'mly drinked and jawed p 28
    They carved in a way that all admired . . . p 29
    Girls went that winter, as a rule . . . p 30
    Golyer p 31
    I reckon my old friend Golyer's Ben . . . p 33
    Caught in the shower of lead and flint p 34
    The old stage p 35
    Over hill and holler p 37
    And he carried his thanks to God p 38
    The Pledge at Spunky Point p 39
    So toddle along with your pledge, Squire p 41
    Then Abner Fry he killed a man p 43
    But ez fur myself, I thank ye . . . p 44
    The End p 45

¹ The illustration also appears in The American Book Collector, May 1968, for the article "Tentative Bibliographic Lists of Western Illustrators" by Jeff C. Dykes.
    Also appears in *American Artist* magazine, December 1966, for the article "The Brandywine Tradition" by Henry C. Pitz.

Hewes, Agnes Danforth

GLORY OF THE SEAS / [illustration] / Painting by N. C. Wyeth / AGNES DANFORTH HEWES / [ornament] / NEW YORK • ALFRED • A • KNOPF • 1933

12 mo. Collation: Author's book list; half title; title (first line printed over color illustration) (second line and ornament in red); copyright (1933) (FIRST EDITION); dedication; historical note; half title; text (1–315); type note and imprint.
Size of leaf trimmed 5³⁄₁₆ x 7⁹⁄₁₆ inches.
Issued in full cloth (blue). Front cover stamped in gray with decorations: (decoration) / GLORY OF THE / SEAS / (ornament) / decoration at bottom). Spine stamped in gray with decorations and ornaments: Glory / of the / Seas / AGNES / DANFORTH / HEWES / (at bottom) KNOPF

Title page illustration in color. (Repeated on the dust wrapper.)
    Description: A manacled black man silhouetted against a clipper ship in full sail.

Glory / of the / Seas / Agnes Danforth Hewes / Junior Literary Guild / and / Alfred A. Knopf / New York • • • 1933

12 mo. Collation: Half title; frontispiece (in color); title (surrounded by double boxed rules); copyright (1933) (FIRST EDITION); dedication; historical note; half title; text (1–315); type note and imprint.
Size of leaf trimmed 5³⁄₁₆ x 7⁹⁄₁₆ inches.
Issued in full cloth (green). Front cover stamped in dark green with decorations: (decoration) / GLORY OF THE / SEAS / (ornament) / (decoration at bottom). Spine stamped in dark green with decorations and ornaments: Glory / of the / Seas / Agnes / Danforth / Hewes / (at bottom) Junior / Guild

Frontispiece illustration in color. Same as in the blue cloth edition.

Hoyt, Charles B.

Heroes of the Argonne / [rule] / An Authentic History of the / Thirty-fifth Division / -By- / Charles B. Hoyt / [rule] / Arranged and Compiled by / C. B. Lyon, Jr. / [rule] / Published by / Franklin Hudson Publishing Company / Kansas City, Mo. / Copyright 1919

8 vo. Collation: Frontispiece (in color) (2); half title (3); title (5); dedication (6); contents (7); illustrations, maps, and diagrams (8); foreword (9); biography—Major General William M. Wright (10); (photograph) (11); biography—Major General Peter E. Traub (12); (photograph) (13); biography—Brigadier General Charles I. Martin (14); (photograph) (15); diagram (17); text (19–259).
Size of leaf trimmed 5¾ x 8¾ inches.
Issued in full cloth (olive green). Front cover stamped in gold: Heroes / of the / Argonne / (pictorial design—grenade) / Charles / B. Hoyt. Spine stamped in gold: Heroes / of the / Argonne / (pictorial design—grenade) / Hoyt.

Frontispiece in color by N. C. Wyeth.
And They Thought We Couldn't Fight
    Victory Loan Poster—Permission by the Treasury Department. (repeated on the dust wrapper)

Huneker, James

The / STEINWAY COLLECTION / of PAINTINGS by / AMERICAN ARTISTS / Together With / PROSE PORTRAITS / of the Great Composers by / James Huneker

/ [decoration] / Published by / Steinway & Sons / MCMXIX

The edition is limited to Five Thousand copies for presentation.

Folio. Collation: Presentation label; half title (with decorations); title (surrounded by ornamental decorations); copyright (1919); prelude (with decorations); text (pages unnumbered).

Size of leaf uncut 9½ x 12⁹⁄₁₆ inches.

Issued in boards (brown) with vellum spine. Front cover stamped in gold with ornamental decorations: THE STEINWAY / COLLECTION (enclosed in boxed rules).

Illustrated with mounted plates (with tissue insets) in color by N. C. Wyeth, Harvey Dunn, A. I. Keller, C. E. Chambers, H. McCarter, C. Anderson, H. Townsend, F. L. Mora, Ernest Blumenschein and J. G. Johansen.

Two paintings in color by N. C. Wyeth.
Wagner & Liszt
Beethoven and Nature[1]

Note: The paintings were executed for Steinway & Sons and used extensively in their advertising campaigns. In addition, they appear in color in the books *Music of Many Lands and Peoples* and *Music Highways and Byways,* edited by McConathy, etc., published by Silver Burdett and Company, New York, 1932 and 1936.
[1] Also appears as a frontispiece in color in the book *Beethoven Master Musician* by Madeleine Goss, Doubleday, Doran & Company, Inc., New York, 1931.

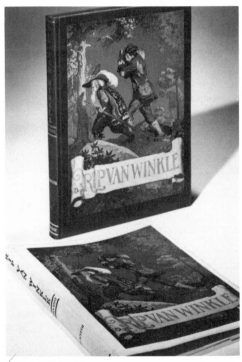

Irving, Washington

RIP VAN WINKLE / by / Washington Irving / [pictorial design] / Pictures & Decorations / by / N. C. Wyeth / Philadelphia / David McKay Company / Publishers

Large 8 vo. Collation: Half title (with drawing); frontispiece (in color with tissue inset); title (over pictorial decoration in colors) (first six lines in tint); drawing; copyright (1921) and imprint; drawing; colored illustrations; half title; text (1–86).

Size of leaf trimmed 7⅛ x 9¾ inches. Gilt top.

Issued in full cloth (brown). Pictorial cover

label in color with decorative banner, printed in light brown: RIP VAN WINKLE. Spine stamped in gold: (rule) / RIP VAN WINKLE / (rule) / Irving / (rule) / N. C. Wyeth / (rule) / McKay / (rule).

Eleven illustrations in color including cover label, endpapers and title page (decoration) drawing. The cover label illustration is repeated on the dust wrapper.

Twenty-six illustrations in pen and ink.
Numbered scroll design in pen and ink. (Repeated on all numbered pages.)
Illustrations (plates) in color:

A village in the Catskill Mountains. (Frontispiece with tissue inset.)
"A termagant wife may, therefore, in some respects, be considered a tolerable blessing; and if so, Rip Van Winkle was thrice blessed."[1] fp 10
"Here they used to sit in the shade through a long lazy summer's day, talking listlessly over village gossip or telling endless sleepy stories about nothing." fp 21
"On nearer approach he was still more surprised at the singularity of the stranger's appearance."[2] fp 32
". . . Though these folks were evidently amusing themselves, yet they maintained the gravest faces, the most mysterious silence."[3] fp 38
"On waking he found himself on the green knoll whence he had first seen the old man of the glen."[4] fp 44
"It was with some difficulty that he found his way to his own house, which he approached with silent awe, expecting every moment to hear the shrill voice of Dame Van Winkle."[1] [5] fp 54
". . . And preferred making friends among the rising generation, with whom he grew into great favor."[6] fp 76

Illustrations (drawings) in pen and ink.
A dwarf
Rip Van Winkle and his dog Wolf
A Dutch colonial house
Diedrich Knickerbocker p 1
. . . farmhouse under a spreading sycamore . . . pp 2–3
Biscuit with imprint of Diedrich Knickerbocker p 4
Woden, God of Saxons p 5
. . . time-worn and weather-beaten . . . p 8
. . . and fish all day without a murmur . . . p 12
He would carry a fowling-piece on his shoulder . . . p 13
Rip Van Winkle, however, was one of those happy mortals . . . p 16
. . . he would fly to the door with yelping precipitation p 19
Nicholas Vedder p 23
Here he would sometimes seat himself at the foot of a tree . . . pp 26–27
During the whole time Rip and his companion had labored on in silence . . . pp 34–35
One taste provoked another . . . pp 40–41
. . . and he fell into a deep sleep pp 42–43
he was only answered by the cawing of a flock of idle crows . . . p 48
They all stared at him with equal marks of surprise . . . pp 50–51
He found the house gone to decay . . . p 52
. . . it was fluttering a flag . . . p 56
. . . a lean, bilious-looking fellow . . . p 59
Here lies Nicholas Vedder p 63
She had a chubby child in her arms, which, frightened at his looks, began to cry p 69
. . . she broke a blood-vessel in a fit of passion at a New England peddler p 70
. . . the wildest recesses of the Catskill Mountains . . . p 86

[1] Also appear in color in *Time* magazine, November 18, 1957, for the article "The Greatest Illustrators."

[2] Also appears as a cover in color for *The New York State Conservationist,* August-September 1954.
[3] Also appears in color in *American Heritage* magazine, December 1961, for the article "The Sunny Master of Sunny Side" by Curtis Dahl.
[4] Also appears in color in *Life* magazine, December 9, 1957, for the article "The Stouthearted Heroes of a Beloved Painter."
[5] Also appears in *This Is America's Story* by Howard B. Wilder, published by Houghton Mifflin Company, Boston, 1948.
[6] Also appears in color in The Beck Engraving Company brochure, "Where's Nicholas Vedder?" In addition, a scratchboard drawing, after Wyeth's pen-and-ink drawing on page 63, appears as a cover design for this brochure.
The endpaper illustration also appears in *Antiques* magazine, November 1967, for the article "Collecting American Nineteenth-century Art" by J. William Middendorf II.

Jackson, Helen Hunt

RAMONA / A Story By / Helen Hunt Jackson / With Illustrations by / N. C. Wyeth / Introduction by / May Lamberton Becker / [publisher's colophon] / Boston / Little, Brown / and Company / 1939

8 vo. Collation: Half title; frontispiece (in color); title (surrounded by ornamental boxed rules); copyright (various dates) (1939); introduction; half title; text (1–424).

Size of leaf trimmed 5⅜ x 8 inches.

Issued in full cloth (blue). Front cover stamped in orange with bands stamped in orange and green: RAMONA / HELEN HUNT JACKSON. Spine stamped in orange with design in green: RAMONA / (design—Indian pottery) / HELEN / HUNT / JACKSON / Little, Brown / and Company

Four illustrations in color.
Descriptions:
Senora Gonzaga Moreno and Ramona. (frontispiece)
Father Salvierderra and Ramona. (repeated on the dust wrapper) fp 44
Alessandro and Ramona on the narrow trail. fp 234
The shooting of Alessandro. fp 370

Johnson, Edna and Scott, Carrie E. (Compiled by)

Anthology of / CHILDREN'S / LITERATURE / [pictorial design] / Compiled by Edna Johnson & Carrie E. Scott / Illustrations In Full Color By N. C. Wyeth / Houghton • Mifflin • Company • Boston / The Riverside Press Cambridge 1940

Large 8 vo. Collation: Title (with pictorial design in color) (I); copyright 1935 (1940 by Newell C. Wyeth) and imprint (II); dedication (III); foreword and acknowledgments (V–IX); contents and appendixes (XI–XXIII); illustrations (XXV); introduction (XXVII–XXIX); books of general criticism and on children's reading (XXXI); illustration; half title (1); text (3–840); appendixes (843–905); pronouncing glossary (906–8); index (909–17).

Size of leaf trimmed 6¾ x 9¾ inches.

Issued in full cloth (light blue). Front cover stamped in silver over brown inset with pictorial designs (Alice, the White Rabbit and Robin Hood): Anthology / of / Children's / Literature. Spine stamped in silver over brown inset: Anthology / of / Children's / Literature / Johnson / • / Scott / (at bottom in silver) Houghton / Mifflin Co.

Seventeen illustrations in color, including endpapers and title page design.

Illustrations (plates with titles printed on paper insets) in color:
Hark, Hark, the Dogs do Bark. fp xxxii
The Old Woman Tost up in a Basket. fp 30
Snow-Drop. fp 60
Jack the Giant-Killer.[1] fp 90
Thumbelisa. fp 184
Arion and the Dolphin. fp 278
The Three Friends. fp 340
Robin Hood and Little John. (repeated on the dust wrapper) fp 370
Oisin in the Land of Youth. fp 400
David and Goliath. fp 430
Heidi.[1] fp 588
Adventure with a Giant Squid. fp 618
"Peculiarsome" Abe. fp 712
The Admiral's Ghost. fp 774
Give Me the Splendid Silent Sun. fp 836

[1] Also appeared in color in *Life* magazine, December 9, 1957, for the article "The Stouthearted Heroes of a Beloved Painter."

Johnston, Mary

THE LONG ROLL / by Mary Johnston / With Illustrations / By N. C. Wyeth / [publisher's colophon] Houghton Mifflin Company / Boston and New York::The / Riverside Press Cambridge / 1911

8 vo. Collation: Author's book list; half title; frontispiece (in color with tissue inset) (II); title (surrounded by boxed rules) (III); copyright (1911) (published May 1911) (Of this First Edition five hundred copies have been autographed by the author and bound entirely uncut with paper label) (IV); Autograph Edition (author's signature); dedication (V); to the reader (VII); contents (IX–X); illustrations (XI); text (1–683); imprint; six pages of publisher's advertising.

Size of leaf uncut 5¼ x 7¾ inches.

Issued in full cloth (gray). Paper label on spine with ornaments and rules in reddish brown: (ornaments) / (rule) / THE / LONG / ROLL / (rule) / BY MARY / JOHNSTON / (rule) / First Edition / (rule) / (ornaments).

Four illustrations in color.
Stonewall Jackson (frontispiece)[1] p II

The Lovers. fp 220
The Battle.[2] fp 456
The Vedette. fp 642

[1] Appeared as a cover in color for *Civil War Times Illustrated*, November 1964.
[2] Also appeared in color in *The Illustrator in America 1900–1960's* by Walt Reed, published by Reinhold Publishing Corporation, New York, 1966. In addition, it appeared as a cover in color for *Civil War Times Illustrated Magazine*, February 1966.

THE LONG ROLL / By Mary Johnston / With Illustrations / By N. C. Wyeth / [publisher's colophon] Houghton Mifflin Company / Boston and New York::The / Riverside Press Cambridge / 1911

(The First Trade Edition)

12 mo. Collation: Author's book list; half title; frontispiece (in color with tissue inset) (II); title (surrounded by boxed rules) (III); copyright (1911) (published May 1911) (IV); dedication (V); to the reader (VII); contents (IX–X); illustrations (XI); text (1–683); imprint (684); six pages of publisher's advertising.

Size of leaf trimmed 5 1/16 x 7 3/8 inches.

Issued in full cloth (gray). Front cover stamped in gold with pictorial design and ornamental borders and rules stamped in dark gray: THE LONG / ROLL / (pictorial design–drum over flags and weapons, etc.) / By / MARY JOHNSTON. Spine stamped in gold with ornaments and rules stamped in dark gray: (rule) / THE / LONG / ROLL / (ornament) / Mary / Johnston / (ornament) / (ornament) / Houghton / Mifflin Co. / (rule).

Four illustrations in color. Same as in the autographed First Edition. Stonewall Jackson (repeated on the dust wrapper).

Johnston, Mary

CEASE FIRING / By Mary Johnston / With Illustrations / By N. C. Wyeth / [publisher's colophon] / Houghton Mifflin Company / Boston and New York::The / Riverside Press Cambridge / 1912

8 vo. Collation: Author's book list; half title; frontispiece (in color with tissue inset) (II);

title (surrounded by boxed rules) (III); copyright (1912) (published November 1912) (Of this First Edition five hundred copies have been autographed by the author and bound entirely uncut with paper label) (IV); Autograph Edition (author's signature); dedication (V); contents (VII–VIII); illustrations (IX); text (1–457); imprint.

Size of leaf uncut 5¼ x 7¾ inches.

Issued in full cloth (gray). Paper label on spine with ornaments and rules in reddish brown: (ornaments) / (rule) / Cease / Firing / (rule) / BY MARY / JOHNSTON / (rule) / First Edition / (rule) / (ornaments).

Four illustrations in color.
The Road to Vidalia (frontispiece).[1] p II
Sharpshooters. fp 128
The Bloody Angle.[2] fp 302
The Scout. fp 392

[1] Also appeared as color cover for *Civil War Times Illustrated*, January 1967.
[2] Also appeared as cover label in color for *The Boy's Book of Battles*, published by Houghton Mifflin Company, Boston, October 1914.

CEASE FIRING / By Mary Johnston / With Illustrations / By N. C. Wyeth / [publisher's colophon] / Houghton Mifflin Company / Boston and New York::The / Riverside Press Cambridge / 1912

(The First Trade Edition)

12 mo. Collation: Author's book list; half title; frontispiece (in color with tissue inset) (II); title (surrounded by boxed rules) (III); copyright (1912) (published November 1912) (IV); dedication (V); contents (VII–VIII); illustrations (IX); text (1–457); imprint (458); two pages of publisher's advertising.

Size of leaf trimmed 5 1/16 x 7 3/8 inches.

Issued in full cloth (gray). Front cover stamped in gold with pictorial design and ornamental borders and rules stamped in dark gray: CEASE / FIRING / (pictorial design–drum over flags and weapons, etc.) / By / MARY JOHNSTON. Spine stamped in gold with ornaments and rules stamped in dark gray: (rule) / CEASE / FIRING / (ornament) / Mary / Johnston / (ornament) / (ornament) / Houghton / Mifflin Co. / (rule).

Four illustrations in color. Same as those in the autographed First Edition.
The Scout (repeated on dust wrapper)

THE WITCH / By / Mary Johnston / [publisher's colophon] / Boston and New York / Houghton Mifflin Company / The Riverside Press Cambridge / 1914

12 mo. Collation: Author's book list: frontispiece (in color with tissue inset) (II); title (III); copyright (1914) (published October, 1914) (IV); contents (V–VI); half title (VII); text (1–442); imprint.

Size of leaf trimmed 5⅛ x 7⅜ inches.

Issued in full cloth (brown). Front cover stamped in gold (title enclosed in stamped box rules): The / WITCH / (rule) / (rule) / BY MARY JOHNSTON. Spine stamped in gold: (rule) / The / WITCH / — / MARY / JOHNSTON / (rule) / (rule) / HOUGHTON / MIFFLIN CO. / (rule).

Frontispiece illustration in color.
"Good-bye, Mistress Friendly-Soul!" p II

Kingsley, Charles

WESTWARD HO! / or, the Voyages and Adventures of / Sir Amyas Leigh, Knight,

of Burrough, / in the County of Devon—
In the reign of / Her Most Glorious Majesty / Queen Elizabeth / By / Charles Kingsley / [design] / Pictures by N. C. Wyeth / New York / Charles Scribner's Sons / MCMXX

Large 8 vo. Collation: Half title (I); title (with pictorial design) (III); copyright (1920) (published October 1920) and imprint (IV); contents (V–VI); illustrations (VII–VIII); half title; text (1–413).

Size of leaf uncut 7 x 9¼ inches. Tinted top.

Issued in full cloth (black). Pictorial cover label in color: WESTWARD HO! / by / Charles Kingsley. Spine Stamped in gold: WESTWARD HO! / (ornament—ship's lantern) / CHARLES / KINGSLEY / Illustrated / By / N. C. WYETH / SCRIBNERS

Seventeen illustrations in color including cover label, endpapers, and title page design.
Illustrations (plates) in color:

John Oxenham
He seemed in the eyes of the schoolboy a very magnifico,—some prince or duke at least.[1] fp 4
Rose of Torridge
. . . and not a week passed but, by mysterious hands, some nosegay, or languishing sonnet, was conveyed into The Rose's chamber. fp 24
The Encounter on Freshwater Cliff
"Give me your papers, letters, whatever Popish devilry you carry, or, as I live, I will cut off your head, and take them myself. . . ." fp 58
Rose Salterne and the White Witch
But before the Jesuits came, two other persons were standing on that lonely beach. fp 66
John Brimblecombe
And now behold him brought in red-hand to judgement. fp 104
The Mourner in the Bog
There she sat upon a stone, tearing her black dishevelled hair, and every now and then throwing up her head, and bursting into a long mournful cry. fp 138
The Duel on the Beach
. . . the devil's game is begun in earnest. fp 158
The Departure of the Rose
. . . and Mrs. Leigh went to the rocky knoll outside the churchyard wall, and watched the ship glide out between the yellow dunes. fp 204
At the Governor's House in Guayra
The cavalier sprang forward, lifted his hat courteously, and joined her, bowing low. fp 230
The Daughter of the Forest
Amyas had seen hundreds of those delicate dark-skinned daughters of the forest, but never such a one as this. fp 278
The City of the True Cross
That great galleon, The City of the True Cross. fp 320
Salvation Yeo Finds His Little Maid Again
"Oh dear! oh dear! my sweet young lady! my pretty little maid! and don't you know me?" fp 348
The Battle with the Armada
And so, with variable fortune, the fight thunders on the livelong afternoon, beneath the virgin cliffs of Freshwater. fp 382
The Despair of Amyas
"Shame!" cried Amyas, hurling his sword, far into the sea, "to lose my right, my right! when it was in my very grasp! Unmerciful!" fp 402

A Scribner Illustrated Classic

[1] The illustration was distributed as a print in color, through the courtesy of the Beck Engraving Company, at the N. C. Wyeth exhibition in The William Penn Memorial Museum, Harrisburg, Pa., 1965.

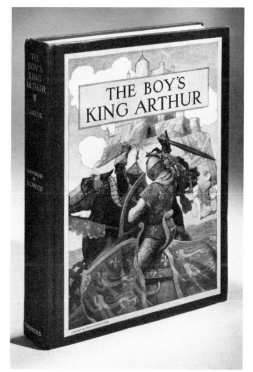

Lanier, Sidney (Edited for boys by)

The / Boy's / KING / ARTHUR [over pictorial design in color]
THE / BOY'S / KING / ARTHUR / Sir Thomas Malory's History / of / King Arthur and His Knights of the Round Table / Edited for boys / by Sidney Lanier / Illustrated by N. C. Wyeth / New York / Charles Scribner's Sons / 1917

Large 8 vo. Collation: Half title; title (enclosed in pictorial design in color); title; copyright (various dates) (1917) and publisher's colophon; explanation; contents; illustrations; text (1–321).

Size of leaf uncut 7 x 9¼ inches. Gilt top.

Issued in full cloth (black). Pictorial cover label in color with gray inset, printed in black: THE BOY'S / KING ARTHUR (title surrounded by gold border rules). Spine stamped in gold: THE / BOY'S / KING / ARTHUR / (ornament—shield) / LANIER / Illustrated / By / N. C. WYETH / SCRIBNERS

Seventeen illustrations in color including cover label, endpapers and title page design.
Illustrations (plates) in color:
So the child was delivered unto Merlin, and so he bare it forth. fp 4
And when they came to the sword that the hand held, King Arthur took it up.[1] fp 16
"I am Sir Launcelot du Lake, King Ban's son of Benwick, and knight of the Round Table." fp 38
And lived by fruit and such as he might get. fp 52
It hung upon a thorn, and there he blew three deadly notes. fp 82
The lady Lyoness . . . had the dwarf in examination. fp 102
"Oh, gentle knight," said la Belle Isolde, "full woe am I of thy departing." fp 130
"They fought with him on foot more than three hours, both before him and behind him." fp 162
King Mark slew the noble knight Sir Tristram as he sat harping before his lady la Belle Isolde. fp 190
When Sir Percival came nigh the brim, and saw the water so boisterous, he doubted to overpass it. fp 214

Sir Mador's spear brake all to pieces, but the other's spear held.[2] fp 246
He rode his way with the queen unto Joyous Gard. fp 278
Then the king . . . ran towards Sir Mordred, crying, "Traitor, now is thy death day come." fp 306
Then Sir Launcelot saw her visage, but he wept not greatly, but sighed. fp 316

A Scribner Illustrated Classic

[1] Also appears in color in Life magazine, December 9, 1957, for the article "The Stouthearted Heroes of a Beloved Painter."
[2] Also appears as a frontispiece in color in The Stream of History, Volume III, by Geoffrey Parsons, published by Charles Scribner's Sons, New York, 1929.

Lawler, Thomas Bonaventure

ESSENTIALS OF / AMERICAN HISTORY / by / Thomas Bonaventure Lawler, A.M., LL.D. / Author of "The Story of Columbus and Magellan" and "A Primary History of the United States" / With Illustrations in Colors By / N. C. Wyeth / [verse] / Revised Edition / Ginn and Company / Boston • New York • Chicago • London / Atlanta • Dallas • Columbus • San Francisco

12 mo. Collation: Frontispiece (in color); title (I); copyright 1902, (1918) (code number 5228) and imprint (II); preface to the revised edition (III–IV); contents (V); map (VI); text (1–471); appendix, etc. (I–XLVIII); index (XLIX–LXV).

Size of leaf trimmed 5⅛ x 7⁹⁄₁₆ inches.

Issued in full cloth (brown). Front cover and emblem stamped in dark brown: ESSENTIALS OF / AMERICAN / HISTORY / (emblem) / LAWLER. Spine and decoration stamped in dark brown: ESSENTIALS / OF / AMERICAN / HISTORY / (decoration) / LAWLER / REVISED / EDITION / (at bottom) GINN AND / COMPANY

Four illustrations in color by N. C. Wyeth.
Columbus Landing in the New World (frontispiece lunette)[1]
On the Way to the Front in '76[2] [4] fp 182
A California Mission[4] fp 326
Driving the Last Spike in the Transcontinental Railroad[3] [4] fp 398

[1] Also appears in color in the book The American People and Nation by Tryon and Lingley, published by Ginn and Company, 1927. In addition, it appears in color in the book The American Nation Yesterday and Today by Tryon, Lingley and Morehouse, published by Ginn and Company, Boston, 1930.
[2] Also appears in the book A School History of the United States by Nathaniel W. Stephenson and Martha Tucker, published by Ginn and Company, Boston, 1921.
[3] Also appears in color in the book America by William J. Long, published by Ginn and Company, Boston, 1923.
[4] Also appears in the book Standard History of America by the same author. Published by Ginn and Company, Boston 1933.

THE GATEWAY / TO AMERICAN HISTORY / By / Thomas Bonaventure Lawler / [publisher's colophon] / Ginn and Company / Boston • New York • Chicago • London / Atlanta • Dallas • Columbus • San Francisco

12 mo. Collation: Frontispiece (in color); title (I); copyright (1924) and imprint (II); preface (III–VI); contents (VII–IX); introduc-

tion (XI–XL); text (1–356); index (357–366).
Size of leaf trimmed 5⅛ x 7⁵⁄₁₆ inches.

Issued in full cloth (light green). Front cover stamped in green enclosed in pictorial design: THE / GATEWAY / TO / AMERICAN / HISTORY / (ornament) / LAWLER / (ornament). Spine stamped in green: (rule) / THE / GATEWAY / TO AMERI- / CAN / HISTORY / (ornament) / LAWLER / GINN AND / COMPANY / (rule).

Illustrated with numerous paintings, photographs, etc.

Frontispiece illustration in color by N. C. Wyeth.
The Crusaders Before Jerusalem

Note: The illustration also appears in the book *The American People and Their Old World Ancestors* by Grace Vollintine, published by Ginn and Company, Boston, 1930.

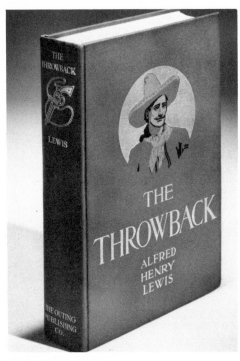

Lewis, Alfred Henry

THE / THROWBACK / A Romance of the Southwest / By / Alfred Henry Lewis / Author of "Wolfville," "Peggy O'Neal," "The President," / "The Sunset Trail," etc. / Illustrated With a Frontispiece in Color / and Three Other Pictures From Paintings / By N. C. Wyeth / New York / The Outing Publishing Company / 1906

12 mo. Collation: Half title; frontispiece (with tissue inset) (II); title (surrounded by double boxed rules) (III); copyright 1905 (1906) and imprint (IV); contents (V–VI); list of illustrations (VII); text (1–347); two pages of publisher's advertising.
Size of leaf trimmed 5 x 7⁵⁄₁₆ inches.

Issued in full cloth (green). Front cover stamped in gold with oval pictorial design (head of cowboy) stamped in gold and colors: THE / THROWBACK / Alfred / Henry / Lewis. Spine stamped in gold with design (rope and revolver): THE / THROWBACK / (design) / LEWIS / THE OUTING / PUBLISHING / CO.

Four illustrations. One (frontispiece) in color and three in black and white.
"Pedro of the Ear," cried Moonlight, "I owed you that." (frontispiece in color) p II

Moonlight was lost in a contemplation of the Cross. fp 78
Threw the bridle rein on Sathanthers' neck, and rolled and lighted a cigarette. fp 136
Behind, not two hundred yards away, were two Indians. fp 252

Lincoln, Joseph C., and Lincoln, Freeman

BLAIR'S ATTIC / by Joseph C. Lincoln / and / Freeman Lincoln / End Papers By N. C. Wyeth / [pictorial design] / Published In New York By / Coward-McCann, Inc. / In The Year 1929

12 mo. Collation: Half title; Author's list; title (pictorial design and eighth line in green) (surrounded by double boxed rules and ornamental border in green); copyright (1929); contents; half title (1); text (3–369)
Size of leaf uncut 5⅛ x 7½ inches. Pale green top.

Issued in full cloth (blue). Front cover stamped in black (title outlined in green) with small pictorial decoration (fishing village) within border outlined in green: BLAIR'S ATTIC / by / Joseph C. Lincoln / and Freeman Lincoln / pictorial decoration. Spine stamped in black: BLAIR'S / ATTIC / by Joseph / C. / Lincoln / and / Freeman / Lincoln / Coward / Mc-Cann.

Endpaper illustrations in colors. (Yellow, blue, black and white)
Description: Seagulls and waves.
Dust wrapper illustration in color.
Description: The old Blair house.

Long, John Luther

WAR / or / What Happens When One Loves One's Enemy / by / John Luther Long / Author of / Madame Butterfly / The Fox-Woman, Etc., Etc. / Illustrations by / N. C. Wyeth / Indianapolis / The Bobbs-Merrill Company / Publishers

12 mo. Collation: Half title; frontispiece (in color with tissue inset); title (surrounded by double boxed rules); copyright (1913) and

imprint; dedication; contents; half title; text (1–371).
Size of leaf trimmed 4⅞ x 7¼ inches.

Issued in full cloth (red). Front cover stamped over gold inset and stamped decoration with border rules: WAR / (ornament) / JOHN / LUTHER / LONG. Spine stamped in gold with stamped decoration: WAR / (stamped rules and decoration) / LONG / (stamped rules and decoration) / BOBBS / MERRILL

Four illustrations in color.
He never caught a thing and he ruined Jon's reputation as a fisherman. (Frontispiece)
Then he looked in her face, playing softer and softer. fp 44
He stopped two or three steps up and sang me a little song—quite like the old Dave. fp 304
War.[1] fp 346

[1] Also reproduced in color on the dust wrapper of the book *The Drums of the 47th* by Robert J. Burdette, published by The Bobbs-Merrill Company, Indianapolis, 1914.

WAR / or / What Happens When One Loves One's Enemy / By / John Luther Long / Author of / Madame Butterfly / The Fox-Woman, Etc., Etc. / Illustrations By / N. C. Wyeth / Indianapolis / The Bobbs-Merrill Company / Publishers

(Variant binding)
12 mo. Collation: Half title; frontispiece (in color); title (surrounded by double boxed rules); copyright (1913) and imprint; dedication; contents; half title; text (1–371).
Size of leaf trimmed 5 x 7⅜ inches.

Issued in boards (light blue). Front cover stamped over dark blue inset and stamped decoration with border rules: WAR / (ornament) / JOHN / LUTHER / LONG. Spine stamped in dark blue: WAR / LONG / BOBBS / MERRILL

Frontispiece illustration in color.
Then he looked in her face, playing softer and softer.

Long, William J.

AMERICA / A History of Our Country / By / William J. Long / Illustrations By / N. C. Wyeth, Sears Gallagher and Rodney Thomson / [verse by Whitman] / [publisher's colophon] / Ginn and Company / Boston • New York • Chicago • London / Atlanta • Dallas • Columbus • San Francisco

12 mo. Collation: Frontispiece (in color); title (I); copyright (1923) (code number 823.4) and imprint (II); foreword (III); acknowledgment (IV); contents (V–VI); colored plates and maps (VII); text (1–531); appendix (I–XXI); bibliography (XXIII–XXX); index (XXX–XLVIII).
Size of leaf trimmed 5⁵⁄₁₆ x 7¾ inches.

Issued in full cloth (maroon). Front cover stamped in black surrounded by pictorial design (the Capitol) and decorations: AMERICA / A HISTORY / • OF OUR • / COUNTRY. Spine stamped in gold: AMERICA / (ornament) / LONG / (pictorial design—Liberty's torch) / GINN AND COMPANY

Three illustrations in color by N. C. Wyeth.
Beginning of the American Union
Washington salutes the flag as he takes command of the Continental Army at Cambridge, 1775. (frontispiece)[1]

He Saved the Union
Lincoln delivers his second inaugural address as President of the United States, March 4, 1865. fp 336

The Last Spike
The West is bound to the East by ties of steel. Completion of the first transcontinental railroad, 1869.[2] fp 410

Idem: Except for spine stamped in black.

[1] Also appears in black and white in the book *Builders of America* by Thomas Bonaventure Lawler, published by Ginn and Company, 1927.
[2] Originally appeared in color in the book *Essentials of American History* by Thomas Bonaventure Lawler, published by Ginn and Company, 1918.

Longfellow, Henry Wadsworth

THE CHILDREN'S LONGFELLOW / Illustrated / Houghton Mifflin Company / Boston & New York / 1908

8 vo. Collation: Half title (surrounded by boxed rules in green with design in green and yellow); frontispiece (in color with titled tissue inset) (II); title (plus pictorial design in colors surrounded by boxed rules in brown) (III); copyright (1908) (IV); publisher's note (V); contents (VII–X); illustrations (XI); half title (surrounded by boxed rules in green with design in green and yellow) (1); text (3–324); indexes (325–34); imprint.
Size of leaf trimmed 6 x 8⅞ inches. Full green edges. Boxed.
Issued in full cloth (olive green). Front cover stamped in gold with pictorial cover label in color by N. C. Wyeth surrounded by decorative rules and borders: THE / CHILDREN'S / LONGFELLOW. Spine stamped in gold with decorations: (decorative rules) / THE / CHILDREN'S / LONG- / FELLOW / (decoration) / HOUGHTON / MIFFLIN CO. / (decorative rules).
Illustrated in color by N. C. Wyeth, F. E Schoonover, Stanley Arthurs, C. W. Ashley, Olive Rush, Howard Smith, and R. Shrader.

One illustration in color by N. C. Wyeth.
Hiawatha's Fishing
And he dropped his line of cedar
Through the clear, transparent water.
(repeated on the cover label) fp 136

Idem: A. Issued in cream cloth. B. Except for pictorial cover label in color by Howard Smith.

Note: The illustration also appears as a frontispiece in color in the book *The Song of Hiawatha* by Longfellow, published by Houghton Mifflin Company, Boston, 1911 (New Holiday Edition and English Edition). In edition, it appears in a trade edition, published by Houghton Mifflin Company, Boston, 1929.

THE SONG OF / HIAWATHA / By Henry Wadsworth Longfellow / With Illustrations And / Designs By / Frederic Remington / Maxfield Parrish / And N. C. Wyeth / [publisher's colophon] / Boston and New York / Houghton Mifflin Company / The Riverside Press Cambridge

(New Holiday Edition)
Large square 8 vo. Collation: Frontispiece (in color, surrounded by boxed rules and title in orange, with tissue inset); title (second line in orange) (I); copyright 1890, 1908 (edition published 1911) (II); publisher's note (with drawing by Remington) (III–IV); contents and list of illustrations (with drawing by Remington) (V–VII); text (1–242).

Size of leaf trimmed 6¾ x 9¹⁄₁₆ inches. Gilt top.
Boxed with pictorial label in color by Maxfield Parrish.
Issued in full cloth (Indian red). Front cover stamped in gold over pictorial label in color by Maxfield Parrish: HIAWATHA. Spine stamped in gold: HIAWATHA / HENRY WADSWORTH / LONGFELLOW / HOUGHTON / MIFFLIN CO.

Frontispiece illustration in color by N. C. Wyeth.
Hiawatha's Fishing

Idem: Issued in black cloth.

Note: The illustration originally appeared in color in the book *The Children's Longfellow*, published by Houghton Mifflin Company, Boston, 1908.

THE SONG OF / HIAWATHA / By Henry Wadsworth Longfellow / With Illustrations And / Designs By / Frederic Remington / Maxfield Parrish / And N. C. Wyeth / [publisher's colophon] George G. Harrap & Co., Ltd., London / 1911

(English Edition)
Large square 8 vo. Full morocco; embossed cover design by Maxfield Parrish; lettering on spine stamped in gold; gilt top; uncut; 242 pp.

Frontispiece illustration in color by N. C. Wyeth. Same as in the New Holiday Edition.

THE SONG OF / HIAWATHA / By / Henry Wadsworth Longfellow / With Illustrations And / Designs By / Frederic Remington / and N. C. Wyeth / [publisher's colophon] / Boston and New York / Houghton Mifflin Company / The Riverside Press Cambridge

8 vo. Collation: Frontispiece (in color surrounded by boxed rules in red); title (second line in red) (I); copyright 1890, 1908 (edition published 1929) and imprint (II); publisher's note (with drawing by Remington) (III–IV); contents and list of illustrations (with drawing by Remington) (V–VII); text (1–242).
Size of leaf trimmed 5¾ x 8½ inches. Green top.
Issued in full cloth (tan). Front cover and pictorial design surrounded by border decoration stamped in green: The / Song / of / Hiawatha / henry Wadsworth Longfellow. Spine stamped in green: The Song / of / Hiawatha / (ornament) / Longfellow / Illustrated / by / Frederic / Remington / Houghton Mifflin Co.

Frontispiece illustration in color by N. C. Wyeth. Same as New Holiday Edition.

THE COURTSHIP OF / MILES STANDISH / By / Henry Wadsworth Longfellow / With an Introduction by / Ernest W. Longfellow / And with pictures by / N. C. Wyeth / [coat of arms] / Boston and New York / Houghton Mifflin Company / The Riverside Press Cambridge / 1920

Large 8 vo. Collation: Half title (Tercentenary Edition with pictorial decoration) (I); title (drawing of Miles Standish's coat of arms) (III); copyright (1920) and imprint (IV); 1620–1920 ter•centennial dedication (with pictorial decoration) (V); contents (with pictorial decoration) (VII); list of pictures (with pictorial decoration) (IX–X); introduction (with

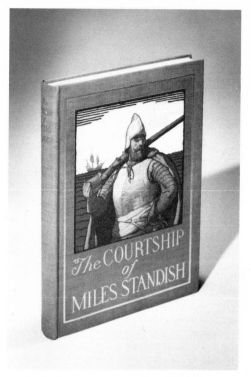

pictorial decoration) (XI–XII); half title (with pictorial decoration) (1); text (3–148).
Size of leaf trimmed 6¹³⁄₁₆ x 9⅝ inches.
Issued in full cloth (gray green). Front cover stamped in gold with pictorial cover label in color: (illustration) THE COURTSHIP / of MILES STANDISH (surrounded by boxed rules). Spine stamped in gold: The / COURTSHIP / of / MILES / STANDISH / (at bottom) HOUGHTON / MIFFLIN CO. Back cover stamped in gold: (Miles Standish's coat of arms).
The Introduction by Ernest W. Longfellow refers to N. C. Wyeth and his illustrations.

Ten illustrations in color including cover label and endpapers. The cover label illustration is repeated on the dust wrapper.
Sixteen illustrations (drawings and decorations) in pen and ink.
Illustrations (plates) in color:
Long at the window he stood, and wistfully gazed on the landscape.[1] fp 10
So through the Plymouth woods John Alden went on his errand. fp 34
Said, in a tremulous voice, "Why don't you speak for yourself, John?"[1] fp 48
Near them was standing an Indian, in attitude stern and defiant.[1] fp 64
Eager, with tearful eyes, to say farewell to the Mayflower, Homeward bound o'er the sea, and leaving them here in the desert.[1][2] fp 76
So the maiden went on, and little divined or imagined what was at work in his heart, that made him so awkward and speechless.[3] fp 98
Headlong he leaped on the boaster, and, snatching his knife from its scabbard.[1] fp 114
So through the Plymouth woods passed onward the bridal procession.[1] fp 146

Illustrations (drawings and decorations) in pen and ink.
Descriptions:
Rose (decoration) p I
Miles Standish's coat of arms (decoration) p III
Banner over pine bough with bells (decoration) p V
Banner over pine trees and birds (decoration) p VII
Banner and Pilgrim (decoration) p IX
The Mayflower within scroll (decoration) p XI

Banner and dogwood bough (decoration) p 1
Pilgrims leave primitive dwelling p 3
Captain Standish reading p 17
Priscilla p 31
John Alden p 51
Pilgrims on the march p 71
The seacoast p 91
An Indian encampment p 105
Hewing and building p 121
Pilgrim settlement p 137

[1] Illustrations and cover label appear in sepia tint in *The Mentor,* July 1926, for the article "The Wooing of Priscilla."
[2] Also appears as a frontispiece in color in the book *Ways to Better English* by Thomas H. Briggs, published by Ginn & Company, Boston, 1924.
[3] Also appears in black and white in *The Artgum,* April 1926, for the article "N. C. Wyeth, Painter and Illustrator," by Anton Kamp.
In addition, the endpaper illustration appears in colors in the book *Captain Blood* by Rafael Sabatini, published by Houghton Mifflin Company (Riverside Bookshelf), Boston, 1927.

Matthews, Brander

POEMS / OF / AMERICAN / PATRIOTISM / Chosen By / Brander / Matthews / An Edition Revised And Extended / Illustrated By / N. C. Wyeth / New York / Charles Scribner's Sons / 1922

Large 8 vo. Collation: Half title; frontispiece (in color with tissue inset) (II); title (printed over pictorial design) (III); copyright (1922) (published October, 1922) and publisher's colophon (IV); dedication (V); poem—James Russell Lowell (VII); prefatory note (IX–X); acknowledgements (XII); table of contents (XIII–XV); illustrations (XVII–XVIII); half title (1); text (3–222); poem—Henry Wadsworth Longfellow.
Size of leaf uncut 7 x 9¼ inches. Tinted top.
Issued in full cloth (black). Pictorial cover label in color: Poems / Of / AMERICAN PATRIOTISM (illustration) / Chosen By / Brander Matthews / Illustrated By / N. C. Wyeth (enclosed in box borders). Spine stamped in gold; POEMS / OF / AMERICAN / PATRIOTISM / (ornament–shield) / Chosen By / BRANDER MATTHEWS / Illustrated / By / N. C. WYETH / SCRIBNERS

Seventeen illustrations in color including cover label, endpapers and title page design. The title page design is repeated on the dust wrapper.
Illustrations (plates) in color:
The Old Continentals (frontispiece with tissue inset)
That is best blood that hath most iron in't
To edge resolve with, pouring without stint
For what makes manhood dear. p II
Paul Revere
And yet, through the gloom and the light,
The fate of a nation was riding that night.[1][2] fp 12
Warren's Address
In the God of battles trust!
Die we may, —and die we must.[1] fp 32
Nathan Hale
By starlight and moonlight,
He seeks the Briton's camp. fp 38
Washington
Dumb for himself, unless it were to God,
But for his barefoot soldiers eloquent. fp 52
The Picket Guard
His musket falls slack—his face, dark and grim,
Grows gentle with memories tender,
As he mutters a prayer for the children asleep—
For their mother—may Heaven defend her! fp 90

Barbara Frietchie
"Shoot, if you must, this old, gray head,
But spare your country's flag," she said. fp 124
John Burns of Gettysburg
And some of the soldiers since declare
That the gleam of his old white hat afar,
Like the crested plume of the brave Navarre,
That day was their oriflamme of war. fp 140
O Captain! My Captain!
O Captain! My Captain! our fearful trip is done,
The ship has weather'd every rock, the prize we sought is won. fp 170
Grant
But lo, the man was here, and this was he;
And at his hands Faith gave us victory. fp 180
Sherman
Who fought for freedom, not glory; made war that war might cease.[3] fp 182
The Regular Army Man
He ain't no Mama's darling, but
He does the best he can,
And he's the chap that wins the scrap,
The Regular Army Man. fp 186
Our Mother
And great gray ships go down the tide
And carry her sons away. fp 206
The Unknown Soldier
He is hailed by the time-crowned brotherhood. fp 222

A Scribner Illustrated Classic

[1] The illustrations also appear in black and white in *The Artgum,* April 1926, for the article "N. C. Wyeth, Painter and Illustrator," by Anton Kamp.
[2] Also appears in the book (Volume I) *History of the United States* by James Truslow Adams, published by Charles Scribner's Sons, New York, 1933. In addition, it appears in numerous textbooks on American history published by Scribner's.
[3] Also appears as a cover in color for *American History Illustrated,* January 1967.

Miller, Olive Beaupré

[pictorial design] / THE TREASURE CHEST / of My Bookhouse / Edited by / Olive Beaupré Miller / [pictorial design] / Chicago / The Bookhouse for Children / Publishers

(The Deluxe Edition)
Volume four.
Large 8 vo. Collation: Half title (1); the treasure chest (surrounded by rules in green) (2); title (with pictorial designs in colors enclosed in box rules) (3); copyright (1920) and imprint (4); list of stories and poems (with pictorial designs in colors and black and white) (5–8); blank page (9–10); text (11–448).
Size of leaf trimmed 6⅞ x 9⅛ inches. Gilt top.
Issued in full cloth (simulated light green leather). Front cover stamped in dark green with pictorial cover label in color enclosed in box rules stamped in dark green: MY BOOKHOUSE / (pictorial cover label) / THE TREASURE CHEST. Spine stamped in gold over decorations and rules in dark green: My / BOOK / HOUSE / Olive / Beaupré / Miller / FOUR / (at bottom) The / BOOKHOUSE / for CHILDREN

Cover label illustration in color by N. C. Wyeth.
Description: A frontier trapper.

[pictorial design] / THE TREASURE CHEST / of / My Bookhouse / Edited by / Olive Beaupré Miller / [pictorial design] / Chicago / The Bookhouse for Children / Publishers

(The First Trade Edition)
Volume four
Large 8 vo. Collation: Half title (1); the treasure chest (2); title (with pictorial designs in colors enclosed in boxed rules) (3); editorial acknowledgements, copyright (1920) and imprint (4); contents (with pictorial designs in colors and black and white) (5–8); text (11–448).
Size of leaf trimmed 6⅞ x 9⅛ inches.
Issued in full cloth (black). Front cover stamped in gold with pictorial cover label in color by N. C. Wyeth: MY BOOKHOUSE / THE TREASURE CHEST (surrounded by stamped double boxed rules). Spine stamped in gold with title surrounded by decoration: (double rules) / MY / BOOK- / HOUSE / (ornament) / THE / TREASURE / CHEST / FOUR / The BOOK- / HOUSE for / CHILDREN / (double rules).

Cover label illustration in color by N. C. Wyeth. Same as in the Deluxe Edition.

Idem: Except for slight variations in the binding and list of contributing artists on the copyright page.

Morse, Willard S., and
Brincklé, Gertrude (Compiled by)

HOWARD PYLE / A Record of / His Illustrations and Writings / Compiled by Willard S. Morse / and Gertrude Brincklé / [rule] / Foreword by N. C. Wyeth / Wilmington, Delaware / The Wilmington Society of the Fine Arts / 1921

Large 8 vo. Collation: Original pen-and-ink drawing by Howard Pyle; frontispiece photograph portrait of Howard Pyle (tipped in with tissue inset); title (I); copyright 1921 (Published January 1921) and imprint (II); This is copy No.___ / of a / special limited edition of twelve copies of this work / printed on Alexandra Japan paper, each containing / an original drawing by Howard Pyle, each signed by / the compilers, and the Foreword signed by N. C. Wyeth (III); Howard Pyle (brief biography) (IV); An Impression of Howard Pyle—the Man by N. C. Wyeth (Foreword with signature) (V–IX); Compiler's Explanation (with signature) (XI–XII); Table of Contents (XIII–XIV); text 3–242; addenda 245.
Size of leaf trimmed 6⅛ x 9½ inches. Gilt top.
Issued in full levant (dark blue) stamped in gold. Front and back covers stamped with gold box rule. Spine stamped in gold: (rule) / (rule) / HOWARD / PYLE / (rule) / A / Record of / his / illustrations / and writings / (rule) / (rule) / (rule)

Note: An edition of 500 copies of this work was published without the foreword by N. C. Wyeth.

Nordhoff, Charles, and
Hall, James Norman

THE / BOUNTY TRILOGY / Comprising the Three Volumes / Mutiny On The Bounty / Men Against The Sea / & Pitcairn's Island / By Charles Nordhoff / & James Norman Hall / [drawing] / Illustrations by N. C. Wyeth / Boston / Little, Brown and Company • 1940

(Wyeth Edition)
Thick 8 vo. Collation: Half title (Wyeth Edition); author's book list; frontispiece (in color) (II); title (with drawing) (III); copy-

right (various dates) (1940) (published October 1940) (IV); preface (V–VIII); contents (IX); illustrations (XI); half title (XIII); dedication (1); list of officers and crew of H.M.S. Bounty (2); text (3–903).

Size of leaf trimmed 5⅝ x 8⅛ inches.

Issued in full cloth (blue). Front cover design (H.M.S. Bounty) stamped in gold. Spine stamped in gold enclosed in decorations and rules: THE / BOUNTY / TRILOGY / (ornament) / NORDHOFF & HALL / Mutiny / On The / Bounty / Men / Against / The Sea / Pitcairn's Island / ATLANTIC / LITTLE, BROWN

Title page drawing in pen and ink.
Description: The H.M.S. Bounty p III
Thirteen illustrations in color including the dust wrapper.

Illustrations (plates) in color:
H.M.S. Bounty (frontispiece) p II
They made a handsome couple. fp 90
Captain Bligh was standing by the mizzenmast. fp 126
For a long time neither of us spoke. fp 178
This was the only bit of land above water anywhere about. fp 254
Well we knew what was happening there. fp 354
Our lives depended upon our helmsman. fp 432
He advanced resolutely toward the carpenter. fp 508
"She makes a grand light." fp 628
The chief raised his musket and fired. fp 758
He looked worse than any naked savage. fp 840
The Topaz, with all sails set, was now far out. fp 900
Dust wrapper illustration in color.
Description: H.M.S. Bounty on the high seas.

Palmer, George Herbert (Translated by)

THE ODYSSEY / OF / HOMER / Translated by / George Herbert Palmer / With Illustrations by / N. C. Wyeth / [pictorial design] / Houghton Mifflin Company / The Riverside Press / Cambridge / MDCCCCXXIX

4 to. Collation: Frontispiece (in color with title printed on tissue inset); title (pictorial design in pen and ink printed in green); copyright (various dates) (1929) and imprint; This Edition is Limited to Five Hundred and Fifty Numbered Copies, of Which Five Hundred are for Sale (copy number and autographs of translator and artist); inscription (Greek) (I); facsimile of a letter to the publisher from the translator (with tissue inset) (III); a note by the artist (V); preface (VII); contents (IX); illustrations (XI–XII); introduction (XIII–XXVIII); drawing (with title printed on tissue inset); text (1–314).

Size of leaf uncut 7⅝ x 10⅜ inches.

Boxed (black) with paper label on front. Cellophane wrapper.

Issued in cloth sides (green) with pigskin spine (ivory). Front cover pictorial design stamped in gold (repeated from the title page design). Leather label (dark green) on spine stamped in gold: (double rules) / THE / ODYSSEY / OF / HOMER / – / Translated / By / Palmer / – / Illustrated / By / Wyeth / (double rules).

Accompanying this Limited Edition is an envelope containing a separate set of illustrations (plates) from the book.

Sixteen illustrations in color. The illustrations (plates) are mounted with titles printed on tissue inserts.

Endpaper illustration (drawing) printed in gray green.

Title page design (drawing in pen and ink printed in green).

Final sketch (drawing) made for the painting: Odysseus and Calypso

Illustrations (mounted plates) in color:
The Mourning Penelope (frontispiece)
Athene
'Then she went dashing down the ridges of Olympus.' fp 4
Telemachus in the Chariot of Nestor
'Not unwillingly the pair flew off into the plain, left the steep citadel of Pylos, and all day long they shook the yoke they bore between them.' fp 4
Proteus, the Old Man of the Sea
'When he is come, he lays him down under the caverned cliffs; while round him seals, the brood of a fair sea nymph, huddle and sleep.' fp 46
Odysseus and Calypso
' "Unhappy man, sorrow no longer here, nor let your days be wasted, for I at last will freely let you go." ' fp 62
The Raft of Odysseus
'Earth-shaking Poseidon raised a great wave, gloomy and grievous, and with bending crest, and launched it on him.' fp 68
Polyphemus, the Cyclops
'Tearing off the top of a high hill, he flung it at us.' fp 116
Circe and the Swine
'Now after she had given the cup and they had drunk it off, straight with a wand she smote them and penned them up in sties; and they took on the heads of swine, the voice, the bristles, and even the shape.' fp 126
Odysseus in the Land of the Dead
'I myself, drawing my sharp sword from my thigh, sat still and did not let the strengthless dead approach the blood till I had made inquiry of Teiresias.' fp 136
The Sirens
'So spoke they, sending forth their glorious song, and my heart longed to listen.'[1] fp 156
Eumaeus, the Swineherd
'The noble swineherd, who guarded his estate more carefully than any man royal Odysseus owned.' fp 174
The Beggars Fight
'So when they raised their fists, Irus struck the right shoulder of Odysseus; but he struck

Irus on the neck below the ear and crushed the bones within.' fp 232
The Boar Hunt
'And now Odysseus, by a downward blow, struck the right shoulder of the boar; clean through it the bright spear-point passed.' fp 252
The Trial of the Bow
'Then, laying the arrow on the arch, he drew the string and arrow notches, and forth from the bench on which he sat let fly the shaft.' fp 276
The Slaughter of the Suitors
'So the four chased the suitors down the hall and smote them right and left.' fp 286
Odysseus and Penelope Reunited
'As when the welcome land appears to swimmers, whose sturdy ship Poseidon wrecked at sea, confounded by the winds and solid waters; a few escape the foaming sea and swim ashore; thick salt foam crusts their flesh; they climb the welcome land, and are escaped from danger; so welcome to her gazing eyes appeared her husband.' fp 296

[1] Appears in color in *American Artist* magazine, January 1945, for the article "N. C. Wyeth—A Giant on a Hilltop" by Ernest W. Watson.
In addition, the endpaper illustration appears in the book *Contemporary Illustrators of Children's Books,* compiled by Bertha E. Mahony and Elinor Whitney, published by The Bookshop for Boys and Girls, Boston, 1930.

THE ODYSSEY / OF / HOMER / Translated by / George Herbert Palmer / With Illustrations by / N. C. Wyeth / [pictorial design] / Houghton Mifflin Company / The Riverside Press, Cambridge / MDCCCCXXIX

(The Deluxe Edition)
4 to. Collation: Frontispiece (in color); title (pictorial design in pen and ink) (I); copyright (various dates) (1929) and imprint (II); inscription (Greek) (III); a note by the artist (V); preface (VII); contents (IX); illustrations (XI–XII); introduction (XIII–XXVIII); half title (XXIX); text (1–314).

Size of leaf trimmed 7½ x 10⅛ inches. Tinted top (speckled).

Slipcase (red) with pictorial label in color. Cellophane wrapper.

Issued in full cloth (red). Front cover stamped in gold with pictorial design and ornament: THE / ODYSSEY / (pictorial design—Zeus by Wyeth) / OF / HOMER / (ornament). Spine stamped in gold: (double rules) / THE / ODYSSEY / OF / HOMER / – / Translated / By / Palmer / – / Illustrated / By / Wyeth / (double rules) / (at bottom) Houghton / Mifflin Co.

Sixteen illustrations (plates) in color.
Endpaper illustration (drawing) printed in brown.
Title page design (drawing in pen and ink).
Illustrations (plates) in color: The same as in the Limited Edition but without mounted plates and tissue insets.
The Raft of Odysseus (repeated as the slipcase label)

THE ODYSSEY / OF / HOMER / Translated by / George Herbert Palmer / With Illustrations by / N. C. Wyeth / [pictorial design] / Houghton Mifflin Company / The Riverside Press, Cambridge / MDCCCCXXIX

(The First Trade Edition)
Large 8 vo. Collation: Frontispiece (in color); title (pictorial design in pen and ink)

(I); copyright (various dates) (1929) (edition published 1933) and imprint (II); inscription (Greek) (III); a note by the artist (V); preface (VII); contents (IX); illustrations (XI–XII); introduction (XIII–XXVIII); half title (XXIX); text (1–314).

Size of leaf trimmed 7 x 9¼ inches.

Issued in full cloth (black). Pictorial cover label in color: THE ODYSSEY / Illustrated By N. C. Wyeth. Spine stamped in white: (double rules) / THE / ODYSSEY / OF / HOMER / – / Translated / By / Palmer / – / Illustrated / By / Wyeth / (double rules) / (at bottom) Houghton / Mifflin Co.

Sixteen illustrations (plates) in color.

Endpaper illustration (drawing) printed in brown.

Title page design (drawing in pen and ink).

Illustrations (plates) in color. Same as in the Limited and Deluxe editions.

The trial of the Bow (repeated on the cover label)

Parkman, Francis

THE OREGON TRAIL: / Sketches of Prairie and / Rocky-Mountain Life / By / Francis Parkman / Boston / Little, Brown, and Company / 1925

(The Wyeth-Remington Edition)

Large 8 vo. Collation: Half title; Nine Hundred and Seventy-five copies of the Wyeth-Remington Edition of THE OREGON TRAIL have been printed, of which Nine Hundred and Fifty are for sale (and copy number); frontispiece (mounted plate in color) (II); title (first and seventh lines in red) (III); copyright (various dates) (1925) (IV); dedication (V); publisher's preface (VII–IX); contents (XI); illustrations (XIII); text (1–364).

Size of leaf uncut 6 x 9 inches. Gilt top. Slipcase with paper label.

Issued with board covers (light brown), cloth spine and corners (Indian red). Front cover design (drawing) after Wyeth printed in brown. Spine stamped in gold: THE / OREGON / TRAIL / (decoration—bison head) / FRANCIS / PARKMAN / LITTLE, BROWN / AND COMPANY

Illustrated by N. C. Wyeth and Frederic Remington.

Six illustrations including dust wrapper in colors by N. C. Wyeth.
Illustrations (mounted plates) in color:
Francis Parkman. (frontispiece) p II
The Parkman Outfit. Henry Chatillon, Guide and Hunter.[1][2] fp 14
An Indian War Party.[3] fp 108
Trappers. fp 226
Buffalo Hunt.[1] fp 312

Note: The pen-and-ink drawing reproduced on the front cover is after Wyeth's illustration titled Buffalo Hunt.

[1] The illustrations also appear in black and white in *The Artgum*, April 1926, for the article "N. C. Wyeth, Painter and Illustrator" by Anton Kamp.
[2] Also appears in color in *American Heritage* magazine, October 1965, for the article "N. C. Wyeth" by Henry C. Pitz.
[3] Also appears in black and white in *Transmission* magazine, 1968, for the article "Taming a Frontier."

Parkman, Francis

The Beacon Hill Bookshelf / [ornament] / THE OREGON TRAIL / Sketches of / Prairie and Rocky-Mountain Life / By / Francis Parkman / With Illustrations in Color by / N. C. Wyeth / [publisher's colophon] / Boston / Little, Brown and Company / 1925

8 vo. Collation: Half title; frontispiece (in color) (II); title (surrounded by boxed rules with second and tenth lines in orange) (III); copyright (various dates) (1925) (IV); dedication (V); contents (VII); illustrations (IX); text (1–364).

Size of leaf trimmed 5½ x 8½ inches. Yellow top.

Issued in full cloth (black). Pictorial cover label in color with title enclosed in box rules, etc.: THE OREGON / TRAIL / Francis Parkman. Spine stamped in gold: (rules) / THE / OREGON / TRAIL / (ornament) / (rules) / FRANCIS / PARKMAN / LITTLE, BROWN / AND COMPANY / (rules).

Six illustrations in color, including the endpapers.
Illustrations (plates) in color. Same as in the Wyeth-Remington Edition.
Buffalo Hunt (repeated on the cover label and dust wrapper)

Parrish, Randall

BETH NORVELL / A Romance Of The West / By / Randall Parrish / Author of "When Wilderness Was King," "My Lady of the / North," "Bob Hampton of Placer," etc. / With Frontispiece in Color by N. C. Wyeth / [publisher's colophon] / Chicago / A. C. McClurg & Co. / 1907

8 vo. Collation: Half title; author's book list; frontispiece (in color) (II); title (first and tenth lines in orange) (III); copyright (1907) (published September 21, 1907) and imprint (IV); contents (V–VI); half title (7); text (9–341); recent Western Fiction, ten pages of publisher's advertising.

Size of leaf trimmed 5⅜ x 8 inches.

Issued in full cloth (light tan). Front cover stamped in yellow with pictorial design and decorations stamped in colors: BETH / NORVELL / RANDALL PARRISH (stamped in black outline). Spine stamped in yellow and

black with decorations in colors: BETH / NORVELL (surrounded by decoration) / PARRISH / (decoration) / A. C. / McCLURG / & CO. (surrounded by decoration).

Frontispiece illustration in color.
The woman never changed her posture, never seemed to realize the approach of dawn; but Winston roused up, lifting his head to gaze wearily forward. p II

Idem: Except for the author's name stamped on spine in green.

Pier, Arthur Stanwood

BOYS OF / ST. TIMOTHY'S / By / Arthur Stanwood Pier / Author of "The Pedagogues," "The Sentimentalists," "The Triumph," Etc. / New York / Charles Scribner's Sons / 1904

12 mo. Collation: Half title; frontispiece (with tissue inset); title; copyright (published September 1904) and imprint; dedication; note; contents; list of illustrations; text (1–284).

Size of leaf trimmed 5 x 7⅜ inches.

Issued in full cloth (green). Front cover stamped in gold over pictorial design (boy with football) in colors: Boys / of St. Timothy's. Spine stamped in gold: Boys / of (ornamented) / St. Tim- / othy's / (ornament) / (two colored bands) / Arthur / Stanwood / Pier / Scribners

Illustrated by N. C. Wyeth, Thomas Fogarty and Rosenmeyer.

Three illustrations in black and white by N. C. Wyeth.
He received the ball, rushed forward, and sprang up and out, with all his might. (frontispiece)
"Oh, Randolph," she cried, "I cannot have you play that game any more!" fp 58
"Don't mind me, fellows! keep right on!" he shouted. fp 214

Note: This is the first book in which N. C. Wyeth's illustrations appear.

Porter, Jane

The / SCOTTISH CHIEFS / By Jane Porter / Edited By Kate Douglas Wiggin and / Nora A. Smith / Illustrated by N. C.

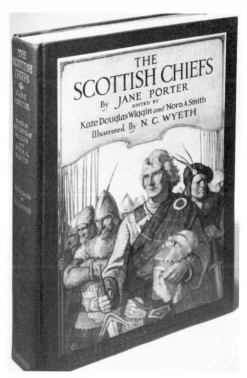

Wyeth / New York / Charles Scribner's Sons / 1921

Large 8 vo. Collation: Half title (I); title (printed over pictorial design—banners) (capital S in Scottish surrounded by scroll in red) (III); copyright (1921) and publisher's colophon (IV); introduction (V–XI); contents (XIII–XIV); illustrations (XV–XVI); half title; text (1–503).

Size of leaf uncut 7 x 9¼ inches. Tinted top.

Issued in full cloth (black). Pictorial cover label in color with decorative gray banner, printed in black: The / SCOTTISH CHIEFS / By JANE PORTER / Edited by / Kate Douglas Wiggin and Nora A. Smith / Illustrated By N. C. Wyeth (title surrounded by gold borders). Spine stamped in gold: THE / SCOTTISH / CHIEFS / (ornament—sprig of holly) / Jane / Porter / Edited By / KATE DOUGLAS / WIGGIN / and / NORA A. / SMITH / Illustrated / By / N. C. WYETH / SCRIBNERS

Seventeen illustrations in color including cover label, endpapers, and title page design. Illustrations (plates) in color:

Wallace and Marion
Being resigned to bury his youth,—since its strength could no longer be serviceable to his country,—books, his harp, and the sweet converse of his Marion, became the occupations of his days. fp 2

The Pledge
"Death and Lady Marion!" was echoed with shouts from mouth to mouth.[1] fp 36

Helen Descends the Glen of Stones
As they mounted the wall of this immense amphitheatre, Helen watched the sublime uprise of the king of light. fp 94

The Storm on the Firth of Clyde
The wind blew a violent gale from that part of the coast, and the sea became boisterous. fp 160

The Battle of Stirling Castle
But all his promptitude proved of no effect. The walls were giving way in parts, and Wallace was mounting by scaling-ladders and clasping the parapets with bridges from his towers.[2] fp 198

The Wounded Helen
He hastened through the dark passage, and almost flying along the lighted galleries entered the hall. fp 248

Wallace and the Children
It was a clear frosty day, and the keenness of the air brightened the complexion of Wallace, while it deepened the roses of his infant companions. fp 264

King Edward. fp 278

Wallace Draws the King's Sword
"This sword I made the arm of the usurper yield to me; and this sword shall defend the regent of Scotland." fp 318

Wallace Rescues Helen
She was in a profound sleep . . . her countenance seemed troubled, her brows frequently knit themselves, and she started as she dreamt, as if in apprehension. fp 368

Bruce on the Beach
When Bruce leaped upon the beach, he turned to Wallace and said with exultation, though in a low voice, "Scotland now receives her king. This earth shall cover me, or support my throne." fp 386

Wallace's Vision
Wallace paused, and stopping at some distance from this apparition, looked on it in silence. fp 424

Death of Edwin
Edwin lay extended on the ground, with an arrow quivering in his breast; his closing eyes still looked upwards to his friend. fp 450

In the Tower of London
At the further end of the apartment, lit by a solitary taper, lay the body of Wallace on a beir, covered with a soldier's cloak. Kneeling by its side, with her head on its bosom, was Helen. fp 480

A Scribner Illustrated Classic

[1] Also appeared in color in *Life* magazine, June 17, 1946, for the article "N. C. Wyeth" (Art Section).

[2] Also appeared in *Life* magazine, December 9, 1957, for the article "The Stouthearted Heroes of a Beloved Painter."

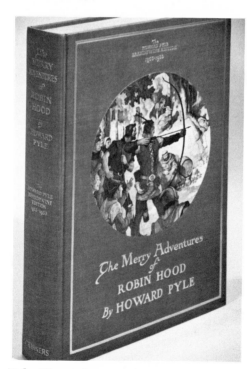

Pyle, Howard

THE / MERRY / ADVENTURES / of / ROBIN HOOD / of Great Renown, / in Nottinghamshire / The / Howard Pyle / Brandywine Edition / 1853–1933

Large 8 vo. Collation: Title (first seven lines surrounded by pen decorations); copy-

right (pen decoration) (Each of the five volumes in the Howard Pyle Brandywine Edition bears a frontispiece in color and a note, the work of former Pyle pupils. The pen decorations are by Robert Ball. Frontispiece and note in this volume by N. C. Wyeth); copyright (1933); frontispiece (in color with title printed on tissue inset); (headpiece decoration by Andrew Wyeth) A recollection by N. C. Wyeth (initial and tailpiece decorations by Andrew Wyeth) (I–III); (From this point, the book follows the format of the original first edition.) frontispiece (IV); title (1933) (surrounded by ornamental border) (V); copyright 1883, 1911 and imprint (VI); preface (VII–VIII); table of contents (IX–XVI); list of illustrations (XVII–XX); second frontispiece (XXII); prologue (1–10); illustration (12); text (13–296).

Size of leaf trimmed 6¾ x 9⅜ inches. Tinted top.

Issued in full cloth (red). Front cover stamped in gold with pictorial cover label in color (surrounded by boxed borders stamped in gold): The / Howard Pyle / Brandywine Edition / 1853–1933 / (pictorial cover label) / The Merry Adventures / of / ROBIN HOOD / By HOWARD PYLE. Spine stamped in gold: The / MERRY / ADVENTURES / of / ROBIN / HOOD / by / HOWARD / PYLE / The / Howard Pyle / Brandywine / Edition / 1853–1933 / SCRIBNERS

Frontispiece illustration in color by N. C. Wyeth.
Robin Hood and His Merry Men in Sherwood Forest (repeated on the circular cover label).

Note: The four companion volumes of the Howard Pyle Brandywine Edition series included a frontispiece and note by his foremost pupils. The contributing artists were Harvey Dunn, Frank E. Schoonover, Stanley Arthurs, and William J. Aylward.

Rawlings, Marjorie Kinnan

THE / YEARLING / by / Marjorie Kinnan Rawlings / With Illustrations by / N. C. Wyeth / [pictorial decoration] / New York / Charles Scribner's Sons / 1939

Large 8 vo. Collation: Of This Edition Seven Hundred and Seventy Copies Have Been Printed Of Which Seven Hundred and Fifty Are For Sale (signed by the author and illustrator) (II); half title (III); title (pictorial decoration in blue) (V); copyright 1938 (1939) (code letter A) and publisher's colophon (VI); illustrations (VII–VIII); facsimile of a letter from N. C. Wyeth (IX and XI); half title (XIII); text (1–400).

Size of leaf uncut 7 x 9¼ inches. Gilt top.

Slipcase with wrapper (green). Paper label (black) on spine stamped in gold.

Issued in full cloth (green). Pictorial decoration (same as title page) within circle on front cover stamped in gold. Spine stamped in gold: (rule) / THE / YEARLING / (ornament) / MARJORIE / KINNAN / RAWLINGS / (ornament) / (at bottom) SCRIBNERS / (rule).

Three drawings. Title page decoration in pen and ink (printed in blue) and two special illustrations for the Limited Edition in charcoal and wash.

Title page decoration in pen and ink.
Description: Flag. p V

Two drawings in charcoal and wash.
Fodder-Wing. fp 44
Pa and Ma Forrester. fp 184

Fifteen illustrations in color including endpapers.

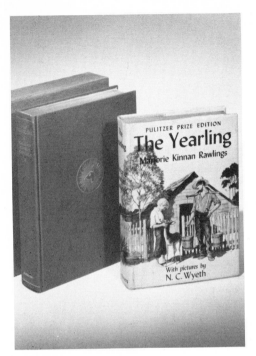

Illustrations (plates) in color:

Jody and the Flutter-Mill
He threw himself on the weedy sand close to the water and abandoned himself to the magic of motion. fp 6

The Fight with Old Slewfoot
Penny ran desperately into the heart of the fracas.[1][2] fp 34

Penny Tells the Story of the Bear Fight
Penny Baxter, no bigger than a dirt-dauber, could outhunt the best of them. And he could sit, as he sat now, weaving a spell of mystery and magic, that held these huge hairy men eager and breathless. fp 54

The Dance of the Whooping Cranes
The cranes were dancing a cotillion as surely as it was danced at Volusia. fp 88

The Fight at Volusia
The fight was in the sandy road in front of the Boyles' store.[2] fp 120

The Vigil
It seemed to Jody that he was alone with his father.[2] fp 144

Jody Finds the Fawn
It was quivering. It made no effort to rise or run. Jody could not trust to move. fp 158

The Burial of Fodder-Wing
Buck set out toward the south hammock. Ma Forrester followed him. Mill-wheel took hold of her arm. The others dropped in behind them. fp 196

The Storm
The familiar pines were like trees at the bottom of the sea, washed across not with mere rain, but with tides and currents.[2] fp 218

Penny Teaches Jody His Sums
Penny would start him on his reading lesson, or his sums, and then before either of them knew it, would be off on a tale.[2] fp 258

The Forresters Go to Town
Buck and Mill-wheel and Lem were crowded together on the wagon seat. fp 288

The Death of Old Slewfoot
They capered together and shouted and yipped until their throats were hoarse and the squirrels were chattering all about them. fp 330

Jody and Flag
One cold night at the end of January, Penny and Ma Baxter had gone to bed while Jody lingered with Flag by the fire.[2][3] fp 352

Jody Lost
The shore had receded alarmingly. Ahead of

him, the open water seemed to stretch without an end. fp 390

Idem: Except for blue cloth binding and slipcase.

A Scribner Illustrated Classic (Limited Edition)

[1] Also appears in color in *Life* magazine, June 17, 1946, for the article on N. C. Wyeth.
[2] The illustrations appear in *Condensed Books Volume 1*, The Reader's Digest Association, Pleasantville, N. Y., 1966.
[3] Also appears as a cover in color for *Woman's Day* magazine, February 1947. In addition, it appears in color in *Life* magazine, December 9, 1957, for the article "The Stouthearted Heroes of a Beloved Painter."

THE YEARLING / by / Marjorie Kinnan Rawlings / With pictures by / N. C. Wyeth / [drawing] / Charles Scribner's Sons • New York / 1939

(Pulitzer Prize Edition)
8 vo. Collation: Author's book list (II); Pulitzer Prize Edition, half title (III); title (with drawing printed in brown) (V); copyright (1939) with Scribner code letter A and publisher's colophon (VI); illustrations (VII–VIII); half title (IX); text (1–400).
Size of leaf uncut 6 x 8⁹⁄₁₆ inches. Green top.
Issued in full buckram (oatmeal). Front cover with pictorial design stamped in brown: The Yearling / Marjorie / Kinnan / Rawlings / (pictorial design–palm tree). Spine stamped in brown with pictorial design (deer head) after Wyeth: The / Yearling / (pictorial design) / Marjorie / Kinnan / Rawlings / Scribners

Sixteen illustrations in color including endpapers and dust wrapper. The dust wrapper appears on this edition only.
Title page illustration in pen and ink, printed in brown.
Description: Old Slewfoot. p V
Illustrations (plates) in color are the same as those in the Limited Edition.

Note: A portion of a quote by N. C. Wyeth appears on the dust wrapper.

THE YEARLING / by / Marjorie Kinnan Rawlings / With pictures by / N. C. Wyeth / [drawing] / Charles Scribner's Sons • New York / 1940

Large 8 vo. Collation: Author's book list (II); half title (III); title (with drawing) (V); copyright 1938 (1939) and publisher's colophon (VI); illustrations (VII–VIII); half title (IX); text (1–400).
Size of leaf uncut 7 x 9¼ inches. Tinted top.
Issued in full cloth (black). Pictorial cover label (Jody and Flag) in color, printed in olive green: THE / YEARLING / MARJORIE KINNAN RAWLINGS (title surrounded by double boxed borders in yellow and olive green). Spine stamped in gold: THE / YEARLING / (ornament) / MARJORIE / KINNAN / RAWLINGS / Illustrated / By / N. C. WYETH / SCRIBNERS

Fourteen illustrations in color including cover label and endpapers.
Title page illustration in pen and ink.
Description: Old Slewfoot p V
Illustrations (plates) in color are the same as those in the Limited Edition with one exception. The illustration Jody Finds the Fawn is not reproduced in this volume.

A Scribner Illustrated Classic

Roberts, Kenneth

Trending / INTO / MAINE / By Kenneth Roberts / With Illustrations by N. C. Wyeth / [drawing] / Boston / Little, Brown and Company / 1938

Large 8 vo. Collation: Half title; frontispiece (in color); title (with drawing printed in green); copyright (1938) (FIRST EDITION) (published May 1938) and imprint; One thousand and seventy-five numbered copies of the ARUNDEL EDITION have been printed on all-rag paper, bound in natural finish cloths and autographed by the author and by the artist; dedication; acknowledgements; Trending Into Maine: quotation—James Rosier; June, 1605; poem; contents (with drawing); illustrations (with drawing); half title (1); text (3–384); index (385–394); author's book list.
Size of leaf uncut 6⅝ x 9½ inches.
Slipcase (pale blue green). Paper label on spine stamped in dark green. Parchment wrapper.
Issued in cloth sides (blue green) and spine (ivory). Leather label (black) on spine stamped in gold: (rule) / Trending / Into / Maine / (ornament) / Kenneth / Roberts / (rule).
Accompanying this Limited Edition is an envelope containing a separate set of illustrations (plates) from the book.

Fifteen illustrations in color including endpapers.
Three illustrations in pen and ink including title page drawing (printed in green), contents page and illustrations page.
Illustrations (drawings) in pen and ink.
Osprey and pine trees (title page)
Road to the village (contents page)
Clipper ship passing lighthouse (illustrations page)
Illustrations (plates) in color:
Captain George Waymouth on the Georges River (frontispiece)
The First Maine Fisherman. fp 18
Dan'l Nason, Sailing Master, 1814. fp 102
They Took Their Wives with Them on Their Cruises. fp 114
A Maine Sea Captain's Daughter
(Based on a portrait, painted in 1842 by an unknown artist, of Jane Nason, youngest daughter of Captain Daniel Nason, when she was twenty-one.)[1] fp 138
The Sea Serpent. fp 178
The Building of a Ship. fp 202
The Lobsterman (Hauling in a Light Fog). fp 228
Trout Fishing. fp 250
Gunning for Partridge. fp 256
A Young Maine Fisherman. fp 280
Arnold's March to Quebec.[2] fp 298
The Doryman (Evening). fp 348
The Aroostook Potato Harvest. fp 360

[1] Also appears as a cover in black and white for *The Yankee* magazine, August 1938.
[2] Appears as a cover in color for *American History Illustrated*, November 1968. In addition, it appears in color in *The Revolution*, Volume 3, by Robert G. Athearn, published by Dell Publishing Co., Inc., New York.

Trending / INTO MAINE / By Kenneth Roberts / With Illustrations by N. C. Wyeth / [drawing] / Boston / Little, Brown and Company / 1938

(The First Trade Edition)
Large 8 vo. Collation: Half title; frontispiece (in color); title (with drawing printed in green); copyright (1938) (published June 1938) and imprint; dedication; acknowledge-

ments; Trending Into Maine: quotation—James Rosier; June, 1605; poem; contents (with drawing); illustrations (with drawing); half title (1); text (3–384); author's book list.

Size of leaf uncut 5¾ x 8¹¹⁄₁₆ inches. Dark gray top.

Issued in buckram (tan). Front cover stamped in green: Trending / INTO MAINE / (pictorial design after Wyeth's title page drawing) / KENNETH ROBERTS (surrounded by double boxed rules). Spine stamped in green: (double rules) / Trending / INTO / MAINE / (ornament—Osprey) / ROBERTS / LITTLE, BROWN / AND COMPANY / (double rules).

Fifteen illustrations in color including endpapers.

Three illustrations in pen and ink including title page drawing (printed in green), contents page and illustrations page.

Illustrations (drawings) in pen and ink. Same as in the Arundel Edition.

Illustrations (plates) in color are the same as those in Arundel Edition.

A Young Maine Fisherman. (repeated on the dust wrapper)

Note: An illustrated advertising brochure printed for the first trade edition states: This edition consisted of only 2500 copies and was published June 20th, 1938. The illustrations, reproduced in black and white, include the title page drawing; A Maine Sea Captain's Daughter; Dan'l Nason, Sailing Master, 1814; and The Building of a Ship.

Rollins, Philip Ashton

JINGLEBOB / By / Philip Ashton Rollins / With Illustrations In Colors / By / N. C. Wyeth / [bronze] / Charles Scribner's Sons / New York • London / 1930

8 vo. Collation: Half title (I); title (title, author and artist surrounded by boxed rules) (bronze by Mahonri M. Young) (III); copyright 1927 (1930) and imprint (IV); dedication (V); preface to second edition (VII); preface (IX–XI); contents (XIII); illustrations (XV); half title (XVII); text (1–263).

Size of leaf uncut 6½ x 8¾ inches. Tinted top.

Issued in full cloth (black). Pictorial cover label in color: JINGLEBOB / by / Philip Ashton Rollins / With Pictures By / N. C. Wyeth. Spine stamped in gold: JINGLEBOB / (ornament—longhorns) / PHILIP A. ROLLINS / Illustrated / By / N. C. WYETH / SCRIBNER'S

Seven illustrations in color including cover label and endpapers. Title page: An American Knight, "Rolling His Own" from a bronze by Mahonri M. Young.
Illustrations (plates) in color:
Vamoose! (cover label)
Chuck wagon. (endpaper printed in brown)[1][2]
"Settin' Pretty" (endpaper printed in brown)[3]
Cutting Out. (Repeated as a label in color on the dust wrapper.) fp 32
The Pullman of the plains.[4] fp 92
In the corral. fp 162
Night herding.[1][3][5] fp 218

A Scribner Illustrated Classic

Note: The Preface to Second Edition by Rollins refers to N. C. Wyeth and his illustrations.
All illustrations (except The Pullman of the plains) originally appeared in color and black and white in *Scribner's Magazine*, March 1906 for the story "A Day with the Round-up" by N. C. Wyeth.

[1] The illustrations also appeared in the book *The Cowboy* by Philip Ashton Rollins, Charles Scribner's Sons, New York, 1922.
[2] Also appears as a frontispiece in the book *A History of Collingsworth County* by The Wellington Leader, Leader Printing Co., Wilmington, Texas, 1925.
[3] Reproduced as a print in color by Charles Scribner's Sons, 1906, under the title Bucking.
[4] Originally appeared in color in *Scribner's Magazine*, August 1910, under the title *The Pay Stage*.
[5] The illustration also appears in *The History of the United States,* volume III, by James Truslow Adams, published by Charles Scribner's Sons, New York, 1933.

Sabatini, Rafael

CAPTAIN BLOOD / His Odyssey / By / Rafael Sabatini / Author of "Scaramouche" / With Frontispiece By / N. C. Wyeth / [publisher's colophon] / Boston and New York / Houghton Mifflin Company / The Riverside Press Cambridge / 1922

12 mo. Collation: Frontispiece (in color); title (I); copyright (1922) and imprint (II); contents (III–IV); half title (1); text (3–356).
Size of leaf trimmed 5 x 7⅜ inches.

Issued in full cloth (black). Front cover stamped in red: CAPTAIN BLOOD / (double rule) / By Rafael / Sabatini. Spine stamped in red: CAPTAIN BLOOD / (double rule) / RAFAEL / SABATINI / HOUGHTON / MIFFLIN CO.

Frontispiece illustration in color.
Description: A portrait of Captain Blood (Repeated on the dust wrapper.)

Shepard, Odell (Selected and Edited by)

The Journals of / BRONSON / ALCOTT / [decoration] / Selected and Edited by / Odell Shepard / Author of "Pedlar's Progress" / Boston / [rule] / Little, Brown and Company / 1938

Large 8 vo. Collation: Half title; frontispiece (in color) (II); title (decoration and rule in green) (III); copyright (1938) (published September 1938) (FIRST EDITION) (IV); dedication (V); preface (VII–IX); introduction (XI–XXVIII); chronological table (XXIX–XXX); illustrations (XXXI); half title (1); text (3–537); index (539–59).

Size of leaf trimmed 6¼ x 9¼ inches. Reddish brown top.

Issued in full cloth (tan). Front cover stamped in gold: A. Bronson Alcott (facsimile signature). Spine stamped in gold over black with ornamental decoration: (rules) / (ornament) / The Journals / of / BRONSON / ALCOTT / (rule) / EDITED BY / ODELL SHEPARD / (ornaments) / LITTLE, BROWN / (rules).

Illustrated from engravings and photographs.
Frontispiece illustration in color by N. C. Wyeth.

Portrait: A. Bronson Alcott (Repeated on the dust wrapper.)

Spearman, Frank H.

WHISPERING / SMITH / [rule] / By / Frank H. Spearman / Illustrated By / N. C. Wyeth / [rule] / Charles Scribner's Sons / New York : : : : : : 1906

12 mo. Collation: Half title; author's book list; frontispiece (in color with tissue inset) (II); title (III); copyright (published September 1906) (IV); dedication (V); contents (VII–IX); illustrations (XI); text (1–421); two pages of publisher's advertising.

Size of leaf trimmed 5 x 7⅜ inches.

Issued in full cloth (red). Front cover stamped in white with pictorial design (Whispering Smith) by Wyeth stamped in colors: WHISPERING / SMITH / FRANK H. SPEARMAN. Spine stamped in gold: WHISPERING / SMITH / FRANK H. / SPEARMAN / SCRIBNERS

Four illustrations in color.
Following the trail itself, Whispering Smith rode slowly. (frontispiece)[1] p II
"And whom may I say the message is from?" fp 26
These three carried rifles slung across their

pommels, and in front of them rode the stranger. fp 132
Wheeling at arm's length, shot again. fp 302

[1] The illustration was reproduced on a poster in color, printed by Charles Scribner's Sons to advertise the book *Whispering Smith*.

NAN OF / MUSIC MOUNTAIN / By / Frank H. Spearman / Illustrated by / N. C. Wyeth / Charles Scribner's Sons / New York:::::::1916

12 mo. Collation: Author's book list; half title; frontispiece in color (with tissue inset) (II); title (III); copyright (1916) (published April 1916) and publisher's colophon (IV); dedication (V); contents (VII–VIII); illustrations (IX); text (1–430); two pages of publisher's advertising.

Size of leaf trimmed 4⅞ x 7⁵⁄₁₆ inches.

Issued in full cloth (green). Front cover stamped in gold with stamped pictorial design (rifle and saddle) surrounded by stamped borders: NAN / of / MUSIC MOUNTAIN / (pictorial design) / FRANK H. / SPEARMAN. Spine stamped in gold: NAN OF / MUSIC / MOUNTAIN / FRANK H. / SPEARMAN / SCRIBNERS

Four illustrations in color.
De Spain covered a hardly perceptible black object on the trail. (frontispiece) p II
Hugging his shield, de Spain threw his second shot over Sandusky's left shoulder.[1] fp 134
"Stand away from that girl!" repeated de Spain harshly, backing the words with a step forward. fp 202
"I've promised you I would. I will promise every time you ask me." fp 414

[1] Appears in color in the book *Harmsen's Western Americana* by Dorothy Harmsen, published by Northland Press, 1971.

Stevenson, Robert Louis

TREASURE ISLAND / By Robert Louis Stevenson / Illustrated / By / N. C. Wyeth / [pictorial design] / New York / Charles Scribner's Sons / M·C·M·X·I

Large 8 vo. Collation: Half title (I); title (printed over pictorial design in color) (III); copyright (1911) (published September 1911) and publisher's colophon (IV); dedication (V); to the hesitating purchaser (VII); contents (IX–XI); illustrations (XIII–XIV); map of Treasure Island (inset); text: part I The Old Buccaneer (3–49); part II The Sea Cook (53–94); part III My Shore Adventure (97–119); part IV The Stockade (123–164); part V My Sea Adventure (167–212); part VI Captain Silver (215–273).

Size of leaf uncut 7 x 9¼ inches. Gilt top.

Issued in full cloth (black). Pictorial cover label in color with light brown inset, printed in black: TREASURE ISLAND / By / Robert Louis Stevenson. Spine stamped in gold: TREASURE / ISLAND / (ornament—spade and pieces of eight) / ROBERT / LOUIS / STEVENSON / Illustrated / By / N. C. WYETH / SCRIBNERS

Seventeen illustrations in color including cover label, endpapers, and title page design.[10]
Illustrations (plates with titles printed on tissue insets) in color:
Captain Bill Bones
All day he hung round the cove, or upon the cliffs, with a brass telescope.[1][10] fp 4
Captain Bones Routs Black Dog
One last tremendous cut which would certainly have split him to the chin had it not

been intercepted by our big signboard of Admiral Benbow.[2][10] fp 16
Old Pew
Tapping up and down the road in a frenzy, and groping and calling for his comrades.[3][4][5][6][10] fp 38
Jim Hawkins Leaves Home
I said good-bye to mother and the cove. fp 58
Long John Silver and Hawkins
To me he was unweariedly kind; and always glad to see me in the galley.[7][8] fp 76
Preparing for the Mutiny
Loaded pistols were served out to all the sure men. fp 102
Ben Gunn
I saw a figure leap with great rapidity behind the trunk of a pine. fp 112
Captain Smollet Defies the Mutineers
Then, climbing on the roof, he had with his own hand bent and run up the colors. fp 138
The Attack on the Block House
The boarders swarmed over the fence like monkeys. fp 162
The Fight in the Cabin
It showed me Hands and his companion locked together in deadly wrestle. fp 178
Israel Hands
"One more step, Mr. Hands," said I, "and I'll blow your brains out."[3] fp 204
The Black Spot
About half way down the slope to the stockade, they were collected in a group.[3][10] fp 226
The Hostage
For all the world, I was led like a dancing bear.[9][10] fp 244
The Treasure Cave!
I was kept busy all day in the cave, packing the minted money into bread-bags. fp 268

A Scribner Illustrated Classic

This was the first volume in a series of Scribner's juvenile classics. This series of books all followed a similar format.

Idem: Except for the tissue insets.

Note: In the contents, Part IV The Stockade, page 23 is misprinted and should read page 123. In subsequent printings, this error is corrected.

[1] The illustration appears in color in the book *Discovering Literature* by Janeway, McFarland, Jewett and Lowery, published by Houghton Mifflin Company, 1968. The illustration also is reproduced

both as a poster and print in color for the Brandywine River Museum, 1971.
[2] Also appears in color in the book *Contemporary Illustrators of Children's Books* by Bertha E. Mahony and Elinor Whitney, published by The Bookshop for Boys and Girls, Boston, 1930.
[3] Also appears in color in *Life* magazine, December 9, 1957, for the article "The Stouthearted Heroes of a Beloved Painter."
[4] Appears in color in the book *The Brandywine Tradition* by Henry C. Pitz, published by Houghton Mifflin Company, Boston, 1969.
[5] Also appears in color in *The Saturday Evening Post,* Fall issue 1971, for the article "Brandywine: A Triumph of Spirit and Strength."
[6] Also appears in color in *The Wyeths* by N. C. Wyeth (edited by Betsy James Wyeth), published by Gambit, Boston, 1971.
[7] Also appears in color in *American Heritage,* October 1965, for the article "N. C. Wyeth" by Henry C. Pitz.
[8] Also appears in color in *American Heritage,* December 1956, for the article "The Books We Got for Christmas" by Ellen Wilson.
[9] The illustration appears in color in *American Artist* magazine, December 1961, for the article "Millions of Pictures" by Henry C. Pitz.
[10] The illustrations also appear in black and white in *The Twentieth Century Book* by John Lewis, published by Reinhold Publishing Corporation, 1967.

The illustrations also appear in color in a Latin edition of *Treasure Island*, Mount Hope Classics, Vol. V, published in cooperation with Charles Scribner's Sons by E. Parmalee Prentice, New York, 1922.

KIDNAPPED / The Adventures Of David Balfour / ROBERT LOUIS STEVENSON / Illustrated / By / N. C. WYETH / New York / Charles Scribner's Sons / MCMXIII

KIDNAPPED / Being Memoirs Of The Adventures Of David / Balfour In The Year 1751 / How he was kidnapped and cast away; his sufferings in a / desert isle; his journey in the wild highlands; his ac- / quaintance with Alan Breck Stewart and other notorious / highland jacobites; with all that he suffered at the hands / of his uncle, Ebenezer Balfour of Shaws, falsely so called / Written By Himself / and now set forth by / Robert Louis Stevenson / New York / Charles Scribner's Sons / 1913

Large 8 vo. Collation: Half title; title (printed over pictorial design) (III); title (V); copyright 1905, (1913) (published October, 1913) and publisher's colophon (VI); dedication (VII–VIII); contents (IX–X); illustrations (XI–XII); half title (1); map: Sketch of the Cruise of the Brig Covenant and the probable course of David Balfour's Wandering (inset); text (3–289).

Size of leaf uncut 7 x 9¼ inches. Gilt top.

Issued in full cloth (black). Pictorial cover label in color with gray inset, printed in black: KIDNAPPED / By / Robert Louis Stevenson (title surrounded by black border rules). Spine stamped in gold: KIDNAPPED / The Adventures / Of / David / Balfour / (ornament) / ROBERT / LOUIS / STEVENSON / Illustrated / By / N. C. WYETH / SCRIBNERS

Seventeen illustrations in color including cover label, endpapers, and title page design.
Illustrations (plates with tissue insets) in color:
Mr. Campbell, the Minister of Essendean
With that he prayed a little while aloud, and in affecting terms, for a young man setting out into the world. fp 6

Mr. Balfour, of the House of Shaws
What he was, whether by trade or birth, was more than I could fathom. fp 18

At Queen's Ferry
And the spirit of all that I beheld put me in thoughts of far voyages and foreign places. fp 48

The Brig "Covenant" in a Fog
All afternoon, when I went on deck, I saw men and officers listening hard over the bulwarks. fp 72

The Siege of the Round-House
It came all of a sudden when it did, with a rush of feet and a roar, and then a shout from Alan.¹ fp 84

The Wreck of the "Covenant"
It was the spare yard I had got hold of, and I was amazed to see how far I had travelled from the brig. fp 112

On the Island of Erraid
But the second day passed; and as long as the light lasted I kept a bright look-out for boats on the sound or men passing on the Ross.² fp 122

The Blind Beggar on the Isle of Mull
In about half an hour of walk, I overtook a great, ragged man, moving pretty fast but feeling before him with a staff. fp 134

The Murderer of Roy Campbell of Glenure
At that the murderer gave a little, quick look over his shoulder, and began to run. fp 154

The Torrent in the Valley of Glencoe
I had scarce time to measure the distance or to understand the peril before I had followed him, and he had caught and stopped me. fp 178

At the Cards in Cluny's Cage
But Alan and Cluny were most of the time at the cards. fp 214

Two Pipers in Balquhidder
All night long the brose was going and the pipes changing hands. fp 238

Mr. Rankeillor, the Lawyer
Here he sat down, and bade me be seated. fp 258

The Parting
For we both knew without a word said that we had come to where our ways parted. fp 286

Endpaper illustration.
The Covenant of Dysart passing the headlands of Western Scotland

A Scribner Illustrated Classic

THE BLACK ARROW / A Tale Of The Two Roses / — / Robert Louis Stevenson / Illustrated by N. C. Wyeth / [pictorial design] / New York / Charles Scribner's Sons / MCMXVI

Large 8 vo. Collation: Half title (I); title (pictorial design in color with lettering printed over banners) (III); copyright (1916) (published October, 1916) and publisher's colophon (IV); critic on the hearth—R.L.S. (V); contents (VII–VIII); illustrations (IX–X); text: prologue (3–22), book I (25–94), book II (97–143), book III (147–194), book IV (197–257), book V (261–328).

Size of leaf uncut 7 x 9¼ inches. Gilt top.
Issued in full cloth (black). Pictorial cover label in color with decorative banner, printed in black: THE BLACK ARROW / By / Robert Louis Stevenson. Spine stamped in gold: THE BLACK / ARROW / (ornament—crossbow) / ROBERT / LOUIS / STEVENSON / Illustrated / By / N. C. WYETH / SCRIBNERS

Seventeen illustrations in color including cover label, endpapers and title page design.
Illustrations (plates) in color:
"They cannot better die than for their natural lord," said Dick. fp 4
"Now, mark me, mine host," Sir Daniel said, "follow but mine orders and I shall be your good lord ever." fp 26
So the change was made, and they went forward as briskly as they durst on the uneven causeway. fp 40
In the fork, like a mastheaded seaman, there stood a man in a green tabard, spying far and wide.¹ fp 56
And putting their mouths to the level of a starry pool, they drank their fill. fp 82
Lastly, a little before dawn, a spearman had come staggering to the moat side, pierced by arrows. fp 98
"We must be in the dungeons," Dick remarked. fp 128
They were now fighting above the knees in the spume and bubble of the breakers. fp 160
The little cockle dipped into the swell and staggered under every gust of wind. fp 174
The Lawless, keeping half a step in front of his companion and holding his head forward like a hunting-dog upon the scent . . . studied out their path.² fp 198
First came the bride, a sorry sight, as pale as the winter, clinging to Sir Daniel's arm. fp 234
There were seven or eight assailants, and but one to keep head against them. fp 262
"Go, Dutton, and that right speedily," he added. "Follow that lad." fp 272
"But be at rest; the Black Arrow flieth nevermore." fp 324

A Scribner Illustrated Classic

¹ Also appears as a cover in color in *The Independent*, December 4, 1916. It was titled "The Man In The Green Tabard."
² Also appears in the book *Illustrating Children's Books* by Henry C. Pitz, published by Watson-Guptill Publications, New York, 1963.

DAVID BALFOUR / [illustration] / by / Robert Louis Stevenson / With Pictures by N. C. Wyeth / New York / Charles Scribner's Sons / MCMXXIV

DAVID BALFOUR / Being Memoirs Of The Further / Adventures Of David Balfour / At Home And Abroad / in which are set forth his misfortunes anent the / Appin murder; his troubles with Lord Advocate / Grant; captivity on the Bass Rock; journey into / Holland and France; and singular relations with / James More Drummond or Macgregor, a son of the / notorious Rob Roy, and his daughter Catriona / Written By Himself, And Now / Set Forth By / Robert Louis Stevenson / Illustrated By N. C. Wyeth / New York / Charles Scribner's Sons / 1924

Large 8 vo. Collation: Half title (I); title (with illustration in color) (III); title (V); copyright (various dates) (1924) and imprint (VI); dedication (VII–VIII); contents (IX–X); illustrations (XI–XII); summary (XIII–XV); half title; chapter heading (1); text (3–356).

Size of leaf uncut 7 x 9¼ inches. Tinted top.
Issued in full cloth (black). Pictorial cover label in color: DAVID BALFOUR (red) / by / Robert Louis Stevenson / (illustration) / With Pictures by N. C. Wyeth (artist in red). Spine stamped in gold: DAVID / BALFOUR / (ornament—thistle) / ROBERT / LOUIS / STEVENSON / Illustrated / By / N. C. WYETH / SCRIBNERS

Twelve illustrations in color including cover label, endpapers and title page. The cover label illustration is repeated as a label in color on the dust wrapper.
Illustrations (plates) in color:
The Gibbet
The sight coming on me suddenly, like an illustration of my fears, I could scarce be done with examining it and drinking in discomfort. fp 28
Prestongrange
At this he rose from his chair, lit a second candle, and for a while gazed upon me steadily. fp 42
David and Catriona
Catriona came with me as far as the garden gate. fp 108
Gillane Sands
"Davie," said he, "this is a kittle passage! as long as we lie here we're safe; but I'm nane sae muckle nearer to my ship or the coast of France." fp 136
Tam on the Craig Face
But whaur Tam hung there was neathing but the craig, and the sea belaw, and the solans skirling and flying.¹ fp 162
Catriona's Leap
The patroon humoured his boat nearer in than was perhaps wholly safe, and Catriona leaped into the air. fp 254
The Walk in the Snow
That was the best walk yet of all of them; she clung near to me in the falling snow. fp 284
On the Brae by Dunkirk
This was on the summit of a brae, the place was windy and conspicuous, we were to be seen there even from the English ship. fp 342
The Duel
. . . and the next wink of time their blades clashed together. fp 350

A Scribner Illustrated Classic

¹ Also appears in black and white in *The Artgum* April 1926, for the article "N. C. Wyeth, Painter and Illustrator" by Anton Kamp.

Stewart, Elinore Pruitt

LETTERS / OF A WOMAN / HOMESTEADER / By / Elinore Pruitt Stewart / With Illustrations by N. C. Wyeth / [publisher's colophon] / Boston and New York / Houghton Mifflin Company / The Riverside Press Cambridge / 1914

12 mo. Collation: Half title (I); frontispiece (with tissue inset) (II); title (surrounded by boxed rules) (III); copyright 1913 (1914) (published May 1914) (IV); publisher's note (V); contents (VII–VIII); illustrations (IX); half title (1); text (3–282); imprint.

Size of leaf trimmed 4¾ x 7³⁄₁₆ inches.

Issued in full cloth (tan). Front cover stamped in black over reddish brown box (surrounded by stamped boxed rules in black): Letters of / A Woman / Homesteader / Elinore Pruitt / Stewart. Spine (title only) stamped in black over reddish brown box (surrounded by stamped boxed rules in black): Letters of / A Woman / Homesteader / Elinore Pruitt / Stewart / Houghton / Mifflin Co.

Six illustrations in black and white.
The Woman Homesteader. (frontispiece, repeated on the dust wrapper) p II
Jerrine was always such a Dear Little Pal. fp 30
Zebulon Pike. fp 112
The Stewart Cabin. fp 138
Gavotte. fp 180
Mrs. Louderer and Mrs. O'Shaughnessy. fp 258

The preface by Francis H. Allen contains a reference to N. C. Wyeth and his illustrations.

Twelve illustrations in color including endpapers and dust wrapper.
Twenty-four illustrations in pen and ink including the title page drawing.°
Illustrations (plates) in color:
Plate   I.   A man of certain probity and worth, immortal and natural! (frontispiece)
Plate   II.   Thoreau Fishing.¹ (repeated as box label)
Plate III.   The Carpenters Repairing Hubbard's Bridge.¹
Plate   IV.   Thoreau and Miss Mary Emerson.
Plate   V.   Mr. Alcott in the Granary Burying Ground in Boston.
Plate   VI.   Thoreau and the Three Reformers.
Plate VII.   The Muskrat-Hunters, Goodwin and Haynes.
Plate VIII.   Fishing Through the Ice.
Plate   IX.   Barefooted Brooks Clark Building Wall.
Plate   X.   Johnny and His Woodchuck-Skin Cap.²

Note: ° Contrary to the title page credit, the twenty-four pen and ink illustrations were drawn by Andrew Wyeth under his father's supervision.
Note: The endpaper illustration also appears as a dust wrapper in color and an illustration in black and white in the book Thoreau by Henry Seidel Canby, published by Houghton Mifflin Company, Boston, 1939. In addition the endpaper illustration appears as endpapers in color in The Wyeths by N. C. Wyeth (edited by Betsy James Wyeth) published by Gambit, Boston, 1971.

¹ Two illustrations (Plates III and IV) are repeated on the back of the dust wrapper in black and white.
² Also appears in The Living Wilderness magazine, Winter 1959, for the article "Single-mindedness in Concord" by Harvey Broome.

Towne, Charles Hanson (Edited by)

FOR / FRANCE / [emblem in color] / [excerpts from La Marseillaise] / Garden City New York / Doubleday, Page & Company / MCMXVII

8 vo. Collation: Half title (I); frontispiece (with tissue inset) (IV); title (V); copyright (1917) (VI); editor's note (VII–VIII); foreword (IX–XII); contents (XIII–XXI); half

Thoreau, Henry David

MEN of CONCORD / and some others As Portrayed / In The Journal Of Henry / David Thoreau Edited By / Francis H. Allen With Il- / lustrations By N. C. Wyeth / [drawing] / [rule] / Houghton Mifflin Company • Boston / The Riverside Press Cambridge

Large 8 vo. Collation: Frontispiece (in color); plate I (frontispiece title); title (I); copyright (1936) and imprint (II); preface (III–IV); illustrations in color (V); introduction (VII–XI); text (1–244); index (245–55).
Size of leaf uncut 6¼ x 9⅜ inches. Boxed (green) with pictorial label in color.
Issued in full cloth (green). Front cover stamped in silver over dark blue band: MEN of CONCORD. Spine stamped in silver over dark blue: MEN / of / CONCORD / THOREAU

title (1); photograph (Richard Harding Davis) (3); facsimile tribute (4–5); an appreciation (6); a posthumous poem (7); memoir (8); illustration (9); from America's greatest living novelist (11); an address (12–13); illustration (14); text (15–412); publisher's colophon and imprint.

Size of leaf trimmed 5⅞ x 8¾ inches.

Issued in full cloth (blue gray). Pictorial cover label design with title (by Wyeth) in color: FOR FRANCE. Spine stamped in black (with paper emblem in color): FOR / FRANCE / (paper emblem) / DOUBLEDAY / PAGE & CO.

Illustrated with numerous paintings, drawings, sculpture, etc.
Cover label in color by N. C. Wyeth. (Repeated on the dust wrapper.)
    Description: Design with title, American flag, eagle and marching French infantry (WWI).

Turkington, Grace A.

MY COUNTRY / A Textbook In Civics And Patriotism / For Young Americans / By / Grace A. Turkington / Frontispiece In Color / By / N. C. Wyeth / Ginn and Company / Boston • New York • Chicago • London / Atlanta • Dallas • Columbus • San Francisco

12 mo. Collation: Frontispiece (in color); title (I); copyright (1918) (code number 318.11) and imprint (II); preface (III–IV); contents (V); map (VI); text (1–371); appendix (373–88); index (389–94).
Size of leaf trimmed 5 x 7⅛ inches.
Issued in full cloth (reddish brown). Front cover stamped in black with stamped pictorial design (arch): MY COUNTRY / (arch) / TURKINGTON. Spine stamped in black with stamped ornament surrounded by garland: MY / COUNTRY / (ornament) / TURKINGTON / GINN AND / COMPANY

Frontispiece illustration in color by N. C. Wyeth.
    Description: Children saluting the American flag.

Idem: Except for binding (brown cloth without stamped pictorial design on front cover).

Van Dyke, Henry

LITTLE RIVERS / A Book of Essays / In Profitable Idleness / By / Henry Van Dyke / [quotation—Col. Robert Venables: The Experienc'd Angler.1662] / [design in colors] / New York / Charles Scribner's Sons / 1920

(Published in eighteen volumes)
8 vo. Collation: This Autograph Edition, printed on Old Stratford paper, is limited to five hundred and four copies, of which this is No.___ (signed Charles Scribner's Sons); The Works of Henry Van Dyke, Avalon Edition, Volume I (ornament), Outdoor Essays I; frontispiece (autographed photograph of Henry Van Dyke in brown tint with tissue inset); title (first and seventh lines in red) (design in colors); copyright (various dates) (1920); foreword to the Avalon Edition; half title; dedication and re-dedication; contents; prelude. An Angler's Wish in Town (1–5); half title (7); quotation—Robert Louis Stevenson: Prince Otto (8); illustration (in brown tint with tissue inset); text (9–280); index (281–90).

Size of leaf uncut 5½ x 8⅜ inches. Gilt top. Tissue wrapper.

Issued in cloth covers (olive green), morocco spine and corners (dark green). Spine stamped in gold with ornamental decorations: (rule) / (ornament surrounded by double rules) / (rule) / THE WORKS / OF / HENRY / VAN DYKE / — / 1 (surrounded by rules) / (rule) / (ornament surrounded by rules) / (rule) / LITTLE RIVERS (surrounded by rules) / (rule) / (ornament surrounded by double rules) / (rule) / 1920 / (rule)

One illustration (autographed in pencil by N. C. Wyeth) in brown tint.
> Every river that flows is good, and has something worthy to be loved.

Idem: Issued in cloth covers (blue), morocco spine and corners (dark blue).

Note: Approximately one hundred sets of this, the limited Edition, were elaborately bound and signed by both the author and the artist.

LITTLE RIVERS / A Book of Essays / In Profitable Idleness / By / Henry Van Dyke / [quotation—Col. Robert Venables: The Experienc'd Angler.1662] / [design in colors] / New York / Charles Scribner's Sons / 1920

(Published in eighteen volumes)
8 vo. Collation: This Autograph Edition, printed on Old Stratford paper, is limited to five hundred and four copies, of which this is No._____ (signed Charles Scribner's Sons); The Works of Henry Van Dyke, Avalon Edition, Volume I (ornament), Outdoor Essays I; frontispiece (autographed photograph of Henry Van Dyke in brown tint with tissue inset); title (first and seventh lines in red) (design in colors); copyright (various dates) (1920); foreword to the Avalon Edition; half title; dedication and rededication; contents; prelude: An Angler's Wish in Town (1–5); half title (7); quotation—Robert Louis Stevenson: Prince Otto (8); illustration (in brown tint with tissue inset); text (9–280); index (281–90).
Size of leaf uncut 5½ x 8⅜ inches. Tissue wrapper.
Issued with board covers (tan), cloth spine and corners (red). Paper label on spine with double rules in red: (double rules) / HENRY / VAN DYKE / I / (double rules) / LITTLE / RIVERS / (double rules)

One illustration in brown tint.
> Every river that flows is good, and has something worthy to be loved.

LITTLE RIVERS / A Book of Essays / In Profitable Idleness / By / Henry Van Dyke / [quotation—Col. Robert Venables: The Experienc'd Angler.1662] / [design in colors] / New York / Charles Scribner's Sons / 1920

(Published in eighteen volumes)
8 vo. Collation: The Works of Henry Van Dyke, Avalon Editions, Volume I (ornament) Outdoor Essays I; frontispiece (in brown tint with tissue inset); title (first and seventh lines in red) (design in colors); copyright (various dates) (1920); foreword to the Avalon Edition; half title; dedication and rededication; contents; prelude (1–5); half title (7); quotation—Robert Louis Stevenson: Prince Otto (8); text (9–280); index (281–90).
Size of leaf uncut 5½ x 8⅜ inches. Gilt top.
Issued in full cloth (blue). Front cover ornament (author's initials) stamped in gold. Spine stamped in gold with ornamental decorations:

THE / WORKS OF / HENRY / VAN DYKE / • I • / LITTLE / RIVERS / SCRIBNERS

Frontispiece illustration in brown tint. Same as in the autographed editions.

FISHERMAN'S LUCK / And Some Other Uncertain / Things / By / Henry Van Dyke / [quotation—M. de Montaigne: Divers Events] / [design in colors] / New York / Charles Scribner's Sons / 1920

(Published in eighteen volumes.)
8 vo. Collation: This Autograph Edition, printed on Old Stratford paper, is limited to five hundred and four copies, of which this is No._____; The Works of Henry Van Dyke, Avalon Edition, Volume II (ornament), Outdoor Essays II; frontispiece (in brown tint with tissue inset); title (first and seventh lines in red) (design in colors); copyright (various dates) (1920); dedication; contents; half title (1); (quotation—Charles Lamb: *Essays of Elia.*) (2); text (3–246); index (247–56).
Size of leaf uncut 5½ x 8⅜ inches. Gilt top. Tissue wrapper.
Issued in cloth covers (olive green), morocco back and corners (dark green). Spine stamped in gold with ornamental decorations: (rule) / (ornament surrounded by double rules) / (rule) / THE WORKS / OF / HENRY / VAN DYKE / — / 2 (surrounded by rules) / (rule) / (ornament surrounded by rules) / (rule) / FISHERMAN'S / LUCK (title surrounded by rules) / (rule) / (ornament surrounded by double rules) / (rule) / 1920 / (rule)

Frontispiece illustration (autographed in pencil by N. C. Wyeth) in brown tint.
> The attraction of angling for all the ages of man, lies in its uncertainty. Tis an affair of luck.

Idem: Issued in cloth covers (blue), morocco spine and corners (dark blue).

Note: Approximately one hundred sets of this, the Limited Edition, were elaborately bound and signed by both the author and the artist.

Van Dyke, Henry

FISHERMAN'S LUCK / And Some Other Uncertain / Things / By / Henry Van Dyke / [quotation—M. de Montaigne: Divers Events] / [design in colors] / New York / Charles Scribner's Sons / 1920

(Published in eighteen volumes)
8 vo. Collation: This Autograph Edition, printed on Old Stratford paper, is limited to five hundred and four copies, of which this is No._____; The Works of Henry Van Dyke, Avalon Edition, Volume II (ornament), Outdoor Essays II; frontispiece (in brown tint with tissue inset); title (first and seventh lines in red) (design in colors); copyright (various dates) (1920); dedication; contents; half title (1); (quotation—Charles Lamb: *Essays of Elia.*) (2); text (3–246); index (247–56).
Size of leaf uncut 5½ x 8⅜ inches. Tissue wrapper.
Issued with board covers (tan), cloth spine and corners (red). Paper label on spine with double rules in red: (double rules) / HENRY / VAN DYKE / II / (double rules) / FISH-ERMAN'S / LUCK / (double rules)

Frontispiece illustration in brown tint.
> The attraction of angling for all the ages of man lies in its uncertainty. Tis an affair of luck.

FISHERMAN'S LUCK / And Some Other Uncertain / Things / By / Henry Van Dyke / [quotation—M. de Montaigne: Divers Events] / [design in colors] / New York / Charles Scribner's Sons / 1920

(Published in eighteen volumes)
8 vo. Collation: The Works of Henry Van Dyke, Avalon Edition, Volume II (ornament), Outdoor Essays II; frontispiece (in brown tint with red); title (first and seventh lines in red) (design in colors); copyright (various dates) (1920); dedication; contents; half title (1); (quotation—Charles Lamb: *Essays of Elia.*) (2); text (3–246); index (247–56).
Size of leaf uncut 5½ x 8⅜ inches. Gilt top.
Issued in full cloth (blue). Front cover ornament (author's initials) stamped in gold. Spine stamped in gold with ornamental decorations: THE / WORKS OF / HENRY / VAN DYKE / • II • / FISHERMAN'S / LUCK / SCRIBNERS

Frontispiece illustration in brown tint, same as in the autographed editions.

"EVEN UNTO / BETHLEHEM" / The Story of Christmas / By / Henry Van Dyke / New York / Charles Scribner's Sons / 1928

Thin 12 mo. Collation: Half title; frontispiece (in color with tissue inset); title; copyright (1928); dedication; a word to the reader; continued; contents; text (1–103); publisher's colophon. (all pages enclosed in box rules)
Size of leaf uncut 5¼ x 7¾ inches.
Issued in full cloth (blue). Front cover stamped in gold: (rule) / "EVEN UNTO / (rule) / BETHLEHEM" / (rule) / THE STORY OF CHRISTMAS / (rule) / HENRY VAN DYKE / (rule). Spine stamped in gold: (rule) / "EVEN / UNTO / BETH- / LE-HEM" / (ornament) / HENRY / VAN DYKE / (rule) / (at bottom) (rule) / SCRIBNERS / (rule).

Frontispiece illustration in color.
> Mary rode on Thistles . . . and Joseph waded the stream below. (Repeated on the dust wrapper.)

Verne, Jules

The MYSTERIOUS / ISLAND / By Jules Verne / [pictorial design] / Pictures by N. C. Wyeth / New York / Charles Scribner's Sons / 1918

Large 8 vo. Collation: half title (I); title (pictorial design in color) (III); copyright 1918 (published October 1918) and publisher's colophon (IV); contents (V); illustrations (VII–VIII); text (1–493).
Size of leaf uncut 7 x 9¼ inches. Tinted top.
Issued in full cloth (black). Pictorial cover label in color with gold inset, printed in black: THE MYSTERIOUS / ISLAND / By Jules Verne (title surrounded by black border rules). Spine stamped in gold: THE / MYSTERIOUS / ISLAND / (ornament—balloon) / JULES / VERNE / Illustrated / By / N. C. WYETH / SCRIBNERS

Seventeen illustrations in color including cover label, endpapers and title page design.
Fifty-one illustrations (drawings) in pen and ink.
Illustrations (plates) in color:
The Castaways Await the Lifting of the Fog
> While the gaze of the reporter and Neb were

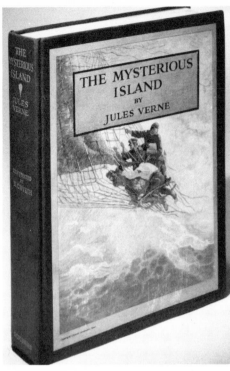

cast upon the ocean, the sailor and Herbert looked eagerly for the coast in the west. fp 20

The Rescue of Captain Harding
However, after traveling for two hours, fatigue overcame him, and he slept. fp 56

Marooned
The island was displayed under their eyes, like a plan in relief with different tints, green for the forests, yellow for the sand, blue for the water. fp 78

Top Is Saved from the Dugong
Thrown in the air by some unknown power, he rose ten feet above the surface of the lake. fp 118.

The Seal Hunt
The seals were numerous, and the hunters, armed with their iron-tipped spears, easily killed half-a-dozen. fp 144

The Discovery of the Chest
Pencroft was not mistaken. Two barrels were there, half buried in the sand, but still firmly attached to a large chest.[1] fp 180

The Capture of the Orang
Nevertheless, they threw themselves on the orang, who defended himself gallantly, but was soon overpowered and bound. fp 214

The Courier of the Air
This little bag was fastened to the neck of the albatross . . . ; then liberty was given to this swift courier of the air. fp 250

The Wild Man of Tabor Island
They did well to hasten, for at a turn of the path near a clearing they saw the lad thrown on the ground and in the grasp of a savage being, apparently a gigantic ape, who was about to do him some great harm. fp 278

The Bonadventure
Every caprice of Nature, still more varied than those of the imagination, appeared on this grand coast, which extended over a length of eight or nine miles. fp 320

Ayrton's Fight with the Pirates
Ayrton was on deck in two bounds, and three seconds later, having discharged his last barrel in the face of a pirate who was about to seize him by the throat, he leaped over the bulwarks into the sea. fp 350

Captain Harding Slays a Convict
In a few seconds, before he had even time to fire his second barrel, he fell, struck to the heart by Harding's dagger, more sure even than his gun. fp 388

Captain Nemo
At these words the reclining figure rose, and

the electric light fell upon his countenance.[2] fp 454

The Last Hope
On this barren rock they had now existed for nine days. fp 490

Illustrations (drawings) in pen and ink. Descriptions:
Captain Cyrus Harding. p 15
Neb fighting the current. p 21
The "Chimneys." p 28
Despairing Neb. p 35
Herbert and Pencroft. p 42
The volcano. p 72
Mt. Franklin. p 81
Kangaroos. p 89
Pencroft shooting bow. p 98
The cliffs at Mandible Cape. p 106
The kiln. p 113
Top. p 120
The outlet. p 128
Exploring the cavern. p 135
Granite House. p 142
The explorers. p 155
Pounding surf at Union Bay. p 165
Herbert in his observatory. p 177
First trial of the canoe. p 184
Monkeys springing among the trees. p 192
Mercy River. p 199
The remains of the balloon. p 208
Master Jup, the Orang. p 216
The cart. p 224
Jup in the kitchen. p 232
Granite House and Prospect Heights. p 239
Harding descending into the well. p 255
The Bonadventure. p 265
The empy hut. p 273
The wild man. p 282
The castaway. p 289
The Bonadventure returns to Lincoln Island. p 298
Ayrton. p 307
Top on the Bonadventure. p 323
Cyrus Harding sighting a vessel through telescope. p 332
The brig Speedy. p 347
Ayrton swims from the brig. p 351
Bob Harvey. p 361
Destruction of the Speedy. p 370
Cannon fire from Granite House. p 377
Convict firing rifle. p 385
Top delivers the note. p 391
Pencroft and wounded Herbert. p 396
The burning of the poultry-yard. p 404
The dead convicts. p 425
The colonists explore a crater. p 434
The awakening of the volcano. p 443
The Nautilus in it subterranean cavern. p 460
The sinking of the Nautilus. p 476
The eruption of Mt. Franklin. p 488
The death of Lincoln Island. p 493

A Scribner Illustrated Classic

[1] Also appears in color on the dust wrapper of the book *The Mysterious Island* by Jules Verne, published by Grosset and Dunlap Publishers, New York.
[2] Also appears in black and white in *The Mentor*, June 1928, for the article "One Hundred Years of Jules Verne" by Richard Dean.

The cover label illustration appears in *Life* magazine, December 9, 1957, for the article "The Stouthearted Heroes of a Beloved Painter."

MICHAEL STROGOFF / A COURIER of THE CZAR / [pictorial design] / Alexander II / by Jules Verne / Illustrated by N. C. Wyeth / New York Charles Scribner's Sons London

Large 8 vo. Collation: Half title (I); title (pictorial design in color surrounded by banners) (first, fourth and fifth lines in red) (III); copyright (1927) and imprint (IV); contents (V–VI); illustrations (VII); text (1–397).

Size of leaf uncut 7 x 9¼ inches. Tinted top.

Issued in full cloth (black). Pictorial cover label in color: MICHAEL STROGOFF / BY JULES VERNE / PICTURES BY N. C. WYETH (blue) / (illustration). Spine stamped in gold: MICHAEL / STROGOFF / (ornament—double eagle) / JULES / VERNE / ILLUSTRATED / BY / N. C. WYETH / (at bottom) SCRIBNERS

Twelve illustrations in color including cover label, endpapers, and title page design.
Illustrations (plates) in color:
When he was fourteen, Michael Strogoff had killed his first bear, quite alone. (Repeated as a label in color on the dust wrapper.) fp 32
Michael Strogoff went forward and took her hand. fp 90
"Defend yourself, for I shall not spare you!" fp 140
He perceived, at some yards from the ruin of the building, an old man surrounded by weeping children. fp 180
Michael was running across the steppe endeavoring to gain the covert of some trees when a detachment of Tartar cavalry appeared on the right. fp 196
Notwithstanding her age she was compelled to follow the convoy of prisoners on foot, without any alleviation of her suffering. fp 230
Marfa, seized by two soldiers, was forced on her knees on the ground.[1] fp 248
The horse fell with his rider to the bottom of the cliff.[2] fp 312
At a touch from Michael's knife . . . the sword flew in splinters, and the wretch, stabbed to the heart, fell lifeless on the ground. fp 388
Endpaper illustration: The Kremlin (title printed on banner)

A Scribner Illustrated Classic

[1] Also appears in color in the book *Achievement in Photo-Engraving and Letter-Press Printing* by Louis Flader, published by The American Photo-Engravers Association, Chicago, 1927.
[2] Also appears in color in *Life* magazine, December 1957, for the article "The Stouthearted Heroes of a Beloved Painter."

Ward, Christopher

THE DUTCH / & SWEDES / on the DELA- / WARE 1609–64 / [double rule] / By Christopher Ward / [double rule] /

[decoration] / [double rule] / University of Pennsylvania Press / Philadelphia • MCMXXX

4 to. Collation: Half title (I); page from original manuscript written in the hand of Christopher Ward (III); frontispiece (in color) (IV); title (with decoration in blue) (V); copyright (1930) (VI); dedication (VII); preface (with ornaments in blue) (IX–X); contents (with ornaments in blue) (XI–XIII); text (1–378); the principal authorities (379–380); index (381–93); This Edition of THE DUTCH & SWEDES ON THE DELAWARE consists of twenty-five lettered copies for private distribution and one hundred numbered copies, all of which are printed on rag paper and signed by author and illustrator (copy number and imprint).

Size of leaf uncut 8¼ x 10⅜ inches.

Issued in buckram sides (light gray) and leather spine (blue). Spine stamped in gold: The / DUTCH / And / SWEDES / On The / DELAWARE / 1609–64 / (ornament) / WARD / (at bottom) publisher's colophon.

Frontispiece illustration (mounted plate) in color.

Johan Printz
  Governor of New Sweden 1643–53.

THE DUTCH / & SWEDES / on the DELA- / WARE 1609–64 / [double rule] / By Christopher Ward / [double rule] / [decoration] / [double rule] / University of Pennsylvania Press / Philadelphia • MCMXXX

8 vo. Collation: Half title; frontispiece (in color) (II); title (with decoration in blue) (III); copyright (1930) (IV); dedication (V); preface (with ornaments in blue) (VII–VIII); contents (with ornaments in blue) (IX–XI); text (1–378); the principal authorities (research) (379–80); index (381–93)

Size of leaf uncut 6¼ x 8¼ inches.

Issued in full cloth (blue). Spine stamped in gold over light blue: (ornamented rules) / The / DUTCH / And / SWEDES / On The / DELAWARE / 1609–64 / (rule) / Ward / (ornamental rules) / (at bottom) (publisher's colophon).

Frontispiece illustration in color.
Johan Printz, Governor of New Sweden, 1643–53. (Repeated on the dust wrapper.)

Note: The illustration also appears in the book *America Marches Past* by George Willard Bonte, published by D. Appleton-Century Company, New York, 1936.

DELAWARE / Tercentenary / Almanack / & Historical / Repository / 19 [ornament] 38 / Being a valuable Compendium of / Historical Information / concerning the State of Delaware / lavishly embellished and enlivened with felicitous / Illustrations by the most eminent Artists and / accurate Maps and Plans by the most ingenious / Cartographers, imprinted for and published by the / Delaware Tercentenary Commission / in the month of December, A.D.1937 and to be sold / by it at One Dollar a copy of this, the First Edition

Thin large 8 vo. Collation: Title (enclosed in double box rules); text (pages unnumbered); acknowledgements and copyright (First

Edition printed December 1937); one page listing the Delaware Tercentenary Commission.

Size of leaf trimmed 6 x 8¹⁵⁄₁₆ inches.

Issued in full cloth (oatmeal). Spine stamped in black: DELAWARE TERCENTENARY ALMANACK 1938

Illustrated with numerous pen-and-ink drawings by N. C. Wyeth, Andrew Wyeth, Howard Pyle, and Frank E. Schoonover, Stanley Arthurs, Clifford W. Ashley, and Albert Kruse.

One illustration in pen and ink by N. C. Wyeth.
  General Washington Reconnoitering from Iron Hill, Delaware, Aug. 26, 1777.

Wiggin, Kate Douglas

SUSANNA AND SUE / By Kate Douglas Wiggin / With Illustrations by Alice Barber Stephens / and N. C. Wyeth / [publisher's colophon] / Houghton Mifflin Company / Boston and New York / The Riverside Press / Cambridge: MDCCCCIX

8 vo. Collation: Author's book list; half title; frontispiece (in color enclosed in decorative borders in orange); title (publisher's colophon in orange) (enclosed in decorative borders in orange); copyright (1909) (published October 1909); contents (with decoration in orange); illustrations (with decoration in orange); text (1–225) (with decorations at top and bottom in orange); imprint; four pages of publisher's advertising.

Size of leaf uncut 5¾ x 8⁹⁄₁₆ inches. Gilt top.

Issued in full cloth (gray). Front cover with pictorial decorations stamped in colors and pictorial label (circular) surrounded by ornamental borders all enclosed in ornamental box rules: SUSANNA AND SUE / (label in colors) / Kate Douglas Wiggin. Spine with pictorial decorations and ornamental rules stamped in colors: (ornamental rules) / SUSANNA / AND / SUE / (ornamental rules) / (decoration) / Kate / Douglas / Wiggin / (decoration) / Houghton / Mifflin Co. / (ornamental rules).

Illustrated by N. C. Wyeth and Alice Barber Stephens.

Twelve chapter headpiece illustrations in pen and ink by N. C. Wyeth.

Chapter I headpiece illustration repeated as Chapter XII tailpiece.

Illustrations (drawings) in pen and ink.
Albion village. p 3
Hathaway farm. p 25
Country road. p 45
Bringing in the cows. p 69
Shaker women burning leaves. p 89
Hay mounds. p 109
Harvesting the hay. p 123
Cow and calf. p 143
Covered bridge. p 165
Winding brook. p 179
Spring plowing. p 197
Farnham village. p 213
Albion village. p 225

Willis, Elizabeth

LESBY / [ornamental line] / By / Elizabeth Willis / Frontispiece by N. C. Wyeth / [ornamental line] / Charles Scribner's Sons / New York 1931

12 mo. Collation: Half title; frontispiece (in color with tissue inset); title (ornamental lines in red); copyright 1930 (1931) with Scribner code letter A and publisher's colophon; dedication; half title; text (1–178).

Size of leaf uncut 5⅛ x 7½ inches.

Issued in cloth sides (orange) and cloth spine

(black). Front cover stamped in gold (enclosed in box rules) over black label: Lesby / (rule) / Elizabeth Willis. Spine stamped in gold: Lesby / (rule) / Willis / (at bottom) Scribners

Frontispiece illustration in color.
Anne, Stephen, and Lesby. (repeated on the dust wrapper)

Note: A reference to N. C. Wyeth appears on the flap of the dust wrapper.

Wyeth, N. C. (Edited and with Introduction by)

MARAUDERS of the SEA / Being a Compilation of Stories / both HISTORICAL & FICTIONAL of / various Exploits of the most Notor- / ious Corsairs, Buccaneers, Pirates, / Mutineers, Privateers, Marooners & ᶜ / [illustration] / Edited & With An Intro / duction by N•C• Wyeth / Illustrated by Peter Hurd / G. P. Putnam's Sons • New York

Large 8 vo. Collation: Half title (with illustration) (I); title (with illustration) (III); copyright (1935) (with illustration), publisher's colophon and imprint (IV); introduction (V–VIII); contents (with illustration) (IX–X); illustrations (with illustration) (XI); illustration (XII); half title (XIII); text (1–319); illustration (320).

Size of leaf uncut 7 x 9¼ inches. Blue gray top.

Issued in full cloth (black). Front cover and pictorial design in black with stamped cream color: MARAUDERS / OF THE SEA / (pictorial design). Spine stamped in cream color: MARAUDERS / OF THE / SEA / – / WYETH / – / HURD / (at bottom) PUTNAM

Illustrated in color (dust wrapper) and black and white by Peter Hurd.

GREAT STORIES / OF THE SEA & SHIPS / Edited and With Intro / duction by N•C• Wyeth / [illustration] / Illustrated In Color and In / Black & White By Peter Hurd / Philadelphia / David McKay Company / Publisher

Large 8 vo. Collation: Half title (1); title (with illustration and corner decorations) (3); copyright (1940) and imprint (4); foreword (5–6); contents (with illustration) (7–8); illustrations (with illustration) (9–10); passage from the Bible (11); text (13–431).

Size of leaf trimmed 7¹⁵⁄₁₆ x 9⅛ inches. Green top.

Issued in full cloth (light oatmeal). Front cover and pictorial design (sailing ship) by Hurd stamped in green: GREAT STORIES OF / THE SEA AND SHIPS / (pictorial design) / Edited by N. C. WYETH. Spine stamped in green: GREAT / STORIES OF / THE SEA / AND SHIPS / Edited by / N. C. WYETH / Illustrated / by / Peter Hurd / McKAY

Illustrated in color (endpapers and cover design) and black and white by Peter Hurd.

Dust wrapper in color (sailing ship) by Peter Hurd.

Wyeth, N. C. (Edited by Betsy James Wyeth)

THE / WYETHS / The Letters of / N. C. Wyeth, 1901– 1945 / edited by Betsy James Wyeth / Gambit Boston / 1971

Large 8 vo. Collation: Half title (I); title (III); copyright (reproduction credits) FIRST PRINTING (1971) Library of Congress Catalog Card Number: 73–137021, International Standard Book Number: 0–87645–046–X (color plate credit) (IV); (dedication) (V); contents (VII); list of illustrations (IX–XII); color plates (XIII); genealogical chart (XIV–XV); text (1–845); index (847–858).

Size of leaf trimmed 9⅛ x 6⅛ inches. Yellow top.

Issued in buckram sides and cloth spine (blue). Front cover stamped in gold: *N. C. WYETH* (facsimile signature). Spine stamped in gold: N. C. / Wyeth / The Wyeths (over dark blue inset) / GAMBIT

Illustrated with numerous photographs.

Nine illustrations (plates) in color including the endpapers.
"Winter" 1909.[1] fp (304)
"Blind Pew" 1911 (*Treasure Island*) (repeated on the dust wrapper). fp 400
"Their arrows flew together . . ." 1917 (*Robin Hood*). fp 544
"Self Portrait" 1918.[2] fp 576
"The Giant" 1923.[3] fp 704

"Portrait of My Mother" 1929. fp 736
"Springhouse" 1944.[4] fp 800
"Nightfall" 1945.[4] fp 832
"The Fox" 1936 (endpapers)[5]

Twenty-nine illustrations in black and white.
Ink drawing (1901). p 8
Sketch of figure on cot. p 19
Sketch of playbill. p 57
Sketch of figure in medieval costume. p 59
A Wilmington street scene (pen and ink). p 68
Sketch: To The West. p 90
Stage driver (pen and ink). p 95
". . . proceeded to make a few color sketches of the adobe house." (sketch) p 102
Sketch: portrait of a Navajo. p 115
Where the Mail Goes Cream of Wheat Goes. p 188
Sketch on envelope (pen and ink). p 245
Sketch of gate-lock. p 259
Pencil drawing for haystack picture. p 278
Baby Carolyn (pen and ink). p 291
The sheriff (pen and ink). p 295
"Babe," 1909. p 304
N.C. standing in stream (pen and ink). p 316
Winter scene: "Dear Folks: Happy New Year! for all!!" (pen and ink). p 331
Stone house in Chadds Ford, Pa. (pen and ink). p 337

"The Ford" Monday morning (drybrush). p 342
Map (pen and ink). p 351
Confederate soldiers (pen and ink). p 361
The Vedette (pen and ink). p 363
N. C. Wyeth, self-portrait, 1913. p 426
Wild strawberries: from Chadds Ford, 1913 (wash drawing). p 436
Hospital sketch (pen and ink). p 561
The Barney place from Pyles hill (pen and ink). p 590
The old barn (pen and ink). p 605
The Christmas hearth (pen and ink). p 613

[1] Originally appeared in color in *Scribner's Magazine*, December 1909, for the poem "The Moods" by George T. Marsh.
[2] Also appears in color in *American Heritage*, October 1965, for the article "N. C. Wyeth" by Henry C. Pitz.
[3] The mural decoration originally appeared in color in *The Ladies' Home Journal*, July 1923.
[4] The paintings also appear in color in *Life* magazine, June 17, 1946, for the article "N. C. Wyeth."
[5] Originally appeared as endpapers in color for the book *Men of Concord* edited by Francis H. Allen, published by Houghton Mifflin Company, Boston 1936.

Dust-wrapper Illustrations

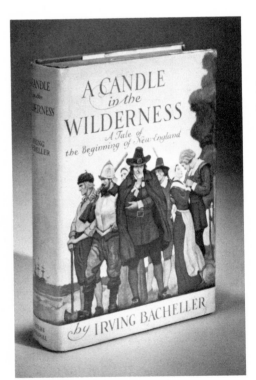

Bacheller, Irving
A CANDLE / IN THE WILDERNESS / A tale of the Beginning / of New England / by / Irving Bacheller / [ornament] / The Bobbs-Merrill Company / Publishers

Copyright 1930 by Irving Bacheller.
First Edition, so stated on the copyright page.
12 mo. Green cloth; lettering on cover and spine stamped in gold; maroon top; 318 pp. (including author's note)

Dust wrapper illustration in color.
Description: An apotheosis of the Massachusetts Bay Colony.

(Beith, John Hay)
DAVID / And / DESTINY / By / Ian Hay / [publisher's colophon] / Boston and New York / Houghton Mifflin Company / 1934 [surrounded by broken and boxed rules]

12 mo. Red cloth; design (piano) on cover stamped in gold; lettering on cover and spine stamped in gold; 317 pp.

Dust wrapper illustration in color.
Description: David playing the piano within a background of tall buildings.

Buchan, John
SALUTE TO / ADVENTURERS / by / John Buchan / [publisher's colophon] / Boston and New York / Houghton Mifflin Company / The Riverside Press Cambridge

Copyright 1917 (1930) by Houghton Mifflin Company.
12 mo. Green cloth; lettering on cover and spine stamped in red; uncut; 348 pp.

Dust wrapper illustration in color.
Description: Two figures stalking through a forest. One, a buckskin man with a pistol and one, an Indian carrying a knife.

By John Buchan / [rule] / THE MAN FROM / THE NORLANDS / [publisher's colophon] / [rule] / Boston • Houghton Mifflin Company • New York / The Riverside Press Cambridge / 1936

12 mo. Gray cloth; lettering on cover and spine stamped in black; 292 pp.

Dust wrapper illustration in color.
Description: Two men standing near cliff edge surveying a wind-scourged sea.

By John Buchan / Adventures of / Richard / Hannay / [rule] [publisher's colophon] [rule] / Containing / The Thirty-Nine Steps / Greenmantle / Mr. Standfast / Houghton Mifflin Company—Boston / The Riverside Press Cambridge / 1939

Copyright 1915, 1916, and 1919 by Houghton Mifflin Company.

12 mo. Green cloth; lettering on cover and spine stamped in dark blue; 374 pp.

Dust wrapper illustration in color.
Description: Man holding revolver.

Note: The illustration also appears as the dust wrapper in color for the book *The Thirty-Nine Steps* by John Buchan, published by Houghton Mifflin Company, Boston, a Book Club Edition.

THE / THIRTY-NINE / STEPS / Houghton Mifflin Company—Boston [date not established]

Book Club Edition
12 mo. Tan cloth; lettering on spine stamped in black; 231 pp.

Dust wrapper illustration in color.
Description: Man holding revolver.

Note: The illustration originally appeared as a dust wrapper in color for the book *The Adventures of Richard Hannay* by John Buchan, published by Houghton Mifflin Company, Boston, 1915.

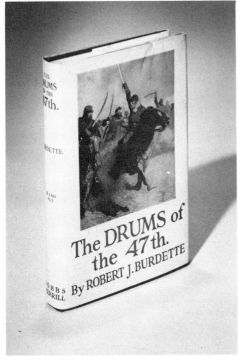

Burdette, Robert J.

THE / DRUMS OF THE 47th / By / Robert J. Burdette, D.D., LL.D. / Author of / Smiles Yoked With Sighs, Chimes From A Jester's Bells / Old Time and Young Tom, etc. / [publisher's colophon] / Indianapolis / The Bobbs-Merrill Company / Publishers

Copyright 1914 by Clara B. Burdette.
12 mo. Green cloth; small design (drum) stamped on cover; lettering on cover and spine stamped in gold; 212 pp.

Dust wrapper illustration in color.
Description: A Union cavalry charge.

Note: The illustration originally appeared in color in the book *War* by John Luther Long, published by The Bobbs-Merrill Company, Indianapolis, 1913. The illustration was titled War.

Burroughs, Edgar Rice

THE / RETURN of TARZAN / By Edgar Rice Burroughs / Author of "Tarzan of the Apes" / [ornament] / With Decorations by

/ J. Allen St. John / A. L. Burt Company, Publishers / 114–120 East Twenty-third Street—New York / Published By Arrangement With A. C. McClurg & Company [title enclosed and surrounded by double boxed rules]

Copyright A. C. McClurg & Co., Chicago 1915.
Published March 1915, so stated on the copyright page.
12 mo. Light green cloth; lettering on cover and spine stamped in black; 365 pp; ten pages of publisher's advertising.

Dust wrapper illustration in color.
Description: Tarzan holding bow and arrow, climbing through treetop jungle growth.

Note: The illustration originally appeared as a cover in color for *New Story Magazine*, August 1913.

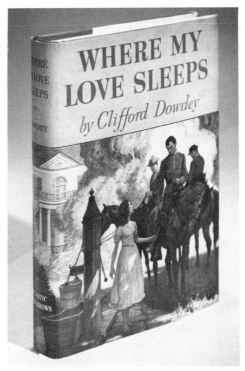

Dowdey, Clifford

WHERE / MY LOVE / SLEEPS / by / Clifford Dowdey / An Atlantic Monthly Press Book / Little, Brown and Company • Boston / 1945

First Edition (published November 1945), so stated on the copyright page.
12 mo. Green cloth; lettering on cover and spine stamped in gold; 298 pp.

Dust wrapper illustration in color.
Description: Three Confederate officers on horseback with woman standing in foreground near a pump.

Forester, C. S.

COMMODORE / HORNBLOWER / By C. S. Forester / [publisher's colophon] / Boston / Little, Brown and Company / 1945 [title surrounded by double boxed rules and ornamental border]

12 mo. Blue green cloth; spine stamped in gold; 384 pp.

Dust wrapper illustration in color.
Description: Commodore Hornblower with telescope.

(Long, Gabrielle Margaret Vere)

DARK ROSALEEN / By / Marjorie Bowen / [publisher's colophon] / Boston and New York / Houghton Mifflin Company / The Riverside Press Cambridge / 1933

12 mo. Orange cloth; lettering on cover and spine stamped in black; green top; 296 pp.

Dust wrapper illustration in color.
Description: Lord Edward Fitzgerald and Pamela.

Nordhoff, Charles, and Hall, James Norman

THE HURRICANE / By / Charles Nordhoff / and / James Norman Hall / [publisher's colophon] / Boston / Little, Brown and Company / 1936

Published February 1936, so stated on the copyright page.
8 vo. blue green cloth; cover (with design) and spine stamped in silver; lettering on spine stamped in silver; 257 pp.

Dust wrapper illustration in color.
Description: South Sea Islanders seek safety in tree during hurricane.

Note: This edition comes with a paper advertisement band over the wrapper stating: The New Novel by the Authors of Mutiny On The Bounty, Nordhoff and Hall—A modern story of the South Seas—First Printing Twenty Thousand.

BOTANY BAY / By / Charles Nordhoff / and / James Norman Hall / [publisher's colophon] / Boston / Little, Brown and Company / 1941

First Edition (published November 1941), so stated on the copyright page.
8 vo. Blue green cloth; pictorial designs on cover and spine stamped in silver; lettering on spine stamped in silver; reddish brown top; 374 pp.

Dust wrapper illustration in color.
Description: Chained convicts in longboats with convict ships moored in background.

Raine, William MacLeod

ROARING RIVER / By / William Mac-Leod Raine / [brand colophon] / Boston And New York / Houghton Mifflin Company / The Riverside Press Cambridge / 1934

12 mo. Orange cloth; lettering on cover and spine stamped in purple; gray tinted top; 297 pp.

Dust wrapper illustration in color.
Description: The fight between Jim Grey and Russell Hughes. Quote: Panther swift, Jim lashed out with his right and caught the protruding jaw.

Rawlings, Marjorie Kinnan

Marjorie Kinnan Rawlings / THE YEAR-LING / [pictorial decoration—Jody and Flag] / Decorations by Edward Shenton / [double rule] / Charles Scribner's Sons / New York : 1942

(The Palmetto Edition)
8 vo. Blue green cloth; pictorial design (Jody & Flag by Shenton) on cover stamped in blue; lettering on cover and spine stamped in blue; 428 pp.
Illustrated with pen-and-ink decorations by Edward Shenton.

Dust wrapper illustration in color by N. C. Wyeth.
Description: Jody and the fawn.

Note: The dust wrapper illustration originally appeared in color as the endpapers for both The Pulitzer Prize Limited Edition and The Pulitzer Prize Trade Edition of *The Yearling*.

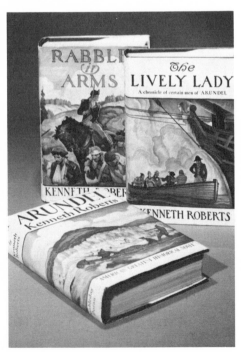

Roberts, Kenneth

ARUNDEL / [double rules with decoration] [orange] / Being / The Recollections of Steven Nason of Arundel, / In the Province of Maine, Attached to the / Secret Expedition Led by Colonel Ben- / edict Arnold

Against Quebec and / Later a Captain in the Con- / tinental Army Serving at / Valcour Island, Bemis / Heights, and / Yorktown / By / Kenneth Roberts / 1930 / [double rule with decoration] [orange] / Doubleday, Doran & Company, Inc. / Garden City, N.Y.

First Edition, so stated on the copyright page.
12 mo. Dark blue cloth; pictorial design (Colonial soldier) on cover and spine stamped in orange; lettering on cover and spine stamped in orange; reddish brown top; 618 pp.

Dust wrapper illustration in color.
Description: Bateaus on the Dead River.

THE LIVELY LADY / [rule] [green] / A Chronicle of Certain Men of Arundel / in Maine, of Privateering During / the War of Impressments, and / of the Circular Prison on / Dartmoor / [publisher's colophon] [green] / [rule] [green] / By Kenneth Roberts / [rule] [green] / Doubleday, Doran & Company, Inc. / Garden City, New York / 1931

First Edition, so stated on the copyright page.
12 mo. Black cloth; pictorial designs on cover and spine stamped in green; lettering on cover and spine stamped in green; 374 pp.

Dust wrapper illustration in color.
Description: Longboat approaching bow of ship adorned with figurehead.

RABBLE IN ARMS / [rule] [blue] / A Chronicle of Arundel / and the Burgoyne / Invasion / [publisher's colophon] [blue] / Doubleday, Doran & Company, Inc. / Garden City, New York / 1933

First Edition, so stated on the copyright page.
Thick 12 mo. Dark blue cloth; cover design stamped in gold (over stamped crossed rules and stars); lettering on spine stamped in gold; 870 pp.

Dust wrapper illustration in color.
Description: Colonials retreating before the British.

Sabatini, Rafael

THE KING'S MINION / Being the Rise and Fall of Robert Carr / of Ferniehurst, Earl of Somerset, Vis- / Count Rochester, Baron Winwick, Baron / Brancepeth, Knight of the Most Noble / Order of the Garter, A Member of His / Majesty's Most Honorable Privy Council / etc., etc., etc. / By / Rafael Sabatini / [publisher's colophon] / Boston and New York / Houghton Mifflin Company / The Riverside Press Cambridge / 1930

12 mo. Black cloth; lettering on cover and spine stamped in orange; orange top 445 pp.

Dust wrapper illustration in color.
Description: Intrigue in the court of King James.

THE BLACK SWAN / By / Rafael Sabatini / [publisher's colophon] / Boston and New York / Houghton Mifflin Company / The Riverside Press Cambridge

Copyright 1931 (1932) by Rafael Sabatini.
12 mo. Black cloth; lettering on cover and spine stamped in orange; orange top; 311 pp.

Dust wrapper illustration in color.
Description: The duel on the beach.

Note: The illustration originally appeared in *The Ladies Home Journal*, September 1931, for the story "The Duel on the Beach" by Rafael Sabatini.

THE STALKING HORSE / By / Rafael Sabatini / [publisher's colophon] / Boston and New York / Houghton Mifflin Company / The Riverside Press Cambridge / 1933

12 mo. Black cloth; lettering on cover and spine stamped in orange; orange top; 304 pp.

Dust wrapper illustration in color.
Description: Swordsman in hedged gardens.
The jacket picture by N. C. Wyeth is reproduced from a painting in the collection of Carl G. Fisher, so stated on the dust wrapper.

VENETIAN MASQUE / A Romance / By / Rafael Sabatini / [publisher's colophon] / Boston and New York / Houghton Mifflin Company / The Riverside Press Cambridge / 1934

8 vo. Black cloth; lettering on cover and spine stamped in orange; orange top; 323 pp.

Dust wrapper illustration in color.
Description: Marc Antoine drawing his sword. The architecture and canals of Venice dominate the background.

Verne, Jules

THE / MYSTERIOUS ISLAND / By / Jules Verne / Author of / Twenty Thousand Leagues Under / The Sea, The Lighthouse At The / End Of The World, Etc. / [publisher's colophon] / Grosset & Dunlap / Publishers — New York [date not established]

8 vo. Light brown cloth; pictorial design on cover stamped in green; lettering on cover and spine stamped in green; green top; 500 pp.

Dust wrapper illustration in color by N. C. Wyeth.

Description: The Discovery of the Chest.

Note: The illustration originally appeared in color in the book *The Mysterious Island* by Jules Verne, published by Charles Scribner's Sons, New York, 1918. It was titled The Discovery of the Chest.

Williams, Ben Ames

ALL THE BROTHERS / WERE VAL- IANT / By / Ben Ames Williams / New York / The Macmillan Company / 1919 / All rights reserved

Published May 1919, so stated on the copyright page.

12 mo. Maroon cloth; lettering and design on cover stamped in green; lettering on spine stamped in gold; 204 pp.

Dust wrapper illustration in tint by N. C. Wyeth.

Description: The battle upon the tumbling decks of the *Nathan Ross.*

Note: The illustration appeared simultaneously in *Everybody's Magazine*, May 1919, for the story "All the Brothers Were Valiant" by Ben Ames Williams.

AMATEURS / AT / WAR [title within flag design in red] / The American Soldier / In Action / Edited by / Ben Ames / Williams / [publisher's colophon] / Houghton Mifflin Company • Boston / The Riverside Press Cambridge / 1943

8 vo. Red cloth; lettering on cover and spine stamped in blue; 498 pp.

Dust wrapper illustration in color.

Description: Uncle Sam leading the American soldier, past and present, into battle.

Books Containing Illustrations Reprinted from Books and Periodicals

Adams, James Truslow

HISTORY / of / THE UNITED STATES / [ornament] / James Truslow Adams / Volume I / The Rise of the Union / [rule] / [publisher's colophon—blue] / [rule] / New York / Charles Scribner's Sons / MCMXXXIII

Of the Federal Edition of the History of the United States by James Truslow Adams only seven hundred and seventy sets have been printed and signed by the author—twenty sets are for presentation and seven hundred and fifty sets are for subscription
(Published in an edition of four volumes.)

Scribner code letter A on the copyright page.

Large 8 vo. Red cloth with white cloth spine; lettering stamped in gold over red leather label (on spine); gilt top; uncut; 306 pp; end-of-volume illustrations.

Boxed in slipcase (red) with cellophane wrapper.

Volume I

Illustrated with numerous paintings, drawings, engravings, photographs, etc.

One end-of-volume illustration in black and white by N. C. Wyeth.
Paul Revere

Note: The illustration originally appeared in color in *Poems of American Patriotism* chosen by Brander Matthews, published by Charles Scribner's Sons, New York, 1922.

HISTORY OF THE / UNITED STATES / By / James Truslow Adams / Volume I / The Rise of the Union / [ornamental decoration—blue] / New York / Charles Scribner's Sons / 1933 [title surrounded by ornamental decorations in blue]

Scribner code letter A on the copyright page.
The First Trade Edition. A four-volume set with a fifth loose-leaf volume for continual revision.

Large 8 vo. Blue cloth; pictorial decorations with rules on cover and spine stamped in gold; stamped rules with ornaments on cover; lettering on spine stamped in gold; 306 pp; end-of-volume illustrations.

Volume I. Same illustration as in the Federal Edition.

HISTORY / of / THE UNITED STATES / [ornament] / James Truslow Adams / Volume II / A Half-Century of Expansion / [rule] / [publisher's colophon—blue] / [rule] / New York / Charles Scribner's Sons / MCMXXXIII

Of the Federal Edition of the History of the United States by James Truslow Adams only seven hundred and seventy sets have been printed and signed by the author—twenty sets are for presentation and seven hundred and fifty sets are for subscription
Scribner code letter A on the copyright page.
Published in an edition of four volumes.

Large 8 vo. Red cloth with white cloth spine; lettering stamped in gold over red leather label (on spine); gilt top; uncut; 346 pp; end-of-volume illustrations.

Boxed in slipcase (red) with cellophane wrapper.

Volume II

Illustrated with numerous paintings, drawings, engravings, photographs, etc.

One end-of-volume illustration in black and white by N. C. Wyeth.
Pioneers—The Opening of the Prairies

Note: The illustration originally appeared as a frontispiece in color in *Scribner's Magazine*, January 1916.

HISTORY OF THE / UNITED STATES / By / James Truslow Adams / Volume II / A Half-Century of Expansion / [ornamental decoration—blue] / New York / Charles Scribner's Sons / 1933 [title surrounded by ornamental decorations in blue]

Scribner code letter A on the copyright page.
The First Trade Edition. A four-volume set with a fifth loose-leaf volume for continual revision.
Large 8 vo. Blue cloth; pictorial decorations with rules on cover and spine stamped in gold; stamped rules with ornaments on cover; lettering on spine stamped in gold; 346 pp; end-of-volume illustrations.

Volume II. Same illustrations as in the Federal Edition.

HISTORY / of / THE UNITED STATES / [ornament] / James Truslow Adams / Volume III / Civil War and Reconstruction / (rule) / [publisher's colophon—blue] / [rule] / New York / Charles Scribner's Sons / MCMXXXIII

Of the Federal Edition of the History of the United States of James Truslow Adams only seven hundred and seventy sets have been printed and signed by the author—twenty sets are for presentation and seven hundred and fifty sets are for subscription
(Published in an edition of four volumes.)

Scribner code letter A on the copyright page.

Large 8 vo. Red cloth with white cloth spine; lettering stamped in gold over red leather label (on spine); gilt top; uncut; 312 pp; end-of-volume illustrations.

Boxed in slipcase (red) with cellophane wrapper.

Volume III

Illustrated with numerous paintings, drawings, engravings, photographs, etc.

One end-of-volume illustration in black and white by N. C. Wyeth.
The Night Herder on Watch During the Round-Up

Note: The illustration originally appeared in *Scribner's Magazine*, March 1906, for the article "A Day with the Round-up" by N. C. Wyeth.

HISTORY OF THE / UNITED STATES / By / James Truslow Adams / Volume III / Civil War and Reconstruction / [ornamental decoration—blue] / New York / Charles Scribner's Sons / 1933 [title surrounded by ornamental decorations in blue]

Scribner code letter A on the copyright page.
The First Trade Edition. A four-volume set with a fifth loose-leaf volume for continual revision.
Large 8 vo. Blue cloth; pictorial decorations with rules on cover and spine stamped in gold; stamped rules with ornaments on cover; letter-

ing on spine stamped in gold; 312 pp; end-of-volume illustrations.

Volume III. Same illustrations as in the Federal Edition.

Adams, James Truslow, and
Vannest, Charles Garrett

THE RECORD OF / AMERICA / By / James Truslow Adams / Author of "The March of Democracy," "The Epic of America," / "America's Tragedy" / and Charles Garrett Vannest / [coauthor's credits] / [rule] / [decoration] / [rule] / Charles Scribner's Sons / New York (etc.)

Copyright 1935 by Charles Scribner's Sons.
Thick 8 vo. Blue cloth (simulated leather); lettering on cover and spine stamped in gold over red; 941 pp. (including index).
Illustrated with paintings, drawings, photographs, maps, etc.

Two illustrations by N. C. Wyeth. One in color and one in black and white.
The Pioneers—The Opening of the Prairies (color).[1] fp 580
Paul Revere's Ride (black and white).[2] p 97

[1] Originally appeared as a frontispiece in color in *Scribner's Magazine,* January 1916.
[2] Originally appeared in color in *Poems of American Patriotism,* edited by Brander Matthews, published by Charles Scribner's Sons, New York, 1922.

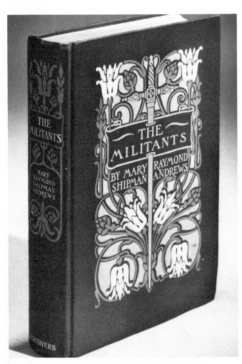

Andrews, Mary Raymond Shipman

THE MILITANTS / Stories of Some Parsons, Soldiers / and Other Fighters in the World / By / Mary Raymond Shipman Andrews / Illustrated / New York / Charles Scribner's Sons / 1907

Published May 1907, so stated on the copyright page.
12 mo. Dark green cloth; cover (with sword design) and spine stamped in gold over floral designs in colors; gilt top; 378 pp.; two pages of publisher's advertising.
Illustrated by N. C. Wyeth, A. I. Keller, etc.

Two illustrations in black and white by N. C. Wyeth.
"I took her in my arms and held her." (frontispiece)
"I got behind a turn and fired as a man came on alone." fp 214

Note: The illustrations originally appeared in color in *Scribner's Magazine,* February 1907, for the story "The Aide-de-Camp" by Mary Raymond Shipman Andrews.

Art Directors Club of Chicago

ADCC record / OF ADVERTISING ART / A record of the exhibition of Advertising Art / sponsored by the Art Directors Club of Chicago / and presented at the Chicago Art Institute / A. Kroch and Son • Publishers • Chicago • 1944

Copyright 1944 by A. Kroch & Son • Chicago.
Folio. Oatmeal cloth; lettering on cover over stamped bands in red and black; lettering on spine stamped in red and black; 258 pp. (including index of artists and advertisers); numerous pages of agencies and advertisers.
Illustrated with the works of numerous artists, photographers, and their exhibitors.

Two illustrations in color by N. C. Wyeth.
Harvest Home
  Minnesota Valley Canning Company
  Leo Burnett Company, Inc. p 24
From the land of Hiawatha
  Minnesota Valley Canning Company
  Leo Burnett Company, Inc. pp 60 & 61
Also shown is a reduced illustration of each advertisement in its final commercial form.

Art Directors Club of New York

ANNUAL / OF ADVERTISEMENT ART / In The / UNITED STATES / 1921 / A Catalogue for the First Annual Exhibition of / Advertising Paintings and Drawings / Held by the Art Directors Club / at the Galleries of the National Arts Club / New York, from March 2 to 31 / [club emblem] / Published for / The Art Directors Club by / Publishers Printing Company / New York

Copyright 1921 by The Art Directors Club, Inc., New York.
4 to. Gray boards with cloth spine (blue gray); club emblem stamped on cover in gold; lettering and date (1921) on cover and spine stamped in gold; 118 pp (plus index of artists and advertisers).
Illustrated with the works of numerous artists and their exhibitors.

Two illustrations in black and white by N. C. Wyeth.
Aunt Jemima Pancake Flour
  Loaned by the Aunt Jemima Mills Co.
  Exhibited by J. Walter Thompson Co. (plate 78). p 25
  Description: Gray Morn.
Aunt Jemima's Pancake Flour
  Loaned by the Aunt Jemima Mills Co.
  Exhibited by J. Walter Thompson Co. (plate 135). p 45
  Description: The Night the Emily Dunston Burned.

THE SECOND / ANNUAL OF / ILLUSTRATIONS / For / ADVERTISEMENTS / In The / UNITED STATES / Published By / The Art Directors Club / New York / Distributed By / The Book Service Company / 15 East 40th Street, New York

Copyright 1923 by The Art Directors Club, Inc., New York.
4 to. Brown boards with cloth spine (dark brown); club emblem on cover stamped in gold; lettering on cover and spine stamped in gold; 171 pp (including index of artists and advertisers).
Illustrated with the works of numerous artists and their exhibitors.

One illustration in black and white by N. C. Wyeth.
Beethoven and Nature
  Loaned and exhibited by Steinway & Sons
  Prepared by N. W. Ayer & Son. pp 51 & 145

Note: The illustration was painted for Steinway & Sons and used extensively in their advertising campaigns, and originally appeared in color in *The Steinway Collection* by James Huneker, published by Steinway & Sons, New York, 1919.

SIXTH ANNUAL OF / ADVERTISING ART / From advertisements shown at the / Exhibition of the Art Directors Club, / Art Center, New York, May 4 to 31 / [club emblem] / 1927 / The Annual is published for the Art Directors Club of New York / By The Book Service Company, 15 E. 40th Street, New York

Copyright, December 1927, by Art Directors Club, Inc.
4 to. Blue cloth; lettering on cover (with ornaments) and spine stamped in gold; 152 pp (plus index of artists and advertisers).
Illustrated with the works of numerous artists and their exhibitors.

One illustration in black and white by N. C. Wyeth.
The Widened Vision
  Loaned and exhibited by N. W. Ayer & Son. pp 34 & 121

Note: The advertisement appeared in *The Saturday Evening Post,* March 6, 1926.

SEVENTH ANNUAL / OF / ADVERTISING ART / From advertisements shown at the / Exhibition of the Art Directors Club, / Art Center, New York, May 5 to 19 / [club emblem] / 1928 / The Annual is published for the Art Directors Club of New York / By The Book Service Company, 15 E. 40th Street, New York

Copyright, November 1928, by the Art Directors Club, Inc.
4 to. Black cloth; lettering and rules on cover stamped in gold; lettering on spine stamped in gold; 136 pp (plus advertising and index).
Illustrated with the works of numerous artists and their exhibitors.

Two illustrations by N. C. Wyeth. One in color and one in black and white.
Christmas in Old Virginia (color)
  Loaned and exhibited by Interwoven Stocking Co. pp 56 & 57
The King's Henchman (black and white)
  Loaned by Steinway & Sons and exhibited by N. W. Ayer & Son. pp 23 & 130

EIGHTH ANNUAL OF / ADVERTISING ART / From Advertisements Shown At the Exhibition of the Art Directors Club, Art Center, New York, May 4 to 29 / [club emblem] / 1929 / The Annual is published for the Art Directors Club of New York / by The Book Service Company, 15 East 40th Street, New York

Copyright, November 1929, by Art Directors Club, Inc.

4 to. Black cloth; lettering on cover (with ornaments) and spine stamped in gold; 134 pp (plus index of artists and advertisers).

Illustrated with the works of numerous artists and their advertisers.

Photograph (opposite Foreword)
Description: At the end of one exhibition gallery hangs the original painting, The Christmas Ship In Old New York.

One illustration in color by N. C. Wyeth.
The Christmas Ship In Old New York
Interwoven Stocking Company (double page illustration). pp 52 & 53

TWENTY-SECOND ANNUAL OF / AD-Vertising / ART / [rule] / Reproductions from the Exhibition / of the Art Directors Club of New York / at the Public Library, Spring 1943

4 to. Brown cloth; number (22) and decorations on cover stamped in black and white; lettering on spine stamped in black; 192 pp (plus studio advertisements, index of artists and advertisers).

Illustrated with the works of numerous artists, photographers, and their exhibitors.

One illustration in black and white by N. C. Wyeth.
From the land of Hiawatha
Minnesota Valley Canning Company
Leo Burnett Company, Inc. pp 126 & 127

24 / ANNUAL OF ADVERTISING ART / Reproductions from the National Exhibition of Advertising Art Shown at Rockefeller Center Galleries in the Spring of Nineteen Hundred and Forty-Five, by the Art Directors Club of New York

Copyright 1945 by the Art Directors Club of New York.

4 to. Reddish brown cloth; number (24) and lettering on cover and spine stamped in black; 314 pp (plus studio advertisements, index of artists and advertisers).

Illustrated with the works of numerous artists, photographers, and their exhibitors.

One illustration in black and white by N. C. Wyeth.
Have a "Coke" = How are things goin? . . . or being friendly in Newfoundland
The Coca-Cola Co.
D'Arcy Advertising Co., Inc. (number 29). p 22

Atwood, Wallace W.

The Earth and its People • Book One / HOME LIFE / IN / FAR-AWAY LANDS / By / Wallace W. Atwood / and / Helen Goss Thomas / with the collaboration of / Isabelle K. Hart / [decoration] / Ginn and Company / Boston • New York • Chicago • London / Atlanta • Dallas • Columbus • San Francisco [title surrounded by decorative boxed rules]

Copyright 1929 by Wallace W. Atwood and Helen Goss Thomas.

4 to. Orange cloth; pictorial design on cover in black; lettering on cover and spine in black; 252 pp (including index).

Illustrated with numerous paintings, photographs, maps, etc.

Frontispiece illustration in color by N. C. Wyeth.
Leaving Port in a Distant Land

Note: This mural painting originally appeared in color in the Ladies' Home Journal, August 1925.

Barnard, Eunice Fuller, and
Tall, Lida Lee

HOW THE OLD WORLD / FOUND THE NEW / By / Eunice Fuller Barnard / and / Lida Lee Tall / [two lines of authors' credits] / Under the Editorship of / J. Montgomery Gambrill / [two lines of editor's credits] / [pictorial decoration—sailing ship] / Ginn & Company / Boston, New York, Chicago, London / Atlanta, Dallas, Columbus, San Francisco

Copyright 1929 by Eunice Fuller Barnard, Lida Lee Tall, and J. Montgomery Gambrill.
8 vo. Light blue cloth; pictorial design (sailing ship and globe) on cover stamped in dark blue; lettering on cover and spine stamped in dark blue; 251 pp.
Illustrated with numerous paintings, photographs, maps, etc.

Frontispiece illustration in color by N. C. Wyeth.
Henry Hudson's Ship, the Half-Moon
(Courtesy of the Hotel Roosevelt, New York)

Barton, Bruce

THE MAN / NOBODY KNOWS / A Discovery of the Real Jesus / By / Bruce Barton / Author of / What Shall It Profit a Man / With frontispiece in color / By N. C. Wyeth / Indianapolis / The Bobbs-Merrill Company / Publishers [title enclosed in orange rules]

Copyright 1925 by The Bobbs-Merrill Company.

Square 8 vo. Blue cloth; lettering on cover and spine stamped in gold (enclosed by ornamental designs); 220 pp.

Frontispiece illustration in color.
The Boy Jesus (Repeated as a label on the dust wrapper.)

Note: The illustration originally appeared in color in the Woman's Home Companion, December 1924, for the story "The Man Nobody Knows" by Bruce Barton.

Beard, Charles A., and Beard, Mary R.

A BASIC HISTORY / of the / UNITED STATES / By Charles A. Beard / and / Mary R. Beard / [design] / Doubleday, Doran & Company / New York, 1944 [title and authors surrounded by boxed rules]

8 vo. Light brown cloth; lettering on cover stamped in brown; small design stamped in brown on spine; lettering on spine stamped in gold over brown; brown top; 554 pp (including index, etc.).
Illustrated with numerous paintings by noted American artists.

Two illustrations in black and white by N. C. Wyeth. Reproduced through the courtesy of the Pennsylvania Railroad.
Descriptions:
Ring Out For Liberty (July 4, 1776)
Building the "President's House."

Note: The illustrations were first published (with two others) as posters in color for the Pennsylvania Railroad.

Blanchard, Ferdinand Q.

HOW ONE MAN / CHANGED THE WORLD / A Story Told for Boys and Girls / with Questions and Topics / for Study / Ferdinand Q. Blanchard / [publisher's colophon] / The Pilgrim Press / Boston Chicago

Copyright 1928, (1935) by Sidney A. Weston.

Thin 8 vo. Orange boards; pictorial design on cover and spine printed in black; lettering on cover and spine printed in black; 119 pp.

Frontispiece illustration in black and white.
The Boy Christ in the Carpenter's Shop

Note: The illustration originally appeared in color in the Woman's Home Companion, December 1924, for the story "The Man Nobody Knows" by Bruce Barton.

Bonte, George Willard

AMERICA MARCHES PAST / A Pictorial Review of America / Through the Years / by / George Willard Bonte / with the editorial assistance of / Samuel E. Forman / [coauthor's credits] / [publisher's colophon] / D. Appleton-Century Company / Incorporated / New York 1936 London [surrounded by boxed rules]

4 to. Dark blue cloth; cover design (eagle) and lettering on spine stamped in silver; 196 pp (including index).
Illustrated with numerous paintings, engravings, photographs, etc.

One illustration in black and white by N. C. Wyeth.
Johan Printz, Governor of Delaware in 1643. p 43

Note: The illustration originally appeared as a frontispiece in color in The Dutch and Swedes on the Delaware 1609–64 by Christopher Ward, published by the University of Pennsylvania Press, Phila., 1930.

THE BOYS' / BOOK OF BATTLES / With Illustrations From Famous Paintings / [publisher's colophon] / Boston and New York / Houghton Mifflin Company / The Riverside Press Cambridge / 1914

Published October 1914, so stated on the copyright page.

Thick 8 vo. Red cloth; cover label in color; lettering on cover in black; lettering on spine stamped in gold; 410 pp.
Illustrated from famous paintings, etc.

Cover label illustration in color by N. C. Wyeth.
Description: The Bloody Angle

Note: The illustration originally appeared in color in Cease Firing by Mary Johnston, published by Houghton Mifflin Company, Boston, November 1912.

Briggs, Thomas H.

WAYS TO / BETTER ENGLISH / Enlarged Course / By / Thomas H. Briggs / Teachers College, Columbia University / and Isabel McKinney / Eastern Illinois State Teachers College / [publisher's colophon] / Ginn & Company / Boston, New

York, Chicago, London / Atlanta, Dallas, Columbus, San Francisco / 1924

8 vo. Blue cloth; lettering on cover and spine stamped in dark blue; 416 pp.
Illustrated with numerous paintings, photographs, etc.

Frontispiece illustration in color by N. C. Wyeth.
The Departure of the Mayflower

Note: The illustration originally appeared in color in the book *The Courtship of Miles Standish* by Henry Wadsworth Longfellow, published by Houghton Mifflin Company, 1920.

Burt, Maxwell Struthers

CHANCE / ENCOUNTERS / By Maxwell Struthers Burt / Author of "John O'May and Other Stories" / With a Frontispiece by / N. C. Wyeth / New York / Charles Scribner's Sons / 1921

12 mo. Dark Blue cloth; lettering on cover and spine stamped in light blue; 287 pp.

Frontispiece illustration in black and white.
"My first sight of Mr. Piece was impressive."

Note: The illustration originally appeared in *Scribner's Magazine*, April, 1920, for the story "Devilled Sweetbreads" by Maxwell Struthers Burt.

Canby, Henry Seidel

THOREAU / By Henry Seidel Canby / With Illustrations / [publisher's colophon] [red] / Boston / Houghton Mifflin Company / The Riverside Press Cambridge / 1939 [title also printed in red]

8 vo. Red cloth; lettering on cover and spine stamped in gold over black (surrounded by boxed rules stamped in gold); yellow top; 508 pp.
Illustrated from early photographs, drawings, etc.

One illustration in black and white by N. C. Wyeth. Repeated in color on the dust wrapper.
Snow fields of Concord. fp 310

Idem: Except for a different dust wrapper.

Note: The illustration originally appeared as endpapers in color for the book *Men of Concord*, edited by Francis H. Allen, published by Houghton Mifflin Company, Boston, 1936.

CHATTERBOX / For 1929 / Founded by J. Erskine Clarke, M.A. / London: Published for the proprietors by / Wells Gardner, Darton & Co. Ltd. / 3 & 4 Paternoster Buildings

Printed in Great Britain—Athenaeum Printing Works—Red Hill—Surrey, so stated on the copyright page.
Large 8 vo. Red morocco; ornamental designs stamped on cover in black; lettering and date (1929) on cover stamped in black over gold inset; lettering on spine stamped in black; 321 pp (including index).
Illustrated with numerous drawings, etc.

Cover label illustration in color by N. C. Wyeth.
Description: Eseldorf was a paradise for us boys.

Note: The illustration originally appeared as a frontispiece in color in *Harper's Monthly Magazine*, May 1916, for the story "The Mysterious Stranger" by Mark Twain.

Clark, Marion G.

WESTWARD / TO THE PACIFIC / By / Marion G. Clark / [author's credits] / Charles Scribner's Sons / New York Chicago Boston Atlanta / San Francisco Dallas

Copyright (various dates) (1935) by Charles Scribner's Sons.
Scribner code letter A on the copyright page.
12 mo. Orange cloth: lettering and rules on cover and spine stamped in black; 514 pp (including index).
Illustrated with paintings, photographs, maps, etc.

One illustration in black and white by N. C. Wyeth.
The Flight Across the Lake. p 299

Note: The illustration originally appeared in color in *The Last of the Mohicans* by James Fenimore Cooper, published by Charles Scribner's Sons, New York, 1919.

Clark, William H.

The American Cavalcade Series / FARMS / AND / FARMERS / The Story of American Agriculture / [drawing] / William·H· Clark / Author of / "Ships and Sailors" and "Railroads and Rivers" / Illustrated from Photographs and Old Prints / L. C. Page & Company (Inc.) / Boston—Publishers

Copyright 1945 by L. C. Page & Company.
8 vo. Green cloth; lettering on cover and spine (with design) stamped in gold; 346 pp. (including index, etc.)
Illustrated by N. C. Wyeth (frontispiece) plus numerous photographs and old prints.

Frontispiece illustration in black and white with tint by N. C. Wyeth.
McCormick's Reaper
This reaper, first publicly demonstrated in July 1831, marked the beginning of the emancipation of the American farmer.

Note: The illustration was painted for the 100th Anniversary of International Harvester Company (1831–1931) and appeared in color in leading periodicals during the year 1931.

Cody, Colonel W. F.

AN AUTOBIOGRAPHY OF / BUFFALO BILL / (Colonel W. F. Cody) / Illustrated by / N. C. Wyeth / [publisher's colophon] / New York / Cosmopolitan Book Corporation / 1920

8 vo. Brown cloth; pictorial design by N. C. Wyeth on cover stamped in red and black; lettering on cover and spine stamped in black; 328 pp.
Photograph of Buffalo Bill (frontispiece).

Cover design is repeated on the dust wrapper (front and back) in colors.
Seven illustrations in black and white.
He Shoved a Pistol in the Man's Face and Said: "I'm Calling the Hand That's in Your Hat." fp 54
Chief Santanta Passed the Peace-Pipe to General Sherman and Said: "My Great White Brothers." fp 86
Winning My Name—"Buffalo Bill." fp 124
It Was No Time for Argument. I Fired and Killed Him. fp 174
Pursued by Fifteen Bloodthirsty Indians, I Had a Running Fight of Eleven Miles. fp 208
A Shower of Arrows Rained on Our Dead Horses from the Closing Circle of Red-Men. fp 282
Stage-Coach Driving Was Full of Hair-Raising Adventures. fp 322

Note: The illustrations originally appeared in *Hearst's Magazine*, August thru December 1916, for the story *The Great West That Was* by Col. William F. Cody. In addition, they appeared in colors in the publication of the same title, published by The Star Company, New York, 1916.

The Collier Classics

PRIZE STORIES from COLLIER'S / [rule] / Selected by / Henry Cabot Lodge • Theodore Roosevelt / Walter H. Page • William Allen White / Ida M. Tarbell • Mark Sullivan / [rule] / [publisher's colophon] / Volume One / [rule] / The Collier Classics / [rule]

Copyright 1916 by P. F. Collier & Son.
12 mo. Cloth. 381 pp.

Frontispiece illustration in brown, black and white.
Slowly and Thoughtfully, Absolutely Without Bravado, Drift Shuffled the Cards.

Note: The illustration originally appeared in *Collier's Weekly*, April 24, 1915, for the story "Anent A Biscuit Shooter" by Francis Hill.

Connolly, James Brendan

THE / CRESTED SEAS / By / James Brendan Connolly / Author of "Out of Gloucester," "The Seiners," "The Deep Sea's Toll," Etc. / With Illustrations / Charles Scribner's Sons / New York:::::1907 [title enclosed in double box rules]

Published September 1907, so stated on the copyright page.
12 mo. Green cloth; pictorial designs on cover and spine in colors; lettering on cover and spine stamped in gold; gilt top; 311 pp.; four pages of publisher's advertising.
Illustrated by N. C. Wyeth, W. J. Aylward, C. W. Ashley, and George Harding.

Two illustrations in black and white by N. C. Wyeth.
"There was no such monstrous lock as that last night, Ollie?"[1] fp 174
"Twas me that stowed them in the dory." fp 182

Note: The illustrations originally appeared in *Scribner's Magazine*, April 1907, for the story "The Smugglers" by James B. Connolly.
[1] The illustration was published as a print by Charles Scribner's Sons, New York, 1907.

WIDE COURSES / [rule] / By / James Brendan Connolly / Author of "Out of Gloucester," "The Seiners," "The / Deep Sea's Toll," "The Crested Seas," "An Olympic / Victor," "Open Water," Etc. / With Illustrations / [rule] / Charles Scribner's Sons / New York:::::1912 [title enclosed in double box rules]

Published April 1912, so stated on the copyright page.
12 mo. Gray green cloth; pictorial design (figure with telescope after Wyeth) on cover stamped in colors; circular design on spine stamped in colors; lettering on cover and spine stamped in gold; uncut; 336 pp.; four pages of publisher's advertising.
Illustrated by N. C. Wyeth, Howard Pyle, Gordon McCouch, F. C. Yohn, etc.

Two illustrations in black and white by N. C. Wyeth.

> After a long look I saw that he did not resume his narrative. By that I knew that the stranger was troubling him. fp 154
>
> There she was, the Dancing Bess, holding a taut bowline to the eastward. And there were the two frigates, but they might as well have been chasing a star. fp 168

Note: The illustrations originally appeared in *Scribner's Magazine*, August 1911, for the story "Captain Blaise" by James B. Connolly.

HEAD WINDS / By / James B. Connolly / Illustrated / Charles Scribner's Sons / New York::::::1916 [title enclosed in double box rules]

Published September 1916, so stated on the copyright page.

12 mo. Green cloth; lettering on cover and spine stamped in gold; uncut; 299 pp.; four pages of publisher's advertising.

Illustrated by N. C. Wyeth, Frank E. Schoonover, and F. C. Yohn.

Two illustrations in black and white by N. C. Wyeth.

> An imaginative boy, with great dreams in his head. fp 38
>
> Without a word he began to shoot. fp 50

Note: The illustrations originally appeared in color in *Scribner's Magazine*, August 1916, for the story "Chavero" by James B. Connolly.

RUNNING FREE / By James B. Connolly / With Illustrations / Charles Scribner's Sons / New York:::::1917 [title enclosed in double box rules]

Published September 1917, so stated on the copyright page.

12 mo. Green cloth; lettering on cover and spine stamped in gold; uncut; 302 pp.; four pages of publisher's advertising.

Illustrated by N. C. Wyeth, F. C. Yohn, and W. J. Enright.

Two illustrations in black and white by N. C. Wyeth.

> "An' the bridal couple'd be holdin' hands an' gazin' over the spanker-boom at the full moon." (frontispiece)
>
> "'Quiscamo vascamo mirajjar,' which is Yunzano for 'I am satisfied, I can now die happy.'" fp 242

Note: The illustrations originally appeared in *Scribner's Magazine*, December 1915, for the story "The Medicine Ship" by James B. Connolly.

HIKER JOY / By / James B. Connolly / With Illustrations By / N. C. Wyeth / New York / Charles Scribner's Sons / 1920 [title enclosed in double box rules]

Published May 1920, so stated on the copyright page.

12 mo. Red cloth; cover and spine stamped in gold; uncut; 244 pp.

Four illustrations in black and white.

> "Couldn't he write about common people—about cops and bums and sailors and crooks and places where reg'lar people lived?" (frontispiece)
>
> All this time Bill and the other guy are dodging and sidestepping. fp 50
>
> "I know what you're thinking of, old General," says Lefty. "Your dream it was to go —when it come your time to go—" fp 116
>
> The ocean just sort o' breathing in on the

sand—Bill'n' me sit here and count the breaths like. fp 240

Note: The illustrations originally appeared in *Collier's Weekly* for the issues of June 28, July 5, July 26, and August 16, 1919.

TIDE RIPS / By / James B. Connolly / With Illustrations / New York / Charles Scribner's Sons / 1922

Published March 1922, so stated on the copyright page.

12 mo. Blue gray cloth; lettering on cover and spine stamped in dark blue; uncut; 246 pp.

Illustrated by N. C. Wyeth and others.

Two illustrations in black and white by N. C. Wyeth.

> "Takes one swing'f his battle-ax 'n' up flies the cover' 'n' there's a dragon black as ink with one eye." (frontispiece)
>
> "The pirates, seein' how it was, puts off in boats." fp 208

Note: The illustrations originally appeared in color in *Scribner's Magazine*, August 1914, for the story "The Rakish Brigantine" by James B. Connolly.

Davis, Charles Belmont

THE / LODGER OVERHEAD / AND OTHERS / By / Charles Belmont Davis / Author Of "The Stage Door," Etc. / Illustrated / New York / Charles Scribner's Sons / 1909 [title enclosed in and surrounded by boxed rules]

Published April 1909, so stated on the copyright page.

12 mo. Green cloth; pictorial designs (candelabra and staircase) on cover stamped in gold and dark green; decoration on spine stamped in dark green; lettering on spine stamped in gold; 370 pp.; one page of publisher's advertising.

Illustrated by N. C. Wyeth, A. I. Keller, James Montgomery Flagg, etc.

Two illustrations in black and white by N. C. Wyeth.

> He glanced furtively at the faces of the four men about him. fp 134
>
> "And I cursed the men who grinned at me across the table." fp 138

Note: The illustrations originally appeared in black and white in *Scribner's Magazine*, for the story "Tommy" by Charles Belmont Davis, December 1904.

Doyle, Arthur Conan

THE LAST GALLEY / Impressions and Tales / By / Arthur Conan Doyle / With Illustrations / [publisher's colophon] / Garden City New York / Doubleday, Page & Company / 1911

12 mo. Red cloth; pictorial designs on cover and spine stamped in colors; lettering on cover and spine stamped in black; 321 pp.

Frontispiece illustration in color by N. C. Wyeth.

> All day held spell bound by this wonderful sight, the hermit crouched in the shadow of the rocks.

Note: The frontispiece illustration originally appeared in color in *Scribner's Magazine*, November 1910, for the tale "The Coming of the Huns" (Through the Mists), Part I by Arthur Conan Doyle.

Faris, John T.

REAL STORIES OF THE / GEOGRAPHY MAKERS / By / John T. Faris / [author's credits] / [publisher's colophon] / Ginn and Company / Boston • New York • Chicago • London / Atlanta • Dallas • Columbus • San Francisco

Copyright 1925 by John T. Faris.

Publisher's code number 630.11, so stated on the copyright page.

12 mo. Blue cloth; pictorial designs on cover and spine stamped in black; lettering on cover and spine stamped in black; 332 pp (including index).

Illustrated with numerous paintings, photographs, maps, etc.

One illustration in black and white by N. C. Wyeth.
Landing of Columbus. p 72

Note: The illustration originally appeared as a frontispiece in color in the book *Essentials of American History* by Thomas Bonaventure Lawler, published by Ginn & Company, Boston, 1918.

Flader, Louis (Compiled & Edited by)

ACHIEVEMENT / IN / PHOTO-ENGRAVING / and / LETTER-PRESS / PRINTING / • / 1927 / • / Compiled and Edited By Louis Flader / Published By The / American Photo-Engravers Association / Chicago, Illinois

Copyrighted 1927 by the American Photo-Engravers Association.

Thick folio. Dark blue morocco stamped with pictorial design (Eagle with banner in red and yellow) and stamped corners (ornamental hinges); spine stamped with ornamental designs; lettering on spine stamped in gold; gilt top; 488 pp (including Index to Contents).

Illustrated in color and black and white with numerous paintings, drawings, advertising illustrations, sculpture, architectural designs, photographs, etc.

Insert of twelve pages designed, engraved and printed by the Powers Reproduction Corporation, New York City (pages A–L).

One illustration in color by N. C. Wyeth.
Illustration from "*Michael Strogoff*" p F

> Description: Marfa, seized by two soldiers, was forced on her knees on the ground.

Note: The illustration originally appeared in color in the book *Michael Strogoff* by Jules Verne, published by Charles Scribner's Sons, N. Y., 1927.

Forester, C. S.

COMMODORE / HORNBLOWER / By / C. S. Forester / [publisher's colophon] / Boston / Little, Brown and Company / 1946 [surrounded by ornamental boxed rules]

12 mo. Blue green cloth; lettering on spine stamped in gold; 384 pp.

Frontispiece illustration in pen and ink.

> Description: A ship of the line in full sail. (Repeated on the dust wrapper.)

Note: This book is one of a four-volume set. The pen-and-ink illustrations in the remaining three books originally appeared in *Captain Horatio Hornblower* by C. S. Forester. (Both the single book and three-volume set.)

Freeland, George Earl; Walker, Edward Everett; and Williams, Helen Esther

The New Frontier Social Science Series / [rule] / AMERICA'S BUILDING / The Makers of Our Flag / George Earl Freeland / [author's published titles] / Edward Everett Walker / [author's published titles] / and / Helen Esther Williams / [author's credits] / Charles Scribner's Sons / New York Chicago Boston Atlanta / San Francisco Dallas

Copyright 1937 by Charles Scribner's Sons.
8 vo. Orange cloth; pictorial designs on cover and spine stamped in red; lettering on cover and spine stamped in black; 425 pp (including index).
Illustrated with numerous paintings, drawings, photographs, maps, etc.

Eight illustrations by N. C. Wyeth. One in color and seven in black and white.

Paul Revere's Ride.[1] p 81
Washington at Valley Forge (color).[1] fp 84
Nathan Hale.[1] p 99
John Paul Jones.[1] p 99
Treasure Island.[1] p 180
The Flight Across the Lake.[1] p 184
The Trial of McCormick's Reaper, At Steele's Tavern, Virginia, in July 1831.[2] p 223
Armed stagecoach carriers of the mail.[3] p 368

[1] The illustrations originally appeared in Scribner publications and are reproduced from the following books: *Poems of American Patriotism, Treasure Island, The Last of the Mohicans.*
[2] Painted for International Harvester Company to commemorate the 100th anniversary of the invention of the McCormick reaper.
[3] The illustration originally appeared in *Scribner's Magazine*, August 1910, and was titled "The Pay-stage."

Frye, Alexis Everett

First Steps In Geography / THE BROOK-LET'S STORY / A New Edition Of / Brooks And Brook Basins / By / Alexis Everett Frye / Come forth into the light of things; / Let Nature be your teacher. / William Wordsworth / Ginn And Company / Boston • New York • Chicago • London / Atlanta • Dallas • Columbus • San Francisco

Copyright 1927 by Ginn & Company.
12 mo. Brown cloth; pictorial cover design (woodland brook) stamped in dark brown and yellow; lettering on cover and spine stamped in dark brown; 189 pp.
Illustrated with paintings and drawings.

Frontispiece illustration (painting) in color by N. C. Wyeth.
The Meadow Brook

Note: The illustration originally appeared in black and white in *The American Art Student*, November-December 1916 for the article, "The Illustrator And His Development" by N. C. Wyeth.

Gabriel, Ralph Henry (Editor)

The Pageant Of America / [ornament] / THE LURE OF / THE FRONTIER / A Story Of Race Conflict / By / Ralph Henry Gabriel / [publisher's design] / New Haven • Yale University Press / Toronto • Glasgow, Brook & Co. / London • Humphrey Milford / Oxford University Press / 1929 [second, third and seventh lines in red]

Washington Edition • Volume II (Published in fifteen volumes.)

4 to. Half morocco with corners; ornamental designs on spine stamped in gold; lettering on spine stamped in gold; gilt top; 309 pp.; notes on the pictures (311–12); index (313–27).
Illustrated with numerous paintings, engravings, photographs, maps, etc.
Frontispiece illustration in color by N. C. Wyeth.
The Pathfinder

Note: The illustration originally appeared as a frontispiece in color in *Scribner's Magazine*, January 1916, under the title of The Opening of the Prairies.

The Pageant Of America / [ornament] / THE LURE OF / THE FRONTIER / A Story Of Race Conflict / By / Ralph Henry Gabriel / [publisher's design] / New Haven • Yale University Press / Toronto • Glasgow, Brook & Co. / London • Humphrey Milford / Oxford University Press / 1929 [second, third and seventh lines in red]

Independence Edition • Volume II (Published in fifteen volumes.)

4 to. Dark brown simulated leather; pictorial designs on cover embossed in gold; lettering on spine stamped in gold; gilt top; 309 pp.; notes on the pictures (311–12); index (313–27).
Illustrations are the same as those in the Washington Edition.

The Pageant Of America / [ornament] / THE LURE OF / THE FRONTIER / A Story of Race Conflict / By / Ralph Henry Gabriel / [publisher's design] / New Haven • Yale University Press / Toronto • Glasgow, Brook & Co. / London • Humphrey Milford / Oxford University Press / 1929 [second, third and seventh lines in red]

Independence Edition • Volume II (Published in fifteen volumes.)

4 to. Blue cloth; pictorial design (Liberty) on cover stamped in gold; ornamental designs and rules on spine stamped in gold; lettering on cover stamped in gold; 309 pp.; notes on the pictures (311–12); index (313–27).
Illustrations are the same as in the Washington Edition.

Goss, Madeleine

BEETHOVEN / MASTER MUSICIAN / By / Madeleine Goss / [pictorial decoration] / Illustrated With / Reproductions of Paintings / and Photographs / Doubleday, Doran & Company, Inc. / Garden City 1931 New York [title enclosed in box rules]

12 mo. Purple cloth; lettering on cover and spine stamped in yellow; yellow top; uncut; 290 pp.
Illustrated with paintings, photographs, etc.

Frontispiece illustration in color by N. C. Wyeth.
Ludwig Van Beethoven

Note: The illustration was painted for Steinway & Sons and used extensively in their advertising campaigns. The painting originally appeared in color in *The Steinway Collection* by James Huneker, published by Steinway & Sons, New York, 1919.

Grinnell, George Bird

BLACKFEET / INDIAN STORIES / By / George Bird Grinnell / Author of / "Blackfeet Lodge Tales," "Trails of the Pathfinders," etc. / New York / Charles Scribner's Sons / 1913

Published September 1913, so stated on the copyright page.
12 mo. Olive green cloth; cover label in color; lettering on cover and spine stamped in white; 214 pp.

Two illustrations in color. The cover label illustration is repeated on the dust wrapper.
Cold Maker (frontispiece)
Cover label.
    Description: Woodland Indian playing flute.

Note: The illustrations originally appeared in color in *Scribner's Magazine*, December 1909, for "The Moods" by George T. Marsh and were titled Winter and Spring.

Hough, Emerson

HEART'S / DESIRE / The Story of a Contended Town / Certain Peculiar Citizens / and Two Fortunate Lovers / A Novel by Emerson Hough / Author of The Mississippi Bubble • • • • The Law of / The Land • • • • The Girl at the Half Way House Etc / Illustrated / The Macmillan Company / [ornament] New York MCMV [ornament] / London: Macmillan & Co., Ltd. [Title enclosed in box rules.]

Published October 1905, so stated on the copyright page.
12 mo. Yellow tan cloth; pictorial design on cover stamped in colors; design on spine stamped in colors; lettering on cover stamped in reddish brown; lettering on spine stamped in gold; gilt top; 367 pp.; two pages of publisher's advertising.
Illustrated by N. C. Wyeth, Howard Giles, F. B. Masters, etc.

One illustration in black and white by N. C. Wyeth.
> "And just whangs old Pinto over the head with it . . . To show him there ain't no coldness." fp 218

Note: This illustration originally appeared in *The Saturday Evening Post,* October 1, 1904 for the story "Science at Heart's Desire" by Emerson Hough.

Judge (magazine)

GEMS / from / JUDGE / [ornament] / Humor, Wit And Satire / From The World's Keenest / Wits. Pictures By Amer- / ica's Cleverest Artists / And Cartoonists. Prose, / Verse, Epigram And Jingle / [ornament] The Leading Anthology / Of Fun and Humor / Judge [ornament] New York / Copyright 1922 [surrounded by box rules in orange]

4 to. Red cloth; pictorial label on cover in color; lettering (with words, Captain Kid) on cover stamped in gold.

Frontispiece illustration in color by N. C. Wyeth.
> "Your legs are all right if they are long enough to reach the ground."

Note: The illustration originally appeared as a cover in color for *Judge* magazine, February 11, 1922.

Kupper, Winifred

Winifred Kupper / [rule] / THE GOLDEN HOOF / The Story of the Sheep of the Southwest / [rule] / [publisher's colophon] / [rule] / New York: Alfred•A•Knopf / 1945

FIRST EDITION, so stated on the copyright page.
Thin 8 vo. Reddish brown cloth; decorations on spine in brown; lettering on spine stamped in gold; printed on yellow paper; dark gray top; 203 pp.

Frontispiece illustration in black and white with tint.
> Description: A Sheep-herder.

Note: The illustration originally appeared in *Scribner's Magazine,* January 1909, for the story "A Sheep-Herder of the South-West" by N. C. Wyeth, and was titled "The Plains Herder."

Landis, Frederick

THE ANGEL OF / LONESOME HILL / A Story of a President / By Frederick Landis / Author of "The Glory of His Country" / [double rules] / New York / Charles Scribner's Sons / 1910

Published April 1910, so stated on the copyright page.
Thin 12 mo. Gray boards; brown cloth backstrip; lettering on cover in brown; drawing (Theodore Roosevelt) on cover printed in brown; 40 pp.

Frontispiece illustration in black and white.
> Those who passed by night were grateful for the lamp.

Note: The frontispiece illustration originally appeared in *Scribner's Magazine,* March 1910, for the story "The Angel of Lonesome Hill" by Frederick Landis.

Langdon, William Chauncy

EVERYDAY THINGS / IN / AMERICAN LIFE / 1607–1776 / By / William Chauncy

Langdon / [drawing] / Charles Scribner's Sons • New York / Charles Scribner's Sons • Ltd • London / 1937

Scribner code letter A on the copyright page.
Large 8 vo. Light red cloth; lettering on cover and spine stamped in dark blue; small design on spine stamped in dark blue; blue top; 334 pp.
Illustrated by N. C. Wyeth, Stanley Arthurs (frontispiece in color, etc.), and with numerous drawings, engravings, and photographs.

Five illustrations in black and white by N. C. Wyeth.
> On horseback with his few belongings on pack-saddles the settler invaded the western slope of the Alleghenies. (pen-and-ink drawing). fp 115
> A settler listens to the warning of a friendly Indian. fp 118
> Colonial forces recruited from the people of the mountain regions. fp 119
> Study on the frontier by light from the open fireplace. (pen-and-ink drawing). fp 121
> Many Southern planters located on banks or bays to insure easy transportation for their crops. (pen-and-ink drawing). fp 244

Note: The illustrations originally appeared in *Drums* by James Boyd, published by Charles Scribner's Sons, New York, 1928.

Law, Frederick Houk

MODERN PLAYS / Short And Long / By / Frederick Houk Law, Ph.D. [author's credits] / [publisher's colophon] / New York & London / The Century Co. / 1924

Thick 12 mo. Maroon cloth; publisher's colophon stamped on cover; lettering on spine stamped in gold; 429 pp.
Illustrated with a painting, a drawing, and photographs.
One illustration in black and white by N. C. Wyeth.
> In his hand was a great fat roll, and he was eating it! fp 90

Note: The illustration originally appeared as a frontispiece in color in *The Pictorial Life of Benjamin Franklin,* published by Dill & Collins Co., Philadelphia, 1923.

Lawler, Thomas Bonaventure

[rule] / BUILDERS OF AMERICA / Revised Edition / [rule] / By Thomas Bonaventure Lawler / Author of / Standard History of America / Essentials of American History / Primary History of the United States / Elementary History of the United States / Gateway to American History / Historia General del Mundo / [publisher's colophon] / Ginn and Company / Boston • New York • Chicago • London / Atlanta • Dallas • Columbus • San Francisco / [rule]

Copyright 1927, 1936 by Thomas Bonaventure Lawler.
12 mo. Brown cloth; cover designs in colors; lettering on cover and spine stamped in black; 371 pp (including index).
Illustrated with numerous paintings, drawings, photographs, maps, etc.

One illustration in black and white by N. C. Wyeth.
> Washington Taking Command of the Army at Cambridge. p 195

Note: The illustration originally appeared as the frontispiece in color in the book *America* by William J. Long, published by Ginn and Company, Boston, 1923.

[broken rule] / STANDARD HISTORY / OF AMERICA / [rule] / By THOMAS BONAVENTURE LAWLER / [six lines of author's credits] / [biblical quote] / [publisher's colophon] / GINN AND COMPANY / Boston • New York • Chicago • London / Atlanta • Dallas • Columbus • San Francisco / [broken rule]

Copyright 1933 by Thomas Bonaventure Lawler.
8 vo. Red cloth; pictorial design (eagle) and lettering stamped on cover; rules, ornaments (stars) and lettering on spine stamped in gold; 625 pp.; appendix and index (I–LXVI).
Illustrated with numerous paintings, engravings, maps, photographs, etc.

Three illustrations in color by N. C. Wyeth.
On the Way to the Front in '76. fp 220
A California Mission. fp 378
Driving the Last Spike in the Transcontinental Railroad. fp 460

Note: The illustrations originally appeared in color in the book *Essentials of American History* by Thomas Bonaventure Lawler, published by Ginn and Company, Boston, 1918.

Marriott, Crittenden

SALLY CASTLETON / SOUTHERNER / By / Crittenden Marriott / Author of "The Isle of Dead Ships," "Out of Russia," etc. / With Illustrations By / N. C. Wyeth / [publisher's colophon] / Philadelphia & London / J. B. Lippincott Company / 1913 [first, second and ninth lines printed in orange]

Published January 1913, so stated on the copyright page.
12 mo. Red cloth; lettering on cover and spine stamped in white; 312 pp.; seven pages of publisher's advertising.

Six illustrations. One (frontispiece) in color and five in black and white.
> The door behind Radcliffe crashed open and a dozen men crowded in, rifles in hand. (frontispiece in color)
> The sentry stared, Radcliffe's manner of address took him by surprise. fp 102
> "Send him back? Not a bit of it! We're going to hang him higher than Haman." fp 138
> "You are mine, and neither life nor death shall take you from me!" fp 204
> Was it indeed he? Or was it a dummy put there to deceive? fp 226
> Suddenly the bag opened and a torrent of letters cascaded to the floor. fp 258

Idem: Except for lettering on cover and spine stamped in black.

Note: The illustrations originally appeared in *Everybody's Magazine,* June thru October 1912, for the story *Sally Castleton, Southerner* by Crittenden Marriott.

Merwin, Samuel

SILK / A Legend / As Narrated In The Journals And / Correspondence of Jan Po / By / Samuel Merwin / Illustrated by / N. C. Wyeth / [Chinese characters] [red] / Boston and New York / Houghton Mifflin Company / The Riverside Press Cambridge / 1923

12 mo. Red cloth; lettering on cover and spine stamped in gold; 266 pp.

Frontispiece illustration in color.
Before Me Sat the Virgin Queen (repeated on the dust wrapper)

Idem: Except for green cloth binding.

Note: The frontispiece illustration also appears in *McCall's Magazine,* September 1923, for the story "Silk" by Samuel Merwin.

Mulford, Clarence Edward

BAR-20 / Being a record of certain happenings that / occurred in the otherwise peaceful lives of one Hopalong Cassidy / and his companions on the range / by / Clarence Edward Mulford [orange] / Illustrated by N. C. Wyeth and F. E. Schoonover / [publisher's colophon] [orange] / New York / The Outing Publishing Company / MCMVII [title also printed in orange]

12 mo. Red cloth; pictorial design (Hopalong Cassidy, after Schoonover) on cover stamped in black and white; lettering on cover stamped in gold and black; lettering on spine stamped in gold; 382 pp.
Illustrated by N. C. Wyeth and Frank E. Schoonover.

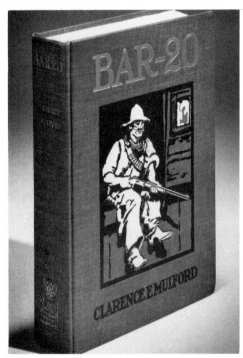

Two illustrations in black and white by N. C. Wyeth.
"Sitting up cross-legged, with each hand holding a gun." fp 106
"Saw a crimson rider sweep down upon him . . . heralded by a blazing star." fp 256

Note: The illustrations originally appearede in *The Outing Magazine* issues of May 1906 and December 1906 for the story "Bar 20 Range Yarns" by Clarence Edward Mulford.

The S. S. McClure Company

McClure's— / The Marketplace of the World / A Brief for Advertisers / Its object being to show that / McClure's Magazine carries / more advertising than any / other magazine, and why / [publisher's colophon] / The S. S. McClure Company / Fourth Avenue and Twenty-Third Street / New York

Thin 12 mo. Green gray boards; cover label (photograph); lettering on cover stamped in gold; (28 pp).

Frontispiece illustration in color by N. C. Wyeth.
The Last Stand

Note: The illustration originally appeared as a cover for *McClure's Magazine,* September 1906.

McConathy, Osbourne; Beattie, John W.; and Morgan, Russell V. (Edited by)

MUSIC / Of Many Lands And Peoples / Edited by / Osbourne McConathy / (credits) / John W. Beattie / [credits] / Russell V. Morgan / [credits] / New York / Chicago / San Francisco / Silver Burdett and Company [border decoration in blue]

Copyright 1932 by Silver Burdett and Company.
4 to. Silver cloth (simulated leather): designs and lettering embossed on cover; lettering embossed on spine; 268 pp (including index).
Illustrated with paintings, photographs, etc.

Frontispiece illustration in color by N. C. Wyeth.
Wagner and Liszt

MUSIC / Highways and Byways / Edited by / Osbourne McConathy / [credits] / John W. Beattie / [credits] / Russell V. Morgan / [credits] / New York / Newark / Boston / Chicago / San Francisco / Silver Burdett Company [border decoration with publisher's colophon in blue]

Copyright 1936 by Silver Burdett Company.
4 to. Brown cloth (simulated leather); design and lettering embossed on cover; lettering embossed on spine. 252 pp (including index).
Illustrated with paintings, photographs, etc.
Frontispiece illustration in color by N. C. Wyeth.
Beethoven and Nature

Note: The illustrations were painted for Steinway & Sons and used extensively in their advertising campaigns. The paintings originally appeared in color in the book *The Steinway Collection* by James Huneker, published by Steinway & Sons, New York, 1919.

The National Geographic Society

AN INVITATION / To / EXPLORE / is cordially invited to visit Washington / to see and sense / THE NATIONAL GEOGRAPHIC / in its home

Published in 1933 by The National Geographic Society.
Thin folio. Light blue boards; pictorial cover label (dirigible) printed in dark blue surrounded by silver borders; molding designs (top and bottom) on cover stamped in dark blue; lettering on cover stamped in dark blue; (32 pp).
Illustrated with The National Geographic mural paintings by N. C. Wyeth, plus numerous photographs, etc.
Photograph: The office of Dr. La Gorce. In the center background, framed in the door entrance, hangs the original painting by N. C. Wyeth, used as an illustration in *Collier's Weekly,* July 17, 1915, for the story, "At the World's Outposts" by James Francis Dwyer.

Seven illustrations by N. C. Wyeth. Endpapers printed in blue and five illustrations in black and white.
Beyond Uncharted Seas Columbus Finds a New World (Repeated as an endpaper and printed in blue.)

The Discoverer
Map of Discovery Eastern Hemisphere
Map of Discovery Western Hemisphere
Through Pathless Skies to the North Pole (Repeated as an endpaper and printed in blue.)

Note: The illustrations (mural paintings) originally appeared as special color supplements in *The National Geographic Magazine,* March, May, June, November 1928, and January 1929.

Packard, Leonard O.; Sinnot, Charles P.; and Overton, Bruce

THE NATIONS TODAY / A Physical, Industrial, and / Commercial Geography / [rule] / Leonard O. Packard / [credits] / Charles P. Sinnott / [credits] / Bruce Overton / [credits] / [rule] / 1939 / The Macmillan Company / New York

Large 8 vo. Blue cloth with pictorial designs stamped on cover and spine in gray and black; lettering on spine stamped in black; 727 pp (including index).
Illustration with numerous paintings, photographs, maps, etc.

One illustration in black and white by N. C. Wyeth.
The world's first reaper—invented by Cyrus Hall McCormick—in a public test at Steele's Tavern, Virginia, in July 1831. p 58

Note: The illustration was painted for the 100th Anniversary of International Harvester Company (1831–1931) and appeared in color in leading periodicals during the year 1931.

Page, Thomas Nelson

UNDER THE CRUST / By / Thomas Nelson Page / Illustrated / New York / Charles Scribner's Sons / 1907 [title and publisher printed in red]

Published November 1907, so stated on the copyright page.
12 mo. Dark green cloth; designs on cover and spine stamped in colors (surrounded by ornamental boxed rules); lettering on cover and spine stamped in gold; gilt top; 307 pp.
Illustrated by N. C. Wyeth, Marchand, Pfeifer, etc.

One illustration in black and white by N. C. Wyeth.
"Here I am, the richest man in all America, if not in the world." fp 132

Note: This illustration originally appeared in *Scribner's Magazine,* March 1906, for the story "A Brother to Diogenes" by Thomas Nelson Page.

THE / LAND OF THE SPIRIT / By / Thomas Nelson Page / Illustrated / Charles Scribner's Sons / New York::::1913 [title surrounded by boxed rules]

Published April 1913, so stated on the copyright page.
12 mo. Dark blue cloth; lettering on cover stamped in gold (surrounded by double boxed rules with stamped ornamental borders); lettering (with ornament) on spine stamped in gold; uncut; 257 pp.
Illustrated by N. C. Wyeth, Walter Biggs, etc.

Two illustrations in black and white by N. C. Wyeth.
Behind them streamed the mingled traffic of a road that led to a great city. fp 84

It was, then, not a dream. This was the sign unto them. fp 104

Note: The illustrations originally appeared in color in *Scribner's Magazine*, December 1912, for the story "The Stable of the Inn" by Thomas Nelson Page.

Palmer, George Herbert (Translated by)

The Riverside Literature Series / [rule] / THE ODYSSEY OF HOMER / Translated by / George Herbert Palmer / [publisher's colophon] / Houghton Mifflin Company / Boston (etc.)

[Date not established.]

16 mo. Tan cloth; small design (publisher's colophon) on cover stamped in dark brown surrounded by double boxed rules; small design (R.L.S. seal) on back cover stamped in dark brown; lettering on spine stamped in dark brown; 402 pp (including Questions and Pronouncing Vocabulary).

Two illustrations in color.
The Raft of Odysseus (frontispiece)
The Trial of the Bow. fp xxxii

Note: The illustrations originally appeared in color in the Limited and Deluxe editions.

Parker, Gilbert

NORTHERN LIGHTS / By / Gilbert Parker / Illustrated / [publisher's colophon] / Harper & Brothers Publishers / New York and London / MCMIX (title surrounded by double boxed rules)

Published September 1909, so stated on the copyright page.

12 mo. Green cloth; pictorial design on cover in colors; ornament on spine stamped in gold; lettering on cover and spine stamped in gold; 353 pp.

Illustrated by N. C. Wyeth, Harvey Dunn, Frank E. Schoonover, Allen True, Will Crawford, etc.

Two illustrations in black and white by N. C. Wyeth.
The start on the north trail.[1] fp 36
"Pauline," he said, feebly, and fainted in her arms.[2] fp 114

[1] Originally appeared in *The Saturday Evening Post*, February 1, 1908, for the story "Once at Red Mans River" by Gilbert Parker.
[2] Originally appeared in *Red Book Magazine*, September 1908, for the story "Who Calls?" by Sir Gilbert Parker.

Parsons, Geoffrey

The / Stream of History / By / Geoffrey Parsons / Volume III / New York / Charles Scribner's Sons / 1929
This edition is limited to five hundred and thirty copies of which five hundred are for sale and thirty for presentation (Volume I numbered and signed by the author)

(Published in four volumes)
Large 8 vo. Brown boards; dark brown cloth spine and corners; morocco label on spine stamped in gold; 342 pp.
Illustrated with paintings, photographs, maps, etc.

Frontispiece illustration in color (mounted plate) by N. C. Wyeth.
A Tournament in the Days of King Arthur

Note: The illustration originally appeared in color in *The Boy's King Arthur* by Sidney Lanier, Charles Scribner's Sons, New York, 1917.

The / Stream of History / By / Geoffrey Parsons / Volume III / New York / Charles Scribner's Sons / 1929

(Published in four volumes)
Large 8 vo. Blue cloth (simulated leather); pictorial designs on cover and spine stamped in gold; lettering on cover and spine stamped in gold; 342 pp.
Illustrated with paintings, photographs, maps, etc.

Frontispiece illustration in color by N. C. Wyeth. Same as in the Limited Edition but illustration not mounted.

The / Stream of History / By / Geoffrey Parsons / Volume IV / New York / Charles Scribner's Sons / 1929
This edition is limited to five hundred and thirty copies of which five hundred are for sale and thirty for presentation (Volume I numbered and signed by the author)

(Published in four volumes)
Large 8 vo. Brown boards; dark brown cloth spine and corners; morocco label on spine stamped in gold; 354 pp (including index 355–72).
Illustrated with paintings, photographs, maps, etc.

One illustration in black and white by N. C. Wyeth.
The Opening of the Prairies. p 251

Note: The illustration originally appeared as a frontispiece in color in *Scribner's Magazine*, January 1916.

The / Stream of History / By / Geoffrey Parsons / Volume IV / New York / Charles Scribner's Sons / 1929

(Published in four volumes)
Large 8 vo. Blue cloth (simulated leather); pictorial designs on cover and spine stamped in gold; lettering on cover and spine stamped in gold; 354 pp (including index 355–72)

Illustrated with paintings, photographs, maps, etc.

One illustration in black and white by N. C. Wyeth. Same as in the Limited Edition.

Phelps, Elizabeth Stuart

THE STORY OF / JESUS CHRIST / By / ELIZABETH STUART PHELPS / [publisher's colophon] / Boston and New York / HOUGHTON MIFFLIN COMPANY / The Riverside Press Cambridge / 1926

8 vo. Dark blue cloth; cover label in color; rules on cover stamped in gold; lettering on spine stamped in gold; 413 pp.
Illustrated with paintings in color and black and white.

Cover label illustration in color by N. C. Wyeth.
Description: "When He Comes He Will Rule over the Whole World"

Note: The illustration originally appeared in color in *Harper's Monthly Magazine*, December 1913, for the story "The Lost Boy" by Henry Van Dyke.

Phillips, Henry Wallace

[double rules] / MR. SCRAGGS / Introduced by Red Saunders [red] / [rules] / By / Henry Wallace Phillips / Author of

"Red Saunders," "Plain Mary Smith," etc. / [publisher's colophon] [red] / [double rules] / The Grafton Press / Publishers New York [title also printed in red]

Published January 1906, so stated on the copyright page.

12 mo. Maroon cloth; cover label in colors (with white border); lettering on cover and spine stamped in white; design on spine stamped in white; uncut; 188 pp.
Illustrated by N. C. Wyeth, Martin Justice, etc.

One illustration in black and white by N. C. Wyeth.
"So we rode in, right cheerful." fp 150

Note: The illustration originally appeared in *The Saturday Evening Post*, May 20, 1905, for the story "Mr. Scraggs Intervenes" by Henry Wallace Phillips.

Quick, Herbert

VANDEMARK'S FOLLY / By / Herbert Quick / With Illustrations by / N. C. Wyeth / [publisher's colophon] / Indianapolis / The Bobbs-Merrill Company / Publishers

Copyright 1922 by Herbert Quick.
12 mo. Maroon cloth; lettering on cover and spine (with rules) stamped in gold; 420 pp.

Eight illustrations in black and white.
"I must think!" I said. "Let me be!" (frontispiece)
When the fight grew warm enough I began to see red. fp 30
I shall never forget the sight. It was like a great green sea. fp 110 (Repeated in color on the dust wrapper.)
That endless stream was flowing on.[1] fp 152
"Don't let me fall," she begged. fp 190
"It's only a single-barrel gun," said he. "Grab him!" fp 246
Rowena buried her face in her shawl.[1] fp 354
That fearful moving flood of wind and frost and snow.[1] fp 406

Note: The illustrations originally appeared in the *Ladies' Home Journal*, September 1921 thru February 1922, for the story *Vandemark's Folly* by Herbert Quick.

ONE MAN'S LIFE / An Autobiography by / Herbert Quick / With Illustrations / [ornament] / Indianapolis / The Bobbs-Merrill Company / Publishers [title surrounded by double boxed rules, and ornament printed in red]

Copyright 1925 by Ella Corey Quick.
8 vo. Reddish brown cloth; cover and spine stamped in gold (cover surrounded by stamped rule border); uncut; 408 pp.
Illustrated by N. C. Wyeth and E. F. Ward, with numerous newspaper excerpts and photographs.

Three illustrations in black and white by N. C. Wyeth.

The Iowa Prairie. fp 76
A Prairie Fire. fp 94
A Snow Scene on the Prairie. fp 118

Note: The illustrations originally appeared in the Ladies' Home Journal, September 1921 through February 1922 for the story Vandemark's Folly by Herbert Quick.

Richmond, Leonard

The / Technique / of the / Poster / Edited by / Leonard Richmond•R•B•A•R•O•I / Author of The Technique of Oil Painting / The Art of Landscape Painting / etc. / [ornament] / London / Sir Isaac Pitman & Sons • Ltd. / 1933

4 to. Cloth; 216 pp (including index).
Illustrated with posters in color and black and white, plus photographs showing types of printing presses.

One illustration (mounted plate) in color by N. C. Wyeth.
Ringing Out Liberty (Plate XVII)
Chapter VII American Posters
A reference to "Ringing Out Liberty" p 71

Note: The illustration was first published (with three others) as a poster in color for the Pennsylvania Railroad.

Roberts, Kenneth

TRENDING INTO MAINE / With Illustrations by N. C. Wyeth / [publisher's colophon] / Doubleday & Company, Inc. / Garden City, New York / 1944

8 vo. Dark blue cloth; pictorial design (clipper ship passing lighthouse) stamped on front cover in black; lettering on spine stamped in gold over black; dark blue top; 430 pp (including index and publisher's advertising).

Two illustrations in pen and ink.
Road to the village (contents page)
Clipper ship passing lighthouse (illustrations page and cover design)
Fifteen illustrations in color including the endpapers.
Illustrations (plates) in color. Same as in the Limited Edition and First Trade Edition.
The Doryman (Evening) (repeated on the dust wrapper).

Rollins, Philip Ashton

THE COWBOY / His Characteristics, His Equipment, and His Part / in the Development of the West / By / Philip Ashton Rollins / New York / Charles Scribner's Sons / 1922

Published April 1922, so stated on the copyright page.

8 vo. Maroon cloth; lettering on cover and spine stamped in gold; 353 pp.
Illustrated by N. C. Wyeth and Charles M. Russell (frontispiece), plus numerous diagrams and photographs.

Two illustrations in black and white by N. C. Wyeth.
The Chuckwagon. fp 218
Night Herding. fp 254

Note: The illustrations originally appeared in Scribner's Magazine, March 1906, for the story "A Day with the Round-Up" by N. C. Wyeth.

Russell, W. Clark

THE WRECK / OF THE / GROSVENOR / By W•Clark•Russell / Grosset and Dunlap / Publishers • New York / By arrangement with Dodd, Mead and Company [title surrounded by boxed rules] [date not established]

Large 8 vo. Blue cloth; lettering on cover (with small design) and spine stamped in yellow; yellow top; uncut; 349 pp.

Frontispiece illustration in color.
They Had Shipped the Mast in the Long-boat (Repeated on the dust wrapper.)

Note: The illustration originally appeared in color in Scribner's Magazine, August 1917, for the story "The Golden Galleon" by Paul Hervey Fox.

Sabatini, Rafael

Riverside Bookshelf [within banner] / CAPTAIN BLOOD / His Odyssey / By / Rafael Sabatini / With Illustrations / [drawing] / Boston and New York / Houghton Mifflin Company / The Riverside Press Cambridge [red] / 1927 [title also printed in red]

8 vo. Dark blue cloth; cover label in color; decoration and lettering on spine stamped in gold; 437 pp.
Illustrated in color by Clyde O. De Land.

Endpaper illustrations in colors (blue, black and white) by N. C. Wyeth.
Description: A sailing ship at sea.

Note: The endpaper illustrations originally appeared as endpapers in the book The Courtship of Miles Standish (Tercentenary Edition) by Henry Wadsworth Longfellow, published by Houghton Mifflin Company, Boston, 1920.

Stephenson, Nathaniel Wright and Martha Tucker

A SCHOOL HISTORY OF / THE UNITED STATES / By / Nathaniel Wright Stephenson / And / Martha Tucker Stepehenson / [publisher's colophon] / Ginn and Company / Boston • New York • Chicago • London / Atlanta • Dallas • Columbus • San Francisco

Copyright 1921, (1924) by Nathaniel Wright Stephenson.
8 vo. Blue cloth; pictorial design (soaring eagle) on cover stamped in dark blue; lettering on cover and spine stamped in dark blue; 548 pp.; appendix (I–XXIV); index (XXV–XIL).
Illustrated with numerous paintings, engravings, drawings, maps, etc.

Frontispiece illustration in color by N. C. Wyeth.
On the Way to the Front in '76

Note: The illustration originally appeared in color in the book Essentials of American History by Thomas Bonaventure Lawler, published by Ginn and Company, Boston, 1918.

Stevenson, Robert Louis (Edition in Latin)

Mount Hope Classics / Vol. V. / INSVLA THESAVRARIA / Ab Avctore / Roberto Lvdovico Stevenson / [rule] / Latine Interpretatvs Est / Arcadivs Avellanvs / Prostat apud / E. Parmalee Prentice / 37 Wall Street, / New York City, N. Y.

Copyright 1922 by E. Parmalee Prentice.
Large 8 vo. Green buckram; lettering on cover stamped in blind; lettering on spine stamped in gold; 361 pp.

Fourteen illustrations in color.
Illustrations (plates with titles printed on tissue insets) in color:
Navarchus Bill Bones fp 6
Navarchus Bones profligat Canem Nigrum fp 21
Senecio Pew fp 52
Iacobellus Hawkins Domum Relinquit fp 78
Longus Ioannes Silver atque Hawkins fp 104
Praeparatio contra Seditionem fp 136
Ben Gunn fp 149
Navarchus Smollett Seditiosis refragatur fp 183
Assultus in Vallum fp 213
Lucta in Cabana fp 234
Israel Hands fp 269
Macula Nigra fp 300
Obses fp 326
Antrum Thesaurarium fp 353

Note: The illustrations originally appeared in color in the book Treasure Island by Robert Louis Stevenson, published by Charles Scribner's Sons, New York, September 1911.
This volume is part of the Edwin J. Beinecke Collection of Writings by and about Robert Louis Stevenson, presented to the Yale University Library, New Haven, Connecticut.

KIDNAPPED / Being Memoirs Of The Adventures Of David / Balfour In The Year 1751 / How he was kidnapped and cast away; his sufferings in a / desert isle; his journey in the wild highlands; his ac / quaintance with Alan Breck Stewart and other notorious / highland jacobites; with all that he suffered at the hands / of his uncle, Ebenezar Balfour of Shaws, falsely so called / Written By Himself / and now set forth by / Robert Louis Stevenson / New York / Charles Scribner's Sons / 1933 [Made for members of Limited Editions Club of New York, 1938]

Large 8 vo. Black cloth; pictorial cover label in color with gray inset, printed in black; lettering on spine stamped in gold; 289 pp.

Eleven illustrations in color including cover label, endpapers, and title page design.
Mr. Balfour, of the House of Shaws fp 18
At Queen's Ferry fp 48
The Siege of the Round-House fp 84
The Wreck of the "Covenant" fp 112
On the Island of Erraid fp 122
The Murderer of Roy Campbell of Glenure fp 154
At the Cards in Cluny's Cage fp 214
Two Pipers in Balquhidder fp 238
The Parting fp 286
Endpaper illustration
The Covenant of Dysart passing the headlands of Western Scotland.

Note: The illustrations originally appeared in the book Kidnapped by Robert Louis Stevenson, pub-

lished by Charles Scribner's Sons, New York, October 1913.
This volume is part of the Edwin J. Beinecke Collection of Writings by and about Robert Louis Stevenson, presented to the Yale University Library, New Haven, Connecticut. This copy was used as a guide in designing the edition of *Kidnapped* for the Limited Editions Club.

Swan, Oliver G. (Edited by)

DEEP WATER DAYS / Edited by Oliver G. Swan / Macrae • Smith • Company / Philadelphia [title and author printed within pictorial design]

Copyright 1929 by Macrae • Smith • Company.
First Edition, so stated on the copyright page.
Large 8 vo. Black cloth; pictorial designs stamped on cover and spine in colors plus gold; lettering on cover and spine stamped in gold; blue top; 506 pp (including acknowledgements).

Illustrated in color by N. C. Wyeth, Frank E. Schoonover, Stanley Arthurs, Charles Hargens, and Manning de V. Lee, plus numerous drawings in black and white.

One illustration in color by N. C. Wyeth.
Whenever a ship was boarded and robbed or whenever a fishing-vessel was laid under contribution, Blackbeard was known to be at the bottom of the business. fp 160

Idem: Except for green cloth with pictorial designs and lettering stamped in blue and green.

Note: The illustration originally appeared in color in *Scribner's Magazine*, August 1917, for the story "The Golden Galleon" by Paul Hervey Fox.

ANCHORS AWEIGH! / . . . Tales of Wooden Ship Days . . . / [drawing enclosed in border] / Edited by / Oliver G. Swan / Grosset & Dunlap / Publishers • New York [date not established]

Copyright 1929 by Macrae • Smith • Company.
Originally published under the title *Deep Water Days*, so stated on the copyright page.
Large 8 vo. Green cloth; pictorial designs on cover stamped in colors; lettering on cover and spine (with rules) stamped in brown; green top; 235 pp.
Illustrated in color by N. C. Wyeth, Stanley Arthurs, Charles Hargens, and Manning de V. Lee, plus numerous illustrations in black and white.
Frontispiece illustration in color by N. C. Wyeth. The same as illustration in *Deep Water Days*.

Tobey, Walter L.

Volume • VI • [over banner decoration] / THE / GRAPHIC ARTS / AND CRAFTS / YEAR BOOK / American Annual Review / of the Printing and / Allied Industries / Walter L • Tobey—Editor / Graphic Arts Press—Hamilton • Ohio [enclosed in decorations in colors]

Copyright 1913 by The Republican Publishing Company, Hamilton, Ohio.
Thick 4 to. Brown cloth (simulated leather) with dark brown leather spine; lettering on spine stamped in gold.
Divided into ten sections with index.
Section III: Engraving and Plate Making:

One illustration in black and white by N. C. Wyeth.
Description: The three were wading recklessly through the muskeg that oozed to the tops of their elk-hide boots. p 100

Note: The illustration originally appeared in *Scribner's Magazine*, February 1912, for the story "My Love Dwelt in a Northern Land" by Mary Synon.

Tryon, Rolla M., and Lingley, Charles R.

THE AMERICAN PEOPLE / AND NATION / By / Rolla M. Tryon / [author's credits] / And / Charles R. Lingley / [author's credits] / [publisher's colophon] / Ginn and Company / Boston • New York • Chicago • London / Atlanta • Dallas • Columbus • San Francisco

Copyright 1927 by Rolla M. Tryon and Charles R. Lingley.
Ginn code number 827.5 on the copyright page.
8 vo. Tan cloth; pictorial designs on cover and spine stamped in colors; lettering on cover and spine stamped in dark brown; 654 pp (plus appendix and index I–XXXVII).
Illustrated with numerous paintings, photographs, and maps.

One illustration in color by N. C. Wyeth.
The Landing of Columbus. fp 2
Idem: Except for two-volume set with code numbers 828.8. The illustration by N. C. Wyeth appears in Volume One.

Note: The illustration originally appeared as a frontispiece in color in *Essentials of American History* by Thomas Bonaventure Lawler, published by Ginn and Company, Boston, 1918.

Tryon, Rolla M.; Lingley, Charles R.; and Morehouse, Frances

[rule] / The • Tryon • And • Lingley • History • Series / [rule] / THE AMERICAN NATION / YESTERDAY AND TODAY / By / Rolla M. Tryon / [author's credits] / Charles R. Lingley / [author's credits] / And / Frances Morehouse / [author's credits] / [decoration] / Ginn and Company / Boston • New York • Chicago • London / Atlanta • Dallas • Columbus • San Francisco

Copyright 1930 by Rolla M. Tryon, Charles R. Lingley and Frances Morehouse.
Ginn code number 531.3 on the copyright page.
8 vo. Blue cloth; pictorial designs on cover and spine stamped in colors; lettering on cover and spine stamped in black; 625 pp; appendix and index (I–XL).
Illustrated with numerous paintings, photographs, maps, etc.
One illustration in color by N. C. Wyeth. Same as illustration in *The American People and Nation*.

Van Dyke, Henry

THE LOST BOY / By / Henry Van Dyke / Illustrated / [publisher's colophon] / Harper & Brothers Publishers / New York and London / MCMXIV

Published September 1914, so stated on the copyright page.
Harper code letters G-O on the copyright page.
Thin 8 vo. Green cloth; pictorial designs on cover and spine stamped in gold; lettering on cover and spine stamped in gold; 44 pp.

Three illustrations (mounted plates) with tissue insets. Two illustrations in color and one in black and white with tint.
"When He Comes He Will Rule over the Whole World." (frontispiece in color)
The Boy was the Joy of the Journey. (black and white with tint.) fp 4
"Come, Live with Us, for I Think Thou Art Chosen." (color) fp 25

Note: The illustrations originally appeared in color in *Harper's Monthly Magazine*, December 1913, for the story "The Lost Boy" by Henry Van Dyke.

THE LOST BOY / By / Henry Van Dyke / Illustrated / [publisher's colophon] / Harper & Brothers Publishers / New York and London / MCMXIV

Published September 1914, so stated on the copyright page.
Harper code letters G-O on the copyright page.
Thin 12 mo. Full levant (black) decoration (publisher's colophon) on cover stamped in gold; ruled spine stamped in gold; lettering on cover stamped in gold; gilt top; uncut; 69 pp (title surrounded by boxed rule stamped in goal).
Three illustrations in black and white by N. C. Wyeth. Same as illustrations in octavo edition.

THE LOST BOY / By / Henry Van Dyke / Illustrated / [publisher's colophon] / Harper & Brothers Publishers / New York and London / MCMXIV

Published September 1914, so stated on the copyright page.
Harper code letters G-O on the copyright page.
Thin 12 mo. Green cloth; pictorial cover design stamped in gold; lettering on cover and spine stamped in gold; uncut; 69 pp.
Three illustrations in black and white. Same as illustrations in octavo edition.

Vollintine, Grace

[rule] / The • Tryon • and • Lingley • History • Series / [rule] / THE AMERICAN PEOPLE / AND / THEIR OLD WORLD ANCESTORS / By / Grace Vol-

lintine / Francis W. Parker School, Chicago / [decoration] / Ginn and Company / Boston • New York • Chicago • London / Atlanta • Dallas • Columbus • San Francisco

Copyright 1930 by Grace Vollintine.
12 mo. Reddish brown cloth; pictorial designs on cover and spine stamped in colors; lettering on cover and spine stamped in black; 576 pp (including index, etc.).
Illustrated with numerous paintings, drawings, photographs, maps, etc.

Two illustrations in black and white by N. C. Wyeth.
Phoenician Biremes.[1] fp 4
Crusaders Before Jerusalem.[2] fp 240

[1] The illustration is from the mural panel *The City of Tyre,* painted by N. C. Wyeth for the First National Bank of Boston. It originally appeared in color in the *Ladies Home Journal,* July 1925.
[2] The illustration originally appeared as a frontispiece in color for *The Gateway to American History* by Thomas Bonaventure Lawler, published by Ginn and Company, Boston, 1930.

The Staff of the Wellington Leader

A / HISTORY / of / COLLINGSWORTH / COUNTY / and Other Stories / By / The Staff of the Wellington Leader / [ornament] / 1925 / Leader Printing Co., Inc. / Wellington, Texas [title surrounded by broken boxed rules]

12 mo. Light brown paper wrappers; pictorial designs (pen and ink) on cover printed in black; lettering on cover and spine printed in black; 234 pp.; advertisers (I–IV).

Frontispiece illustration in black and white.
Description: The lee of the grub-wagon.

Note: The illustration originally appeared in *Scribner's Magazine,* March 1906, for the story "A Day with the Round-Up" by N. C. Wyeth.

Wertenbaker, Thomas Jefferson, and Smith, Donald E.

The / UNITED STATES / OF AMERICA / A History / By / Thomas Jefferson Wertenbaker / [author's credits] / and / Donald E. Smith / [author's credits] / [publisher's colophon] / Charles Scribner's Sons / New York   Chicago   Boston   Atlanta / San Francisco   Dallas

Copyright 1931 by Charles Scribner's Sons.
Scribner's code letter (A), so stated on the copyright page.
12 mo. Red cloth; lettering on cover and spine stamped in gold; 712 pp (including index, etc.)
Illustrated with paintings in color and maps.

Three illustrations in color by N. C. Wyeth.
Paul Revere.[1] fp 114
Washington At Valley Forge.[1] fp 134
The Pioneers—The Opening of the Prairies.[2] fp 256

Idem: Except for green cloth binding.

[1] The illustrations originally appeared in *Poems of American Patriotism,* edited by Brander Matthews, published by Charles Scribner's Sons, N. Y., October, 1922.
[2] Originally appeared as a frontispiece in color in *Scribner's Magazine,* January 1916.

White, Stewart Edward

ARIZONA NIGHTS / By / Stewart Edward White / [decoration] / Illustrations

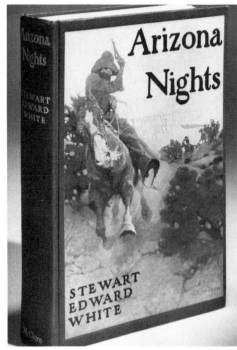

by N. C. Wyeth / New York / The McClure Company / MCMVII

Published October 1907, so stated on the copyright page.
12 mo. Green cloth; cover label in color; lettering on spine stamped in gold; 351 pp; four pages of publisher's advertising.

Seven illustrations in color.
Called him out and shot him in the stomach. (frontispiece) p II
We joined the second expedition. fp 50
An almighty exciting race. (repeated on the cover label and dust wrapper) fp 54
We had to "shoot the rapids." fp 70
I saw his horse jump back dodgin' a rattlesnake or somethin'. fp 84
"Look here!" he yells. "Listen to what I'm tellin' ye!" fp 132
They got to fighten on which should get the first hoss, so I bent my gun on them and made them draw lots. fp 140

Note: The illustrations originally appeared in *McClure's Magazine,* March thru May 1906, for the story "Arizona Nights" by Stewart Edward White.

ARIZONA NIGHTS • The / Works of / Stewart / Edward / White / Garden City, New York / Doubleday, Page & Co. / 1916 [title printed over drawing with green tint]

Copyright 1907 by The McClure Company.
12 mo. Green cloth; pictorial designs on cover and spine stamped in black; lettering on cover and spine stamped in gold; gilt top; 351 pp.
Frontispiece illustration in black and white.
Description: A gunfight.

Note: The illustration originally appeared in *McClure's Magazine,* April 1906, for the story "Arizona Nights" by Stewart Edward White and was titled "At the same time Hahn pulled his gun and shot him through the middle."

CAMP AND TRAIL / By / Stewart Edward White / Author of "The Blazed Trail," "The Pass," etc. / Frontispiece in color by Fernand Lungren / and many other illustrations / from photographs, etc. / [pub-

lisher's colophon] [orange] / New York / The Outing Publishing Company / MCMVII [title also printed in orange]

8 vo. Blue cloth; pictorial design on cover and spine stamped in colors; lettering on cover and spine stamped in white; uncut; 236 pp (including index)
Illustrated by N. C. Wyeth and Fernand Lungren (frontispiece in color); plus numerous drawings and photographs.
One illustration in black and white by N. C. Wyeth.
On the Trail. fp 16

Note: The illustration originally appeared in *The Outing Magazine,* September 1907, for the story "Mountaineering in North America" by Robert Dunn.

THE RIVERMAN / By / Stewart Edward White / [decoration] / Illustrations by N. C. Wyeth and / Clarence F. Underwood / New York / The McClure Company / MCMVIII

12 mo. Gray green cloth; cover label in colors; lettering on cover and spine stamped in white; 368 pp; four pages of publisher's advertising.
Illustrated by N. C. Wyeth and Clarence F. Underwood.
Cover label illustration in colors by N. C. Wyeth (repeated on the dust wrapper).
Twelve illustrations in black and white by N. C. Wyeth.
Several Bad Jams Relieved the Monotony. fp 52
The Doctor. fp 56
"I Say, Orde, I Want to Apologize to You." fp 68
"I'd Like to See You Get Any Three Men to Agree to Anything on This River." fp 76
And Looked Out Beyond the Tumbled Shore Ice to the Steel-Gray Angry Waters. fp 192
Leaned Against Their Peavies and Were Swept Away by the Swift Current. fp 198
"And How Are Ye, Ye Ould Darlint?" fp 206
Quite Oblivious to the Keen Wind. fp 298
He Fell Upon the Woodwork with Unparalleled Ferocity. fp 302
After Them Wafted the Rather Disorganized Strains of "Whoa, Emma!" fp 316
His Eyes Burned Bright as Though from Some Internal Fire. fp 348
"I'm Going to Give You About the Worst Licking You Ever Heard Tell Of." fp 364

Note: The illustrations originally appeared in *The Saturday Evening Post* issues of December 14, 1907, February 15, 22, 29, March 7, 14, and 21, 1908.

THE WESTERNERS • The / Works of / Stewart / Edward / White / Garden City, New York / Doubleday, Page & Co. / 1913 [title printed over drawing with green tint]

Copyright 1900 and 1901 by Stewart Edward White.
12 mo. Light green cloth; pictorial designs on cover and spine stamped in green; lettering on cover and spine stamped in gold; gilt top; 344 pp.

Frontispiece illustration in black and white.
Description: Two cowboys on horseback following wagon-train.

Note: The illustration originally appeared in *McClure's Magazine,* March 1906, for the story "Arizona Nights" by Stewart Edward White and was titled We Joined the Second Expedition.

THE CLAIM JUMPERS • The / Works of / Stewart / Edward / White / Garden City, New York / Doubleday, Page & Co. / 1916 [title printed over drawing with green tint]

Copyright 1901 by Stewart Edward White.
12 mo. Light green cloth; pictorial designs on cover and spine stamped in green; lettering on cover and spine stamped in gold; gilt top; 284 pp.

Frontispiece illustration in black and white. Description: Two men walking past street-light.

Note: The illustration originally appeared in *The Saturday Evening Post*, December 14, 1907, for the story "The Brace Game" by Stewart Edward White and was titled "I say, Orde, I want to apologize to you."

Wood, William, and Gabriel, Ralph Henry

The Pageant Of America / [ornament] / IN DEFENSE / OF LIBERTY / By / William Wood / Ralph Henry Gabriel / [publisher's design] / New Haven • Yale University Press / Toronto • Glasgow, Brook & Co. / London • Humphrey Milford / Ox-ford University Press / 1928 [second, third and seventh lines in red]

Washington Edition • Volume VII
(Published in fifteen volumes)
4 to. Half morocco with corners; ornamental designs on spine stamped in gold; lettering on spine stamped in gold; gilt top; 351 pp.; notes on the pictures (353–54); index (355–70).
Illustrated with numerous paintings, engravings, photographs, maps, etc.
Two illustrations in black and white by N. C. Wyeth.
Battle of Wilson's Creek. p 29
The Mine Creek Charge. p 167

Note: The illustrations are reproduced from the mural paintings in the Missouri state capitol building, Jefferson City, Missouri. The mural paintings originally appeared in color in *The Ladies Home Journal*, March 1921.

The Pageant Of America / [ornament] / IN DEFENSE / OF LIBERTY / By / William Wood / Ralph Henry Gabriel / [publisher's design] / New Haven • Yale University Press / Toronto • Glasgow, Brook & Co. / London • Humphrey Milford / Oxford University Press / 1928 [second, third and seventh lines in red]

Independence Edition • Volume VII
(Published in fifteen volumes)

4 to. Dark brown simulated leather; pictorial designs on cover embossed in gold; lettering on spine stamped in gold; gilt top; 351 pp.; notes on the pictures (353–54); index (355–70).
Illustrated with numerous paintings, engravings, photographs, maps, etc.
Two illustrations in black and white by N. C. Wyeth. Same as those in Washington Edition.

The Pageant Of America / [ornament] / IN DEFENSE / OF LIBERTY / By / William Wood / Ralph Henry Gabriel / [publisher's design] / New Haven • Yale University Press / Toronto • Glasgow, Brook & Co. / London • Humphrey Milford / Oxford University Press / 1928 [second, third and seventh lines in red]

Independence Edition • Volume VII
(Published in fifteen volumes)
4 to. Blue cloth; pictorial design (Liberty) on cover stamped in gold; ornamental designs and rules on spine stamped in gold; lettering on cover stamped in gold; 351 pp.; notes on the pictures (353–54); index (355–70).
Illustrated with numerous paintings, engravings, photographs, maps, etc.
Two illustrations in black and white by N. C. Wyeth. Same as those in the Washington Edition.

Books Published Since 1946 Containing
Illustrations by N. C. Wyeth

American Heritage (By the Editors of)

By the Editors of American Heritage / The Magazine of History / Editor in Charge: Richard M. Ketchum / Narrative by Bruce Lancaster / with a chapter by J. H. Plumb / Introduction by Bruce Catton / The / AMERICAN HERITAGE / Book of / THE REVOLUTION [red] / Published by American Heritage Publishing Co., Inc., New York Book Trade Distribution by Simon & Schuster, Inc. [book title surrounded by scroll with pictorial designs in color]

Copyright 1958 by American Heritage Publishing Company, Inc.
4 to. Maroon cloth; spine stamped in gold; boxed (with pictorial label, front and back in color); 384 pp (including index).
Illustrated with paintings, drawings, engravings, maps, etc.
One illustration in color by N. C. Wyeth.
Arnold began his drive on Quebec with 1,100 men. About half of them sick and nearly starved, conquered the boiling rapids and brutal portages, the flooded swamps and numbing cold. The 350 miles march took six weeks. p 129

Idem: Except for deluxe edition issued with slip-case.

Note: The illustration originally appeared in color in *Trending into Maine* by Kenneth Roberts, published by Little, Brown and Company, Boston, 1938. It was titled Arnold's March to Quebec.

Athearn, Robert G.

[quotation: John F. Kennedy—four lines] / THE AMERICAN HERITAGE / NEW ILLUSTRATED HISTORY / OF THE UNITED STATES / Volume 3 / The REVOLUTION / pictorial design in color [carved eagle] / By Robert G. Athearn / Professor of History, University of Colorado / created and designed by the editors of / American Heritage / the magazine of history / Published By / Dell Publishing Co., Inc., New York

Copyright 1963 by American Heritage Publishing Co., Inc.
(Published in sixteen volumes)
4 to. White cloth with illustration printed in color on front and back; lettering on cover and spine stamped in red, yellow and white; 269 pp.
Illustrated with numerous paintings, drawings, maps and photographs in color and black and white.

One illustration in color by N. C. Wyeth.
Benedict Arnold began his 350-mile march from Boston to Quebec with 1,100 men. He lost half to cold and hunger as he went through the wilds of Maine. p 211

Note: The illustration originally appeared in *Trending into Maine* by Kenneth Roberts, published by Little, Brown and Company, 1938. It was titled Arnold's March to Quebec.

Ball, Bernice M.

[drawings—historic houses] / CHESTER COUNTY & ITS DAY / Bernice M. Ball / [publisher's colophon] / Published by / The Chester County Day Committee / of the / Women's Auxiliary / [rule] / The Chester County Hospital / West Chester, Pennsylvania / [drawing—hospital]

Copyright 1970 by The Chester County Hospital.
Published in a Limited Edition of 3000 copies, signed by the author.
4 to. Red cloth; seal (Chester County) stamped on cover in gold; lettering on spine stamped in gold; 225 pp.
Illustrated with numerous paintings, drawings, photographs, etc.

One illustration in black and white by N. C. Wyeth.
"Fence Builders" courtesy of Mr. Carl D. Pratt p 20

Brotze, Emma Mae, and Lehmbers, A. E.

THE HISTORY of / Teaxs / Emma Mae Brotze / [author's credits] / A. E. Lehmbers / [author's credits] / Noble and Noble, Publishers, Inc., 707 Browder St., Dallas, Texas

Copyright 1954 by J. Kendrick Noble
8 vo. Black and yellow cloth; photograph

mounted on cover; lettering on cover and spine stamped in yellow, outlined in black; 199 pp.
Illustrated with paintings and photographs.

One illustration in black and white by N. C. Wyeth.

> This painting by N. C. Wyeth shows the brave defenders of the Alamo fighting desperately to hold back the enemy. p 83

Note: The illustration originally appeared in the 1944 calendar "Flags in America's History" published by John Morrell & Co., Ottumwa, Iowa.

Butterfield, Roger (and the editors of *The Saturday Evening Post*)

The Saturday Evening / POST / Treasury / Selected From / the Complete Files / By Roger Butterfield and / The Editors of the Saturday Evening Post / [publisher's colophon] / Simon and Schuster • New York [enclosed in double box rules and printed on blue paper]

Copyright 1954 by Curtis Publishing Company.
4 to. Boards (rose) with gray cloth spine; pictorial design (Benjamin Franklin) stamped on cover in gold; lettering and rules on spine stamped in gold (title over black); rose top; 544 pp (including index).
Illustrated with paintings, drawings, etc.

One reduced illustration in black and white by N. C. Wyeth (as it appeared with text from an early *Post* story).

> Description: He filled both hands and cut loose at one of the four horsemen. p xv

Note: The illustration originally appeared in *The Saturday Evening Post*, November 23, 1912, as a title-piece for the story "The Three Godfathers" by Peter B. Kyne.

Carmer, Carl (Edited by)

CAVALCADE / OF AMERICA / The Deeds and Achievements / of the Men and Women / Who Made Our Country Great / Edited by Carl Carmer / [pictorial design in color] / New York / Crown Publishers, Inc. • Lothrop, Lee & Shepard Co., Inc.

Copyright 1956 by Lothrop, Lee & Shepard Co., Inc.
4 to. Blue-gray boards; red cloth spine; pictorial design (American flag) stamped on cover; lettering and ornaments on spine stamped in white; 382 pp (including index).
Illustrated in color and black and white with paintings, engravings, photographs, etc.

One illustration in black and white by N. C. Wyeth.

> Description: First public test of the McCormick reaper. p 229

Idem: Except for red cloth (simulated leather) with cover and spine stamped in gold.

Note: The illustration was painted for the 100th Anniversary (1831–1931) of International Harvester Company and was used extensively in their advertising campaigns. It appeared in color in leading periodicals during the year 1931.

Carroll, H. Bailey

The Story of / Texas / by / H. Bailey Carroll / Professor of History, The University of Texas / [author's credits] / [author's credits] / Frances Nesmith / [credits] / Mary Jane Gentry / [credits] / Noble & Noble, Publishers, New York

Copyright 1963 by Noble and Noble, Publishers, Inc.
8 vo. Light blue cloth; pictorial designs (outline of Texas, etc.) stamped on cover and spine in silver; lettering on cover and spine stamped in silver; 362 pp.
Illustrated with paintings and photographs.

One illustration in black and white by N. C. Wyeth.

> This painting by N. C. Wyeth shows the brave defenders of the Alamo fighting desperately to hold back the enemy. p 119

Note: The illustration originally appeared in the 1944 calendar "Flags in America's History" published by John Morrell & Co., Ottumwa, Iowa.

Cook, Fred

The Golden Book / of / THE AMERICAN / REVOLUTION / Adapted for Young Readers / by Fred Cook / from The American Heritage Book of The Revolution / by the Editors of American Heritage / with narrative by Bruce Lancaster / Introduction by Bruce Catton / Golden Press [publisher's colophon] New York [lettering, THE AMERICAN REVOLUTION, surrounded by pictorial decorations in color]

Copyright 1958, (1959) by American Heritage Publishing Company, Inc.
4 to. Pictorial cloth (front and back covers in color); lettering on cover printed in red, black and white; lettering on spine printed in black; red top; 191 pp.
Illustrated with numerous paintings, engravings, maps, etc.

One illustration in color by N. C. Wyeth.

> Arnold began his march to Quebec with 1,100 men. About half of them, sick and nearly starved, conquered the rapids, swamps, and the numbing cold. The 350-mile march took six weeks. p 32

Note: The illustration originally appeared in color in *Trending into Maine* by Kenneth Roberts, published by Little, Brown and Company, Boston, June 1938. It was titled Arnold's March to Quebec.

Elder, Donald (and the editors of *Good Housekeeping*)

The / Good Housekeeping / Treasury / Selected From The Complete Files / By Donald Elder And / The Editors Of Good Housekeeping / Simon And Schuster 1960

4 to. Brown boards with white cloth spine; lettering on cover stamped in gold; lettering and ornaments on spine stamped in dark brown and gold; brown top; 638 pp (including index).
Illustrated with a portfolio of *Good Housekeeping* illustrations, advertisements, interiors, architecture, etc., from past to present.

One illustration in black and white by N. C. Wyeth.

> Night Scene (illustration from "Children of the Bible," a series by Bruce Barton, November 1929). p 29

Fielder, Mildred

WILD BILL and / DEADWOOD / by / Mildred Fielder / [photographic descriptions] / Superior Publishing Company—Seattle

Copyright 1965 by Superior Publishing Company, Seattle, Washington.

FIRST EDITION, so stated on the copyright page.
4 to. Gray cloth; lettering on cover and spine stamped in black; 160 pp.
Illustrated with drawings, engravings, and photographs.

One illustration (charcoal drawing) by N. C. Wyeth.

> Description: Wild Bill Hickok with drawn revolvers. p 50 (Repeated on the dust wrapper in colors.)

Janeway, Elizabeth; McFarland, Philip; Jewett, Arno; and Lowery, Josephine

Elizabeth Janeway / Philip McFarland / Arno Jewett / Josephine Lowery / [photograph] / DISCOVERING / LITERATURE / Houghton Mifflin Company • Boston / New York • Atlanta • Geneva • Illinois / Dallas • Palo Alto

(Copyright 1968 by Houghton Mifflin Company.)
4 to. Cloth (tan); pictorial decoration on cover stamped in reddish brown and black; lettering on cover stamped in red; lettering on spine stamped in yellow over red band and in black; lettering on back cover stamped in black; 626 pp.
Illustrated with numerous paintings, drawings, photographs, etc.

One illustration in color by N. C. Wyeth.
N. C. Wyeth did this painting of the old buccaneer who stayed with Jim Hawkins and his family at Admiral Benbow Inn and set in motion the exciting events of Stevenson's *Treasure Island*. p 560

Note: This illustration originally appeared in *Treasure Island* by Robert Louis Stevenson, published by Charles Scribner's Sons, New York, September 1911. It was titled "Captain Bill Bones."

Lewis, John

THE TWENTIETH CENTURY BOOK / Its illustration and design / John Lewis / Reinhold [publisher's colophon] Publishing Corporation / A subsidiary of Chapman-Reinhold, Inc.

Copyright 1967 by John Claude Lewis.
4 to. Red cloth; lettering on cover and spine stamped in gold; 272 pp (including index).
Illustrated in color and black and white with numerous paintings, drawings, wood engravings, etc.

Six illustrations in black and white by N. C. Wyeth.

> All day he hung round the cove p 204
> Title page from *Treasure Island* p 205
> One last tremendous cut p 206
> Tapping up and down the road in a frenzy p 207
> About half way down the slope to the stockade, they were collected in a group p 212
> For all the world, I was led like a dancing bear p 213

References to N. C. Wyeth on pages 139, 142, 207 and 208.

Note: The illustrations originally appeared in color in *Treasure Island* by Robert Louis Stevenson, published by Charles Scribner's Sons, New York, September 1911.

Mackey, Margaret G.

The • Tiegs-Adams • Social • Studies • Series / [rule] / YOUR COUNTRY'S

STORY / Pioneers • Builders • Leaders / By Margaret G. Macky / with / Ernest W. Tiegs and Fay Adams / Ginn and Company / Boston • New York • etc. [titles printed over photographs of the U.S. Capitol and Minute Man statue]

Copyright 1953 by Ginn and Company.
4 to. Cloth (yellow and brown); illustration on front cover printed in color; lettering on cover printed in brown and white; lettering on spine printed in brown and white; lettering on back cover printed in brown; 552 pp (including index and Pronouncing Vocabulary)
Illustrated with numerous paintings, drawings, photographs, maps, graphs, etc.

Five illustrations in color and black and white by N. C. Wyeth.
Coronado searches for the riches of the Seven Cities of Cibolo.[1] (color) p 31
Signing the "Mayflower Compact."[1] (black and white) p 54
General Washington at Yorktown.[1] (black and white) p 123
Sacajawea guides the exploring party of Lewis and Clark through the Rocky Mountains.[1] (color) p 175
A public test of Cyrus McCormick's reaper.[2] p 242

[1] The illustrations originally appeared in color for the 1940 "America In The Making" calendar, published by John Morrell & Company, Ottumwa, Iowa.
[2] Painted for the 100th Anniversary of International Harvester Company (1831–1931). It appeared in color in leading periodicals during the year 1931.

Pitz, Henry C.

A Treasury of / AMERICAN / BOOK ILLUSTRATION / by / Henry C. Pitz / [pictorial design] / American Studio Books / and Watson-Guptill Publications, Inc. / New York and London.

Copyright 1947 by the Holme Press, Inc.
Folio. Red cloth; pictorial decoration on cover stamped in gold; lettering on cover and spine stamped in gold; 128 pp.
Illustrated with the works of numerous artists.

One illustration in black and white by N. C. Wyeth.
Description: On the sea wall with John Paul Jones. p 94

Note: The illustration originally appeared in color in Drums by James Boyd, published by Charles Scribner's Sons, N. Y., 1928.

ILLUSTRATING / CHILDREN'S BOOKS / History—Technique—Production / Henry C. Pitz / [publisher's colophon] / New York / Watson-Guptill Publications

Copyright 1963 by Watson-Guptill Publications, Inc.
4 to. Blue cloth; spine stamped in gold; 207 pp (including index).
Illustrated with book illustrations, drawings, diagrams, etc.

One illustration in black and white by N. C. Wyeth.
Description: The Lawless, keeping half a step in front of his companion. . . . p 71
References to N. C. Wyeth on pages 72 and 74.

Note: The illustration originally appeared in color in the book The Black Arrow by Robert Louis Stevenson, published by Charles Scribner's Sons, New York, October 1916.

Pourade, Richard F.

Volume Four of a Series / on the Historic Birthplace of California / The History of San Diego / THE GLORY YEARS / Written By / Richard F. Pourade / [credits] / Commissioned By / James S. Copley / [credits] / Published By The Union-Tribune Publishing Company.

Copyright 1964 by The Union-Tribune Publishing Company, San Diego, California.
First Edition, so stated on the copyright page.
4 to. Dark blue cloth; stamped design on cover; lettering on spine stamped in gold; 274 pp (including index).
Illustrated with numerous paintings, photographs, engravings and maps.

One illustration in color by N. C. Wyeth.
The boom also brought an era of lawlessness and saloons were scenes of nightly brawling. p 173

Note: The illustration originally appeared in black and white in Collier's Weekly, January 1, 1916, for the story "Punderson Waite" by Ceylon Hollingsworth.

Rawlings, Marjorie Kinnan

The / YEARLING / By / Marjorie Kinnan Rawlings / Decorations by / Edward Shenton / Charles Scribner's Sons • New York

Copyright 1938, 1941, (1947) by Marjorie Kinan Rawlings.
(School Edition)
8 vo. Pale yellow cloth; illustration (Jody and Flag) printed on cover in color; lettering on cover and spine printed in black; 428 pp.
Illustrated with pen-and-ink decorations by Edward Shenton.

Cover illustration in color by N. C. Wyeth.
Description: Jody and Flag.

Ray, Frederic (Compiled by)

O! / SAY / CAN / YOU / SEE / The Story of America through great paintings / Jacket and Design by Earl R. Blust [inset] / Color Reproductions by Edward Wilson [inset] / Compiled and Narrated by Frederic Ray [inset] / Introduction by Robert H. Fowler [inset] / Epilogue by Dr. Charles C. Sellers [inset] / Stackpole Book [inset] / a National Historical Society book [inset]

Copyright 1970 by The National Historical Society.
Folio. Gray cloth; cover and spine stamped in gold; 189 pp.
Illustrated with works by noted American artists and illustrators plus biographical sketches on the artists represented.
N. C. WYETH (page 171)
Photograph of N. C. Wyeth at work on "The Landing of Columbus" for John Morrell & Company.

Six illustrations in color by N. C. Wyeth.
The Indian in his Solitude.[1] p 19
The Landing of Columbus.[2] p 24
At Concord Bridge.[3] p 43
Bombardment of Tripoli.[2] p 69
By the Dawn's Early Light.[4] p 75
The Battle.[5] p 109

[1] Originally appeared in color for the series "The Indian In His Solitude," The Outing Magazine, June 1907. It was titled The Silent Burial.
[2] The illustrations originally appeared in color for the 1944 "Flags In American History" calendar,

published by John Morrell & Company, Ottumwa, Iowa.
[3] Originally appeared in color as a Bank Holiday Poster—Independence Day, printed for the U.S. Treasury Department, 1921.
[4] Originally appeared as a calendar and poster for the New York Life Insurance Company, 1941.
[5] Originally appeared in color in The Long Roll by Mary Johnston, published by Houghton Mifflin Company, Boston, 1911.

The Reader's Digest Association

[rule] / Reader's Digest [green] / CONDENSED / BOOKS / Volume 1 • 1966 [green] / [rule] / The Reader's Digest Association [green] / Pleasantville, New York

First Edition, so stated on the copyright page.
Edition of Winter Selections: Six condensed books.
The Yearling (white) / A Condensation Of The Book By / Marjorie Kinnan Rawlings / Illustrations By N. C. Wyeth / The original edition of "The Yearling" is published at $5.00 by Charles Scribner's Sons / and is copyright 1938 by Marjorie Kinnan Rawlings. / Illustrations by N. C. Wyeth, copyright 1939 by Charles Scribner's Sons, used by permission. (Title printed over illustration in color.)
Pages 210–346.
Thick 12 mo. Green decorative cloth covers with dark green spine (simulated leather); lettering on spine stamped in gold over maroon insets; gilt top; 598 pp.

Seven illustrations in color.
Endpaper illustration. pp (210-211)
The Fight with Old Slewfoot. p (225)
The Fight at Volusia. p (248)
The Vigil. p (261)
The Storm. p (289)
Penny Teaches Jody His Sums. p (299)
Jody and Flag. p (327)

Note: The illustrations originally appeared in color in both The Pulitzer Prize Limited Edition and The Pulitzer Prize Trade Edition of The Yearling.

Reynolds, Quentin

The Story Of / 100 Years Of Publishing At Street & Smith / THE / FICTION FACTORY / Or / From Pulp Row To Quality Street / By Quentin Reynolds / [publisher's colophon] / Random House / New York

Copyright 1955 by Street & Smith Publications, Inc.
Published in a Limited Edition of 50 copies. Slipcase.
Large 8 vo. Reddish brown cloth with morocco spine (black); pictorial design on cover stamped in gold; lettering on spine stamped in gold; gilt top; uncut; 283 pp (including index).
Illustrated with numerous paintings, engravings, photographs, etc.

One illustration in color by N. C. Wyeth.
Description: Bear hunter in canoe. p 100

Note: The illustration originally appeared as a cover in color for The Popular Magazine, November 15, 1909.

The Story Of / 100 Years of Publishing at Street & Smith / THE / FICTION FACTORY / Or / From Pulp Row To Quality Street / By Quentin Reynolds / [publisher's colophon] / Random House / New York

Copyright 1955 by Street & Smith Publications, Inc.

First Printing, so stated on the copyright page.

Large 8 vo. Reddish brown cloth with morocco spine (black); publisher's colophon stamped on cover in gold; lettering and rules on spine stamped in gold; uncut; 283 pp (including index).

Illustrated with numerous paintings, engravings, photographs, etc.

One illustration in color by N. C. Wyeth. Same as in the Limited Edition.

Rossi, Paul A., and Hunt, David C.
(Selections and Text by)

THE ART Of The OLD WEST / From The Collection Of The Gilcrease Institute / Selections And Text By Paul A. Rossi and David C. Hunt / Illustration by Frederic Remington [Indian Warfare] (1971)

Published by Alfred A. Knopf, Inc.
FIRST EDITION, so stated on the copyright page.

Folio. Gray buckram; pictorial design (Frederic Remington's bronze: The Mountain Man) stamped on front cover in brown; lettering on spine stamped in gold; 336 pp (including Listing of Artists and Works, Bibliography, etc.)

Illustrated in color and black and white with works of the noted artists who portrayed the West.

One illustration in black and white by N. C. Wyeth.
The James Gang pp 258–59

Note: The illustration originally appeared in *The Ladies Home Journal*, November 1921, for the story "Vandemark's Folly" by Herbert Quick. It was titled "For a moment he seemed to be looking right at me. This was my first sight of Bowie Bushyager."

Shuman, Eleanore Nolan

THE TRENTON STORY / By / Eleanore Nolan Shuman / [seal of the city of Trenton] / MacCrellish & Quigley Company / Trenton, New Jersey

Copyright 1958 by Eleanore Nolan Shuman.
Large 8 vo. Blue cloth; lettering on spine

stamped in gold; 385 pp (including appendix)
Illustrated with numerous paintings, drawings, and photographs.

One illustration (mural painting) in black and white by N. C. Wyeth.
Washington's Reception at Trenton p 72
The reception to Washington on April 21, 1789, at Trenton on his way to New York to assume the duties of the presidency of the United States.

Note: The mural painting was commissioned by The Trenton Trust Company (First-Mechanics National Bank) completed in 1930. It adorns the west wall of the main office building at State and Warren streets in Trenton, New Jersey.

THE / SILVER BURDETT / STORY

24 mo. Collation: Title; to our guests (II); contents (III); foreword; text (VI–10); (56) blank note pages.

Size of leaf trimmed 3¾ x 5 inches.
Issued in full cloth. Front cover stamped in silver with pictorial decoration (Silver Burdett tower): (pictorial decoration) The / Silver Burdett / Story / (rule). Spine stamped in silver: THE SILVER BURDETT STORY. Back cover stamped in silver: (rule) / OUR WAYS / AND TIMES / (rule).

Illustrated with graphs and photographs.

One illustration (mural painting) in black and white by N. C. Wyeth.
The Spirit of Education p 6
Pages 6 and 7 describe the mural briefly and present a key for help in identifying the figures depicted in the painting.

Note: The mural was painted by N. C. Wyeth in 1935 to commemorate the company's first half century of service to education.

Van Duyn Southworth, Gertrude and John

The Story of / OUR / AMERICA / by / Gertrude Van Duyn Southworth / and / John Van Duyn Southworth / [six lines of authors' credits] / Co-Authors of / Long Ago in the Old World / Early Days in the New World / etc. / Iroquois Publishing Company, Inc. / Syracuse, New York

Copyright 1955 by Iroquois Publishing Company, Inc.

8 vo. Red cloth; front cover stamped in silver with pictorial design (minuteman) stamped in black; lettering on spine stamped in silver; 868 pp (including index, etc.)

Illustrated in color and black and white with numerous paintings, drawings, photographs, maps, etc.

Six illustrations in color by N. C. Wyeth.
Leif the Lucky Discovers North America. p 2
Columbus Discovers the New World. p 6
The Battle of Bunker Hill. p 100
The Constitution Bombarding Tripoli. p 175
The Defense of the Alamo. p 264
General Robert E. Lee and His Troops. p 324

Note: The illustrations originally appeared in the 1944 "Flags of American History" calendar, published by John Morrell & Company, Ottumwa, Iowa.

Wilder, Howard B.

THIS IS / AMERICA'S STORY / [pictorial design] / Howard B. Wilder [credits] / Robert P. Ludlum [credits] / Harriet McCune Brown [credits] / Howard R. Anderson [credits] / Houghton Mifflin Company • Boston • New York • Chicago / Dallas • Atlanta • San Francisco • The Riverside Press Cambridge

Copyright 1948 by Howard B. Wilder, Robert P. Ludlum, and Harriet McCune Brown.

Large 8 vo. Gray cloth with pictorial design stamped in red and blue; lettering on cover stamped over red inset; lettering on spine stamped in red and black; 712 pp (including acknowledgments, picture credits, etc.).

Illustrated with numerous paintings, drawings, engravings, and photographs.

One illustration in black and white by N. C. Wyeth.
Rip Van Winkle p 322

Note: The illustration originally appeared in color in *Rip Van Winkle* by Washington Irving, published by David McKay Company, Phila., 1921. It was titled "It was with some difficulty that he found his way to his own house, . . ."

Books Containing Biographical Information and References to N. C. Wyeth

Ainsworth, Ed

by Ed Ainsworth / [pictorial design] / [double rules] / THE COWBOY IN ART / [double rules] / The World Publishing Company • New York and Cleveland / [publisher's colophon]

Copyright 1968 by Ed Ainsworth.
First Printing, so stated on the copyright page.
4 to. Brown cloth; pictorial design on cover stamped in gold; spine stamped in gold; 242 pp (including index and acknowledgments).
Illustrated with numerous paintings, drawings, bronzes, photographs, etc.

References to N. C. Wyeth on pages 57, 99, 182–84.

Apgar, John F., Jr.

FRANK E. SCHOONOVER / Painter-Illustrator • A Bibliography / By John F. Apgar, Jr.

(Privately printed)
Copyright 1969 by John F. Apgar, Jr.
Printed in an edition of five hundred and fifty copies of which 50 are limited and signed by the author and artist.
8 vo. White cloth; pictorial label on cover

in brown tint; lettering on cover and spine stamped in gold; (65 pp).
References to N. C. Wyeth.
Idem: The trade edition has tan cloth with lettering stamped in dark brown.

Arbuthnot, May Hill

CHILDREN AND BOOKS / May Hill Arbuthnot / [author's credits] / [rule] / Scott, Foresman and Company / Chicago (etc.)

Copyright 1947 by Scott, Foresman and Company.
Large 8 vo. Light blue cloth; lettering on

cover and spine stamped in gold over brown; 626 pp (including index).

Reference to N. C. Wyeth and his work for the book *The Yearling*.

Illustrated with numerous book illustrations, drawings, and photographs, etc.

Two illustrations in black and white by N. C. Wyeth.

    Illustration from *Robinson Crusoe* p 19
    Illustration from *The Odyssey* p 270

Beitz, Lester

TREASURY / OF / FRONTIER / RELICS / A Collectors Guide / By / Les Beitz / Edwin House : New York / trade distribution by / Crown Publishers, Inc.

Copyright 1966 by Lester Beitz.

8 vo. Light gold cloth; designs on cover stamped in brown; lettering on spine stamped in red; 246 pp (including index)

A chapter dealing in Western Art discusses the works of N. C. Wyeth on pages 196–211.

    Photograph of N. C. Wyeth on horseback. p 200

Eleven illustrations in black and white by N. C. Wyeth

    The lee of the grub-wagon.[1] p 23
    The glowing iron stuck in his hand. . . .[2] p 35
    The little posse started out on its journey. . . .[2] p 41
    Hopalong Cassidy.[3] p 83
    The Captain and Danvers.[4] p 103
    Cutting Out.[1] p 121
    Racing for Dinner.[1] p 165
    In the Corral.[1] p 203
    The Silent Fisherman.[5] p 205
    As the mail goes Cream of Wheat Goes.[6] p 207
    Bucking.[1] p 209

[1] The illustrations originally appeared in color in *Scribner's Magazine*, March 1906, for the article "A Day with the Round-Up" by N. C. Wyeth.
[2] The illustrations originally appeared in color in the book *Langford of the Three Bars* by Kate and Virgil D. Boyles, published by A. C. McClurg & Co., Chicago, 1907.
[3] Originally appeared in color in *The Outing Magazine*, May 1906, for the story "Bar 20 Range Yarns" by Clarence Edward Mulford.
[4] Originally appeared in black and white in *Scribner's Magazine*, August 1907, for the story "Lascar" by Hugh Johnson.
[5] Originally appeared as a frontispiece in color in *Scribner's Magazine*, October 1907.
[6] Originally appeared as an advertisement for Cream of Wheat 1908–18.

Bimson, Walter Reed

THE WEST AND WALTER BIMSON / Paintings, Watercolors, Drawings and Sculpture / collected by / Mr. Walter Reed Bimson / Published By / The University Of Arizona Museum Of Art / Tucson, Arizona [surrounded by ornamental boxed rules painted in blue]

Copyright 1971 by Walter Reed Bimson.

4 to. Red cloth; lettering (initials) on cover stamped in gold over black inset; lettering on spine stamped in gold; 223 pp.

Illustrated with numerous paintings in color and black and white plus bronze sculpture by noted artists of the West.

Accompanied by a biographical text on the artists represented.

Biographical text on N. C. Wyeth 1882–1945 (page 156)

Two illustrations in color by N. C. Wyeth. Indian Brave Fishing (repeated on the dust wrapper).[1] p 157
Holdup in the Canyon.[2] p 158

[1] Originally appeared as a cover in color for *The Popular Magazine*, June 7, 1923.
[2] Originally appeared as a frontispiece in color in *McClure's Magazine*, August 1906.

Bolton, Theodore

AMERICAN / BOOK ILLUSTRATORS / Bibliographic Check Lists / of 123 Artists / by Theodore Bolton / [decoration] / New York • R. R. Bowker Company / 1938

Printed in a LIMITED EDITION of One Thousand Copies.

Large 8 vo. Collation: Half title (I); author's book list (II); title (III); copyright (1938) (printed in a Limited Edition of one thousand copies) and imprint (IV); introduction (V–VII); contents (IX–XII); half title; text (1–209); index (211–90).

Size of leaf trimmed 6 x 9⅜ inches.

Issued in full cloth (reddish brown). Front cover stamped with decoration. Spine stamped in gold: American / Book / Illustrators / By / Theodore / Bolton / (at bottom) Bowker

A bibliographical record of books illustrated by one hundred and twenty-three American artists.

The works of Newell Convers Wyeth listed on pages 206–9.

Burke, W. J., and Howe, Will D.

American / Authors and Books / [publisher's colophon] / New York / Gramercy Publishing Co. / 419 Fourth Avenue / New York / 1943

Thick large 8 vo. Reddish brown cloth; lettering on spine stamped in gold over stamped dark blue insets; 858 pp.

Biographical information on N. C. Wyeth on page 850.

Burlingame, Roger

OF MAKING / MANY BOOKS / [rule] / A Hundred Years of Reading, Writing and Publishing / [rule] / by / Roger Burlingame / MDCCCXLVI (ornamental design) MDCCCXLVI / [rule] / New York / Charles Scribner's Sons / 1946

Scribner code letter A on the copyright page.

Large 8 vo. Brown cloth; lettering on cover and spine stamped in gold (surrounded by double boxed rules); brown top; 347 pp (including index).

References to N. C. Wyeth on pages 235 and 237.

Byrnes, Gene (Selected and Compiled by)

A Complete Guide to / DRAWING / ILLUSTRATION / CARTOONING / AND PAINTING / Selected and Compiled by / Gene Byrnes / with editorial assistance and text / by A. Thornton Bishop / [publisher's colophon] / Simon and Schuster, New York

Copyright 1948 by Gene Byrnes.

4 to. Red boards with cloth spine; lettering on cover stamped in gold over black inset; lettering stamped on spine in gold (title over black inset); dark gray top; 354 pp (plus one page of author's credits).

A volume on drawing and painting shown through examples from the works of 138 outstanding artists.

DECORATIVE PAINTING (pages 327–29)

Discussed are N. C. Wyeth's mural paintings for the Home Office of the Metropolitan Life Insurance Company, New York

    Two photographs of the murals.
    Going to Church (in process of completion in the artist's studio). p 328
    Thanksgiving Feast (as completed and hung in the Metropolitan Life Insurance Company). p 328

Canby, Henry Seidel

THE / BRANDYWINE / by Henry Seidel Canby / Illustrated by / Andrew Wyeth / [drawing] / Farrar & Rinehart / Incorporated / New York   Toronto

Copyright 1941 by Henry Seidel Canby.

8 vo. Light brown cloth; R of A (Rivers of America) series seal stamped on cover; lettering on spine stamped in gold (title over plum colored band); plum colored top; 285 pp (including index).

Illustrated with dry brush drawings by Andrew Wyeth.

Reference to N. C. Wyeth on page 253.

Carlson, Raymond (Edited by)

Gallery of / Western Paintings / Edited by / Raymond Carlson / McGraw-Hill Book Company, Inc. / New York   London   Toronto

Copyright 1951 by Hobson & Herr, Inc.

First Edition, so stated on the copyright page.

Folio. Reddish brown cloth with small pictorial cover label in color; lettering on spine stamped in silver and black; 85 pp.

Illustrated with numerous works in color and black and white by noted painters of the western scene.

Reference to N. C. Wyeth on page 65.

Carr, James F. (Compiled by)

MANTLE FIELDING'S / DICTIONARY / of / American Painters, Sculptors, and Engravers / With an Addendum / Containing Corrections and / Additional Material on the / Original Entries / Compiled by / James F. Carr / James F. Carr / Publisher / New York 1965

Large 8 vo. Brown cloth; lettering on spine stamped in gold; 529 pp.

Newell Convers Wyeth

Listing of awards, mural decorations, etc. on page 420.

Dineen, Michael P. (and the editors of Country Beautiful Foundation)

GREAT ART TREASURES IN AMERICA'S SMALLER MUSEUMS / [oval painting] / By The Editors Of Country Beautiful / Editorial Direction : Michael P. Dineen • / Edited by Robert L. Pollery • Text by / Harold Haydon, Associate Professor of Art / and Director of the Midway Studios, / University of Chicago / [sculpture] / Published by G. P. Putnam's Sons, New York / In association with Country Beautiful Foundation, Inc., Waukesha, Wisconsin

Copyright 1967 by Country Life Beautiful Foundation, Inc.

First Edition, so stated on the copyright page.

4 to. Red cloth; lettering on cover and spine stamped in gold; 194 pp.

Illustrated with reproductions in color and black and white from the collections of America's finest smaller museums.

From the collection of the New Britain Museum of American Art.

One illustration in black and white by N. C. Wyeth.

One more step, Mr. Hands. p 27

Note: The illustration originally appeared in color in the book *Treasure Island* by Robert Louis Stevenson, published by Charles Scribner's Sons, N. Y., September 1911.

Dunn, Harvey

AN EVENING / In The Classroom / [woodcut] / Being Notes Taken By / Miss Taylor In One / Of The Classes Of / Painting Conducted / By Harvey Dunn / And Printed At The / Instigation Of / Mario Cooper.

Copyright 1934 by Harvey Dunn.

This The First Edition Of AN EVENING IN THE CLASSROOM Consists Of One Thousand Copies.

Thin large 8 vo. Issued in paper wrappers; 55 pp.

Illustrated with woodcuts by Harvey Dunn. N. C. Wyeth quoted on page 50.

Eckman, Jeannette

DELAWARE / A Guide to the First State / [ornament] / Compiled and Written by the Federal Writers' Project / of the Work Progress Administration / for the State of Delaware / New and Revised Edition / By Jeannette Eckman / Edited By Henry G. Alsberg / American Guide Series / Illustrated / [publisher's colophon] / Hastings House / Publishers   New York 22

First published in June 1938, so stated on the copyright page; second printing December 1948; Second Edition extensively revised May 1955; Copyright 1955 by Hastings House Publishers, Inc.

Illustrated with photographs, engravings, etc.

8 vo. Gray cloth; lettering on cover and spine stamped in dark blue; 562 pp (including index).

References to N. C. Wyeth on pages 142, 143, and 304.

Eliot, Alexander

Three Hundred Years / of / AMERICAN PAINTING / by / Alexander Eliot / art editor of Time / with an introduction by John Walker / director of the National Gallery / Time Incorporated • New York • 1957

Folio. White cloth covers with maroon cloth spine (simulated leather); cover and spine stamped in gold; 318 pp (including index).

Illustrated with numerous paintings in color by noted American artists.

Reference to N. C. Wyeth on page 288.

Exman, Eugene

THE / HOUSE / OF / HARPER / [publisher's colophons] One Hundred and Fifty Years of Publishing / Eugene Exman / Harper & Row, Publishers / New York, Evanston, and London

Copyright 1967 by Eugene Exman.

First Edition, so stated on the copyright page.

Large 8 vo. Red cloth; publisher's colophon stamped on cover; lettering and colophon on spine stamped in gold (title over stamped inset in black); 326 pp (including index).

Reference to N. C. Wyeth on page 117.

Field, Carolyn W. (Edited by)

SUBJECT / COLLECTIONS / IN CHILDREN'S / LITERATURE / Edited by Carolyn W. Field, / Consultants: Virginia Haviland, Elizabeth Nesbitt, / for the National Planning Commitee for Special Collections, / Children's Services Division, American Library Association / [woodcut—Chapbook: Sir Bevis of Hampton] / R. R. Bowker Company   New York & London 1969

8 vo. Orange cloth; woodcut (Sir Bevis of Hampton) stamped on cover in black; lettering on cover and spine stamped in white; 142 pp (including index).

Illustrated with a few woodcuts and engravings.

Reference to N. C. Wyeth on page 59.

Fielding, Mantle

DICTIONARY / of / American Painters, Sculptors / and / Engravers / By / Mantle Fielding / Author of Gilbert Stuart and his / Portraits of Washington / Printed for the Subscribers / Philadelphia [1926]

Limited to an edition of seven hundred copies, printed for the subscribers.

Illustrated with numerous paintings by noted 18th century American artists.

4 to. Cloth; 433 pp (including a brief bibliography).

N. C. Wyeth
    Listing of credits, awards, and mural decorations on page 420.

Gallatin, Albert Eugene

ART / AND THE GREAT WAR / By / Albert Eugene Gallatin / [credits—eight lines] / With One Hundred Illustrations / [ornament—brown] / New York / E. P. Dutton & Company / 1919 [first line printed in brown]

Folio. Green boards; dark green cloth spine; lettering on cover and spine stamped in gold; uncut; 288 pp.

Reference to N. C. Wyeth on page 39.

Note: N. C. Wyeth and Henry Reuterdahl collaborated in the painting of a large poster mural measuring 25' x 90'. It was executed for the Third Liberty Loan and was displayed on the Sub-Treasury Building in New York City.

Harmsen, Dorothy

HARMSEN'S WESTERN AMERICANA / [painting in color] / A collection of / one hundred western paintings / with biograph-ical profiles / of the artists / By Dorothy Harmsen / Foreword By Robert Rockwell / Northland Press / Flagstaff, Arizona [publisher's colophon]

Copyright 1971 by Harmsen's Western Americana.

4 to. White buckram covers with dark blue spine; spine stamped in gold; 213 pp (including list of artists and selected bibliography).

Illustrated with numerous paintings in color by noted artists of the West.

N. C. Wyeth, N.A.
    1882–1945
    Biographical study (page 204).

One illustration in color by N. C. Wyeth. Gunfight. fp 204
(Illustration from *Nan of Music Mountain*)

Reference to N. C. Wyeth in chapter on Gerard Curtis Delano (page 62).

Haviland, Virginia

CHILDREN'S LITERATURE / A Guide to Reference Sources / Prepared Under the Direction of / Virginia Haviland / [publisher's colophon] / Library of Congress / Washington : 1966

Large 8 vo. Blue cloth; designs on cover stamped in white; lettering on spine stamped in white; 341 pp (including index).

References to N. C. Wyeth on pages 92 (number 312) and 117 (number 392).

Horwitt, Nathan George (Written and arranged by)

A Book of / Notable American / Illustrators / [double rules] / Vol. 2, 1927 / [ornament] / [introduction]

Published by The Walker Engraving Corporation, New York.

Volume 2

Thin folio. Boards (black) with orange cloth spine; orange cover label with lettering in black (surrounded by scrollwork); (31 pp).

A series of critical appreciations of notable American Illustrators.

No. 17 N. C. WYETH

Photograph of Wyeth at work on the mural painting *Elizabethan Galleons* for the First National Bank of Boston.

One illustration in black and white.
    Description: A Spanish Galleon (p 17)

Note: The illustration originally appeared as a cover in color for *Scribner's Magazine*, September 1923.

Howard, Frances R. (Editor)

AMERICAN ART ANNUAL / Founded 1898 by Florence N. Levy / Volume XVIII / The American Federation of Arts / 1741 New York Ave., Washington, D.C. / 1921

Copyright 1922 by The American Federation of Arts.

Large 8 vo. Green cloth; lettering on cover and spine stamped in gold; 680 pp.

Illustrated with numerous paintings, sculpture, and photographs.

N. C. Wyeth listed among the artists on page 634.

Hydeman, Sid

HOW TO / ILLUSTRATE / FOR MONEY / By Sid Hydeman / Art Editor, Redbook Magazine / Foreword By / Edwin Balmer / [publisher's colophon] Harper & Brothers Publishers / New York and London / 1936

First Edition, so stated on the copyright page. Harper code letters B–L on the copyright page.

Large 8 vo. Light brown boards; brown cloth spine; lettering on cover and spine labels printed in brown; 173 pp (including index).

References to N. C. Wyeth on pages 21 and 83.

Irwin, Grace

TRAIL-BLAZERS / OF AMERICAN ART / By / Grace Irwin / [publisher's colophon] / Harper & Brothers, Publishers / New York and London / 1930

First Edition, so stated on the copyright page. Harper code letters H-E on the copyright page.

8 vo. Cloth; 228 pp.

Illustrated in color and black and white.

Chapter XI: Howard Pyle and Some Others (pages 208–26)

References to N. C. Wyeth on pages 221 and 224.

Karolevitz, Robert F.

[decoration] / [illustration in color surrounded by boxed rule] / WHERE YOUR HEART IS / The Story Of Harvey Dunn, Artist / by Robert F. Karolevitz

Copyright 1970 by North Plains Press, Aberdeen, S. Dak.

Folio. Gray blue cloth; lettering on cover and spine stamped in gold; 208 pp (including index).

References to N. C. Wyeth on pages 32, 37, 51, 93, 109, 122, and 129.

Klemin, Diana

The Illustrated Book: Its Art and Craft / by Diana Klemin / [publisher's colophon] Clarkson N. Potter, Inc. Publisher • New York / Distributed by Crown Publishers, Inc.

Copyright 1970 by Diana Klemin.

First Edition, so stated on the copyright page.

4 to. White cloth; lettering on cover and spine stamped in black; 159 pp (including index).

Illustrated in color and black and white with the works of noted illustrators.

One illustration in black and white by N. C. Wyeth.

The Lobsterman. p 90

References to N. C. Wyeth on pages 18, 71, and 91.

Note: The illustration originally appeared in color in the book *Trending into Maine* by Kenneth Roberts, published by Little, Brown and Company, Boston, 1938.

Krakel, Dean

TOM RYAN / A painter in Four Sixes country / by Dean Krakel / Northland Press / Flagstaff, Arizona

Copyright 1971 by Dean Krakel.

8 vo. Brown cloth; pictorial design (calf) on cover stamped in gold; lettering on spine stamped in gold; 111 pp (including bibliography).

Illustrated in color and black and white with the artist's paintings and drawings.

References to N. C. Wyeth on pages 6, 16, 23, 25, 26, 27, 30, 31, and 100.

Kunitz, Stanley J., and Haycraft, Howard

The Junior Book / of Authors / An Introduction to the Lives of Writers and Illustrators / for Younger Readers from Lewis Carroll and Louisa Alcott to the Present Day / Edited by / Stanley J. Kunitz and Howard Haycraft Assisted by / Wilbur C. Hadden / Julia E. Johnsen / Illustrated with 260 Photographs / and Drawings / With an Introduction by / Effie L. Power / (publisher's colophon) / New York / The H. W. Wilson Company / Nineteen Hundred Thirty-Four

Copyright November 1934, so stated on the copyright page.

4 to. Orange cloth; pictorial cover stamped in black designs (surrounded by rules); lettering on cover stamped in black (surrounded by boxed rules); lettering on spine stamped in black; 430 pp (including index, Authors' Names —How To Pronounce Them and The Children's Almanac of Books and Holidays).

Illustrated with photographic portraits, etc.

N. C. Wyeth

A biographical study of the artist's life (pages 386–87).

One illustration in black and white by N. C. Wyeth.

Self-Portrait p 387

A reference to N. C. Wyeth's illustrations is found in the biographical study on Robert Louis Stevenson (pages 346–47).

Note: The illustration originally appeared as a frontispiece in black and white in *Scribner's Magazine*, August 1928.

Larkin, Oliver W.

Oliver W. Larkin / ART AND LIFE / IN AMERICA / Rinehart & Company, Inc. New York

Copyright 1949 by Oliver W. Larkin.

4 to. Cloth; 547 pp (including the index).

Illustrated with numerous paintings, drawings, etc.

References to N. C. Wyeth on page 332.

Latimer, Louise P. (Compiled by)

ILLUSTRATORS / A Finding List / Compiled By / Louise P. Latimer / The Public Library, Washington, D. C. / Boston / The F. W. Faxon Company / 83–91 Francis Street / 1929

Thin 8 vo. Green cloth; lettering on cover stamped in gold (surrounded by boxed rules); lettering on spine stamped in gold; 47 pp.

A listing of books illustrated by N. C. Wyeth appears on pages 28 and 29.

Logsdon, Gene

Wyeth People / A Portrait of Andrew Wyeth / as He Is Seen by / His Friends and Neighbors / Gene Logsdon / Illustrated with Photographs by the Author / Doubleday &

Company, Inc., Garden City, New York / 1971

Copyright 1969, 1971 by Farm Journal, Inc.

8 vo. Green cloth; lettering on spine stamped in gold; 159 pp (including index).

References to N. C. Wyeth on pages 25, 27, 28, 34, 38, 53, 55–56, 67, 99, 109, 123, 127, and 131.

Lykes, Richard Wayne

HOWARD PYLE / TEACHER OF ILLUSTRATION / Richard Wayne Lykes / Graduate School of Arts and Sciences / University of Pennsylvania / 1947

College thesis paper; 65 pp.

References to N. C. Wyeth on pages 24, 25, 28, 29, 37, 38, 45, 46, 47, 49, 50, 52, 55, 56, 63, 64, and 65.

Mahony, Bertha E., and Whitney, Elinor (Compiled by)

CONTEMPORARY / ILLUSTRATORS / OF CHILDREN'S / BOOKS / Compiled By / Bertha E. Mahony / and Elinor Whitney / [pictorial decoration] / The Bookshop For Boys and Girls / Women's Educational / and Industrial Union / Boston 1930

4 to. Light brown cloth; pictorial design (repeat of the title page decoration) on cover stamped in gold; small leather labels on spine stamped in gold; 135 pp (including appendix).

The Illustrators

A brief biographical study and check listing of books illustrated by N. C. Wyeth. p 81

The Brandywine Tradition—Howard Pyle and N. C. Wyeth by Dudley Cammett Lunt.

With illustrations by N. C. Wyeth and Howard Pyle (pages 126–30).

Two illustrations by N. C. Wyeth. One in color and one in pen and ink.

Illustration from *Treasure Island* fp 128

Endpaper illustration from *The Odyssey* p 130

REALMS / of / GOLD / In Children's Books / Compiled by / Bertha E. Mahony and / Elinor Whitney / The Fifth Edition of "Books for Boys and Girls—A / Suggestive Purchase List" previously published / by The Bookshop for Boys and Girls, / Women's Educational and Industrial / Union, Boston, Massachusetts / [publisher's colophon] / 1929 / Doubleday, Doran & Company, Inc. / Garden City, New York

First Edition, so stated on the copyright page.

Large 8 vo. Gold cloth; lettering on cover and spine stamped in dark brown; gold top; 796 pp (including index)

This guide to the best children's books of all types covers a number of the books illustrated by N. C. Wyeth. References to these books are found on pages 233, 245, 250, 253, 260, 433, 473, 485, 486, 502, 509, 512, 514, 515, 532, 535, 536, 547, 548, 691, and 692.

FIVE YEARS OF / Children's Books / A Supplement to / Realms of Gold / Compiled by / Bertha E. Mahony and / Elinor Whitney / 1936 / Doubleday, Doran & Company, Inc. / Garden City, New York

Large 8 vo. Brown cloth; stamped lettering on cover; lettering on spine stamped in gold; brown top; 599 pp (including index).

References to books illustrated by N. C. Wyeth on pages 182 and 283.

Mahony, Bertha E.; Latimer, Louise Payson; and Folmsbee, Beulah

(Compiled by)

ILLUSTRATORS / of / Children's Books / 1744–1945 / Compiled by / Bertha E. Mahony / Louise Payson Latimer / Beulah Folmsbee / [drawing—John Tenniel] / The Horn Book Inc. Boston

Copyright 1947 by the Horn Book, Inc.
4 to. Blue cloth; lettering on cover and spine stamped in gold; 527 pp (including index).
References to N. C. Wyeth on pages 115, 121, 184, 187, 191, and 229.

Meigs, John (Editor)

Peter Hurd / THE LITHOGRAPHS / Introduction / By / Andrew Wyeth / Editor / John Meigs / 1968 / Baker Gallery Press

First Printing 1968, so stated on the copyright page.
4 to. Black cloth; lettering on spine stamped in gold; 23 pp; plates (I–LVIII)
References to N. C. Wyeth in the Introduction by Andrew Wyeth, the Foreword by John Meigs, and the text.

Mellon, Gertrud A., and Wilder, Elizabeth F.

Gertrud A. Mellon, Co-ordinating Editor / Elizabeth F. Wilder, Editor / MAINE and Its Role in American Art / [double rules] / 1740–1963 / Under the Auspices of Colby College, Waterville, Maine   A studio Book • The Viking Press • New York

Copyright 1963 by The Viking Press, Inc.
4 to. Gray boards with cloth back (gray green); lettering on spine stamped in gold; 178 pp (including index).
Illustrated in color and black and white with the works of numerous American artists.

One illustration (painting) in black and white by N. C. Wyeth.
Dark Harbor Fishermen p 110
    Oil, 30 × 35 inches. Collection of Robert F. Woolworth
References to N. C. Wyeth on page 116.

Mellquist, Jerome

The / Emergence / of an / American Art / By / Jerome Mellquist / [publisher's colophon] / New York / Charles Scribner's Sons / 1942 [title surrounded by ornamental boxed rules]

Scribner code letter A on the copyright page.
Large 8 vo. Red cloth; lettering on spine stamped in gold; 421 pp (including appendix and index).
Reference to N. C. Wyeth on page 152.

Meryman, Richard

Richard Meryman / ANDREW WYETH / 1968 : Houghton Mifflin Company : Boston

Copyright 1968 by The Mill Incorporated.
First Printing, so stated on the copyright page.

Folio: Beige buckram sides with buckram spine (dark brown); initials AW on cover stamped in dark brown; lettering on spine stamped in white; 174 pp (including index of paintings and drawings).
Illustrated in color and black and white with numerous tempera paintings, watercolors, drybrush drawings, working drawings, and pencil studies by Andrew Wyeth.
The text contains many references to N. C. Wyeth.

Moore, Annie Carroll

ROADS TO / CHILDHOOD / Views and Reviews of / Children's Books / By / Annie Carroll Moore / New [publisher's colophon] York / George H. Doran Company

Copyright 1920 by George H. Doran Company.
12 mo. Light brown boards with brown cloth spine; small paper label on spine printed in black; 240 pp (including index).
Comments and references to books illustrated by N. C. Wyeth on pages 63, 89, and 153.

Moore, Anne Carroll

THE / THREE OWLS / A Book About Children's Books / Their Authors / Artists and Critics / Written and Edited By / Anne Carroll Moore / New York / The Macmillian Company / 1925 / All Rights Reserved

Published November 1925, so stated on the copyright page.
12 mo. Green cloth; designs (owls) and rules on spine stamped in black; lettering on cover and spine stamped in black; 376 pp (including index).
References to N. C. Wyeth on pages 235, 236, 322, 323, and 324.
Idem: Except for orange cloth binding.

Note: The articles originally appeared in the *New York Herald Tribune*'s weekly literary review titled "The Three Owls" by Anne Carroll Moore, 1924.

CROSS-ROADS / TO CHILDHOOD / By / Anne Carroll Moore / New [publisher's colophon] York / George H. Doran Company

Copyright 1926 by George H. Doran Company.
12 mo. Cloth; 292 pp (including index).
Comments and references to books illustrated by N. C. Wyeth on pages 88, 92, 93, 96, and 97.

MY ROADS / TO CHILDHOOD / Views and Reviews of / Children's Books / By / Anne Carroll Moore / Decorations by Arthur Lougee / [publisher's colophon] / New York / Doubleday, Doran & Company, Inc. / 1939 [title surrounded by boxed rules]

First edition, so stated on the copyright page.
8 vo. Blue cloth; author's initials stamped on cover; lettering on spine stamped in gold; 399 pp (including index).
A repeat of the text in the earlier volumes by Anne Carroll Moore titled *Cross-Roads to Childhood* and *Roads to Childhood*.

Morse, Willard S., and Brincklé, Gertrude (Compiled by)

HOWARD PYLE / A Record of / His Illustrations and Writings / Compiled by

Willard S. Morse / and Gertrude Brincklé / Wilmington, Delaware / The Wilmington Society of the Fine Arts / 1921

An edition of 500 copies of this work has been issued and distributed to the contributing members of the society and to the public libraries of the principal cities of this country

Large 8 vo. Boards (blue) with vellum spine; paper label on cover stamped in black; 242 pp; tissue wrapper.
Reference to N. C. Wyeth on page 242.

Note: The foreword by N. C. Wyeth which appears in the special limited edition is deleted from this volume.

Nesbitt, Elizabeth

Howard Pyle / [decorative double rules] / Elizabeth Nesbitt / A Walck Monograph / General Editor: Kathleen Lines / Henry Z. Walck, Incorporated / New York

First American edition 1966, so stated on the copyright page.
12 mo. Blue cloth; lettering on cover and spine stamped in black; 72 pp.
References to N. C. Wyeth on pages 24, 32, and 35.

Oakley, Amy

OUR / PENNSYLVANIA / Keys / To The / Keystone State / by / Amy Oakley / Illustrations by / Thornton Oakley / [design] / The Bobbs-Merrill Company, Inc. / Publishers / Indianapolis   New York

Copyright 1950 by Amy and Thornton Oakley.
8 vo. Blue cloth; lettering and ornaments on cover and spine stamped in gold; 467 pp (including index).
Reference to N. C. Wyeth on page 105.

Pitz, Henry C.

THE / BRANDYWINE / TRADITION / Henry C. Pitz / [publisher's colophon] / Illustrated with 16 color / and 32 black-and-white plates / Houghton Mifflin Company   Boston / 1969

4 to. Light olive cloth; lettering on cover stamped in black; title stamped on spine in gold over black inset; author and publisher stamped in black; 252 pp (including bibliography and index).
Newell Convers Wyeth (pages 188–207.) (Chapter XVI)
Other references to N. C. Wyeth on pages 106, 111, 127, 128, 136, 176, 182, 208, 209, and 210.
Two photographs of N. C. Wyeth.
Photographic portrait.
N. C. Wyeth painting a mural (Metropolitan Life Insurance Company)
Illustrated in color and black and white with the works of Howard Pyle, noted students of Pyle, Andrew Wyeth, etc.

Two illustrations in color by N. C. Wyeth.
Blind Pew[1]
The Ore Wagon[2]

[1] Originally appeared in color in the book *Treasure Island* by Robert Louis Stevenson, published by Charles Scribner's Sons, September 1911. It was titled Old Pew.
[2] Originally appeared in color in *McClure's Magazine*, May 1908, for the story "The Misadventures of Cassidy" by Edward S. Moffat.

Randall, David A.

David A. Randall / [rule and ornaments] / DUKEDOM / LARGE / ENOUGH / (quotation) / [publisher's colophon] / Random House   New York

Copyright 1962 (1969) by David Randall. Large 8 vo. Maroon cloth; lettering on spine stamped in gold; green top; 368 pp (including index).
Reference to N. C. Wyeth on page 180.

Reed, H. Clay, and Reed, Marion B. (Compiled by)

A BIBLIOGRAPHY OF DELAWARE / THROUGH 1960 / Compiled By H. Clay Reed / professor of history emeritus / University of Delaware / and / Marion Bjornson Reed / formerly executive secretary / Historical Society of Delaware / Published for / The Institute Of Delaware History and Culture / by the / University of Delaware Press / Newark • 1966

Large 8 vo. Blue paper wraps; lettering on cover and spine stamped in black; 196 pp.
References to Dudley Lunt's article on N. C. Wyeth in *Delaware History* and the N. C. Wyeth Memorial Exhibition at The Wilmington Society of the Fine Arts in 1946.

Reed, Walt (Compiled and edited by)

(drawing) / The Illustrator in America / 1900–1960's / Compiled and edited by / Walt Reed / (publisher's colophon) Reinhold Publishing Corporation / New York

Copyright 1966 by Walt Reed.
Folio: white cloth; spine stamped in gold; 272 pp (including bibliography).
This pictorial history of American illustration (1900–1960's) contains numerous works and a biographical sketch of the artists represented.
N. C. Wyeth (pages 72–73)
Four illustrations. One in color and three in black and white.
The Battle[1] (color) p 72
In the Crystal Depths[2] p 73
Illustrations from *Arizona Nights* p 73
Description: An Almighty exciting race.
Illustration from *Treasure Island* p 73
Description: Israel Hands

[1] Originally appeared in color in the book *The Long Roll* by Mary Johnston, published by Houghton Mifflin Company, Boston, May 1911.
[2] Originally appeared in color in *The Outing Magazine*, June 1907, a part of the series "The Indian in His Solitude."

Richardson, E. P.

PAINTING / IN / AMERICA / The story of 450 years / E. P. Richardson / The Detroit Institute of Arts / Thomas Y. Crowell Company, New York

Copyright 1956 by E. P. Richardson.
4 to. Tan cloth; lettering on cover stamped in gold over black inset; lettering on spine stamped in gold over black insets; 447 pp (including selected bibliography and index).
Reference to N. C. Wyeth on page 369.

Rockwell, Norman

NORMAN ROCKWELL / My Adventures as an Illustrator / by / Norman Rockwell / As Told To Thomas Rockwell / Doubleday & Company, Inc. / Garden City, New York / 1960

First Edition, so stated on the copyright page.
Large 8 vo. Black cloth; cover and spine stamped in gold over brown insets; 448 pp (including a Portfolio).
Reference to N. C. Wyeth on page 69.

Saint-Gaudens, Homer

THE / AMERICAN / ARTIST / And His Times / [rule] / By Homer Saint-Gaudens / Director, Department of Fine Arts / Carnegie Institute / [ornament—red] / With Frontispiece In Color And / Sixty-Four Halftone Illustrations / [rule] / Dodd, Mead & Company / Publishers • New York / 1941 [title, publisher and date printed in red]

First Edition, so stated on the copyright page.
4 to. Black cloth; facsimile signature on cover stamped in gold; lettering on spine stamped in gold over red inset; ornaments and rules on spine stamped in gold; tinted top; uncut; 332 pp (including index).
References to N. C. Wyeth on pages 163 and 164.

Simon, Howard

500 YEARS OF ART / IN ILLUSTRATION / From Albrecht Dürer to Rockwell Kent / By Howard Simon / Garden City Publishing Co. Inc. / Garden City, New York

Copyright 1949 by Garden City Publishing Company.
4 to. Black cloth with gray cloth spine; title stamped on spine in gold over black inset; publisher stamped on spine in black; tinted top; 476 pp (including index).
Reference to N. C. Wyeth on page 395.

Watson, Ernest W.

[rule] / COLOR / AND METHOD / IN PAINTING / [double rule] / As seen in the work of / 12 American Painters / by / Ernest W. Watson / (rule) / [publisher's colophon] / [double rule] / Watson-Guptill / Publications, Inc. / New York

Copyright 1942 by Watson-Guptill Publications, Inc.
4 to. Black cloth; cover label in color; lettering on cover and spine stamped in silver; 141 pp.
ANDREW WYETH (pages 61–71)
Illustrated with paintings, drawings, etc., by Andrew Wyeth.
Numerous references to N. C. Wyeth.

[rule] / FORTY / ILLUSTRATORS / And how they work / [double rule] / by / Ernest W. Watson / Author of / Pencil Drawing / Color And Method In Painting / Watercolor Demonstrated / The Relief Print / [rule] / [publisher's colophon] / Watson-Guptill Publications, Inc. / New York / 1946

First Edition, so stated on the copyright page.
4 to. Black cloth; lettering on cover label

printed in white over colors; lettering on spine stamped in silver; 318 pp.
An illustrated series of interviews with forty leading American illustrators.
N. C. WYETH *Giant On a Hilltop* (pages 310–18).
Portrait of N. C. Wyeth (photograph) p 310.
N. C. Wyeth in his Chadds Ford Studio (drawing by Andrew Wyeth) p 312.
Eight illustrations. Three in color and five in black and white.
Illustration from *Drums*. p 311
Johnny Fraser and John Paul Jones standing on the sea wall overlooking the Harbor of Brest.[1] (color)
A random collection of N. C. Wyeth illustrations. Nine illustrations represented. (black and white) p 313
SUMMER NIGHT. p 315
Egg tempera painting (color)
SUMMER NIGHT (detail) (color). p 315
Caldwell's Island (black and white). p 316
Corn Harvest[2] (black and white). p 316
Lobsterman[3] (black and white). p 316
Pencil study for an illustration by N. C. Wyeth[4] (black and white). p 317

Note: The text and most of the illustrations in this article originally appeared in *American Artist* magazine, January 1945.
[1] Originally appeared in *Drums* by James Boyd published by Charles Scribner's Sons, New York, 1928.
[2] The painting was reproduced as a calendar in color for Brown and Bigelow, 1944, and it was titled "Give Us This Day."
[3] The painting was reproduced as a calendar in color for Brown and Bigelow, 1944.
[4] The preliminary drawing for the illustration was titled "Gold." The finished painting was reproduced in color in the 1941 "Romance of Commerce" calendar, published by John Morrell & Company, Ottumwa, Iowa.

Whiting, John D.

PRACTICAL / ILLUSTRATION / A Guide for Artists / By / John D. Whiting / Illustrated / [publisher's colophon] / Harper & Brothers Publishers / New York and London

Copyright 1920 by Harper & Brothers.
Published November 1920, so stated on the copyright page.
Harper code letters (K–U) on the copyright page.
Large 8 vo. Gray boards; dark gray cloth spine; pictorial cover label in color; lettering on cover printed in green; lettering on spine stamped in gold; uncut; 153 pp.
N. C. Wyeth mentioned on pages 27, 29, and 133.

Young, William (Edited and compiled by)

A DICTIONARY / of / AMERICAN ARTISTS, / SCULPTORS and ENGRAVERS / From the beginnings through the turn of the Twentieth Century / Edited and compiled by / William Young / Research Editor: Phillip Baker Jr. / Associate Editors: Janet M. Conn and Dorothy M. Young / Published by William Young and Co. / 1077 Massachusetts 02138

Copyright 1968 by William Young.
Large 8 vo. Brown cloth; design on cover stamped in gold; lettering on spine stamped in gold; 515 pp.
Newell Convers Wyeth
A brief biography and list of awards.

II. Periodicals

All Around Magazine
(formerly **New Story**)

1915

December
"The Return of the Four" by Edwin Bliss. Cover illustration in color. Description: A man in desert outfit.

1916

January
Cover illustration in color. Description: Chinese horesman riding down man armed with knife.

February
"The Lost Vein" by Edwin Bliss. Cover illustration in color. Description: A prospector carrying dead man, with dog following.

March
Cover illustration in color. Description: Ambushed on the trail.

All-Arts Magazine

1925

September   Vol. I No. 4
"N. C. Wyeth" by Isabel Hoopes. Pages 6–13. Photograph of N. C. Wyeth painting mural decoration for the First National Bank of Boston.

Three illustrations in black and white of the mural panels executed for the Hotel Roosevelt.
The Half Moon (left panel) p 9
The Half Moon (center panel)[1] p 11
The Half Moon (right panel) p 13

[1] The mural painting appears in color in *The World* (New York) color gravure magazine section, September 26, 1926. In addition, it appears as a frontispiece in color in the book *How the Old World Found the New* by Barnard and Tall, published by Ginn and Company, Boston, 1929.

All Outdoors

1913

Autumn
Cover illustration in color. Description: The Hunter.

Note: The illustration originally appeared as a cover in color for *The Outing Magazine,* June 1907. It is one of the five paintings that made up the Solitude Series.

The American Architect

1926

November 20   Vol. CXXX No. 2509
Frontispiece illustration in black and white. A Vision of New York

Description: In *Diedrich Knickerbocker's History of New York,* Washington Irving tells of the vision that came to Oloffe Van Kortlandt, one of the Dutch pioneers who had reached New York harbor seeking a place to settle.

Note: The illustration was commissioned by The New York Telephone Company for use in an advertising campaign.

The American Art Student

1916

September   Volume 1 Number I
"From An Art Editor": An interview with Mr. F. D. Casey, art editor of *Collier's Weekly.* Pages 4, 5 and 6. Discussed are two of N. C. Wyeth's illustrations which appeared in current *Collier's* issues.

Two illustrations in black and white.
Description: Stannard sat on that lonely island like a bloated spider.[1] p 4
Description: We just naturally fights like a pair of friends and gentlemen.[2] p 5

[1] Appeared in *Collier's Weekly,* July 17, 1915, for the story "At the World's Outposts" by James Francis Dwyer.
[2] Appeared in *Collier's Weekly,* March 25, 1916, for the story "A Matter of Friendship" by Roy Norton.

1916

**November—
December**   Volume 1 Numbers 3 & 4
"The Illustrator and His Development" by N. C. Wyeth. Pages 3–6 and 12.
Eight illustrations in black and white.
Portrait study (self-portrait). p 3
Illustration for Poem.[1] p 4
Study of composition sketch "for Poem" (drawing). p 4
Final composition sketch "for Poem" (drawing). p 4
Landscape study (Chadds Ford woodland). p 5
Still life (candlestick, crock, and book). p 5
Landscape study[2] (cows in a pasture). p 6
Still life (pipe, pitcher, and plate). p 6

[1] The illustration originally appeared in color in *The Delineator,* November 1915, for the story "Autum Dawn: A Poem Of The Indian Harvest" by Constance Skinner.
[2] The illustration (painting) also appears as a frontispiece in color in the book *The Brooklet's Story* by Alexis Everett Frye, published by Ginn and Company, Boston, 1927.

1926

June 30   Volume 9 Number 9
"Commercial and Industrial Art." Pages 26 and 27. Article on The Second Annual Exhibition of the Philadelphia Chapter of the Art Directors Club. Comprising the jury was N. C. Wyeth, mural painter, and Earl Horter, etcher.

American Artist

1942

September   Volume 6 Number 7
"Andrew Wyeth: One of America's Youngest and Most Talented Artists." Pages 18–24. Illustrated with numerous paintings, watercolors, and drawings by Andrew Wyeth. References to N. C. Wyeth.

1945

January   Volume 9 Number 1
"N. C. Wyeth: Giant On A Hilltop." Interviewed by Ernest W. Watson. Pages 16–22 and 28.

Portrait of N. C. Wyeth (photograph). p 16
N. C. Wyeth in his Chadds Ford Studio (drawing by Andrew Wyeth). p 17
Fifteen illustrations. Three in color and twelve in black and white.
"Summer Night" (egg tempera) (color). p 18
"Summer Night" Exact size detail (color). p 19
A random collection of N. C. Wyeth illustrations. p 20
Illustration from *The Odyssey* The Sirens (color). p 21
Caldwell's Island. p 22
Corn Harvest. p 22
Lobsterman. p 22

Note: The article and most of the illustrations appear in the book *Forty Illustrators and How They Work* by Ernest W. Watson, published by Watson-Guptill Publications, Inc., New York, 1946.

1951

December   Volume 15 Number 10
Issue 150
"Howard Pyle: Father of American Illustration" by Henry C. Pitz. Pages 44–47 and 81–83. Illustrated in color and black and white with paintings and pen and inks by Pyle. Reference to N. C. Wyeth on page 82.

1958

November   Volume 22 Number 9
Issue 219

"Andrew Wyeth: As the famous son of a famous father who belonged to the Pyle Circle, Andrew Wyeth has added luster to the tradition he inherited" by Henry C. Pitz. Pages 27–33, 65, and 66. Illustrated in color and black and white with paintings, watercolors, and drawings by the artist. References to N. C. Wyeth on page 27.

1961

December   Volume 25 Number 10
Issue 250

"Millions of Pictures" (Part II) by Henry C. Pitz. Pages 52–57 and 85–88. Illustrated in color and black and white by noted American illustrators. Reference to N. C. Wyeth on page 54.

One illustration in color by N. C. Wyeth.
The Hostage (*Treasure Island*). p 53

1966

December   Volume 30 Number 10
Issue 300

"The Brandywine Tradition: A rich inheritance that began over a half century ago and shows no signs of abatement" by Henry C. Pitz. Pages 43–49 and 74–77. Illustrated in color and black and white by Howard Pyle, his pupils, etc.

Two illustrations by N. C. Wyeth.
Illustration from *The Pike County Ballads*
Description: The Deacon and Parson Skeeters in the tail game of Draw (black and white). p 46
Illustration from *Treasure Island*
Description: The Hostage. p 47

1967

June   Volume 31 Number 6
Issue 306

"The Illustrations of Steven Kidd" by Henry Gasser. Pages 38–43, 72, 73, and 78–80. Illustrated in black and white with works by Steven Kidd. Reference to N. C. Wyeth on page 73.

The American Book Collector

1968

May   Vol. XVIII No. 9
"Tentative Bibliographic Check Lists of Western Illustrators" by Jeff C. Dykes. Pages 19–24. Newell Convers Wyeth (1882–1945), Part One.

One illustration in black and white.
Description: Golyer.[1] p 19

[1] The illustration originally appears in color in the book *The Pike County Ballads* by John Hay, published by Houghton Mifflin Company, Boston, October 1912.

June   Vol. XVIII No. 10
"Tentative Bibliographic Check Lists of Western Illustrators" by Jeff C. Dykes. Pages 30–34. Newell Convers Wyeth (1882–1945), Part Two.

The American Boy

1921

September   Volume 22 Number 11
Cover illustration in colors (red, brown, black and white). Description: Indian chief on charging pony.

Note: The illustration also appears in color in the booklet *A Livestock Heritage* by Frank Harding, published by The American Livestock Insurance Company, Geneva, Illinois, 1971.

The American Gun

1961

Spring   Volume 1 Number 2
"The Long Long Rifle" by Herb Glass. Pages 42–48.
One illustration in color by N. C. Wyeth.
Daniel Boone. p 42

Note: The illustration originally appeared in the calendar *America in the Making*, published by John Morrell & Company, Ottumwa, Iowa, 1940.

American Heritage

1956

December   Vol. VIII No. 1
"The Books We Got for Christmas" by Ellen Wilson. Pages 26–37. Illustrated with pictures by N. C. Wyeth, Howard Pyle, Arthur Rackham, Jessie Wilcox Smith, A. B. Frost, etc.

One illustration in color by N. C. Wyeth.
Description: Long John Silver and Hawkins. p 35

Note: The illustration originally appeared in *Treasure Island* by Robert Louis Stevenson, published by Charles Scribner's Sons, N. Y., September 1911.

1961

December   Vol. XIII No. 1
"The Sunny Master of Sunny Side" by Curtis Dahl. Pages 36–55, 92, and 93. A portfolio of illustrations titled An Illustrated Washington Irving (pages 41–55). Illustrated with works in color and black and white by N. C. Wyeth, Arthur Rackham, Maxfield Parrish, F. O. C. Darley, etc.

One illustration in color by N. C. Wyeth.
Description: ". . . Though these folks were evidently amusing themselves, yet they maintained the gravest faces, the most mysterious silence." p 53

Note: The illustration originally appeared in *Rip Van Winkle* by Washington Irving, published by David McKay, Philadelphia, 1921.

1964

December   Vol. XVI No. 1
Frontispiece illustration in color. Description: Children surprising dad in the act of playing Santa. p 2

Note: The illustration originally appeared as a cover in color for *The Popular Magazine*, December 1915.

1965

October   Vol. XVI No. 6
Cover illustration in color. The Last Stand (An outlaw at bay).[1]

"N. C. Wyeth: The great illustrator found giants in clouds and inspiration in the classics

of fiction and history. And, like old Charles Willson Peale, he founded and trained a dynasty of fine artists" by Henry C. Pitz.

Four photographs.
Howard Pyle with students N. C. Wyeth, Thornton Oakley, and Henry Peck (oval). p 39
N. C. Wyeth working on the Metropolitan Life Insurance Company mural. p 45
N. C. Wyeth early in his career at work on an illustration for *Arizona Nights* by Stewart Edward White. p 47
Henriette Wyeth at work on a portrait of her father. p 50

Sixteen illustrations in color and black and white by N. C. Wyeth.
The Giant (memorial decoration—Westtown School, Westtown, Penna.) (color). p 36
Self-portrait (easel painting)[2] (color). p 37
Jim Hawkins and Long John Silver (illustration from *Treasure Island*) (color). p 42
The Battle at Glens Falls (illustration from *The Last of the Mohicans*) (color). p 43
Battle of Wilson's Creek (mural decoration—Missouri State Capitol) (double page illustration in color). pp 44–45
Ore Wagon (illustration from *McClure's Magazine*, May 1908) (color). p 46
The Parkman Outfit (illustration from *The Oregon Trail*) (color). p 47
A shower of arrows rained on our dead horses from the closing circle of red-men. (illustration from *The Great West That Was*) (double page illustration in color). p 48–49
Nightfall (easel painting) (color). p 50
Andrew Wyeth as a boy (easel portrait) (color). p 51
In Penobscot Bay (easel painting) (color). p 51
Navajo woman (sketch). p 47
Navajo man (sketch). p 47
Hind legs of horse (sketch). p 47
Indian ambush (sketch). p 55
Illustration from *Rip Van Winkle* (pen and ink). p 83

Five reduced illustrations in black and white.
Cover illustration, *Tarzan of the Apes* for *New Story Magazine*, August 1913. p 42
Cover illustration for *Commodore Hornblower*. p 42
Cover illustration for *Drums*. p 42
Cover illustration for *Robinson Crusoe*. p 42
Cover illustration for *Rip Van Winkle*. p 42

A Painting Family (Wyeth family tree), accompanied by one photograph and numerous illustrations in color and black and white.

[1] The illustration originally appeared as a cover in tint for *McClure's Magazine*, September 1906.
[2] The self-portrait also appears in color in *Life* magazine, December 17, 1971, for the article "The Wyeths' Kind of Christmas Magic" by Richard Meryman.

1971

December   Vol. XXIII No. 1
Cover illustration in color. Description: Children sledding.

Note: The illustration originally appeared as a cover in color for *The Popular Magazine*, March 20, 1923.

American History Illustrated

1966

April   Vol. I No. 1
"Pyle Inspired a Generation of Illustrators" by Frederic Ray. Page 34. N. C. Wyeth mentioned among a list of Howard Pyle's accomplished students.

May   Vol. I No. 2
Cover illustration in color. The Call of the Wild

Note: This illustration was originally titled The Hunter, and was part of The Solitude Series, published in *The Outing Magazine*, June 1907.

August   Vol. I No. 5
"The Indian and the Horse" by David Bonney. Pages 44–54. Illustrated with photographs and from works by N. C. Wyeth, Charles F. Wimar, Frederic Remington, and Charles M. Russell.

One illustration in black and white by N. C. Wyeth.
> The plains Indians never saw horses until the appearance of Spanish explorers such as Coronado. p 47

Note: The illustration originally appeared in color in the calendar *America in the Making*, published by John Morrell & Company, Ottumwa, Iowa, 1940. It was titled Francisco Vasquez De Coronado.

1967

January   Vol. I No. 9
Cover illustration in color. Sherman

Note: The illustration originally appeared in the book *Poems of American Patriotism*, published by Charles Scribner's Sons, N. Y., October 1922.

June   Vol. II No. 3
Cover illustration in color. At Concord Bridge

Note: The illustration originally appeared as a Banking Poster, published by the Canterbury Company, Inc., Chicago, 1921. It was titled Independence Day.

October   Vol. II No. 6
"Remember the Alamo" by William C. Davis. Pages 4–11 and 53–57.
One illustration in two colors (brown, black and white).
The Siege of the Alamo p 9

Note: The illustration originally appeared in color in the calendar *Flags in American History*, published by John Morrell & Company, Ottumwa, Iowa, 1944.

December   Vol. II No. 8
Cover illustration in color. By the Dawn's Early Light

Note: The illustration originally appeared as a calendar in color for the New York Life Insurance Company, 1941.

1968

February   Vol. II No. 10
Cover illustration in color. The "Constitution" Bombarding Tripoli

Note: The illustration originally appeared in color in the calendar *Flags in American History*, published by John Morrell & Company, Ottumwa, Iowa, 1944.

June   Vol. II No. 3
Cover illustration in color. Black Beard, Buccaneer

Note: The illustration originally appeared in *Scribner's Magazine*, August 1917, for the story "The Golden Galleon" by Paul Hervey Fox.

November   Vol. III No. 7
Cover illustration in color. Arnold's March to Quebec

Note: The illustration originally appeared in *Trending into Maine* by Kenneth Roberts, published by Little, Brown and Company, Boston, June 1938.

1969

May   Vol. IV No. 1
Cover illustration in color. The Indian in His Solitude

Note: This illustration was originally titled The Silent Burial and was part of The Solitude Series, published in *The Outing Magazine*, June 1907.

June   Vol. IV No. 3
Back cover illustration in black and white with tint. Ethan Allen–Forerunner of Independence.

Note: The illustration was originally painted as an advertisement for the Joseph Dixon Crucible Company, Jersey City, N. J., 1934.

July   Vol. IV No. 4
Back cover illustration in black and white with tint. "Ringing Out Liberty"

Note: The illustration originally appeared (with three others) as a poster in color for the Pennsylvania Railroad.

1970

May   Vol. V No. 2
Cover illustration in color. Fremont the Pathfinder

Note: The illustration originally appeared in color in the calendar *Flags in American History*, published by John Morrell & Company, Ottumwa, Iowa, 1944.

1971

May   Vol. VI No. 2
The Concise Illustrated History of the Civil War from the editors of *American History Illustrated*. Narrative by Dr. James I. Robertson, Jr. Illustrated with numerous paintings, engravings, drawings, photographs, maps, etc.

One illustration in black and white by N. C. Wyeth.
Battle of Wilson's Creek, August 10, 1861 p 12

Note: Mural painting in the Missouri State Capitol, Jefferson City, Missouri. It originally appeared in color in the *Ladies' Home Journal*, March 1921.

July   Vol. VI No. 4
Cover illustration in color. "General George Washington"

Note: The illustration originally appeared as an advertisement for Strawbridge & Clothier Co., Philadelphia, in commemoration of the 200th Anniversary of the birth of George Washington (1732–1932).

American Legion Magazine

1944

February   Volume 36 Number 2
Cover illustration in color.
> Description: Abraham Lincoln writing the famous Bixby letter, November 21, 1864.

Note: The illustration originally appeared as a calendar in color, published by Shaw-Barton Company, 1943.

The American Magazine

1907

August   Vol. IX No. 4
"The Awakening" by Joe H. Ranson. Pages 403–11.
Two illustrations in black and white.
> He staggered to his feet and gazed wildly about him
> He raised his arms in silent worship

1908

March   Vol. LXV No. 3
"The Brutal Fact" by John G. Neihardt. Pages 517–27.
Four illustrations in black and white.
> Mike Fallon (charcoal and wash). p 521
> The tall, patient Dane–the kind, the trusting Dane–waiting bravely for the treacherous blow with the tin cup on his head. p (523)
> As he proceeded, he breathed humble, fervent prayers into the silence of the dawn. p (525)
> Description: Little Jean following the trail of Fallon. (charcoal and wash) p 526

1914

June   Vol. LXXVII No. 6
"A Modern Opium Eater: A Newspaper Man's Story of His Own Experience With The Drug" by No. 6606. Pages 30–35.
Three illustrations. Two (including frontispiece) in color and one in black and white.
> I was overworked. Every line of copy in our ten-page sheet passed through my hands. (frontispiece in color)
> After that I visited Lee, first at intervals of several days, then, by degrees, more frequently, until finally I became a daily user of opium.[1] (color) p 30
> I had many friends among professional thieves. From the very first I had been "right." (black and white) p 33

[1] References to the illustration appear in *The International Studio* (Studio Talk) February, 1915.

July   Vol. LXXVIII No. 1
"Boston Blackie Stories" by No. 6606.
"The Price of Principle." Pages 10–15.
Three illustrations in color and black and white.
> Unhurried and without excitement, but quickly, Boston Blackie forced drawer after drawer (frontispiece in color). p 10
> I planted the layout and "lamped" out through the transom. I could see them at the head of the stairs, hammering on Kelly's door, and every man had his gun out[1] (black and white). p 13
> Mac's wife and child hear the news[1] (black and white). p 15

[1] The illustrations are reproduced as prints (plates 50 and 51) in the portfolio *Pictures by Prominent Artists*, United Y.M.C.A. Schools, N. Y., 1921.

August   Vol. LXXVIII No. 2
"Boston Blackie Stories" by No. 6606. "The Story About Dad Morgan." Pages 42–46.

Three illustrations in black and white.
> "She didn't come–she didn't come," he said over and over to himself. "She didn't come to see her old dad–and it's Christmas Day." p 42
> "But, Father, I can't go to Rob without clothes like a beggar girl. I wish I were dead." p 45

"If there is such a thing as justice or right anywhere, here or in some other world, that old man has a lot coming to him," said Cushions reverently. p 46

September   Vol. LXXVIII No. 3
"Boston Blackie Stories" by No. 6606. "Death Cell Visions." Pages 47–51.

Three illustrations in black and white.
> Description: Woman writing a letter (head-piece illustration). p. 47
> "That's right," said the old captain, "take your time and get a good look round. It's your last chance, son!" p 49
> "Look, look!" he whispered from behind teeth that clicked like castanets. "See! He's coming!" p 50

October   Vol. LXXVIII No. .4
"Boston Blackie Stories" by No. 6606. "A Thief's Daughter." Pages 34–38.

Two illustrations in black and white.
> "She still cooked for us when Tom asked her, but she never touched a pill herself. If there is any harder test for will power, you'll have to show it to me." p 34
> "I left the two there together, both crying. She went West that night, and Dayton Tom was never the same man afterward." p 37

November   Vol. LXXVIII No. 5
Photograph of N. C. Wyeth. Page 6.
Description: N. C. Wyeth, the great illustrator, who has illustrated all the "Boston Blackie" stories. Next month he has a frontispiece in colors—and he also illustrates a Christmas story by Moroso.

December   Vol. LXXVIII No. 6
"The Sandwich-Man" by Nina Wilcox Putnam. Pages 10 and 11.

One illustration in color.
> "I am advertising the Brotherhood of Man, Simplicity, Truth, and Freedom from Possessions." (double page illustration) pp 10–11

"Alias Santa Claus" by John A. Moroso. Pages 18–23.

Three illustrations in colors (red, brown, black and white).
> Ten thousand dollars! Why, even one thousand dollars would keep him clothed, housed and fed for the few remaining years of his life and there would be enough left over to keep his old body out of Potter's Field. His hands trembled and the white fire of the diamonds flashed more temptingly. p 18
> When he left prison for the second time he was an old man, penniless and friendless (headpiece illustration). p 19
> He had earned enough for a fifteen-cent lodging and a ten-cent meal and still had half his stock. He was grateful. p 22

American Magazine of Art

1917

August   Vol. VIII No. 10
"War Posters by Well-Known Illustrators." Page 420. Recorded from the Official Bulletin—Washington, D.C., N. C. Wyeth is listed among artists who contributed designs to Herbert C. Hoover's Food Commission.

1921

July   Vol. XII No. 7
"Decorations in the Missouri State Capitol, Jefferson City." Pages 243–49. Illustrated with numerous mural decorations by various artists.

Two illustrations (mural paintings) in black and white.
Battle of Westport, 1864 p 244
Battle of Wilson's Creek p 245

Note: The mural paintings originally appeared in color in the *Ladies' Home Journal*, March 1921.

December   Vol. XII No. 12
Notes: Philadelphia Art Alliance. Page 425. An exhibition of illustrations by N. C. Wyeth from the following books: *The Courtship of Miles Standish*, *Westward Ho!*, *The Boy's King Arthur*, and *Rip Van Winkle*, with a number of mural paintings, the sketches for which were included in the show.

1923

December   Vol. XIV No. 12
Items: Pennsylvania Museum. Pages 690–92. An exhibition of work by Philadelphia illustrators, to open November 1 at the Pennsylvania Museum, Fairmount Park and to continue through November 26. N. C. Wyeth is mentioned as one of the contributing artists.

1933

February   Vol. XXVI No. 2
"Three Winter Shows" by Edward Alden Jewell. Pages 61–72.

One illustration in black and white.
> In a Dream, I Meet General Washington. p 63
The work was awarded the Fourth William A. Clark Prize, The Corcoran Biennial, 1932. Accompanying the work is a commentary by the critic.

Note: The illustration originally appeared in *The Art Digest*, December 1, 1932, for the article "1932 Corcoran Biennial (review)."

Antiques

1957

November   Vol. LXXII No. 5
Shop talk. Page 402. A note on the forthcoming N. C. Wyeth exhibition at Knoedler's Gallery.

One illustration in black and white.
> Description: "I may never see this spot again, Deerslayer," she said. . . . p 402

Note: The illustration originally appeared in color in *The Deerslayer* by James Fenimore Cooper, published by Charles Scribner's Sons, N. Y., 1925.

1964

December   Vol. LXXXVI No. 6
James Graham & Sons (Art Galleries) Page 649.

One illustration in black and white by N. C. Wyeth.
> Children Sledding

Note: The illustration originally appeared as a cover in color for *The Popular Magazine*, March 20, 1923.

1966

May   Vol. LXXXIX No. 5
James Graham & Sons (Art Galleries) Page 682.

One illustration in black and white by N. C. Wyeth.
> The Moose Hunt

Note: The illustration originally appeared as an advertisement for Winchester Arms Company.

1967

November   Vol. XCII No. 5
"Collecting American nineteenth-century art" by J. William Middendorf II. Pages 680–88. Illustrated in color and black and white with works by noted artists of the period.

One illustration in black and white by N. C. Wyeth.
> Rip Van Winkle and the Moonlight Bowlers. p 684

Note: The illustration originally appeared in colors as the endpapers for *Rip Van Winkle* by Washington Irving, published by David McKay Company, Phila., 1921.

November   Vol. XCII No. 5
James Graham & Sons (Art Galleries) Page 606.

One illustration in black and white by N. C. Wyeth.
> Indians on Otsego Rock

Note: The illustration originally appeared in colors as the endpapers in *The Deerslayer* by James Fenimore Cooper, published by Charles Scribner's Sons, N.Y., 1925.

1969

July   Vol. XCVI No. 5
James Graham & Sons (Art Galleries) Page 57.

One illustration in black and white by N. C. Wyeth.
> Naval Engagement (detail)

Note: The illustration originally appeared as a cover in color for *The Popular Magazine*, February 20, 1923.

October   Vol. XCII No. 4
Berry Hill Galleries Page 4.

One illustration in black and white by N. C. Wyeth.
> The Decoy

Note: The illustration originally appeared as a cover in color for *New Story Magazine*, February 1913.

The Chadds Ford Gallery Page 436.

One illustration in black and white by N. C. Wyeth.
> The Beekeeper

Note: The illustration originally appeared in black and white in *Scribner's Magazine*.

Architecture

1921

June   Vol. XLIII No. 6
Frontispiece illustration in black and white.
Battle of Wilson's Creek
Mural decoration for the Missouri State Capitol.
Tracy and Swartwout, Architects.

Note: The mural decoration originally appeared in the *Ladies' Home Journal*, March 1921.

Argosy

1962

February   Volume 354 Number 2
Cover illustration in color. Description: Winchester Model 1895 rifle over background painting by N. C. Wyeth of Theodore Roosevelt and hunting companion confronting grizzly bear on rocky ridge.

Note: The illustration originally appeared as a calendar and a print in color, published by Winchester Repeating Arms Co. (1912)

Arizona Highways

1953

November   Vol. XXIX No. 11
"A Southwestern Heritage" by Peter Hurd. Pages 14–27. Photograph portrait of Peter Hurd. Illustrated in color (including cover, front and back pages) and black and white by Peter Hurd. In the article are numerous references to N. C. Wyeth.

The Arizonian

1969

November 13   Volume 17 Number 46
Cover illustration in color. The Outlaw

Note: The illustration originally appeared as a cover for *McClure's Magazine*, September 1906.

Art and Archaeology

1933

January–February   Vol. XXXIV No. 1
"The New Corcoran Biennial" by Arthur Stanley Riggs. Pages 29–42. Illustrated with the works of Wyeth, Glackens, Luks, Tarbell, Redfield, Grabach, etc.

One illustration in black and white by N. C. Wyeth.
    In a Dream I Meet General Washington.[1]
    p 34
The painting received the 4th William A. Clark Prize of $500, accompanied by The Corcoran Honorable Mention Certificate.

Red Cross Poster (back of contents page).
One illustration in black and white.
    Description: Massed Red Cross flags.

[1] The illustration originally appeared in *The Art Digest*, December 1, 1932, for the article "1932 Corcoran Biennial (review)."

The Art Digest

1932

December 1   Vol. VII No. 5
1932 Corcoran Biennial (review). Page 3. Illustrated with award winning paintings by various artists.

One illustration in black and white by N. C. Wyeth.
    "In a Dream, I Meet General Washington." p 3
The painting was awarded the Fourth William A. Clark Prize.

Note: The illustration also appears in *Art and Archaeology*, January–February 1933, for the article "The New Corcoran Biennial" by Arthur Stanley Riggs. In addition it appears in the *American Magazine of Art*, February 1933, for the article

"Three Winter Shows" by Edward Alden Jewell. Also appears as a cover for the *Philadelphia Forum*, February 1933. Also appears in *The Art Digest*, December 1, 1934, for the "Grand Central Art Galleries Second Annual Exhibition of Illustrations."

1934

December 1   Vol. IX No. 5
Grand Central Art Galleries (Exhibition Notice). The Second Annual Exhibition of Illustrations.

One illustration in black and white (inside front cover).
    "In a Dream, I Meet General Washington."

Note: Originally appeared in *The Art Digest*, December 1, 1932, for the article "1932 Corcoran Biennial (review)."

1939

December 15   Vol. XIV No. 6
"The Clan Wyeth Presents Its Famed Patriarch." Page 8. An article on a recent exhibition of N. C. Wyeth's works at the Macbeth Gallery, New York. Photograph of the Wyeth family.

One illustration in black and white.
Deep Cove Lobsterman. p 8
(lent by the Pennsylvania Academy)

December 15   Vol. XIV No. 6
Macbeth Gallery (Exhibition Notice). Exhibition of paintings by N. C. Wyeth entitled, "In the Georges Islands, Maine"—Through December 30, 1939. Page 26.

1940

June 1   Vol. XIV No. 17
Wyeth Represents Delaware. International Business Machines contemporary American painting exhibition at the New York World's Fair. Page 13.

One illustration in black and white.
Three Fisherman. p 13

1943

December   Volume 18 Number 6
Carnegie Institute Exhibition (review). Page 9. Noted in the review is N. C. Wyeth's painting "Portrait of a Farmer."

Art Direction

1957

February   Vol. VIII No. 2
"We Have Lost Excitement . . . Magazine Illustration, with all its full-color and splashy techniques, just isn't vibrant" by Kirk Wilkinson. Pages 76 and 77. Illustrated in black and white with works by Howard Pyle. Reference to N. C. Wyeth.

Art in America

1964

June   Volume 52 Number 3
The Season Surveyed by Hilton Kramer. Pages 108–114. Among numerous reviews the author mentions illustrations by N. C. Wyeth which were exhibited by James Graham & Sons Gallery.

One illustration in black and white by N. C. Wyeth.
Children on Sleds. p 112

Note: The illustration originally appeared as a cover in color for *The Popular Magazine*, March 20, 1923.

James Graham & Sons (Art Galleries)
Page 141.

One illustration in black and white by N. C. Wyeth.
    The Lost Vein

Note: The illustration originally appeared as a cover in color for the *All Around Magazine*, February 1916.

Art News

1946

January 15–31   Vol. XLIV No. 19
N. C. Wyeth—A Veteran Illustrator: In Memoriam. Page 14. Photograph portrait of N. C. Wyeth.

Two illustrations in black and white.
Thoreau and the Fox (illustration from *Men of Concord*). p 14
Nightfall. p 14

The Art Quarterly

1968

Winter   Vol. XXXI No. 4
James Graham & Sons (Art Galleries). Page ix

One illustration in black and white by N. C. Wyeth.
    Tractors and Massed Flags

Note: The illustration originally appeared as a calendar in color for Brown & Bigelow, 1943.

The Artgum (Mass. Normal Art School, Boston)

1926

April   Vol. IV No. 4
            Junior Number
N. C. Wyeth, Painter and Illustrator by Anton Kamp. Pages 2–20.

Two photographs of N. C. Wyeth.
    Description: N. C. Wyeth working on a mural painting for the First National Bank of Boston. fp 2
    Description: N. C. Wyeth on horseback, Colorado, 1904. p 13

Eleven illustrations in black and white.
    "The Parkman Outfit. Henry Chatillon, Guide and Hunter" (illustration from *The Oregon Trail*). p 5
    "The Courtship of Miles Standish" (illustration from *The Courtship of Miles Standish*). p 6
    "Buffalo Hunt" (illustration from *The Oregon Trail*). p 10
    "The Indian War Party" (illustration from *The Oregon Trail*). p 11
    "City of Tyre" (The First National Bank, Boston). p 14
    "The Modern Tramp Steamer" (The First National Bank, Boston). p 15
    Pilgrim head (pen and ink from *The Courtship of Miles Standish*). p 16
    The Fight at Glens Falls (illustration from *The Last of the Mohicans*). p 17

Paul Revere (illustration from *Poems of American Patriotism*). p 18
Photograph of book *David Balfour*. 18
Tam on the Craig Face (illustration from *David Balfour*). p 19
Photograph of book *The Deerslayer*. p 19
Warren's Address (illustration from *Poems of American Patriotism*). p 20

Atlantic Monthly

1964

June   Volume 213 Number 6
"Andrew Wyeth: An Atlantic Portrait" by E. P. Richardson. Pages 62–71. Photograph of Andrew Wyeth. Illustrated in color and black and white with the works of Andrew Wyeth. N. C. Wyeth mentioned on pages 64, 67, 68, and 69.

The Beacon (Ohio Oil Company)

1951
July   Vol. XVI No. 7
Cover illustration in color. Cutting Out Broncs for Breaking. Cover information on Page 2.

Note: Originally intended for the series of illustrations to accompany the article "A Day with the Round-Up" by N. C. Wyeth, *Scribner's Magazine*, March 1906. The painting was never reproduced prior to its appearance as a cover for *The Beacon*.

The Bookman

1918

July   Volume 47 Number 5
"Making Posters Fight" by Montrose J. Moses. Pages 504–12. Reference to N. C. Wyeth on page 508. Photograph of N. C. Wyeth and Henry Reuterdahl on scaffold putting finishing touches on great poster on Sub-Treasury Building, New York. p 509

Bowdoin Alumnus (Bowdoin College)

1945
August   Vol. XIX No. 4
"Bowdoin's One Hundred Fortieth." Professor Thayer Reviews Our Fourth Wartime Commencement. Pages 2–6. An honorary degree of Master of Arts was conferred on Newell C. Wyeth, noted artist and illustrator. (page 3)

The Burroughs Clearing House

1926
"Colorful Assets In The Murals—How the Artists Accomplish the Purpose of Paintings on the Wall to Express the Individuality of the Bank" by John Walker Harrington. Pages 19–21. Illustrated with mural paintings by various artists.

Two illustrations in black and white by N. C. Wyeth.
    "The Apotheosis of Franklin"[1]
      Franklin Savings Bank, N. Y.
    "The Clipper Ships"[2]
      First National Bank of Boston.

[1] The mural painting originally appeared in color in the *Ladies' Home Journal*, July 1926.
[2] The mural painting originally appeared in color in the *Ladies' Home Journal*, August 1925, for the article "Mural Paintings In The First National Bank Of Boston."

Carnegie Magazine

1946

January   Vol. XIX No. 7
"The People's Choice." Pages 209 and 210. N. C. Wyeth's painting "Nightfall" was chosen by the public as the third most popular work in the recent Carnegie exhibition.

The Cathedral Age
(National Cathedral, Washington, D.C.)

1939
Spring   Vol. XIV No. 1
"A Brief Cathedral Commentary." Pages 42 and 43.

One illustration in black and white by N. C. Wyeth.
    Central Panel of Reredos. p 43

1940
Spring   Vol. XV No. 1
Frontispiece illustration in black and white
"Song of the Air Mail"

Note: The illustration originally appeared in color in the book *Adventure* (The World of Music-Song Programs For Youth) Edited by Glenn, Leavitt, Rebmann, and Baker, published by Ginn and Company, Boston, 1938.

1942
Winter   Vol. XVI No. 4
"A Brief Cathedral Commentary" by Herald L. Stendal. Pages 22–27. Illustrated in color and black and white with numerous decorations, statuary, etc.

One illustration in color by N. C. Wyeth. One of three reredos panels.
    Description: Choir of Attendant Angels. p 22

Century Magazine

1907
May   Vol. LXXIV No. 1
"The Education of Trooper Brown" by Will Adams. Pages 11–18.

One illustration in black and white.
    "Keep your arms folded!" p (10)

July   Vol. LXXIV No. 3
"In the Dark of the Moon" by Emma Ghent Curtis. Pages 386–97.

One illustration in black and white.
    "We paused in the square of generous light." p (393)

1908
September   Vol. LXXVI No. 5
"A Night Raid at Eagle River" by Hamlin Garland. Pages 725–34.

One illustration in black and white.
    "You're pretty swift, aren't you? she said cuttingly." p (733)

1909
January   Vol. LXXVII No. 3
"The Flat-Game Man" by G. W. Ogden. Pages 364–73.

One illustration in black and white.
    "After their manner, they had turned their tails to the wind, and were drifting ahead of the storm." p (371)

1910
February   Vol. LXXIX No. 4
"An All-Time All-American Foot-Ball Team" by Walter Camp. Pages 594–606.

Two illustrations in black and white.
    Between halves—the head coach braces up the team. p (595)
    The victorious captain. p (596)

1913
April   Vol. LXXXV No. 6
"A Monte Flat Pastoral: How Old Man Plunkett Went Home" by Bret Harte. Pages 828–37.

One illustration in black and white.
    "There was only one to whom the rain had not brought blessing, and that was Plunkett." p (835)

July   Vol. LXXXVI No. 3
"How Beelzebub Came to the Convent" by Ethel Watts Mumford. Pages 323–30.

One illustration in black and white.
    "The five white-clad ancient women who morning and evening crossed the patio to the chapel." p (325)

November   Vol. LXXXVII No. 1
"The Woman from Yonder" by Stephen French Whitman. Pages 1–11.

Frontispiece illustration in color.
"The Woman from Yonder"
    "Madame Grimaux rose to her feet, slightly pale, but with a smile of apology. . . . Alexandre remonstrated in an unfamiliar language. She anwsered him softly in the same tongue. How I strove to analyze those sounds! They were no doubt the key to everything."

1914
September   Vol. LXXXVIII No. 5
"The Sheep Woman" by Sarah Comstock. Pages 764–73.

Two illustrations in black and white.
    "So it came to pass that S'bina was known as the sheep-woman." p 765
    "She watched the oncoming rider." p 767

1915
September   Vol. XC No. 5
"Mary Postgate . . . How does your garden grow?" by Rudyard Kipling. Pages 641–49.

Frontispiece illustration in color.
    "Her long pleasure was broken by a sound that she had waited for"

Civil War Times Illustrated

1964
November   Volume 3 Number 7
Cover illustration in color. Stonewall Jackson
"Editorially Speaking" by Robert H. Fowler. Page 26. A brief biographical sketch on N. C. Wyeth and a reference to the cover painting.

Note: The illustration originally appeared as a frontispiece in color in the book *The Long Roll* by Mary Johnston, published by Houghton Mifflin Company, Boston, May 1911.

1966

February Volume 4 Number 10
Cover illustration in color. The Battle

Note: The illustration originally appeared in color in the book *The Long Roll* by Mary Johnston, published by Houghton Mifflin Company, Boston, May 1911.

July Vol. V No. 4
Cover illustration in color. "The Battle of Westport"

"The Battle of Westport": Sterling Price's bold raid across Missouri ended here in the biggest battle of the war west of the Mississippi by D. Alexander Brown. Pages 4–11 and 40–43. Illustrated with numerous paintings, engravings, maps, and photographs.

One illustration in black and white by N. C. Wyeth.
"The Battle of Westport" pp 4–5

Note: The mural painting originally appeared in the *Ladies' Home Journal,* March 1921.

1967

January Vol. V No. 9
Cover illustration in color. The Road to Vidalia

Note: The illustration originally appeared as a frontispiece in color in the book *Cease Firing* by Mary Johnston, published by Houghton Mifflin Company, Boston, November 1912.

1969

July Volume VIII Number 4
Cover illustration in color. "Troops by the hundreds were passing by."

Note: The illustration originally appeared in *Everybody's Magazine,* August 1912, for the story "Sally Castleton, Southerner" by Crittenden Marriott.

Collier's Weekly

1904

February Vol. XXXII No. 20
"The Great Baltimore Fire" by David Graham Phillips. Baltimore Fire Extra. Pages 1–8. Illustrated by N. C. Wyeth, H. J. Peck, A. E. Becher, and Allen True, plus a number of photographs.

One illustration (charcoal drawing) in black and white by N. C. Wyeth.
Fighting the fire from the telephone poles. p 3

1912

January 27 Volume 48 Number 19
"The Harvest Moon at Lolo" by Justus Miles Forman. Pages 15, 16, and 30.

Two illustrations in colors. (orange, blue, brown, black and white)
Description: Pirate about to fire pistol at man charging him. (headpiece illustration). p 15
Round the dead man's neck, suspended by a cord, hung the Harvest Moon. p 16

February 17 Volume 48 Number 22
"The Strength of Men" by James Oliver Curwood. Cover illustration in color.
"And Jan felt the throb and pulse of a giant life under him—"

Three illustrations in colors (green, orange, brown, black and white). Pages 20, 21, 35, and 36.
In a single flash four paddles struck the water, and the two canoes shot bow and bow up the stream. (double page illustration). pp 20–21
. . . the cedar-capped ridge. p 20
Up there . . . he could see . . . Marie. p 21

July 27 Volume 49 Number 19
"Sir Henry" by R. W. Hofflund. Pages 18, 19, 27, and 28.

Two illustrations. One in brown, black and white and one in black and white.
"Just out," says Sir Henry. "In fact, we don't keep it. Try a lemon soda." The Mexican pointed his finger at him. "If you have no whiskey, says he, go out and get some." (brown, black and white). p 18
"But Sir Henry never stopped. He kept right on. When he reached the top step he braced his foot on it and gave a mighty spring and caught the Greaser around the waist and swung him clean out of the saddle." (black and white). p 19

October 12 Volume 50 Number 4
"Somewhere Safe to Sea" by Courtney Ryley Cooper. Pages 18, 19, 28, 30, and 31.

Two illustrations in colors. (orange, blue, brown, black and white)
Silently we threaded our way along the slippery trail and down toward the valley. p 18
There the Sweetwater rushed into its greatest pool, and there Mr. Jordan took his flies from the book and got ready to cast. p 19

1913

March 8 Volume 50 Number 25
"A Son of Hagar" by Jane Anderson. Pages 18, 19, and 36.

Three illustrations in black and white.
Description: Racing on horseback. (headpiece illustration). p 18
He turned over and crawled around back of the bush, trying to make a wide circle around the fire. The bullets followed him. p 18
Man with revolver crouched behind cactus. p 19

April 5 Volume 51 Number 3
"The Country Up-In-Back" by Charles Tenney Jackson. Pages 18, 19, and 36–40.

Two illustrations in black and white.
Description: A man and woman facing one another. (headpiece illustration) p 18
She clung to his neck, looking up at the hot sky, then closed her eyes, for it seemed that the yellow devils of the flood were on them. p 19

1915

March 27 Volume 55 Number 2
"Mike the Vagabone—and the Root of Evil" by Peter B. Kyne. Pages 8, 9, 44, and 45.

One illustration in black and white.
"I ran aft to the clear space abaft the funnel; and there I found the spiggoties shtandin', holdin' a council av war. I fired into the thick av them and had five av them down when that thievin' engineer came

sneakin up behind me and shtruck me on the back av the head wit' a monkey wrench. p 9

April 3 Volume 55 Number 3
"Mike the Vagabone—and the Root of Evil" by Peter B. Kyne. Pages 18, 19, and 22.

One illustration in black and white.
"We'll lave it up to the termites," says he, and he sat down and lit another cigarette. He'd smoked three before wan av the termites arrived and bit the poor lip av me. 'Twas like bein' branded wit' a hot iron, and I was for goin' mad, until thinks I: "This is undignified av you, Michael Josuph Killerher, Be a man." p 18

April 24 Volume 55 Number 6
"Anent a Biscuit Shooter" by Francis Hill. Pages 8, 9, 25, and 26.

One illustration in black and white.
Slowly and thoughtfully, absolutely without bravado, Drift shuffled the cards. "Keep ca'm Dawse," he advised. "Set down, why don't you?" p 9

Note: The illustration also appears in the book *Prize Stories from Collier's,* Volume One, published by P. F. Collier & Son, N. Y., 1916.

May 22 Volume 55 Number 10
"The Virtue of Neils Hansen" by Vingie E. Roe. Pages 10, 11, 31, and 33.

One illustration in black and white.
Back and forth across it we went, twisting, straining, holding our strength, each striving to break the grip of the other's fingers on his wrist. I felt his breath upon my face, saw his cold eyes like blue fire burning me. p 10

July 17 Volume 55 Number 18
"At the World's Outposts" by James Francis Dwyer. Pages 17–19 and 34.

Two illustrations. One in black and white and one in color.
They said that Stannard sat on that lonely island like a bloated spider, watching the yellow current that tore past Blerveaux Light and carried doomed vessels down to the Isle of Lost Ships.[1] (black and white) p 17
When I tried with cracked lips and swollen tongue to babble of what I had witnessed, he called me liar and threw stones at me so that I had to crawl into a crevice in the rocks to dodge the missiles. (double page illustration in orange, brown, black and white) pp 18–19

Note: The illustration also appears in *The American Art Student,* September 1916 for the article "From an Art Editor" (an interview).
[1] The cover in colored inks is copied after Wyeth's illustration on page 17.

July 24 Volume 55 Number 19
"At the World's Outposts" by James Francis Dwyer. Pages 11 and 32–34.

One illustration in black and white.
Sitting in the bow of the boat, with his eyes fixed upon the woman who was nursing the Dane, was Stannard the Terrible! p 11

October 9 Volume 56 Number 4
"Twice in the Same Place" by Wilbur Hall. Pages 9–11 and 29–31.

Two illustrations in black and white.
> Tub Fanning traveled around a little and learned geography from the top of a freight string. In Pennsylvania there were but slim oil pickings for little fellows. p 10
>
> In the ancient two-cylinder tug which he had acquired Fanning waved cheerily at a trainman, and at that identical moment the broker got a tail hold on an inspiration. p 11

December 18   Volume 56 Number 14
"What Happened at El Rancho Verde" by Vingie E. Roe. Pages 7, 8, and 30–34.

One illustration in black and white.
> It was a magnificent finale, a sight for men and gods. Like the wind he flung by the other horse, and two lengths ahead he went by the corral gate. p 8

1916

January 1   Volume 56 Number 16
"Punderson Waite" by Ceylon Hollingsworth. Pages 9, 10, and 22–24.

One illustration in black and white.
> Waite seized him and swung him on high amid a volley of terrified oaths and then dashed him down and away. p 10

Note: The illustration also appears in *True West* magazine, December 1967, for the article "N. C. Wyeth: Painter of Men . . . In Action" by Les Beitz. In addition, the illustration appears in color in the book *The Glory Years* by Richard F. Pourade, published by The Union-Tribune Publishing Co., 1964.

February 19   Volume 56 Number 23
"Captain Bill" by Roy Norton. Pages 9, 10, 34, 35, 37, and 38.

One illustration in black and white.
> From the stern to the pilot house they danced and struck and howled: the one yelling venomously, the other whooping with gleeful vehemence. p 10

March 25   Volume 57 Number 2
"A Matter of Friendship" by Roy Norton. Pages 12, 13, 39, and 40.

One illustration in black and white.
> "We just naturally fights like a pair of friends and gentlemen. Bite, kick, and gouge; but no hard feelin's between me and you!" p 13

Note: The illustration also appears in *The American Art Student*, September 1916, for the article "From an Art Editor" (an interview).

April 22   Volume 57 Number 6
"Captain Bill, Rebel" by Roy Norton. Pages 19, 20, and 38–40.

Two illustrations in black and white.
> Description: Eskimo in kayak watching a passing riverboat. (headpiece illustration) p 19
>
> He was caught, turned about and turkey-trotted aft toward Captain Bill's cabin, into which he was unceremoniously heaved like a sack of cabbage. p 20

May 27   Volume 57 Number 11
Cover illustration in color. Description: Border soldier with rifle standing beside his horse. Desert terrain in background.

July 22   Volume 57 Number 19
"The Confidence Game" by Charles Trethewey. Pages 9, 10, 24, 25, and 28.

One illustration in black and white.
> The man's query was so startlingly abrupt that it caught Slim with his guard down. p 10

October 21   Volume 58 Number 6
"Blue Lock, the Queen" by Vingie E. Roe. Pages 12, 13, and 40–42.

One illustration in black and white.
> The rifle came down through the empty air. Like the wind itself silver queen shot into flight. p 13

December 2   Volume 58 Number 12
"The Stakes" by Vingie E. Roe. Pages 19, 20, and 33–35.

Two illustrations in black and white.
> Description: Man and woman on horseback with canyon background. (headpiece illustration) p 19
>
> The sun beat down upon him. The dry, white dust beat up around him. The girl sagged and lolled on his shoulder. p 20

1917

January 6   Volume 58 Number 17
"The Fourth Man" by John Russell. Pages 12–14, 16, and 17.

Three illustrations in black and white.
> Description: Men adrift on a raft. (headpiece illustration) p 12
>
> But the Parrot's big grip closed quietly around his wrist and pinioned him. p 13
>
> He spread his sail of pandanus leaves and headed back toward New Caledonia. p 14

January 27   Volume 58 Number 20
"The Wicks of Macassar" by John Russell. Pages 12, 13, 32, and 33.

Two illustrations in black and white.
> Description: Natives chasing man through swamp. (headpiece illustration) p 12
>
> They were eight, and no man ever saw the like before nor will again. p 13

February 24   Volume 58 Number 24
"Jetsam" by John Russell. Pages 14, 15, 36–38, and 41.

Two illustrations in black and white.
> Description: Two men sitting on beach. (headpiece illustration) p 14
>
> For an instant the three seemed to hang suspended, like some many-limbed polyp. p 15

June 9   Volume 59 Number 13
"Smoky Face" by Vingie E. Roe. Pages 17–21, 24, 27, and 28.

Two illustrations in black and white.
> In ten seconds his gun was leveled in their gaping faces. "Back!" he yelled, his blue eyes black like a maniac's; "fall back!" p 17
>
> It was the first time Smoky Face had given that particular call, but the band understood. p 18

October 20   Volume 60 Number 6
"East of Eastward" by John Russell. Pages 15, 16, 38–40, and 42.

Two illustrations in black and white.
> Description: Ape chained to tree. (title-piece illustration) p 15
>
> She belonged in this garden, in the checker of light and shadow and exotic color, slender like a young bamboo and rounded as a purple passion fruit. p 16

1919

June 28   Volume 63 Number 26
"The Jack-o'-Lanterns" by James B. Connolly. Pages 7, 8, 22, 34, and 35.

Three illustrations in black and white.
> "Couldn't he write about common people —about cops and bums and sailors and crooks and places where reg'lar people lived?"[1] p 7
>
> I see the cheeks are powder-burnt and there's a mark acrost his forehead like it was one time split open. p 8
>
> I'm just going to swing the light away from the coal bin. p 22

[1] Also appears as the frontispiece in the book *Hiker Joy* by James B. Connolly, published by Charles Scribner's Sons, N.Y., 1920.

July 5   Volume 64 Number 1
"The Lumber Boat" by James B. Connolly. Pages 7, 8, 24, 32, and 33.

Two illustrations in black and white.
> Description: Two men on raft fighting with knives.[1] (headpiece illustration) p 7
>
> "Ah say, bredren, who's agwine abo'd de ship wid all dem angles? Is you, brudder?" p 8

[1] The headpiece illustration also appears in the book *Hiker Joy* by James B. Connolly, published by Charles Scribner's Sons, N.Y., 1920.

July 12   Volume 64 Number 2
"The Undersea Man" by James B. Connolly. Pages 7, 8, and 36–38.

Two illustrations in black and white.
> I step nearer and see a pistol under the seat and another pistol alongside him. I have a nidea o' grabing one o' them. p 7
>
> "Don't! My wrist—it is cracking!" I hear Worts say. p 8

July 19   Volume 64 Number 3
"The U-212" by James B. Connolly. Pages 7, 8, and 34–37.

Two illustrations in black and white.
> . . . they'd seen me shooting about five feet into the air. p 7
>
> I looked up for my land and see instead something like a bird playing tag against the moonshine. p 8

July 26   Volume 64 Number 4
"Good-bye the Horse Boat" by James B. Connolly. Pages 11, 12, 24, and 26.

Two illustrations in black and white.
> "I know what you're thinking of, old General," says Lefty. "Your dream it was to go—when it come your time to go—"[1] p 11
>
> I climbed up over the bow, trying to make no noise. But Clews heard me. p 12

[1] The illustration appears in the book *Hiker Joy* by James B. Connolly, published by Charles Scribner's Sons, N.Y., 1920.

August 9   Volume 64 Number 6
"The Flying Sailor" by James B. Connolly. Pages 12, 13, 26, and 27.

One illustration in black and white.

A dozen bullets I must've pumped out and we sweeping nearer to her every second. p 13

August 16   Volume 64 Number 7

"London Lights" by James B. Connolly. Pages 10, 11, and 28–31.

One illustration in black and white.

The ocean just sort o' breathing in on the sand—Bill 'n' me sit here and count the breaths like. p 11

Note: The illustration also appears in the book *Hiker Joy* by James B. Connolly, published by Charles Scribner's Sons, N.Y., 1920.

October 4   Volume 64 Number 14

"The Wreck on Deliverance" by John Russell. Pages 5, 6, 40, 42, 44, and 45.

Two illustrations in black and white.

The stream began to bear us away from those ranks of fortunate folks who stood to listen to Jennie May. p 5

"But still," Logroscino stammered, "but still—this does not got to be true . . . What kind of a surgeon are you?" p 6

December 13   Volume 64 Number 24

"The Devil's Whisper" by James Francis Dwyer. Pages 11, 12, and 57–60.

Two illustrations in black and white.

Prince Lermontor fired at Peter Smith; Kilmair, directly behind, could not use his revolver. Elfrida Carlingford sprang up, but realized her powerlessness to help. p 11

"Four different sizes o' shoes," said Peter Smith. "Right," agreed Kilmair; "four hombres and one senorita. I don't think we'll be welcomed." p 12

1920

April 10   Volume 65 Number 15

"Nooning at the Devilbrew" by Holman Day. Pages 10, 11, 26, 28, and 32.

Two illustrations in black and white.

Description: Elise in canoe. (headpiece illustration) p 10

Octave plunged down the chute, leaning forward on the three huge logs chained together. p 11

Columbia (Knights Of Columbus)

1958

October

Cover illustration in color. Description: Columbus Discovers America.

Note: The illustration originally appeared in color in the calendar *Flags In American History*, published by John Morrell & Company, Ottumwa, Iowa, 1944.

The Country Gentleman

1918

January 26   Vol. LXXXIII No. 4

Cover illustration in two colors (brown, black and white).

Description: Lumberjack with axe.

March 2   Vol. LXXXIII No. 9

Cover illustration in two colors (red, black and white).

Description: Mexican sheepherder on horseback holding a young lamb.

1925

September   Vol. XC No. 35

Cover illustration in color. Description: A lumberjack standing among cut trees.

December   Vol. XC No. 38

Cover illustration in color. " 'Twas the night before Christmas, when all through the house/ not a creature was stirring, not even a mouse." Description: Santa Claus.

Editor's note: There's an elfin quality about N. C. Wyeth's Santa Claus. His pack is made, so Wyeth says, from a bit of winter sky, and twenty minutes past twelve (as shown on the clock in the picture) is the real mystic hour in children's minds. (page 138)

Note: The illustration also appears in color in *Life* magazine, December 17, 1971, for the article "The Wyeths' Kind of Christmas Magic" by Richard Meryman.

1926

July   Vol. XCI No. 7

Cover illustration in color. Description: Cowboy on bucking horse shooting two revolvers. Firecrackers exploding about horse.

November   Vol. XCI No. 11

Cover illustration in color. Description: A Pilgrim family offering a Thanksgiving Day prayer.

1927

March   Vol. XCII No. 3

Cover illustration in color. Description: Tapping sugar maples.

1944

June   Vol. CXIV No. 6

Cover illustration in color. On the Hay Load. Photograph of N. C. Wyeth posing with the completed cover painting on page 3. Editor's talk about the cover plus a brief biographical sketch on the artist on page 3.

November   Vol. CXIV No. 11

Cover illustration in color. The Old Timer. Editor's note: Wyeth talks about the cover illustration.

1946

February   Vol. CXVI No. 2

"First Farmer of the Land" by Donald Culross Peattie. Page 18, 19, and 56–58.

One illustration in color.

First Farmer of the Land. p 19

A brief description of the painting and mention of N. C. Wyeth's death on page 18.

Note: This illustration was on Wyeth's easel and in the process of completion at the time of his tragic accident.

Delaware History

1953

March   Vol. V No. 3

"The Howard Pyle School of Art" by Dudley Lunt. Pages 151–77. Frontispiece photograph of Howard Pyle.

Seven pen and ink drawings by N. C. Wyeth.

Wilmington Street Scene. fp 151

The Artist at His Easel. (sketch) p 151

Halloween Costume. (sketch) p 157

Old Grist Mill. (sketch) p 157

The Diver. (sketch) p 165

Chased by a Bull. (sketch) p 167

To the West. (sketch) p 177

Note: The pen-and-ink drawings appear through the courtesy of Mrs. N. C. Wyeth and are among many sketches in the collection of Mr. Wyeth's manuscript letters that are in the possession of Mrs. Wyeth.

Delaware History is published semiannually by the Historical Society of Delaware.

Delaware Today

1967

February–March   Volume 5 Number 6

Cover illustration in color. Center portion of the mural "The Apotheosis of the Family," gracing the entire south wall of the Wilmington Savings Fund Society building. N. C. Wyeth Mural. Pages 2, 3, and 23.

The Delineator

1905

October   Vol. LXII No. 10

"The Minute Man" Familiar Quotations Pictured. Page 576.

One illustration in black and white.

"Here once the embattled farmers stood/ and fired the shot heard round the world" —Emerson. p 576

Note: The pictorial content of this illustration again appeared in 1921, when Wyeth was commissioned to design a banking poster for Independence Day.

1912

February   Vol. LXXIX No. 2

"The Prairie" by Clarice Vallette McCauley. Pages 85 and 86.

Frontispiece illustration in black and white. At the door of their little cabin he kissed her. p 84

1915

November   Vol. LXXXII No. 11

"An Artist's Appreciation" (Editorial). Page 3. N. C. Wyeth expresses his thoughts about the poem "Autumn Dawn."

November   Vol. LXXXII No. 11

"Autumn Dawn" A Poem Of The Indian Harvest by Constance Skinner. Page 16.

One illustration in color.

Description: Indian fisherman with his family standing on a ridge with lake below and mountainous background. p 16

Note: The illustration also appears with two of the preliminary drawings in *The American Art Student* November-December 1916, for the article "The Illustrator and His Development" by N. C. Wyeth.

1919

April   Vol. LXXXVI No. 4

"The Planting of the Trees: The Story of Sceanba's Love" by Eleanor Cox. Pages 14, 15, and 70.

One illustration in two colors. (green, black and white)

So Hate That is Brother to Death Was in the Heart of Craftainy the Harper for Cormac Conloingias. (double page illustration) pp 14–15

D'A'C News (Official Publication of
Detroit Athletic Club)

1931

April

Cover illustration in color. "Man's Aspiration to
Conquer the Skies." (Reproduced by courtesy
of the owner, Edward S. Evans.)

Note: The illustration originally appeared in color
in *Redbook Magazine*, January 1930, and was titled
The Answer of the Skies.

DuPont Magazine

1948

September–October   Volume 42 Number 5
Page 32. Photograph of the main dining room
in the Hotel duPont, Wilmington, Del. On the
wall hangs Wyeth's painting "Island Funeral."

Everybody's Magazine

1912

June   Vol. XXVI No. 6
Sally Castleton, Southerner by Crittenden Marriott. Pages 754–69.

Two illustrations in black and white.
> Too tired and weak to guide his horse, he
> could only hang to his saddle and trust to
> the beast instinct to avoid destruction! And
> to spur—ever to spur—praying that he
> might reach help before brain and body
> failed together. (double page illustration)
> pp 756–57
> In imagination she could hear the rattling
> of drums, the ring of bugles, the low
> thunder of rumbling batteries. p 762

July   Vol. XXVII No. 1
Sally Castleton, Southerner by Crittenden Marriott. Pages 18–32.

Three illustrations in black and white.
> At the same moment the door behind Rad-
> cliffe crashed open and a dozen men
> crowded in, rifles in hand.[1] (frontispiece)
> "The plan is to have your cavalry cut a
> hole through the Confederate lines, and
> for me to slip through it . . . put me across
> to-night and I'll be in Richmond day after
> to-morrow." p 21
> He stopped his horse within a few paces of
> the sentry. "Good morning, brother!" he
> exclaimed. "Lord! I'm glad to see some-
> body! This is Rockfish, isn't it?"[1] (double
> page illustration) pp 26–27

August   Vol. XXVII No. 2
Sally Castleton, Southerner by Crittenden Marriott. Pages 256–70.

Three illustrations in black and white.
> "Send him back? Not a bit of it! We're
> going to hang him higher than Haman."[1]
> p 256
> Troops by the hundred were passing—tat-
> tered, war-hardened, lean, efficient troops,
> whose road-pace was eagerness itself.[2]
> (double page illustration) pp 260–61
> The girl's heart seemed to stop beating.
> The horses plodded through the leafy
> aisles, glorious with colors of the Autumn
> woods, but she saw none of them.[1] p 267

September   Vol. XXVII No. 3
Sally Castleton, Southerner by Crittenden Marriott. Pages 398–412.

Three illustrations in black and white.
> Step by step she forced herself to move
> across the floor till she stood above the
> bed.[1] p 399
> Day was breaking as, unhindered, Rad-
> cliffe passed the barrier. p 403
> Suddenly the bag opened, and a torrent of
> letters fell to the floor. 'Genie's face flushed
> red as fire.[1] p 407

October   Vol. XXVII No. 4
Sally Castleton, Southerner by Crittenden Marriott. Pages 546–58.

Two illustrations in black and white.
> 'Genie had grasped Phillip's saddle, and
> was clinging there. "Please! Please!" she
> begged. "Oh, my God, Phillip, he'll kill
> you!" p 547
> Deep in hollow sockets his hot eyes burned,
> red with fever. He sat his horse like an
> old man, haggard and bent. p 553

[1] The illustrations for this series also appear in the
book *Sally Castleton, Southerner* by Crittenden
Marriott, published by J. B. Lippincott Company,
Phila., January 1913.
[2] Also appears as a cover in color for *Civil War
Times Illustrated*, July 1969.

1919

January   Vol. XL No. 1
"The Mildest-Mannered Man" by Ben Ames
Williams. Pages 31–36 and 92–95.

Three illustrations in black and white.
> Her eyes were blue, with the blue of the
> sky at dawn. p 31
> Slag was a figure for sculptors. p 33
> Slag charged with the momentum of an
> avalanche across the shed; and Hulda,
> watching, thought he must sweep Eben
> back into the flaming stack. (double page
> illustration) pp 34–35

April   Vol. XL No. 4
"All the Brothers Were Valiant" by Ben Ames
Williams. Pages 15–22 and 83–89.

Three illustrations. One in sepia tint and two
in black and white.
> Description: Colonial house. (headpiece
> illustration in sepia tint) p 15
> To prove how much she hated him she
> nestled against his side, and his arm in-
> folded her. p 17
> "I sat there in the sun, drifting with the
> wind, and held her in my arms till she
> died." p 19

May   Vol. XL No. 5
"All the Brothers Were Valiant" by Ben Ames
Williams. Pages 38–42 and 110–14.

Three illustrations in black and white.
> Description: The Whaler, Nathan Ross.
> (headpiece illustration) p 38
> She was like nothing in his grasp; she
> could not stir. p 39
> The story of the battle upon the tumbling
> decks of the Nathan Ross was to be retold
> at many a gam upon the whaling-grounds.[1]
> p 41

[1] The illustration was reproduced on the dust
wrapper of *All the Brothers Were Valiant* by Ben
Ames Williams, Macmillan Company, N. Y., 1919.

Fortune

1939

January   Vol. XIX No. 1
"Cream of Wheat's Cream" . . . has been a consistent profit, skimmed off every year since

1900. Pages 68–72, 74, 76, and 79. Reference
to N. C. Wyeth on page 79.

One illustration in color by N. C. Wyeth.
> Where The Mail Goes Cream of Wheat
> Goes
>> Cream of Wheat's most famous adver-
>> tisement was painted in 1906 by N. C.
>> Wyeth for $800. p 71

Note: The illustration originally appeared in color
in the leading periodicals during the year 1907
and was reproduced for many years thereafter.

Forward

Records indicate N. C. Wyeth accepted commissions to illustrate articles for *Forward* during the early months of 1903. Extensive research
has failed to turn up any of the issues to date.

The Garnet and White
(West Chester High School,
West Chester, Pa.)

1935

November   Vol. XXVIII No. 1
Interviews: "An Intimate Glimpse of N. C.
Wyeth" by Janet M. Miller. Pages 10 and 11.

Good Housekeeping

1929

January   Vol. LXXXVIII No. 1
Children of the Bible by Bruce Barton. Part I
"The First Children." Pages 34, 35, and 169.

One illustration in color.
> When temptation came, and Adam and
> Eve fell out of their sinless and virtueless
> Eden, they began to be worth while. They
> fell from innocence into manhood and
> womanhood. They fell from shiftlessness
> into work. They fell from a drifting irre-
> sponsibility into worry and trouble and
> despair, but also into ambition and courage
> and hope. p 35

February   Vol. LXXXVIII No. 2
Part II "The Boy Who Established a Nation."
Pages 50, 51, and 168.

One illustration in color.
> The boy, Moses, clad in princely garments,
> witnessed the bitter suffering of his people
> at the hands of the Egyptian taskmasters.
> As he grew in years he became increas-
> ingly conscious of his kinship with the
> oppressed and exploited workers. p 51

March   Vol. LXXXVIII No. 3
Part III "The Boy Who Anointed Two Kings."
Pages 50, 51, and 224.

One illustration in color.
> Kindly but sternly Eli watched the little
> Samuel. Had he been too indulgent with
> his own boys? He must not make the same
> mistake with this young life. Earnestly he
> taught and admonished and corrected, and
> "the child Samuel grew on, and was in
> favor both with the Lord, and also with
> men." p 51

April   Vol. LXXXVIII No. 4
Part IV "The Boy Who Became King." Pages
50, 51, and 340.

One illustration in color.

Finally, the great scene of boyhood, the scene which will endear its hero to every generation of boys forever, the original of all the Jack the Giant Killer stories—David and Goliath. p 51

May   Vol. LXXXVIII No. 5
Part V "The Little Maid in the Captain's House." Pages 50, 51, and 312.

One illustration in color.

Naaman's wife brought the little maid that he himself might hear her. A glow of conviction shines in her face. She knows this prophet of whom she speaks. With childish eagerness, her words tumbling over each other, she urges Naaman to implore his aid. p 51

June   Vol. LXXXVIII No. 6
Part VI "The First Caddy." Pages 58, 59, and 259.

One illustration in color.

Jonathan shot, as he walked along, and the boy, running ahead, picked up the arrows and brought them back. And when they were out of sight of the court, they went toward a rock named Ezel, accessible from the wilderness and not far from the road. There David had hidden, straining his ears for the words that might mean life or death. p 59

July   Vol. LXXXIX No. 1
Part VII "The Prince Who Was Hidden." Pages 58, 59, and 165.

One illustration in color.

While the soldiers pressed for a closer view, and a thrill of expectancy ran through them all, Jehoiada led Joash out from behind the pillar. A trembling little fellow, a wondering, wide-eyed lad, but a son of the line of David, every inch a king! p 59

August   Vol. LXXXIX No. 2
Part VIII "The Sons of the Prophet Isaiah." Pages 66, 67, and 176.

One illustration in color.

The Assyrians had camped on the plains beyond the walls, and the whole city was paralyzed with fear. Only Isaiah was unterrified. In majestic calm he stood and hurled his defiance at the enemy. p 67

September   Vol. LXXXIX No. 3
Part IX "The Boy With the Basket." Pages 50, 51, and 278.

One illustration in color.

Age grows calculating, but youth is spendthrift in its generosity. Even if the boy trudged home hungry, he intended that Jesus should be fed. He gave his evening meal to the Master. p 51

October   Vol. LXXXIX No. 4
Part X "The Daughter of Jairus." Pages 50, 51, and 230.

One illustration in color.

That night a thankful father and mother knelt down beside the bed where their only daughter lay in healthful sleep. A little girl had come back to her parents from the very gates of death. The Galilean stars looked down and smiled their benediction. p 51

November   Vol. LXXXIX No. 5
Part XI "The Boy Who First Wrote the Story of Jesus." Pages 50, 51, 237, and 238.

One illustration in color.

A little after midnight, Jesus and his disciples came down the stair and went out. Mark got up and followed. He had heard rumors of plots and schemes, and he was curious to know what would happen next.[1] p 51

[1] Also appears in black and white in the book *The Good Housekeeping Treasury* by Donald Elder, published by Simon and Schuster, 1960.

December   Vol. LXXXIX No. 6
Part XII "The Royal Child of Bethlehem." Pages 50, 51, and 130.

One illustration in color.

Jesus lived the life of a Galilean boy. He went to the village school, which was kept in the local synagogue by a local rabbi. He learned the clumsy letters of the Hebrew alphabet according to current methods of instruction. p 51

1931

December   Vol. XCIII No. 6
"A Story of the Man Whose Birthday We Call Christmas" by Coningsby Dawson. Pages 16, 17, 114, and 116.

One illustration in color.

A boy spoke. "The camels the wise men rode—what color were they?" Jesus smiled, remembering that this was the question he, himself, had asked in Nazareth. (double page illustration) pp 16–17

1932

November   Vol. XCV No. 5
"Black Falcon" by Herbert Ravenel Sass. Pages 35, 38, and 210–15.

One illustration in color.

Genghis Khan's eyes were fixed upon the dark scarred face of the young man in front of him. Little could be hidden from those eyes, and suddenly the young man knew that he stood revealed. The inscrutable eyes gave no sign, but at last Genghis Khan beckoned to the girl, and she came and stood beside him. (double page illustration) pp 36–37

Harper's Monthly Magazine

1905

August   Vol. CXI No. 663
"Covered Embers" A Story by Elizabeth Stuart Phelps. Pages 351–62.

Three illustrations in sepia tint.

"There is one thing better than money—and that is a human home." fp 352
He heard her sob her way up-stairs. fp 356
One might have thought that he did not care. fp 360

October   Vol. CXI No. 665
"Back to Indiana" by Elmore Elliott Peake. Pages 658–67.

Two illustrations in black and white.

Often the road was hot and dusty. p (661)
"It was such a warm little house, there," said she, huskily. p (663)

November   Vol. CXI No. 666
"Homing Tides" A Story by Edith Macvane. Pages 859–72.

Two illustrations in black and white.

For what, after all, were they fishing? p (861)
"Who is it, please?" she asked. p (866)

1906

January   Vol. CXII No. 668
"The Road to Europe" by Grace Ellery Channing. Pages 266–75.

Two illustrations in black and white.

"We must hope for the best," Miss Luella faltered. p (269)
Out on the gravel walk they came to a standstill. p (273)

1911

November   Vol. CXXIII No. 738
"Growing Up" A Story by Gouverneur Morris. Pages 881–87.

Two illustrations in colors (ochre, blue, black and white).

The children were playing at marriage-by-capture. fp 882
Nothing would escape their black, jewel-like, inscrutable eyes. fp 886

1913

December   Vol. CXXVIII No. 763
"The Lost Boy" by Henry Van Dyke. Pages 3–15.

Three illustrations. Two (including frontispiece) in color and one in black and white.

"When He comes He will rule over the whole world"[1] (frontispiece in color).
Leaping from Rock to Rock in sheer delight (black and white) fp 4
"Come, live with us, for I think thou art chosen" (color) fp 10

Note: The illustrations appear in the book *The Lost Boy* (three editions), published by Harper & Brothers, N. Y., September 1914.
[1] The illustration also appears as a cover label in color for the book *The Story of Jesus Christ* by Elizabeth Stuart Phelps, published by Houghton Mifflin Company, Boston, 1926.

1914

May   Vol. CXXVIII No. 768
"The Tobacco Famine at Tamarac" A Story by Forrest Crissey. Pages 826–35.

Two illustrations. Frontispiece in color, and one in black and white.

Looking longingly into the gray eyes of peachy the unattainable. (frontispiece)
"He was the sickest-lookin' thing that ever escaped death" (black and white). fp 834

1915

August   Vol. CXXXI No. 783
"Sea-Green" by Katherine Fullerton Gerould. Pages 327–39.

Two illustrations in black and white.

Mr. Fenby always sat with his wife after supper. fp 330
"And you will stay on—after last night?" fp 338

1916

May   Vol. CXXXII No. 792

The Mysterious Stranger A Romance by Mark Twain. Part I Pages 813–18.

Three illustrations. Frontispiece in color and two in pen and ink.
> Eseldorf was a paradise for us boys[1] (frontispiece)
> Titlepiece illustration in pen and ink (castle viewed from a forest) p (813)
> Initial (I) design in pen and ink. p (813)

June   Vol. CXXXII No. 793

The Mysterious Stranger A Romance by Mark Twain. Part II Pages 38–43.

One illustration in color.
> The lightning blazed out flash upon flash and set the castle on fire. fp 40

July   Vol. CXXXIII No. 794

The Mysterious Stranger A Romance by Mark Twain. Part III Pages 236–41.

Frontispiece illustration in color.
> On the fourth day comes the astrologer from his crumbling old tower.

August   Vol. CXXXIII No. 795

The Mysterious Stranger A Romance by Mark Twain. Part IV Pages 441–46.

One illustration in color.
> Marget was cheerful by help of Wilhelm Meidling. fp 444

September   Vol. CXXXIII No. 796

The Mysterious Stranger A Romance by Mark Twain. Part V Pages 574–81.

One illustration in color.
> The astrologer emptied the whole of the bowl into the bottle. fp 576

October   Vol. CXXXIII No. 797

The Mysterious Stranger A Romance by Mark Twain. Part VI Pages 749–58.

One illustration in color.
> There was a sound of tramping outside and the crowd came solemnly in. fp 752

November   Vol. CXXXIII No. 798

The Mysterious Stranger A Romance by Mark Twain. Part VII. Pages 883–92.

Frontispiece illustration in color.
> "Life itself is only a vision, a dream."

Note: All the illustrations for this seven part serial appear in the book *The Mysterious Stranger,* published by Harper & Brothers, N. Y., October 1916. [1] The illustration also appeared on a cover label in color for the book *Chatter Box,* published by Wells Garder, Darton & Co. Ltd. London, 1929.

1927

November   Vol. CLIV

The National Association of Book Publishers (Book Week, November 13–19, 1927). Page 2.

One illustration in black and white.
> Description: Seventeenth century adventurer on deck of ship, with heavy seas and galleon in background. p 2

Hearst's

1916

August   Volume 30 Number 2

The Great West That Was "Buffalo Bill's Life Story" by Col. William F. Cody. Pages 74, 75, 129, and 130.

Two illustrations in black and white.
> "I remember," writes Buffalo Bill, "the next day father began trading with the Indians who were so pleased over the bargains we offered that they sent their friends back to us after they cantered away."[1] p 74
> When the moon arose there was silhouetted across its face the dusky figure of a war-bonneted Sioux, rifle at shoulder, aiming at one of our party. Raising my gun I fired and the brave came crashing down the bank. (headpiece vignette) p 75[1][2]

September   Volume 30 Number 3

The Great West That Was by Col. William F. Cody. Pages 158, 159, and 197–99.

Two illustrations in black and white.
> One day a band of fifteen Indians jammed me in a sand ravine. I made a running fight for eleven miles, but went unscathed and had a lead of two miles at Sweetwater Bridge.[1][2] (headpiece illustration) p 158
> Behind Simpson's dead-mule barricades we made ready for attack from the circling redskins. The carcases were soon stuck full of arrows, and Woods was winged in the shoulder.[1][2][3] p 159

October   Volume 30 Number 4

The Great West That Was by Col. William F. Cody. Pages 244, 245, and 254–57.

Three illustrations in two colors (brown, black and white).
> Wheeling about I saw that the other man, hearing the fall, had turned, his hand upon his revolver. It was no time for argument. I fired and killed him (headpiece illustration).[1][2] p 244
> Dropping one of the sage-hens I asked the man behind me to pick it up. As he was groping for it I pulled one of my Colt's revolvers, and hit him over the head. He dropped senseless. (headpiece illustration) p 245
> The man with the hatful of cards picked out of his reserves, put the hat on his head and raised Bill a hundred. Bill came back with a raise of two hundred and as the other covered it he shoved a pistol into his face observing; "I'm calling the hand that is in your hat."[1][2] p 245

November   Volume 30 Number 5

The Great West That Was by Col. William F. Cody. Pages 309, 310, and 373–75 .

Two illustrations in black and white.
> "My great white brothers," said Chief Santanta, after loading the peace-pipe and passing it to General Sherman, "I welcome you to my camp and to my people!"[1][2] p 309
> "For a time, there being no scouting to do," says Colonel Cody, "I drove stage between Plum Creek and Fort Kearney, with plenty of hair-raising adventures thrown in."[1][2] p 310

December   Volume 30 Number 6

The Great West That Was by William F. Cody. Pages 396 and 461–64.

One illustration in black and white.
> Description: Bison herd drinking at a waterhole.[1][2] (headpiece illustration) p 396

[1] The illustrations for this serial, *The Great West That Was,* also appear in the book (paper wraps) *The Great West That Was* by William F. Cody, published by The Star Company, N. Y., 1916.
[2] The illustrations appear in the book *An Autobiography of Buffalo Bill* by Colonel W. F. Cody, published by the Cosmopolitan Book Corporation, N. Y., 1920.
[3] In addition, the illustration appears in color in *American Heritage,* October 1965, for the article "N. C. Wyeth" by Henry C. Pitz.

Hearst's International

1923

June   Vol. XLIII No. 6

"Buffalo Swamp" A Ballad of the Moonshine Belt by Damon Runyon. Page 52.

One illustration in two colors (black and white with green tint).
> Description: A group of armed horsemen. p 52

July   Vol. XLIV No. 1

"The Grace of the Dim Strain" A story of the wild outdoors where humans are courageous and beasts seem human by Vingie E. Roe. Pages 22–27, 145, and 146.

Three illustrations in colors.
> The father kept the children near him, but always young Olaf looked with tragic eyes toward the slope where Padfoot waited. (double page illustration in green, orange, black and white) pp 22–23
> This dangerous wild thing was undecided whether to leap in or back out. Eye to eye boy and wolf stared at each other for one terrible moment. (double page illustration in blue, black and white) pp 24–25
> Just as the baby's feet cleared the ground Padfoot leaped into the air and buried his teeth in the feathers of his old enemy. (orange, black and white) p 26

August   Vol. XLIV No. 2

"Foolish Like a Fox" A swinging tale of human, salty, hard-bitten Cappy Ricks by Peter B. Kyne. Pages 12, 17, and 141–44.

Four illustrations. Three in two colors and one in black and white.
> "I'm not going," Randall told the men in the overcrowded boat. "I'll stick here and when you get to San Francisco ask Cappy Ricks to send a tug out to look for me." (double page illustration in blue, black and white) pp 12–13
> "The sea breeds fighters and that's what I want in the employ of the Blue Star. You two just naturally make me sick at the stomach. Get out!" (double page illustration in red, brown, black and white) pp 14–15
> The life-boat pulled away, leaving Randall loyally clinging to the boom of the drifting hulk. (blue, black and white) p 16
> A gust, fiercer than any of its predecessors, heeled the Wanderer over and the lip of a comber climbed in over her counter and swept aft to the break of the poop. (black and white) p 17

Hercules Chemist

1942

Cover illustration in color. Primal Chemistry.

Note: The illustration originally appeared as a Hercules Powder Co. calendar for the year 1942.

The Hercules Mixer
(Hercules Powder Company)

1935
January
Cover illustration in color. "New Trails"

1938
February
Cover illustration in color. "The Alchemist"

1939
January
Cover illustration in color. "A New World"

1940
January
Cover illustration in color. "The Pioneers"

1942
January
Cover illustration in color. "Primal Chemistry"

1944
January
Cover illustration in color. "Sweet Land of Liberty"

1946
January
Cover illustration in color. "The Spirit Of '46"

Note: All illustrations originally appeared as Hercules calendars for the years stated. In addition, Hercules Powder Company issued color prints of these works.

The Home Office
(Metropolitan Life Insurance Co.)

1941
December   Volume 23 Number 7
"The Days of the Pilgrims Live Again in Our Murals." In rich colors Artist Wyeth recaptures the lyrical side of New England life as early colonists lived it. Pages 8 and 9. Photographic portrait of N. C. Wyeth. p 8

One illustration in black and white.
  Description: The Wedding Procession. p 8

Note: The mural paintings depict four activities in the lives of the Pilgrims—The Thanksgiving Feast, The Wedding Procession, The Turkey Hunters, and Going to Church.

Horn Book

1946
September—October   Vol. XXII No. 5
"N. C. Wyeth 1882–1945" by Dudley Lunt. Pages 332–38. Photographic portrait of N. C. Wyeth by William E. Phelps. p 332

The Independent
(Incorporated with *Harper's Weekly*)

1916
December 4
Cover illustration in color by N. C. Wyeth. The Man In The Green Tabard.

Note: The illustration originally appeared in color in *The Black Arrow* by Robert Louis Stevenson, published by Charles Scribner's Sons, New York, October 1916. It was titled "In the fork, like a mastheaded seaman, there stood a man in a green tabard, spying far and wide."

The International Studio

1914
January   Vol. LI No. 203
Wilmington Fine Arts Exhibition. Pages CLXI–CLXII.

One illustration in black and white.
  The Invaders p CLXI
This work received the First Prize for Illustration in the Wilmington Society of the Fine Arts Exhibition in 1913.

Note: The illustration originally appeared as a frontispiece in black and white in *Everybody's Magazine*, July 1912, for the serial *Sally Castleton, Southerner* by Crittenden Marriott.

1915
January   Vol. LIV No. 215
"A Tribute to Howard Pyle" by J. B. Carrington. Page LXXXV. In the article are references to N. C. Wyeth.

One illustration in black and white by Howard Pyle.

January   Vol. LIV No. 215
"Decorative Pictures at the Pennsylvania Academy of Fine Arts" by Theodore L. Fitzsimons. Pages LXXXVII–XC. The review discusses N. C. Wyeth's most striking illustration entitled The Black Dragon.

One illustration in black and white.
  The Black Dragon p LXXXIX

Note: The illustration appeared in color in *Scribner's Magazine*, August 1914, for the story "The Rakish Brigantine" by James B. Connolly.

February   Vol. LIV No. 216
Studio Talk: "The Twelfth Annual Exhibition of Watercolors, Pastels, and Black & White Work at the Pennsylvania Academy of the Fine Arts. Pages 292–316. The review refers to N. C. Wyeth's noteworthy illustration, Opium Smoker. (page 314)

Note: The illustration appeared in color in *The American Magazine*, June 1914, for the story "A Modern Opium Eater" by No. 6606.

1917
February   Vol. LX No. 240
Studio Talk. Pages 201–6. A reference to N. C. Wyeth's work in the 14th Annual Water Color Exhibition at The Pennsylvania Academy of Fine Arts (page 204)

1923
May   Vol. LXXVII No. 312
"Art in Missouri's Capitol" Historic events and persons of the State made subjects of mural decorations by famous painters by Emily Grant Hutchins. Pages 96–100. Illustrated with numerous decorations by various artists. Reference to mural paintings on page 99.
Two illustrations (mural paintings) in black and white by N. C. Wyeth.
Battle of Wilson's Creek p 98
Battle of Westport Landing p 99

Note: The mural paintings originally appeared in color in the *Ladies' Home Journal*, March 1921.

Judge

1921
November 19   Vol. LXXXI No. 2090
Thanksgiving Number
Cover illustration in color. Description: A drifter—In a night scene with quarter moon, black man, carrying bag and holding stick, is looking back over his shoulder at farm building. Wild turkey sitting on tree limb above.

December 17   Volume 81 Number 2094
Christmas Number
Cover illustration in color. "Hey, Kiddies, here we are again!" Description: Santa Claus in a gift-filled sleigh flying through the skies.

1922
February 11   Volume 82 Number 2102
Cover illustration in color. "Your legs are all right if they are long enough to reach the ground."

  Lincoln's genial humor typified the spirit of the National Smile week.

Ladies' Home Journal

1906
August   Vol. XXIV No. 9
"The War Maiden of the Sioux" The Valiant Story of the Most Beautiful Girl of Two Indian Tribes by Charles A. Eastman. Page 14.

One illustration in black and white.
  "Look! Look! The War Maiden Comes!"

1907
December   Vol. XXV No. 1
"A Christmas Venture" A Story of the Days of Washington at Valley Forge by S. Weir Mitchell. Pages 11, 12, and 71.

One illustration in black and white.
  "The Drifts Became Heavier. There Were No Marks of Recent Travel." p 11

1908
January   Vol. XXV No. 2
"A Christmas Venture" by S. Weir Mitchell. Pages 21 and 53.

One illustration in black and white.
  "Why, This Map is Invaluable. What is Your Name, My Boy?" p 21

May   Vol. XXV No. 6
"The Outlaw and the Girl" A Singular Romance of a Girl in the Rocky Mountains by Hamlin Garland. Pages 7, 8, 70, and 71

Three illustrations in black and white.
  Description: The Outlaw (spot illustration). p 7
  "She Rode on for Nearly Half an Hour, Bravely Enduring Her Pain." p 7
  Description: The Girl (spot illustration). p 7

June   Vol. XXV No. 7
"The Outlaw and the Girl" by Hamlin Garland. Pages 17, 18, and 55.

Two illustrations in black and white.
  "As He Sat in the Doorway Looking at the Storm He Realized that He was Shaken by a Wild, Crude Lyric of Passion." p 17
  "Take Me Back—Inside," Alice Said to the Man Who Had Her in His Arms. "I Feel Cold Here." p 17

1919
August   Vol. XXXVI No. 8
"The White Admiral of the Woods" And the Gloomy Ghost From the City Who Carried a

Blight in His Face by Herbert D. Ward. Pages 9, 90, and 92–94.

One illustration in color.
Description: Man with butterfly perched upon his finger with background scene of lake and mountains. p 9

October   Vol. XXXVI No. 10
From the Battlefields of France to the Wheat Fields of America. p 16

One illustration in color.

1921

March   Vol. XXXVIII No. 3
"New Mural Paintings by N. C. Wyeth for the Missouri State Capitol." Page 20.

Two lunette paintings in color.
The Battle of Westport.[1] p 20
The Battle of Wilson's Creek.[2] p 20

Note: The mural paintings also appear in black and white in *The American Magazine of Art,* July 1921, and *The International Studio,* May 1923. In addition, they appear in black and white in volume 7 of *The Pageant of America* by Ralph Henry Gabriel, published by Yale University Press, New Haven, 1925–29. They also appear in color in a Souvenir Guide To Missouri's Capitol.
[1] The Battle of Westport appears as a cover in color for *Civil War Times Illustrated,* July 1966. It is also repeated in this issue in black and white.
[2] The Battle of Wilson's Creek appears in color in the article "N. C. Wyeth" by Henry C. Pitz, *American Heritage,* October 1965. In addition, it appears in *Architecture,* June 1921.

September   Vol. XXXVIII No. 9
Vandemark's Folly by Herbert Quick. Pages 3–6, 72, 75, 76, 78, and 81.

Four illustrations in black and white.
It was the newest, strangest, most delightful, sternest, most wonderful thing in the world—the Iowa prairie.[1] p 3
John Rucker had become the dark cloud in my life. I think now that I was afraid of him because my mother was. p 4
He crowded me too far one day and pushed me to the point of one of those frenzied revolts for which the Dutch are famous.[2] p 5
It was not signed. I read it slowly, because I was not very good at reading, and turned my eyes west—where my mother had gone. p 6

October   Vol. XXXVIII No. 10
Vandemark's Folly by Herbert Quick. Pages 21–23, 107, 108, and 110–12.

Three illustrations in black and white.
That endless stream across the Dubuque ferry was flowing on ahead of me, and the fast-going part of it was passing me every hour like swift schooners outstripping a slow, round-bellied Dutch square-rigger.[2] p 21
The last morning Rowena came to my fire and, snatching the spider away from me, took the job off my hands, baking the cakes while I ate.[3] p 22
If the woman in the wagon was scared to death at the sight of the prairie, I surely had cause to be afraid: but I was not. I was uplifted.[2] p 23

November   Vol. XXXVIII No. 11
Vandemark's Folly by Herbert Quick. Pages 21–23, 98, 101, 102, and 104.

Three illustrations in black and white.
I jumped down into the stream and caught her in my arms as she was losing her hold.[2] p 21
For a moment he seemed to be looking right at me. This was my first sight of Bowie Bushyager.[4] p 22
I turned cold as I thought of her playing with her doll while I had been out on the prairie laying poison plots against her innocence, her trust in me. p 23

December   Vol. XXXVIII No. 12
Vandemark's Folly by Herbert Quick. Pages 20–22, 106, 108, 109, 111, and 112.

Two illustrations in black and white.
I remember how Rowena looked back at us, as the Gowdy buggy went off like the wind, with Buck's arm behind the girl to keep her from jouncing out. p 20
I was scared by the report of the gun—so I clinched with the fellow and threw him out.[2] p 21

1922

January   Vol. XXXIX No. 1
Vandemark's Folly by Herbert Quick. Pages 18, 19, 77, 79, 80, 83, and 85.

Two illustrations in black and white.
As I turned I saw her kneeling there, her hair all about her face, with her hands stretched out to me: and then I walked blindly away into the long grass of the marsh.[2] p 18
"Oh," exclaimed Magnus, "you shouldn't talk so! Ve got plenty to eat. Dere bane lots people in Norvay would yump at de shance to yange places wit' us." p 19

February   Vol. XXXIX No. 2
Vandemark's Folly by Herbert Quick. Pages 18–20, 137, 139, 140, 143–46, and 149.

Three illustrations in color and black and white.
We sweltered and almost suffocated. Rowena buried her face in her shawl and swayed as if falling.[1][2] (color) p 18
They trampled over me as they drove our men off the field. (color) p 19
Two or three times one of the mares fell in the drifts, and nothing but the courage bred into them in the blue-grass fields of Kentucky saved us from stalling out in that fearful moving flood of snow.[1][2] (black and white) p 20

[1] The illustrations also appear in the book *One Man's Life* by Herbert Quick, published by The Bobbs-Merrill Company, 1925.
[2] The illustrations for this serial also appear in the book *Vandemark's Folly* by Herbert Quick, published by The Bobbs-Merrill Company, Indianapolis, 1922.
[3] The illustration also appears in black and white in the article "Cookery In The Mississippi Valley" by Caroline B. King, published in the *Ladies' Home Journal,* November 1924.
[4] The illustration also appears in the book *The Art of the Old West* by Paul A. Rossi and David C. Hunt, published by Alfred A. Knopf, New York, 1971.

March   Vol. XXXIX No. 3
Cover illustration in color. Description: A Boy's Fantasy. While reading, a boy envisions a pirate attack on a galleon.

June   Vol. XXXIX No. 6
"Surf" by Stephen Morehouse Avery. Pages 10, 11, 152–54, 157, and 158.

Two illustrations in color.
Description: Duel across a table. p 10
"I seek him called Splinters," she said. "I heard your story from the window. Come with me." p 11

1923

February   Vol. XL No. 2
"In the Dark Days of the Civil War." Page 18.

One illustration in color reproduced through the courtesy of the Federal Reserve Bank of Boston.
One of N. C. Wyeth's new decorations for the Federal Reserve Bank in Boston, depicting Lincoln and his Secretary of the Treasury, Salmon P. Chase, discussing the financial problems of the war. Uniform in size with this, the Washington decoration forms the central motif of the opposite wall of a magnificent room in Boston's newest bank building. It will be reproduced in a later issue of the *Journal.* Featuring the most famous Presidents of our country, these two mural decorations are a notable addition to America's historical paintings. p 18

Note: The mural painting also appears in *Scribner's Magazine,* July 1928.

March   Vol. XL No. 3
"Snake and Hawk" by Stephen Vincent Benét. Pages 10, 11, and 128–30.

Two illustrations in color.
Description: Illustration (within oval) of a galleon at full sail on the high seas. p 10
We were three days taking out even what gold and gems we could load on ourselves, and our beasts, the treasure of three queens pardons. p 11

July   Vol. XL No. 7
The Giant. Pages 14 and 15. Reproduced from the mural decoration by N. C. Wyeth in the Westtown School, Westtown, Pa.

One illustration in color.
The Giant p 14

Note: The Giant also appears in color in the article "N. C. Wyeth" by Henry C. Pitz in *American Heritage,* October 1965. In addition, it appears in color in the book *The Wyeths* by N. C. Wyeth (edited by Betsy James Wyeth), published by Gambit, Boston, 1971.

December   Vol. XL No. 12
"The Collier and the King" by Edwin Markham. Page 9.

One illustration in color.
Description: Holding a burning brand in air, he saw the tired king standing there. p 9

1924

February   Vol. XLI No. 2
"The Founders of Our National Financial Policies." Page 19.

One illustration in color reproduced through the courtesy of the Federal Reserve Bank of Boston.
Washington, Hamilton, and Robert Morris are credited with planning the financial rock upon which our nation's security is built. These three, grouped in conference, form the subject of a mural decoration by N. C. Wyeth which, together with the panel representing Lincoln and Salmon P. Chase, his Secretary of the Treasury, adorns

the Junior Bankers' Lobby of the Federal Reserve Bank of Boston. p 19

Note: The mural painting also appears in *Scribner's Magazine,* July 1928.

November Vol. XLI No. 11
Cover illustration in color. Description: Portrait of Henriette Wyeth.[1]

"Cookery in the Mississippi Valley" by Caroline B. King. Page 135.

One illustration in black and white.
Description: Woman cooking by a campfire.[2] p 135

[1] The painting also appears in black and white in the article "Wyeths by Wyeths," published in *Town & Country* magazine, November 1946.
[2] The illustration originally appeared in *Vandemark's Folly* by Herbert Quick, published in the *Ladies' Home Journal,* October 1921.

December Vol. XLI No. 12
"On Christmas Night by Bethlehem Town" by Robert P. Tristram Coffin. Pages 9 and 155.

One illustration in color.
Description: Shepherds in the hills viewing with awe the star over Bethlehem town. p 9

1925

July Vol. XLII No. 7
"Mural Paintings in the First National Bank of Boston." Pages 16 and 17.

Two illustrations in color.
The City of Tyre.[1] p 16
Elizabethan Galleons. p 17

[1] The mural painting also appears in *Scribner's Magazine,* July 1928.

"Biremes and Galleons" by N. C. Wyeth. Page 54. The artist's interpretation of the mural paintings.

"Our Family Album" by the Editors. Pages 21 and 138. Photograph and article on N. C. Wyeth.

August Vol. XLII No. 8
"Mural Paintings in the First National Bank of Boston." Pages 16 and 17.
Two illustrations in color.
Clipper Ships.[1] p 16
The Pack Mule of the Sea. p 17

"Tramps and Clippers" by N. C. Wyeth. Page 38. The artist's interpretation of the mural paintings.

Note: The mural paintings also appear in *Scribner's Magazine,* July 1928.
[1] The mural painting also appears in black and white in *The Burroughs Clearing House,* 1926, for the article "Colorful Assets in the Murals" by John Walker Harrington.

1926

July Vol. XLIII No. 7
"An Apotheosis of Franklin" A Mural Decoration by N. C. Wyeth. Page 13. An interpretation of the mural painting by N. C. Wyeth. Mural decoration for the Franklin Savings Bank of New York City.

One illustration in color.
Description: The central figure is of Benjamin Franklin, surrounded by his great contemporaries, the builders of this nation. In the background stands Independence

Hall in Philadelphia—symbol of Liberty. p 13

Note: The mural decoration also appears in black and white in *The Burroughs Clearing House,* 1926, for the article "Colorful Assets in the Murals" by John Walker Harrington.

1927

May Vol. XLIV No. 5
"The Legend of Kogal and Azin" by Donald and Louise Peattie. Pages 23 and 71.

Three illustrations in color.
Description: Ducks flying (spot illustration). p 23
Description: Ducks swimming (spot illustration). p 23
Out of the sky to her fell Kogal, with a great cry, scattering a spray of silver over the lotus blossoms. p 23

December Vol. XLIV No. 12
"A Desert Santa Claus" by Harold Bell Wright. Pages 6, 7, 103, and 104.

One illlustration in color.
"Coming toward the camp was a regulation Santa Claus—red breeches, boots, pack and all. For a minute or two we were too paralyzed to move." p 7

1928

September Vol. XLV No. 9
Elizabeth and Essex by Lytton Strachey. Pages 6, 7, 190, 192, 195, 196, 198, 200, 201, and 203–5.

Two illustrations in color.
Description: Elizabeth I (titlepiece illustration) p 6
Description: The earl of Essex riding horse and holding a falcon. p 7

October Vol. XLV No. 10
Elizabeth and Essex by Lytton Strachey. Pages 9, 10, 171, 172, 174, 177, and 179.

One illustration in color.
Description: Essex sails for Cádiz. p 9

November Vol. XLV No. 11
Elizabeth and Essex by Lytton Strachey. Pages 16, 17, 205, 206, 209, and 210.

One illustration in color.
And there, quite close to him, was Elizabeth among her ladies, in a dressing gown, unpainted, without her wig, her gray hair hanging in wisps about her face, and her eyes starting from her head. p 17

December Vol. XLV No. 12
Elizabeth and Essex by Lytton Strachey. Pages 17, 139, 141, 143, 144, and 146.

One illustration in color.
Description: Essex imprisoned in the Tower. (headpiece illustration) p 17

1929

May Vol. XLVI No. 5
"Amber's Mirage" by Zane Grey. Pages 5, 6 and 250–53.

Two illustrations in black and white.
One long gaze filled Jim Crawford with sustaining strength. This was a possession of his soul. p 5
"Oh, Al!" she wailed . . . "I didn't know I loved you so or I'd been different." p 6

June Vol. XLVI No. 6
"Amber's Mirage" by Zane Grey. Pages 7, 73, 75, and 78.

One illustration in color.
"Look!" cried Crawford exultantly. "What you see? . . . Jim!" "Amber's mirage!" p 7

July Vol. XLVI
"Amber's Mirage" by Zane Grey. Pages 13 and 119–21.

One illustration in black and white.
"Howdy, Shade. I see your hunt for gold hasn't improved your manners," he said mockingly. p 13

1930

September Vol. XLVII No. 9
"Green Vigil" A Saga of the West by Wilbur Daniel Steele. Pages 3–5 and 79.

Three illustrations. One in color, one in black and white, and one in two colors.
Where there had been no tree, now there was a tree. It changed the plain. (color) p 3
She thought a poet was a man who made rimes; she did not guess that this man when he said: "There'll be fences here, and fields and roofs and chimneys," was talking poetry. (black and white) p 4
Ivy shut her eyes when she hit now. Those gibbering monkey men did not know it, but Ivy in her terror knew it; no longer was it arms swinging a vindictive ax, but it was an ax of panic swinging helpless arms. (reddish brown, black and white) p 5

1931

September Vol. XLVIII No. 9
"The Duel on the Beach" by Rafael Sabatini. Pages 3–5.

One illustration in color.
"Allons!" said De Bernis. "It is time to make an end. So!" He parried. "So!" p 3

Note: The Duel on the Beach is reproduced on the dust wrapper of the book *The Black Swan* by Rafael Sabatini, published by Houghton Mifflin Company, Boston, 1932.

Leslie's Popular Monthly

1903

August Vol. LVI No. 4
"Working for Fame" by John M. Oskison. Pages 372–8.

Four illustrations in black and white.
"It may be I'll some time be arrested,/But we're all of us working for fame;/What care I how that is accomplished?/For the end of all men is the same." (titlepiece pen and ink drawing) p (372)
Into town from the south.[1] p (375)
As Broadwell raced West.[1] p (377)
Description: A smoking revolver with bags of gold. (tailpiece pen and ink drawing) p 378

[1] The illustrations also appear in *True West,* December 1967, for the article "N. C. Wyeth, Painter of Men . . . In Action" by Les Beitz.

1904

August Vol. LVIII No. 4
"The Trouble at Bishop's House" by Holman F. Day. Pages 340–50. With Drawings by the

Howard Pyle School. Illustrated by N. C. Wyeth, H. C. Peck, and Allen True. Frontispiece illustration in black and white by N. C. Wyeth. Merely three children.

Life

1921

September 22   Volume 78 Number 2029
Cover illustration in color. "Stand and Deliver!"

Life (Magazine)

1944

April 24   Volume 16 Number 17
Carnegie Show (Art Section). Exhibit titled "Painting in the United States." Pages 74–79. Illustrated with paintings by Wayman Adams, Fletcher Martin, John Koch, N. C. Wyeth, etc.

One painting in color by N. C. Wyeth.
"Portrait of a Farmer" p 78

1946

June 17   Volume 20 Number 24
"N. C. Wyeth" (Art Section). Pages 78–81. Photo of N. C. Wyeth in his studio at Chadds Ford, Pa. (p 78). Three pen and ink drawings by Howard Pyle from his book *The Merry Adventures of Robin Hood*.
Eight illustrations in color by N. C. Wyeth.
Mrs. Cushman's House. p 79
The Spring House. p 79
Nightfall. p 80
Summer Night. p 80
    Illustration from *Drums*. p 81
    Illustration from *The Scottish Chiefs*. p 81
    Illustration from *The Yearling*. p 81
    Illustration from *Robin Hood*. p 81

1957

December 9   Volume 43 Number 24
"The Stouthearted Heroes of a Beloved Painter" —N. C. Wyeth, the great American illustrator, created a world that lives on in his classics for children. Pages 88–100. Portrait of N. C. Wyeth at his easel by daughter Henriette. (p 88)

Nineteen illustrations in color by N. C. Wyeth.
    Illustration from *Kidnapped*. p 89
    Illustrations (three) from *Robin Hood*. pp 90–91
    Illustration from *The Yearling*. p 93
    Illustration from *Hans Brinker*. p 93
    Illustrations (two) from *Anthology of Children's Literature*. pp 92–93
    Illustration from *The Mysterious Island*. p 94
    Illustration from *Rip Van Winkle*. p 94
    Illustration from *Robinson Crusoe*. p 95
    Illustration from *Michael Strogoff, A Courier of the Czar*. p 95
    Illustrations (four) from *Treasure Island*. pp 96–97
    Illustration from *The Scottish Chiefs*. p 98
    Illustration from *The Boy's King Arthur*. p 99
    Illustration from *The Last of the Mohicans*. p 100

1965

May 14   Volume 58 Number 19
"Andrew Wyeth" An Interview by Richard Meryman. Pages 92–106, 108, 110, 112, 114, 116, 121, and 122. Photograph of N. C. Wyeth on page 108. References to N. C. Wyeth on pages 3, 93, 104, 108, and 110.

1971

December 17   Special Double Issue
"The Wyeths' Kind of Christmas Magic" by Richard Meryman. Pages 122–29. Including in the article are excerpts from letters N. C. Wyeth wrote to his parents, his daughter Henriette, and close friend and fellow artist Sidney Chase. Illustrated with paintings and drawings in color and black and white by N. C. Wyeth, Andrew Wyeth, and James Wyeth.
Three illustrations in color by N. C. Wyeth.
Ole St. Nick. p 122[1]
A self-portrait. p 123[2]
The Magician and the Maid of Beauty. p 124[3]

[1] Originally appeared as a cover in color for *The Country Gentleman*, December 1925.
[2] The self-portrait also appears in color in *American Heritage*, October 1965, for the article "N. C. Wyeth" by Henry C. Pitz.
[3] Originally appeared in color in the book *The Sampo* by James Baldwin, published by Charles Scribner's Sons, N. Y., 1912.

The Living Wilderness

1959

Winter   Vol. XXIII No. 67
"Single-Mindedness in Concord" (reviewed) by Harvey Broome. Pages 15–21.

One illustration in black and white.
    Thoreau meeting "a very little boy in the street . . . who had on a home-made cap of a woodchuckskin." p 17

Note: The illustration originally appeared in color in *Men of Concord* (edited by Francis H. Allen), Houghton Mifflin Company, 1936. The original painting is now the property of the Concord Free Public Library, Concord, Massachusetts.

McCall's

1923

September   Vol. L No. 12
Silk by Samuel Merwin. Pages 7–9, 50, 56, and 59.

Two illustrations. One in black and white and one in two colors.
    Before me sat the Virgin Queen of Balkh; with a shock I realized that her face was wholly unveiled. (black and white) p 7
    My confusion, I think, derived from my complete unfamiliarity with this sort of thing. I sat breathless, watching the strange exotic creature before me. She was as slim as a boy, and danced with a lightness and suppleness of body and arms and hands unlike anything I have ever seen. (double page illustration in brown, black and white) pp 8–9

[1] The illustration also appears as a frontispiece in color in the book *Silk* by Samuel Merwin, published by Houghton Mifflin Company, Boston, 1923.

October   Vol. LI No. 1
Silk by Samuel Merwin. Pages 16, 28, 42, 47, and 49.
One illustration in two colors. (green, black and white)
    The pale, moonlit city lay all about us in a ghostly circle. Mosulla and I had never been so close in spirit. p 16

November   Vol. LI No. 2
Silk by Samuel Merwin. Pages 8 and 62. Illustrated by N. C. Wyeth and decorations by Willy Pogany.

One illustration in two colors (blue, black and white).
    The queen lounged restfully on the divan among the cushions, looking out at him under lowered lashes, like one who dreams. p 8

December   Vol. LI No. 3
Silk by Samuel Merwin. Pages 12, 13, 27, and 30.
One illustration in two colors. (reddish brown, black and white)
    We rode quietly until the suburbs had dropped behind, and then lashed out furiously. (double page illustration) pp 12–13

1924

December   Vol. LII No. 3
"The Midnight Revel" by Thomas Hardy. Pages 8 and 9.

One illustration in two colors. (reddish brown, black and white)
    "There Stood a Figure Beneath the Moon!" (double page illustration) pp 8–9

1925

April   Vol. LII No. 7
A Son of His Father by Harold Bell Wright. Pages 5–7, 64–66, 69–71, and 76.

Two illustrations. One in black and white and one in colors.
    "When my brother Larry had a chance to come to America . . ." (black and white) p 5
    "I've seen him ride broncs that had piled the best of them, and as for roping—even the Mexican vaqueros have had to hand it to him more than once." (double page illustration in red, brown, black and white) pp 6–7

May   Vol. LII No. 8
A Son of His Father by Harold Bell Wright. Pages 15–17, 72, 81–83, 102, 104–6, and 108.

Two illustrations in colors. (red, brown, black and white)
    The sweet strains of music . . . stole into the consciousness of the tired girl. p 15
    The effect was startling. The man's feet left the ground and he fell with a thud as if dropped from some height. Morgan whirled to face the others, the fire of his wrath still aflame. pp 16–17

June   Vol. LII No. 9
A Son of His Father by Harold Bell Wright. Pages 15–17, 45, 46, and 51.

Two illustrations in two colors. (blue, black and white)
    For some time the dark form remained motionless, listening to the girl singing her Irish songs. p 15
    And so the man of books and the Irish girl, that morning, found the bond of the friendship—a friendship that was to be to them, all the years of their lives, a very beautiful thing. (double page illustration) pp 16–17

July   Vol. LII No. 10
A Son of His Father by Harold Bell Wright. Pages 13–15, 45, and 46.
Two illustrations in two colors.
    "Mr. Gray, who had been chatting with Wing Foo, offered to go along and help." (black and white with yellow tint) p 13

"Do you mean that you do not care—that you do not hate and despise me? I have never known a woman like you. I have never believed that there were such women." (double page illustration in red, black and white) pp 14–15

August   Vol. LII No. 11

A Son of His Father by Harold Bell Wright. Pages 15–17, 30, 44, and 72.

Two illustrations in two colors. (red, black and white)

"He'd left his horse an' was climbin' down into the canyon." p 15

Suddenly the restful quiet of the morning was broken by Pablo . . . Gray paused in the middle of a sentence and with Morgan and Jo started for the gate. Bill dropped his paper and got to his feet. (double page illustration) pp 16–17

September   Vol. LII No. 12

A Son of His Father by Harold Bell Wright. Pages 19–21, 60, and 68.

Two illustrations in two colors.

"All right," he said harshly. "You understand that you are a prisoner here now, don't you?" (brown, black and white) p 19

"It ees in the night, too, that men with the Pack mules go from Black Canyon across the line into Mexico. All the time it ees in the night." (double page illustration in green, black and white) pp 20–21

October   Vol. LIII No. 1

A Son of His Father by Harold Bell Wright. Pages 19–21, 107, and 108.

Two illustrations in two colors.

In a hospital room Nora found her brother with Big Boy Morgan watching beside his bed. (black and white with red tint) p 19

Pablo swung the girl behind him. "Who ees there?" he called sharply and repeated the challenge in Spanish. A familiar voice answered from behind the corner of the wall. "Don't shoot, Pablo; it is all right." (double page illustration in blue, black and white) pp 20–21

1926

January   Vol. LIII No. 4

"Slim" by James Boyd. Pages 9–11 and 75.

Two illustrations. One in black and white and one in two colors.

"Say Pardner," He Ventured To A Hairy Old Timer On A Pea-Green Landau, "What's The Chance For A Job Around Here?" (black and white) p 9

Far Off a Voice Said, "All Right, Slim, Hop Him!" Then There Were Dim Cries Of "Sock It To Him!" . . . Barred By Long Shadows Of The Stockade A Little Puff Of Dust Drifted Up. Through It He Saw A Row Of White Faces Like Beads On A String. A Cloud Of Dust Poured Over Him, He Lashed Down Wildly. After That There Was Nothing But Spinning Haze In Which He And His Saddle Rocked And Spun. And All Along It Just Seemed Like A Play. There Was No Sense To It. He Knew He'd Come Off. (black and white with yellow tint) pp 10–11

December   Vol. LIV No. 3

"Queen Esther" by W. L. George. Pages 21 and 85.

One illustration in colors. (red, brown, black and white)

Esther's White Arm Loaded With Jewels, Pointed Towards Haman. p 21

1928

August   Vol. LV No. 11

"You Shall Have Homes" by Carl Sandburg. Page 7.

One illustration (decoration) in colors. (blue, brown, black and white)

Description: Girl standing among reeds with wild geese, ducks, and herons flying overhead.

October   Vol. LVI No. 1

"Song of the Road's End" by H. Sewall Bailey. Page 7.

Two illustrations. One (decoration) in colors and one in pen and ink.

Description: Gypsies sitting around campfire under a starlit sky. A violinist plays in the center of the group. (decoration in red, blue, brown, black and white)

Description: A Gypsy wagon following the winding road. (pen and ink drawing with dark blue tint)

1929

February   Vol. LVI No. 5

The Romantic Prince For king, for country, for liege lady! a new novel of faith and valor by Rafael Sabatini. Pages 13–15, 76, 78, 80, 82, 85, 86, 88, and 90.

Five illustrations. Three in colors and two in pen and ink.

The young Zealander was not the man to receive kicks with inpunity. (red, brown, black and white) p 13

Somewhere at some dim time he and this girl, as yet unnamed to him, had been indissolubly united. (red, blue, brown, black and white) p 14

Description: Grazing cattle (pen-and-ink drawing with red tint) p 14

Description: A Flemish street scene (pen-and-ink drawing with red tint) p 15

The gentleman, young and fair and good to look upon, took in the situation at a glance. (red, blue, brown, black and white) p 15

March   Vol. LVI No. 6

The Romantic Prince As colorful as a richly woven tapestry against a fifteenth century background by Rafael Sabatini. Pages 17–19, 84, 86, 88, 90, 94, 97, and 138. Photograph of N. C. Wyeth plus a paragraph mentioning his work for *The Romantic Prince*. p 4

Two illustrations in colors (red, blue, brown, black and white)

Count Anthony placed his gloved hand on hers. "Do you recall, Johanna, our first meeting?" p 17

"God's light! I'll question him: ay, and wring an answer from him if I have to put a length of whipcord round his temples! Now go your way," the governor informed him. (double page illustration in red, blue, brown, black and white) pp 18–19

April   Vol. LVI No. 7

The Romantic Prince Honor and treason meet in the lists of Rafael Sabatini. Pages 22, 23 and 106–11.

One illustration in colors (red, brown, black and white)

The Governor, infuriated by the attack upon him, thundered: "Stand where you are, or, on my oath, my men shall cut you down!" (double page illustration) pp 22–23

May   Vol. LVI No. 8

The Romantic Prince High romance in the days of chivalry by Rafael Sabatini. Pages 27, 28, and 123–30.

Two illustrations in colors.

"At daybreak, mistress, in execution of the sentence passed upon him yesterday in the Governor's court." (red, blue, brown, black and white) p 27

For answer Rhymsault picked up a flagon from the table and hurled it at the Fool. (red, green, brown, black and white) p 28

June   Vol. LVI No. 9

The Romantic Prince by Rafael Sabatini. Pages 26, 27, 111, 112, and 115–18.

Two illustrations in colors.

Description: Man embracing woman. (headpiece illustration in red, green, brown, black and white) p 26

"Are you mad? With what am I charged?" (red, blue, brown, black and white) p 27

1931

July   Vol. LVIII No. 10

The Lindberghs. The family's own story by Lynn and Dora B. Haine. Pages 7–9, 103, 107, and 110. Photograph on page 2 of N. C. Wyeth, plus a brief biographical sketch by the editors.

Three illustrations in colors.

Description: Seagulls. (titlepiece decoration) p 7

Like that flight to Paris, theirs was a Viking advenure, too. (red, green, brown, black and white) p 7

At a bend in the Sauk River, the Lindbergh saga in America began. (double page illustration in red, blue, brown, black and white) pp 8–9

August   Vol. LVIII No. 11

The Lindberghs. The family's own story by Lynn and Dora B. Haine. Pages 14–17, 35, and 36.

Two illustrations in colors.

From his father Charles Augustus learned one golden truth—no degree of adversity can conquer the unconquerable. (blue, brown, black and white) p 14

The boyhood of C. A. Lindbergh yields many clues to his personality as a man. (red, brown, green, black and white) p 15

September   Vol. LVIII No. 12

The Lindberghs. The family's own story by Lynn and Dora B. Haine. Pages 20–22, 54–56, and 62.

One illustration in colors (red, green, brown, black and white)

"That trip with Charles was one of the happiest times in my whole life. I got acquainted with my boy in those two weeks, as I never knew him before. I found the man in him." (double page illustration) pp 20–21

October   Vol. LIX No. 1

The Lindberghs. The family's own story by Lynn and Dora B. Haine. Pages 24, 25, 104, and 110.

One illustration in colors (green, brown, black and white)

"I have my own way of doing things . . . Opposition is good to try one's metal on." p 25

McClure's Magazine

1906

March   Vol. XXVI No. 5
Arizona Nights by Stewart Edward White. "The Cattleman's Yarn: The Remittance Man Story." Pages 515–22.

Two illustrations. One (frontispiece) in color and one in black and white.
    "An almighty exciting race."[1] (frontispiece)
    We joined the second expedition. p (521)

April   Vol. XXVI No. 6
Arizona Nights by Stewart Edward White. "The Ranch Foreman's Yarn: The Cattle Rustler Story." Pages 646–54.

Three illustrations in black and white.
    "At the same time Hahn pulled his gun and shot him through the middle." p 646
    Description: Riders on a mountain trail. (headpiece illustration) p 647
    "I saw his horse jump back dodgin' a rattlesnake or somethin'." p 648

May   Vol. XXVII No. 1
Arizona Nights by Stewart Edward White. "Cyclone Bill's Yarn: The Mining Camp Story." Pages 63–69.

Two illustrations in black and white.
    "Look here!" he yells. "Listen to what I'm tellin ye!" p 64
    "They got to fightin' on which should get the first hoss: so I bent my gun on them and made them draw lots." p 68

Note: This series of illustrations also appears in color in the book *Arizona Nights* by Stewart Edward White, published by The McClure Company, N. Y., October 1907.
[1] The illustration also appears in black and white in the book *The Illustrator in America* (Wyeth chapter) by Walt Reed, published by Reinhold Publishing Corp., N. Y., 1966.

August   Vol. XXVII No. 4
"The Story of Montana" by C. P. Connolly. Pages 347–61.

Frontispiece illustration in color.
    "Hands up"

Note: The illustration also appears in color in the book *The West and Walter Bimson* published by the University of Arizona Museum of Art, Tucson, 1971. It is titled "Holdup in the Canyon."

September   Vol. XXVII No. 5
Cover illustration in black and white with tint. The Last Stand "Montana"[1]

"The Story of Montana" by C. P. Connolly. Pages 451–65. Frontispiece illustration in black and white. The Prospector

[1] The illustration appears as the frontispiece in color in the book *McClure's The Market Place of the World*, published by The McClure Company, N.Y., 1906. In addition, it appears in color on the cover of *American Heritage*, October 1965. It also appears as a cover in color for *The Arizonian*, November 13, 1969.

November   Vol. XXVIII No. 1
Cover illustration in color. Description: Indian chief on pony with hand raised in sign of friendship.

1908

May   Vol. XXXI No. 1
"The Misadventures of Cassidy" by Edward S. Moffat. Pages 3–15.

Four illustrations in color.
    "For four long summer months of dust and heat Cassidy had been a freighter."[1] (frontispiece)
    "I've sold them wheelers!" p (4)
    "Nearest to the rough pine box stood the widow, with lowered eyes." p (5)
    "I hereby pronounce yuh man and wife!" p (7)

[1] The illustration also appears in color in the book *The Brandywine Tradition* by Henry C. Pitz, published by Houghton Mifflin Company, Boston, 1969. In addition, it appeared in *American Heritage*, October 1965, for the article "N. C. Wyeth" by Henry C. Pitz.

1912

June   Vol. XL No. 2
"The Shooting at Raeder" by Edith Ronald Mirrielees. Pages 187–94.

Two illustrations in black and white.
    "Who's afraid of his guns?" shouted McFarlane. "He daren't shoot in a square fight!" p 190
    The Swede's innocent all right. And he's got two guns. p 191

1916

February   Vol. XLVI No. 4
"The Great Understanding" by Mary Heaton Vorse. Pages 19, 20, 76, and 77.

One illustration in black and white.
    Artist's description: "In this illustration I have endeavored to convey the mood of this powerful story–to interpret that potential, ominous spirit. To me the tale appeals as a fragment of Tolstoy or Turgeneff." N.C.W. p 19

June   Vol. XLVII No. 2
"Alfalfa" by Lyman Bryson. Pages 31 and 50.

One illustration in black and white.
    The girl watched her lover a little anxiously because he was moody. The visitor ate with his eyes down. p 31

July   Vol. XLVII No. 3
"The Desert Rat" Another in a Series of Exciting Mexican Border Stories by B. M. Bower and Buck Connor. Pages 40–42, 62, and 63.

One illustration in black and white.
    "Take a drink—maybe you'll feel better," he urged huskily, and unscrewed the canteen top. "We all——." p 40

The Mentor

1923

December   Volume 11 Number 11
"Six Immortals and How They Grew into Books" by Arthur Bartlett Maurice. Pages 1–16. Illustrated from paintings and photographs.

Two illustrations in black and white by N. C. Wyeth.
    Robin Hood leading his gallant band of outlaws through Sherwood Forest. p 2
    The outlaw and his archers meet a foe in the dappled glades of the forest. p 9

Note: The illustrations originally appeared in color in *Robin Hood* by Paul Creswick, published by David McKay Company, Phila., 1917.

1926

July   Volume 14 Number 6
"The Wooing of Priscilla." With Illustrations Reproduced from Paintings by N. C. Wyeth for Longfellow's *Courtship of Miles Standish*. Pages 41–47. There is also a brief biography of N. C. Wyeth on page 41.
Seven illustrations in sepia tint.
    Miles Standish, the Captain of Plymouth. p 41
    Miles Standish cherishes the thought of Priscilla. p 42
    John Alden bears the offer of Miles Standish to Priscilla. p 43
    The Indians issue defiance. p 44
    How Miles Standish fought the Indians. p 45
    The sailing of the Mayflower. p 46
    The wedding of John Alden and Priscilla. p 47

Note: The illustrations originally appeared in color in *The Courtship of Miles Standish* (Tercentenary Edition) by Henry Wadsworth Longfellow, published by Houghton Mifflin Company, Boston, 1920.

1927

June   Volume 15 Number 5
"Howard Pyle, Artist, Author, Founder of a School of Illustration" by John W. Vandercook. N. C. Wyeth is mentioned among the list of Pyle's pupils on page 9. "Howard Pyle as I Knew Him" by N. C. Wyeth. Pages 15–17.

Note: A large portion of this article originally appeared in *The Christian Science Monitor*, November 13, 1912.

1928

June   Volume 16 Number 5
"One Hundred Years of Jules Verne" by Richard Dean. Pages 18 and 19.

One illustration in black and white by N. C. Wyeth.
Captain Nemo—The Man of Mystery. p 19

Note: The illustration originally appeared in color in *The Mysterious Island* by Jules Verne, published by Charles Scribner's Sons, N. Y., October 1918.

The Metropolitan

1904

October   Vol. XXI No. 1
"Skiffington's Pony" by George Hibbard. Pages 106–12.
Three illustrations in black and white.
    The animal upon which Skiffington cantered forward was a sorry enough spectacle. (headpiece illustration) p (106)
    The ball rolled straight to No. 2, who was hovering on the outside. p (109)
    The ball, speeding from under the animals' feet, had rolled straight toward the goal. p (111)

1905

August   Vol. XXII No. 5
"When the Wilderness Relents" by Philip Verrill Mighels. Pages 552–62. Illustrated by N. C. Wyeth and Charles Sarka (headpiece pen and ink drawing)
Three illustrations in black and white by N. C. Wyeth.
    A Sturdy Bit of a Pioneer. p 553
    While he debated the boy was coming on. p (557)
    "They'd git you, Jack, if you did," suggested the law-man grimly. p (559)

Modern Packaging

1943

April Volume 16 Number 8
Twelfth Annual All-American Package Competition. Award for window displays to Hiram Walker Inc. Page 105.

One illustration in black and white.
Christopher Columbus p 105
  In commemoration marking the 450th anniversary of the discovery of America by Christopher Columbus. (1492–1942)

Note: This illustration appeared as a window display poster.

National Geographic Magazine

In 1928 the National Geographic Society published full color prints of the five mural paintings executed by N. C. Wyeth for the Hubbard Memorial Building (society headquarters), Washington, D.C. These prints appeared as supplement inserts in five issues during 1928 and continuing into 1929.

1928

March Vol. LIII No. 3
Special Color Supplement, "The Discoverer" by N. C. Wyeth.
Title: The Discoverer
Size: 10 x 32 inches.

May Vol. LIII No. 5
Special Color Supplement, "Commander Byrd at the North Pole" by N. C. Wyeth.
Title: Through Pathless Skies to the North Pole
Size: 9½ x 13 inches.

July Vol. LIV No. 1
Special Color Supplement, "The Caravels of Columbus" by N. C. Wyeth.
Title: Beyond Uncharted Seas Columbus Finds a New World
Size: 9½ x 13 inches.

November Vol. LIV No. 5
Special Color Supplement, "Map of Discovery—Eastern Hemisphere" by N. C. Wyeth.
Title: Map of Discovery—Eastern Hemisphere
Size: 16¾ x 18½ inches.

1929

January Vol. LV No. 1
Special Color Supplement, "Map of Discovery—Western Hemisphere" by N. C. Wyeth.
Title: Map of Discovery—Western Hemisphere
Size: 16¾ x 18½ inches.

1949

April Vol. XCV No. 4
"The British Way" Great Britain's Major Gifts to Freedom, Democratic Government, Science, and Society by Sir Evelyn Wrench. Pages 421–552. Illustrated with paintings by noted artists, plus numerous photographs.

One illustration in color by N. C. Wyeth.
  "For a Mile or Thereabouts, My Raft Went Very Well" p 481
"The Late N. C. Wyeth Represented." Pages 544 and 545. A brief biographical sketch of the artist and his background.

Note: The illustration originally appeared in color in *Robinson Crusoe* by Daniel Defoe, published by The Cosmopolitan Book Corporation, New York, 1920.

1960

March Volume 117 Number 3
"Colleague of the Golden Years: John Oliver La Gorce" by Gilbert Grosvenor. Pages 440–44. Photograph of the office of John Oliver La Gorce on page 443. In the entrance hall hangs a painting by N. C. Wyth which originally appeared as an illustration in *Collier's Weekly*, June 17, 1915, for the story "At the World's Outposts" by James Francis Dwyer.

1965

July Volume 128 Number 1
"First Lady of the National Geographic" by Gilbert Hovey Grosvenor. Pages 100–21. Needlepoint design in color on page 105. Design in needlepoint executed by Mrs. Elsie May Grosvenor for her son. The design is taken from a mural painting by N. C. Wyeth, his Map of Discovery—The Western Hemisphere in Hubbard Hall.

1966

November Volume 130 Number 5
"The Living White House" by Lonnelle Aikman. Pages 593–643. Illustrated with numerous paintings, engravings, and photographs.

One illustration in color by N. C. Wyeth.
"President's Palace." p 600

Note: The illustration was originally done for the Pennsylvania Railroad as one of a series of four posters.

1968

June Volume 133 Number 6
"Character Marks the Coast of Maine" by John Scofield. Pages 798–843. A reference to the N. C. Wyeth mural paintings done for The National Geographic Society on pages 823 and 825.

1970

June Volume 137 Number 6
"Exciting New Books for 1970–71" by Gilbert M. Grosvenor. Pages 880–84. Illustrated with paintings and photographs.

One illustration in color by N. C. Wyeth.
  Description: The McCormick Reaper. p 884

Note: The illustration originally appeared as an advertisement for the 100th Anniversary (1831–1931) of the International Harvester Company.

National Republic

1927

March Vol. XIV No. 11
Cover illustration in black and white. Benjamin Franklin's Entry Into Philadelphia.

Note: The illustration originally appeared as a frontispiece in color in the book *The Pictorial Life of Benjamin Franklin*, published by Dill & Collins Co., Philadelphia, 1923.

New Story Magazine

1912

October
"McKeon's Graft" by Luke Thrice.
Cover illustration in color. Description: Two outlaws holding up a train.

December
"On the Wings of Evening" by Wright Beach Paulhan.
Cover illustration in color. Description: Figure of man holding revolver and shielding woman, with a dead figure lying in the foreground.

1913

January
"Little Gal" by Charles Neville Buck.
Cover illustration in color. Description: Man and girl confronted by man holding rifle.

February
"The Decoy" by Frank Blighton.
Cover illustration in color. Description: Two men in tree, the figure in the foreground is firing a pistol.

June
"The Return of Tarzan" by Edgar R. Burroughs.
Cover illustration in color. Description: Man in desert garb and Arab on horseback.

July
"The Breaking Point" by Robert J. Pearsall.
Cover illustration in color. Description: Two men fighting on rocky beach.

August
"The Return of Tarzan" by Edgar Rice Burroughs.
Cover illustration in color. Description: Tarzan holding bow and arrow, climbing through tree-top jungle growth.

Note: The illustration is repeated as a dust wrapper in color for the book *The Return of Tarzan* by Edgar Rice Burroughs, published by A. L. Burt Company, Publishers, N.Y., 1915.

October
"The Burglar" by Edward Rutledge.
Cover illustration in color. Description: "The Burglar."

November
"The Million Dollar Hour" by John Fleming Wilson.
Cover illustration in color. Description: Figure of a man on ship's bridge.

1914

January
"Alan and the Holy Flower" by H. Rider Haggard.
Cover illustration in color. Description: Men carrying supplies ashore on tropical island led by bearded old man with butterfly net.

February
"The Story of Allan Quartermain" by Rider Haggard.
Cover illustration in color. Description: Figure of African warrior.

March
"Lizard's Gold" by Preston Ward.
Cover illustration in color. Description: Prospectors and thieves.

April
"The Gun Man" by Preston Ward.
Cover illustration in color. Description: Mexican vaquero on bucking horse.

Note: This illustration also appears as the cover illustration for *The Popular Magazine* of March 30, 1926.

1915

October
"Father Teasdale Again" by Arthur Preston.
Cover illustration in color. Description: Figure
of Mexican vaquero leaning against horse.

Note: This illustration also appears as the cover
illustration for *The Popular Magazine* of September 20, 1926.

The New York State Conservationist

1954

August–September   Vol. IX No. 1
Cover illustration in color. Rip Van Winkle.

Note: The illustration originally appeared in the
book *Rip Van Winkle* by Washington Irving, published by David McKay Company, Phila., 1921. It
was titled "On nearer approach he was still more
surprised at the singularity of the stranger's appearance."

Newsweek

1939

December 18
"Pa Wyeth and His Clan." Pages 40 and 42.
Photographs of the Wyeth family. Portrait of
N. C. Wyeth by daughter Henriette.
    Description: N. C. Wyeth at his easel
    posed with the painting "Island Funeral."

1957

November 4
Art Section. Page 111.
One illustration in black and white.
    Description: The Sea Serpent. p 111

Note: The illustration originally appeared in color
in *Trending into Maine* by Kenneth Roberts, published by Little Brown and Company, Boston, June
1938.

1971

June 28   Vol. LXXVII No. 26
The Brandywine School Art Section. Page 93.
A Review of the opening of the Brandywine
River Museum by Douglas Davis. Numerous
references to N. C. Wyeth. Illustrated with
paintings and a photograph of the museum.
One illustration in black and white by N. C.
Wyeth.
Blind Pew. p 93

Note: The illustration originally appeared in color
in *Treasure Island* by Robert Louis Stevenson,
published by Charles Scribner's Sons, N.Y., September 1911.

The Northwestern Miller

1923

Anniversary Number.
One illustration in color. Painting by N. C.
Wyeth, Needham, Massachusetts.
The Miller's Wooing.

1927

May 18
Cover illustration in color. The Miller's Wooing.

The Outing Magazine

1906

May   Vol. XLVIII No. 2
Bar 20 Range Yarns by Clarence Edward Mulford. Part III "Trials of a Peaceful Puncher."
Pages 200–5.

One illustration in color.
    "Sitting up cross-legged, with each hand
    holding a gun from which came thin wisps
    of smoke." fp 200

Note: The illustration also appears in the book
Bar 20 by Clarence E. Mulford, published by The
Outing Publishing Company, N. Y., 1907.

August   Vol. XLVIII No. 5
The Buccaneers "When Pierre Le Grand Set
This Pace" by John R. Spears. Pages 523–27.

One illustration in color.
    The cattle killers were the original cowboys of America. fp 524

September   Vol. XLVIII No. 6
The Buccaneers "Drake and the 'Golden Hind'"
by John R. Spears. Pages 742–46.

Frontispiece illustration in black and white.
"When Drake saw for the first time the waters
of the South Sea."

Advertisement in the Outing Magazine Advertiser section for *Outing Magazine,* the October
issue. One reduced illustration in black and
white by N. C. Wyeth for *The Buccaneers.*

October   Vol. XLIX No. 1
The Buccaneers "Half-Forgotten Captains Of
The Buccaneer Crews" by John R. Spears. Pages
57–64.

Frontispiece illustration in color. ". . . with
stones . . . he shaped them into rude knives."

November   Vol. XLIX No. 2
"Love in the Wilderness" by Lawrence Mott.
Pages 153–8.

Frontispiece illustration in black and white. "A
rounded shape on a little hillside caught his
eyes."

Advertisement in The Outing Advertiser section
for *Outing Magazine,* the December issue. One
reduced illustration in black and white by N.
C. Wyeth for "Cassidy at Cactus." Also mentioned is Wyeth's painting titled Christmas
Mail for the Camp to appear in the December
issue.

December   Vol. XLIX, No. 3
Frontispiece illustration in color. Christmas Mail
for the Ranch.
Bar 20 Range Yarns by Clarence Edward Mulford. Part VII "Cassidy at Cactus." Pages 329–34.

One illustration in two colors (green, black and
white).
    "Mr. Cassidy . . . saw a crimson rider
    sweep down upon him . . . heralded by a
    blazing 41."[1] p (337)

The article "An interview with Caspar Whitney" includes a photograph of N. C. Wyeth.
Advertisement in the Outing Magazine Advertiser section for *Outing Magazine,* the January
issue. One reduced illustration in black and
white by N. C. Wyeth for "How They Opened
the Snow Road."

[1] Also appears in the book *Bar 20* by Clarence E.
Mulford, published by The Outing Publishing
Company, N.Y., 1907.

1907

January   Vol. XLIX No. 4
Photograph of N. C. Wyeth (back of frontispiece illustration)

"How They Opened the Snow Road" by W. M.
Raine and W. H. Eader. Pages 447–52.

Four illustrations in color (bound between
pages 448–49).
    "The eight miners followed the treacherous
    trail cautiously, the wind whipping the red
    and blue into their faces." fp 448
    "From an upper snow platform to which
    the hard blocks were thrown, a second
    man heaved them over the bank."
    "Long Henry drove cautiously across the
    scene of yesterday's accident and up the
    approach to the rocky point."
    "He rose to his feet and flung the six
    pounds of powerful explosive far out into
    the great snow comb."

Advertisement in The Outing Magazine Advertiser section for *Outing Magazine,* the February
issue. One reduced illustration in black and
white by N. C. Wyeth for "The Best Man Out
of Labrador."

February   Vol. XLIX No. 5
"The Best Man Out of Labrador" by Lawrence
Mott. Pages 585–93.

Frontispiece illustration in black and white.
"Keep him off fur God's sake! he screamed."

May   Vol. L No. 2
Advertisement in The Outing Magazine Advertiser section for *Outing Magazine,* the June issue. One illustration in black and white by N.
C. Wyeth of the June cover painting.

June   Vol. L No. 3
"The Indian in His Solitude"
A series of five paintings in color (including
the cover) by N. C. Wyeth. Headpiece and
tailpiece designs (pen-and-inks initialed GMB).

Cover illustration in color. Description: The
Hunter.[1]
Four illustrations in color (three bound between
pages 301–5).
    The Magic Pool[2] (frontispiece)
    The Spearman
    In the Crystal Depths[3]
    The Silent Burial[4]

Note: The five paintings that make up The Indian
in His Solitude were published as a portfolio of
prints by The Outing Publishing Company, N. Y.,
1907.
[1] In addition, it appears as a cover in color for *All
Outdoors,* Autumn 1913. Also appears as a cover
in color for *American History Illustrated,* May 1966.
[2] Also appears as a calendar in color. (publisher
unknown)
[3] Also appears in black and white in the book
The Illustrator in America (Wyeth chapter) by
Walt Reed, published by Reinhold Publishing
Corp. N. Y., 1966.
[4] Also appears as a cover in color for *American
History Illustrated,* May 1966. In addition, it appears in color in the book, *O! Say Can You See*
compiled by Frederic Ray, published by National
Historical Society (Stackpole).

July   Vol. L No. 4
The Buccaneers "Mansvelt the Bluffer" by John
R. Spears. Pages 481–84.

One illustration in black and white.
    "To the last he would pose and swagger."
    p (480)

September   Vol. L No. 6
"Mountaineering in North America." Deeds and
opportunities on the world's best continent for
climbing by Robert Dunn. Pages 714–22.

One illustration in black and white.
    On the trail. p (715)

Note: The illustration also appears in the book *Camp and Trail* by Stewart Edward White, published by The Outing Publishing Company, N. Y., 1907.

Pennsylvania Magazine of History and Biography

1947

January   Vol. LXXI No. 1
"Remarks on Illustration and Pennsylvania's Contributors to Its Golden Age" by Thornton Oakley. Pages 3–18. References to N. C. Wyeth.

Persimmon Hill (National Cowboy Hall of Fame)

1971

A Quarterly of the West   Vol. II No. 1
Cover illustration in color. "A Word of Precaution to the Passengers."

Note: The illustration originally appeared in black and white in *Scribner's Magazine*, November 1906, for the story "The Admirable Outlaw" by M'Cready Sykes.

The Philadelphia Forum

1933

February   Volume 12 Number 6
Cover illustration in black and white. "In a Dream I Meet General Washington"

"The Academy Exhibition" by Harvey M. Watts. Pages 8, 9, 22, and 24. Critique and comments on "In a Dream I Meet General Washington" by N. C. Wyeth.

Note: The illustration originally appeared in *The Art Digest*, December 1, 1932, for the article "1932 Corcoran Biennial (review)."

1946

May
"N. C. Wyeth—an Appreciation" by Henry Pleasants, Jr., M.D. Pages 7 and 8.

Pictorial Review

1919

March
The Fifth of *Pictorial Review*'s Series of Great War Paintings.

One illustration in color. "Kamerad!"
    The fierce fighting at Cantigny, Bois Belleau, and Chateau-Thierry was enough to show the Germans the kind of soldiers the Americans were, and that their cause was hopeless. After the lesson of those glorious days, whenever the Americans met the enemy, German hands flew up and German lips cried "Kamerad!" because they realized the Americans were not playing at war, but were dead earnest. It was the beginning of the end. p 20

April
The Ninth of *Pictorial Review*'s Series of War Paintings.

One illustration in color. The Americans at Chateau-Thierry
    "Shatoo Theery? Was it some fight? I'll say so!" After the Botches hammered us for seven hours with high explosives we

was pretty much nuts, an' we went tearin' into that old burg like mad. Some hadn't any shirts on, or tin hats, leggins, nor nothin'—just the bayonet. p 12

The Pilgrim Elementary Teacher

1926

July   Vol. X No. 6
One illustration in sepia tint (fold out).
Boy Christ, Carpenter

Note: This illustration originally appeared in color in the *Woman's Home Companion*, December 1924, for the serial *The Man Nobody Knows* by Bruce Barton.

The Popular Magazine

1909

November 15   Vol. XIV No. 3
Month-End Edition
Cover illustration in color. Description: Bear hunter in canoe returning from a successful hunt. Mountain peaks dominate the background.

Note: The illustration also appears in color in the book *The Fiction Factory* by Quentin Reynolds, published by Random House, New York, 1955.

1910

February 1   Vol. XV No. 2
First February Number
Cover illustration in color. Caribou Hunters

May 15   Vol. XVI No. 3
Month-End Edition
Cover illustration in color. "The Return from the Plow"
A Chat With You (Editor's note). Reference to N. C. Wyeth and the cover illustration.

September 1   Vol. XVII No. 4
First September Number
Cover illustration in color. Description: Polo players.

December 15   Vol. XVIII No. 4
First December Number
Cover illustration in color. Description: Three hunters with hounds.

1911

February 15   Vol. XIX No. 3
Month-End Edition
Cover illustration in color. Description: Man skiing down slope with snow-covered peaks in background.

March 15   Vol. XIX No. 5
Month-End Edition
Cover illustration in color. "The Poacher"

June 1   Vol. XX No. 4
First June Number
Cover illustration in color. "The Call of The Spring." Description: Old farmer and grandson going fishing.

August 1   Vol. XXI No. 2
First August Number
Cover illustration in color. Description: Pennsylvania farmer gathering in the hay.

November 1   Vol. XXII No. 2
First November Number
Cover illustration in color. Description: Woodcutter with oxteam.

1912

March 15   Vol. XXIII No. 5
Month-End Edition
Cover illustration in color. Description: The frontiersman.

June 1   Vol. XXIV No. 4
First June Number
Cover illustration in color. Description: Salmon fisherman.

August 1   Vol. XXV No. 2
First August Number
Cover illustration in color. Description: Farmer and daughter on a hay wagon.

November 1   Vol. XXVI No. 2
First November Number
Cover illustration in color. Description: Cowboy on horseback confronted by a grizzly bear on narrow mountain trail.

Note: The illustration also appears as a cover in color for *Western Story Magazine*, October 1948.

December 15   Vol. XXVI No. 5
Month-End Edition
Cover illustration in color. Description: Prospector with burro on mountaintop.

1913

January 1   Vol. XXVI No. 6
First January Number
Cover illustration in color. Description: A Hindu mystic.

Note: This illustration is signed Pearson Barnes, a pseudonym Wyeth used on occasion.

August 1   Vol. XXIX No. 2
First August Number
Cover illustration in color. Description: Two farm boys berry picking.

November 1   Vol. XXX No. 2
First November Number
Cover illustration in color. Description: Farmer with pumpkin.

1914

April 15   Vol. XXXII No. 1
Month-End Edition
Cover illustration in color. Description: Plowboy drinking from brook.

September 1   Vol. XXXIII No. 4
First September Number
Cover illustration in color. Description: Young farmer and girl standing near wagon.

1915

February 7   Vol. XXXV No. 4
Cover illustration in color. Description: Two hunters.

April 7   Vol. XXXVI No. 2
Cover illustration in color. Description: Man in sailboat spots figure on beach.

August 7   Vol. XXXVIII No. 4
Cover illustration in color. Description: Two farm boys in flatboat among lilies. Pennsylvania farm country.

December 20   Vol. XXXIX No. 1
Cover illustration in color. Description: Children surprising dad in the act of playing Santa.

Note: The illustration also appears as the frontispiece in *American Heritage,* December 1964.

1916

February 20   Vol. XXXIX No. 5
Cover illustration in color. Description: Two cowpunchers sitting on corral fence watching the antics of a cowboy on a bucking horse.

March 7   Vol. XXXIX No. 6
Cover illustration in color. Description: A repeat of the February 20 cover.

1922

December 20   Vol. LXVI No. 5
Cover illustration in color. Description: Bringing home the Christmas tree. Figure of man with freshly cut evergreen tree over shoulder.

1923

February 20   Vol. LXVII No. 4
Cover illustration in color. Description: Two seventeenth century sailing ships in combat.

March 20   Vol. LXVII No. 5
Cover illustration in color. Description: Children sledding.

Note: The illustration appears in black and white in the article "The Season Surveyed" by Hilton Dramer, published in *Art in America,* June 1964. In addition, it appears as a cover in color for *American Heritage,* December 1971.

June 7   Vol. LXVIII No. 4
Cover illustration in color. Description: Indian spear fisherman.

Note: The illustration appears in color in the book *The West and Walter Bimson* published by the University of Arizona Museum of Art, Tucson, 1971, and is repeated on the dust wrapper.

1926

March 30   Vol. LXXIX No. 5
Cover illustration in color. Description: Mexican vaquero on bucking horse.

Note: The illustration originally appeared as a cover in color for *New Story Magazine,* April 1914.

September 20   Vol. LXXXI No. 5
Cover illustration in color. Description: Mexican vaquero and horse.

Note: The illustration originally appeared as a cover in color for *New Story Magazine,* October 1915.

The Progressive Farmer

1936

November   Volume 51 Number 11
Cover illustration in color. Autumn in the Hill Country

Note: The illustration is repeated as a cover in color for *The Progressive Farmer,* October 1946.

1937

March   Volume 52 Number 3
Cover illustration in color. Bringing in the Sheep

November   Volume 52 Number 11
Cover illustration in color. Bringing in the Cows[1]

December   Volume 52 Number 12
Cover illustration in color. Christmas in the Old South[1]

[1] Contrary to the cover credits, the illustrations were in fact painted by Andrew Wyeth.

1938

August   Volume 53 Number 8
Cover illustration in color. Lunch for Daddy

1942

March   Volume 57 Number 3
Cover illustration in color. The Farmer's Call to the Colors.

1943

November   Volume 58 Number 11
Cover illustration in color. "Soldiers of the Home Front"

1945

January   Volume 60 Number 1
Cover illustration in color. Humanity Looks for a New World—Sunrise in 1945

October   Volume 60 Number 10
Cover illustration in color. Corn Harvest in the Hill Country

1946

October   Volume 61 Number 10
Cover illustration in color. Autumn in the Hill Country

Note: The illustration originally appeared as a cover in color for *The Progressive Farmer,* November 1936.

The Red Barrel (The Coca-Cola Company)

1936

January   Vol. XV No. 1
Cover illustration in color. Description: Old clamdigger and girl drinking Cokes near sea.

Inside front cover is a reduced illustration of the cover and a photograph of Wyeth, plus a biographical sketch of the artist.

1939

December 15   Vol. XIX No. 12
"Commercial Art as a Careeer" by Horace W. Hardy. Pages 22–28. Illustrated with the works of N. C. Wyeth, Donald Teague, Norman Rockwell, Bradshaw Crandell, etc. In the article are references to N. C. Wyeth and his work in the illustration field.

One illustration in black and white by N. C. Wyeth.
   Description: Bowmen of the White Company.

Note: The illustration originally appeared as the endpaper illustration in *The White Company* by Arthur Conan Doyle, published by Cosmopolitan Book Corporation, New York, 1922.

Redbook Magazine

1908

September   Vol. XI No. 5
"Who Calls?" by Sir Gilbert Parker. Pages 641–53.

Three illustrations in black and white.
   —A careless, strong willful, white man who had lived the Indian life for many years. (frontispiece in brown tint)
   The Indian in her had found its way to Portage la Drome. p 645
   "Pauline," he said feebly, and fainted in her arms.[1] p 651

[1] The illustration appears in the book *Northern Lights* by Gilbert Parker, published by Harper & Brothers, N. Y., 1909.

1909

January   Vol. XII No. 3
"The Recoil" by William Macleod Raine. Pages 465–73.

Three illustrations. One in brown tint and two in black and white.
   No wild rose of the mountain could have been purer, fresher, than she (frontispiece in brown tint)
   "I came to see you about that ditch of yours, Chisholm" p 467
   "I aint through with you yet," the forester called back p 471

October   Vol. XIII No. 6
"Svenson" by Michael Williams and Kenneth MacNichol. Pages 913–28.

Three illustrations in two colors (blue, black and white).
   Under Svenson's charge the spell of the desert took hold. p 917
   He rode away, following a dim trail among the sage. p 921
   On the cross she hung a tiny sack of eagle's skin. p 925

1910

April   Vol. XIV No. 6
"*The Sheriff of Granite*" by William Macleod Raine. Pages 1036–45.

Three illustrations. One (frontispiece) in brown tint and two in black and white.
   There was a flash of circling steel, a report, and the little Sheriff crumpled like a jackrabbit. (frontispiece)
   "I aint done right by you, honey; I sure aint." p 1039
   Each frozen minute brought them both nearer to death in the blizzard. p 1043

1929

November   Vol. LIV No. 1
"Miles Standish"—An important but forgotten episode of our early history. Page 22.

One illustration in black and white.
   Description: The fight between Miles Standish and Pecksuot. p 22

1930

January   Vol. LIV No. 3
"The Answer of the Skies." Page 17.

One illustration in color.
   Up from Earth's Centre through the Seventh Gate I rose, and on the Throne of Saturn sat, And many a Knot unravell'd by the Road; But not the Master-Knot of Human Fate. p 17

Note: The illustration also appears as a cover in color for *D'A'C News,* April 1931.

July   Vol. LV No. 3
"Belleau Wood, June 1918"—A high moment in America's history. Pages 30 and 31.

One illustration in color.

It was after this attack that the High Command published to the German army: "The moral effect of our own gunfire cannot seriously impede the advance of the American Infantry" (double page illustration). pp 30–31

1931

July Vol. LVII No. 3
"Lion Heart" When chivalry set the stage for modern civilization by Konrad Bercovici. Pages 34–37, 94, 96, and 98.

Two illustrations in colors.

"Since when is a heathen wench's word better than that of twenty Christians?" asked one of the monks. "It is I who will decide whether she alone speaketh the truth, or all of you," Richard said sternly. (double page illustration in orange, brown, black and white) pp 34–35
The enemy had re-formed the line and bounced forward as if thrown by a spring. Richard had thrown the helmet over the Saracens' heads. "Look at me!" (double page illustration in red, brown, black and white) pp 36–37

August Vol. LVII No. 4
"The Captive Queen" And the conqueror in his hour of triumph by Conrad Bercovici. Pages 44–48, 120, and 121.

Two illustrations. One in colors and one in black and white.

At sundown Alexander was still sitting on his improvised throne looking fixedly at the splotch of blood and the pieces of crimson-spotted linen. (orange, brown, black and white) p 45
Now he knew–the gods had reserved her for him! He leaped at her like a lion, shouting: "I too have found what I wanted–my share of the wealth of Asia!" (double page illustration in black and white) pp 46–47

The Red Cross Magazine

1918

June Vol. XIII No. 6
"The New Crusaders Enter Jerusalem" General Allenby and his soldiers welcomed with joy. Pages 16–20.

Four illustrations in color.

The Twentieth Century and the First–The Dramatic Contrast of an English Tank in the Streets of Jerusalem. p (17)
What the Crusaders Dreamed of Has Now Come True–The English Troops Descending the Mount of Olives. p (18)
The Sign in the Heavens Which the Judean Shepherds Watching Their Flocks See This Year. p (19)
The Golden Gate in the Wall of Jerusalem With a Jewish Cemetery in the Foreground. p (20)

July Vol. XIII No. 7
Cover illustration in color. Description: American soldier supporting wounded French comrade.

1919

January Vol. XIV No. 1
"Chasing a Victorious Army" How the American Red Cross threw in the high-speed gear to keep up with our troops at Chateau-Thierry. Pages 5–10.

One illustration in sepia tint.

"The advance was rapid, amazingly so . . . A national vigor flowered afresh at Chateau-Thierry . . . They outdistanced their artillery and supply trains . . . in fact, they outstripped everything, including their commanders' calculations." p (6)

March Vol. XIV No. 3
Cover illustration in color. Description: The victorious allies. Represented are the soldiers of Belgium, The United States, France, Great Britain, and Italy.

1920

February Vol. XV No. 2
"Memgumban Gets the Idea" by Walter B. Pitkin. Pages 42–47 and 70–72.

Two illustrations in black and white.

"Ahi! If he hurts so much as the little finger of my captain," Memgumban screamed, "I shall tie you to an ant hill!" And he leaped at the Chinaman with his kris. p 42
Memgumban, back in the steamy hills, was unhappy. The hills were sadly unimproved real estate. Trees full of pythons, jungles swarming with nasty little hill dwarfs who blew poisoned arrows at you as a pastime. (double page illustration) pp 46–47

St. Nicholas

1927

November
"The Watch Tower" A Review of Current Events by Edward N. Teall. Page 48.

One illustration in black and white.

Poster for Children's Book Week, November 13 to 19.

Description: Seventeenth century adventurer on deck of ship, with heavy seas and galleon in background.

The Saturday Evening Post

1903

February 21 Volume 175 Number 34
Cover illustration in two colors (red, black and white). Description: Cowboy on bucking bronco.

Note: This was N. C. Wyeth's first magazine cover, executed at the age of twenty-one. The original study painting is in the permanent collection of the Wilmington Society of the Fine Arts, Wilmington, Delaware.

1904

October 1 Volume 177 Number 14
"Science at Heart's Desire" The Story of a Cowpuncher, an Osteopath and a Cross-Eyed Horse by Emerson Hough. Pages 6, 7, and 22.

Four illustrations in black and white.

"And Just Whangs Old Pinto Over the Head With It."[1] (headpiece drawing) p 6
"And He'd Stop And Disentangle Hisself From All Kinds Of Ridin" (headpiece drawing). p 6
"Doc, He Walks Up To Old Pinto And Has A Look At Him, Frontways, Sideways And All Around." p 7
"He Falls To Buckin' Sincere And Conscientious Up There Among The Benches." p 7

[1] Also appears in the book *Heart's Desire* by Emerson Hough, published by The Macmillan Company, N. Y., October 1905.

1905

February 18 Volume 177 Number 34
"Five Dog Limit at 65°N." The Story of a North Pole Freeze Out by Hugh Pendexter. Pages 10, 11, and 20.

Three illustrations in black and white.

"And We Were In Our Own Sight As Grasshoppers" (headpiece illustration). p 10
"And They Were Abominably Given To Song." p 10
"The Interpreter Cheering Us On The Way With A Dirge." p 11

March 4 Volume 177 Number 36
"The Reform at Red Ant" How Trading-Stamps Proved a Power for Good in the Yukon Country by Hugh Pendexter. Pages 4 and 5.

Two illustrations in black and white.

"He Even Asked If It Would Be All Right To Retain His Pipe And Tobacco" (headpiece illustration). p 4
"Jest Tryin' A Little Innercent Game." p 5

March 25 Volume 177 Number 39
"The Passing of a Graft" and What the Trolley Had to Do with it by Karl Edwin Harriman. Pages 2 and 3.

Two illustrations in black and white.

The Carnival Barker (headpiece illustration). p 2
"Me And My Little Old Torch And My Spiel." p 3

April 8 Volume 177 Number 41
"Why the Weekly Planet Died" The Story of the Women and the Pies that Killed It by Alfred Henry Lewis. Pages 9–11.

Four illustrations in black and white.

Several Gentlemen Joined In This Sprightly Pastime (headpiece illustration). p 9
The Weekly Planet Was In A State Of Siege. p 10
What Could One Boy Do Against Two Hundred Pies. p 10
"Ride Hard!" Shouted Mr. Wright, "To Be Captured Is Death By Torture!" p 11

May 20 Volume 177 Number 47
Cover illustration in two colors (orange, black and white). Description: A Chinese pirate with pistols.

"Mr. Scraggs Intervenes" by Henry Wallace Phillips. Pages 6, 7, and 29.
Three illustrations in black and white.

He Landed On Top Of A Quakin' Asp (headpiece illustration). p 6
"There Ain't A Person In These United States That Kin Slide A Flatiron Over Dry Goods The Way My Pete Kin" (drawing). p 6
"So We Rode In, Right Cheerful."[1] p 7

[1] Also appears in the book *Mr. Scraggs* By Henry Wallace Phillips, published by The Grafton Press, N. Y., January 1906.

June 3 Volume 177 Number 49
"Taken at the Flood" The Heap Big Potlatch of Major Dalkeith, Remittance Man by Vincent Harper. Pages 6, 7 and 24.
Two illustrations in black and white.

Then The Tide Ebbed, And One Night The Major Decamped (headpiece illustration). p 6
"An Exhibition, Sir, Of Self-Effacement Which Shamed Our Puny Civilized Philanthropy." p 7

July 15   Volume 178 Number 3
"The Pneumogastric Nerve" A Story of Physical Pressure and Moral Reaction Afloat by Morgan Robertson. Pages 3–6, 15, and 16. Illustrated by N. C. Wyeth and Oliver Kemp.

Two illustrations in black and white by N. C. Wyeth.
> "Can Ye Talk Yet, Mr. Beresford?" p 4
> Literally Wiping The Deck With Him. p 5

August 5   Volume 178 Number 6
"A Round-up in Central Park" In Which Cupid Follows a Trans-Continental Trail by Eleanor Gates. Pages 2–4.
Three illustrations in black and white.
> Description: Woman on galloping horse (headpiece drawing). p 2
> People was a-taken Me for Bill Cody (drawing). p 3
> She Seemed About Four Miles Off from Me, and There was a Right Cold Current Blowin' in My Direction. p 4

October 14   Volume 178 Number 16
"The Wasteful West" How America's Most Wasteful Blunder Cost the West a Great Opportunity and the Country a Food-Supply by Emerson Hough. Pages 1–3 and 18.
Five illustrations in black and white.
> Description: Indian on galloping horse (headpiece illustration). p 1
> Description: American Bison (headpiece illustration). p 1
> The White Man Did Nothing but Waste. p 1
> How Many Millions One Can Only Guess. p 2
> Sometimes Two or Three Would Make Up a Partnership for the Sake of Greater Safety. p 3

November 11   Volume 178 Number 20
"An Antiente Greate Companie" by Arthur E. McFarland. Pages 1–3 and 27.
Four illustrations in black and white.
> Description: Indian breed with musket (headpiece drawing). p 1
> Description: Old man smoking pipe. p 1
> And They Did Their Trading from the Top of Battlemented Walls. p 2
> They Did Not Want "Civilized," Field-Tilling Indians. p 3

November 18   Volume 178 Number 21
"Mart Haney's Mate: The Girl and the Gambler" by Hamlin Garland. Pages 1, 2, 3, 28, and 32.
Three illustrations in black and white.
> "Roll Up a Couple of Big Melons," Said Haney Largely. "We're All Drying to Cinders Over Here" (headpiece drawing). p 1
> Mrs. Gilman Took to Keeping Boarders—the Refuge of Widows (drawing). p 2
> "I Want You, My Girl. Sure I do!" p 3

"The Nor'westers" by Arthur E. McFarland. Pages 14, 15, 33, and 34.
Two illustrations in black and white.
> Description: A Nor'wester exploring the forests of the northern Rockies (headpiece drawing). p 4
> The Nor'westers Built Canoes that Would Carry Twelve Men. p 15

December 9   Volume 178 Number 24
Cover illustration in colors (red, brown, black and white). Description: Buffalo hunters.

"On the Trail of the First Trust" Astor, the Free Traders and the Rocky Mountain Men by Arthur E. McFarland. Pages 7, 8, 9, 26, and 27.
Three illustrations in black and white.
> Description: A frontier fort (headpiece illustration). p 7
> From the Upper Lakes Astor's Mackinaw Boats Could Make Their Way into the Mississippi. p 7
> Jim Bridger was Little Used to the Phenomena of Towns and Cities.[1] p 8

[1] The illustration later appears in *The Saturday Evening Post*, November 15, 1913, for the article "Wealth on Wings" by Emerson Hough.
The illustration is very similar in content to the painting The Sheriff, which appeared in *Scribner's Magazine*, June 1912.

1906

January 20   Volume 178 Number 30
"The Imitation Bad Man" A Chronicle of Long Hair and Short Nerve by Emerson Hough. Pages 6, 7, and 20.
Four illustrations in black and white.
> Description: Billy the Kid. (headpiece pen-and-ink drawing) p 6
> Description: Bob Ollinger. (headpiece pen-and-ink drawing) p 6
> The Skilled Use of Weapons was Once Desirable in the West. p 6
> Hungry, but Stern, on the Depot Platform. p 7

February 10   Volume 178 Number 33
"The Tenderfoot" by Emerson Hough. Pages 6, 7, 25, and 26.

Three illustrations in black and white.
> Description: Cowboy on barrel shooting with tenderfoot jumping. (drawing) p 6
> "Feet a Little Tender, Eh?" (drawing) p 6
> The Tenderfoot Will Learn in Time. p 7

1907

November 30   Volume 180 Number 22
Cover illustration in colors (orange, brown, black and white). Description: Portrait of an outlaw.

December 14   Volume 180 Number 24
"The Brace-Game" by Stewart Edward White. Pages 10, 11, and 27.

Three illustrations in black and white.
> Description: John Orde, Lumberjack. (headpiece illustration) p 10
> The Doctor. p 10
> "I Say, Orde, I Want to Apologize to You."[1] p 11

Note: The illustrations also appear in the book *The Riverman* by Stewart Edward White, published by The McClure Company, 1908.
[1] The illustration appears in the book *The Claim Jumpers*, The Works of Stewart Edward White, published by Doubleday, Page & Co., Garden City, N. Y., 1916.

1908

February 1   Volume 180 Number 31
"Once at Red Man's River" A Tale of the Early Days on the Border by Gilbert Parker. Pages 18–20.

Three illustrations in black and white.
> Saw Him Set Adrift in a Canoe Without a Paddle. (headpiece illustration) p 18
> The Next Morning at Sunrise Abe Hawley and the Girl He had Waited for so Long Started on the North Trail Together.[1] p 18
> He was the One Desperate Figure of the Night. p 19

[1] The illustration also appears in the book *Northern Lights* by Gilbert Parker, published by Harper & Brothers, N. Y., September 1909.

February 15   Volume 180 Number 33
The Partners by Stewart Edward White. Pages 3–5 and 30–32.

Three illustrations in black and white.
> Description: A tent camp. (headpiece illustration) p 3
> A Very Rotund, Cautious Person of German Extraction. p 4
> I'd like to See You Get Any Three Men to Agree to Anything on This River.[1] p 5

February 22   Volume 180 Number 34
Cover illustration in two colors (red, black and white). Description: Portrait of a lumberjack.[1]

The Partners by Stewart Edward White. Pages 12–14 and 22–24.

Three illustrations in black and white.
> Description: Logging on a river.[1] (headpiece illustration) p 12
> And Looked Out Beyond the Tumbled Short Ice to the Steel-Gray Angry Waters.[1] p 13
> "And How Are Ye, Ye Ould Darlint?"[1] p 14

February 29   Volume 180 Number 35
The Partners by Stewart Edward White. Pages 13–15, 23, and 24.

Three illustrations in black and white.
> "Joe, I'm Going to Cut that Whole Forty Million We Have Left." (headpiece illustration) p 13
> "The Little Rascal Fills the Wood-Box for a Cent a Time." p 14
> Quite Oblivious to the Keen Wind.[1] p 15

March 7   Volume 180 Number 36
The Partners by Stewart Edward White. Pages 12, 13, and 27.

Two illustrations in black and white.
> Description: Rolling the felled trees into the river.[1] (headpiece illustration) p 12
> After Them Wafted the Rather Disorganized Strains of "Whoa, Emma!"[1] p 13

March 14   Volume 180 Number 37
The Partners by Stewart Edward White. Pages 12, 13, 19, and 20.

Two illustrations in black and white.
> "I Guess That'll be All." p 12
> His Eyes Burned Bright as Though from Some Internal Fire.[1] p 13

March 21   Volume 180 Number 38
The Partners by Stewart Edward White. Pages 12, 13, and 30–32.

Two illustrations in black and white.
> All Day Long He Gazed Steadily on the Shifting Shadows. (headpiece illustration) p 12
> "I'm Going to Give You About the Worst Licking You Ever Heard Tell Of."[1] p 13

[1] The illustrations for this series also appear in the book *The Riverman* by Stewart Edward White, published by The McClure Company, N.Y., 1908.

July 18   Volume 181 Number 3
Cover illustration in colors (orange, brown, black and white). Description: Indian fishing.

August 1   Volume 181 Number 5
Cover illustration in colors (orange, brown, black and white). Description: The Sheriff.

Number 9009 by James Hopper and Fred R. Bechdolt. Pages 3–5, 27, and 28.

Four illustrations in black and white.
> Description: The convict. (headpiece illustration) p 3
> Description: The guard. (headpiece illustration) p 3
> Each Carried in His Hand a Rifle, Loosely, Like a Hunter. p 4
> His Right Wrist Linked to a Garroter. p 5

August 8   Volume 181 Number 6
Number 9009 by James Hopper and Fred R. Bechdolt. Pages 8, 9, and 27–29.

Three illustrations in black and white.
> At the Little Patch of Blue Sky. (headpiece illustration) p 8
> Aimed Carefully at His Breast, Each with His Index Finger Upon His Rifle-Trigger. p 8
> He Talked with His Eyes—a Single Sharp Shifting of the Eyeballs and a Flash of Light from Them. p 29

August 15   Volume 181 Number 7
Number 9009 by James Hopper and Fred R. Bechdolt. Pages 13–15 and 25–27.

Three illustrations in black and white.
> A Long, Lean, Hard Man with a Lead-Hued Face. (headpiece illustration) p 13
> "Put Down that Gun!" p 14
> Instantly He Slid Out into the Luminous Space. p 15

August 22   Volume 181 Number 8
Number 9009 by James Hopper and Fred R. Bechdolt. Pages 12, 13, 30, and 31.

Three illustrations in black and white.
> "Ahead Rode a Keen Eyed Man." (headpiece illustration) p 12
> "Put Down that Axe!" p 12
> There was No Shout, No Cry, Not a Breath, Not a Sigh. p 13

September 26   Volume 181 Number 13
Cover illustration in two colors (red, black and white). Description: Boy on a donkey.

1909

November 20   Volume 182 Number 21
"Magazine Illustrators" Unconventional Snapshots of Well-Known Artists at Play. Page 36. Illustrated with photographs. Photograph: Allen True in Suspense, N. C. Wyeth and H. T. Dunn, the Suspenders. (The photograph shows the mock hanging of Allen True by N. C. Wyeth and H. T. Dunn.)

1910

February 12   Volume 182 Number 33
"On the Other Side of the Ridge" by James Hopper. Pages 20, 21, and 50.

Two illustrations in black and white.
> "I Take You to Witness—They're Traveling in a Circle." (headpiece illustration) p 20
> "They're Still Wandering About Here—Men, Oxen, Wagons and All." p 21

August 13   Volume 183 Number 7
The Line of Least Resistance by Eugene Manlove Rhodes. Pages 3–5 and 30–32.

Three illustrations in black and white.
> Kennedy, Riding Bareback and Sidewise. (headpiece illustration) p 3
> Hiram Yeast Was Deeply in Love With Life. p 4
> "Do You Happen to Be Looking for Me?" p 5

August 20   Volume 183 Number 8
The Line of Least Resistance by Eugene Manlove Rhodes. Pages 15–17.

Three illustrations in black and white.
> "Take That One!" (headpiece illustration) p 15
> Matters Were Going Ill With Red-Faced Kim Ki. p 16
> "I see at Last Why It is Always the Western Man and the Eastern Girl Who Fall in Love—in the Novels." p 17

August 27   Volume 183 Number 9
The Line of Least Resistance by Eugene Manlove Rhodes. Pages 16–18 and 50–52.

Three illustrations in black and white.
> Kennedy Had the Girl in the Saddle Before Him, Shielded by His Body. (headpiece illustration) p 16
> From Behind His Back Indians Bounded Down Toward Him, Eager to Capture Him Alive. p 17
> "Do You See it—Sticking Up Right in the Middle of Moongate Pass?" p 18

September 3   Volume 183 Number 10
"The Line of Least Resistance" by Eugene Manlove Rhodes. Pages 22, 23, 53, and 54.

Two illustrations in black and white.
> "They'll See the Fire at Dundee in Short Dots or Long Dashes." (headpiece illustrations) p 22
> "I Thank Him for the Knowledge That I Shall Not Tell! . . . And, Perhaps . . . I Shall Not Wholly Die . . . Perhaps." p 23

1912

November 23   Volume 185, Number 21
"The Three Godfathers" by Peter B. Kyne. Pages 8–11 and 53–58.

Four illustrations in black and white.
> He Filled Both Hands and Cut Loose at One of the Four Horseman.[1] (headpiece illustration) p 8
> The Trailing Brutes Grew Bolder. p 9
> He Leaned Heavily Against the Animal, Which Half Led, Half Dragged Him Along. p 10
> The Three Bad Men Had No Blankets. p 11

[1] The illustration also appears in *The Saturday Evening Post Treasury* by Roger Butterfield, published by Simon and Schuster, N.Y., 1954.

1913

November 15   Volume 186 Number 20
"Wealth on Wings" by Emerson Hough. Pages 8, 9, and 29–31.

One illustration in black and white.
> Description: Jim Bridger was Little Used to the Phenomena of Towns and Cities. p 9

Note: The illustration originally appeared in *The Saturday Evening Post*, December 9, 1905, for the article "On the Trail of the First Trust" by Arthur E. McFarland.

1917

March 10   Volume 189 Number 37
"The Ideal of His Dreams" by Ida M. Evans. Pages 74, 77, 80, 82, 85, and 86. Illustrated by N. C. Wyeth and W. B. King.

One illustration in black and white by N. C. Wyeth.
> Description: Woman standing on hilltop. p 85

1971

Fall
"Brandywine: A Triumph Of Spirit And Strength." Pages 68–73. Photographs of the Brandywine River Museum (rearview). Illustrated with works by N. C. Wyeth, Andrew Wyeth, and James Wyeth.

Three illustrations in color by N. C. Wyeth.
The Fence Builders. p 69
He Blew Three Deadly Notes.[1] p 70
Blind Pew.[2] p 73

[1] Originally appeared in color in *The Boy's King Arthur* by Sidney Lanier, published by Charles Scribner's Sons, N.Y., 1917.
[2] Originally appeared in color in *Treasure Island* by Robert Louis Stevenson, published by Charles Scribner's Sons, N.Y., September 1911.

Saturday Review

1962

May 5
"A Man of Few Affairs" A Centenary Appreciation of Henry David Thoreau by Lewis Leary. Pages 12 and 13.

One illustration in black and white.
> Thoreau (*second from left*) and Emerson (*wearing top hat*) with Concord townspeople. p 12

Note: The illustration originally appeared in color on the dust wrapper of the book *Men of Concord* by Henry David Thoreau (edited by Francis Allen), published by Houghton Mifflin Company, Boston, 1936.

Scribner's Magazine

1904

December   Vol. XXXVI No. 6
"Tommy" by Charles Belmont Davis. Pages 713–21.

Three illustrations in black and white.
> The old friends sat about the fireplace and told stories. p 713
> He glanced furtively at the faces of the four men about him.[1] p 717
> "And I cursed the men who grinned at me across the table."[1] p 719

[1] The illustrations also appear in black and white in the book *The Lodger Overhead and Others* by Charles Belmont Davis, published by Charles Scribner's Sons, N.Y., April 1909.

1905

November   Vol. XXXVIII No. 5
Scribner's Art Features. Pages x–xi. Editorial note: N. C. Wyeth will contribute a series of original and vigorous illustrations in color, ac-

companying an article by himself, on a typical Western cattle round-up.

One reduced illustration in black and white.
    Description: "Cutting Out"

1906

January   Vol. XXXIX No. 1
Scribner's Magazine Notes. Pages 37 and 38. Editorial note: Refers to Wyeth's trip to the West, actively working as a cowboy in the cattle country. Also his soon to be published article, "Day With The Round-Up." Photograph of N. C. Wyeth in cowboy costume. p 38

March   Vol. XXXIX No. 3
"A Day with the Round-Up" An Impression by N. C. Wyeth. Pages 285–90.

Seven illustrations. Four (including frontispiece) in color and three in black and white.
    Above the sea of round, shiny backs the thin loops swirled and shot two volumes of dust.[1] fp 257
    "Rounding Up"[1] (color). fp 285
    The lee of the grub-wagon.[1][2][3] p 285
    The wild, spectacular race for dinner (color).[4][6] fp 286
    "Bucking."[1][4] p 287
    "Cutting out"[1] (color). fp 288
    A night herder.[1][2][5] p 289

[1] The illustrations also appear in color in the book *Jinglebob* by Phillip Ashton Rollins, published by Charles Scribner's Sons, N. Y., 1930.
[2] Also appear in black and white in the book *The Cowboy* by Phillip Ashton Rollins, published by Charles Scribner's Sons, N. Y., 1922.
[3] Also appears in black and white in the book *A History of Collingsworth County*, edited by The Staff of the Wellington Leader, published by the Leader Printing Co., Wellington, Texas, 1925.
[4] The illustrations were published as prints in color by Charles Scribner's Sons, 1906.
[5] Also appears in black and white in Volume III of *History of the United States* by James Truslow Adams. published by Charles Scribner's Sons, 1933.
[6] Also appears in black and white in *True West*, December 1967, for the article "N. C. Wyeth Painter of Men . . . In Action" by Les Beitz.

"A Brother to Diogenes" by Thomas Nelson Page. Pages 290–99.

One illustration (charcoal and wash) in black and white.
    "Here I am, the richest man in all America if not in the world." p 291

Note: The illustration also appears in the book *Under the Crust* by Thomas Nelson Page, published by Charles Scribner's Sons, N. Y., 1907.

October   Vol. XL No. 4
One illustration in black and white.
The Moose Call p 480

Note: The illustration was published as a print by Charles Scribner's Sons, 1906.

November   Vol. XL No. 5
"The Admirable Outlaw" by M'Cready Sykes. Pages 627–34.

Two illustrations in black and white.
    My English friend thought it was a hold-up.[1] p 629
    Arranged the line of march so that there should be no possibility of escape. p 631

[1] The illustration was published as a print by Charles Scribner's Sons, 1906. In addition, it appears as a cover in color for *Persimmon Hill*, 1971, Vol. II, No. 1.

December   Vol. XL No. 6
"Passing" by W. L. Alden. Pages 703–12.

Three illustrations in black and white.
    He was searching the Old Testament for some strong and bitter text. p 705
    Sat all night by his bedside. p 707
    Mr. Scroggs lifted up his voice in a passionate prayer. p 711

1907

February   Vol. XLI No. 2
"The Aide-de-Camp" by Mary Raymond Shipman Andrews. Pages 209–19.

Two illustrations in color.
    "I got behind a turn and fired as a man came on alone." fp 212
    "I took her in my arms and held her." fp 216

Note: The illustrations also appear in the book *The Militants* by Mary Raymond Shipman Andrews, published by Charles Scribner's Sons, N. Y., 1907.

April   Vol. XLI No. 4
"The Smugglers" by James B. Connolly. Pages 402–12.

Two illustrations in black and white.
    "There was no such monstrous lock as that last night, Ollie?" p (409)
    "Twas me that stowed them in the dory." p (411)

Note: The illustrations also appear in the book *The Crested Seas* by James B. Connolly, published by Charles Scribner's Sons, N. Y., 1907.
[1] The illustration was published as a print by Charles Scribner's Sons, 1907.

July   Vol. XLII No. 1
Scribner's Magazine Advertiser. Page 3. One reduced illustration in black and white by N. C. Wyeth for *Lascar* to be published in the August Number.

August   Vol. XLII No. 2
"Lascar" by Hugh Johnson. Pages 173–83.

Four illustrations in black and white.
    The Captain and Danvers.[1] p 177
    It was mumbled into a slender, pointed ear. p 179
    He was actually fretting with the bit. p (181)
    He thrust a dirty, crumpled wad of bills into the gasping mouth. p (182)

[1] The illustration also appears in the book *A Treasury of Frontier Relics* by Lester Beitz, published by Edwin House, N.Y., 1966.

October   Vol. XLII No. 4
Frontispiece illustration in color.
The Silent Fisherman

Note: The illustration The Silent Fisherman was published as a print by Charles Scribner's Sons, 1907, and was titled The Lone Fisherman. The illustration also appears in black and white in the book *A Treasury of Frontier Relics* by Lester Beitz, published by Edwin House, N.Y., 1966.

November   Vol. XLII No. 5
"Art and Artists." Artists whose work will appear in Scribner's Magazine during 1908. Page 2.
One reduced illustration in black and white by N. C. Wyeth.
    Description: On The October Trail p 2

1908

February   Vol. XLIII No. 2
"For the Honor of the Balloon Corps" by Fredrick Palmer. Pages 131–37.

Four illustrations in black and white.
    Freloar slowly descended, shouting aloud to himself. (frontispiece)
    Day and night he labored joyously with a plan of one of the enemy's balloons before him. p 133
    "The Chief," trimmed for flight, sprang downward at all speed. p (135)
    "It didn't work," he managed to say. p 136

April   Vol. XLIII No. 4
"Bart Harrington, Genius" by Elizabeth Jordan. Pages 456–65.

Two illustrations in black and white.
    The busy world itself might well hush its noisy activities long enough to hear of it. p (461)
    Spent his days browsing in libraries, where he read omnivorously. p (463)

August   Vol. XLIV No. 2
"Back to the Farm" by Martha Gilbert Dickinson Bianchi. Pages 164–71.

Four illustrations in color.
    Descriptions:
    Driving the cattle where the meadow brook is brawling. p (165)
    Down in the hayfield where scythes glint through the clover. p (167)
    Plowing the cornfield. p (169)
    Bringing home the pumpkins. p (171)

Eight illustrations (drawings) in pen and ink.
    Descriptions:
    Cows in the meadow. p 164
    The farmhouse and barn. p 164
    Fields. p (166)
    The hay wagon. p (166)
    Country lane. p (168)
    Plowing. p (168)
    Farmer with axe. p (170)
    Cornfield. p (170)

September   Vol. XLIV No. 3
"The Contracting Engineer" by Benjamin Brooks. Pages 259–73.

One illustration in black and white.
    The locating engineer—the first man on the ground who often risks his life to approximate possible routes. p (261)

October   Vol. XLIV No. 4
Frontispiece illustration in color. On the October Trail (A Navajo family)

"The Old Canoe" by George T. Marsh. Pages 446–47.

One illustration in black and white.
    In Phantom guise my spirit flies
    As the dream-blades dip and swing. p (446)

December   Vol. XLIV No. 6
Magazine Notes. Page 64f. Editorial note: Refers to N. C. Wyeth's article and illustrations for "A Sheep-Herder of the South-West," to appear in the January *Scribner's Magazine*.

1909

January   Vol. XLV No. 1
"A Sheep-Herder of the South-West" by N. C. Wyeth. Pages 16–21.

Four illustrations in black and white with tint.
The Plains Herder.[1] (frontispiece)
Navajo herder in the foothills. fp 17
The Mexican Greaser. fp 18
Pastoral of the South-west. fp 20

[1] Also appears as the frontispiece in the book *The Golden Hoof* by Winifred Kupper, published by Alfred A. Knopf, N. Y., 1945.

March Vol. XLV No. 3
Frontispiece illustration in colors (blue, ochre, black and white).
The War Clouds

December Vol. XLVI No. 6
"The Moods" by George T. Marsh. Pages 680–84. Title design (pen and ink) by Franklin Booth.
Four illustrations in color by N. C. Wyeth.
Spring. "Song"[1] p (681)
Sing the breezes in the birches.
Hymn the runnels as they journey.
Pipes the warbler where he perches
Challenging to vocal tourney
Brook and breeze—What sylvan spirit
Trolls those magic staves that hover?
Hark! 'tis fairy fluting, hear it?
Of some vanished Huron lover.

Summer. "Hush"[2] p (682)
Long the mating season's over;
Motionless lie meadow grasses;
Mute the throat of feathered rover;
Mirrored in the still pools' glasses
Hang the hot clouds' shimmering fleeces.
Are they runes of summers perished
That the fisher hears—and ceases—
Or the voices of one he cherished?

Autumn. "Waiting"[2][3] p (683)
Through the mists that veil the valley,
Blazoned by the Frost King's brushes,
Vanguards of gray legions sally;
Flaps the heron from the rushes.
In the haze that hides the ranges
Lurks the breath of white wind creeping
With a shroud—the forest changes
Its gay garments, and is sleeping.

Winter. "Death"[1][4] p (684)
When the wild blasts whip the passes;
In the tepees Famine tarries.
Sore the stinging sleet harasses
Where the snow-swirls sweep the prairies.
The Great Spirit's face is clouded:
Hears he not the women wailing
From his Hunting-Grounds enshrouded?
Shall our prayers rise unavailing?

[1] The illustrations also appeared in color in *Blackfeet Indian Stories* by George Bird Grinnell, published by Charles Scribner's Sons, N.Y., 1913.
[2] The illustrations inspired two mural paintings which N. C. Wyeth executed for The Hotel Utica, Utica, N. Y., in 1911–12.
[3] In addition, a similar design appeared on the Hotel Utica service plates.
[4] Also appears in color in the book *The Wyeths* by N. C. Wyeth, edited by Betsy James Wyeth, published by Gambit, Boston, 1971.

December
Scribner's Magazine Advertiser. Page 6.
One illustration in black and white.
Description: The Pay Stage. p 6

1910

March Vol. XLVII No. 3
"The Angel of Lonesome Hill" by Frederick Landis. Pages 302–11.

Four illustrations in black and white.
Description: The house on Lonesome Hill. p 302
Those who passed by night were grateful for the lamp.[1] p (304)
The policeman walked a few paces away to turn anon and survey the waiting pilgrim. p 309
"Mother, you sent me for a clothes-line—I've been delayed—but here it is." p 310

[1] The illustration also appears in the book *The Angel of Lonesome Hill* by Frederick Landis, published by Charles Scribner's Sons, N.Y., April 1910.

August Vol. XLVIII No. 2
One illustration in color.
The Pay-Stage. p (164)

Note: The illustration also appears in the book *Jinglebob* by Phillip Ashton Rollins, published by Charles Scribner's Sons, N. Y., 1930.

November Vol. XLVIII No. 5
"The Coming of the Huns" by Arthur Conan Doyle. *Through the Mists* Part I. Pages 548–53.

Two illustrations. One (frontispiece) in color and one in black and white.
All day, held spell-bound by this wonderful sight, the hermit crouched in the shadow of the rocks[1] (frontispiece).
The Huns (black and white). p 548

[1] The illustration appeared as the frontispiece in color in *The Last Galley* by Arthur Conan Doyle, published by Doubleday, Page & Company, N.Y., 1911.

December Vol. XLVIII
"The First Cargo" by Arthur Conan Doyle. *Through the Mists*. Part II. Pages 655–59.

Two illustrations. One (frontispiece) in color and one in pen and ink.
The First Cargo (frontispiece).
Description: The Saxon Fleet (headpiece pen and ink drawing). p 655

Scribner's Magazine Advertiser. Page 11. Advertisement for the continuing series of *Through the Mists* articles by Arthur Conan Doyle and illustrated by N. C. Wyeth.

1911

January Vol. XLIX No. 1
"The Red Star" by Arthur Conan Doyle. *Through the Mists* Part III. Pages 24–28.

Two illustrations. One in color and one in pen and ink.
Description: Marauding Arab warriors riding camels (headpiece pen-and-ink drawing). p 24
It was hard to remember that he was only the wandering leader of an Arab caravan (color). fp (24)

March Vol. XLIX No. 3
"The Artist" by Dorothy Canfield. Pages 288–93.

One illustration in black and white.
"He turned and faced the rising sun, the light full on his face." p 288

April Vol. XLIX No. 4
"Portrait of a Philosopher" by Dorothy Canfield. Pages 447–56.

Three illustrations in black and white.
Description: The Campus (headpiece pen-and-ink drawing). p 447

His queer shabby clothes, his big stooping frame, his sad black eyes, absent almost to vacancy. p 449
"Sure, it's Professor Grid to the life!" he said admiringly. p 451

August Vol. L No. 2
"Captain Blaise" by James B. Connolly. Pages 129–50.

Seven illustrations in black and white.
Description: The bark, Nereid. p (129)
After my dinner in town was through with, I rode hard. p 131
I found him sitting out under the moon, smoking a cheroot as usual. p 133
It was a short, very stout, and very black negro who stood at attention before Captain Blaise. p 135
I had half seen how he had rested his elbow on the hedge and carried his head to one side when he fired that first shot. p 136
After a long look I saw that he did not resume his narrative. By that I knew that the stranger was troubling him.[1] p 145
There she was, the Dancing Bess, holding a taut bowline to the eastward. And there were the two frigates, but they might as well have been chasing a star.[1] p 147

[1] The illustrations also appear in the book *Wide Courses* by James B. Connolly, published by Charles Scribner's Sons, N.Y., 1912.

December Vol. L No. 6
"Allemande Left!" A Story of the North Country by Mary Synon. Pages 723–34.

Two illustrations in black and white.
For three months he worked as an axeman . . . his only companion a dour Scotchman who never spoke. p (729)
She leaned toward him with eyes shining more brightly than the moonlight in the wake of their canoe. "Oh, you're splendid." p (731)

1912

January Vol. LI No. 1
"Saving Donald Ferguson" A Story of the North Country by Mary Synon. Pages 36–45.

Two illustrations in black and white.
The next morning Kenyon found her just outside Ferguson's shack, prone on the fallen leaves. p (36)
"Can't we even stay friends?" he pleaded. p (45)

February Vol. LI No. 2
"My Love Dwelt in a Northern Land" by Mary Synon. Pages 191–99.

Two illustrations in black and white.
There fell a long silence through which O'Hara read and Kenyon kept watch at the window. p (193)
The three were wading recklessly through the muskeg that oozed to the tops of their elk-hide boots.[1] p (195)

[1] Also appears in *The Graphic Arts and Crafts Year Book, Volume VI*, edited by Walter L. Tobey, published by The Republican Publishing Company, Hamilton, Ohio, 1913.

June Vol. LI No. 6
Frontispiece illustration in colors (blue, ocher, brown, black and white). The Sheriff

"Cobalt Bloom" A Story of the North Country by Mary Synon. Pages 666–72.

One illustration in colors. (blue, ocher, brown, black and white)

> They fell into abuse of all engineering in general, and Bush engineering in particular. fp (666)

July   Vol. LII No. 1
"Six Sons of Ossian" A Story of the North Country by Mary Synon. Pages 81–91.

One illustration in black and white.

> There in a white world of mist, . . . he stood alone, fighting his battle between love for a girl and a standard of honor in the friendship of men. p (89)

October   Vol. LII No. 4
One illustration in color.

> The Moose Hunter. A Moonlight Night. fp (468)

December   Vol. LII No. 6
"The Stable of the Inn" by Thomas Nelson Page. Pages 641–47.

Two illustrations in color.

> Behind them streamed the mingled traffic of a road that led to a great city. (frontispiece)
> It was, then, not a dream. This was the sign unto them. fp (644)

Note: The illustrations also appear in the book *The Land of the Spirit* by Thomas Nelson Page, published by Charles Scribner's Sons, N.Y., 1913.

1913

March   Vol. LIII No. 3
"Madame Robin" by Perceval Gibbon. Pages 334–46.

Five illustrations in black and white, two of which are reproduced in yellow tint.

> From his place at the farther side of the café, the shabby stranger looked on with furtive intentness. (charcoal and wash) p 336
> While the Arab, majestic in all his attitudes, smoked dreamily over his coffee-cup. (charcoal and wash) p 337
> "Enter, madame," said the Arab to the mother, and stood aside against the open door to let her pass in. (yellow tint) p 339
> "Then what are you going to do with me?" (yellow tint) p 343
> Description: A camel caravan. p 346

June   Vol. LIII No. 6
"Mrs. Van Anden Sings" A story of the North Country by Mary Synon. Pages 678–85.

One illustration in black and white.

> We all listened breathless even after the last chord of it had ceased to throb. p 678

October   Vol. LIV No. 4
Frontispiece illustration in color.

> A Primitive Spearman

The New Scribner Bookstore. Pages 33–36. N. C. Wyeth's *Treasure Island* paintings on view in the new Exhibition Gallery.

December   Vol. LIV No. 6
Frontispiece illustration in color. Christmas Morning

"The Great Minus" by Gilbert Parker. Pages 665–77.

Five illustrations in black and white.

> The stranger, Tsaga, had appeared sud-

denly at the fort with neither dogs nor gun, nor anything soever save the Indian costume that he wore. p 667
> At last, however, she had let Pascal Sarrotte see her mind. p 669
> They travelled all day through the ever-increasing cold, speaking but little, their faces covered from the deadly frost. p 670
> For a long time the three brothers smoked on in silence. p 671
> When, next night, two horror-stricken faces peered through this doorway, the three still sat where Tsaga had left them. p 672

1914

March   Vol. LV No. 3
"The Bravest Son" by Mary Synon. Pages 380–93.

Four illustrations (charcoal and wash) in black and white.

> He rubbed his fire-smartened eyes to read . . . the Haileybury Commercial Club's invitation to the public. p 381
> The man watched the tussle for a time with apparently concentrated interest. p 382
> But Rodney stepped back, his hand rising to his forehead in salute. "Captain Hurst," he said. p 391
> Wild creatures passed him in their panic rush. p 393

August   Vol. LVI No. 2
"The Rakish Brigantine" by James B. Connolly. Pages 214–23.

Four illustrations. Three in color (including frontispiece) and one in pen and ink.

> "Yes, 'N', He'd Let a Roar Outer Him, An' Mebbe He'd Sing, "Hail Columbia, Happy Land!"[1] (frontispiece)
> The brigantine and sea serpent (headpiece pen-and-ink drawing) p 214
> "'N' the pirates, seein' how it was, puts off in boats."[2] (color) p 217
> "One swing 'f his battle-axe chops off the lock, 'n there's a dragon black as ink wi' one eye."[2][3] (color) p 221

[1] The frontispiece illustration also appears in *Scribner's Magazine* (Fiftieth Anniversary Issue 1887–1937), January 1937.
[2] The illustrations also appear in the book *Tide Rips* by James B. Connolly, published by Charles Scribner's Sons, N.Y., 1922.
[3] The illustration appears in *The International Studio*, January 1915, for the article, "Decorative Pictures At The Pennsylvania Academy Of Fine Arts" by Theodore L. Fitzsimons.

December   Vol. LVI No. 6
"The Waif Woman" by Robert Louis Stevenson. Pages 687–701. Cover illustration in color.

Five illustrations. Three (including frontispiece) in color and two in black and white.

> Thorgunna, The Waif Woman. (frontispiece)
> Description: A procession across the glacier. (headpiece illustration) p 687
> The first walking of Thorgunna. Great fear fell upon them: The marrow of their back grew cold. (color and repeated on the cover) p 689
> It was a rough day, the sea was wild, the boat labored exceedingly. p 692
> The death of Finnward Keelfarer. This was the first vengeance of Thorgunna. (color) p 695

Scribner's Magazine Advertiser. Page 16. One illustration (Pioneers) by N. C. Wyeth in black

and white to appear as a frontispiece for *Scribner's* in 1915.

1915

March   Vol. LVII No. 3
"Panama (A Poem)" by Joseph Mills Hanson. Pages 282–83.

Two illustrations (including frontispiece) in black and white.

> These swamps, where fever-maddened men have pressed/To fight and die for gold. . . . (frontispiece) p 264
> Description: Freighter passing through canal. p 283

July   Vol. LVIII No. 1
Scribner's Magazine Advertiser. Page 9. Photograph of N. C. Wyeth. p 9

Magazine Notes. Page 7. Wyeth's pictures mentioned for Stephen Phillips "No. 6".

August   Vol. LVIII No. 2
"No. 6". A Dramatic Sketch in Three Scenes by Stephen Phillips. Pages 130–38.

Nine illustrations. One in color, two in black and white, and the remaining six are pen-and-ink decorations.

> Description: Angel singing. (headpiece pen-and-ink drawing for Scene I) p 130
> Description: Letter A. (pen-and-ink decoration) p 130
> The Youth. Master, I shall not fail you. (color) p 131
> Description: Angel and Death. (headpiece pen-and-ink drawing for Scene II) p 134
> Description: Letter A. (pen-and-ink decoration) p 134
> Andrea. Stop this one! Him—the Sixth! (black and white) p 135
> Description: Death offering a drink. (headpiece pen-and-ink drawing for Scene III) p 136
> Description: Letter O. (pen-and-ink decoration) p 136
> Andrea. I implore you not to move. (black and white) p 137

November   Vol. LVIII No. 5
Scribner's Magazine Advertiser. Page 8. One illustration in black and white for *The Medicine Ship* by James B. Connolly to appear in *Scribner's Magazine*, December 1915.

December   Vol. LVIII No. 6
"The Medicine Ship" by James B. Connolly. Pages 652–63.

Three illustrations. One in color and two in black and white.

> "An' the bridal couple'd be holdin' hands an' gazin' over the spanker-boom at the full moon." p 652
> "However, after six days o'restin up, with salubrious fruits an' wines an' the most melojus concerts, my capt'n broaches the cause of why we're callin' on the Don Hidalgo Rodreego Cazamma." (color) p 657
> "'Quiscanto vascamo mirajjar'; which is Yunzano for 'I am satisfied, I can now die happy'."[1] p 661

[1] The illustrations also appear in the book *Running Free* by James B. Connolly, published by Charles Scribner's Sons, N.Y., 1917.

1916

January   Vol. LIX No. 1
Frontispiece illustration in color. Pioneers–The Opening of the Prairies.

Note: This painting appears as the frontispiece illustration in Volume II of *The Pageant of America* edited by Ralph Henry Gabriel, published by The Yale University Press, New Haven, 1925–29. In addition, it also appears in numerous books on American history.

May   Vol. LIX No. 5
"The Quest of Narcisse Lablanche" by George T. Marsh. Pages 608–20.
Four illustrations. Two in color and two in black and white.
> Description: The meeting in the canoes. p 608
> Description: Letter Q. (decoration) p 608
> "My son, when will you put this revenge from your heart?" (color) p 613
> One January afternoon, at dusk, the Matagami winter mail jingled up to the tradehouse. (color) p 617

Magazine Notes. Page 10. Mentions Wyeth's pictures appearing in the story by George T. Marsh.

August   Vol. LX No. 2
"Chavero" by James B. Connolly. Pages 146–53.

Two illustrations. One (frontispiece) in color and one in black and white.
> He was a fine boy–an imaginative boy, with great dreams in his head. (frontispiece)
> Without a word he began to shoot. p 146

Note: The illustrations also appear in the book *Head Winds* by James B. Connolly, published by Charles Scribner's Sons, N.Y., 1916.

December   Vol. XL No. 6
"The Wild Woman's Lullaby" by Constance Lindsay Skinner. Page 701.

Frontispiece illustration in color. Song of the Eagle That Mates with the Storm!

"The Garden of Bee-man John" by Margaret Adelaide Wilson. Pages 736–41.

One illustration in black and white.
> Miss Margery and Bee-Man John. p 736

1917

February   Vol. LXI No. 2
Frontispiece illustration in color. The Fight in the Peaks
> The experience of a Norwegian locating engineer, on the lone of the Canadian Pacific Railway, who, being an experienced skirunner, packed mail over the mountains before the railroad was completed.

Magazine Notes. Page 5. Photograph of N. C. Wyeth. Mentions Wyeth's painting of the frontispiece.

August   Vol. LXII No. 2
"The Golden Galleon" by Paul Hervey Fox. Pages 166–67.

Three illustrations. One (frontispiece) in color and two in black and white.
> "Oh, Morgan's men are out for you; and Blackbeard–buccaneer!"[1] (frontispiece)
> Description: The Golden Galleon. p 166
> Description: Treasure for the mighty King of Spain! p 167

[1] The frontispiece illustration also appears in color in the book *Deep Water Days* by Oliver Swan, published by Macrae Smith Pub. Co., Phila., 1929. In addition, the illustration appears in the books *Anchors Aweigh!* by Oliver G. Swan, published

by Grosset & Dunlap Publishers, N.Y., and *The Wreck of the Grosvenor* by W. Clarke Russell, published by Grosset & Dunlap Publishers, N.Y. It also appears as a cover in color for *American History Illustrated*, June 1968.

1918

March   Vol. LXIII No. 3
"Man Primeval" by G. B. Lancaster. Pages 336–47.

Three illustrations in black and white.
> "Two year we've had o' this life . . . Two blarsted God-forsaken year, an' another yet." p 341
> Here, in his own element, the message of the trails was strongest . . . It surged about him. p 343
> "I'm going away," she said in tremulous defiance. p 345

October   Vol. LXIV No. 4
"Bill Green Puts Out to Sea" by James B. Connolly. Pages 474–81.
One illustration in black and white.
> Next morning came a clear day–a hot day. p 481

December   Vol. LXIV No. 6
"Rural America in War-time" by Theodore Dreiser. Pages 734–46.

One illustration (charcoal drawing) in black and white.
> The letter from "Over There".[1] p 735

Book Notes. Page 12. N. C. Wyeth's Choice. Jules Verne's *The Mysterious Island* was proposed by Wyeth to follow in the Scribner's classics series.

[1] The illustration also appeared in a repeat of this article in *Scribner's Magazine* (Fiftieth Anniversary Issue 1887–1937), January 1937.

1919

August   Vol. LXVI No. 2
"The Swallow" by Mary Raymond Shipman Andrews. Pages 153–64.

Frontispiece illustration in colors (blue, ocher, brown, black and white). He turned and pinned the thing which men die for on the shabby coat of the guide.

November   Vol. LXVI No. 5
"For Better Illustration" by N. C. Wyeth. Pages 638–42.

Three illustrations in black and white.
> Still life study. p 639
> Landscape study. p 640
> September afternoon. p 641

Magazine Notes. Page 20. N. C. Wyeth mentioned as one of the foremost American illustrators.

1920

April   Vol. LXVII No. 4
"Devilled Sweetbreads" by Maxwell Struthers Burt. Pages 411–21.

One illustration in black and white.
> They were entirely absorbed in their primitive pastime. p 413

Note: The illustration also appears as a frontispiece in the book *Chance Encounters* by Maxwell Struthers Burt, published by Charles Scribner's Sons, N.Y., 1921.

1922

February   Vol. LXXI No. 2
"Eilean Erraid" The Beloved Isle of Robert Louis Stevenson by Llewellyn M. Buell. Pages 184–95.

One illustration in black and white.
> David Balfour on the Island of Erraid. p 189

Note: This illustration originally appeared in *Kidnapped* by Robert Louis Stevenson, published by Charles Scribner's Sons, N.Y., October 1913.

1923

September   Vol. LXXIV No. 3
Cover illustration in color. Description: A Spanish Galleon.

1924

July   Vol. LXXVI No. 1
"Tides" by Henry Meade Williams. Pages 58–61.

Frontispiece illustration (charcoal drawing) in black and white. The Tide! And the stones were wet where the water had been. p 2

1928

July   Vol. LXXXIV No. 1
"Boston of the Future" by F. J. Stimson. Pages 1–12.

Five illustrations in black and white.
> Phoenician Biremes. (frontispiece)
> Mural painting in the First National Bank of Boston.
> The panel represents three Phoenician biremes pulling out to sea from under the embattlements and the towering city of Tyre. The artist writes, "Although we are certain of Tyre's existence, its exact location, and we know of its dynamic force in industry and politics, yet it looms through the dim reaches of history like a dream city, a dream life, the mere dawn of the present stupendous age."

> Salmon P. Chase conferring with Lincoln.
> Mural painting in The Federal Reserve Bank of Boston. p (9)
> Salmon P. Chase conferring with Lincoln in the cabinet room of the White House about the National Bank Act of 1863.

> The Clippers 1843–1870.
> Mural painting in The First National Bank of Boston. p (10)
> "The period of the clipper ship forms perhaps the most important epoch in maritime history. This era witnessed the highest development of the wooden sailing ship in construction, speed, and beauty. One might say that the clipper type represents the swan-song of the master designer and builder. It is significant that New England was in the forefront of designing these splendid craft and reached the maximum of production just as steam navigation was made practical."–N. C. Wyeth.

> The Tramp Steamer
> Mural painting in The First National Bank of Boston. p (11)
> "The modern cargo carrier, the dependable, patient, colossal pack-mule of the sea! A craft that has suffered much in the eyes of all who refuse to read beauty and

romance into her daily toil and majestic bulk.

"Wandering alone over the water wastes of the world, steaming quietly into remote and unheard-of ports, opening her gaping hatches, swallowing vast quantities and varieties of the world's merchandise, steaming away again, stoically meeting storm and sunshine, high seas and calm."–N. C. Wyeth.

A conference between Alexander Hamilton, George Washington, and Robert Morris.
    Mural painting in The Federal Reserve Bank of Boston. p (12)
    A conference between three friends, Alexander Hamilton, Secretary of the Treasury, President George Washington, and Robert Morris, in Washington's Philadelphia residence–a house built and owned by Robert Morris and given over for Washington's use while in office.

Note: The two mural paintings in The Federal Reserve Bank of Boston originally appeared in color in the *Ladies' Home Journal*, February 1923 and February 1924.
    The four mural paintings in The First National Bank of Boston originally appeared in color in the *Ladies' Home Journal*, July and August 1925.

August   Vol. LXXXIV No. 2
Newell Convers Wyeth A self-portrait. fp (133). Frontispiece illustration in black and white.
    "The stovepipe and the cape belonged to my paternal grandfather, who, I have every right to think, often walked down Brattle Street, Cambridge, arrayed in this apparel with Oliver Wendell Holmes, Louis Agassiz, Longfellow, and others of that splendid group. At any rate, he was a near neighbor and knew them all."–The artist.

1937

January   Vol. CI No. 1
Fiftieth Anniversary Issue 1887–1937. A representative group of illustrations by some of the great Scribner artists. Pages 65–80.
One illustration in color by N. C. Wyeth.
    "Yes'n'he'd let a roar outer him, an' mebbe he'd sing, 'Hail Columbia, Happy Land!'" p (76)
    Illustration by N. C. Wyeth for "The Rakish Brigantine" by James B. Connolly. Previously published in *Scribner's Magazine*, August 1914.

"The 1910's: Rural America in War-Time" by Theodore Dreiser. Pages 99–103. Illustrated by N. C. Wyeth and Capt. John W. Thomason, Jr.

One illustration (charcoal drawing) in black and white by N. C. Wyeth.
    The Letter from "Over There" p 100

Note: The illustration originally appeared in the same article in *Scribner's Magazine*, December 1918.

1938

April   Vol. CIII No. 4
"Andrew Wyeth's Maine Water Colors." Pages 33–35. In the article is a reference to N. C. Wyeth.

1939

March   Vol. CV No. 3
Editor's Note: Straws in the Wind. Page 4. Along with the editor's comments on Peter Hurd's cover painting are references to N. C. Wyeth.

Show

May   Vol. V No. 4
"Andrew Wyeth" by Brian O'Doherty. Pages 46–55, 72, 73, and 75. Three photographs of Andrew Wyeth. Illustrated with numerous paintings in color and black and white by Andrew Wyeth. References to N. C. Wyeth on pages 48, 50, and 52.

Success

1903

March   Vol. VI No. 106
"The Romance of the 'C.P.'" by Edwin Markham. The story of the construction of the Central Pacific Railroad, during the early sixties. The great undertaking that joined the West and the East. Pages 127–30 and 174.

One illustration in black and white.
    Description: Two surveyors (titlepiece illustration) p (127)

November   Vol. VI No. 114
The Duke of Cameron Avenue or, the Settlement Fight in "The Seventh" by Henry Ketchell Webster. Pages 629–31. Illustrated by N. C. Wyeth and Arthur Jameson.

One illustration in black and white by N. C. Wyeth.
    "It's a scientific, historic, precise '–and at every word his big hand made the glasses jump,–' designation of him!" (headpiece illustration) p 629

December   Vol. VI No. 115
The Duke of Cameron Avenue by Henry Ketchell Webster. Pages 749–52.

Three illustrations in black and white.
    "Well," he said, slowly, "I believe you're right." p 749
    "He found Schmeckenbecker solemnly throwing dice." p 750
    "Come out, man, with me, and have a look." p 751

1904

January   Vol. VII No. 116
The Duke of Cameron Avenue by Henry Kitchell Webster. Pages 30–34.

Three illustrations in black and white.
    "The lines on Father Lauth's face settled deeper. He folded his arms and waited." (headpiece illustration) p 30
    "Schmeckenbecker was more amusing than instructive." p 31
    "You have used Carter Hall to further your personal ambitions." p 33

February   Vol. VII No. 117
The Duke of Cameron Avenue by Henry Kitchell Webster. Pages 106–8.

Two illustrations in black and white.
    "Ramsay scrambled over the rail to the orchestra pit, and over the piano and the footlights." (headpiece illustration) p 106
    "Schmeckenbecker faced the mob, gallantly shouting his defiance." p 107

Time (The Weekly Newsmagazine)

1937

November 15   Vol. XXX No. 20
"Pyles and Wyeths." Page 57.

1946

January 28   Vol. XLVII No. 4
"Four to Carry On." Page 44. References to N. C. Wyeth's career and the memorial exhibition at the Wilmington Society of the Fine Arts. To carry on his artistic heritage were three of his children, Henriette, Carolyn, and Andrew, plus son-in-law Peter Hurd.

1957

November 18   Vol. LXX No. 21
"The Greatest Illustrator." Pages 94–96. Photograph of N. C. Wyeth (circa 1944) p 94

Two illustrations in color from *Rip Van Winkle* by Washington Irving.
    Rip Van Winkle Leaving. p 95
    Rip Van Winkle Returning. p 96

Note: The illustrations originally appeared in color in *Rip Van Winkle* by Washington Irving, published by David McKay Company, 1921.

1962

November 2   Volume LXXX No. 18
"Above the Battle." Page 70. Article on Andrew Wyeth. Numerous references to N. C. Wyeth.

1963

December 27   Volume 82 No. 26
"Andy's World." Pages 44–52. Seven photographs, two drawings in black and white, three illustrations in black and white, and nine illustrations in color by Andrew Wyeth. Numerous references to N. C. Wyeth.

Town & Country

1946

November   Volume 100 Number 4290
"Wyeths" by Wyeths. Pages 126–27. Illustrated in color and black and white with paintings, watercolors, and drawings by members of the Wyeth family.

Two illustrations in black and white by N. C. Wyeth.
    Portrait of Henriette Wyeth[1] p 126
    Andrew Wyeth (drawing–1939) p 127

Among the works illustrated are two examples by Wyeth's children of their father.
    Portrait of N. C. Wyeth by Henriette Wyeth (color)
    N. C. Wyeth at work in his studio by Andrew Wyeth. (drawing–1944)

[1] The portrait was reproduced as a cover in color for the *Ladies' Home Journal*, November 1924.

Transmission (Northern Natural Gas Company)
Published Quarterly   Vol. XVII No. 1

1968

"Taming a Frontier" New View of The Old West Through Art. Pages 11–14. Illustrated in color and black and white with paintings by noted artists who portrayed the Old West.

One illustration in black and white by N. C. Wyeth.
    "Indian Attack" p 14
Reference to N. C. Wyeth on page 11.

Note: The illustration originally appeared in color in *The Oregon Trail* by Francis Parkman, published by Little, Brown & Company, Boston, 1925.

True West

1967

December Volume 15 Number 2
"N. C. Wyeth Painter of Men . . . In Action" by Les Beitz. Pages 20, 21, and 68.

Two photographs of N. C. Wyeth.
N. C. Wyeth. (portrait) p 20
N. C. Wyeth on horseback. (Colorado 1904) p 21

Five illustrations in black and white.
Description: A wild spectacular race for dinner.[1] p 20
Description: Into town from the south.[2] p 21
Description: As Broadwell raced West.[2] p 21
Bar-room Brawl[3] p 21
"Rounding Up"[1] p 68

[1] The illustrations originally appeared in color in *Scribner's Magazine,* March 1906, for the article "A Day With the Round-Up by N. C. Wyeth.
[2] The illustrations originally appeared in *Leslie's Popular Monthly,* August 1903, for the story "Working for Fame" by John M. Oskison.
[3] The illustration originally appeared in *Collier's Weekly,* January 1, 1916, for the story "Punderson Waite" by Ceylon Hollingsworth.

Western Story

1948

October Vol. CCXIX No. 6
Cover illustration in color. Description: Cowboy on horseback confronted by a grizzly bear on narrow mountain trail.

Note: The illustration originally appeared as a cover in color on *The Popular Magazine,* November 1912.

Woman's Day

1937

November Volume 1 Number 2
Cover illustration in color. "The Cornhuskers"

The Cornhuskers—The story of the painting on the cover of this magazine (the editors). Page 28. Photograph of N. C. Wyeth.

1945

August
"The Peach-Brandy Leg" by Mabel Thompson Rauch. Pages 22, 23, 52, 54, and 57–60.

One illustration in color.
Description: Union troops boarding Mississippi River steamers. p 22

November
Cover illustration in color. Description: A soldier returns from the war.

1946

March
"Ann Story" by Dorothy Canfield Fisher. Pages 22, 23, and 74–79.

One illustration in color.
As they paddled away, they could see the Indians come whooping into the clearing. pp 22–23

October
Cover illustration in color. "The Husking Bee"

1947

February
Cover illustration in color. Description: Jody and Flag

Cover Talk: A short article on N. C. Wyeth by the editors of *Woman's Day.*

Note: The cover illustration originally appeared in color in the book *The Yearling* by Marjorie Kinnan Rawlings, published by Charles Scribner's Sons, N.Y. 1939.

September
"Grandmothers Are Back in Style" by Sidonie Matsner Gruenberg. Pages 48, 49, and 77–79.

One painting in color.
A quiet summer day along the Brandywine. p 49

1948

February
"What Would Lincoln Do Today?" by Carl Sandburg. Page 27.

One illustration (charcoal and wash) in black and white.
Description: A portrait of Abraham Lincoln.

1963

August
"The Wonderful World of Andrew Wyeth." Pages 33–37, 67, and 68. Illustrated with paintings by Andrew Wyeth. Reference to N. C. Wyeth on page 67.

1964

August
"Maine and her Artists" by Roul Tunley. Pages 62–66 and 68. Illustrated from paintings by noted American artists.

One painting in color by N. C. Wyeth.
Dark Harbor Fishermen. p 64

Woman's Home Companion

1909

June Vol. XXXVI No. 6
"To the Highest Bidder" by Maude Radford Warren. Pages 5 and 6.

Two illustrations in black and white.
"But Jean Baptiste and Cecile were left to dreams more beautiful than most, for they were real." p 5
"But no", said Jean Baptiste, with a sudden forward step, 'I offer Cecile five hundred dollars'." p 5

1924

July Vol. LI No. 7
"Time and Tide" A story of the hour when the tide was right by Adriana Spadoni. Pages 7–9.

One illustration in color.
Big Black Beppo and Little Black Beppo. They drew in the lines, sagging with fish. p 9

December Vol. LI No. 12
"The Man Nobody Knows" by Bruce Barton. Pages 7, 8, 125, and 126. Illustrated by N. C. Wyeth with decorations by J. Flanagan.

One illustration in color by N. C. Wyeth.
The books that are written about Him as the Son of God almost forget that His favorite title for Himself was the Son of Man. p 9

Note: The illustration also appears as a *frontispiece* in color in the book *The Man Nobody Knows* by Bruce Barton, published by The Bobbs-Merrill Company, Indianapolis, 1925. In additioin, it appears as a frontispiece in black and white in the book *How One Man Changed the World* by Ferdinand Q. Blanchard, published by The Pilgrim Press, Boston, 1928 (1935). It also appears in sepia tint in *The Pilgrim Elementary Teacher,* July 1926.

1929

November Vol. LVI No. 11
Cimarron A novel by Edna Ferber. Pages 7–11, 169–76, and 178–80. Illustrated by N. C. Wyeth and Charles S. Chapman.

Two illustrations in color by N. C. Wyeth.
Sabra, filled with a dizzy mixture of fright and exhilaration, forgot to look back at everything she was leaving. (titlepiece vignette) p 7
"Next to me was a girl who looked about eighteen. On the other side was an old fellow with a long gray beard." p 8

December Vol. LVI No. 12
Cimarron A brilliant novel of our last frontier by Edna Ferber. Pages 20–24, 58, 61, and 62. Illustrated by N. C. Wyeth and Charles S. Chapman.

Two illustrations by N. C. Wyeth. One in color and one in two colors.
His eyes looked as Sabra had never seen them look, merciless, cold, hypnotic. "A three-cornered piece, you'll find it, Lon. The Cravat sheep-brand." (color) p 21
Sabra thought privately that two women could have finished the job in half the time with one tenth the fuss. (ocher, black and white) p 23

1930

January Vol. LVII No. 1
Cimarron The last frontier, where divine worship is held in a gambling tent, by Edna Ferber. Pages 9–13, 72, 74, and 76. Illustrated by N. C. Wyeth and Charles S. Chapman.

Two illustrations in colors by N. C. Wyeth.
They seemed actually to know Yancey. They called him Buffalo Head. (orange, brown, black and white) p 11
Yancey's ardent eyes took on their most melting look. (orange, brown, black and white) p 13

February Vol. LVII No. 2
Cimarron Yancey gets the Kid, the most famous desperado of the Southwest, by Edna Ferber. Pages 26–30, 52, 54, 57, and 58. Illustrated by N. C. Wyeth and Charles S. Chapman.

Two illustrations in two colors by N. C. Wyeth.
"I'll drill the first one of you that fires another shot." (vignette illustration in pale green, black and white) p 27
Doctor Valliant often vanished for days and would reappear as inexplicably as he had vanished. (reddish brown, black and white) p 29

March Vol. LVII No. 3
Cimarron The return of Yancey and the trial of Dixie Lee, by Edna Ferber. Pages 33–36, 132, 134, 136, 138, and 140. Illustrated by N. C. Wyeth and Charles S. Chapman.

Two illustrations in black and white by N. C. Wyeth.

> She was in his arms with an inarticulate cry. (with yellow tint) p 33
>
> "Your father—" Sabra would begin courageously, resolved to make him live again in the minds of the children. (vignette illustration) p 36

April   Vol. LVII No. 4

Cimarron Prosperity and decadence; the coming of oil in Oklahoma, by Edna Ferber. Pages 26–30, 176, 177, 188–90, 192–96, 198, and 200. Illustrated by N. C. Wyeth and Charles S. Chapman.

Two illustrations by N. C. Wyeth. One (headpiece vignette) in black and white and one in colors.

> "When you take that down, Sabra honey, you'll be the editor of this newspaper. Until you do that I am." (headpiece vignette) p 26
>
> She knew she must not lose her dignity before this Indian woman—before her son. (reddish brown, black and white) p 29

May   Vol. LVII No. 5

Cimarron Conclusion by Edna Ferber. Pages 28–30 and 174–76. Illustrated by N. C. Wyeth and Charles S. Chapman.

One illustration in two colors by N. C. Wyeth.

> She flung herself on the ground and lifted the magnificent head gently. (reddish brown, black and white) p 29

1940

May   Vol. LXVII No. 5

"Laughing Lady" by Constance Wagner. Pages 16, 17, 99, 100, 102, and 103. Illustrated by N. C. Wyeth and Hardie Gramatky.

One illustration in color by N. C. Wyeth.

> "Sit down," says the stranger. "I take what I have a mind to, sir." p 17

Yankee

1938

August   Vol. XI No. 8

Cover illustration in black and white. A Sea Captain's Daughter.

Note: The illustration originally appeared in color in *Trending into Maine* by Kenneth Roberts, published by Little, Brown & Company, Boston, June 1938.

1947

May   Vol. XI No. 5

Page 24. Two paintings in black and white.
"Sunglint." p 24
"The Red Dory." p 24

1970

September   Volume 34 Number 9

Sole Witness to "The Wyeth Canal" by Francis W. Hatch. Pages 46–49.

Two photographs in brown tint.

> Description: Mural panel of the Western Hemisphere. p 46
> Description: N. C. Wyeth standing before the mural panel, Elizabethan Galleons. p 46

Note: The mural panels were executed for the First National Bank of Boston.

III. Newspapers

Boston Herald (Rotogravure Section)

1938

June 19
A group of illustrations from Kenneth Roberts' latest book *Trending Into Maine*.
Five illustrations by N. C. Wyeth.
  The first Maine fisherman.
  They took their wives with them in their cruises.
  Captain George Waymouth on the Georges River.
  Daniel Nason sailing master, 1814.
  Arnold's march to Quebec.

Boston Sunday Post

1921

November 27
Article on N. C. Wyeth by Muriel Caswall.
King of the Pirates, Armed to the Teeth, Discovered in Needham • Stacks His Cutlasses and Daniel Boone's Gun in Old Homestead—N. C. Wyeth Ends Roving Days—His Pirate Sketches Won Him Fame
One photograph
N. C. Wyeth and self-portrait.
Two pen-and-ink drawings.
Pirate—Such boy-worshipped heroes as this—who looks as if he'd just stepped out of "Treasure Island"—Sketched for the *Sunday Post* by Mr. Wyeth.
Indian—Ooh, look, boys! Betcha that redskin is up to something awful—Sketched by Mr. Wyeth especially for the *Sunday Post*.

Boston Post
(Color Gravure Section)

1922

December 12
"Wyeth's Paintings on Show at the City Club"
One illustration in black and white.
Illustration from "Courtship of Miles Standish"
  This incident in Longfellow's poem, where Priscilla asks John Alden why he does not speak for himself, is one of 30 original oil paintings by N. C. Wyeth, now on exhibition in the art gallery of the Boston City Club.

The Christian Science Monitor

1912

November 13
"Pupils of Pyle Tell Of His Teaching" by N. C. Wyeth and Sidney M. Chase.
N. C. Wyeth Gives Glimpse of Twilight Talks and of Life of Colony at Chadds Ford Near Wilmington

Note: A large portion of this article was used in the introduction to *Howard Pyle: A Chronicle* by Charles D. Abbott, published by Harper & Brothers, N.Y., 1925. In addition, portions were also used in the article "Howard Pyle As I Knew Him" by N. C. Wyeth, published in *The Mentor*, June 1927.

1950

June 21
"N. C. Wyeth, Illustrator"
Article focuses on the illustrated classics.

Cleveland Plain Dealer
(Color Gravure Section)

1922

December 10
"Paints Awhile, Then Milks Cow" Artist Alternates Minutes at Easel With Chores on Farm
Article on N. C. Wyeth.

The Coastal Courier (Color Gravure Section)
(Edition of The Courier-Gazette, Rockland, Maine)

1966

July 31   Volume 7 Number 7
Cover illustration in black and white by N. C. Wyeth.
"Bill Bones On The Cliff"

Daily Local News (West Chester, Pa.)

1931

February 8
Wyeth Opens Westtown Exhibit at Art Center
Talk given by N. C. Wyeth.

1932

November 11
Famous Artist Lays Aside His Brushes to Chat With Interviewer in His Studio
An interview with N. C. Wyeth.

The Dearborn Independent

1923

January 20
Article on N. C. Wyeth.
One photograph.
N. C. Wyeth and his family.
Two illustrations in black and white.
  Conference between Abraham Lincoln and his Secretary of the Treasury, Salmon P. Chase.
  Alleyne's Ride With a Message to the Prince—*The White Company*

The Delmarva Star
(Wilmington, Delaware)

1934

August 19
"Children's Artist"—A Painter and Muralist of World Renown, N. C. Wyeth Likes Best To Paint for Youth, Hopes and Dreams.
Page 12
Photograph of N. C. Wyeth at his easel.
Pen-and-ink illustration by Franklin Booth after N. C. Wyeth's mural painting "The Apotheosis of the Family."

Evening Journal (Color Gravure Section)
(Wilmington, Del.)

1933

November 4   Saturday
Cover illustration in color.
The American Red Cross / Carries on / Join! (poster)

Inter-State Milk Products Review
(Color Gravure Section)

1944

October   Vol. XXV No. 6
Cover illustration in black and white.
William Penn—Man of Vision, Courage, Action.

Note: The illustration is reproduced from a mural decoration by N. C. Wyeth in the Penn Mutual Insurance Company, main office, Philadelphia.

The New York Herald
(Literary and Art Section)

1907

December 8
"Illustration in Museum Galleries"
Page 3.
Comments by noted illustrators on the development of a proposed collection of American Illustration to be exhibited permanently at The Metropolitan Museum of Art.
A paragraph by N. C. Wyeth.

The New York Herald

1920

December 5
"Wyeth Illustrates the Classics
This Painter Recreates in Color the Scenery of Great Fiction-Drama"
Three illustrations in black and white.
Why don't you speak for yourself, John?
  (*The Courtship of Miles Standish*)
"Westward Ho!" (endpapers)
The Footprint (*Robinson Crusoe*)

New York Herald Tribune
(Book Section)

1925

May 10   Sunday
The Three Owls edited by Anne Carroll Moore.
"Robin Hood's Country."
One illustration by Howard Pyle.
> Robin Hood meeteth the tall stranger on the
> bridge.
Article on N. C. Wyeth.

New York Journal American
(Pictorial Living)

1963

October 6
Cover illustration in color.
Columbus Discovers America

Note: The illustration originally appeared in color
in the *Flags of American History* calendar, published by the John Morrell Company, Ottumwa,
Iowa, 1944.

New York Mirror

1958

April 13
April in '75
The 183rd Anniversary of Paul Revere's Ride.
Pages 10 and 11.
One illustration in color.
> "A hurry of hoofs in a village street, / a shape
> in the moonlight, a bulk in the dark, / and be-
> neath, from the pebbles, in passing, a spark /
> struck out by a steed flying fearless and fleet . . ."

Note: The illustration originally appeared in the
book *Poems of American Patriotism* edited by
Brander Matthews, published by Charles Scribner's
Sons, N.Y., October 1922.

1959

February 22
George Washington—In Fact and Legend
Pages 10 and 11.
Two illustrations in color.
> Rip Van Winkle comes home after his long
> sleep.[1]
> General Washington, the landowner, forfeited
> an easy life to lead a ragged army—voluntarily
> without pay.[2]

[1] The illustration originally appeared in color in
Rip Van Winkle by Washington Irving, published
by David McKay Company, Phila., 1921.
[2] The illustration originally appeared as a cover in
color on *The Country Gentleman* magazine, February 1946. It was titled First Farmer Of The
Land.

New York Sunday News
(Coloroto Magazine)

1958

April 20
One illustration in color.
Page 20.
> America's First Standing Army

1959

June 14
One illustration in color.
Page 38.
> The Flag at Bunker Hill

Note: The illustrations originally appeared in color
in the calendar Flags in American History, published by John Morrell & Company, Ottumwa,
Iowa, 1944.

The New York Times

1912

October 13
"On Illustrations" A Suggestion and a Comment
on Illustrating Fiction by N. C. Wyeth.
Page 574.

The New York Times
(Color Gravure Section)

1924

September 14
One illustration in brown tint.
The First Albany "Day Boat": The Halfmoon
> With the Palisades in the Background a Por-
> tion of a Mural Decoration by N. C. Wyeth
> for the Dining Room of the New York Roose-
> velt Hotel.

The New York Times
(Book Review)

1969

February 2   Section 7
The Brandywine Tradition by Henry C. Pitz.
A Review by Donelson F. Hoopes.
Pages 7 and 28.
Two illustrations by Howard Pyle and N. C.
Wyeth.
One illustration in black and white.
Blind Pew (illustration from *Treasure Island*)

The New York Times
(Sunday Magazine)

1957

October 27
"Wyeth: Adventure in Art"
Pages 40 and 41.
Five illustrations in black and white.
Illustration from *The Boy's King Arthur*
Illustration from *Rip Van Winkle*
Illustration from *The Oregon Trail*
Illustration from *Treasure Island*
Illustration from *The Bounty Trilogy*

The New York Tribune
(Sunday Magazine)

1906

November 4
"The White Man's Way" by Jack London.
Pages 3 and 4.
Two illustrations in black and white.
Description: Indian with ax (titlepiece illustra-
tion). p 3
> "He would say, only do I care to eat the grub
> of the white man." p 4

1910

March 6
"The Sun King" by Herman Scheffauer.
Pages 3, 4, and 18.
One illustration in black and white.
> "You should have seen that son of the Vik-
> ings step out of the hut!" p 3

1913

August 3
Hardpan & Co. by Roy Norton.
Cover illustration in color.
Description: He waved his hand indefinitely
toward the valley that lay at their feet. . . .
Hardpan & Co., Chapter 1.
Pages 3, 4, 15, 16, and 17.
One illustration in black and white.
> "Think what might happen if it was not pro-
> tected by those hills!" p 3

August 10
Hardpan & Co. by Roy Norton.
Pages 12–15.
One illustration in black and white.
> Even as Jim looked, two men, locked and strik-
> ing furiously at each other, swayed through
> the opening. p 13

August 17
Hardpan & Co. by Roy Norton.
Pages 10–12 and 18.
One illustration in black and white.
> "See here, Harges, don't you ask me to do
> any of your dirty work—because I won't do
> it!" p 11

August 24
Hardpan & Co. by Roy Norton.
Pages 14–17.
One illustration in black and white.
> Again, at the mouth of the shaft, they shook
> hands in congratulation. p 14

August 31
Hardpan & Co. by Roy Norton.
Pages 15–18.
One illustration in black and white.
> "Up with your hands or we'll make this a
> shambles, now that we've started." p 16

September 7
Hardpan & Co. by Roy Norton.
Pages 11–14.
One illustration in black and white.
> "Is there anything in this Coroner's investiga-
> tion we've got to be careful of?" he asked.
> p 11

Note: All Wyeth illustrated articles appearing in
The New York Tribune were also syndicated in *The
Philadelphia Press*.

The Philadelphia Inquirer
(Picture Parade Section)

1944

June 11
Cover illustration in color.
JOIN The Blood Donor Service TODAY
Description: Marines landing on Japanese-held
island during World War II.
(painting courtesy of Sharp & Dohme)

Philadelphia Public Ledger

1932

April 17
Washington in Dream Fights Battle, by N. C.
Wyeth.

St. Louis Post-Dispatch
(Rotogravure Picture Section)

1921

January 9   Sunday Morning
Stirring Scene in Missouri History Depicted by
Noted Artists—Eight of the Paintings Just Placed
in the State Capitol.
Two mural paintings by N. C. Wyeth.
Battle of Wilson's Creek, near Springfield, Mo.
Battle of Westport Landing

The Star
(Wilmington, Delaware)

1910

January 23
"Wilmington's Colony of Artists"
A Series of Interesting and Timely Articles

About the Many Popular Illustrators and Painters in This City and Vicinity.
No. 12
"N. C. Wyeth"
Photograph of N. C. Wyeth standing before his painting "The Contracting Engineer."

Note: The illustration originally appeared in *Scribner's Magazine*, September 1908, for the story "The Contracting Engineer" by Benjamin Brooks.

The Sunday Bulletin (Philadelphia)
(Magazine Section)

1966

July 3
"The Wyeth Who Doesn't Paint" Nathaniel, Member of a Family Famed in Art, Has Made his Own Brilliant Reputation as an Engineer by Pete Martin.
Pages 10–12.
Illustrated with photographs.
Nathaniel and grandson Andrew in front of N. C. Wyeth's painting, In a Dream I Meet General Washington.

Sunday Globe Magazine (Boston)

1921

"Wyeth, Noted Illustrator, Back in Needham Home by Joseph F. Dinneeen."
Pages 12 and 13.
Photograph of N. C. Wyeth.
Three illustrations in black and white.
Cavalry Charge, a 20-foot lunette in the Missouri State Capitol, depicting a critical moment in one of the great Civil War battles fought on Missouri soil.
Everybody in America Will Remember This Thrift Campaign Poster (Thanksgiving)
Raiders—one of Mr. Wyeth's striking paintings of Civil War Days

The Sunday Herald (Boston)
(Rotogravure Section)

1922

August 6
"N. C. Wyeth Completes His Historical Mural Paintings For New Boston Federal Reserve Bank"
Two mural paintings.
Abraham Lincoln and Salmon Chase.
Alexander Hamilton addressing George Washington and Robert Morris.

Washington Post

1926

May 9
Article on N. C. Wyeth.
One illustration in black and white.
The Duel on the Beach
A new oil painting by N. C. Wyeth, which is on view at the Mayflower Hotel. The painting was made for Carl G. Fisher of Miami Beach, Fla.

The World (New York)
(Color Gravure Section)

1926

September 26
The Half Moon in the Hudson—By N. C. Wyeth. Third of a Series of Famous Paintings Depicting Important Events in the History of the United States
One illustration in color by N. C. Wyeth.
The Half Moon in the Hudson

Note: The illustration originally appeared in black and white in *All Arts Magazine*, September 1925, for the article "N. C. Wyeth" by Isabel Hoopes.

IV. Prints and Portfolios

John Oxenham
Engraved and printed by The Beck Engraving Company, Philadelphia, Pennsylvania, 1965.
Print in color: print size 15³⁄₁₆ × 11¹³⁄₁₆ inches; picture size 12 × 8¹³⁄₁₆ inches.

Note: The illustration originally appeared in color in the book *Westward Ho!* by Charles Kingsley, published by Charles Scribner's Sons, New York, 1920. This print was distributed through the courtesy of the Beck Engraving Company, during the opening of the N. C. Wyeth exhibition in The William Penn Memorial Museum, Harrisburg, Pennsylvania, 1965.

Captain Bill Bones
Copyright 1971 by the Brandywine River Museum.
Print in color: print size 34¾ × 28 inches; picture size 29¾ × 24 inches.

Note: The print is duplicated as a poster in color advertising the Opening Show of the Brandywine River Museum. The illustration originally appeared in color in *Treasure Island,* published by Charles Scribner's Sons, New York, September 1911.

Where The Mail Goes Cream of Wheat Goes
Copyright 1907 by the Cream of Wheat Corporation.
Print in color: picture size 12⅝ × 9¼ inches.

Note: Cream of Wheat's most famous advertisement was used extensively in their advertising campaigns over the period of 1907–18.

Alaska
Copyright 1907 by the Cream of Wheat Corporation.
Print in color: print size 16 × 11 inches; picture size 14½ × 9⅛ inches.

Description: Trapper standing on sled, loaded with boxes of Cream of Wheat, defends his cargo against a pack of wolves.

Ethan Allen, Forerunner of Independence
(Ticonderoga, May 10, 1775)
Copyright 1934 by Joseph Dixon Crucible Company.
Print in color: published in two sizes:
Print size 13½ × 9½ inches; picture size 7⅛ × 9¼ inches.
Print size 31½ × 24 inches.

Lobstering Off Black Spruce Ledge
Copyright by Forbes Lithograph Manufacturing Co., Boston, 1944.
Print in color: print size 23½ × 27¼ inches; picture size 16 × 20½ inches.

Note: This is the second painting executed by Wyeth of almost identical content.

The Seeker
Copyright 1933 (1934) by Hercules Powder Company Incorporated.
Print in color: paper mount (light yellow with printed title and boxed rules) 21½ × 15⅞ inches; picture size 17 × 11⅝ inches.

Note: The illustration originally appeared on the Hercules Powder Company calendar for the year 1934.

New Trails
Copyright 1935 by Hercules Powder Company.
Print in color: paper mount (light brown with printed title) 20⅞ × 15 inches; picture size 16⅞ × 11⅜ inches.

Note: The illustration originally appeared on the Hercules Powder Company calendar for the year 1935.

The Alchemist
Copyright 1938 by Hercules Powder Company Incorporated.
Print in color: print size (with title and border rules) 20 × 13 inches; picture size 16⅞ × 11½ inches.

Note: The illustration originally appeared on the Hercules Powder Company calendar for the year 1938.

A New World
Copyright 1939 by Hercules Powder Company Incorporated.
Print in color: print size (with border rules) 17¾ × 12⁷⁄₁₆ inches; picture size 16⅞ × 11½ inches.

Note: The illustration originally appeared on the Hercules Powder Company calendar for the year 1939.

Pioneers
Copyright 1940 by Hercules Powder Company Incorporated.
Print in color: cardboard mount (with title and boxed rules) 19¾ × 14 inches; picture size 16⅞ × 11½ inches.

Note: The illustration originally appeared on the Hercules Powder Company calendar for the year 1940.

Primal Chemistry
Copyright 1942 by Hercules Powder Company Incorporated.
Print in color: paper mount (with title and boxed rules printed in green) 19¾ × 13⅞ inches; print size 17¾ × 11¼ inches.

Note: The illustration originally appeared on the Hercules Powder Company calendar for the year 1942.

Alaskan Mail Carrier (Wall Hanger)
Published by The Adsply Factors, Inc.
Print in color: print size (with floral clay model border) 20 × 15 inches; picture size (with black and red borders) 14¾ × 11⅝ inches.
Descriptive text for the Alaskan Mail Carrier appears at the bottom left corner.
This picture represents an incident in the life of an Alaskan mail carrier, Henderson, who it is now claimed was the first to really locate that great mining district that caused what is known as the "Klondike Stampede." He never realized a cent for his discovery, and for some time packed mail for the government from Nome across the hills some forty miles to a series of mining camps. In this way he was able to eke out a living. The story of a particularly terrific fight he once had with a pack of wolves is told by many that knew of his wonderful shooting ability—all but two of the wolves he killed and they finally slunk away, leaving him a victor on the frozen lake.

Note: The illustration is reproduced in reverse from the original painting commissioned by International Harvester Co. of America. It originally appeared as a poster in color published for Champion Harvesting Machines, a Division of International Harvester Co. of America in 1909.

Sweet Land of Liberty
Copyright 1944 by Hercules Powder Company Incorporated.
Print in color: picture size 18⅛ × 13 inches.

Note: The illustration originally appeared on the Hercules Powder Company calendar for the year 1944.

The Spirit of '46
Copyright 1945 (1946) by Hercules Powder Company Incorporated.
Print in color: paper mount with title (red) and pictorial decoration (Spirit of '76 in green) 24 × 17 inches; picture size 19¹⁄₁₆ × 13 inches.

Note: The illustration originally appeared on the Hercules Powder Company calendar for the year 1946. In addition, it was published as a poster.

The Island Funeral
Print in color: print size 30½ × 35 inches; picture size 26⅝ × 31 inches.
The print is contained in a gold cardboard frame. It is accompanied by a descriptive folder which reproduces the painting in black and white on the cover. The painting is owned by the Hotel DuPont in Wilmington, Delaware, and is displayed in the Christiana Room.

(Roping a Runaway Bronc)
Copyright 1904 by Edgar S. Nash.
Print in black and white with tint: board mount

16¾ × 21⅝ inches; picture size 12½ × 17⅜ inches.

Note: To my knowledge, this is the earliest known print of a work by N. C. Wyeth and was probably painted about 1903. The print was untitled but is described above.

The Discoverer

First of a series of five murals—The Romance of Discovery—painted for the National Geographic Society Headquarters in Washington, D.C.
Copyright 1928 by the National Geographic Society.
Supplement insert for the *National Geographic Magazine*, March 1928.
The Discoverer
Urged ever onward by the Quest of the Unknown, the Dauntless Leader, symbolic of Man's age-old struggle to Master the Earth, has Braved the Sea, Conquered the Desert, Pierced the Jungle, Scaled the Mount. At last his tired eyes behold the Goal of his Dream. It is his gift to World Knowledge.
Print in color: print size 10 × 32 inches; picture size 8 x 30 inches.
The print was also advertised and sold individually through the National Geographic Society. The print size remained the same except for a tan border added to enhance the presentation. Print size 12½ × 34 inches; tan border 11½ × 33 inches; picture size 8 × 30 inches.

Through Pathless Skies to the North Pole

Second of a series of five murals—The Romance of Discovery—painted for the National Geographic Society Headquarters in Washington, D.C.
Copyright 1928 by the National Geographic Society.
Supplement insert for the *National Geographic Magazine*, May 1928.
Through Pathless Skies to the North Pole
Under the golden glow of a midnight sun, the valiant Byrd, employing Geography's newest ally in exploration, is the first to reach, with winged speed, that goal which his compatriot, the intrepid Peary, had won, foot by foot.
Print in color: print size 9½ × 13¼ inches; picture size 8 × 11¾ inches.
The print was also advertised and sold individually through the National Geographic Society. The print size remained the same except for a tan border added to enhance the presentation. Print size 12⅜ × 16 inches; tan border 11¼ × 15 inches; picture size 8 × 11¾ inches.

Beyond Uncharted Seas Columbus Find a New World

Third of a series of five murals—The Romance of Discovery—painted for the National Geographic Society Headquarters in Washington, D.C.
Copyright 1928 by the National Geographic Society.
Supplement insert for the *National Geographic Magazine*, July 1928.
Beyond Uncharted Seas Columbus Finds a New World.
Into the setting sun, conquering tempest, mutiny and terrors of the unknown, the Great Admiral steers his tiny caravels to give civilization a new hemisphere—and gain fame everlasting.
Print in color: print size 9½ × 13⅛ inches; picture size 8 × 11¾ inches.
The print was also advertised and sold individually through the National Geographic Society. The print size remained the same except for a tan border added to enhance the presentation. Print size 12⅜ × 16 inches; tan border 11¼ × 15 inches; picture size 8 × 11¾ inches.

Map of Discovery: Eastern Hemisphere

Fourth of a series of five murals—The Romance of Discovery—painted for the National Geographic Society Headquarters in Washington, D.C.
Copyright 1928 by the National Geographic Society.
Supplement insert for the *National Geographic Magazine*, November 1928.
Map of Discovery: Eastern Hemisphere
While simulating the illuminated mariners' charts of the Sixteenth Century, which pictorially dramatized the deeds of dauntless explorers, this map of the Eastern Hemisphere records present-day political boundaries. It also traces the routes of the great discoverers who sailed strange seas and penetrated misty continents to add new areas to the known world.
Print in color: print size 16¾ × 18⅝ inches; picture size 15⅞ × 18⅛ inches.

Map of Discovery: Western Hemisphere

Fifth of a series of five murals—The Romance of Discovery—painted for the National Geographic Society Headquarters in Washington, D.C.
Copyright 1928 by the National Geographic Society.
Supplement insert for the *National Geographic Magazine*, January 1929.
Map of Discovery: Western Hemisphere
Painted in quaint Sixteenth Century style, this chart of the Western Hemisphere suggests the imagination that launched intrepid explorers to the ends of the earth, yet records accurately the boundaries of to-day. On it are traced the paths, plowed through virgin seas and blazed across unknown continents, that gave to man a realization of the true magnitude of his world.
Print in color: print size 16¾ × 18⅝ inches; picture size 15⅞ × 18 inches.

The Star Spangled Banner

Copyright 1941 by New York Life Insurance Company.
Lithographed by Ketterlinus.
Print in color: print size 20½ × 17⅞ inches; picture size 14⅜ × 12¼ inches.
The Star Spangled Banner
Francis Scott Key writing the immortal verses which became our National Anthem.

Note: The illustration was reproduced as a calendar in color for the New York Life Insurance Co., 1941.

The Solitude Series

Copyright 1907 by The Outing Publishing Company.
A portfolio of five prints in color, boxed: board mounts with printed titles and quotations 20 × 15 inches; print size 16⅝ × 11½ inches; picture size 16 1/16 × 10 15/16 inches.
The Hunter
The Magic Pool
The Spearman
In the Crystal Depths
The Silent Burial

Note: The paintings originally appeared in color in *The Outing Magazine*, June 1907, for "The Indian in His Solitude." The paintings soon after appeared as a series (set) of prints and was advertised extensively in *The Outing Magazine* for a number of years.

A Fighting Chance

Copyright by W. M. Sanford.
Published by The Knapp Co., N.Y.
Mounted print in color: board mount 12¼ × 14⅞ inches; print size 11½ × 14⅞ inches.

The Moose Call

Copyright 1906 by Charles Scribner's Sons, New York.
Print in black and white with tint: board mount 20 × 14 inches; print size 15⅝ × 11 inches; picture size 14⅛ × 10 inches.

Note: The illustration also appeared in black and white in *Scribner's Magazine*, October 1906.

Cow-Punchers by N. C. Wyeth

Copyright 1906 by Charles Scribner's Sons, New York.
Two prints in color: board mounts 20 × 15⅞ inches; picture size 14¾ × 10 inches.
Bucking
Racing for Dinner

Note: The illustrations originally appeared in color and black and white in *Scribner's Magazine*, March 1906, for the article "A Day with the Round-Up" by N. C. Wyeth.

The Admirable Outlaw

Copyright 1906 by Charles Scribner's Sons, New York.
Print in brown, black and white; board mount 22½ × 15 inches; print size 18 5/16 × 11 5/16 inches.

Note: The print originally appeared as an illustration in black and white in *Scribner's Magazine*, November 1906, for the story "The Admirable Outlaw" by M'Cready Sykes. It was titled "My English Friend Thought it Was a Hold-up."

The Smugglers

Copyright 1970 by Charles Scribner's Sons, New York.
Print in brown, black and white: print size 17⅛ × 11 3/16 inches.

Note: The print originally appeared as an illustration in black and white in *Scribner's Magazine*, April 1907, for the story "The Smugglers" by James B. Connolly. It was titled "There was no such monstrous lock as that last night, Ollie?"

The Lone Fisherman

Copyright 1907 by Charles Scribner's Sons, N. Y.
Print in black and white with green tint; print size 12⅞ × 10 13/16 inches; picture size 11 11/16 × 9⅞ inches.

Note: The print originally appeared as a frontispiece in color in *Scribner's Magazine*, October 1907, and was titled "The Silent Fisherman."

Little Rivers

Autographed by the artist, N. C. Wyeth.
Copyright 1920 by Charles Scribner's Sons, New York.
Print in brown, black and white: print size 14 × 11 inches.
Description: Every river that flows is good, and has something worthy to be loved.

Note: The illustration appeared as a frontispiece in *Little Rivers* (Avalon Edition) by Henry Van Dyke, published by Charles Scribner's Sons, N.Y., 1920. The print was given to those purchasing the Van Dyke Avalon Editions.

The Spirit of Education

Silver, Burdett and Company 1885–1935
Print in color: print size 20½ × 25 inches.
The print is accompanied by a descriptive folder, "The Spirit Of Education, An Interview with the Artist, Newell C. Wyeth."

Note: The mural painting The Spirit of Education adorns the entrance lobby walls of the Silver, Burdett Publishing Company, Morristown, New Jersey.

Portfolio of Prints

PICTURES / By / Prominent Artists / (ornament) / Courtesy of / Harper and Brothers / Charles Scribner's Sons / The American Magazine / The Century Company / Seventy Pictures / by / (list of artists) / (ornament) / Selected By / Frank R. Southhard / for the / Ex-Service Men, Students / of the / Commercal Art Courses (red) / of the / Extension Division / United Y.M.C.A. Schools / J. Foster Hill, Director / (emblem) / 1921 (title also printed in red)

Folio. Boards with cloth spine (blue).

Print size 12¾ × 9¾ inches.

Seventy plates in black and white.

Plate 50 and 51 by N. C. Wyeth.

> I planted the layout and "camped" out through the transom. I could see them at the head of the stairs, hammering on Kelly's door, and every man had his gun out. (Plate 50)

> Mac's wife and child hear the news (Plate 51)

Note: The illustrations originally appeared in *The American Magazine*, July 1914, for *Boston Blackie Stories*, "The Price of Principles" by No. 6606.

The Apotheosis of the Family

Mural painting Unveiled on the One Hundreth Anniversary of Wilmington Savings Fund Society.

With description of the mural and biographical summary of the artist.

Print in color: print size 11½ × 20⅛ inches; picture size 5 × 18 inches (all enclosed in double box and border rules).

The Apotheosis of the Family

With description of the mural and biographical summary of the artist. (detachable)

Print in color: print size 6⅞ × 26 inches; picture size 5 × 18 inches.

(Hunting the Grizzly)

Copyright by Winchester Repeating Arms Co. (1912)

Print in color: print size 16¾ × 13⅝ inches.

Description: Theodore Roosevelt and hunting companion confronting grizzly bear on rocky ridge.

Note: The illustration was reproduced as a calendar in color for Winchester Repeating Arms Co., New Haven, Conn.

V. Posters

American Red Cross poster, World War I (1918)
Poster in color.
Description: Medic supporting wounded soldier on battlefield with infantry advancing in the background.

1933 American Red Cross Fund
Poster in color: poster size 18¾ × 15 inches.
Description: Unfurled Red Cross flags with clouds in background.

Note: This poster was again used in the 1953 Red Cross Fund Drive.

Answer the Call! • 1953 Red Cross Fund
Poster in color: poster size 18¾ × 15 inches; picture size 18¼ × 14½ inches.
Description: Unfurled Red Cross flags with clouds in background.

Note: The illustration was originally commissioned by The American Red Cross for their advertising campaign of 1933.

Bank Holiday Poster
Published by the Canterbury Company, Inc., Chicago, Illinois.
Copyright 1921 by Charles Daniel Frey Company, New York and Chicago.
Poster in color; published in two sizes:
    Poster size 35⅛ × 21 inches; picture size 34 × 20 inches.
    Poster size 17 × 11½ inches; picture size 14¾ × 10 inches.
New Year's Day
Description: Medieval revelers welcoming the New Year as the old year "Father Time" passes.

Bank Holiday Poster
Published by the Canterbury Company, Inc., Chicago, Illinois.
Copyright 1921 by Charles Daniel Frey Company, New York and Chicago.
Poster in color; published in two sizes:
    Poster size 35⅛ × 21 inches; picture size 34 × 20 inches.
    Poster size 17 × 11½ inches; picture size 14¾ × 10 inches.
Independence Day
Description: The minutemen at Concord Bridge.

Note: The illustration appears as a cover in color for *American History Illustrated Magazine*, June 1967.

Bank Holiday Poster
Published by the Canterbury Company, Inc., Chicago, Illinois.
Copyright 1921 by Charles Daniel Frey Company, New York and Chicago.

Poster in color; published in two sizes:
    Poster size 35⅛ × 21 inches; picture size 34 × 20 inches.
    Poster size 17 × 11½ inches; picture size 14¾ × 10 inches.
Thanksgiving Day
Description: A pilgrim family give a Thanksgiving prayer.

Bank Holiday Poster
Published by the Canterbury Company, Inc., Chicago, Illinois.
Copyright 1921 by Charles Daniel Frey Company, New York and Chicago.
Poster in color; published in two sizes:
    Poster size 35⅛ × 21 inches; picture size 34 × 20 inches.
    Poster size 17 × 11½ inches; picture size 14¾ × 10 inches.
Christmas
Description: Santa Claus on a rooftop about to climb down the chimney.

Brandywine River Museum
Opening Show June 19th, 1971 Chadds Ford, Pennsylvania
N. C. Wyeth, Andrew Wyeth, James Wyeth, Howard Pyle & Students
Copyright 1971 by the Brandywine River Museum.
Printed by the Triton Press Inc., N.Y.C.
Poster in color: poster size 40⅛ × 26 inches; picture size 29¾ × 24 inches.
    Description: Captain Bill Bones

Note: The illustration originally appeared in color in *Treasure Island* by Robert Louis Stevenson, published by Charles Scribner's Sons, N.Y., 1911.

Children's Museum of Art at Carnegie Institute.
Poster with tipped-on color illustration: poster size 20 × 14 inches.
Description: The castaways await the lifting of the fog.

Note: The illustration originally appeared in color in *The Mysterious Island* by Jules Verne, published by Charles Scribner's Sons, New York, October 1918.

Children's Museum of Art at Carnegie Institute.
Poster with tipped-on color illustration: poster size 20 × 14 inches.
Description: "Go, Dutton, and that right speedily," he added. "Follow that lad."

Note: The illustration originally appeared in color in *The Black Arrow* by Robert Louis Stevenson, published by Charles Scribner's Sons, New York, October 1916.

Lumber
Advertising Poster for The Coca-Cola Company.
Copyright MCMXLIII (1943) by The Coca-Cola Company.
Poster in color: poster size 16 × 11 inches; picture size 14⅜ × 9¹³⁄₁₆ inches.
Description: Lumberjacks cutting and sawing timber in winter.

Educational Poster:
Our America • Transportation
Number 1 (Chart for First Week) Bridges the Oceans and Spans the Land—The Development of Transportation
Distributed by The Coca-Cola Bottling Company.
Copyright MCMXLIII by The Coca-Cola Company.
Poster in color (fold out): poster size 22 × 32 inches.
A New World in View
Description: The three vessels of Columbus.

Note: A number of small inset sketches are found on the right and left borders of the Wyeth illustration depicting different forms of transportation.

Educational Poster:
Our America • Lumber
Number II (Chart for Second Week) Distribution . . . From Raw Material To Workable Product—The Transporting and Preparing of Lumber
Distributed by The Coca-Cola Bottling Company.
Copyright MCMXLIII by The Coca-Cola Company.
Poster in color (fold out): poster size 22 × 32 inches.
Breaking a Log Jam

Note: A number of small inset sketches are found on the right and left borders of the Wyeth illustration depicting the development and distribution of paper.

The Cream of Wheat Corporation, Minneapolis, Minnesota.
Easel supports designed by The J. D. Lewis Company, First National Bank Building—Chicago
Display poster in color; poster size 34 × 23 inches; picture size 29½ × 20⅛ inches.
The poster is designed with wooden supports, which, when fitted, form an easel displaying the full poster. It also has a small loop at top for hanging.
Illustration in color.
Where The Mail Goes CREAM OF WHEAT Goes

N. C. WYETH, N. A. / MEMORIAL EXHI-
BITION / (Illustration in color) / JANUARY
8 to JANUARY 27 / Week Days 10–5 Sundays
/ 2–6 Admission Free / DELAWARE ART
CENTER / Park Drive and Woodlawn Avenue
/ Take No. 10 Bus to Woodlawn Avenue Walk
North to Park Drive
Published 1946
Poster in color: poster size 14 × 11 inches.
Mounted illustration in color.
Description: The Hostage (illustration from
Treasure Island)

Advertising Poster for the book *The Lost Boy*
by Henry Van Dyke.
Harper & Brothers, New York
Poster in colors (yellow, blue, black and white):
poster size 21 × 14⅜ inches; picture size
19½ × 13¾ inches.
Description: "Come, Live With Us, For I
Think Thou Art Chosen."

Note: The illustration originally appeared in color
in *Harper's Monthly Magazine*, December 1913,
for the story "The Lost Boy" by Henry Van Dyke.

The Spirit of '46
Copyright 1945 (1946) by Hercules Powder
Company Incorporated.
Poster in color: poster size 44 × 27½ inches;
picture size 37 × 25¾ inches.

Note: The illustration originally appeared on the
Hercules Powder Company calendar for the year
1946. In addition, it was published as a print.

Christopher Columbus
The Distillers of Canadian Club—Hiram Walker
Inc., 1942.
Display by Ketterlinus Lithographic Mfg. Co.
Display poster in color: poster size 44 × 35
inches; picture size 26¼ × 23¼ inches.
Description: Columbus sights the New World.
Surrounding the painting is an ornate frame,
draped in the ancient flag of Ferdinand and
Isabella of Spain. The ornamental banner above
the painting displays the dates 1492–1942.

Note: The illustration commemorates the 450th
anniversary of the discovery of America by Christopher Columbus (1492–1942).

Advertising Poster for the book *Pike County
Ballads* by John Hay (Houghton Mifflin Com-
pany)
Poster in colors (blue, black and white): poster
size 22 × 14 inches.
Description: The carpetbaggers

Note: The illustration appeared as the endpapers
in *Pike County Ballads* by John Hay, published
by Houghton Mifflin Company, Boston, October
1912.

Advertising Poster for the book *Captain Blood*
by Rafael Sabatini (Houghton Mifflin Company)
Poster in color: poster size 20 × 14 inches;
picture size 8½ × 8⅞ inches.
Description: Captain Blood

Note: The poster illustration originally appeared as
a frontispiece in color in *Captain Blood* by Rafael
Sabatini, published by Houghton Mifflin Company,
Boston, 1922.

Alaskan Mail Carrier
Advertising Poster for Champion Harvesting
Machines.
Copyright 1909 by International Harvester Co.
of America.
Poster in color: poster size 15¼ × 12 inches.

Description: An Alaskan mail carrier, having
fought off an attack by wolves, stands amidst
the dead animals with a smoking revolver.

Note: The Alaskan Mail Carrier is also reproduced
as a wall hanging display.

Advertising Poster (banner):
Christmas in Old Virginia
Copyright by the Interwoven Stocking Com-
pany.
Printed by the Sweeney Lith. Co., Belleville,
N.J.
Poster in color, printed on cloth: poster size
20½ × 60 inches; picture size 15½ × 60
inches; brass eyelets for hanging.
Printed below illustration: Interwoven Socks
For Christmas
Description: President and Mrs. George Wash-
ington greeting the arrival of the Christmas tree
and holiday guests at Mt. Vernon, Virginia.

Note: The illustration appears in color in the
Seventh Annual of Advertising Art, published by
The Book Service Company, 1928, for the Art
Directors Club of New York.

Advertising Poster (banner):
The Christmas Ship In Old New York
Copyright by the Interwoven Stocking Com-
pany.
Printed by the Sweeney Lith., Co., Belleville,
N.J.
Poster in color, printed on cloth: poster size
20½ × 60 inches; brass eyelets for hanging.
Description: Seventeenth Century New Amster-
dam settlers grouped about the snow-covered
harbor welcoming seamen unloading a ship.

Note: The illustration appears in color in the
Eighth Annual of Advertising Art, published by
The Book Service Company, 1929, for the Art
Directors Club of New York.

Advertising Poster for Ketterlinus Co., Philadelphia, New York, Chicago, Boston.
America Must Go Forward
Description: George Washington on horseback
followed by his army bearing battle flags.
Poster in color: poster size 24 × 17¾ inches;
picture size (mounted) 13¾ × 12¼ inches.

Note: The illustration also appears on a poster in
color published for Strawbridge & Clothier by Ketterlinus Co. to commemorate the 200th Anniversary of the birth of George Washington.

Poster (Giant)
Third Liberty Loan Drive (1918)
A collaboration of the artists N. C. Wyeth and
Henry Reuterdahl.
Poster in color: poster size 25 × 90 feet.
Description: American troops going over the
top (*left half section by N. C. Wyeth*)
The War at Sea (*right half section by Henry
Reuterdahl*)
Displayed on the front of the Sub-Treasury Build-
ing, N.Y., N.Y. during April 1918.

Advertising Poster for the book *Arizona Nights*
by Stewart Edward White.
Published by The McClure Company, New
York.
Poster in colors (orange, brown, black and
white): poster size 17⁵⁄₁₆ × 13¼ inches; pic-
ture size 14¹⁵⁄₁₆ × 11⅛ inches.
Description: "An Almighty Exciting Race."

Note: The illustration originally appeared as a
frontispiece in color in *McClure's Magazine*, March
1906, for the story "Arizona Nights" by Stewart
Edward White.

Advertising Poster for *McClure's Magazine*.
Copyright 1906 by The S. S. McClure Co.
Poster in brown tint; poster size 18 × 12 inches.
Description: Indian chief on pony with hand
raised in a sign of friendship.

Note: The illustration appeared as a cover in color
for *McClure's Magazine*, November 1906.

Advertising Poster for the book *Beth Norvell* A
Splendid New Romance of the West by Randall
Parrish.
A. C. McClurg & Co. Publishers.
Poster in colors (orange, green, black and
white): poster size 20½ × 14½ inches; picture
size 20 × 14 inches.
Description: Portion of cover design—Beth Nor-
vell.

Romance, History, Travel
Copyright 1928 by the National Association of
Book Publishers.
Poster in color: poster size 15 × 12 inches.
Description: Seventeenth century adventurer on
deck of ship, with heavy seas and galleon in
background.

Note: The illustration appeared in a number of
periodicals in 1927–28. In addition, it was published as a mailing card.

Historic Pageant of Needham
Printed under the auspices of The New Century
Club to be held November 5th and 6th, 1911.
Poster (charcoal drawing) in brown tint; poster
size 17⅞ × 14 inches.
Description: Drawing of Indian chief "Nehoi-
den" with decorative banners above and below
containing printed information.

Pennsylvania Railroad Patriotic Posters No. 1
Copyright 1930 by the Pennsylvania Railroad,
Philadelphia.
Poster in color: poster size 41 × 17 inches;
picture size 30½ × 25 inches.
Ringing Out Liberty
    July 8, 1776, Philadelphia
    Home City of the Pennsylvania Railroad

Note: The poster is also reproduced as a calendar
in color for The Forbes Lithograph Mfg. Co.,
Boston, 1932. It also appears in color in the book
The Technique of the Poster by Leonard Richmond, published by Sir Isaac Pitman & Son, Ltd,
1933. In addition, it appears in black and white
in the book *A Basic History of the United States*
by Charles A. and Mary R. Beard, published by
Doubleday, Doran & Co., New York, 1944.

Pennsylvania Railroad Patriotic Posters No. 2
Copyright 1930 by the Pennsylvania Railroad,
Philadelphia.
Poster in color: poster size 41 × 27 inches;
picture size 30½ × 25 inches.
In Old Kentucky
Modern Kentucky
    Is Served By The Pennsylvania Railroad

Note: The poster is reproduced as a calendar in
color for The Forbes Lithograph Mfg. Co., Boston,
1932.

Pennsylvania Railroad Patriotic Posters No. 3
Copyright 1930 by the Pennsylvania Railroad,
Philadelphia.
Poster in color: poster size 41 × 27 inches;
picture size 30½ × 25 inches.
Pittsburgh in the Beginning
    Fort Prince George
    Established February 17, 1754

Modern Pittsburgh
      Is Served By The PENNSYLVANIA RAIL-
      ROAD

Note: The poster is reproduced as a calendar in color for The Forbes Lithograph Mfg. Co., Boston, 1932.

Pennsylvania Railroad Patriotic Posters No. 4
Copyright 1930 by the Pennsylvania Railroad, Philadelphia.
Poster in color: poster size 41 × 27 inches; picture size 30½ × 25 inches.
Building the First White House
Washington, D.C. 1798

Note: The poster is reproduced as a calendar in color for The Forbes Lithograph Mfg. Co., Boston, 1932. In addition, it appears in color in the *National Geographic Magazine,* November 1966.

Advertising Poster for the book *Whispering Smith* by Frank H. Spearman.
Copyright 1906 by Charles Scribner's Sons, N.Y.
Poster in color: poster size 22¾ × 14¾ inches.
Description: Following the trail itself, Whispering Smith rode slowly.

Note: The poster illustration originally appeared as a frontispiece in color in *Whispering Smith* by Frank H. Spearman, published by Charles Scribner's Sons, New York, September 1906.

Display Poster
Copyright 1944 by E. R. Squibb & Sons.
Poster in color.
Description: Doctor and nurse standing at bedside of patient administering blood plasma.

Display Poster
Copyright 1944 by E. R. Squibb & Sons.
Poster in color.
Description: Marines landing on Japanese-held island. Figure in foreground supports a wounded comrade.

Display Poster
Copyright 1944 by E. R. Squibb & Sons.
Poster in color.
Description: Wounded soldier on stretcher being administered blood plasma. Beach with jungle growth in background.

Display Poster: Public Health and Morale
Copyright 1944 by E. R. Squibb & Sons.
Poster in color: poster size 34 × 26 inches.
Description: Family group (father, mother, son, and daughter) with factories in background and aircraft overhead.

Display Poster: The American Mother
Copyright 1945 by E. R. Squibb & Sons.
Poster in color: poster size 41⅛ × 30 inches.
Description: Mother weighing her child on scale.

In commemoration of the 200th Anniversary of the birth of George Washington.
George Washington (1732–1932)
Whose magnificent achievements in spite of pessimism and indifference should ever prove an inspiration to American courage and confidence
Published for Strawbridge & Clothier by Ketterlinus Co.

Poster in color: poster size 21 × 17 inches; picture size 14½ × 12⅜ inches.

Note: The illustration also appears as a mounted advertising poster in color for Ketterlinus Co., Philadelphia. In addition, the illustration was reproduced as a calendar for the New York Life Insurance Co., 1940.

Buy War Bonds
Published by the U.S. Government Printing Office, 1942.
Poster in color published in two sizes: poster size 14 × 11 inches, 28 × 22 inches; picture size 12½ × 11 inches.

Description: Uncle Sam carrying American flag directing troops to battle as Air Force planes fly overhead.

United States Naval Department (1917)
Poster in color.
Neptune

Note: References to N. C. Wyeth painting a 6′ × 9′ poster illustration of Neptune are recorded, but the compiler has been unable to locate the work.

Exhibition Poster (Wilmington Savings Fund Society)
Poster in black and white: poster size 12 × 17½ inches; photograph size 5 × 6⅜ inches.
Tribute to N. C. Wyeth October 21–November 1 (1968)
      Paintings by the Famed Artist-Illustrator, from Private Collections, Many to be Shown Publicly for the First Time
Photograph of Newell Convers Wyeth at his easel.

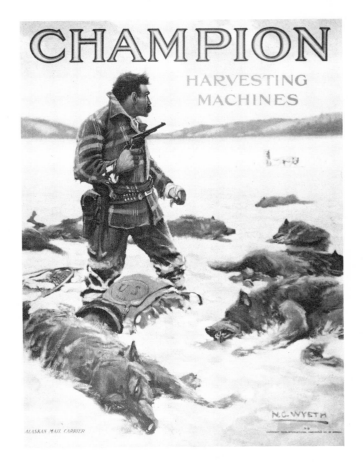

VI. Calendars

Berwind-White Coal Mining Company
Designed, Engraved and Printed By The Beck Engraving Co., New York Philadelphia Chicago
Copyright 1922 (1923) by The Beck Engraving Co.
Calendar in color: calendar size 12⅜ × 10 inches; picture size (cover design) 9⅞ × 8 inches; picture size 8¼ × 8 inches (other plates)
Cover design in color.
Description: An imaginary sea creature with flying fish.
Four illustrations in color.
The Viking Ship
The Ships of Columbus
The Golden Galleon
The Conquerer

"Spring Plowing For The Allies"
Copyright 1943 by Brown & Bigelow.
Calendar in color: picture size 6¼ × 4⅝ inches.
Description: Tractors plowing fields with Allied flags unfurled in clouds above.

Lift Up Your Hearts
Copyright 1943 by Brown & Bigelow
Calendar in color; published in two sizes:
    Calendar size 33 × 16 inches; picture size 18 × 13½ inches.
    Calendar size 20 × 10½ inches; picture size 11 × 8¼ inches.
Description: Elderly couple standing near picket fence looking at a rainbow.

Calendar: A Soldier's Return
Copyright 1944 by Brown & Bigelow
Calendar in color.

"Give Us This Day"
Copyright 1944 by Brown & Bigelow.
Calendar in color: calendar size 30 × 16 inches; picture size 14 × 14 inches.
Description: View of the cornfields of Pennsylvania during the fall harvest. A large bank barn stands in the middle distance.

Note: Reproduced from the painting titled Corn Harvest.

"Time and Tide . . ."
Copyright 1944 by Brown & Bigelow.
Calendar in color: calendar size 16½ × 19 inches; picture size 13⁵⁄₁₆ × 16⅞ inches.

Note: Reproduced from the painting titled Lobstering Off Black Spruce Ledge.

Our Emblem
Copyright 1944 by Brown & Bigelow
Calendar in color; published in two sizes:
    Calendar size 33½ × 16 inches; picture size 17¼ × 13½ inches.
    Calendar size 19½ × 10 inches; picture size 10½ × 7⅞ inches.
Description: Bald eagle flying over country village.

Coca-Cola 50th Anniversary 1886–1936
Calendar in color: calendar size 25 × 12 inches; picture size 16¾ × 11 inches.
Description: Old lobsterman, leaning against dory, and young girl drinking Cokes. Ocean background.

Copyright 1937 by Coca-Cola Company.
Calendar in color: calendar size 24¾ × 12 inches; picture size 16½ × 11 inches.
Description: Boy, carrying two Cokes, going fishing with his dog.

GENERAL ELECTRIC COMPANY • Mazda Lamp • Nela Park, Cleveland, Ohio — Sales Promotion Department, 1935.
Copyright General Electric Company, 1934.
Calendar size 19⅛ × 8½ inches; picture size 18½ × 7½ inches (including border design)
One illustration in color.
The Carvers of the Sphinx

GENERAL ELECTRIC COMPANY • Mazda Lamp • Nela Park, Cleveland, Ohio — Sales Promotion Department, 1936.
Copyright General Electric Company, 1935.
Calendar size 19⅛ × 8½ inches; picture size 18½ × 7½ inches (including border designs)
One illustration in color.
The Torch Race
    The Grecian Olympics of 1000 B.C.

The Three Hunters
Copyright 1933 by Hercules Powder Company.
Calendar in color: calendar size 30 × 13 inches; picture size 17 × 11½ inches.

Note: The illustration was reproduced as a print in color by Hercules Powder Company in 1933.

The Seeker
Copyright 1934 by Hercules Powder Company Incorporated.
Calendar in color: calendar size 30 × 13 inches; picture size 17 × 11¾ inches.

Note: The illustration was reproduced as a print in color by Hercules Powder Company in 1933 (1934).

New Trails
Copyright 1934 (1935) by Hercules Powder Company.
Calendar in color: calendar size 30 × 13 inches; picture size 17 × 11¾ inches.

Note: The illustration was reproduced as a print in color by Hercules Powder Company in 1935.

The Alchemist
Copyright 1937 by Hercules Powder Company Incorporated.
Calendar in color: calendar size 30 × 13 inches; picture size 16¾ × 11½ inches. (mounted on gray green paper)

Note: The illustration was reproduced as a print in color by Hercules Powder Company in 1937.

A New World
Copyright 1939 by Hercules Powder Company Incorporated.
Calendar in color: calendar size 30 × 13 inches; picture size 16⅞ × 11½ inches.

Note: The illustration was reproduced as a print in color by Hercules Powder Company in 1939.

Pioneers
Copyright 1940 by Hercules Powder Company Incorporated.
Calendar in color: calendar size 30 × 13 inches; picture size 16⅞ × 11½ inches.

Note: The illustration was reproduced as a print in color by Hercules Powder Company in 1940.

Primal Chemistry
Copyright 1942 by Hercules Powder Company Incorporated.
Calendar in color: calendar size 30 × 13 inches; picture size 17¾ × 11¼ inches.

Note: The illustration was reproduced as a print in color by the Hercules Powder Company in 1942.

Sweet Land of Liberty
Copyright 1944 by Hercules Powder Company Incorporated.
Calendar in color: calendar size 30 × 13 inches; picture size 18½ × 13 inches.

Note: The illustration was reproduced as a calendar in color by the Hercules Powder Company in 1944.

The Spirit of '46
Copyright 1946 by Hercules Powder Company Incorporated.
Calendar in color: calendar size 30 × 13 inches; picture size 18¾ × 13 inches.

Note: The illustration was reproduced as a print in color by Hercules Powder Company in 1945 (1946).

Seeking the New Home

Fire Insurance Company (undetermined)
Calendar in color: picture size 6 × 8¼ inches.
Description: Pioneer family cooking the evening meal by a campfire. Father stands guard near covered wagon in the background.

Winter at Valley Forge

Fire Insurance Company (undetermined)
Calendar in color: picture size 6 × 8¼ inches.
Description: General Washington and his troops singing around campfire.

The Forbes Lithograph Mfg. Co., Boston, 1932.
Calendar in color: calendar size 25½ × 15 inches; picture size with scroll design 19½ × 14¼ inches.
The paintings are reproduced through the courtesy of the Pennsylvania Railroad.
Four illustrations in color.
Ringing Out Liberty
In Old Kentucky
Pittsburgh in the Beginning, Fort Prince George —Established February 17, 1754
Building the First White House, Washington, D.C. 1798
Accompanying the calendar are descriptions of the paintings and a brief biographical sketch on N. C. Wyeth.

Note: The illustrations were originally painted as a series of four patriotic posters for the Pennsylvania Railroad.

The World's First Reaper

Public Test of Cyrus Hall McCormick's Invention
Steele's Tavern, Virginia, July 1831.
Copyright 1931 by International Harvester Company.
Calendar in color: calendar size 22½ × 13¾ inches; picture size 12⅜ × 12⅝ inches.

Note: The illustration was painted for International Harvester Co. in commemoration of the 100th Anniversary of the McCormick Reaper.

The Magic Pool

"Unkahee, The God of Water"
From *The Song of Hiawatha*
Calendar in color: picture size 10⅞ × 16 inches.

Note: The illustration originally appeared in color in *The Outing Magazine,* June 1907, as one of the series "The Indian in His Solitude."

Twelve Artists Depict America
John Morrell & Company, Ottumwa, Iowa, 1939.
Calendar in color: picture size 7⅞ × 7 inches.
One illustration in color by N. C. Wyeth.
The Homesteaders (April)
Description: A homesteader pauses for a drink during the day's plowing. His wife, holding their young child and a water jug, stands nearby.

America in the Making

John Morrell & Company, Ottumwa, Iowa, 1940.
Copyright 1939 by John Morrell & Co.
Printed by Ketterlinus Litho Mfg. Co., Phila. and Chicago.
Published in two sizes:
Calendar size 30½ × 14 inches; picture size 14 × 12¾ inches.
Calendar size 17¾ × 8¼ inches; picture size 10⅛ × 7⅞ inches.

Twelve illustrations in color.
January	Francisco Vasquez De Coronado[1][2][3]
February	The Mayflower Compact[1]
March	Jacques Marquette
April	Benjamin Franklin
May	Daniel Boone[4]
June	Thomas Jefferson
July	George Washington At Yorktown[1]
August	Captain John Paul Jones
September	Lewis and Clark
October	Covered Wagons
November	Sam Houston[3]
December	Abraham Lincoln

Note: The paper wrapper in which the calendar was issued contains a reference to N. C. Wyeth.
[1] The illustrations also appeared in color and in black and white in the book *Your Country's Story* by Margaret G. Mackey, published by Ginn and Company, Boston, 1953.
[2] Also appears in *American History Illustrated Magazine,* August 1966, for the article "The Indian and the Horse" by David Bonney.
[3] The illustrations also appear in the book *Forty Illustrators and How They Work* by Ernest W. Watson published by Watson-Guptill Publications, Inc., New York, 1946.
[4] Also appears in color in *The American Gun Magazine,* Spring 1961, for the article "The Long Long Rifle" by Herb Glass.

Romance of Commerce

John Morrell & Company, Ottumwa, Iowa, 1941.
Text by John Kieran.
Published in two sizes:
Calendar size 30¼ × 14 inches; picture size 14⅞ × 13⅜ inches.
Calendar size 17⅞ × 8¼ inches; picture size 10⅛ × 7⅞ inches.
Twelve illustrations in color.
January	The Story of Furs
February	The Story of Coffee
March	The Story of Whaling
April	The Story of Glass
May	The Story of Salt
June	The Story of Silk
July	The Story of Perfume
August	The Story of Tin
September	The Story of Cattle
October	The Story of Gold
November	The Story of Rugs
December	The Story of Jewelry

Note: The paper wrapper in which the calendar was issued contains a short biographical sketch on N. C. Wyeth.

Flags in American History

John Morrell & Company, Ottumwa, Iowa, 1944.
Published in two sizes:
Calendar size 30¼ × 14 inches; picture size 14⅞ × 13⅜ inches.
Calendar size 17⅞ × 8¼ inches; picture size 10⅛ × 7⅞ inches.
Twelve illustrations in color.
January	The Viking Flag
	Norsemen Sight America's Shores
February	The Royal Standard Of Spain
	Columbus Discovers America[1]
March	The Bunker Hill Flag
	The Battle Of Bunker Hill
April	The Grand Union Flag
	John Paul Jones Hoists Our First Flag
May	The First Stars And Stripes
	Betsy Ross Making The Flag
June	U.S. Army National Colors
	America's First Standing Army
July	The Star-Spangled Banner
	The Constitution Bombarding Tripoli[2]
August	The U.S. Coast Guard Flag
	Coast Guard To The Rescue
September	The Alamo Flag
	The Last Stand At The Alamo[3]
October	The Fremont Flag
	Fremont And The Pathfinder Flag[4]
November	The Confederate Battle Flag
	Faithful Troops Cheer General Lee

December   The Stars And Stripes Of To-Day
Old Glory, Symbol Of Liberty

Note: The paper wrapper in which the calendar was issued contains a short biographical sketch on N. C. Wyeth, N. A., and the letter written to John Morrell & Company expressing Wyeth's enthusiasm and interest in the project.
[1] The illustration also appears as a cover in color for the *Columbia* [Knights of Columbus] *Magazine,* October 1958. In addition, it appears in a photograph in *Life* magazine, June 17, 1946, for the article on N. C. Wyeth. The photograph shows Wyeth working toward completion of the painting in his studio.
[2] Also appears as a cover in color for *American History Illustrated Magazine,* February 1968.
[3] Also appears in *American History Illustrated Magazine,* October 1967.
[4] Also appears as a cover in color for *American History Illustrated Magazine,* May 1970.
In addition, a number of the illustrations appeared in color in the Coloroto Section of the *New York Sunday News* during 1959.

Drafting the Declaration of Independence—1776

Copyright by the Thomas D. Murphy Co.
Calendar in color; published in two sizes:
Calendar size 18½ × 13¼ inches; picture size 9¼ × 13¼ inches.
Calendar size 16 × 10 inches; picture size 8 × 10 inches.
Description: Thomas Jefferson, John Adams, Benjamin Franklin, Roger Sherman, and Robert R. Livingston drafting the Declaration of Independence.

A Cherished Memory

Copyright by the Thomas D. Murphy Co., 1943
Calendar in color; published in two sizes:
Picture size 14 × 10⅛ inches.
Picture size 10½ × 8 inches.
Description: Abraham Lincoln writing the famous Bixby letter, November 21, 1864.

Note: The illustration was originally commissioned by the Shaw-Barton Company and used in their 1943 calendar line. The illustration also appeared as a cover in color for *The American Legion* magazine, February 1944.

"Sun Glint"

Courtesy New Britain Museum of American Art, New Britain, Connecticut.
1967 Edition; The Fine American Art Calendar Collection
Calendar in color: calendar size 12 × 17; picture size 10¾ × 15.

George Washington

Copyright 1940 by New York Life Insurance Company.
Lithographed by Ketterlinus.
Calendar in color.

Note: The illustration originally appeared as a poster published for Strawbridge & Clothier (Phila.) by Ketterlinus Co.

The Star Spangled Banner

Francis Scott Key writing the immortal verses which became our National Anthem.
Copyright 1941 by F. A. Schneder.
New York Life Insurance Company's Reproduction Of A Painting By N. C. Wyeth.
Lithographed by Ketterlinus.
Calendar in color: calendar size 15 × 9 inches; picture size 8¼ × 7 inches.

Note: The illustration was reproduced as a print in color by the New York Life Insurance Company in 1941.

"Give Me Liberty or Give Me Death!"

Patrick Henry ending his immortal speech to the Second Virginia Convention, St. John's Church, Richmond, Va., March 23, 1775.
Copyright 1942 by New York Life Insurance Company.
Lithograph by Ketterlinus.
Calendar in color: calendar size 18 × 12 inches; picture size 11¾ × 10⅛ inches.

1845 ONE HUNDRED YEARS AGO WHEN THE NEW YORK LIFE WAS FOUNDED 1945
Copyright 1945 by the New York Life Insurance Company.
Lithographed by Ketterlinus, Philadelphia.
Six illustrations in color by N. C. Wyeth, Gayle Hoskins, Stanley M. Arthurs, Frank E. Schoonover and Walter Stewart.
Calendar in color: calendar size 18 × 14 inches; picture size 9⅜ × 11⁹⁄₁₆ inches.
One illustration in color by N. C. Wyeth.
The Mississippi Steamboat

In the year, 1845, when the New York Life was organized, the era of the Mississippi River Steamboat was at its height—a lusty pageant of luxury, adventure and excitement, celebrated in song and story. An indispensable means of transportation and communications, the steamboat contributed greatly toward the development of the nation.

Commemorating the 100th Anniversary of the Philadelphia Sketch Club 1860–1960 (Engagement Calendar)
Calendar in black and white: calendar size 7 × 5 inches.
Illustrated with works by members, past and present, of the Philadelphia Sketch Club, accompanied with a brief biographical sketch and photograph of each artist represented.
One illustration (painting) in black and white by N. C. Wyeth.
Springhouse

Note: N. C. Wyeth became a member of the Philadelphia Sketch Club in 1911. The painting appears in color in *Life* magazine, June 17, 1946, for the article on N. C. Wyeth.

Lincoln's Second Inaugural

"Let us strive on . . . to care for him who shall have borne the battle, and for his widow and his orphan . . . to do all which may achieve a just and lasting peace."
Copyright Shaw-Barton Company.
Calendar in color; published in two sizes:
Calendar size 32½ × 16 inches; picture size 18⅛ × 13¾ inches (including border banner design)
Calendar size 15½ × 8¾ inches; picture size 9 × 6⅞ inches.

A Cherished Memory
Copyright (1943) by Shaw-Barton Company.
Calendar in color: picture size 14 × 10⅛
Description: Abraham Lincoln writing the famous Bixby letter, November 21, 1864.

Note: The illustration also appeared on a 1943 calendar published by the Thomas D. Murphy Co. In addition the painting was also reproduced as a cover in color for *The American Legion* magazine, February 1944.

The Husker
Copyright 1945 by Shaw-Barton, Coshocton, Ohio.
Printed for the McCormick Transportation Company, Wilmington, Delaware.
Calendar in color: calendar size 22½ × 17 inches; picture size (showing) 14½ × 10⅝ inches.
Accompanying the calendar is a printed description of The Husker. It measures 5¼ × 7¼ inches.

Note: The illustration originally appeared as a cover in color for *The Progressive Farmer*, October

1945. The cover was titled Corn Harvest in the Hill Country.

SNYDER & BLACK & SCHLEGEL Incorporated (Lithographers since 1841)
Calendar in color: calendar size 30½ × 12 inches; picture size 9¹⁵⁄₁₆ × 10⅜ inches.
Description: Boy with dog on hilltop envisioning historic figures among the clouds.

Stonewall Jackson
Calendar in color: picture size 15 × 12 inches.

Note: The illustration originally appeared as a frontispiece in color in the book *The Long Roll* by Mary Johnston, published by Houghton Mifflin Company, Boston, May 1911.

Copyright by Winchester Repeating Arms Co., New Haven, Conn. (1912)
Calendar in color: calendar size 30 × 15¼ inches; picture size 16¾ × 13⅝ inches.
Printed below illustration in red: WINCHESTER
Description: Theodore Roosevelt and hunting companion confronting grizzly bear on rocky ridge.

Note: The illustration also appears as a print in color. In addition, it is reproduced as a cover in color for *Argosy Magazine*, February 1962.

Copyright by Winchester Repeating Arms Co., New Haven, Conn.
Calendar in color: picture size 12½ × 15 inches.
Description: Moose hunters. One hunter calling with bark horn, while other readies rifle as moose emerges from behind boulder.

Note: The illustration also appears in black and white in *Antiques Magazine*, May 1966. It is reproduced through the courtesy of James Graham & Sons (gallery), New York, New York.

VII. Advertisements

The American Red Cross

1918

Poster in color.
Description: Medic supporting wounded soldier on battlefield with infantry advancing in the background.

1933

Poster in color.
The American Red Cross carries on—Join!
Description: Unfurled Red Cross flags with clouds in background.

1953

Poster in color.
Answer the Call!
Description: Unfurled Red Cross flags with clouds in background.

Note: The advertisements appeared in various periodicals. The 1933 poster was reissued in 1953.

American Telephone and Telegraph Company

1911

In the Bell Democracy
Illustration in black and white.
Description: Horse and rider in deep snow approaching log cabin.

1912

The Pony Express
Illustration in black and white.
Description: A pony express rider leaving his station depot.

The Right of All the Way
Illustration in black and white.
Description: A group of children waving at a passing train.

1918

The Miracle of the Marne
Illustration in black and white.
Description: Advancing French infantry led by the spirit of the Maid of Orleans.

The Spirit of War Service
Illustration in black and white.
Description: A French soldier of the Signal Corps repairing communication lines at the front.

Note: The advertisements appeared in the following periodicals: *Harper's Monthly, Cosmopolitan, National Geographic, Life, McClure's Scribner's, The Outlook, Everybody's, The Literary Digest,* etc.

American Tobacco Company
(Lucky Strike Cigarettes)

1932

"Nature *in the Raw* is seldom MILD," a series of advertisements created for Lucky Strike Cigarettes—American Tobacco Company.

The Fort Dearborn Massacre
Illustration in color or in black and white.
Description: Massacre of settlers by Miami Indians, August 15, 1812. Buckskinned settler grappling with tomahawk-wielding Indian.

Custer's Last Stand
Illustration in color or in black and white.
Description: Custer's defeat at the Little Big Horn, Montana, June 25, 1876. Custer firing revolver from behind dead horse at attacking Sioux Indians.

The Dark and Bloody Ground
Illustration in color or in black and white.
Description: Two concealed Indians observing from rocky ledge.

The Sea Wolf
Illustration in color or in black and white.
Description: Captain Kidd's fierce raids on the gold-laden galleons (1696) which made him the scourge of the Spanish Main. Captain Kidd running sea captain through with his sword.

The War Whoop
Illustration in color or in black and white.
Description: Indian war dance.

Note: The advertisements appeared in the following periodicals: *American Magazine, Liberty Magazine, Collier's Weekly, Pictorial Review.* In addition, the advertisements appeared in most major newspapers of the period.

Aunt Jemima Mills Company
(Aunt Jemima Pancake Flour)

1920

How Aunt Jemima Saved the Colonel's Mustache and His Reputation as a Host
Two illustrations either in color or in colors (red orange, brown, black and white).
"Good Lawd, massa, Aun' 'Liza's got a mis'ry!"
Description: So happy he was that, when breakfast was over he came immediately to the kitchen. (vignette illustration)

When the Rob't E. Lee Stopped at Aunt Jemima's Cabin
Two illustrations either in color or in colors (red orange, brown, black and white).

For twenty long years he had remembered
Description: Aunt Jemima serving her pancakes to two Confederate officers. (vignette illustration)

The Night the Emily Dunstan Burned
Two illustrations either in color or in colors (red orange, brown, black and white).
"Twas right toward that cabin on the Louisiana side I swung her"
Description: The Emily Dunstan burning. (vignette illustration)

Gray Morn
Two illustrations either in color or in colors (red orange, brown, black and white).
"Yo' sho' did give dem Yanks de slip"
Description: They had lain hidden in bushes on the Mississippi bank. (vignette illustration)

1921

Aunt Jemima Bids Goodbye to the Old Plantation
Two illustrations either in color or in colors (red orange, brown, black and white).
"Farewell! a word that must be, and hath been —a sound which makes us linger; yet—farewell!"
Description: Then the flour was put out in packaged form—in packages with Aunt Jemima's picture on them. (vignette illustration)

At the World's Fair in '93 Aunt Jemima was a Sensation
Two illustrations either in color or in colors (red orange, brown, black and white).
It seemed that everybody wanted to taste those golden-brown cakes.
Description: Aunt Jemima cooking her pancakes in the kitchen. (vignette illustration)

Note: The advertisements appeared in the following periodicals: *The Saturday Evening Post,* the *Ladies' Home Journal, Woman's Home Companion, Pictorial Review,* etc.

N. W. Ayer & Son (Advertising Headquarters, Philadelphia)

1926

The Widened Vision
Illustration in black and white.
Description: Pioneer with oxteam envisions a modern city in the wilderness.

Note: The advertisement appeared in *The Saturday Evening Post,* March 6, 1926.

The Coca-Cola Company

1935

Illustration in color.
Description: Glass of Coca-Cola embedded in snowbank next to a soda fountain.
Illustration in color.
Description: Three bottles of Coca-Cola embedded in drifted snow. Pine trees and mountains in background.

1936

Illustration in color.
Description: Hand holding bottle of Coca-Cola. Coca-Cola dispenser embedded in iceberg surrounded by boxed pack ice.

1937

Illustration in color.
Description: Hand holding glass of Coca-Cola. Snowfields and mountains in background.
Illustration in color.
Description: Bottle of Coca-Cola embedded in drifted snow. Coca-Cola dispenser in background.

1944

Illustration in color.
Description: World War II GIs standing on dock in a Newfoundland harbor. One soldier offering a Coca-Cola to a cod fisherman in dory.

Note: The advertisements appeared in the following periodicals: *The Saturday Evening Post, Life, National Geographic, Cosmopolitan, The American,* etc.

1944

Billboard Display Advertisement
Billboard in color.
Description: Bottle of Coke embedded in an iceberg with background of northern lights.

Cream of Wheat Company

1908

"Where the Mail Goes CREAM OF WHEAT Goes"
Copyright 1907 by Cream of Wheat Company.
Illustration either in color, in two colors (brown, black and white), or in black and white.
Description: Cowboy on horseback at the Cream of Wheat mailbox.

Alaska
Copyright 1907 by Cream of Wheat.
Illustration either in color, in colors (blue, orange, brown, black and white), or in black and white.
Description: Trapper standing on sled, which is loaded with boxes of Cream of Wheat, defends his cargo against a pack of wolves.

1909

The Bronco Buster
Copyright 1907 by Cream of Wheat Company.
Illustration in colors (blue, orange, brown, black and white).
Description: Rodeo rider on bucking horse.

Note: The advertisements appeared in the following periodicals: *The Youth's Companion,* the *Ladies' Home Journal, Collier's Weekly, Cosmopolitan, American Cookery, The Delineator, National Geographic, The Literary Digest, Munsey's, McClure's, Ladies' World, Harper's Bazaar, The Saturday Evening Post,* etc.

Joseph Dixon Crucible Co.
(Ticonderoga Pencil Division)

1934

"Ethan Allen, Forerunner of Independence"
Illustration in color.

Description: Ethan Allen leading the assault in the capture of Fort Ticonderoga.

Note: The advertisement appeared in *The Saturday Evening Post,* September 8, 1934. In addition, the illustration was reproduced as a print in color and was forwarded, upon request, to the interested party.

E. I. du Pont de Nemours & Company

1916

A Great Sport for Good Sports
Illustration in color.
Description: Trap shooting at firing range.

Note: The advertisement appeared in *Redbook Magazine,* April 1916.

Fisk Cord Tires

1918

Fisk Cord Tires • Your Satisfaction • First to Last
Illustration either in color or in black and white.
Description: Natives carrying crude rubber in baskets down hill to anchored ship below.

1919

Illustration in color.
Description: Group of Indians on horseback watch in astonishment as car speeds by.

Note: The advertisements appeared in the following periodicals: *Collier's Weekly,* March 16, 1918, *Country Life.*

Frankfort Distilleries
(Paul Jones Whiskey)

1935

"Now Major, for the best part of the game"
Illustration in color.
Description: Two Southern gentlemen playing pool.

"I would like to have known my grandfather better"
Illustration in color.
Description: Men looking at a portrait of Paul Jones.

The First Kentucky Derby
Illustration in color.
Description: In the winner's circle.

"Tobey, fetch me the key to the springhouse"
Illustration in color.
Description: Two men sitting on porch of Southern mansion.

Note: The advertisements appeared in the following periodicals: *The American, Liberty Magazine, Cosmopolitan, Fortune,* etc.

Goodyear (Aircraft Mfg. Co.)

1943

We've found the Northwest Passage . . . in the Skies
Illustration in color.
Sir Martin Frobisher's expedition ice-locked in Frobisher Bay.

Note: The advertisement appeared in *Life* mazazine, October 4, 1943.

M. Grumbacher

1942

M. Grumbacher Oil Colors.
A photograph of the artist and a brief bio-

graphical sketch of achievement and endorsement of product.

Note: The advertisement appeared in *The Art Digest* magazine, October 1, 1942.

Hiram Walker Inc. (The Distillers of Canadian Club)

1942

Illustration in color.
Description: Christopher Columbus sights the New World.

Note: The illustration commemorates the 450th anniversary of the discovery of America by Christopher Columbus (1492–1942) and was used as a window display poster.

International-Harvester Company

1931

The World's First Reaper
Illustration in color.
Description: Public test of Cyrus Hall McCormick's Invention, Steele's Tavern, Virginia, 1831.

Note: The advertisement was painted for the 100th Anniversary of the McCormick Reaper and appeared in the following periodicals: *The Saturday Evening Post, MacLean's Magazine, The Country Gentlemen,* etc.

Interwoven Stocking Company

1927

Christmas in Old Virginia
Illustration in color or in colors (red, green, brown, black and white).
Description: President and Mrs. George Washington greeting the arrival of the Christmas tree and Christmas guests at Mt. Vernon.

1928

The Christmas Ship in Old New York
Illustration in color.
Description: Seventeenth century New Amsterdam settlers grouped about a snow-covered harbor welcoming seamen unloading a Dutch sailing vessel.

Note: The advertisements appeared in *The Saturday Evening Post.*

Jobbers Overall Co., Inc.
(Blue Buckle OverAlls)

1918

Illustration in colors (red, blue, brown, black and white).
Description: Two farmers watching farmer on tractor plowing field.

1919

Illustration in colors (red, blue, brown, black and white).
Description: Two construction workers standing on girders.
Illustration in colors (red, blue, brown, black and white).
Description: Two farmers talking. One is seated on a plow horse.
Illustration in colors (red, blue, brown, black and white).
Description: Loggers breaking a log jam.

Illustration in colors (red, blue, brown, black and white).
Description: Two steelworkers stoking furnace.

Note: The advetisements appeared in *The Saturday Evening Post*, 1918–1919.

Kellogg's Toasted Corn Flakes

1915

First Aid to the Hungry
Illustration in color.
Description: Children parading in line carrying boxes of corn flakes.

Note: The advertisement appeared in the following periodicals: *Good Housekeeping*, the *Ladies' Home Journal, American Magazine*.

Minnesota Valley Canning Company

1942

Great Spirit of the Cornlands (From the land of Hiawatha)
Illustration in color.
Description: Indian standing among fields of corn.

1943

Bringing in the Ears (Harvest Home)
Illustration in color.
Description: Farmworkers picking corn and loading the ears into wagons.

Note: The advertisements appeared in *Life* magazine.

The New York Telephone Company

1926

A Vision of New York
Inspired from an incident in *Diedrich Knickerbocker's History of New York* by Washington Irving.
Description: The sage Oloffe and the good St. Nicholas.

Note: The advertisement appeared as a frontispiece in black and white in *The American Architect*, November 20, 1926.

Pierce-Arrow Motor Car Company

1917

Illustration in color.
Description: A blacksmith at his anvil.

Note: The illustration appeared in *Country Life*, March 1917.

Pontiac Division (General Motors)

1945

Illustration in color.
Description: Hand of Indian holding bow with arrow.

Note: The illustration appeared in the following periodicals: *Life* magazine, *Look, Better Homes & Gardens, Newsweek*, etc.

Steinway & Sons

1921

Wagner and Lizst
Illustration either in color or in black and white.
Description: Franz Lizst playing a composition on the piano as Richard Wagner listens.
Beethoven and Nature
Illustration either in color or in black and white.
Description: Beethoven standing before stream.

1927

The King's Henchman
Illustration either in color or in black and white.
Description: Knight and maiden in forest.

1928

Die Walküre
Illustration either in color or in black and white.
Description: The Magic Fire Spell: Brünnhilde and Wotan

Note: The advertisements appeared in the following periodicals: *Century, Harper's Monthly, The Literary Digest, Better Homes and Gardens, Good Housekeeping, National Geographic, The Saturday Evening Post, American Mercury, Country Life*, etc.

E. R. Squibb & Sons

1944

Display poster in color.
Description: Wounded soldier on stretcher being given blood plasma. Beach with jungle growth in background.
Display poster in color.
Description: Marines landing on Japanese-held island. Figure in foreground supports a wounded comrade.
Display poster in color.
Description: Doctor and nurse standing near bedside of patient who is being administered blood plasma.

Display poster in color.
Public Health and Morale
Description: Family group standing before factories in full production, with aircraft flying overhead.

1945

Display poster in color.
The American Mother
Description: Mother weighing her child on scale.

Strathmore Paper Company

1945

An endorsement of Strathmore products by N. C. Wyeth accompanied by a photograph of artist at work.

Note: The advertisement appeared in *American Artist Magazine*, January 1945.

United Hotels Company of America

1926

Art in the Modern Hotel—An Important Part of Its Charm
Illustration (triptych) in black and white.
The Hendrick Hudson Mural Painting by N. C. Wyeth in the Main Dining Room, The Roosevelt Hotel, New York

Note: The advertisement appeared in the *International Studio*, February 1926.

F. Weber Co.

1945

Illustrated is N. C. Wyeth's painting Portrait of a Farmer (Pennsylvania Farmer) along with an endorsement of the product, Weber Fine Artists' Colors.

Note: The advertisement appeared in *American Artist Magazine*, January 1945.

The Willys-Overland Company

1915

The Overland Out West
Illustration in colors (orange, brown, black and white)
Description: The west of yesterday and today. Westerners riding in wagon (inset) and in the new Overland automobile.

Note: The advertisement appeared in *Collier's Weekly*, March 20, 1915.

VIII. Exhibition Catalogues

The Art Institute of Chicago

Catalogue of the Forty- / Sixth Annual Exhibition / of American Paintings / and Sculpture / The Art Institute of Chicago / October 24, 1935, to December 8, 1935, / Chicago, 1935

Exhibition Catalogue.
8 vo. Paper covers (tan) with lettering stamped in pink and blue; unnumbered pages.
Illustrated with works by exhibiting artists.
One painting exhibited by N. C. Wyeth.
Dying Winter (page 21, number 233)

Baltimore Museum of Art

FIRST BALTIMORE PAN AMERICAN / EXHIBITION OF / CONTEMPORARY PAINTINGS / January Fifteenth / February Twenty-Eighth / MCMXXXI / [ornament] / BALTIMORE MUSEUM OF ART / Baltimore

Exhibition Catalogue.
8 vo. Paper covers with pictorial design in black and white; 47 pp.
Size of leaf trimmed 5¾ × 8¾ inches.
Illustrated with works by exhibiting artists.

One painting exhibited by N. C. Wyeth.
My Mother
Number 31 (page 17)

The Brandywine River Museum

THE / BRANDYWINE / HERITAGE / Howard Pyle N. C. Wyeth Andrew Wyeth James Wyeth / The Brandywine River Museum / Chadds Ford, Pennsylvania.

Copyright 1971 by The Brandywine River Museum.
Exhibition Catalogue.
Large square 8 vo. Paper covers (with four illustrations in color); 121 pp.
Size of leaf trimmed 9⅜ × 9¹⁵⁄₁₆ inches.
Foreword by Richard McLanathan.
Illustrated with 169 works in color and black and white by those artists represented.

Twenty-two drawings and paintings by N. C. Wyeth exhibited. (pages 44–61, numbers 53–78)
53 Indian Drawings 1904
55 The Navajo Herder 1908
54 Mowing 1907
57 Winter 1909
58 Blind Pew 1911
59 At The "Admiral Benbow" 1911
60 Ben Gunn 1911
66 The Vedette 1911
67 Road to Vidalia 1912
69 Fence Builders 1915

70 Self-Portrait 1915
71 The Black Arrow Flieth Nevermore 1916
72 Fight on The Plains 1916
73 Study for "New Born Calf" 1917
74 New Born Calf 1917
78 The Huron Flew Through the Air 1925
75 He Blew Three Deadly Notes 1917
Idem: Same except issued in brown cloth covers with lettering on spine stamped in white by the New York Graphic Society, Greenwich, Conn., 1971. The exhibition catalogue, published in May 1971, preceded the hard cover edition which was published in September.

Carnegie Institute

DIRECTIONS IN / AMERICAN PAINTING / October Twenty-Third / December Fourteenth / 1941 / Carnegie Institute / Pittsburgh

Exhibition Catalogue.
8 vo. Paper covers (in colors); loose sheets with ringed plastic binder; unnumbered pages.
Size of leaf trimmed 6 × 9 inches.
Illustrated with works by exhibiting artists.

One illustration (painting) in black and white by N. C. Wyeth.
Island Funeral (Plate 31)
Exhibited in Gallery G, Number 297

PAINTING IN THE / UNITED STATES, 1944 / October Twelfth / December Tenth / Carnegie Institute / Pittsburgh

Exhibition Catalogue.
8 vo. Paper covers (in colors); unnumbered pages.
Size of leaf trimmed 5¾ × 8¾ inches.
Illustrated with works by exhibiting artists.

One illustration (painting) in black and white by N. C. Wyeth.
War Letter (Plate 84)
Exhibited in Gallery M, Number 82.

PAINTING IN THE / UNITED STATES 1945 / October Eleventh / December Ninth / Carnegie Institute / Pittsburgh

Exhibition Catalogue.
8 vo. Paper covers (in colors); unnumbered pages.
Size of leaf trimmed 5¾ × 8¾ inches.
Illustrated with works by exhibiting artists.

One illustration (painting) in black and white by N. C. Wyeth.
Nightfall (Plate 58)
Exhibited in Gallery L, Number 26.

Colby College Art Museum

Colby College Art Museum, Waterville, Maine May 4–August 31, 1963 / Museum Of Fine Arts Boston, Massachusetts December 12, 1963– January 26, 1964 / Whitney Museum Of American Art New York City February 10–March 22, 1964 / MAINE / And / ITS / ARTISTS / 1710–1963 / An Exhibition In Celebration Of / The Sesquicentennial Of Colby College, 1813–1963

Exhibition Catalogue.
Thin 4 to. Paper covers (with light blue wrapper printed in dark blue); 47 pp.
Size of leaf trimmed 9 × 12 inches.
Illustrated in color and black and white with the works of noted American artists.

One painting by N. C. Wyeth exhibited.
Sun Glint
tempera 23″ × 31″
New Britain Museum of American Art
New Britain, Connecticut
Page 28, Number 123
Artists of Wider Repute 1865–1916
A reference to N. C. Wyeth (page 10)

The Corcoran Gallery of Art

TWELFTH EXHIBITION / of / CONTEMPORARY AMERICAN / OIL PAINTINGS / November 30, 1930, to January 11, 1931 / (Inclusive) / [ornament] / The Corcoran Gallery of Art / Washington / District of Columbia [all surrounded by boxed rules]

Exhibition Catalogue.
12 mo. Paper covers; 132 pp.
Size of leaf trimmed 5¼ × 7 inches.
Illustrated with works by exhibiting artists.

One illustration (painting) in black and white by N. C. Wyeth.
Pennsylvania Barn
Exhibited in Gallery A, Number 21 (page 29)

THE THIRTEENTH EXHIBITION / of / CONTEMPORARY AMERICAN / OIL PAINTINGS / December 4, 1932, to January 15, 1933 / (Inclusive) / [ornament] / The Corcoran Gallery of Art / Washington / District of Columbia [all surrounded by boxed rules]

Exhibition Catalogue.
12 mo. Paper covers; 123 pp.
Size of leaf trimmed 5¼ × 7 inches.
Illustrated with works by exhibiting artists.

One illustration (painting) in black and white by N. C. Wyeth.

In a Dream I Meet General Washington p 108
Exhibited in Gallery H, Number 207 (page 79)
Awarded the Fourth W. A. Clark Prize ($500) accompanied by the Corcoran Honorable Mention Certificate.

THE FOURTEENTH / BIENNIAL EXHIBITION / of / CONTEMPORARY AMERICAN / OIL PAINTINGS / March 24 to May 5, 1935 / (Inclusive) / [ornament] / The Corcoran Gallery of Art / Washington / District of Columbia [all surrounded by boxed rules]

Exhibition Catalogue.
12 mo. Paper covers; 142 pp.
Size of leaf trimmed 5¼ × 7 inches.
Illustrated with works of exhibiting artists.

One illustration (painting) in black and white by N. C. Wyeth.
Three Fishermen p 116
Exhibited in Gallery A, Number 11 (page 25)

Catalogue of the / FORTY-THIRD / Annual Exhibition / of The Society Of / Washington Artists / January 20 to February 11, 1934 / The Corcoran Gallery of Art / Washington, D. C.

Exhibition Catalogue.
12 mo. Paper covers (light brown lettering); 31 pp.
Size of leaf trimmed 5⅛ × 7⅛ inches.

One painting exhibited by N. C. Wyeth.
The Red Pung
Number 30 (page 15)

THE FIFTEENTH / BIENNIAL EXHIBITION / of / CONTEMPORARY AMERICAN / OIL PAINTINGS / March 18 to May 9, 1937 / (Inclusive) / [ornament] / The Corcoran Gallery of Art / Washington / District of Columbia [all surrounded by boxed rules]

Exhibition Catalogue.
12 mo. Paper covers; 164 pp.
Size of leaf trimmed 5¼ × 7 inches.
Illustrated with works by exhibiting artists.

One illustration (painting) in black and white by N. C. Wyeth.
The Letter p 36
Exhibited in Gallery A, Number 21 (page 31)

THE SIXTEENTH / BIENNIAL EXHIBITION / of / CONTEMPORARY AMERICAN / OIL PAINTINGS / March 26 to May 7, 1939 / (Inclusive) / [ornament] / The Corcoran Gallery of Art / Washington / District of Columbia

Exhibition Catalogue.
12 mo. Paper covers; 107 pp.
Size of leaf trimmed 5¼ × 7 inches.
Illustrated with works by exhibiting artists.

One illustration (painting) in black and white by N. C. Wyeth.
Dark Harbor Lobsterman p 104
Exhibited in Gallery 1, Number 253 (page 59)

THE EIGHTEENTH / BIENNIAL EXHIBITION / of / CONTEMPORARY AMERICAN / OIL PAINTINGS / March 21 to May 2, 1943 / (Inclusive) / [ornament] / The Corcoran Gallery of Art / Washington / District of Columbia [all surrounded by boxed rules]

Exhibition Catalogue.
12 mo. Paper covers; 48 pp.
Size of leaf trimmed 5¼ × 7 inches.
Illustrated with four paintings by exhibiting artists.

One painting exhibited by N. C. Wyeth.
Cornfield in Pennsylvania
Exhibited in the Central Gallery, Number 212 (page 31)

THE NINETEENTH / BIENNIAL EXHIBITION / of / CONTEMPORARY AMERICAN / OIL PAINTINGS / March 18 to April 29, 1945 / (Inclusive) / [ornament] / The Corcoran Gallery of Art / Washington / District of Columbia [all surrounded by boxed rules]

Exhibition Catalogue.
12 mo. Paper covers; 48 pp.
Size of leaf trimmed 5¼ × 7 inches.
Illustrated with works by exhibiting artists.

One painting exhibited by N. C. Wyeth.
The Spring House
Exhibited in Gallery H, Number 201 (page 33)

Exhibition / of reproductions / of paintings / by / Old Masters / and Modern American Painters / and / Illustrators[1]

Exhibition Catalogue.
Size of leaf trimmed 5 × 6¼ inches; (20) pp.
Introduction by N. C. Wyeth.
Prefaces by Edward W. Bok and J. H. Chapin, Art Editor *Scribner's Magazine*.
The exhibition includes 171 works by Old Masters and Contemporary painters and illustrators.

Seven paintings exhibited by N. C. Wyeth.
158. Illustration for *Red Cross Magazine*
159. Illustration for *Robin Hood*
160. Illustration for *Robin Hood*
161. Cover Inlay for *Robin Hood*
162. Illustration for *Red Cross Magazine*
163. Wagner and Liszt
      The Steinway Collection
164. Beethoven
      The Steinway Collection

[1] This catalogue gives neither the location nor date of the exhibition.

William A. Farnsworth Library and Art Museum (Rockland, Maine)
AN EXHIBITION OF PAINTINGS FROM THE WORLD OF N. C. WYETH (Farnsworth emblem—green) / 1966 / SUMMER / EXHIBITION / July 20–September 4

Copyright 1966 by the William A. Farnsworth Library and Art Museum.
Foreword by Wendell S. Hadlock (Director)
Introduction: A letter written to N. C. Wyeth's brother Edwin during World War II.
Exhibition Catalogue.
8 vo. Paper covers (oatmeal with green lettering); (34) pp.
Size of leaf trimmed 6 × 8⅞ inches.

Seventy-eight drawings, illustrations and paintings by N. C. Wyeth exhibited.
Twenty-two illustrations in black and white.
Picture of N. C. Wyeth
Indian drawings (four)
The Wagon Race
The Trapper
The Vedette
Blind Pew
Passing out the Weapons

One Step More, Mr. Hands
At Queen's Ferry
On the Island of Erraid
Fight at the Cross
The Black Arrow Flieth Never More
Discovery of The Chest
In Ambush
Passing of Robin
Carving the Marker
Thoreau and the Fox
Mrs. Cushman's House
In Penobscot Bay

Fogg Art Museum
A Loan Exhibition Organized By The Fogg Art Museum 1963 / ANDREW WYETH Dry Brush and Pencil Drawings / Fogg Art Museum Harvard University Cambridge Massachusetts / The Pierpont Morgan Library New York New York / The Corcoran Gallery Of Art Washington D.C. / William A. Farnsworth Library And Art Museum Rockland Maine

Exhibition Catalogue.
8 vo. Paper covers (The Mill—painting by Andrew Wyeth); 73 pp.
Size of leaf trimmed 8½ × 11 inches.
Introduction by Agnes Mongan
      Assistant Director and Curator of Drawings, Fogg Art Museum
Illustrated with tempera paintings, watercolors, dry brush drawings, pencil drawings, and studies by Andrew Wyeth.
In the Introduction and Catalogue text appear numerous references to N. C. Wyeth.
Idem: Also published in a clothbound edition.

Grand Central Art Galleries
Exhibition Of / Illustrations / Grand Central / Art Galleries

Exhibition Catalogue.
8 vo. Paper covers (gray); unnumbered pages.
Size of leaf trimmed 6½ × 9 inches.
Exhibition of the work of Prominent Illustrators October 31st thru November 11th, 1933

One illustration (painting) in black and white by N. C. Wyeth.
"In a Dream I Meet General Washington"

Knoedler Galleries
EXHIBITION OF PAINTING / By / N. C. WYETH / 1882–1945 / (illustration in color—Cover design from "Treasure Island") / October 29–November 23, 1957 / Knoedler Galleries / 14 East 57th Street / New York

Exhibition Catalogue.
4 to. Paper covers (illustration in color with dark blue lettering); (8) pp.
Size of leaf trimmed 7 × 10 inches.
Biographical sketch / Newell Convers Wyeth, N.A.
The catalogue lists one hundred ten works by N. C. Wyeth.
      Miscellaneous (1–9)
      Still Lifes (10–12)
      Landscapes Chadds Ford, Pennsylvania (13–28)
      Landscapes Port Clyde, Maine (29–34)
Illustrations for magazines
      Outing (35–40)
      Winchester Rifle Advertisement (41–43)
      Woman's Home Companion (44–45)
      The Popular (46–47)
      McCall's—"The Romantic Prince" by R. Sabatini (48)
Illustrations for books (49–110)

The Museum, Lubbock, Texas
Wyeth Family Show / April 15–May 13, 1951 / Sponsored by / Lubbock Junior Welfare League / The Museum / Lubbock, Texas

Exhibition Folder.
Biographical material on members of the Wyeth family.
Biographical sketch on N. C. Wyeth.

Four paintings by N. C. Wyeth exhibited.
No. 6   "Death Mask of Keats"
         Loaned by the Roswell Museum
No. 12   "The Posse"
         Loaned by Mrs. H. S. Griffin, Wichita Falls, Texas
No. 14   "Forest Depths"
         Illustration for *The Deerslayer*
         Loaned by Peter Wyeth Hurd, grandson of N. C. Wyeth
No. 18   "Penobscot Bay"
         Loaned by the Roswell Museum

The National Academy
The National Academy / 215 West 57th Street / New York / [ornament] / Catalogue of the One Hundred and Fourteenth / Annual Exhibition / 1940 / Open March 15th to April 11th / Daily 10 A.M. To 6 P.M. / Sundays 1:30 To 6 P.M. / Copyright 1940 by The National Academy of Design

Exhibition Catalogue.
12 mo. Paper covers (reddish brown with black lettering); 97 pp. (plus 7 pages of advertising)
Size of leaf trimmed 5⅜ × 7⅞ inches.
Illustrated with works by member artists.

One painting exhibited by N. C. Wyeth.
Marshall Farm
Exhibited in Center Gallery, Number 147 (page 19)

THE NATIONAL ACADEMY / 215 West 57th Street / New York / [ornament] / Catalogue of the / One Hundred and Fifteenth / Annual Exhibition / 1941 / Open March 11 to April 9th / Daily 10 A.M. to 6 P.M. / Sundays 1:30 to 6 P.M. / Copyright 1941 by The National Academy of Design

Exhibition Catalogue.
12 mo. Paper covers (gray with brown lettering); 100 pp. (plus 6 pages of advertising)
Size of leaf trimmed 5⅜ × 7¾ inches.
Illustrated with works by member artists.

One painting exhibited by N. C. Wyeth, A.N.A.
The Letter—1918
Exhibited in the Vanderbilt Gallery, Number 267 (page 22)

The / National Academy of Design / presents its / 116th ANNUAL EXHIBITION / of / Contemporary American / Painting And Sculpture / April 8th through May 16th / 1942 / Hours: 1 to 6 p.m. daily / National Academy Galleries / 1083 Fifth Avenue, New York, N.Y. / The Graphic Art and Architecture sections will be / presented from October 16th to November 29th, 1942.

Exhibition Catalogue.
12 mo. Paper covers (gray with dark blue lettering); 89 pp; (plus 6 pages of advertising)
Size of leaf trimmed 5¼ × 7⅝ inches.
Illustrated with works by member artists.

One illustration (painting) in black and white by N. C. Wyeth, N.A.
Walden Pond Revisited p 22
Exhibited in the Second Floor Gallery, Number 90 (page 23)
List of Academicians: N. C. Wyeth elected to the Academy in 1941. (page 71)

The / National Academy of Design / presents its / 118th ANNUAL EXHIBITION / of / Contemporary American / Painting And Sculpture / March 29th through April 25th / 1944 / Hours: 1 to 5 p.m. daily / [ornament] / National Academy Galleries / 1083 Fifth Avenue, New York, N.Y. / The second half of the 118th Annual Exhibition will / be presented from May 29th to June 18th, 1944 / Copyright 1944 by The National Academy of Design

Exhibition Catalogue.
12 mo. Paper covers (gray with dark blue lettering); 76 pp. (plus 4 pages of advertising)
Size of leaf trimmed 5¼ × 7⅝ inches.
Illustrated with works by member artists.

One painting exhibited by N. C. Wyeth, N.A.
Dark Harbor Fisherman
Exhibited in First Floor Gallery B-1, Number 27 (page 13)
List of Academicians: N. C. Wyeth 1941 (page 58)

The / National Academy of Design / presents its / 119th ANNUAL EXHIBITION / of / Contemporary American / Painting, Sculpture and / Graphic Art / March 14 through April 3 / 1945 / Hours: 1 to 5 p.m. daily / [ornament] / National Academy Galleries / 1083 Fifth Avenue, New York, N.Y. / Copyright 1945 by The National Academy of Design

Exhibition Catalogue.
12 mo. Paper covers (blue green with dark blue lettering); 91 pp. (plus 4 pages of advertising)
Size of leaf trimmed 5¼ × 7⅝ inches.
Illustrated with works by member artists.

One illustration (painting) in black and white by N. C. Wyeth, N.A.
In Penobscot Bay p 22
Exhibited in Second Floor Gallery B-2, Number 124 (page 23)
List of Academicians: N. C. Wyeth 1941 (page 74)

The / National Academy of Design / presents its / 120th ANNUAL EXHIBITION / of / Contemporary American Painting and Sculpture / December 4th through December 21st / 1945 / Hours: 1 to 5 p.m. daily / [ornament] / National Academy Galleries / 1083 Fifth Avenue, New York, N.Y. / Copyright 1945 by The National Academy of Design

Exhibition Catalogue.
12 mo. Paper covers (blue green with dark blue lettering); 80 pp. (plus 3 pages of advertising)
Size of leaf trimmed 5¼ × 7⅝ inches.
Illustrated with works by member artists.

One painting by N. C. Wyeth, N.A., exhibited.
(Deceased)
Sun Glint
Exhibited in Fourth Floor Gallery B-5 (page 29)
List of Academicians: N. C. Wyeth 1941–1945 (page 76)

Needham Free Public Library
DEDICATION OF THE N. C. WYETH ROOM / NEEDHAM FREE PUBLIC LIBRARY / October 27, 1968 / PROGRAM / Greetings from the Library Trustees / Mrs. Harriet Brush / The N. C. Wyeth Room / Mr. R. F. Bosworth / My Brother N. C. Wyeth / Mr. Stimson Wyeth / Dedication / Mr. Nathaniel Wyeth

Exhibition Folder.
Size of leaf trimmed 5⅝ × 5⅞ inches.
Photograph of N. C. Wyeth painting from nature printed on cover.
N. C. Wyeth, 1882–1945, by Stimson Wyeth
List of Trustees of The Needham Free Public Library printed on back cover.

Paintings and illustrations exhibited.
1.   The Poacher (magazine cover)
2.   The Black Dragon (illustration)
3.   Boy Waving American Flag
4.   Boy Reading to Mother (illustration)
5.   My Mother
6.   My Brother Stimson
7.   Abandoned (magazine cover)
8.   World War II Bond Poster
9.   Poster for 200th Anniversary of Needham
10. Four Reproductions
11. Winter
12. Attack on the Mailman (illustration)
13. The Pirate (*Captain Blood*, illustration)
14. #3 Babylonian (illustration)
15. Sabatini (illustration)
16. Mandarin (I) (illustration)
17. Dancing Girl (II) (illustration)
18. Man from Northlands (illustration)

North Carolina Museum of Art, Raleigh
AMERICAN PAINTINGS SINCE 1900 / FROM THE PERMANENT COLLECTION / Exhibition / April 1–23, 1967 / NORTH CAROLINA MUSEUM OF ART, RALEIGH

Exhibition Catalogue.
Thin large 8 vo. Paper covers; 46 pp.
Size of leaf trimmed 7⅜ × 9⅞ inches.
Illustrated with works from the museum's permanent collection in color and black and white.

One illustration (painting) in black and white by N. C. Wyeth accompanied by a brief biographical study of the artist.
Corn Harvest on the Brandywine p 44

Note: The painting was reproduced as a cover in color for *The Progressive Farmer*, November 1936 and October 1946. It was originally titled Autumn in the Hill Country.

Panama-Pacific International Exposition
Official Catalogue / [illustrated] / of the / Department of Fine Arts / PANAMA-PACIFIC INTERNATIONAL / EXPOSITION / (with Awards) / San Francisco, California / 1915 / Copyright 1915 by The Wahlgreen Company / – / The Wahlgreen Company / Official Publishers to the Panama-Pacific International Exposition / San Francisco

Exhibition Catalogue.
8 vo. Paper covers; 256 pp. (including notes)
Size of leaf trimmed 6 × 9 inches.
United States Section.
Pages 24 and 25.
Location of N. C. Wyeth's paintings in exhibition.
Biographical Index—Painters, Etc.
Pages 196 and 197.
Reference to N. C. Wyeth (Recipient of the Gold Medal, Panama-Pacific International Exposition, San Francisco 1915) and list of paintings exhibited.

Paintings exhibited as follows:
No. 57   Ebenezer Balfour (*Kidnapped*)
      Gallery 26, Wall C.
No. 58   Chinese Pirates
      Gallery 26, Wall C.
No. 59   Old Pew (*Treasure Island*)
      Gallery 26, Wall C.
No. 64   Captain Bones Routs Black Dog (*Treasure Island*)
      Gallery 26, Wall C.
No. 67   The Picador
      Gallery 26, Wall C.
No. 4214   Roaring Skipper
      Gallery 119, Wall A.

Illustrated Catalogue of the Post- / Exposition Exhibition in the / Department of Fine Arts • / Panama-Pacific International Exposition • San Francisco • / California—January First to / May First • Nineteen Hundred / & Sixteen • Published by the / San Francisco Art Association (1915)

Exhibition Catalogue.
8 vo. Paper covers (tan); pictorial designs and lettering stamped on cover and spine in black; 112 pp.
A listing of paintings exhibited by N. C. Wyeth on page 66.

Paintings exhibited as follows:
No. 6620   Old Pew (*Treasure Island*)
No. 6621   Chinese Pirates
No. 6622   The Picador
No. 6623   Captain Bones Routs Black Dog (*Treasure Island*)
No. 6624   Ebenezer Balfour (*Kidnapped*)

PANAMA-PACIFIC / INTERNATIONAL EXPOSITION / SAN FRANCISCO, 1915 / REPORT OF THE / DEPARTMENT OF FINE ARTS

Exhibition Catalogue.
8 vo. Paper covers (light gray); 24 pp.
Size of leaf trimmed 6 × 9 inches.
The Gold Medal presented to N. C. Wyeth (page 16).

The Parrish Art Museum
Loan Exhibition / of Paintings / by / THE WYETH FAMILY / July 30 to August 22, 1966 / The Parrish Art Museum / 25 Job's Lane, Southampton, New York

Exhibition Catalogue.
12 mo. Paper covers (blue with dark blue lettering).
Size of leaf trimmed 8½ × 6⅜ inches.
Foreword by Nicholas Wyeth.
Illustrated with numerous works by members of the Wyeth family.

One illustration (painting) in black and white by N. C. Wyeth.
Self Portrait (The National Academy of Design)
In this exhibition are eighteen works by N. C. Wyeth.

William Penn Memorial Museum
N. C. WYETH / And / The Brandywine / Tradition / October 13–November 28, 1965 / The Pennsylvania Historical and Museum / Commission / William Penn Memorial Museum / Harrisburg, Pennsylvania [surrounded by boxed rules]

Copyright 1965 by The Pennsylvania State University.
Exhibition Catalogue.

4 to. Paper covers (plum with purple inset, with blue lettering); (40) pp.
Size of leaf trimmed 8¼ × 11 inches.
Text by Henry C. Pitz.
Five photographs:
     Newell Convers Wyeth 1882–1945
     Howard Pyle with some of his pupils
     The Wyeth home in Chadds Ford
     N. C. Wyeth outside his studio at Chadds Ford
     Interior—N. C. Wyeth Studio

N. C. Wyeth letter with sketch.

Seven illustrations in color:
Battle at Glens Falls
Andy With The Fire Engine
The Ore Wagon
In Penobscot Bay
The Giant
The Parkman Outfit
Nightfall
Catalogue of the Exhibition lists one hundred nineteen works by N. C. Wyeth plus paintings by Carolyn Wyeth, Henriette Wyeth Hurd, and Andrew Wyeth.

The Pennsylvania Academy of the Fine Arts
The Pennsylvania / Academy of the Fine Arts / Founded 1805 / [ornament] / The Philadelphia / Water Color Club / CATALOGUE OF THE SEVENTH / ANNUAL PHILADELPHIA WATER / COLOR EXHIBITION, NOVEM- / BER 8 TO DECEMBER 19, 1909 / [ornament] / Philadelphia / MCMIX

Exhibition Catalogue.
12 mo. Paper covers (brown with dark brown lettering, blue emblem); 48 pp; plus advertising I–XI.
Size of leaf trimmed 5 × 6⅞ inches.
Illustrated with works by exhibiting artists.

Two paintings exhibited by N. C. Wyeth.
Mexican Greaser and His Sheep
     Number 579 (page 36)
Pastoral of the South West
     Number 588 (page 36)
All works exhibited in Gallery E.

The Pennsylvania / Academy of the Fine Arts / Founded 1805 / [ornament] / The Philadelphia / Water Color Club / CATALOGUE OF THE EIGHTH / ANNUAL PHILADELPHIA WATER / COLOR EXHIBITION, NOVEM- / BER 14 TO DECEMBER 18, 1910 / [ornament] / Philadelphia / MCMX

Exhibition Catalogue.
12 mo. Paper covers (light brown with black lettering, brown emblem); 75 pp; plus advertising I–XI.
Size of leaf trimmed 5 × 6⅞ inches.
Illustrated with works by exhibiting artists.

Four paintings exhibited by N. C. Wyeth.
Spring
     Number 792 (page 50)
Winter
     Number 794 (page 51)
Summer
     Number 798 (page 51)
Autumn
     Number 800 (page 51)
All works exhibited in Rotunda.
Received Beck Prize for one of the above.

The Pennsylvania / Academy of the Fine Arts / Founded 1805 / [ornament] / CATALOGUE OF THE 106TH ANNUAL EXHIBITION, FEBRUARY 5 / TO MARCH 26, 1911 / Second Edition / Philadelphia / MCMXI

Exhibition Catalogue.
12 mo. Paper covers (gray with ornamental green designs and lettering); 88 pp; plus advertising I–XVI.
Size of leaf trimmed 4½ × 6⅞ inches.
Illustrated with works by exhibiting artists.

One painting exhibited by N. C. Wyeth.
Spring
     Number 563 (page 49)
Exhibited in Gallery I.

The Pennsylvania / Academy of the Fine Arts / Founded 1805 / [ornament] / The Philadelphia / Water Color Club / CATALOGUE OF THE NINTH ANNUAL PHILADELPHIA WATER / COLOR EXHIBITION, NOVEM- / BER 13 TO DECEMBER 17, 1911 / [ornament] / Philadelphia / MCMXI

Exhibition Catalogue.
12 mo. Paper covers (rose with dark brown lettering, black and white emblem); 108 pp; plus advertising I–XII.
Size of leaf trimmed 5 × 6⅞ inches.
Illustrated with works by exhibiting artists.

Two paintings exhibited by N. C. Wyeth.
Three Wise Men
     Number 1006 (page 79)
The Poet
     Number 1044 (page 83)
All works exhibited in South Corridor.

The Pennsylvania / Academy of the Fine Arts / Founded 1805 / [ornament] / The Philadelphia / Water Color Club / CATALOGUE OF THE TENTH / ANNUAL PHILADELPHIA WATER / COLOR EXHIBITION, NOVEM- / BER 10 to DECEMBER 15, 1912 / [ornament] / Philadelphia / MCMXII

Exhibition Catalogue.
12 mo. Paper covers (brown); 56 pp; plus advertising I–XVI.
Size of leaf trimmed 5 × 6⅞ inches.
Illustrated with works by exhibiting artists.

One illustration in black and white by N. C. Wyeth.
Captain Bones
Three paintings exhibited by N. C. Wyeth
Old Pew (Illustrating *Treasure Island*)
     Number 159 (page 16)
Captain Bones (Illustrating *Treasure Island*)
     Number 166 (page 17)
The Coming of the Huns
     Number 174 (page 18)
All works exhibited in the North Transept Gallery.

The Pennsylvania / Academy of the Fine Arts / Founded 1805 / [ornament] / The Philadelphia Water Color Club / The Pennsylvania Society / of Miniature Painters / CATALOGUE OF THE ELEVENTH / ANNUAL PHILADELPHIA WATER / COLOR EXHIBITION, AND THE / TWELFTH ANNUAL EXHIBITION / OF MINIATURES / November 9 to December 14, 1913 / [ornament] / Philadelphia / 1913

Exhibition Catalogue.
12 mo. Paper covers (gray with green lettering, brown emblem); 102 pp; plus advertising I–XII.
Size of leaf trimmed 5 × 6⅞ inches.
Illustrated with works by exhibiting artists.

Four paintings exhibited by N. C. Wyeth.
Draw Poker
     Number 721 (page 47)

Golyer's Ben
  Number 723 (page 47)
Little Breeches
  Number 724 (page 47)
Jim Bludso
  Number 725 (page 47)
  All works exhibited in North Transept Gallery.

The Pennsylvania / Academy of the Fine Arts / Founded 1805 / [ornament] / The Philadelphia Water Color Club / The Pennsylvania Society / of Miniature Painters / CATALOGUE OF THE TWELFTH / ANNUAL PHILADELPHIA WATER / COLOR EXHIBITION, AND THE / THIRTEENTH ANNUAL EXHIBITION / OF MINIATURES / November 8 To December 13, 1914 / [ornament] / Philadelphia / 1914

Exhibition Catalogue.
12 mo. Paper covers (light blue with dark blue lettering and emblem); 102 pp; plus advertising I–XII.
Size of leaf trimmed 5 × 6⅞ inches.
Illustrated with works by exhibiting artists.

One illustration in black and white by N. C. Wyeth.
The Black Dragon
Five paintings exhibited by N. C. Wyeth.
The Black Dragon
  Number 1006 (page 79)
At Queen's Ferry: Illustration for Kidnapped
  Number 1015 (page 80)
With the Blind Beggar on the Isle of Mull: Illustration for Kidnapped
  Number 1029 (page 81)
Opium Smoker
  Number 1040 (page 82)
Book Cover for Kidnapped (page 82)
  All works exhibited in Rotunda and West Corridor.

The Pennsylvania / Academy of the Fine Arts / Founded 1805 / [ornament] / The Philadelphia Water Color Club / The Pennsylvania Society / of Miniature Painters / CATALOGUE OF THE THIRTEENTH / ANNUAL PHILADELPHIA WATER / COLOR EXHIBITION, AND THE / FOURTEENTH ANNUAL EXHIBITION / OF MINIATURES / November 7 To December 12, 1915 / [ornament] / Philadelphia / 1915

Exhibition Catalogue.
12 mo. Paper covers (gray with green lettering and emblem); 118 pp; plus advertising I–XII.
Size of leaf trimmed 5 × 6⅞ inches.
Illustrated with works by exhibiting artists.

One painting exhibited by N. C. Wyeth.
A Beach Tragedy (Oil)
  Number 317 (page 33)
Exhibited in Gallery K.

The Pennsylvania / Academy of the Fine Arts / Founded 1805 / [ornament] / The Philadelphia Water Color Club / The Pennsylvania Society / of Miniature Painters / CATALOGUE OF THE FOURTEENTH / ANNUAL PHILADELPHIA WATER / COLOR EXHIBITION AND THE / FIFTEENTH ANNUAL EXHIBITION / OF MINIATURES / November 5 To December 10, 1916 / [ornament] / Philadelphia / 1916

Exhibition Catalogue.
12 mo. Paper covers (light green with dark green lettering and emblem); 98 pp; plus advertising I–XIV.

Size of leaf trimmed 5 × 6⅞ inches.
Illustrated with works by exhibiting artists.

Four paintings exhibited by N. C. Wyeth.
A Northern Tragedy (Oil Painting)
  Number 819 (page 73)
Decoration for Poem (Oil Painting)
  Number 820 (page 73)
The Roaring Skipper (Oil Painting)
  Number 831 (page 74)
Thorgunna, the Waif Woman (Oil Painting)
  Number 832 (page 74)
  All works exhibited in Central Gallery.

The Pennsylvania / Academy of the Fine Arts / Founded 1805 / The Philadelphia Water Color Club / The Pennsylvania Society / of Miniature Painters / CATALOGUE OF THE FIFTEENTH / ANNUAL PHILADELPHIA WATER / COLOR EXHIBITION, AND THE / SIXTEENTH ANNUAL EXHIBITION / OF MINIATURES / NOVEMBER 4 TO DECEMBER 9, 1917 / Philadelphia / 1917

Exhibition Catalogue.
12 mo. Paper covers (buff with brown lettering, brown emblem); 136 pp; plus advertising I–XVI.
Size of leaf trimmed 5 × 6⅞ inches.
Illustrated with works by exhibiting artists.

Three illustrations (group) in black and white by N. C. Wyeth.
Medieval Courtship
The Wild Woman's Tragedy
Village Tragedy
Six paintings exhibited by N. C. Wyeth.
Illustration for The Story of Robin Hood
  Number 453 (page 47)
The Prophet
  Number 454 (page 47)
Illustration
  Number 456 (page 48)
Medieval Courtship
  Number 468 (page 49)
The Wild Woman's Lullaby
  Number 469 (page 49)
Village Tragedy
  Number 471 (page 49)
  All works exhibited in North Transept.

The Pennsylvania / Academy of the Fine Arts / Founded 1805 / CATALOGUE OF THE 115TH ANNUAL EX- / HIBITION, FEBRUARY 8 / TO MARCH 28, 1920 / Second Edition / Philadelphia / 1920

Exhibition Catalogue.
12 mo. Paper covers (gray with red lettering and ornamental decorations); 112 pp; plus advertising I–XVI
Size of leaf trimmed 4¾ × 6⅝ inches.
Illustrated with works by exhibiting artists.

One illustration (painting) in black and white by N. C. Wyeth.
Buttonwood Farm
One painting exhibited by N. C. Wyeth.
Buttonwood Farm
  Number 39 (page 21)
Exhibited in the South Corridor Gallery.

THE PENNSYLVANIA ACADEMY / OF THE FINE ARTS / Founded 1805 / The Philadelphia Water Color Club / The Pennsylvania Society of / Miniature Painters / Catalogue of the Eighteenth Annual / Philadelphia Water Color Exhibition, / and the Nineteenth Annual / Exhibition of Miniatures / November 7 to December 12, 1920 / Second Edition / Philadelphia / 1920

Exhibition Catalogue.
12 mo. Paper covers (light brown with dark brown lettering, brown emblem); 86 pp; plus advertising I–XIV.
Size of leaf trimmed 5 × 6⅞ inches.
Illustrated with works by exhibiting artists.

One illustration in black and white by N. C. Wyeth.
The Captives, The Last of the Mohicans
Five paintings exhibited by N. C. Wyeth.
The Supplicant (The Last of the Mohicans–Oil)
  Number 562 (page 57)
The Captives (The Last of the Mohicans–Oil)
  Number 628 (page 63)
The Psalmist (The Last of the Mohicans–Oil)
  Number 651 (page 65)
Uncas Slays a Deer (The Last of the Mohicans–Oil)
  Number 683 (page 67)
The Burial of Uncas (The Last of the Mohicans–Oil)
  Number 684 (page 67)
  All works exhibited in Rotunda and West Corridor.

Catalogue Of The One- / Hundred-And-Twenty-First / Annual Exhibition Of The / Pennsylvania Academy / Of The Fine Arts / January 31, 1926 / (Academy seal) / March 21, 1926 / Philadelphia

Exhibition Catalogue.
12 mo. Paper covers (brown with dark brown lettering); 90 pp; plus index of sponsors I–XVI.
Size of leaf trimmed 5¼ × 7¾ inches.
Illustrated with works by exhibiting artists.

One painting exhibited by N. C. Wyeth.
The Harbor at Herring Gut
  Number 123 (page 33)
Exhibited in the Central Gallery.

Catalogue Of / The One-Hundred-And- / Twenty-Sixth Annual / Exhibition Of The / Pennsylvania Academy / Of The Fine Arts / January 25th–March 15th / 1931 / Philadelphia

Exhibition Catalogue.
12 mo. Paper covers (blue with silver lettering); 95 pp; plus advertising I–XII.
Size of leaf trimmed 5¼ × 7¾ inches.
Illustrated with works by exhibiting artists.

One painting exhibited by N. C. Wyeth.
Pennsylvania Barn
  Number 232 (page 39)
Exhibited in Gallery F.

The Pennsylvania / Academy of the Fine Arts / Founded 1805 / CATALOGUE OF THE / 127th ANNUAL EXHIBITION / January 24 to March 13, 1932 / Final Edition / Philadelphia / 1932

Exhibition Catalogue.
12 mo. Paper covers (red with silver lettering); 85 pp; plus advertising I–XII.
Size of leaf trimmed 5 × 7¾ inches.
Illustrated with works by exhibiting artists.

One painting exhibited by N. C. Wyeth.
The Red Pung
  Number 30 (page 15)

The Pennsylvania / Academy of the Fine Arts / Founded 1805 / CATALOGUE of the / 128th ANNUAL EXHIBITION / January 29 to March 19, 1933 / Second Edition / Philadelphia / 1933

Exhibition Catalogue.
12 mo. Paper covers (with gray lettering); 80 pp; plus advertising I–X.
Size of leaf trimmed 5 × 7¾ inches.
Illustrated with works by exhibiting artists.

Two paintings exhibited by N. C. Wyeth.
In a Dream, I Meet General Washington
     Number 92 (page 18)
My Mother
     Number 426 (page 44)
All works exhibited in Gallery B and Gallery 1.

The Pennsylvania / Academy of the Fine Arts / Founded 1805 / Catalogue of the / 130th Annual Exhibition / January 27 to March 3, 1935 / Second Edition / Philadelphia / 1935

Exhibition Catalogue.
12 mo. Paper covers (red with silver lettering); 37 pp; plus advertising I–XIII.
Size of leaf trimmed 5 × 7¾ inches.
Illustrated with works by exhibiting artists.

One painting exhibited by N. C. Wyeth.
The Sounding Sea
     Number 132 (page 17)
Exhibited in Gallery F.

The Pennsylvania / Academy of the Fine Arts / Founded 1805 / CATALOGUE OF THE / 131st ANNUAL EXHIBITION / January 26 to March 1, 1936 / Second Edition / Philadelphia / 1936

Exhibition Catalogue.
12 mo. Paper covers (dark blue with silver lettering); 36 pp; plus advertising I–XI.
Size of leaf trimmed 5 × 7¾ inches.
Illustrated with works by exhibiting artists.

One painting exhibited by N. C. Wyeth.
Corn Harvest
     Number 233 (page 21)
Exhibited in Gallery K.

CATALOGUE OF THE / ONE HUNDRED AND THIRTY-FOURTH / ANNUAL EXHIBITION / OF / PAINTING AND SCULPTURE / January 29 through March 5 / 1939 / Weekdays and Holidays 10 A.M. to 5 P.M. Sundays 1 P.M. to 5 P.M. / Second Edition / The Price of this Catalogue is Twenty-Five Cents / The Pennsylvania Academy / of the Fine Arts / Broad and Cherry Streets Philadelphia

Exhibition Catalogue.
12 mo. Paper covers (bright yellow with gray lettering); pages unnumbered; plus advertising.
Size of leaf trimmed 5 × 7¾ inches.
Illustrated with works by exhibiting artists.

Two paintings exhibited by N. C. Wyeth.
Sundown, Maine Coast
     Number 7
Deep Cove Lobster Man
     Number 268
All works exhibited in Gallery A and Gallery L.

THE PENNSYLVANIA ACADEMY / OF THE FINE ARTS / Presents / The One Hundred and Thirty-Fifth / Annual Exhibition / of / Paintings and Sculpture / January 28 through March 3 / 1940 / Weekdays and Holidays, 10 A.M. to 5 P.M.; Sundays, 1 to 5 P.M. / Catalogue / Second Edition / The Price of this Catalogue is Twenty-Five Cents / Broad and Cherry Streets Philadelphia

Exhibition Catalogue.
12 mo. Paper covers (light green with dark green lettering); pages unnumbered; plus advertising.
Size of leaf trimmed 5 × 7¾ inches.
Illustrated with works by exhibiting artists.

One painting exhibited by N. C. Wyeth.
The Road to the Jones House
     Number 7
Exhibited in Gallery A.

THE PENNSYLVANIA ACADEMY / OF THE FINE ARTS / presents / The One Hundred and Thirty-Sixth / Annual Exhibition / of / Painting and Sculpture / January 26 through March 2 / 1941 / Weekdays, 10 A.M. to 5 P.M.; Sundays and Holidays, 1 to 5 P.M. / Catalogue / Second Edition / The Price of this Catalogue is Twenty-Five Cents / Broad and Cherry Streets Philadelphia

Exhibition Catalogue.
12 mo. Paper covers (brown with light blue lettering); pages unnumbered; plus advertising.
Size of leaf trimmed 5 × 7¾ inches.
Illustrated with works by exhibiting artists.

One painting exhibited by N. C. Wyeth.
John Teel: Fisherman
     Number 30
Exhibited in Gallery B.

THE PENNSYLVANIA ACADEMY / OF THE FINE ARTS / presents / THE ONE HUNDRED AND THIRTY-EIGHTH / ANNUAL EXHIBITION / OF / PAINTING AND SCULPTURE / January 24 through February 28 / 1943 / Tuesdays through Saturdays, 10 A.M. to 5 P.M.; Sundays and Holidays, 1 to 5 P.M. / Closed Mondays / Catalogue / Second Edition / The Price of this Catalogue is Twenty-Five Cents / Broad and Cherry Streets Philadelphia

Exhibition Catalogue.
12 mo. Paper covers (beige with orange lettering); pages unnumbered; plus advertising.
Size of leaf trimmed 5 × 7¾ inches.

Painting exhibited by N. C. Wyeth.
Summer Night
     Number 14
Exhibited in Gallery A.

THE PENNSYLVANIA ACADEMY / OF THE FINE ARTS / presents / THE ONE HUNDRED AND THIRTY-NINTH / ANNUAL EXHIBITION / OF / PAINTING AND SCULPTURE / January 23 through February 27 / 1944 / Tuesdays through Saturdays, 10 A.M. to 5 P.M.; Sundays and Holidays, 1 to 5 P.M. / Closed Mondays / Catalogue / Second Edition / The Price of this Catalogue is Twenty-Five Cents / Broad and Cherry Streets Philadelphia

Exhibition Catalogue.
12 mo. Paper covers (light blue with gray lettering); pages unnumbered; plus advertising.
Size of leaf trimmed 5 × 7¾ inches.
Illustrated with works by exhibiting artists.

One painting exhibited by N. C. Wyeth.
Dark Harbor Fishermen
     Number 16
Exhibited in Gallery A.

The Pennsylvania Academy / Of The Fine Arts / Presents / THE ONE HUNDRED AND FORTY-FIRST / ANNUAL EXHIBITION / OF / PAINTING AND SCULPTURE / January 26 through March 3 / 1946 / Tuesdays through Saturdays, 10 A.M. to 5 P.M.; Sundays and Holidays, 1 to 5 P.M. / Closed Mondays / Catalogue / Second Edition / The Price of this Catalogue is Twenty-Five Cents / Broad and Cherry Streets / Philadelphia

Exhibition Catalogue.
12 mo. Paper covers (light brown with dark green lettering); unnumbered pages.
Size of leaf trimmed 5¼ × 7¾ inches.
Illustrated with works by exhibiting artists.

One painting by N. C. Wyeth exhibited (Mrs. N. C. Wyeth).
Pennsylvania Farmer
     Number 22
Exhibited in Gallery B.

Studio Guild Inc.
[illustration] / Second Annual / Art Display Week / Sponsored By / Studio Guild Inc. New York City / October 25 to 31, 1936

Exhibition Catalogue.
4 to.
Size of leaf trimmed 7½ × 10½ inches.
Illustrated with the works of numerous artists.

One illustration (painting) by N. C. Wyeth.
The Red Pung (Number 93)
Exhibited at the Canadian National Railways and Steamship Lines.

The Toledo Museum of Art
THE TOLEDO MUSEUM OF ART / Founded by Edward Drummond Libbey / Catalogue / [rules] / Eighteenth Annual / Exhibition of Selected / Paintings By Contempo- / rary American Artists / [rules] / June 1 To August 31, 1930

Exhibition Catalogue.
8 vo. Paper covers; 4 pp.
Size of leaf trimmed 6¼ × 9 inches.

One painting exhibited by N. C. Wyeth (Number 70).
Pennsylvania Barn

The Treasury Department
A National Exhibition Of Original Paintings / By American Artists • Designed For Poster Use / Sponsored By The Treasury Department's / National Committee Of Honorary Patrons / [seal] / [ornaments—stars] / Art for Bonds / [ornaments—stars]

Exhibition Catalogue.
Large 8 vo. Paper covers (light blue top half, medium blue bottom half, reverse type)
Size of leaf trimmed 7½ × 10 inches.
Introduction by Henry Morgenthau, Jr.
Foreword by Mrs. Henry Morgenthau, Jr.
Brief biographical sketch on N. C. Wyeth.

One painting exhibited by N. C. Wyeth.
Uncle Sam (number 36)

Note: The painting was reproduced as a poster in color for the War Savings Staff.

Unitarian Laymen's League
The / Parables of Jesus / Illustrated By / N. C. Wyeth / An Announcement / [Unitarian seal] / Unitarian Laymen's League / Seven Park Square, Boston / New York Chicago /

St. Louis San Francisco / December 25, 1923
[all surrounded by double boxed rules]

Exhibition Announcement.
Size of leaf trimmed 4 × 8 inches.
A private viewing of the first six paintings
completed by N. C. Wyeth.
The text contains a history on the develop-
ment of The Parables of Jesus paintings and
Mr. Wyeth's interpretations of the completed
works.

List of paintings exhibited:
The Child
The Leaven
The Net
The Barren Fig Tree
The Hidden Treasure
The Secret Growth of the Seed

U.S. Naval Academy Museum
[three rules] / United States Naval Academy
Museum / Annapolis, Maryland / [ornament]
/ CATALOGUE / –of– / PAINTINGS / [in-
signia] / 1961 / [three rules] [all printed in
blue]

Exhibition Catalogue.
8 vo. Paper covers; 32 pp.
Size of leaf trimmed 5½ × 8½ inches.
Foreword by Wade DeWeese, Capt. U.S.
Navy (Ret.) Director, U.S. Naval Academy
Museum, Published April, 1961.
A listing of works in the collection.

Paintings by N. C. Wyeth.
Flags In America's History (Numbers 212–23)
212 America's First Standing Army
213 Battle of Bunker Hill
214 Betsy Ross Making the Flag
215 Coast Guard to the Rescue
216 Columbus Discovers America
217 U.S.S. Constitution Bombarding Tripoli
218 Faithful Troops Cheer General Lee
219 Fremont and the Pathfinding Flag
220 John Paul Jones Hoists Our First Flag
221 Last Stand at the Alamo
222 Norsemen Sight America's Shores
223 Old Glory, Symbol of Liberty

Note: The illustrations originally appeared for the
Flags In American History calendar, published by
John Morrell & Co., 1944.

Washington National Cathedral
A GUIDE TO / WASHINGTON CATHE-
DRAL / [rule] / The Cathedral Church Of
Saint Peter And Saint Paul / Mount Saint Al-
ban / Washington, District Of Columbia

Copyright 1965 by the National Cathedral
Association.
Catalogue.
8 vo. Paper covers (photograph of the National Cathedral in color); 158 pp.
Size of leaf trimmed 5½ × 8⅜ inches.
Illustrated in color and black and white with
numerous paintings, sculpture and photographs.

One illustration in color.
The Chapel of The Holy Spirit Triptych by
N. C. Wyeth p 48
Description: The triptych features, in the
center panel painting, Christ the Lord. The
panels to the right and left are angels praising the Lord with voice and instruments. In
the small sections below the three panels are
seven small doves, symbolizing the sections
of the confirmation prayer. Patterns of the
needlepoint kneelers are also woven around
the dove as the symbol of the Holy Spirit.

Wilmington Savings Fund Society
[photographic portrait of N. C. Wyeth 1882–
1945] / Tribute to N. C. Wyeth / October 21–
November 1, 1968 / Wilmington Savings Fund
Society / Wilmington, Delaware

Exhibition Catalogue.
12 mo. Paper covers in color (center section
of the mural, The Apotheosis of the Family)
Size of leaf trimmed 5½ × 7 inches.
Collation: Description of mural; title (including photographic portrait); biography by
Henry C. Pitz; catalogue of the exhibition;
excerpts; The Apotheosis of the Family; acknowledgments; title (without photographic
portrait).

Cover illustration in color.
The Apotheosis of the Family (front and
back covers)
List of paintings exhibited:
1. Somewhere They Had Met ("The Romantic
   Prince")
2. He Hurled the Flagon ("The Romantic
   Prince")
3. Robin Hood and Little John (The Anthology
   of Children's Literature)
4. Death of Finnward Keelfarer ("The Waif
   Woman")
5. Fence Builders
6. Title Page Design (David Balfour)
7. The Falls at Brinton's Mill
8. Still Life with Brush
9. A Moonlit Night
10. Herring Gut
11. Wallace and Marion (Scottish Chiefs)
12. Cover Painting (The Yearling)
13. Jody and Flag (The Yearling)
14. Fight with Old Slewfoot (The Yearling)
15. Penny Teaches Jody (The Yearling)
16. Jody Lost (The Yearling)
17. Spearfishing
18. Still Life with Apples
19. Teel's Landing
20. Troops by the Hundreds Were Passing (Sally
    Castleton)
21. Mowing
22. The Seeker
23. Sweet Land of Liberty
24. The Fogbow
25. N. C. Wyeth Self Portrait
26. Howard Pyle's Studio in Wilmington
27. The Flutter-Mill (The Yearling)
28. Portrait of Stanley M. Arthurs
29. Gray Day—Maine Coast
30. Display of N. C. Wyeth sketch, letter, and
    books that he illustrated.

The Wilmington Society of the Fine Arts
(The Delaware Art Museum)
CATALOGUE / of the / Sixth Annual / EX-
HIBITION / of / The Wilmington Society /
of the Fine Arts / [ornament] / New Century
Club / Wilmington, Del. / November 5th to
8th / 1917

Exhibition Catalogue.
Large 8 vo. Paper covers.
Size of leaf trimmed 4¼ × 9½ inches.

Four paintings exhibited by N. C. Wyeth.
Tree Cutters (number 114)
Beethoven (number 120)
Cows in Moonlight (number 142)
Blackbeard (number 163)

CATALOGUE / of the / Seventh Annual /
EXHIBITION / of / The Wilmington Society
/ of the Fine Arts / [ornament] / New Century Club / Wilmington, Del. / February 3rd,
4th, 5th and 6th / 1919

Exhibition Catalogue.
Large 8 vo. Paper covers.
Size of leaf trimmed 4¼ × 9½ inches.

Four paintings exhibited by N. C. Wyeth.
Chateau Thierry! (number 15)
In France, 1918 (number 25)
Brandywine Meadows (number 42)
Self-Portrait (number 89)

[rule] / CATALOGUE / of the / Eighth An-
nual / EXHIBITION / of / The Wilmington
Society / of the Fine Arts / [ornament] /
DuPont Ball Room / Wilmington, Delaware /
April 13th and 14th / 1920 / [rule] / Private
View / Monday Evening, April 12th / [rule]

Exhibition Catalogue.
Large 8 vo. Paper covers.
Size of leaf trimmed 4¼ × 9½ inches.

Three paintings exhibited by N. C. Wyeth.
The Passing of Summer (number 19)
A Little River (number 44)
Buttonwood Farm (number 82)
     Loaned by the Reading Museum

[design—museum] / Preserving / A Priceless
Heritage / [band] / Achieving A / Community
Art Center / [band] / [band] [design and
bands printed in blue]

Printed May 7, 1935.
Catalogue.
4 to. Paper covers.
Size of leaf trimmed 8⅝ × 11 inches.
Illustrated with works in the museum collec-
tion.

One illustration in black and white by N. C.
Wyeth.
Sailor's Fantasy

N. C. WYETH, N.A. 1882–1945 / MEMO-
RIAL EXHIBITION / JANUARY 7 TO 27,
1946 / The Wilmington Society Of The Fine
Arts / Delaware Art Center Building / Wilmington . . . . Delaware

Memorial Exhibition Catalogue.
Limited to 1200 copies.
Printed by C. L. Story Co.
Large 8 vo. Paper covers (light gray); (16)
pp.
Size of leaf trimmed 7⅜ × 9⅜ inches.
Biographical Sketch • Newell Convers Wyeth,
N.A.
Foreword by Paul Horgan.
Mounted photograph of N. C. Wyeth (by
William E. Phelps)

Three mounted illustrations.
"Summer Night" (color)
"Nightfall" (black and white)
Illustration for Treasure Island (color)
     Description: The Hostage

List of Paintings.
1. Self Portrait, 1914
2. Island Funeral
3. In a Dream I Meet General Washington
   awarded 4th W.A. Clark Prize Corcoran Gallery of Art 1932
4. Nightfall
   awarded 3rd Popular Prize Carnegie Institute
   1945
5. Self Portrait, 1940
   loaned by the National Academy
6. In the Kitchen
7. Grandfather's Sleigh
8. Mrs. Cushman's House
9. Mrs. Cushman's House
10. Summer Night
    awarded the Painting Prize, The Wilmington
    Society of the Fine Arts 1943
11. The Spring House
    awarded 1st Popular Prize Corcoran Gallery
    of Art 1945

12. Deep Cove Fisherman
  loaned by the Pennsylvania Academy of Fine Arts
13. Low Tide
  loaned by Mr. and Mrs. A. Felix DuPont
15. Fisherman Family
16. Still Life
  loaned by Mr. and Mrs. Henry T. Bush, Jr.
17. Corn Harvest
18. Dying Winter
19. The Crystal Gazer
20. Rainy Day
21. Fence Builders
22. Woodcutters in the Snow
23. Still Life with Onions
24. Children Bathing
25. My Mother
26. Spring Landscape
27. The Apple Orchard

List of Illustrations.
Anthology of Children's Literature
  Compiled by Johnson and Scott, Houghton, Mifflin & Co. 1940
28. Hark Hark the Dogs Do Bark
29. Jack the Giant Killer
30. The Three Friends
31. St. George and the Dragon
Men of Concord by Henry David Thoreau
  Edited by F. H. Allen Houghton, Mifflin & Co. 1936

32. Johnny and His Woodchuck Skin Cap
33. Thoreau and the Fox
  Loaned by the Canajoharie Library and Art Gallery
64. The Muskrat Hunters
David Balfour By Robert Louis Stevenson
  Charles Scribner's Sons 1924
34. The Gibbet
Drums By James Boyd
  Charles Scribner's Sons 1928
35. The Mother of John Paul Jones
36. Johnny's Defeat at the Dock
65. Johnny's Fight with Cherry
The Scottish Chiefs By Jane Porter
  Charles Scribner's Sons 1926
37. The Pledge
38. Vision of Wallace
39. In the Tower of London
40. Battle of Sterling Castle
The Mysterious Stranger By Mark Twain
  Charles Scribner's Sons 1911
41. Three Boys
42. Satan
43. The Drowning
Michael Strogoff by Jules Verne
  Charles Scribner's Sons 1927
44. Fall of the Blind Horse
45. The Fight with Ivan Ogareff
Trending into Maine By Kenneth Roberts
  Little, Brown and Co. 1938

46. Dan'l Nason, Sailing Master, 1814
47. Charlie Stone
48. The Sea Serpent
The Yearling By Marjorie Kinnan Rawlings
  Charles Scribner's Sons 1939
49. Jacket Design
50. The Bear Story
Westward Ho! By Charles Kingsley
  Charles Scribner's Sons 1920
51. The Mourner in the Bog
52. John Brimblecombe
53. Rose and the White Witch

      o   o   o

54. Illustration for *Scribner's Magazine* 1906
55. Illustration for *Scribner's Magazine* 1906
56. Illustration for *Scribner's Magazine* 1907
57. The Life Boat *Scribner's Magazine* 1907
58. Illustration for *Scribner's Magazine* 1907
59. Illustration for *Scribner's Magazine* 1907
60. Endpapers for *The White Company* By A. Conan Doyle David McKay
61. Illustration for *The Deerslayer* By James Fenimore Cooper Charles Scribner's Sons 1925
62. Parable of the Lost Sheep from *The Parables of Jesus* By S. Parkes Cadman David McKay, 1931
63. Design for Book Cover for *Anthony Adverse* By Hervey Allen
66. Miles Standish

IX. Miscellaneous Catalogues

Great American Editions
BRANDYWINE TRADITION ARTISTS / featuring the works of Howard Pyle, Frank E. Schoonover, The Wyeth Family / Charles Colombo, David Hanna / with Introductory Essay / by Rowland Elzea, Curator of Collections, Delaware Art Museum / October 1971—October 1972 / Exhibitors: / International Art Gallery, Pittsburgh, Pennsylvania / Tennessee Fine Arts Center, Nashville, Tennessee / Wichita Art Association, Wichita, Kansas / Isaac Delgado Museum of Art, New Orleans, Louisiana / Charleston Museum at Sunrise, Charleston, West Virginia

Copyright 1971 by Great American Editions.
First printing—October 1971.
Catalogue.
Size of leaf trimmed 10⅞ × 8⅜ inches.
8 vo. Paper covers (tan) with cut-out center; designs and lettering on cover stamped in brown; 55 pp.
The catalogue contains brief biographical sketches of the artists represented.
Illustrated in sepia tint and black and white with numerous paintings, drawings and photographs.
N. C. Wyeth (1882–1945)
Pages 21–24.
Biographical sketch (page 22)

   p 22 Photograph of N. C. Wyeth on horse with a young friend, 1904 (plate xxi)
      23 Illustration from *Sally Castleton Southerner* (plate xxii)
      23 Johnny fights Cherry (illustration from *Drums*) (plate xxiii)
      24 "Indian Fisherman, Woman and Child" (plate xxiv)
      24 "A Sailor's Fantasy" (plate xxv)

Hotel duPont (Wilmington, Delaware)
[illustration in color] / Paintings in the / Hotel duPont

Catalogue.
Large 8 vo. Paper covers; unnumbered pages.
Size of leaf trimmed 6 × 9 inches.
Illustrated in color with works by various artists.

One illustration (painting) in color by N. C. Wyeth.
The Island Funeral
   Exhibited in the Club Room
A two-page description and biographical sketch accompany the painting.

William A. Farnsworth Library and Art Museum
OILS • WATERCOLORS • DRAWINGS / by / JAMES WYETH / July 11—September 8, 1969 / An exhibition presented by the William A. Farnsworth Library and Art Museum / Rockland, Maine

Copyright 1969 by the William A. Farnsworth Library and Art Museum, Rockland, Maine.
Exhibition Catalogue.
Size of leaf trimmed 7⅝ × 11 inches.
12 mo. Paper covers (painting in color by James Wyeth); (unnumbered pages)
Illustrated with paintings and drawings in black and white by James Wyeth.
Reference to N. C. Wyeth in the Introduction by Priscilla B. Adams (Director of Public Relations for William A. Farnsworth Library and Art Museum)

Los Angeles County Museum of Natural History
W. H. D. KOERNER / Illustrator of the West / (drawing) / An exhibition arranged by the History Division / in cooperation with the artist's daughter, Mrs. / Ruth Koerner Oliver, of Santa Barbara / Los Angeles County Museum of Natural History / February 21st to June 9th, 1968

Catalogue.
4 to. Paper covers with cover illustration in color; 64 pp.
Illustrated in color and black and white with the works of W. H. D. Koerner.
Reference to N. C. Wyeth on page 6.

Missouri's Capitol
Souvenir Guide To / MISSOURI'S / CAPITOL

Catalogue (Guide).
4 to. Paper covers (photographs of Missouri State Capitol in color)
Size of leaf trimmed 8½ × 11 inches.
Illustrated in color with numerous paintings, photographs, diagrams, etc.

Two illustrations (lunette murals) in color by N. C. Wyeth.
   The Battle of Wilson's Creek was a desperate engagement in the Civil War.
   The Battle of Westport has been called the Gettysburg of the West.

National Cathedral Association
Washington Cathedral / A Series of Views / Many In Full Color / [Cathedral seal] / National Cathedral Association / Washington Cathedral / Mount Saint Alban / Washington, D.C. [1939]
Catalogue [Guide]

12 mo. Paper covers (photograph with gold lettering); 30 pp.
Size of leaf trimmed 5¾ × 7¾ inches.
Illustrated in color and black and white with numerous paintings and photographs.

Two mural paintings in color by N. C. Wyeth.
   Chapel of the Holy Spirit
      Central Panel of the Reredos p 5

   Chapel of the Holy Spirit
      North Panel of the Reredos p 14

St. Andrew's School
ST. ANDREW'S SCHOOL / The First Decade / 1930–1940 / (School Emblem)

Brochure.
Size of leaf trimmed 9 × 11¾ inches.

One illustration (mural painting) in black and white by N. C. Wyeth. (front and back covers)
Presented to the School in 1938 by Mrs. Irénée duPont—The painting covers the east wall of the Dining Hall.

The Wilmington Society of the Fine Arts
Catalogue of Pictures / by / Howard Pyle / In The Permanent Collection Of The / Wilmington Society Of The Fine Arts / [ornament] / Public Library Building / Wilmington —Delaware

Catalogue.
Printed by Chas. L. Story Co., Wilmington, Del., 1926.
4 to. Paper covers (gray with cover label in color by Howard Pyle); 32 pp.
Size of leaf trimmed 6⅞ × 9⅞ inches.
N. C. Wyeth is listed among those individuals who contributed to the original fund for the purchase and endowment of the Collection of Pictures by Howard Pyle, and who, in order to further the interests of Art in Delaware, formed the Wilmington Society of the Fine Arts in the year 1912.
Additional Acquisitions.
   Painting by N. C. Wyeth acquired by purchase from one of the Society's annual exhibitions.
   A Sailor's Fantasy (1920)

The Wilmington Society of the Fine Arts
(The Delaware Art Museum)
HOWARD PYLE / Works In The Collection Of The / Delaware Art Museum / 2301 Kentmere Parkway / Wilmington, Delaware 19806 / 1971 / (copyright) The Wilmington Society of the Fine Arts

Catalogue.
Large 8 vo. Paper covers (red); 56 pp.
Size of leaf trimmed 7 × 9⅞ inches.
Photograph of Howard Pyle at his easel.
Howard Pyle Signature Types
Numerous illustrations in color and black and white by Howard Pyle.
Howard Pyle And Late 19th Century American Illustration by Rowland Eliza, Curator of Collections (pages 5–10)
   N. C. Wyeth listed among Pyle's notable pupils plus the Society's N. C. Wyeth research library (page 10)

X. Exhibition Folders

American Lithographic Company, Inc.
(galleries)
[illustration] / A most unusual / collection of original / paintings showing some / of the recent experiments of / N. C. WYETH
On view during the month of July in the galleries of the American Lithographic Company, Inc., 52 East 19th Street, New York, N. Y.

Exhibition Folder.
Size of leaf trimmed 8¼ × 6¼ inches.
One illustration printed in green.
> Description: The endpaper illustrations from *The Odyssey of Homer*.

The Chadds Ford Historical Society
The Chadds Ford / Art Heritage / 1898–1968 / Howard Pyle / N. C. Wyeth / Carolyn Wyeth / John W. McCoy II / Andrew Wyeth / Rea Redifer / George A. Weymouth / James Wyeth

Folder with cover drawing by Andrew Wyeth.
Size of leaf trimmed 8½ × 10¹⁵⁄₁₆ inches.

Thirteen N. C. Wyeth paintings exhibited.
1. The Black Arrow Flieth Never More
2. The Vedette
3. Ben Gunn
4. Portrait of Andy
5. Dobbin
6. Man Fishing
7. Pre-study for Man Fishing
8. Self Portrait
9. First Mark for *Treasure Island*
10. Title Page of *Rip Van Winkle*
11. Blind Pew
12. Four Indian Drawings
13. In a Dream I Meet General Washington

The Chester County Art Association
Second Annual Exhibition / The Chester County / Art Association / at / "North Hill" / West Chester • • • Pennsylvania / May 13th to 21st, 1933 / [rule] / [list of officers] / [list of committee chairmen]

Exhibition Folder (printed in green).
Size of leaf trimmed 6 × 9 inches.

Three paintings exhibited by N. C. Wyeth.
Walden Pond Revisited (number 69)
Old Albert (number 70)
John McVey (number 71)

The / WYETH EXHIBITION / [painting— Roman Horse by Carolyn Wyeth] / Chester County Art Centre / 320 North Church Street, West Chester, Pa. / October 12 to and including October 31, 1935. / Open daily 9 A.M. to 5 P.M. / Wednesdays and Saturdays 9 A.M. to 10 P.M. / Held Under The Joint Sponsorship Of The / Chester County Art Association / and the / School Board of West Chester

Exhibition Folder.
Size of leaf trimmed 6⅛ × 9½ inches.
The Wyeths and Their Exhibition
Biographical sketches by John Frederick Lewis, Jr., and Christian Brinton plus accompanying text with photographs of Newell Convers Wyeth, Henriette Wyeth, Carolyn Wyeth, and Andrew Wyeth.

List of paintings exhibited by N. C. Wyeth.
1. Walden Pond Revisited, 1933
2. My Mother, 1931
3. Old Albert, 1931
4. The Recipe Book, 1933
5. Sounding Sea, 1934
6. Harbour, Port Clyde, 1932
7. Spring, 1918–1933
8. Maine Doryman, 1934
9. My Grandfather's House, 1931
10. Brother Islands, 1934
11. Island Farm, 1935
12. Group of Book Illustrations

The Corcoran Gallery of Art
Memorial Exhibition / of / Paintings and Drawings / By / N. C. WYETH / 1882–1945 / [ornament] / THE CORCORAN GALLERY OF ART / Washington, D.C. / From Sunday, May 19th, through Sunday, June 9th, 1946 / [ornament] / Hours of opening: Sundays and May 30th 2 to 5 P.M.; / Mondays 12 P.M. to 4:30 P.M.; other weekdays 9 A.M.

Exhibition Folder.
Gray paper.
Size of leaf trimmed 5 × 7 inches.
Collation: title; biographical sketch; catalogue (paintings and illustrations)

Paintings:
1. War Letter
2. Nightfall
3. Island Funeral
4. Corn Harvest
5. Mrs. Cushman's House
6. The Crystal Gazer
7. My Mother
8. Still Life with Onions
9. Dying Winter
10. The Apple Branch
11. Self Portrait
12. Grandfather's Sleigh
13. Cannibal Shore
14. Hydrographic Signal, Blubber Island, 1944
15. The Jones House
Illustrations:
16. The Drowning
    The Mysterious Stranger by Mark Twain
17. Washington, the Farmer
(Unfinished, last picture)
18. The Mother of John Paul Jones
    Drums by James Boyd
19. The Duel on the Beach
    The Duel on the Beach by Rafael Sabatini
    Lent by Dr. John Oliver La Gorce
20. Life Boat
    Scribner's Magazine, 1907
21. Johnny and His Woodchuck Skin Cap
    Men of Concord by H. D. Thoreau. Edited by F. H. Allen
22. Muskrat Hunters
    Men of Concord by H. D. Thoreau. Edited by F. H. Allen
23. Dan'l Nason, Sailing Master, 1914
    Trending into Maine by Kenneth Roberts
24. The Sea Serpent
    Trending into Maine by Kenneth Roberts
25. In the *Tower of London*
    The Scottish Chiefs by Jane Porter
26. Hark, Hark, the Dogs do Bark
    Anthology of Children's Literature compiled by Johnson and Scott
27. Fall of the Blind Horse
    Michael Strogoff by Jules Verne
28. Death of Slewfoot
    The Yearling by Marjorie K. Rawlings
29. The Forrester Brothers
    The Yearling by Marjorie K. Rawlings
30. John Brimblecombe
    Westward Ho! by Charles Kingsley

Delaware Art Center (The Wilmington Society of the Fine Arts)
[Portrait of N. C. Wyeth by Henriette Wyeth] / Paintings By Members Of / THE WYETH FAMILY / January 8 to 29, 1951 / DELAWARE ART CENTER / Park Drive At Woodlawn Ave.

Exhibition Folder.
Size of leaf trimmed 7 × 9 inches.

One painting exhibited by N. C. Wyeth.
The Spring House (number 36) Delaware Art Center Collection

Galleries of Charles Daniel Frey Company
[illustration] / An / Exhibition / of Paintings by / N. C. WYETH / at the Galleries of / CHARLES DANIEL / FREY COMPANY / Flatiron Building / New York / [seal] / Commencing August Seventeenth

Exhibition Folder.
Size of leaf trimmed 3¾ × 9¼ inches.
Cover illustration in black and white.
> Description: Slag was a figure for sculptors.[1]

Paintings listed in exhibition:
1. Kitchen Romance
2. The Young Dreamer

3. Spring Landscape
4. Still Life
5. Village Tragedy
6. "Wild Bill" Hickock at the Cards
7. The Villain of the Story
8. Still Life
9. Sea Tragedy
10. Icelandic Tragedy
11. The Viking's Wife
12. Fence Builders
13. The Invaders
14. Beach Drama

[1] The cover illustration originally appeared in *Everybody's Magazine*, January 1919, for the story "The Mildest-Mannered Man" by Ben Ames Williams.

Graham, James & Sons (Gallery)
N. C. WYETH / (illustration—train holdup) / Exhibition: January 15–February 8, 1964

Exhibition Folder.
Size of leaf trimmed 7⅞ × 8⅝ inches.

Three illustrations in black and white.
  Two Bandits Holding Up Train (cover illustration)
  Mexican Cowboy With Horse
  Two Boys On Fence With Berry Pails

The folder is accompanied by a loose insert catalogue which contains the list of illustrations exhibited and a brief biographical sketch on N. C. Wyeth.

Macbeth Gallery
[illustration] / In the Georges Islands, Maine / Paintings By / N. C. WYETH / (rule) / December 5th–30th / 1939 / [rule] / Macbeth Gallery / 11 East 57th Street • New York

Exhibition Folder.
Size of leaf trimmed 4⅜ × 6⅛ inches.
Introduction by Peter Hurd.

One illustration in black and white.
Three Fishermen (title page)
List of Titles.
1. Fox in the Snow
2. The Red Dory
3. Blubber Island
4. Sun Glint
5. Marshall Farm
6. Black Spruce Ledge
7. The Road to the Jones House
8. Island Funeral
9. Deep Cove Lobsterman
   Lend by Pennsylvania Academy of Fine Arts
10. Back Shore
11. Ship Building
12. Three Fishermen

Mendola, Joseph T. (Art Gallery)
(Illustration—Norman Rockwell) / The / American / Illustrator / In cooperation with the Famous Artists School / of Westport, Connecticut, we present "The / American Illustrator," a joint exhibition of / outstanding American illustration art, past and / present. January 28th through February, 1972. / Joseph T. Mendola Art Gallery. / JOSEPH T. / MENDOLA / ART GALLERY

Exhibition Folder.
Size of leaf trimmed 3½ × 8½ inches.
Illustrated with the works of various illustrators, past and present.

One illustration in black and white by N. C. Wyeth.
  Description: Endpaper illustration from *Anthony Adverse*.

Portraits, Inc.
The / WYETH FAMILY / [family lineage chart] / Painter Members / (—) / Portraits, Inc. 460 Park Avenue at 57th Street / October 22nd Through November 9th, 1946

Foreword by Helen Appleton Read.
Exhibition Folder.
Size of leaf trimmed 7 × 8¾ inches.
List of paintings exhibited by the family, preceded by a brief biographical sketch.

Paintings exhibited by N. C. Wyeth, N.A., 1882–1945
1. Self Portrait, 1940
   Lent by the National Academy of Design
2. Night Fall
   Lent by the estate of N. C. Wyeth
3. Spring House
   Lent by the Wilmington Society of the Fine Arts
4. Thoreau and the Fox
   Lent by The Canajoharie Library and Art Gallery
5. Mrs. Cushman's House
   Lent by the estate of N. C. Wyeth
6. Island Funeral
   Lent by the estate of N. C. Wyeth
7. Hydrographic Signal
   Lent by the estate of N. C. Wyeth
8. Summer Night
   Lent by Mrs. Irene duPont
Advertised on the back cover are books illustrated and edited by N. C. Wyeth.

Pratt Institute
Exhibition / Of / PAINTINGS AND ILLUSTRATIONS / By / N. C. WYETH / [seal] / Art Gallery : Pratt Institute / Brooklyn, New York / February 13th to March 6th / Day and evening except Sunday / 1920 / DeKalb Avenue Cars from Manhattan end of Brooklyn Bridge / or from Borough Hall Section of Subway to Ryerson Street [surrounded by ornamental boxed rules]

Exhibition Folder.
Size of leaf trimmed 5 × 6¼ inches.
Brief biographical sketch on N. C. Wyeth.

Catalogue of Paintings and Illustrations.
1. Illustration for Celtic Legend
2. The Magician
3. A Sea Tragedy
4. The Marksman
5. The Black Dragon—A Sailor's Yarn
6. Illustration for Icelandic Saga
7. The Lovers
8. Medieval Tragedy
9. Iron Worker—The Villain in the Story
   King Arthur
10. Sir Launcelot and the Dead Queen Guenevere
11. The Signal to the Castle
12. The Fight Near the Blasted Tree
13. The Death of Tristram
   Kidnapped
14. The Fugitives
15. Mr. Balfour of the House of Shaws
   The Black Arrow
16. Death of Sir Daniel
17. Dick and Lawless in Holyrood Forest
18. Dick Spreads the Alarm
19. The Wedding
20. Crookback Fights Eight Assailants
21. Crossing the Fens
22. The Wounded Spearman
   Mysterious Island
23. Captain Nemo
24. The Flight of the Bird Messenger
25. Cover Lining for the *Mysterious Island*
26. The Rescue of Captain Harding
27. The Survivors

St. Botolph Club
St. Botolph Club / An Exhibition of Illustrations / for the Odyssey / By / N. C. Wyeth / From Friday, January 17, to Saturday, February 1, / both days inclusive / 1930 [all surrounded by boxed rules]

Exhibition Folder.
Size of leaf trimmed 7 × 5 inches.

Exhibited are sixteen illustrations from *The Odyssey*.

List of illustrations:
1. Odysseus and Penelope Reunited
2. Circe and the Swine
3. The Boar Hunt
4. Eumaeus, the Swineherd
5. Odysseus in the Land of the Dead
6. Odysseus and Calypso
7. Polyphemus, the Cyclops
8. Proteus, the Old Man of the Sea
9. The Raft of Odysseus
10. Telemachus in the Chariot of Nestor
11. The Sirens
12. The Trial of the Bow
13. The Beggars Fight
14. The Slaughter of the Suitors
15. Athene
16. The Mourning Penelope

Swarthmore College
THREE / GENERATIONS / OF / WYETHS March 1964

Exhibition Folder.
Size of leaf trimmed 5⅝ × 8⅝ inches.
Contains brief biographical sketches on N. C. Wyeth, Andrew Wyeth, and James Wyeth.

Cover illustration in black and white by N. C. Wyeth.
Blind Pew

Five paintings by N. C. Wyeth exhibited.
Blind Pew
Cow in the Moonlight
Nathan Hale
Paul Revere
The Spring House

The Unitarian Laymen's League
The / Parables of Jesus / Illustrated By / N. C. WYETH / An Announcement / [Unitarian seal] / Unitarian Laymen's League / Seven Park Square, Boston / New York Chicago / St. Louis San Francisco / December 25, 1923 [surrounded by double boxed rules]

Exhibition Folder.
Size of leaf trimmed 8 × 4 inches.
Interpretations by N. C. Wyeth of the Parables and their transition into paintings.

Six paintings exhibited.
The Child
The Leaven
The Net
The Barren Fig Tree
The Hidden Treasure
The Secret Growth of the Seed

Christmas Eve Celebration / Monday, December 24 / The Unitarian Laymen's League / invites you / to join in its celebration on / Christmas Eve / 8:30 at Arlington Street Church / Special Song Service / by the / Laymen's League Chorus / [rule] / 10:30 at Unity House / The Chorus will return to Unity House for / Carol singing, a social hour and the / Exhibition of the / Parables of Jesus / Illustrated by / N. C. Wyeth / Members of the League are cordially invited to / bring their families and friends to join in the / celebration

Exhibition Folder.
Size of leaf trimmed 3¾ × 7⅝ inches.

Six paintings exhibited.
The Child
The Net
Secret Growth of the Seed
The Leaven
The Hidden Treasure
The Fig Tree

The Virginia Museum
ILLUSTRATED BY N. C. WYETH

Exhibition Folder (green).
Size of leaf trimmed 6¼ × 9¼ inches.
Exhibition: Preview Friday evening November 7 from 8 to 10 P.M.

One illustration in green, black and white.
Description: The Sea Serpent (illustration from *Trending into Maine*)

The Wilmington Society of the Fine Arts
(The Delaware Art Museum)
Exhibition of / Paintings / By / Delaware Artists / Members / Of The Society / And Pupils Of / Howard Pyle / [ornament] / Under the auspices of / The / Wilmington Society / of the / Fine Arts / [ornament] / 1927 / New Library Building / Wilmington, Delaware / November 1st to December 17th / Open every afternoon from 1:30 to 5 o'clock [surrounded by boxed rules]

Exhibition Folder (brown paper).
Size of leaf trimmed 4½ × 11⅛ inches.

Three paintings exhibited by N. C. Wyeth.
Portrait (number 14)
Overmantel Decoration (number 73)
  Loaned by Mr. John B. Williams
The Life Mask of John Keats (number 140)

Loan Exhibition of / Portraits / [ornament] / The / Wilmington Society / of the / Fine Arts / March 2nd to March 9th, 1928 [surrounded by boxed rules]

Exhibition Folder.
Size of leaf trimmed 4½ × 7⅞ inches.

One painting exhibited by N. C. Wyeth.
Mr. Charles L. Patterson (number 28)

Fifteenth Annual / Exhibition of / Paintings / By / Delaware Artists / Members Of The Society / And Pupils Of / Howard Pyle / [ornament] / Under the auspices of / The / Wilmington Society / of the / Fine Arts / [ornament] / 1928 / New Library Building / Wilmington, Delaware / October 10th to November 10th / Open every afternoon from 1.30 to 5 o'clock / Wednesday, Saturdays and Sundays Free / The Pictures in this Exhibition are for Sale / Prices on application at the Desk [surrounded by box rules]

Exhibition Folder (brown paper).
Size of leaf trimmed 4½ × 11 inches.

Two paintings exhibited by N. C. Wyeth.
Oak Tree (number 27)
Illustrating Wagner's Fire Music (number 56)
  Loaned by the Steinway Company

Exhibition by / the Society / of Mural Painters / [ornament] / Under the auspices of / The / Wilmington Society / of the / Fine Arts

/ [ornament] / 1928 / New Library Building / Wilmington, Delaware / November 14th to December 15th / Open every afternoon from 1.30 to 5 o'clock / Wednesdays, Saturdays and Sundays Free

Exhibition Folder (brown paper).
Size of leaf trimmed 4½ × 11¼ inches.
Mural paintings by members of the Society.

N. C. Wyeth—Chadds Ford, Pa.
98. Map Sketch with arch top. "Preliminary sketch for Mural Decoration executed for the First National Bank of Boston." 18 × 30 feet
99. Map Sketch Hendrik Hudson. Sketch for Mural Map for Hotel Roosevelt, N. Y.
100. Ornamental, Chinese Legend.
101. A. & B. Eastern and Western Hemisphere Maps Color Reproductions. "Miniature reproductions of Decorative Maps made for the Hubbard Memorial Building," Washington, D.C.
102. Balboa Discovering Pacific. Color reproduction of thirty-foot panel for Hubbard Memorial Building, Washington, D. C.
103. Airplane over Arctic Ice. Color reproduction in miniature for the panel in Hubbard Memorial Building, Washington, D.C.
104. Ship Sailing Toward Sunset. Color miniature of panel for Hubbard Memorial Building, Washington, D.C.
105. Panels executed for the Boston Federal Reserve Bank. Color reproductions.
106. Color reproductions for four panels (16 × 25 feet) executed for the First National Bank of Boston.
107. A. & B. Photographs of two battle picture lunettes. Two wall pictures executed for the Missouri State Capitol.
108. Color reproduction showing Tower of Independence Hall. "Apotheosis of Franklin." Painted for the Franklin Savings Bank, New York City.
109. Color reproduction of Hudson's ship, "Half Moon." Panel painted for the Hotel Roosevelt, New York.
110. "The Giant." Painted for Westover School, Pennsylvania.

Sixteenth Annual / Exhibition of / Paintings / By / Delaware Artists / Members Of The Society / And Pupils Of / Howard Pyle / [ornament] / Under the auspices of / The / Wilmington Society / of the / Fine Arts / [ornament] / 1929 / Library Building / Wilmington, Delaware / December 4th to December 31st / Open every afternoon from 1.30 to 5 o'clock / Wednesday, Saturdays and Sundays Free / The Pictures in this Exhibition are for Sale / Prices on application at the Desk [surrounded by box rules]

Exhibition Folder.
Size of leaf trimmed 4½ × 11 inches.

Five paintings exhibited by N. C. Wyeth.
Essex of England (number 13)
Old House, New England (number 15)
Elizabeth of England (number 16)
Sea Panther (number 95—Gallery E)
The First Family (number 115—Gallery G)

Seventeenth Annual / Exhibition of / Paintings / By / Delaware Artists / Members Of The Society / And Pupils Of / Howard Pyle / [ornament] / Under the auspices of / The / Wilmington Society / of the / Fine Arts / [ornament] / 1930 / Library Building / Wilmington, Delaware / November 3rd to November 25th / Open every afternoon from 1.30 to 5 o'clock / Wednesday, Saturdays and Sundays Free / The Pictures in this Exhibition are for Sale / Prices on application at the Desk [surrounded by box rules]

Exhibition Folder.
Size of leaf trimmed 4½ × 11 inches.

Two paintings exhibited by N. C. Wyeth.
The Crystal Gazer (number 44)
Blue Jug (number 80)

THE WILMINGTON SOCIETY / of the / FINE ARTS / Exhibition of Paintings / by N. C. WYETH / Friday, February twenty-eighth / to / Friday, March fourteenth / 1930 / Library Building, Wilmington, Delaware / open every afternoon from 1:30 to 5:00 P.M. / Sundays, 3:00 to 6:00 P.M. [surrounded by double boxed rules with corner ornaments]

Exhibition Folder.
Size of leaf trimmed 6½ × 8½ inches.

List of paintings exhibited by N. C. Wyeth.
The Odyssey
1. The Slaughter of the Suitors
2. Athene, Daughter of Zeus
3. Odysseus in the Land of the Dead
5. The Trial of the Bow
6. Proteus, The Old Man of the Sea
7. Eumaeus, The Swineherd
18. The Mourning Penelope
19. The Fight of the Beggars
20. The Sirens
21. The Cyclops
22. Calypso and Odysseus
23. Telemachus in the Chariot of Nestor
24. Neptune Battles with Odysseus
25. Circe and the Swine
26. The Boar Hunt
27. Odysseus and Penelope Reunited
The Parables
8. The Barren Fig Tree
9. The Lost Sheep
10. The Net
11. The Sower
12. The Child
13. The Good Samaritan
14. The Prodigal Son
15. The Hidden Treasure
16. The Secret Growth of the Seed
17. The Leaven
Six Paintings
4. Still Life
28. John McVey
29. Old Albert
30. Pennsylvania Barn
31. My Mother
32. My Grandfather's House, New England
Small Gallery—Children of the Bible Series
33. The Little Prince Who Was Hidden
34. The Little Girl in Naaman's House
35. Eli and Samuel
36. David and Goliath
37. Mark
38. The Boy with the Basket of Loaves and Fishes
39. Moses in Egypt
40. The Sons of the Prophet Isaiah
41. Cain and Abel
42. The Boy who Retrieved Jonathan's Arrows
Miscellaneous
43. From Cooper's *Deerslayer*
44. The Buffalo Hunt
45. The Water Hole
46. The War Party
47. From Cooper's *Deerslayer*

NINETEENTH Annual Exhibition / DELAWARE ARTISTS / Pupils of Howard Pyle / Members of the Society [all surrounded by boxed rule] / NOVEMBER SEVENTH Through / November Twenty-Seventh / 1932 / The Wilmington Society / of the Fine Arts / [rule] / Library Building Wilmington, Delaware / Open every afternoon from 1.30 to 5.00 p.m. / Sundays, 3.00 to 6.00 p.m. / Wednesdays, Saturdays, Sundays Free

Exhibition Folder (light brown paper with brown lettering).
Size of leaf trimmed 5¾ × 8¼ inches.

Two paintings exhibited by N. C. Wyeth.
Spring–1918 (number 7)
Kentucky Shepherd (number 50)

Delaware / Water Color Show / Spring 1940
/ The Wilmington Society Of The Fine Arts /
April First To / April Twenty-Eighth / Dela-
ware Art Center / Park Drive At Woodlawn
Avenue / Wilmington, Delaware / Open Week-
days 10 to 5 / Sundays 2 to 6 / Admission
Free

Exhibition Folder (peach paper).
Size of leaf trimmed 5¾ × 8½ inches.

Two paintings exhibited by N. C. Wyeth.
The Explorer (number 51)
The Captain's Bride (number 62)

Twenty-Eighth Annual Exhibition / Paintings
By Delaware Artists / Pupils Of Howard Pyle
/ Members Of The Society / The Wilmington
Society Of The Fine Arts / November Twenty-
Fourth / December Thirty-First / 1941 / Dela-
ware Art Center / Park Drive At Woodlawn
Avenue / Wilmington, Delaware / Open Week-
days 10 to 5 / Sundays 2 to 6 / Admission
Free

Exhibition Folder (light pink paper).
Size of leaf trimmed 5¾ × 8½ inches.

One painting exhibited by N. C. Wyeth.
Black Spruce Ledge (number 24)

DELAWARE / WATER COLOR SHOW /
SPRING 1942 / The Wilmington Society of the
Fine Arts / May Third to / May Twenty-
Fourth / Delaware Art Center / Park Drive at
Woodlawn Avenue / Wilmington, Delaware /
Open Weekdays 10 to 5 / Sundays 2 to 6 /
Admission free

Exhibition Folder.
Water Colors, Prints, Drawings and Illustrations By Delaware Artists, Pupils of Howard
Pyle, and Members of the Wilmington Society
of the Fine Arts.

Two paintings exhibited by N. C. Wyeth.
Jody and Flag (illustration from *The Yearling,*
Number 35)
Jack and the Two-headed Giant (illustration from
The Anthology of Children's Literature, Number
54)

Twenty-Ninth Annual Exhibition / Paintings
By Delaware Artists / Pupils of Howard Pyle /
Members Of The Society / The Wilmington
Society of the Fine Arts / November First /
December Fifth / 1942 / Delaware Art Center
/ Park Drive At Woodlawn Avenue / Wilming-
ton, Delaware / Open Weekdays 10 to 5 / Sun-
days 2 to 6 / Admission Free

Exhibition Folder.
Size of leaf trimmed 5¾ × 8¼ inches.

One painting exhibited by N. C. Wyeth.
Walden Pond (number 37)

THIRTIETH ANNUAL EXHIBITION / Of
The Work Of Delaware Artists / Pupils Of
Howard Pyle / Members Of The Society / The
Wilmington Society Of The Fine Arts / Sep-
tember Twenty-Sixth / October Twenty-Sixth
/ 1943 / Delaware Art Center / Park Drive At
Woodlawn Avenue / Wilmington, Delaware /
Open Weekdays 10 to 5 / Sunday 2 to 6 /
Admission Free

Exhibition Folder (gray paper).
Size of leaf trimmed 5¾ × 8½ inches.

Two paintings exhibited by N. C. Wyeth.
The Corn Husker (number 17)
Summer Night (number 26)
    The prize for painting.

THIRTY-FIRST ANNUAL EXHIBITION /
Of The Work Of Delaware Artists / Pupils Of
Howard Pyle / Members Of The Society / The
Wilmington Society Of The Fine Arts / Novem-
ber Fifth / December Third / 1944 / Delaware
Art Center / Park Drive At Woodlawn Avenue

/ Wilmington, Delaware / Open Weekdays 10
to 5 / Sundays 2 to 6 / Admission Free

Exhibition Folder (rose paper).
Size of leaf trimmed 5¾ × 8½ inches.

Two paintings exhibited by N. C. Wyeth.
Portrait of a Farmer (number 25)
Dark Harbor Fisherman (number 39)

Bulletin No. 69 / February 1947

Size of leaf trimmed 6⅛ × 9¼ inches.

One illustration (painting) in black and white
by N. C. Wyeth.
The Spring House
    Purchased by Popular subscription, March
    1946.

TWENTY-THREE AMERICAN PAINTERS /
Their Portraits and Their Work / 1815–1945 /
October 7 to November 4, 1956 / The Wilming-
ton Society of the Fine Arts / Delaware Art
Center / Park Drive at Woodlawn Avenue

Exhibition Folder.
Size of leaf trimmed 5¾ × 8½ inches.

Two N. C. Wyeth paintings exhibited.
Self Portrait
Nightfall

THE / BRANDYWINE / TRADITION /
February 28 Through March 23, 1969 / The
Wilmington Society Of The Fine Arts / Dela-
ware Art Center / 2301 Kentmere Parkway

Exhibition Folder.
Size of leaf trimmed 5½ × 8½ inches.
Introduction by Bruce St. John (Director—
Delaware Art Center)

Two N. C. Wyeth paintings exhibited.
Old Blind Pew
    Lent by Mr. and Mrs. Andrew Wyeth
Sailor's Fantasy

XI. Folders, Brochures, Booklets, and Pamphlets

The Baker and Taylor Co.
A Christmas Bulletin of the Best Books of 1932,
Published at Book Headquarters
The Baker and Taylor Co., 55 Fifth Avenue,
New York

Advertising Bulletin.
Cover illustration in color by N. C. Wyeth.
Description: Santa Claus on snow-covered
rooftop, about to climb down chimney to
deliver books as Christmas gifts.

Brandywine River Museum
Brandywine River Museum / Opening Show /
[illustration—Captain Bill Bones from *Treasure
Island*] / June 19th, 1971 / Chadds Ford,
Pennsylvania / N. C. Wyeth • Andrew Wyeth
• James Wyeth / Howard Pyle & Students
[printed in brown tint]

Copyright 1971 by The Brandywine River
Museum.
Press Release Folder.
Size of leaf trimmed 9½ × 12 inches.

Note: The cover illustration is a reproduction of
the Brandywine River Museum's Opening Show
Poster.

Chadds Ford Historical Society
Historic / Chadd's Ford Day / Chadds Ford
Mill—Tri-County Conservancy / [illustration] /
Chadds Ford Historical Society / for the benefit
of the / John Chad House Restoration / Satur-
day, September 7, 1968

Folder.
Size of leaf trimmed 5⁹⁄₁₆ × 8½ inches.
Program of Events / Exhibits and Shows
The exhibition is represented by works of
N. C. Wyeth, Howard Pyle, Andrew Wyeth,
and James Wyeth.

The West / and / Walter Bimson (1971)

Advertising Folder. (blue)
Size of leaf trimmed 8½ × 4½ inches.

Illustration by N. C. Wyeth printed in brown.
Description: Indian Fisherman

**Bulletin / Of / The Chester County /
Historical / Society / (seal) / 1936**

Paper covers; 51 pp.
Size of leaf trimmed 6 × 9 inches.
An Artist and History
A brief address given at a meeting of the
Chester County Historical Society on October

16, 1934. Excerpts about N. C. Wyeth on
page 24.

Cosmopolitan Book Corporation
Cosmopolitan Publications / Autumn of 1920 /
[illustration—Dean Cornwell] / Cosmopolitan
Book Corporation / Publishers / 119 West 40th
Street, New York

Advertising Brochure.
Large 8 vo. Paper covers; 10 pp.
Size of leaf trimmed 7 × 10 inches.
Illustrated with works from recently published
Cosmopolitan books.
Advertisement for Wyeth's *Robinson Crusoe,*
"The Gift Book of the Year"—Boxed—Price
$5.00 (page 5)

One illustration in black and white by N. C.
Wyeth.
Description: The despair of Robinson
Crusoe (Cover illustration from the book)
Advertisement for *Buffalo Bill's Life Story* by
Wm. F. Cody. (page 6)
One illustration in black and white by N. C.
Wyeth.
Description: Gunfight between two men.

Dallas Museum of Fine Arts—
Newsletter—September 1960

Size of leaf trimmed 7 × 10 inches.
Famous Families in American Art
A brief biography about the Wyeth family.
One illustration (painting) in black and white
by Henriette Wyeth Hurd.
Portrait of N. C. Wyeth.

Delaware Art Center (The Delaware
Art Museum)
(Wilmington, Delaware)
Calendar for January / Exhibition, Lecture,
Music, Motion Pictures—Delaware Art Center,
January 1946

Folder.
Size of leaf trimmed 5½ × 8¾ inches.
Exhibition: January 8 to January 27
N. C. Wyeth, N.A. 1882–1945 Memorial Ex-
hibition accompanied by a brief biography of
the artist.

The Delaware Art Museum
(The Wilmington Society of the Fine Arts)

Pupils of Howard Pyle
Museum Flier (1971)

Size of leaf trimmed 8⅜ × 11 inches.
Brief biographical sketches on six of Howard
Pyle's pupils accompanied by examples of
their work from the Museum's collection.
N. C. Wyeth (1812–1945)

One reduced illustration in black and white
by N. C. Wyeth.
Johnny Fights Cherry (illustration from
Drums by James Boyd)

Federal Reserve Bank of Boston
Federal Reserve / Society News / April, 1922 /
[ornament] / Boston / Massachusetts (Volume
Four, Number One)

Brochure.
Large 8 vo. Paper covers (gray); 24 pp.
Size of leaf trimmed 6⅞ × 10 inches.
The Hamilton Mural Paintings by N. C.
Wyeth.
Pages 2–4 and 18.
One illustration (mural painting) in black
and white.
The Hamilton Mural

The First National Bank of Boston
Four Mural Paintings in The First National
Bank of Boston (1925)
Folder.
Four mural paintings in color; folder size 14 ×
10½ inches; picture size 11½ × 8¹¹⁄₁₆ inches.
Mural paintings:
The Phoenician Biremes
The Elizabethan Galleons
The Clippers
The Tramp Steamer
The paintings are accompanied by a brief de-
scription by the artist.

Note: The paintings also appeared in color in
the *Ladies' Home Journal,* July and August 1925.

The / Mural Paintings / An Interview with
the Painter / N. C. Wyeth / [pictorial design—
clipper ship] / The First National Bank of Boston [pictorial design printed in blue]

Folder.
Size of leaf trimmed 4⅞ × 7¹¹⁄₁₆ inches.
Text by N. C. Wyeth—Phoenician Biremes,
Elizabethan Galleons, The Clippers, The
Tramp Steamer.

[illustration in color] / It's / Mid-SUMMER /
there today

Folder.
Size of leaf trimmed 3½ × 6 inches.

One illustration (mural painting) in color.
Description: The Tramp Steamer

Ginn and Company, Boston
illustration in color / [rule] / SONG PRO-GRAMS / FOR YOUTH / [rule] / THE WORLD OF MUSIC / [rule]

Advertising Folder.
4 to. Paper covers with illustration in color; unnumbered pages.
Size of leaf trimmed 7 × 10⅛ inches.

Cover illustration in color by N. C. Wyeth.
Description: In a Strange Land
In the advertising text is a reference to N. C. Wyeth's paintings for World Of Music series.

Glenn, Mabelle; Leavitt, Helen S.; Rebmann, Victor L. F.; and Baker, Earl L.
The World of Music / Advance Pages The Three Books Comprising / Song Programs For Youth / TREASURE / ADVENTURE / DIS-COVERY / [decoration and rule] / Edited by / Mabelle Glenn / [credits] / Helen S. Leavitt / [credits] / Victor L. F. Rebmann / [credits] / Earl L. Baker / [credits] / Artist / N. C. Wyeth / [rule and decoration] / Ginn and Company / Boston: New York [etc.]

4 to. Collation: Title (1); copyright (1937) (code numbers 837.5) and acknowledgments (2); text (3-47); index (48).
Size of leaf trimmed 7¾ × 10¼ inches.
Issued in paper covers (black). Front cover in black over stamped gold decoration and green bands: • SONG • PROGRAMS • FOR • YOUTH • / DISCOVERY (over stamped gold decoration) / • THE • WORLD • OF • MUSIC •

One illustration in color.
Indian Prayer fp 20

Harding, Frank
A Livestock Heritage / Animals and People / in Art
Copyright 1971 by Shorthorn World Publication Co., Geneva, Illinois
Published for The American Livestock Insurance Company
Booklet.
4 to. Paper covers in color (photograph); unnumbered pages.
Size of leaf trimmed 8⅛ × 11⅛ inches.
Illustrated in color and black and white with numerous paintings, watercolors, bronzes, etc.

One painting in color by N. C. Wyeth.
Indian Lance

Note: The painting originally appeared as a cover in colors for American Boy, September 1921.

Houghton Mifflin Company
Wyeth's Masterpiece THE COURTSHIP OF MILES STANDISH

Advertising Folder.
Size of leaf trimmed 14¼ × 9½ inches.

Two illustrations by N. C. Wyeth from the book.
Endpaper illustration (blue, black and white)
Description: The Mayflower on the high seas.
Pen-and-ink illustration.
Description: Pilgrims leaving log building.

(illustration) / Holiday Books / Houghton Mifflin Company

Advertising Brochure.
8 vo. Paper covers.
Size of leaf trimmed 6 × 9 inches.
Illustrated with works from current Houghton Mifflin books.

Two illustrations in color by N. C. Wyeth.
The Raft of Odysseus (front cover)
Telemachus in the Chariot of Nestor (back cover)
Advertisement for the book The Odyssey of Homer, edited by Herbert W. Palmer, on page 11. Accompanying the advertisement is a reduced illustration (drawing) of a Greek sailing ship which appears on the title page of the book.

The Spring Piper / Books for April, May, June, (1932)

Advertising Brochure.
8 vo. Paper covers.
Size of leaf trimmed 6 × 9 inches.
Illustrated with works from current Houghton Mifflin books.

Cover illustration in black and white by N. C. Wyeth.
The Duel on the Sands
To be reproduced on the dust wrapper of The Black Swan by Rafael Sabatini.

Note: The illustration originally appeared in color in the Ladies' Home Journal, September 1931, for the story The Duel on the Beach by Rafael Sabatini.

[design–tree] / Books for Gifts [red] / 1936 / Houghton Mifflin Company [red] / 2 Park Street, Boston, Massachusetts

Advertising Catalogue.
8 vo. Paper covers; 32 pp.
Size of leaf trimmed 6 × 9 inches.
Illustrated with works from current Houghton Mifflin books.

One illustration in black and white by N. C. Wyeth.
Description: Building a bridge from Men of Concord (back cover)
Advertisement for the book Men of Concord by Henry David Thoreau, edited by Francis H. Allen and illustrated by N. C. Wyeth (page 23).

Jobbers OverAll Co., Inc.
[pictorial design–factory] / $250,000 / Advertising Campaign / for / Blue Buckle / Union Made / Over Alls

Advertising Brochure.
Folio. Paper covers.
Size of leaf trimmed 11 × 13¾ inches.
Illustrated with paintings and photographs.

Three illustrations in colors by N. C. Wyeth. (red, blue, brown, black and white)
Descriptions: Two steelworkers stoking furnace.
Two construction workers standing on girders.
Two farmers talking.

Little, Brown & Company
TRENDING / INTO / MAINE / By Kenneth Roberts / With Illustrations by N. C. Wyeth / (drawing) / First Trade Edition / Consisting of only 7500 copies / with 14 reproductions of paintings in full color / To Be Published June 20th. Copies May Be Reserved Now.

Advertising Folder.
Large 8 vo. Paper covers; 4 pp.
Size of leaf trimmed 6¼ × 9½ inches.
Brief biographical sketches of Kenneth Roberts and N. C. Wyeth.

Four illustrations in black and white by N. C. Wyeth.
Title page pen-and ink-drawing.
Description: Osprey and pine tree.
A Maine Sea Captain's Daughter
Dan'l Nason, Sailing Master, 1814
The Building Of A Ship

[illustration] / Books / Autumn 1940 / Little, Brown / & Company / Boston

Advertising Catalogue.
8 vo. Paper covers; 28 pp.
Size of leaf trimmed 6 x 9 inches.

Cover illustration in black and white with tint by N. C. Wyeth.
Description: The H. M. S. Bounty
Advertisement for the book The Bounty Trilogy by Nordoff and Hall (Wyeth Edition) on page 5.

John Morrell & Co., Ottumwa, Iowa
[illustration by Wyeth] / Annual Report / John Morrell & Co. / 1943.

Brochure.
8 vo. Paper covers.
Size of leaf trimmed 6 × 9 inches.

One illustration (tipped on) in color by N. C. Wyeth.
Old Glory, Symbol of Liberty (4 × 4¾ inches)

National Cathedral Association
Washington Cathedral / A Series of Views / Many In Full Color / (Cathedral seal) / National Cathedral Association / Washington Cathedral / Mount Saint Alban / Washington, D.C.

First Edition, October 1939.
Catalogue (Guide)
12 mo. Paper covers (photograph with gold lettering); 30 pp.
Size of leaf trimmed 7¾ × 5¾ inches.
Illustrated in color and black and white with paintings, photographs, etc.

Two illustrations (mural paintings) in color by N. C. Wyeth.
Chapel of the Holy Spirit
Central Panel of the Reredos p 5
Chapel of the Holy Spirit
North Panel of the Reredos p 14

The Penn Mutual Life Insurance Company
WILLIAM PENN / Man Of / Vision • Courage • Action / [emblem–blue] / A Mural Painting by / N. C. WYETH / For the Home Office Building of / THE PENN MUTUAL LIFE INSURANCE COMPANY / Independence Square Philadelphia, Pennsylvania [all surrounded by boxed rules printed in blue]

Brochure.
Size of leaf trimmed 8 × 10 inches.
An Interview With The Artist—N. C. Wyeth

One illustration in color. (mural painting surrounded by boxed rules printed in blue)
WILLIAM PENN Man of Vision • Courage • Action

The Pennsylvania Academy of the Fine Arts

Oil Painting and Sculpture / by / Artists of Philadelphia / and its environs / The Pennsylvania Academy Of The Fine Arts / And Its Fellowship / Broad and Cherry Streets, Philadelphia / April 13 through May 12, 1940

Pamphlet.
Size of leaf trimmed 5¼ × 7¾ inches.

One painting exhibited by N. C. Wyeth.
Island Funeral (Gallery E, Number 75)

G. P. Putnam's Sons

FALL BOOKS / 1935 / G. P. Putnam's Sons / Including the Publications of / Minton, Balch & Company / This Catalogue is in Chronological / Order According to Publication Dates

Advertising Catalogue.
8 vo. Paper covers (reddish brown and yellow); 79 pp.
Size of leaf trimmed 6 × 9 inches.
Advertisement for the book *Marauders of the Sea*, edited by N. C. Wyeth, on pages 18 and 24.

The Roosevelt (Hotel)

Copyright 1924 by the New York United Hotels, Inc.

Brochure.
Size of leaf trimmed 7¾ × 10½ inches.
Parchment covers (light blue with embossed silver design and title—The Roosevelt)
Illustrated with paintings, photographs, etc.

One illustration (mural painting) in black and white with tint by N. C. Wyeth.
The Half Moon on the Hudson (center panel)
Photograph of hotel room; at one end is displayed an illustration from the book *The Courtship of Miles Standish*, illustrated by N. C. Wyeth.

Charles Scribner's Sons

BOOKS FOREVER / FOR CHILDREN / Compiled by / Lavinia Russ (title enclosed in drawing)
Published for The Scribner Book Store, 597 Fifth Avenue, New York (1963)

Advertising booklet.
Size of leaf trimmed 5½ × 7½ inches. 62 pp.
A children's book price listing.

One illustration (pen and ink drawing) in black and white by N. C. Wyeth.
Description: The Slave Ship (clouds removed) p 52
(Illustration from *Drums*)

SCRIBNER / HOLIDAY BOOKS / 1924–1925 / (illustration by N. C. Wyeth) / Charles Scribner's Sons / Fifth Avenue at 48th Street, New York (title and illustration surrounded by and enclosed in ornamental rules printed in blue)

Copyright 1924 by Charles Scribner's Sons.
Advertising booklet.
Size of leaf trimmed 6¾ × 10 inches. 32 pp.
Illustrated with numerous paintings, drawings, photographs, etc.

Three illustrations by N. C. Wyeth. One in color and two in black and white.

Cover illustration (in color) for *David Balfour*
Illustration for *David Balfour* p 27
Illustration for *Scottish Chiefs* p 27

The Howard Pyle Brandywine Edition 1853–1933

Advertising Brochure.
8 vo. Paper covers
Size of leaf trimmed 6¼ × 9 inches.

Cover illustration in color by N. C. Wyeth.
Description: Robin Hood and His Merry Men in Sherwood Forest
Back cover illustration in color by Stanley Arthurs.
Five pen-and-ink illustrations by Howard Pyle.
One pen-and-ink illustration by Andrew Wyeth.
Description: Turner's Grist-Mill, Chadds Ford, Pennsylvania, the second floor was used by the students of Howard Pyle (1898–1903).
The brochure is accompanied with a short biography of Howard Pyle.

Silver, Burdett and Company

MUSIC / NOTES / Book Five / [ornamental rule] / Silver, Burdett and Company [surrounded by double boxed rules]

Copyright 1930 by Silver, Burdett and Company.
Booklet.
8 vo. Paper covers (yellow printed in green); 48 pp.
Size of leaf trimmed 6 × 9 inches.
Illustrated in color and black and white with paintings, drawings, and photographs.

Two illustrations in color by N. C. Wyeth.
The Magic Fire Spell
Painted for the Steinway Collection
The King's Henchman
Painted for the Steinway Collection

United Drug Company
THE PARABLES OF JESUS

Advertisement for a DeLuxe edition of Christmas Religious Folders to be sold through the United Drug Company, Boston and St. Louis.

Advertising Folder.
4 to. Paper covers with lettering in brown tint.
Size of leaf trimmed 8½ × 11 inches.

Six illustrations in brown tint.
The Child
The Net
The Leaven
The Secret Growth of the Seed
The Barren Fig Tree
The Hidden Treasure
The illustrations are accompanied by a reproduction of a Christmas folder.

University of Arizona Museum of Art
The West / and / Walter Bimson (printed over illustration by N. C. Wyeth)
Published by the University of Arizona Museum of Art (1971)

Advertising Folder.
Size of leaf trimmed 4½ × 8½ inches.

One illustration printed in brown.
Indian Brave Fishing

Hotel Utica Mural Paintings

Compliments of J. W. and D. M. Johnson.
Two reproductions in color of the Murals in Hotel Utica, Utica, New York.
Folder.
Size of leaf trimmed 3½ × 6 inches.

Note: The mural paintings were based on two illustrations which appeared in color in *Scribner's Magazine*, December 1909, for "The Moods" by George T. Marsh.

The Virginia Museum of Fine Arts
Members' Bulletin.
November 1958, Vol. 19 No. 3

N. C. Wyeth, Illustrator, accompanied by a brief biography of the artist.

One illustration in black and white.
The Sea Serpent (illustration from *Trending into Maine*)

West Virginia Pulp and Paper Company
WESTVACO / INSPIRATIONS / FOR • PRINTERS / NUMBER •• 77

Published by West Virginia Pulp and Paper Company, 1931.
Advertising Brochure.
Folio. Paper covers; pages 1523–38.
Size of leaf trimmed 9¼ × 12⅛ inches.

One illustration in color by N. C. Wyeth.
Public Test of the World's First Reaper

Note: The illustration was painted for the 100th Anniversary of International Harvester Company (1831–1931), and appeared in color in leading periodicals during the year 1931.

Western Union (telegrams)

Thanksgiving Greeting by Western Union.
Copyright 1936 by Western Union Telegraph Co.
Telegram size 6½ × 8¼ inches; picture size 1⅝ × 7⅝ inches.

One illustration in color by N. C. Wyeth.
Description: Pilgrim family at dinner.

Holiday Greeting by Western Union.
Copyright 1936 by Western Union Telegraph Co.
Telegram size 6½ × 8 inches; picture size 1½ × 7½ inches.

One illustration in color by N. C. Wyeth.
Description: Eighteenth century father and children bringing home holly and freshly cut evergreens before Christmas.

Christmas Greeting by Western Union.
Copyright 1936 by Western Union Telegraph Co.
Telegram size 7 × 8½ inches; picture size 1⅝ × 7⅝ inches.

One illustration in color by N. C. Wyeth.
Description: Santa about to climb down chimney to deliver presents.

The Wilmington Institute Free Library
N. C. WYETH / 1882–1945 / Original Illustrations / For / Robinson Crusoe / By / Daniel Defoe / Purchased in 1922 / For / The Wilmington Institute Free Library / Wilmington, Delaware

Folder.
Size of leaf trimmed 4½ × 6¾ inches.
Illustrator's preface by N. C. Wyeth.
N. C. Wyeth by Dudley Lunt.

Note: The illustrator's preface by N. C. Wyeth was originally written for the Wyeth edition of *Robinson Crusoe* by Daniel Defoe, published by The Cosmopolitan Book Corporation, New York 1920.

Wilmington Savings Fund Society
One Hundred Years / In / WILMINGTON / [pictorial design] / Wilmington Savings Fund Society / Wilmington, Delaware / Founded In 1832

Copyright 1932 by the Wilmington Savings Fund Society.
Thin 4 to. Brown paper covers; lettering on cover stamped in black over yellow; 23 pp. Embellishments in pen and ink by Robert Ball.
Tipped-in reproduction in color of the mural painting The Apotheosis of the Family (Reproduced from the preliminary sketch and measuring 9 × 16 inches). The text printed below the painting describes the development of the mural and a brief biographical summary of the artist's life.

Letters 1901–1945
The Wyeths by N. C. Wyeth, Edited by Betsy James Wyeth, 1971.
Distributed by The Brandywine River Museum, Chadds Ford, Pa.

Advertising Flier.
Size 8½ × 13½ inches; folded 8½ × 3⅜ inches.
Illustrated with paintings, sketches, and photographs in black and white.

XII. Sale Catalogues

Baker Collector Gallery
Baker Collector Gallery / Lubbock, Texas / 1301–13th Street

Sale Catalogue.
8 vo. Paper covers; unnumbered pages.
Size of leaf trimmed 5½ × 8½ inches.
Illustrated with numerous paintings, drawings, etc. by various artists.

One illustration (painting) in black and white by N. C. Wyeth.
In Penobscot Bay (1934)
The painting is accompanied by a brief biographical sketch.

J. N. Bartfield Art Galleries, Inc.
Catalogue of / AMERICAN / Paintings and Sculpture / Historical–Western / [painting in color] / O. C. Seltzer (1887–1957) / Cover: Scouting Party 20 × 27 inches / Oil, signed / Number 100 / J. N. Bartfield Art Galleries, Inc. / 45 West 57th Street, New York, N. Y. 10019 / [telephone number]

Sale Catalogue.
Large 8 vo. Paper covers; unnumbered pages.
Size of leaf trimmed 6½ × 9½ inches.
Illustrated with works by various artists in color and black and white.

Four illustrations in black and white by N. C. Wyeth.
52. Mystery Tree
53. Indian with canoe (charcoal drawing)
54a The War Clouds (charcoal drawing)
54b Civil War Battle (charcoal drawing—on reverse side of The War Clouds)

Card, Helen L.
HATS OFF TO THE AMERICAN ILLUSTRATOR! / [photograph] / Teri's Office—photo by Teri / Pictures by Berke, Schoonover, Deming, Pyle, Etc. / Bronze on table by Carl Kauba / Helen L. Card / 714 Madison Avenue, New York 21, N. Y. / [telephone number] / Catalog No. Two

Sale Catalogue.
8 vo. Paper covers; 34 pp.
Size of leaf trimmed 5⅝ × 8½ inches.
Illustrated with works by N. C. Wyeth, Howard Pyle, Frank E. Schoonover, Norman Rockwell, John Clymer, Philip R. Goodwin, etc.

One illustration in black and white by N. C. Wyeth.
Description: A Mountain Man. p 33

Note: The illustration originally appeared as a cover in color for *The Popular Magazine,* March 15, 1912.

TO THE TRUE AMERICAN SPIRIT / [illustration] / At the Recruiting Station, 1861 / [oil painting by Howard Pyle] / Howard Pyle : A Bibliographical Checklist as well as / an Illustrated, Priced Catalog / *Catalog #4* / Helen L. Card, 714 Madison Avenue, New York 21, / New York / [telephone number]

Sale Catalogue.
8 vo. Paper covers; 176 pp.
Size of leaf trimmed 5½ × 8½ inches.
Illustrated with the works of Howard Pyle.
Numerous references to N. C. Wyeth.

HANG ON, FELLERS! WE'RE / [illustration] / OUT ON A LIMB / A splendid oil painting by Tom Ryan, who / calls it "Their First Hide." / [price] / Helen L. Card / 714 Madison Avenue, New York 21, N. Y. / [telephone number] / Catalog No. Five

Sale Catalogue.
8 vo. Paper covers; 98 pp.
Size of leaf trimmed 5½ × 8½ inches.
Illustrated with the works of N. C. Wyeth (book advertisements), Frederic Remington, Frank E. Schoonover, Robert Lougheed, Tom Ryan, etc.
A checklist of books illustrated by N. C. Wyeth. (pages 62–89)

Christie, Manson & Woods
Catalogue / Of / Impressionist, / American and Modern / Paintings and Watercolours / and a Group of Dorothy Doughty Birds / The Property of various owners / from / England Scotland / France Switzerland Norway / United States of America / which will be sold by auction by / Christie, Manson & Woods (New York) / at / The Warwick Hotel / 5701 Main Street, Houston, Texas 77002 / On Monday, April 6, 1970 / at 8 p.m. precisely / [Texas office, address, etc.] / Admission By Catalogue Only

Auction Sale Catalogue.
Large 8 vo. Paper covers in color; 94 pp. (including index)
Size of leaf trimmed 7¼ × 9½ inches.
Illustrated with numerous works in color and black and white.

Two illustrations by N. C. Wyeth. One in color and one in black and white.
The Petition (color)

Exhibited in Harrisburg, Pennsylvania, exhibition N. C. Wyeth and the Brandywine Tradition
The Signal (black and white)

Edward Eberstadt & Sons
Catalogue 134 / AMERICANA / Books, Manuscripts & Paintings / Offered for Sale by / Edward Eberstadt & Sons / 888 Madison Avenue, At 72nd Street / New York 21, N. Y.

Sale Catalogue.
8 vo. Paper covers; 111 pp.
Size of leaf trimmed 6 × 9 inches.
Illustrated with works by various artists in black and white.

One illustration in black and white by N. C. Wyeth.
Jim Bludso and the Prairie Bell (number 442)
Description of painting (page 70)

Catalogue 135 / AMERICANA / (collection data) / Books, Manuscripts & Paintings / Offered for Sale by / Edward Eberstadt & Sons / 888 Madison Avenue, At 72nd Street / New York 21, N. Y.

Sale Catalogue.
8 vo. Paper covers; 160 pp.
Size of leaf trimmed 6 × 9 inches.
Illustrated with works by various artists in black and white.

One illustration in black and white by N. C. Wyeth.
War or Peace (back of back cover)
Description of painting (page 153)

Catalogue 139 / A Distinguished Collection of / WESTERN PAINTINGS / Including such foremost American artists as / Berninghaus, Bierstadt, Borein, Cary, Catlin, / Choris, Colyer, Couse, Dixon, Eastman, / Farny, Frenzeny, Gaul, Hansen, Hays, Hill, / Hudson, Johnson, Keith, Leigh, Miller, Moran, / Paxson, Pierry, Ranney, Raschen, Remington, / Rindisbacher, Russell, Stanley, Sully, Tait, / Wittredge, Wimar, Woodside, Wyeth, etc. / With an Introduction by / Harold McCracken / Offered for Sale by / Edward Eberstadt & Sons / 888 Madison Avenue, at 72nd Street / New York 21, N. Y.

Sale Catalogue.
8 vo. Paper covers.
Size of leaf trimmed 6 × 9 inches.
Illustrated with 129 works in black and white.

One painting in black and white by N. C. Wyeth.
War or Peace (number 126)

Catalogue 146 / 1908–1958 / Our Golden Anniversary / Catalogue of / AMERICAN PAINTINGS / Historical • Genre • Western / Offered for Sale by / Edward Eberstadt & Sons / 888 Madison Avenue, At 72nd Street / New York 21, N. Y.

Sale Catalogue.
8 vo. Paper covers. (126) pp.
Size of leaf trimmed 6 × 9 inches.
Illustrated with 191 works in black and white.

Three paintings in black and white by N. C. Wyeth.
War or Peace (number 187)
Ann Stuyvesant (number 188-a)
Peter Minuit (number 188-b)

Mannados Bookshop
MANNADOS / BOOKSHOP / Rare Books / First Editions / Association Items / [cover design by N. C. Wyeth from *The Last of the Mohicans*]

Sale Catalogue.
12 mo. Paper covers.
Size of leaf trimmed 4¾ × 7⅛ inches.
Description of painting (Item 342) page 54

Maxwell Galleries Ltd.
AMERICAN ART / SINCE 1850 / MAXWELL GALLERIES LTD / SAN FRANCISCO

Sale Catalogue.
8 vo. Paper covers (in color); 84 pp.
Size of leaf trimmed 7 × 10 inches.
Illustrated with numerous paintings by American artists in color and in black and white.

One illustration in black and white by N. C. Wyeth.
The Scout (Number 384) p 35
Painting listed in the index of artists (page 84)

Parke-Bernet Galleries, Inc.
AMERICAN Paintings / Drawings Sculpture / [list of artists–five lines] / ° ° ° / [list of estates and collections–eleven lines] / ° ° ° / Public Auction Thursday March 16 at 8 p.m. / Parke-Bernet Galleries • Inc / Affiliated with Sotheby & Co London / New York • 1967

Auction Sale Catalogue.
Size of leaf trimmed 7 × 10¼ inches.
4 to. Paper covers (blue) with lettering in red; 54 pp.
Illustrated with the works of numerous artists.

Four paintings by N. C. Wyeth for auction sale of which two are reproduced in black and white.

Train Robbery (black and white) (number 87) p 38
A Maine Fisherman's Family (black and white (number 88) p 39
The Fight with the Harpoons (number 89) p 40
Cowboy with Horse (number 90) p 40

AMERICAN PAINTINGS / DRAWINGS & SCULPTURE / [five lines of artists represented] / [ornaments] / [eight lines of various owners] / Public Auction / Wednesday • March 19 at 8 p.m. / Thursday • March 20 at 1:45 p.m. / PARKE-BERNET GALLERIES • INC / (Affiliated with Sotheby & Co London) / New York • 1969 (Sale Number 2822)

Auction Sale Catalogue.
Size of leaf trimmed 6⅞ × 10¼ inches.
4 to. Paper covers (blue) with lettering in dark blue; 158 pp.
Illustrated with the works of numerous artists.

One illustration in black and white by N. C. Wyeth.
Mystery Tree (number 202) p 151

Nineteenth & Twentieth Century / AMERICAN PAINTINGS / & SCULPTURE / [three lines of artists represented] / [ornament] / [six lines of various owners] / Public Auction / Wednesday Evening • October 22 at 8 / PARKE-BERNET GALLERIES • INC / (Affiliated with Sotheby & Co London) / New York • 1969

Auction Sale Catalogue.
Size of leaf trimmed 6⅞ × 10¼ inches.
4 to. Paper covers (light yellow) with lettering in blue; 113 pp.
Illustrated with the works of numerous artists.

Two illustrations in black and white by N. C. Wyeth.
Beach-Scene—Two Men Fighting (number 58) p 58
Corn Husker (charcoal drawing) (number 61) p 61

Sale Number 2914 / Free Public Exhibition / From Friday • October 17th to Date of Sale / Ten a.m. to five p.m. • Closed Sunday and Monday / Public Auction / Wednesday • October 22 at 8 p.m. / Exhibition and Sale at the / Parke-Bernet Galleries • Inc / 980 Madison • 76th–77th Street / New York 10021 / [telephone number] / Sale Conducted by / Peter Wilson • John L. Marion / Charles A. Hellmich • Edward Lee Cave / Edward J. Landrigan III / 1969

Auction Sale Catalogue.
Size of leaf trimmed 7 × 10⅛ inches.
4 to. Paper covers (light yellow) with lettering in blue; 113 pp.
Illustrated with works of numerous artists.

One illustration (charcoal drawing) in black and white by N. C. Wyeth for auction sale.
Corn Husker (number 61) p 61

Sale Number 3079 / Catalogue Price $2 • By Mail $3 / Exhibition From Saturday • September 19 To Date Of Sale / 10 A.M. to 5 P.M. • Closed Saturday and Sunday / AMERICAN & OTHER / WATERCOLORS • DRAWINGS / & SCULPTURE / Of The / Nineteenth & Twentieth Centuries / Including A Group Of / MARINE PAINTINGS / [four lines of artists represented] / [ornament] / Property of Various Owners / Public Auction / Thursday • September 24 at 2 p.m. / PARKE-BERNET GALLERIES • INC / [Affiliated with Sotheby & Co London] / New York • 1970 / [rule] / Cover Illustration: Number 74

Auction Sale Catalogue.
Size of leaf trimmed 6 × 9³⁄₁₆ inches.
Large 8 vo. Paper covers (illustration); 65 pp.
Illustrated with the works of numerous artists.

One illustration (charcoal drawing) by N. C. Wyeth.
Indian Cleaning Fowl

AMERICAN PAINTINGS / DRAWINGS AND SCULPTURE / OF THE / 18th–19th & 20th CENTURIES / [six lines of artists represented] / [ornaments] / [nine lines of various owners] / Public Auction / Thursday Evening • December 10 at 8 p.m. / PARKE-BERNET GALLERIES • INC / ° Affiliated with Sotheby & Co London ° / New York • 1970 / [rule] / Cover Illustration: Number 30 (Sale Number 3133)

Auction Sale Catalogue.
Size of leaf trimmed 7⅞ × 10⅛ inches.
4 to. Paper covers (illustration); 97 pp.
Illustrated with the works of numerous artists in color and black and white.

One painting by N. C. Wyeth.
Coasting (number 46) p 54

Penny Hill Auction Co.
Penny Hill Auction Co. / Presents / for auction / "How Old Man Plunkett Went On" / (Wyeth illustration) / an N. C. Wyeth original / Roland F. Cohen–Auctioneer / 728 Phila. Pike, Wilm., Del. / At: The Montery / Wednesday, April 10, 7:00 p m / Previews: Tuesday April 9, 7:00 p m 'Till 10:00 p m (1967)

Auction Sale Folder.
Size of leaf trimmed 5½ × 8½ inches.

One illustration in black and white by N. C. Wyeth.
"How Old Man Plunkett Went On"

XIII. Cards and Postcards

Cards
A CANDLE / in the / WILDERNESS / A Tale of / the Beginning of New England / by IRVING BACHELLER

Card size $3\frac{5}{8} \times 5\frac{5}{8}$ inches; picture size $3\frac{1}{4} \times 5\frac{1}{4}$ inches.

One illustration in colors. (red, green, brown, black and white)
Description: The apotheosis of the Massachusetts Bay Colony.

(Exhibition mailing)
[illustration—The Red Dory] / In the Georges Islands, Maine / Paintings By / N. C. WYETH / (rule) / December 5th–30th, 1939 / [rule] / Macbeth Gallery / 11 East 57th Street • New York [surrounded by boxed rules]

Card size: $5\frac{1}{2} \times 3\frac{1}{2}$ inches.

A Tribute To Benjamin Franklin (mural)
The Franklin Savings Bank, New York

Card in color: card size $5\frac{7}{8} \times 8\frac{3}{8}$ inches; picture size $2\frac{1}{2} \times 5$ inches.

Printed within the card is a brief description of the mural and a quote from Benjamin Franklin to David Hartley, December 4, 1789.

Romance, History, Travel
Copyright by the National Association of Book Publishers.

Card in color: card size $5\frac{1}{2} \times 3\frac{1}{2}$ inches.
Description: Seventeenth century adventurer on deck of ship, with heavy seas and galleon in background.

Note: The illustration appeared in a number of periodicals in 1927–28. In addition, it was reproduced as a poster in color.

THE SPRING HOUSE
Copyright 1946 by the Wilmington Society of the Fine Arts.

Card size $6\frac{1}{4} \times 5\frac{7}{8}$ inches; picture size $6 \times 4\frac{5}{8}$ inches.
Card in black and white: The Permanent Collection
Delaware Art Center • Wilmington, Delaware

Calendar Cards
The First National Bank of Boston Mural Paintings
Set of five cards in color: card size $3\frac{7}{8} \times 9\frac{1}{4}$ inches.
Set of cards:
The Elizabethan Galleons
The Clipper Ship
The Tramp Steamer
The Phoenician Biremes
A Mural Decoration (Western Hemisphere)

Religious Folders (Christmas cards)

Copyright 1923 by N. C. Wyeth, Chadds Ford, Pa.
Paintings by N. C. Wyeth, Illuminations by T. B. Hapgood.
Religious Folders in color; boxed (quantity of twelve plus envelopes).
Size of leaf trimmed $8\frac{1}{8} \times 6$ inches.

Six paintings.
The Child
The Net
The Secret Growth of the Seed
The Leaven
The Hidden Treasure
The Barren Fig Tree

Note: The paintings depicting The Parables of Jesus were commissioned by The Unitarian Laymen's League. A total of 600,000 cards were printed and distributed. The paintings were reproduced in the book *The Parables of Jesus* by S. Parkes Cadman, published by David McKay Company, Philadelphia, 1931.

Presidential Christmas Card
[stamped Presidential seal] / With all best wishes / from our family / for a Merry Christmas / and a Happy New Year / The President and Mrs. Nixon
Designed by Hallmark (1971)

Card in red with mounted illustration set in card window bordered in gold; card size $5 \times 7\frac{1}{2}$ inches.
Washington, D. C. 1798 Building The First White House
Painted by N. C. Wyeth, this view of the construction of the President's House in the late eighteenth century shows President George Washington and the architect of the White House, James Hoban, inspecting the uncompleted building.

Note: The illustration originally appeared as one of four patriotic posters for the Pennsylvania Railroad.

Christmas Folder
With Greetings of / THE CHRISTMAS SEASON
From Ginn and Company 1923
Illustration (loose in folder) in color: folder size $4\frac{5}{8} \times 6$ inches.
"Suffer The Little Children To Come Unto Me"

Note: The illustration originally appeared as a frontispiece in colors in the book *The Corona Readers* by James H. Fassett, published by Ginn & Company, Boston, 1920.

Christmas Card
Choir of Angels
From a Panel of the Reredos, Chapel of the Holy Spirit, Washington Cathedral

Christmas card in color: card size $3\frac{3}{4} \times 5\frac{3}{4}$ inches.

Christmas Calendar Card
Published by Washington Cathedral, Washington, D.C., 1963

Illustrations in color (two panels).
Choir of Angels
Panels of Reredos, Chapel of the Holy Spirit

American National Red Cross, Washington 13, D.C.
1953 Red Cross Fund—March 1–31

Postcard in colors (red, blue, black and white): postcard size $5\frac{1}{2} \times 3\frac{1}{2}$ inches.
Answer the Call
Description: Red Cross banners with cloud background.

Advertising postcard for the book *The Drums of the 47th* by Robert J. Burdette, published by The Bobbs Merrill Company, 1914.

Postcard in black and white: postcard size $5\frac{3}{8} \times 3\frac{3}{8}$ inches.

Advertising *Vandemark's Folly* by Herbert Quick
The Bobbs-Merrill Co. Indianapolis, Indiana

Set of five cards in black and white: card size $5\frac{1}{2} \times 3\frac{1}{2}$ inches.
Set of cards:

Card with advertising copy.
The Erie Canal Fight Episode.
The Prairie-Fire Scene.
I Jumped Down into the Stream and Caught Her in My Arms.
The Iowa Prairie.

A Tribute to Benjamin Franklin
Mural painting by N. C. Wyeth in The Franklin Savings Bank in the city of New York (Eighth Avenue and 42nd Street)

Postcard in color: postcard size $5\%_{16}$ × $3\%_{16}$ inches; picture size $4\%_{16}$ × $2\%_{16}$ inches (enclosed in blue rule)
On the reverse side is a brief description of the mural painting.

WILLIAM PENN Man of Vision · Courage · Action

Copyright 1944 by the Penn Mutual Life Insurance Company.
A Mural Painting by N. C. Wyeth.
Postcard in color: postcard size $5\frac{1}{2}$ × $3\frac{1}{2}$ inches.

Note: Mural painting in the Home Office building of the Penn Mutual Life Insurance Company, Independence Square, Philadelphia.

Hendrick Hudson Dining Room—The Roosevelt, New York City

Postcard in black and white: postcard size $5\frac{1}{2}$ × $3\frac{1}{2}$ inches.
Description: A photograph of the Hendrick Hudson dining room showing the wall placement of the three Wyeth mural panels.

Triptych painting by N. C. Wyeth in the Chapel of the Holy Spirit, Washington Cathedral, Mount Saint Alban, Washington, D. C.
Postcard in color: postcard size 7 × $5\frac{1}{2}$ inches.

WASHINGTON CATHEDRAL Mount Saint Alban, Washington, D.C.
Altar and Triptych painted by N. C. Wyeth in the Chapel of the Holy Spirit

Postcard in black and white: postcard $3\%_{16}$ × $5\%_8$ inches; picture size 3 × $4\%_8$ inches.

WASHINGTON CATHEDRAL Mount Saint Alban, Washington, D.C.
Altar and Triptych painted by N. C. Wyeth in the Chapel of the Holy Spirit

Postcard in color: postcard size $5\frac{1}{2}$ × $3\frac{1}{2}$ inches.

"The Apotheosis of the Family"

Mural painting by N. C. Wyeth for the Wilmington Savings Fund Society.
Postcard in color: postcard size $3\frac{1}{2}$ × $8\frac{1}{4}$ inches.
On the reverse side is a brief description of the mural painting.

The Spring House

Postcard in color: postcard size 7 × $5\frac{1}{4}$ inches.
Collection of The Wilmington Society of the Fine Arts, Delaware Art Center, Wilmington, Delaware.

Advertising postcard for the book *The Wyeths* by N. C. Wyeth, edited by Betsy James Wyeth, 1971.
Distributed by The Brandywine River Museum, Chadds Ford, Pa.

Postcard in color; postcard size $8\frac{1}{4}$ × $3\frac{1}{2}$ inches; picture size $4\frac{1}{8}$ × $3\frac{1}{2}$ inches.

Painting in color.
"Portrait of My Mother"

XIV. Hotel Utica Plate

Hotel Utica Plate
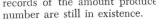
Manufactured by Syracuse China Corporation, Syracuse, New York.
Produced in two sizes: 8 inch and 10 inch (dinner service)

The decoration consists of an overglazed gold band with a maroon color line and the Wyeth painting done by decal is bordered by a gold band. A special back stamp reads as follows: O. P. CO. / SYRACUSE / CHINA / "The Return of the Hunter" / PAINTED BY / *N. C. WYETH* / For / HOTEL UTICA / Reproduction By / ONONDAGA POTTERY CO. / Syracuse, N.Y.
Records show the original order was placed August 14, 1911, with replacements in August 1937 and April 1939. There are no existing records of the amount produced. Only a small number are still in existence.

With Gratitude

A BOOK that must basically depend upon the assistance of others should identify those people whose generosity helped to make it possible. Such is the purpose of the section usually known as Acknowledgments, but that word does not adequately express our feeling toward the many individuals and organizations that assisted us in the completion of this work on N. C. Wyeth. We mention them here with very special gratitude:

Mrs. N. C. Wyeth and Mr. and Mrs. Andrew Wyeth, who gave generously of their own private collections, their time, and their encouragement; also Miss Carolyn Wyeth and Mrs. John McCoy II.

The late Helen L. Card, who supplied invaluable bibliographical material from her extensive files on American illustrators, and Ronald R. Randall, of John Howell—Books, a Wyeth specialist who also supplied bibliographic material.

Richard Layton, former curator of the Brandywine River Museum, whose unfailing support included aid in locating many of the owners of Wyeth paintings.

Henry Chachowski, photographer extraordinary, who devoted much of his time and talent to photographing many of the pictures contained in this book, and to Beatrice Dunn for her assistance in typing the Bibliography, which is so important a compilation.

Mrs. Kathryn Pinney, who edited this book, and George Hornby, who designed it.

Russell Barnet Aitken
Charles Allmond III
American Airlines
  Miss Kathleen Coy
American Tobacco Company
  M. V. Timlen
John F. Apgar, Jr.
Mrs. Sidney Ashcraft
J. N. Bartfield Galleries, Inc., New York
George Beck
Leroy Benge, Sr.
Miss Amanda K. Berls
Walter Bimson
Brandywine River Museum, Chadds
  Ford, Pa.
  Andrew Johnson, Director
  Mrs. Barbara DiFilippo
  Mrs. Anne Mayer
  Miss Jennifer Taylor
Mr. and Mrs. J. Bruce Bredin
Mrs. Gertrude H. Britton
The Brooklyn Museum
  Arno Jakobson
  Susanne P. Sack
Brown & Bigelow
  M. W. Eichers
Mr. and Mrs. R. R. M. Carpenter, Jr.
Civil War Times Illustrated
  Frederic Ray
John Clymer
Coca-Cola Company
  Wilbur G. Kurtz, Jr.
  Marshall H. Lane
Coe Kerr Galleries, Inc., New York
Colby College Art Museum,
  Waterville, Maine
  Hugh J. Gourley III
Mrs. Russell G. Colt
Jerome Connolly
Dallas Museum of Fine Art
  Merrill C. Reuppel
Delaware Art Museum, Wilmington
  Bruce St. John, Director

Roland Elzea, Curator of Collections
Mrs. Phyllis Nixon
Mrs. A. Burton Stanhope
Mr. and Mrs. Richard DeVictor
Diamond M Foundation, Snyder, Texas
  Mrs. Waunita Strayhorn
Hon. James S. Douglas
Downe Publishing, Inc.,
  and *The Ladies' Home Journal*
Edward Eberstadt & Sons, New York
W. S. Farish III
Federal Reserve Bank of Boston
  James T. Timberlake
The First National Bank of Boston
  John W. Calkins
First Trenton National Bank
  John B. Cole, Jr.
The Franklin Savings Bank, New York
  William P. Reuss
Free Public Library of Philadelphia
  Mrs. Carolyn W. Field
  Russell Heaney
General Electric Company
  E. J. Hile
  George F. Way
Ginn and Company
The Armand Hammer Foundation
Harper & Row, Publishers
Dallett Hemphill
Hercules Inc.
  Richard B. Douglas
  Edward L. Grant
Frank Herzog (Photographer)
William Hisgrove
Hotel DuPont, Wilmington
  J. E. Allinger
Houghton Mifflin Company
John Howell—Books, San Francisco
Jay R. Huckabee
Mr. and Mrs. Peter Hurd
Curtis M. Hutchins
International Harvester Company
  of America, Inc.

J. H. Aeschliman
Interwoven, Division of Kayser-Roth
  Corporation
  Randolph C. Bramwell
Iowa State University
  Dr. W. Robert Parks, President
David Jones
Mr. and Mrs. Anton Kamp
Kellogg Company
  A. J. Finley
Kennedy Galleries, Inc., New York
  Eugene Coulon
  Rudolph Wunderlich
Kirk in the Hills, Bloomfield Hills,
  Michigan
  Ralph L. Tweedale
Joseph Klemik (Photographer)
Gerald Kraus (Photographer)
Frank Lerner (Photographer)
Mr. and Mrs. Joseph E. Levine
The Library of Congress
  Dudley B. Ball
Little, Brown and Company
M. Knoedler & Co., Inc., New York
  Bernard Danenberg
John Denys McCoy
David McKay Company, Inc.
C. T. McLaughlin
Chester Marron
Metropolitan Life Insurance Company
  The late C. L. Christiernin
  Paul Mulcahy
The Minneapolis Institute of Arts
  Samuel Sachs II, Curator
Missouri State Museum, Jefferson City
  Donald M. Johnson
John Morrell & Company
  W. F. Anderson
  A. M. Johnson
Dr. and Mrs. William A. Morton, Jr.
Paul D. Myers
Nabisco, Inc.
  Miss Mary Hoban

National Cowboy Hall of Fame and
Western Heritage Center
Dean Krakel
National Geographic Magazine
Dr. Melvin M. Payne
Andrew Poggenpohl
Needham Free Public Library
Mrs. Vivian McIver
The New Britain Museum of
American Art
Mrs. Irving Blomstrann
New York Life Insurance Company
George H. Kelley
The New York Public Library
Edwin S. Holmgren
Joseph T. Rankin
The North Carolina Museum of Art
Benjamin F. Williams, Curator
Oneida Historical Society and
The Munson-Williams-Proctor
Institute, Utica, New York
Jason L. Cox
Penn Central Transportation Company
Ralph F. Timbers
Penn Mutual Life Insurance Company
Wilbur S. Benjamin
Pennsylvania Academy of the Fine Arts,
Philadelphia
Mrs. Elizabeth Bailey
Mr. and Mrs. Edward H. Porter, Jr.
Carl D. Pratt
Princeton University Library
Alexander P. Clark
Quaker Oats Company
Miss Lucille Nitzburg
The Reading Public Museum and
Art Gallery, Reading
James M. K. Waldron
W. C. Roberts
William R. Rollins
Roosevelt Hotel, New York City
Joseph W. McCarthy
Donald P. Ross

B. F. Schlimme
Frank E. Schoonover
John Schoonover
Courtlandt Schoonover
Charles Scribner's Sons
Charles Scribner, Jr.
Joseph E. Seagram & Sons, Inc.
Silver Burdett Company
Mrs. Pauline Coburn
Mr. and Mrs. William V. Sipple, Jr.
C. R. Smith
Mrs. Arthur L. Smythe
Mrs. Andrew J. Sordoni, Jr.
Southern Arizona Bank & Trust
Company, Tucson
A. L. Ruiz
St. Andrew's School, Middletown,
Delaware
Dr. Robert A. Moss
Dr. Walden Pell II
State of Missouri, Division of Commerce
and Industrial Development
Gerald R. Massie
Steinway & Sons, New York
John H. Steinway
Syracuse China Corporation
George E. Springs
Thomas Gilcrease Institute of American
History and Art, Tulsa, Oklahoma
Mrs. Mary Elizabeth Good
Traymore Hotel, Atlantic City
Carroll Knauer
Alexander Ferguson Treadwell
The United Educators, Inc., Lake Bluff,
Illinois
Everett Edgar Sentman
United States Naval Academy,
The Museum
Captain A. J. Ellis, U.S.N.
University of Arizona, Museum of Art,
Tucson
William E. Steadman
University of South Dakota, Vermillion

Dr. Richard L. Bowen, President
U.S. Naval Ordnance Laboratory,
Silver Spring, Maryland
Frank Nichter
Valley National Bank, Phoenix, Arizona
Mrs. Vera Costello
Washington Cathedral, Mount Saint
Alban, Washington, D.C.
John H. Bayless
Charles Waterhouse
Jack Webb
Westtown School, Westtown, Pa.
Miss Margaret Axson
Earl Harrison
Mr. and Mrs. George A. Weymouth
Mr. Donald Widdoes (Photographer)
William A. Farnsworth Library Art
Museum, Rockland, Maine
Wendell S. Hadlock, Director
William Penn Memorial Museum
Harrisburg
Mrs. Patricia Nemser
Wilmington Institute and New Castle
County Libraries
Wilmington Savings Fund Society
Mrs. Frances D. Naczi
Wilmington Trust Company
H. Franklin Baker
Winchester-Western and The Gun
Museum, New Haven, Conn.
T. E. Hall
Mrs. Norman B. Woolworth
R. Frederick Woolworth
Zeal Wright (Photographer)
James B. Wyeth
Nicholas Wyeth
Mrs. Stimson Wyeth
Yale University Library
Mrs. Joyce B. Schneider
YMCA of Wilmington and
New Castle County

Notes

Chapter 1—Howard Pyle's World of Illustration

1. Charles D. Abbott, *Howard Pyle: A Chronicle* (New York: Harper & Brothers, 1925), p. 205
2. Homer Saint-Gaudens, *The American Artist and His Times* (New York: Dodd, Mead, 1941), p. 163.
3. "Circular of The School of Illustration" (Philadelphia: Drexel Institute of Art, Science and Industry, 1896/1897), p. 3.
4. Abbott, *Howard Pyle,* pp. 213–14.
5. Richard Wayne Lykes, "Howard Pyle: Teacher of Illustration" (Diss. University of Pennsylvania, 1947), p. 28.

Chapter 2—Wyeth's Student Years

1. Joseph F. Dinneen, "Wyeth: Noted Illustrator," *Boston Sunday Globe* [n.d.].
2. Muriel Caswall, "King of the Pirates," *Boston Sunday Post* (Nov. 27, 1921).
3. From a speech by Anton Kamp, July 1951.
4. N. C. Wyeth, "For Better Illustration," *Scribner's Magazine* (Nov. 1919): 638–42.
5. N. C. Wyeth, "Pupils of Pyle Tell of His Teaching," *Christian Science Monitor* (Nov. 13, 1912).
6. Ibid.
7. Speech, Anton Kamp.
8. Wyeth, "Pupils of Pyle."
9. Ibid.
10. Sidney M. Chase, "Pupils of Wyeth Tell of His Teaching," *Christian Science Monitor* (Nov. 13, 1912).
11. N. C. Wyeth, "Howard Pyle as I Knew Him," *Mentor Magazine* (July 1927): 15–17.
12. Wyeth, "Pupils of Pyle."
13. Isabel Hoopes, "N. C. Wyeth," *All-Arts Magazine* (Sept. 1925).
14. Wyeth, "Pupils of Pyle."
15. Ibid.

Chapter 3—N.C.'s West

1. A week after Remington's death Wyeth said, during an interview:

    "I have often considered Remington as not so much a painter as a historian. He has recorded the western life conscientiously and truthfully. Remington has always been concerned with the detail and action rather than the bigger spirit of the west, and his work will always last because it is a faithful pictorial account of a life that is fast disappearing.
    "The very fact of Remington's fidelity and photographic truthfulness has always had a great influence on all illustrators taking up the western life. This influence has no doubt had its effect on some of the local artists, though not to an extent that would be noticeable in their work.
    "Remington has been highly respected by all men of the artistic world because of his sincerity, even though he never has reached a real pinnacle in his painting."
    The Star, Wilmington, Del., Jan. 2, 1910

2. *The Star,* Wilmington, Del., Jan. 23, 1910.
3. Muriel Caswall, "King of the Pirates," *Boston Sunday Post* (Nov. 27, 1921).

Chapter 5—Brandywine Country

1. "Wilmington's Colony of Artists—No. 12, N. C. Wyeth," *The Star,* Wilmington, Del., Jan. 23, 1910.
2. *Ladies' Home Journal,* July 1925.

Chapter 6—Religious Painting

1. Isabel Hoopes, "N. C. Wyeth," *All-Arts* (Sept. 1925), p. 7.
2. "The Parables of Jesus" (An Announcement) (Boston: Unitarian Laymen's League, Dec. 25, 1923).

Chapter 7—The Classics

1. Joseph F. Dinneen, "Wyeth, Noted Illustrator," *Boston Sunday Globe* Magazine [n.d.]
2. Letter, undated, Scribner Archive, Princeton University Library, Princeton, N.J.
3. "Book News," *Scribner's Magazine* (Dec. 1918): 12.
4. Letter, undated, Scribner Archive, Princeton University Library, Princeton, N.J.
5. Ibid.
6. Letter dated November 13, 1919, Scribner Archive, Princeton University Library, Princeton, N.J.
7. Ibid.
8. Letter, undated, Scribner Archive, Princeton University Library, Princeton, N.J.
9. Letter dated June 14, 1920, Scribner Archive, Princeton University Library, Princeton, N.J.
10. Letter dated July 19, 1920, Scribner Archive, Princeton University Library, Princeton, N.J.
11. N. C. Wyeth, Preface to *Robinson Crusoe.*
12. Letter dated July 19, 1920, Scribner Archive, Princeton University Library, Princeton, N.J.
13. Letter dated August 17, 1921, Scribner Archive, Princeton University Library, Princeton, N.J.
14. Letter dated August 21, 1921, Scribner Archive, Princeton University Library, Princeton, N.J.
15. Letter dated June 20, 1929, Scribner Archive, Princeton University Library, Princeton, N.J.
16. Letter dated June 25, 1929, Scribner Archive, Princeton University Library, Princeton, N.J.
17. Letter dated August 19, 1929, Scribner Archive, Princeton University Library, Princeton, N.J.
18. Marjorie Kinnan Rawlings, *The Yearling* (New York: Charles Scribner's Sons, 1929). Excerpt from the Wyeth letter was reproduced in the limited edition only.

Chapter 8—From Blackbeard to St. Nick

1. N. C. Wyeth, "On Illustration—A Suggestion and a Comment on Illustrating Fiction," *The New York Times* (Oct. 13, 1912): 574.
2. *The Ladies' Home Journal* (July 1925).
3. The Scribner Archive, Princeton University Library, Princeton, N.J.
4. *A Book of Notable American Illustrators,* Walker Engraving Company, N.Y., 1927

Chapter 9—Commercial Art

1. The Scribner Archive, Princeton University Library, Princeton, N.J.

Chapter 10—Murals, Lunettes, and the Triptych

1. Letter, undated, Scribner Archive, Princeton University Library, Princeton, N.J.
2. "Mural Paintings in the First National Bank of Boston," *The Ladies' Home Journal* (July 1925).
3. Letter, undated, Scribner Archive, Princeton University Library, Princeton, N.J.
4. "N. C. Wyeth Mural," *Delaware Today* (Feb.-March 1967).
5. Information on St. Andrew's School and its mural was furnished in correspondence with the Reverend Walker Pell II, first headmaster of the school.
6. "The Days of the Pilgrims Live Again," *The Home Office* (employee paper of the Metropolitan Life Insurance Company) (Dec. 1941).

Chapter 11—Easel Painting

1. Ernest W. Watson, "N. C. Wyeth, Giant on a Hilltop," *American Artist* (Jan. 1945).
2. Ibid.
3. N. C. Wyeth, "For Better Illustration," *Scribner's Magazine* (Nov. 1919).
4. Harvey Dunn, "An Evening in the Classroom," Privately printed pamphlet, 1934.
5. Letter (circa 1921) to Joseph Chapin, Scribner Archive, Princeton University Library, Princeton, N.J.
6. Letter, undated, to Joseph Chapin, Scribner Archive, Princeton University Library, Princeton, N.J.
7. Isabel Hoopes, "N. C. Wyeth," *All-Arts* (Sept. 1925).
8. Letter dated June 20, 1929, to Joseph Chapin, Scribner Archive, Princeton University Library, Princeton, N.J.

Index

Italic page numbers indicate illustrations.